PRINCETONIANS
1776–1783

PRINCETONIANS

$== 1776-1783 ==$

A BIOGRAPHICAL

DICTIONARY

By RICHARD A. HARRISON

PRINCETON UNIVERSITY PRESS

PRINCETON, NEW JERSEY

1981

Library of Congress Cataloging in Publication Data will
be found on the last printed page of this book

◉ Publication of this book was made possible by a grant from the
New Jersey Committee for the Humanities through the
National Endowment for the Humanities.

This book has been composed in Linotype Baskerville

Clothbound editions of Princeton University Press books
are printed on acid-free paper, and binding materials are
chosen for strength and durability

Printed in the United States of America
by Princeton University Press, Princeton, New Jersey

TO THE MEMORY OF

Wesley Frank Craven
(1905–1981)

CONTENTS

LIST OF ILLUSTRATIONS

PREFACE

THIS third volume in the series of biographical dictionaries of Princetonians takes the record of the alumni of the College of New Jersey through the classes that attended during the American Revolution. As was true of the earlier volumes, which covered the classes of 1748-1768 and 1769-1775 respectively, the amount of information available about the careers of identified Princetonians increased as the lives of these men extended into the period of the Revolution and beyond. The problem of identification itself, however, was greatly complicated by the confusion of the revolutionary era.

This disruption was not a major obstacle to identifying most of the men who actually graduated from Nassau Hall, for their names were generally recorded in the Trustee Minutes, in newspaper reports of commencement exercises, and in the general catalogues of the College. There were years, however, in which even the identity of graduates was obscured as a result of the war. The commencement of 1776 was not reported in newspapers, and there were no formal exercises in 1777. Moreover, the trustees, unable to muster a quorum, could not confer degrees on those two classes until well after the actual graduations, and the clerk who listed the names of the new laureates—and who probably did so some time after the board had acted—occasionally confused the names or forgot to include all of them.

Identifying students who attended the College but did not graduate was much more of a problem. Since the earliest classes, non-graduates tended to have less continuing contact with fellow Princetonians after departing Nassau Hall and thus left a more difficult path for the historian to follow. The war, which forced full suspension of the College from November 1776 to July 1777, cut short the educations of many young men; of the 157 Princetonians included in this volume, 75, or almost 50%, did not take their degrees.

Compounding the problem of identification was the tendency of descendants, genealogists, and local historians to confer a Princeton education on men for whom no evidence of attendance at Nassau Hall has been discovered. As in the earlier volumes, the policy here has been to include only those individuals for whose matriculation persuasive evidence has been found. Thus John Coburn, a graduate of the grammar school in 1774 who, with his fellow graduates, was admitted as a freshman to the College, has not been included because of the absence of proof that he actually enrolled. So too John Bell Tilden (1761-1838) has been excluded. According to family tradition, he left the College at the age of eighteen to join the Pennsylvania Line of the Continental Army. In his case, there is no conclusive proof, as there is with Coburn, that he actually attended either the grammar school or the College; but that he was enrolled in the former is entirely possible. Thomas Patterson, listed in some sources as a member of the Cliosophic Society in the Class of 1783, has been omitted on the supposition that he was, in fact, the merchant whose establishment in Princeton was a favorite store among students before the Revolution and that he perhaps was admitted to the society as an honorary member, being a brother of one of its founders, William Paterson (A.B. 1763). The variant spelling of the family name in this instance presented no difficulty, but in other cases it added a troublesome dimension to the problem of identification. Even more frustrating, usually both the family and the given names were among the most commonplace, so the name of almost any person might be found in many different parts of North America.

The accounts of student payments and charges kept by the College stewards, the latest of which covers the period from November 1774 to April 1775, were of substantial help in identifying non-graduates in the classes of 1776-1778. The ledger maintained in Patterson's store, which survives in fairly complete form for the period of August 1774 to November 1775 but which is very fragmentary thereafter, was also useful, because it frequently identified customers as students. Like the stewards' accounts, however, it was of little help for classes after 1778. The records of the Cliosophic and American Whig societies, which provided valuable information for earlier classes, were much less useful for the war years, because the two literary clubs themselves were virtually dormant during the Revolution and were revived only in 1781 and 1782, respectively.

Confirmation of attendance at the College has often come through diligent research on specific individuals, as was the case with two of the best-known men included here, John Brown of Kentucky and Nathaniel Macon of North Carolina, both of the Class of 1778, and both of whom left brief notations of their attendance at Princeton. But the original suggestions of the identities of many Princetonians came from the Princeton University Archives, in which files on all graduates and some non-graduates were established by Varnum Lansing Collins, one-time Secretary of the University. These archival files were significantly supplemented by James McLachlan, author of *Princetonians, 1748-1768,* and his staff, who compiled lists of possible Princetonians as they did the invaluable groundwork for this project. While a few undue omissions are likely, we have justifiable confidence that the men included in this volume constituted very nearly all of the members of the classes of 1776-1783.

One question of identity deserves separate mention. Among the names found in the non-graduate file of the University Archives were those of two assumed brothers, Guy and Paul Rupert. Their identification became the special passion of every researcher associated with the preparation of this volume until it was discovered that a long-forgotten student hoax was responsible. On February 22, 1884, the *Princetonian* devoted a column and a half to the report of a half-buried gravestone in the Witherspoon Street cemetery which read:

In Memory of
GUY and PAUL RUPERT
Students of the College of New Jersey,
who Departed this Life January 1777.
Their Blood is on the Hands of the British.

The story went on to explain the last line of the inscription by telling of an invasion of Princeton by a British regiment in *February* 1777. The news of its approach had emptied the village of its citizens and the College of its students, except for the Rupert brothers who continued to occupy their room in Nassau Hall for reasons having no explanation. In due course their room was invaded by two Hessians, an officer and a soldier. In the ensuing altercation, Paul was held by the soldier while the officer ran him through with his sword. Guy, who undertook to assist his brother, was fatally wounded. Washington, fresh from a decisive action at Stony Brook that put the British to flight, on hearing of this dastardly deed went to Nassau Hall, where he "listened with a father's pity and tearful eyes" to the dying words of Guy Rupert. It had been Washington who left in the cemetery the "plain slab" that continued to stand as "another monument of his generous and noble heart, and a stigma everlasting throughout all time on the name of the British 'Hessian Hirelings.'" However seriously intended as a paean to the Father of His Country, the story is pure fiction and the Rupert brothers merely inventions of a Washington Birthday fable.*

* The story was printed under the caption of "Mosses from an Old Monument," and it may be worth noting that the issue of the *Princetonian* for March 7, 1884, carried another fictional story headed "Mosses from an Old Monument (Revised)."

As with the previous volumes, the limit on the length of each biography has been waived only for men who were particularly representative of their time and place, or whose careers were clearly connected to the history of the College itself. Like their predecessors, these Princetonians were individuals of generally high achievement in their communities, states, and nation, and most of their lives have gone virtually unrecorded in modern scholarship. Taken together, their biographies not only provide valuable insight into the history of their era but also establish the special contribution of the College of New Jersey.

The writing of this volume has been made possible by funding provided chiefly through matching grants from the National Endowment for the Humanities. While the name of all of the alumni of Princeton whose contributions enabled us to qualify for those grants cannot be mentioned here, the following deserve particular appreciation: Nathaniel Burt '36, Levering Cartwright '26, John K. Jenney '25, Wheaton J. Lane '25, Maurice Lee, Jr. '46, Baldwin Maull '22, Adolph G. Rosengarten, Jr. '27, Edward W. Scudder, Jr. '35, and Richard B. Scudder '35. The completion of the volume has depended upon support generously provided by President William G. Bowen and the Shelby Cullom Davis Center for Historical Studies of the Department of History, of which Professor Lawrence Stone is director, and by the Bicentennial Committee of Princeton University, William H. Weathersby and Jeremiah S. Finch, chairmen.

No less than the earlier two volumes, the composition of this work was immensely facilitated by Earle E. Coleman, Archivist of Princeton University, and Cynthia McClelland, Assistant Archivist, and by the staff of the Firestone Library at Princeton. Several other institutions provided important assistance, and most of those have been acknowledged in the "Sources" section of each applicable biography. The staffs of the following, however, were helpful in so large a number of cases that they must be mentioned here: Presbyterian Historical Society; historical societies of Pennsylvania, Massachusetts, New York, New Jersey, Maryland, and Wisconsin; state libraries of Connecticut and New Jersey; Library of Congress; New York Public Library; National Archives of the United States; Alexander Library at Rutgers

---

Once more, a gravestone had been discovered in the "Withoutaspook Cemetery" inscribed to the memory of two brothers, Obediah and Kaul Hoopit, students of the College of New Jersey who had departed "this life and that Institution" in March 1784. There were no other parallels with the earlier story on the Rupert brothers. For this citation I am indebted to Virginia Creesy.

the State University; Speer Library of Princeton Theological Seminary; Maryland Legislative Historical Project (E. C. Papenfuse and R. W. Jordan, principal investigators), Hall of Records, Annapolis; Harvard University Archives; University of Pennsylvania Archives; American Antiquarian Society; Frick Art Reference Library; and Genealogical Society of Pennsylvania. Individuals who made important contributions of information are also acknowledged in the "Sources," but very special thanks are due David Wise and Nelson R. Burr '27.

Those biographical sketches that are unsigned were written by Richard A. Harrison. Contributing authors of the biographies in this volume, together with the signatures used for identification of their several contributions, are:

> W. Frank Craven—WFC
> Gary S. DeKrey—GSD
> James McLachlan—JMcL
> James M. Rosenheim—JMR
> Jane E. Weber—JW

The members of the Editorial Advisory Committee, as always, have provided expert guidance and sound critical advice. For their hardworking efforts in research assistance and manuscript typing, Jennifer Guberman, Sharon Rodgers, Linda Salvucci, and Ruth L. Woodward are to be highly commended. Once again, Jane Serumgard Harrison volunteered much of her time to assist with uncounted details. Finally, Gail Filion and Tam Curry of Princeton University Press offered invaluable editorial advice.

In February 1981, while this volume was being prepared for publication, W. Frank Craven died. Chairman of the Editorial Advisory Committee since its inception, he also served as director of the project from the autumn of 1977; he devoted his years of ostensible retirement to the completion and perfection of the Princetonians series. His wisdom and encouragement are reflected in each volume, but his contribution to the work is beyond calculation or description. An ornament to his profession, one of the most distinguished American historians of his time, Frank Craven was simultaneously a great teacher, a sage adviser, an inspiring colleague, and a cherished friend. Everyone who knew him has special memories of him, but those who were associated with him in this project know best of all the depth of his devotion and his courage. The dedication of this volume is a woefully inadequate expression of the respect and love we had for him.

R.A.H.

INTRODUCTION

By 1775, after seven years as president of the College of New Jersey, John Witherspoon had led the institution to financial health and academic vitality. The treasury was more than twice as rich as he had first found it; the library, with its more than 2,000 volumes, had grown at nearly the same rate; and the student body had expanded to rival Yale's as second largest among all American colleges. Given continued peace, the prospects for the College seemed unlimited. Yet when the class of 1775 graduated in September, it was clear that the great social and political forces stirring America would envelop Nassau Hall.

Even before the bloodshed at Lexington and Concord, politics had become a passion among the students of the College. This interest in public affairs and sympathy for the colonial cause were encouraged by Witherspoon, who as early as September 1774 had gone personally to observe the deliberations of the First Continental Congress in Philadelphia. In April 1775 his young charges had responded to the news from Massachusetts by forming their own militia company. Princeton, as the headquarters of the provincial government in the summer of 1775 and of the New Jersey Committee of Safety early in 1776, was in the thick of revolutionary activities in New Jersey. Professor of Mathematics and Natural Sciences William Churchill Houston (A.B. 1768), Witherspoon's chief assistant at the College, was a deputy secretary to the Continental Congress in the winter of 1775-1776. And Witherspoon himself served in a variety of provincial and county organizations. Named to the committee to draft a constitution for New Jersey, he was prevented from serving on it by his selection to the Continental Congress on June 22, 1776; he joined the Congress in time to sign the Declaration of Independence. Until his final resignation from Congress in 1782, Witherspoon tried heroically to fulfill his obligations both to the nation and to the College, and he succeeded to a remarkable degree. But the disruptions attendant to the American Revolution were amplified at Nassau Hall by the frequent absences and preoccupations of its president.

Witherspoon's devotion to the College throughout his congressional tenure was nonetheless obvious. He never missed a meeting of the trustees or a commencement, and he presided at the opening of almost every academic term. Until the late fall of 1776, he virtually commuted between Philadelphia and Princeton. But after his reelection in November 1776 and during the hiatus in the operation of the College, his attendance in Congress was fairly constant. A leave of absence from that body in February 1777 and a prolonged absence in the summer of that year were clearly related to preparations for the resumption of classes in Nassau Hall. After a brief period in Congress in the late autumn of 1777, Witherspoon was again reelected, but his attendance was sporadic through the winter of 1777-1778. Reluctant to leave New Jersey with too few delegates to cast its vote, he frequently postponed returning to Princeton until enough of his colleagues had resumed their seats in Congress to assure representation. But his duties at Nassau Hall often kept him away from the Congress for weeks at a time, occasionally with the result that the state's vote could not be cast.[1]

Witherspoon accepted his reelection in November 1778 with the condition that he must have "full liberty to attend only when I could conveniently." He made "a good deal of use of that liberty" in 1779. In May, Professor Houston, for two years a member of the state assembly, was also chosen to sit in Congress. To his apparent relief, Witherspoon was not reelected in November. He had found that members of Congress "not only receive no profit from that office, but . . . five out of six of them, if not more, are great losers in their private affairs." With Houston elected to a full term, the president was "determined to give particular attention to the revival of the College."[2] Houston was discomfited by his double burden as congressman and professor, just as Witherspoon had been, and it is likely that he and Witherspoon agreed that they would both stand for election in November 1780 so that at least one of them could always be at Princeton.[3] Witherspoon did not seek reelection in November 1781, serving instead in the state legislature, but he did agree to fill a partial congressional term from May to November 1782.[4] His attendance continued to be irregular, and after November of that year he did not sit in the Congress again.

In addition to his noteworthy contributions as a member of nearly 120 of the committees through which Congress dealt with the problems of government, Witherspoon used his time in Congress to the advantage of the College. On August 14, 1776, for example, he obtained congressional approval for the exemption of the tutors at Nassau Hall

---

[1] Varnum Lansing Collins, *President Witherspoon* (1925), II, 86; *LMCC*, II, lvi-lvii, 130n; III, lvi, 57-59, 67, 415-16n, 531; IV, lvii, 118.
[2] *LMCC*, IV, liv, lvii, 118n.   [3] Ibid., V, lix, lx, 487n.
[4] Ibid., VI, xlviii.

from military service.[5] And while returning from a congressional inspection tour in 1779, Witherspoon brought with him to Princeton the young patroon Stephen Van Rensselaer (Class of 1782), heir to one of the greatest fortunes in the country. But there was little that the president could do for the institution while he was on the nation's business. It was against his very specific wishes that some of the students left Princeton in August 1776 for Elizabethtown on the New Jersey coast, with the intention perhaps of joining the American forces on Long Island. Tradition holds that the adventurous company was led by William R. Davie (A.B. 1776); and it certainly included John Pintard (A.B. 1776) and probably George W. Hazard (Class of 1777). Most of the young men returned to the College somewhat chastened by their first experience with war.

While they were gone, Princeton had become the virtual seat of the Revolution in New Jersey.[6] The new state government met there that summer, and in September trustee William Livingston was inaugurated there as the state's first governor. It was thus with good reason that both the town and the College were concerned that the British army, by late November pursuing the American forces southward from New York, might be ruthless in pacifying Princeton.

Already the disruptive effects of the war upon the College's fortunes had been foretold by the failure of the board of trustees to gather a quorum for its regular meeting in connection with the scheduled commencement of September 25, 1776. The board therefore could not act officially to confer degrees on the qualified seniors, and it was agreed to postpone that action until a special meeting could be held in November. The members of the Class of 1776 were not formally awarded their degrees until May 24, 1777, when for the first time after the preceding September, the trustees managed to muster a quorum. Historians of the College have been left with no real knowledge of what transpired at the commencement of 1776 until in the research

5 *NJHSP* 50 (1932), 131. Likewise, Witherspoon's experience at the College was useful to Congress, as when he warned that allowing the army's general officers to elect major generals would have the same unhappy results as his one experiment in allowing college seniors to choose the recipients of honors at their own commencement. [See Collins, *President Witherspoon*, II, 64.] Houston resigned his commission in the Somerset County militia on August 17, explaining that his duties at the College "in the absence of Dr. Witherspoon" made it impossible for him to give "due attention to his company" [see *Princetonians, 1748-1768*, 645].

6 The account of CNJ's history during the Revolution may be found in Maclean, *History*; Wertenbaker, *Princeton*; Collins, *President Witherspoon*; Ashbel Green, *Life of . . . Witherspoon* (1973); A. Leitch, *Princeton Companion* (1978), passim; and W. S. Dix, "Princeton University Library," *Princeton University Library Chronicle*, 40 (Autumn 1978), 53-58.

for this volume there was found a letter from William Vernon (A.B. 1776) to his father that described the proceedings of that day. With the curtailed ceremonies ended and the audience dismissed, the president advised the seniors of plans for the later award of their degrees and offered meanwhile to provide any one of them with a certificate attesting to his having completed the requirements for the A.B. Two such certificates, issued to William R. Davie (A.B. 1776) and Joseph W. Henderson (A.B. 1776), have been found. The discovery of a similar certificate belonging to James Crawford (A.B. 1777) indicates that Witherspoon must have made the same offer of temporary certificates in lieu of diplomas the next year.

On November 29, 1776, Witherspoon had been forced to close the College entirely with a dismissal of the students that was movingly described by Joseph Clark (A.B. 1781), then a student but one destined to complete his studies only after military service with the Continental Army. Assisted by Benjamin Hawkins and John Graham of the Class of 1777, the president led his family to Pequea, Pennsylvania and then rejoined the Congress in Philadelphia. Three days after the closing of the College, the retreating American army passed through Princeton, and on December 7 the British arrived. They used the lower floor of Nassau Hall as a stable, wrecked the library, and did some damage to the town and local farms, including Witherspoon's own "Tusculum," less than two miles from the College. On January 3, 1777, the Battle of Princeton brought an end to the British occupation. Nassau Hall, where the redcoats staged their last defense, was battered by cannon balls, one of which, according to tradition, was fired by a battery commanded by Alexander Hamilton, passed through a window, and beheaded the College's portrait of King George II, in whose name the institution's original charter had been issued. For five months militiamen and Continentals occupied the College, doing at least as much damage to the building and the grounds with their vandalism as the British had done. Nassau Hall then became a hospital. It was not returned fully to the use of the College until much later in the war.

Having awarded the seniors of 1776 their degrees in May 1777 at Cooper's Ferry, New Jersey, the trustees moved promptly to reconvene the College. In March Witherspoon and Houston had summoned students to the regular summer session beginning on May 10 in some unspecified place away from Princeton,[7] but the confusion and danger had been too great and the summer session of 1777 was postponed.

[7] *Pennsylvania Packet*, 26 Mar 1777.

Following the board meeting in May, the president issued a new call for students to meet in Princeton on July 8, and the session finally began on that date.[8] Seniors in particular were alerted that they should be prepared for their final examinations. These were given in August, but there was not even a "private" commencement ceremony in 1777, and the trustees did not officially confer degrees upon that year's seniors until April 16, 1778. Among the costs of wartime disruptions in the life of the College was a failure to keep adequate records even of the more important actions by the trustees, as the almost unbelievable confusion in their minutes regarding the award of degrees to members of the Class of 1777, and especially the case of James Ashton Bayard of that class, make abundantly clear.

Naturally, the board took what steps it could to regain complete use of Nassau Hall and to repair the damage done to College property. The Cooper's Ferry meeting of May 1777 created a committee to make plans to restore the building and also called upon Witherspoon to obtain a congressional resolution that no more troops would be quartered at the College. On that question and on claims for reparations the president kept up a constant campaign in Congress. His call for compensation for damages in October 1777 prompted a "universal complaint against our Troops" but did not yet stir the Congress to appropriate the funds.[9] Meanwhile, the College continued, as Benjamin Rush (A.B. 1760) described it in January 1777, a "heap of ruin."[10]

Classes were held in the president's house and students boarded in the town during 1777 and 1778. So few scholars were in residence, however, that in August 1778 Witherspoon announced that any enrolled member of the senior class who could pass his examinations would receive the A.B. degree, whether he had been studying in Princeton or at home. Moreover, the scarcity of students led the president to call upon men eligible for the A.M. degree to volunteer as orators for the commencement of 1778, which was held as scheduled on September 30.[11] By the beginning of the regular session in the fall of 1778, several young men were at least able to occupy rooms in the lower floors of Nassau Hall.

On April 12, 1779, the trustees again considered how best they might restore the building and the College's depleted treasury. Two years earlier they had invested the institution's money in United States Loan Office certificates, and the depreciation of those bonds was

8 Ibid., 26 Jun 1777; 22 Jul 1777.   9 *LMCC*, II, 513.
10 Dix, "Princeton University Library," 55.
11 *N.J. Gazette*, 21 Oct 1778.

grave. Drafts in France helped maintain solvency, but by 1779 a crisis
was imminent. The board appealed for help from friends in Pennsylvania and New England, and it asked once more for some reparations
from Congress, which finally allocated $19,357 (Continental) for the
College of New Jersey in November. The money was worth a mere 5%
of its face value, however, and when Samuel Stanhope Smith (A.B.
1769) joined the faculty in December 1779, he was paid, at the president's suggestion, with one-half of Witherspoon's own salary of £400.
In exchange, the board devoted the revenue from tuition for the coming academic year exclusively to the salaries of Witherspoon, Smith,
and Houston.

Those difficulties aside, the College was actually on the road to recovery by early 1780, when Witherspoon issued an important and
revealing public announcement.[12] Written as advice to the parents and
schoolmasters of potential Princetonians, it warned against some of
the failures in preparation that the president had sadly noted among
students since the war began. He urged preparatory teachers to be
certain that their pupils were thoroughly trained in the classical languages and literature and in English and he lamented the tendency
among parents to rush their sons through these basic subjects without
insuring that the boys had truly learned what they were supposed to
learn. He had discovered the two basic principles of teaching, he
said: "that the learner should be made as perfect as possible in one
thing before he be carried forward to another"; and that "the steps
of transition should be as . . . easy and gentle as possible." Implying
perhaps that he disapproved of the practice, the president reminded
his readers that the trustees permitted students to enter with advanced standing. That, he said, made it all the more important for
the young men to be well grounded in the fundamentals before they
came to Princeton. It is also quite possible that Witherspoon had been
disappointed by the deportment of students during the unsettled
early years of the war, for he admonished parents not only to support
the laws of schools and colleges but also to keep strict rules within the
home.

If that injunction emanated from unhappy experiences at Nassau
Hall, the president might at least have taken some comfort in knowing that discipline was a problem at other colleges during those years.
At Harvard, for example, there was a high number of "misfits and
downright rascals" in attendance.[13] Witherspoon's administration of

---

[12] *NJA* (2 ser.), IV, 223-27.
[13] Samuel Eliot Morison, *Three Centuries of Harvard* (Cambridge, 1936), 152.

discipline, if the experience of John Pintard (A.B. 1776) and George Blewer (Class of 1777) is any indication, was both firm and scrupulously fair before the College closed in 1776. But most institutions had had at least to bend their rules to accommodate the times, and students were relieved of normal residency requirements for the A.B. almost everywhere. It was not surprising that young men, much of whose education had been outside of the classroom and out of the sight of stern tutors, and some of whom had actually served in the army, would not accept the yoke of college discipline with the same docility as earlier students.

It was undoubtedly with some relief, therefore, that Witherspoon was able to announce in September 1781 that the old rules would once again apply in Princeton and that students would henceforth live in the College rather than in town except with the president's permission. Repairs on Nassau Hall had not yet progressed to the extent that such dormitory arrangements would be very comfortable, so the trustees had decreed that every entering student should pay an entrance fee of one guinea in addition to his £6 annual tuition, £2 annual chamber rental, and board charges. The proceeds from the new fee would go toward restoring the building. All charges were to be paid six months in advance, and any student who failed to comply with that requirement would be dismissed, unless the president himself paid the fee. For some time Witherspoon had advanced such personal loans to occasional students, but in September 1781 he declared that the practice was too "expensive and dangerous" and that he would not be so generous in the future.[14] The board also empowered trustees Joseph Reed (A.B. 1757) and Colonel John Bayard to borrow money for immediate repair work. Unable to do so, the two men personally advanced £39 to the College treasury, a sum subsequently repaid by credits toward the education of sons who thereafter attended the College. Ashbel Green (A.B. 1783) later recalled that at the time of his first enrollment early in May 1782 much of Nassau Hall still remained "uninhabited and uninhabitable."[15]

Although the College of New Jersey undoubtedly suffered more severely during the war than did most of the other colonial colleges, all of them experienced serious difficulties. Queen's College at New Brunswick, occupied by the British only a few days before Nassau Hall, was in enemy hands until June 1777. When classes resumed a few months later, they were held in North Branch, at the juncture of the north and south branches of the Raritan River, rather than in

14 NJA (2 ser.), V, 303-305.   15 Maclean, History, 330-31.

New Brunswick. Although commencement exercises in 1778 were conducted at the college itself, Queen's did not permanently resume its
normal operations in New Brunswick until 1781, at which time the
buildings and the college treasury were in equivalent disarray.[16]

King's College in New York City, which had been "conceived . . .
as a bulwark of the established order, not as its critic," had strengthened its ties to the English Crown "on the very eve of the Revolution."[17] The Loyalist college officials fled New York in April 1775 and
returned in May only to have a mob invade the college and put
President Myles Cooper to flight for England. In April 1776 the New
York Committee of Safety converted the college into a military hospital, and classes for the few remaining students were held in the home
of one of the governors. There they continued when the British army
replaced the Americans in the college in 1777. Although President
Benjamin Moore solicited new students that summer, King's probably
closed down soon afterward. It was not reopened until, as Columbia
College, it was incorporated into the new University of the State of
New York at the end of the Revolution.[18]

The College of Philadelphia was a mustering place for provincial
troops as early as 1774, and as a result, no public commencement exercises were held there in 1775 or 1776. In June 1777 the college
officially closed after months of irregular operation, and from September 1777 to June 1778, the British occupied Philadelphia. Although
classes were scheduled to begin again in January 1779, a hostile state
government, which had earlier suspended the authority of the trustees,
waited until that November to reorganize the institution as the University of the State of Pennsylvania, with a new chairman of the board,
Joseph Reed, and a new provost, John Ewing (A.B. 1754). The first
public commencement exercises since 1774 were held in 1780.[19]

Yale College was closed for two weeks on April 22, 1775, and the
commencement exercises that year were conducted privately. There
was not to be another public commencement in New Haven until
1781. Nevertheless, classes continued to meet until August 1776, when
disease at a nearby military camp forced the college to suspend its
operations. Students returned in the autumn only to face severe shortages of food that necessitated another suspension in December. From

16 W.H.S. Demarest, *History of Rutgers College, 1766-1924* (1924), 103, 104, 118-
21, 125-26, 141; R. P. McCormick, *Rutgers: A Bicentennial History* (1966), 15-19.
17 D. C. Humphrey, *From King's College to Columbia, 1746-1800* (1976), 140.
18 Ibid., 140-46, 152-54.
19 E. P. Cheyney, *History of the University of Pennsylvania, 1740-1940* (1940), 89,
116-17, 120-21, 123-24, 137, 140.

January to March 1777 Yale tried to maintain a regular schedule, but persistent shortages led to the scattering of classes to various parts of Connecticut. The assumption of the college's presidency by Ezra Stiles in June 1778 coincided with the resumption of classes in New Haven, and the students remained until July 1779, when the arrival of a British fleet forced their evacuation until October. That winter, with food stocks still dangerously low, Stiles closed the college to all students who could not provide their own board. Not until May 1780 did Yale's wartime troubles end and regular class schedules resume.[20]

There was no public commencement at Harvard in 1774 as a protest by the corporation against the British occupation of Boston, and subsequent exercises were conducted privately until 1781. During the American siege of Boston in 1775, Cambridge served as headquarters for the rebel troops. That May the college buildings were taken by the provincial congress, and the library and scientific apparatus were moved to Andover. In October 1775 Harvard resumed its classes at Concord and continued that exile until June 1776, after which the institution returned to its regular schedule in Cambridge. The college buildings, which had housed over 1,000 troops during the siege, miraculously escaped with only £450 in damages.[21]

At the urging of the students, the commencement exercises at Rhode Island College were private in 1775. And while the graduation of 1776 was a public affair it was the last such until 1783. The arrival of the British navy in Newport in December 1776 made Providence a garrison town for American soldiers, and like most of her sister institutions, Rhode Island College became a barracks and a hospital. Regular classes were suspended until after June 1782, but formal instruction was offered in the homes of tutors, President James Manning (A.B. 1762), or Professor David Howell (A.B. 1766). The corporation managed to meet irregularly to confer degrees or to petition the legislature for funds. The dilapidation of the college buildings when they were finally evacuated in June 1782 made the latter function especially important.[22]

Dartmouth was alone among American colleges in never having been forced to close during the Revolution; its commencements were regular and public. There were hardships, of course, particularly because the college, the most recent to be founded, had relied heavily on financial support from England. When President Eleazar Wheelock

20 B. M. Kelley, *Yale: A History* (1974), 87 & n, 91-102.
21 Morison, *Three Centuries of Harvard*, 139-41, 144-45, 148-53.
22 W. C. Bronson, *History of Brown University* (1914), 62-63, 65-68, 71-72, 76-77.

died in January 1779, he left the institution with an almost empty treasury. Yet Dartmouth managed not only to survive but to grow.[23]

William and Mary was in serious difficulty with many of the leading planters of Virginia through several years before the coming of the Revolution, if only because its close ties to the Church of England and the Society for the Propagation of the Gospel in Foreign Parts tended to identify the college with advocacy of an American bishopric, a proposal hardly more popular in Virginia than it was in New England. The college remained open through most of the war years, in part because Virginia became a main theater of the war only toward its end. It survived the Revolution, even experienced a promising reorganization during its course. But located in one of the earliest states to commit itself to a separation of church and state, the college was never fully free of penalty for its longtime identification with the Anglican establishment.[24]

Predictably, the number of young men who received A.B. degrees from American colleges declined during the war. In the seven years between 1769 and 1775, 830 A.B.s had been conferred, compared with 704 for the seven years from 1776 to 1782. While most colleges seemed well on their way to producing higher numbers of graduates by 1783, the war had a substantial, if temporary, effect on the share of baccalaureates for each college. Table A compares the numbers of graduates from American colleges between 1776 and 1783. Clearly, the years from 1779 to 1781 represented the nadir of collegiate education during the war.

Equally noteworthy is the proportionate share of A.B.s produced by each college. Table B compares the percentage of the total number of graduates for each college during the war years with the percentages during the period 1769-1775.

Not surprisingly, the colleges that suffered the least disruption during the Revolution did proportionately better than the others in producing graduates. Dartmouth more than doubled its productivity. Yale replaced Harvard as the college producing the greatest number of A.B.s.

Nassau Hall's location at the "crossroads of the Revolution" was obviously a major obstacle to student enrollment. But the number of graduates during the war is in no sense a complete measure of the size of the student body, for one important effect of the disruption was

---

[23] M. D. Bisbee, *General Catalogue of Dartmouth College* (1900), 33-36.

[24] R. P. Thomson, "The Reform of the College of William and Mary," *APS Proc.*, 115 (1971), 187-213; J. E. Morpurgo, *Their Majesties' Royall Colledge* (1976), 200-207.

TABLE A[25]

A.B.s Awarded by American Colleges, 1776-1783

	Harvard	Yale	CNJ	R.I.	Phila.	King's	Dart-mouth	Queen's	Total
1776	43	33	27	9	7	7*	12	1	139
1777	42	56	7	7	—	—	12	—	124
1778	32	40	5	—	—	—	17	2	96
1779	26	34	6	—	—	—	17	—	83
1780	30	27	6	1	8	—	10	7	89
1781	27	27	6	—	6	—	5	—	71
1782	35	26	11	7	16	—	4	3	102
1783	30	42	14	6	11	—	14	4	121
Total	265	285	82	30	48	7*	91	17	825

19 3

* One of these 7 members of the King's College class of 1776 actually received his degree in 1793.

TABLE B

Percentages of All A.B.s Awarded by Each College

	Harvard	Yale	CNJ	R.I.	Phila.	King's	Dart-mouth	Queen's
1769-1775 (TOTAL 830)	37	22.6	18.1	5.3	6	5.3	3.7*	1.8†
1776-1783 (TOTAL 825)	32.1	34.5	9.9	3.6	5.8	0.8‡	11	2

* Dartmouth awarded degrees beginning in 1771; for the years 1771-1775, Dartmouth granted 4.9% of all A.B.s.

† Queen's awarded degrees beginning in 1774; for the years 1774-1775, Queen's granted 5.4% of all A.B.s.

‡ King's awarded degrees for the last time during the war in 1776; that year, King's granted 5% of all A.B.s.

that proportionately fewer students remained in college for the full course of study. Table C compares the numbers of graduates of the College of New Jersey in the periods 1748-1768, 1769-1775, and 1776-1783 with the numbers of students who have been identified as having enrolled without graduating.

25 The College of William and Mary is not included in this table and in the subsequent discussion because its records are very incomplete and such as they are indicate that many of its students did not bother to take the degree. Figures are from *Quinquennial Catalogue of Officers and Graduates of Havard University* (1925); Dexter, *Yale Biographies*, III and IV; *Historical Catalogue of Brown University, 1764-1934* (1936); *University of Pennsylvania Catalogue of Matriculates . . . 1749-1783* (1894); M. H. Thomas, *Columbia University Officers and Alumni, 1754-1857* (1936); *General Catalogue of Dartmouth College, 1769-1910* (1910-1911); *Catalogue of Officers and Alumni of Rutgers College, 1766-1916* (1916).

TABLE C

GRADUATES AND NON-GRADUATES OF CNJ

	A.B.s	Non-graduates	Percent Non-graduates
1748-1768	313	25	7.4
1769-1775	150	28	15.7
1776-1783	82	75	47.8

Similar increases in the numbers of non-graduating students undoubtedly occurred at all colleges. For example, the one graduating class at King's College between 1776 and 1783, the class of 1776, had originally included eighteen young men, only six of whom actually received the A.B. degree that year. Of the eleven students who had been members of Rhode Island's class of 1778, none graduated in that year.[26]

Among the students who left Nassau Hall without graduating, six or seven transferred to other institutions, compared with only four transfers from the College between 1769 and 1775. Those earlier four had chosen to move in accordance with the normal criterion by which most students selected a college: they decided to complete their educations closer to home. For most of the later transfers, the same consideration applied: Eliphaz Perkins (Class of 1776), a resident of Connecticut, moved to Yale; Jacob Conant (Class of 1777) from Massachusetts went to Harvard; Tristram Lowther (Class of 1777), who had come to Princeton from North Carolina, had been born in New York to an Anglican family among whom were many Loyalists and went from Nassau Hall to King's College before it closed; Richard Bland Lee (Class of 1779), whose older brothers had graduated from the College in 1773 and 1775, returned to his home state of Virginia to attend William and Mary, as did also John Brown (Class of 1778), later United States senator from Kentucky; William Kennedy (Class of 1782) probably transferred to the College of Philadelphia, near his Pennsylvania home. Only Stephen Van Rensselaer, the young patroon, left the College for reasons not clearly related to his place of residence. He transferred to Harvard because his family was concerned for his safety in New Jersey.

As it had since its inception, Nassau Hall attracted students from a greater geographical range during the Revolution than did any other college. Table D identifies the 157 students included in this volume

---

[26] Thomas, *Columbia University Officers and Alumni, 1754-1857*, 103-104; see also Columbia University Alumni Register, 1754-1931 (1932), 989; *Historical Catalogue of Brown University*.

in terms of the provinces/states in which they resided when they entered the College. It also compares the percentage from each province/state with the percentages among the 338 identified students in the classes of 1748 to 1768 and among the 178 identified students in the classes of 1769 to 1775.

TABLE D

RESIDENCE OF CNJ STUDENTS AT TIME OF ENROLLMENT

Province/State	Number 1776-1783	Percent 1776-1783	Percent 1769-1775	Percent 1748-1768
New Hampshire	0	0	1.1	0.6
Massachusetts	2	1.3	6.7	11.5
Connecticut	2	1.3	2.8	12.7
Rhode Island	3	1.9	1.1	0
New York	23	24.6	13.5	14.8
New Jersey	45	28.7	24.7	26.3
Pennsylvania	28 +1	17.8	21.3	11.9
Delaware	0	0	1.1	1.8
Maryland	6	3.8	3.9	5
Virginia	21	13.4	5	2.7
North Carolina	6(7)*	3.8(4.4)*	7.3	1.2
South Carolina	1(2)*	0.6(1.3)*	1.1	0.6
Georgia	1	0.6	0.6	0
Unknown	18	11.5	9.5	11

* The home of George West (Class of 1779) is identified only as "Carolina."

The largest proportion of students continued to hail from the middle colonies or states (New York, New Jersey, and Pennsylvania), with the largest group of all coming from New Jersey. Yet Nassau Hall was far less dependent on its immediate neighbors for students than were any of its sister institutions. The regional comparison in Table E confirms the shift southward in the College's appeal, already well begun by 1775.

TABLE E

PERCENTAGES OF CNJ STUDENTS BY REGION OF ORIGIN AT TIME OF MATRICULATION

	1748-1768	1769-1775	1776-1783
New England	24.8	11.7	4.4
Middle	54.8	60.6	61.1
South	9.5	17.9	22.9
Unknown	11	9.5	11.5

Witherspoon's early decision to seek students and other support in the south, where there was only one competing college, sharply altered the composition of the student body during the revolutionary era. Especially noticeable was the increased number of young men who came to Princeton from Virginia, and for that Witherspoon must share the credit with several alumni, most notably Samuel Stanhope Smith, who became the first rector of the Prince Edward Academy, later Hampden-Sidney College. Prior to his return to Princeton in 1779, Smith prepared a number of Virginians for study at Nassau Hall. Indeed, one student may have qualified for his degree exclusively on the basis of his education at Prince Edward.

Princetonians in the classes of 1776-1783 had been born in any of ten mainland colonies, the British Isles, or the West Indies, and they resided in any of eleven colonies or states when they enrolled. These figures represent only a slightly less expansive attraction to the College since the classes of 1769-1775, when students born in eleven colonies and resident in thirteen had attended.

One predictable aspect of the increased proportion of southerners at the College was that proportionately more students were the sons of men who might be identified as gentlemen—a vague classification incorporating wealthy landowners, planters, gentlemen farmers, and other groups of higher than average standards of living. By no means, however, were all "gentlemen's" sons from the south, and perhaps even more significant was the overall increase among these 157 students in the number whose fathers were professional men or merchants, as compared with the 178 men in the classes of 1769-1775 (See Table F). Although the number of small farmers among the "unknown" group was probably high, and although none of the categories except "gentlemen" automatically connotes the prosperity of the family, the shift in the social origins of Princetonians in the classes between 1769 and 1783 toward the new national elite was profound.

Concomitant with that shift was the change in the number of graduates who went on to become ordained clergymen. Just as proportionately fewer sons of ministers enrolled in the College, so the number of future ministers declined. Table G compares the numbers and percentages of clergymen among the graduates of American colleges between 1776 and 1783 and illustrates the change in the proportions of clergymen among graduates since 1769-1775:

Among the 338 identified alumni of Nassau Hall in the classes of 1748-1768, no less than 158, or 46.7%, were ordained. Among the 178 identified members of the classes of 1769-1775, that proportion

TABLE F

PROFESSION OF FATHERS OF STUDENTS AT CNJ, CLASSES OF 1776-1783
AND PERCENTAGE COMPARISON WITH CLASSES OF 1769-1775

Professions	Number 1776-1783	Percent 1776-1783	Percent 1769-1775
Farmers	23 + 1	14.6	32
Clergymen	13	8.3	14-14.1
Merchants	26	16.6	13
Gentlemen	35	22.3	10.1
Urban occupations*	9	5.7	7.3
Lawyers	6	3.8	3.4
Physicians	4	2.5	1.7
Soldiers	0	0	1.1
Unknown	41	26	17.4-16.8

* Urban occupations include artisans, innkeepers, local officials, engineers, shop owners, etc.

TABLE G

ORDAINED CLERGYMEN AMONG COLLEGE GRADUATES

College	A.B.s, 1776-1783	Number Clergymen, 1776-1783	Percent 1776-1783	Percent 1769-1775
Harvard	265	41	15.5	13.8
Yale	285	63	22.1	36.2
CNJ	82	17	21	48
Rhode Island	30	8*	26.7	31.8
Philadelphia	48	7	14.6	12
King's	7	0†	0	4.5
Dartmouth	91	37	40.6	74‡
Queen's	17	7	41.2	13.3§

* Two members of the Rhode Island Class of 1778 took A.B.s from Yale and were ordained, as were two non-graduating members of the Rhode Island Class of 1780.
† One non-graduating member of the King's class of 1776 was ordained.
‡ 1771-1775 only.
§ 1773-1775 only.

dropped to 40.4%. For the 157 identified Princetonians in the classes of 1776-1783, it plummeted to 11.5%; and this figure includes Daniel Thatcher (Class of 1778), who was ordained although he did not graduate. The dislocations caused by war cannot alone account for such a dramatic change. Shifts in geographical and social origins of the students must also be considered, along with the greater secular influences of both society and the College. It is equally significant that while the number of ministers who had graduated from Nassau Hall shrank, those who were ordained were now overwhelmingly Presbyterian. In its early years, the College educated potential clergymen in a variety of denominations. Of the 158 ministers in the classes of 1748 to 1768, 97 were Presbyterian, 41 Congregationalist, 10 Anglican/ Episcopalian, 6 Dutch Reformed, 3 Baptist, and 1 Lutheran. The 72 ministers in the classes of 1769 to 1775 included 52 Presbyterians, 17 Congregationalists, and 3 Anglican/Episcopalians. But of the 18 clergymen in the classes of 1776 to 1783, all but 1 were Presbyterian; the other was an Episcopal priest. The proportion of Presbyterians among ordained Princetonians thus rose from 61.4% of all clergymen for the classes of 1748-1768, to 72.2% for 1769-1775, to 94.4% for 1776-1783. As W. Frank Craven has pointed out, "insofar as it can be said that the primary function of the College had been to provide a basic education for clergymen, the College was becoming more closely bound than ever before to the service of the Presbyterian Church."[27]

As fewer Princetonians entered the ministry, so the proportion who were "professional men" after they left the College also declined in comparison with the classes of 1769 to 1775, continuing the downward trend since 1748 to 1768. Between 67 and 70 of the 157 identified students in the wartime classes were either clergymen, physicians, or lawyers—between 42.7% and 44.6% as compared with 66% for 1769-1775, and with 74% for 1748-1768. The figures are uncertain because Joseph F. Lane (A.B. 1776) and Samuel Beach (A.B. 1783) may have been lawyers, and Samuel Thane (Class of 1777) may have been a physician. James L. Wilson (A.B. 1776), the one Episcopal clergyman in this group of Princetonians, was also a physician. None of these professions precluded activities in other fields, and the temper of the times led many young men into public service or into mercantile pursuits with the same fervor, sense of accomplishment, or status that had borne their predecessors into the three professions. Certainly Witherspoon encouraged such diversity.

If fewer sons of clergymen were enrolling in the College than had enrolled before, the number and proportion of scholars who were the sons of earlier Princetonians or relatives of College officers or employees increased. In the classes of 1769 to 1775, fourteen students were the children of trustees or presidents, including Witherspoon's three surviving sons. In the revolutionary years, sixteen scholars were close relatives of College officials, including Aaron D. (A.B. 1779) and George Woodruff (A.B. 1783), sons of steward Elias Woodruff, and James Rock (A.B. 1783), the son of the College handyman. Four or

---

[27] W. F. Craven, "On the Writing of a Biographical Dictionary," *APS Proc.*, 122, no. 2 (April 1978), 74.

five Princetonians in the classes of 1769-1775 were the sons of alumni, whereas nine or ten men in the classes of 1776-1783 had fathers who had attended the College, depending upon the identity of Samuel Thane. The six students whose fathers graduated from other colleges included five sons of Yale alumni, compared with seven sons of Yale graduates and one of a Yale non-graduate in the classes of 1769-1775; and one son of a Harvard graduate, the same number as in the earlier seven classes.

Given the lower percentage of aspiring clergymen among Princetonians from the classes of 1776 to 1783, it is a bit surprising that the average age of the 104 of these 157 students whose ages are known was somewhat higher at graduation (or at what would have been graduation for those who left the College without taking a degree) than that of the 141 of the 178 students identified in the classes of 1769 to 1775 whose ages are known. It was not uncommon for young men who hoped to be ordained to have matriculated later in life than most of their classmates. The oldest student among the classes of 1769-1775 was, indeed, a future minister: Samuel Shannon (A.B. 1776), who was over thirty when he left Nassau Hall. The youngest member of these eight classes was John Y. Noel (A.B. 1777), a mere 15 years of age at the end of his college course. Yet Shannon was younger than the oldest Princetonian who had graduated between 1769 and 1775, and Noel was older than the youngest of that earlier group. The overall average age at graduation of the students in the later eight classes for whom ages are known was more than 22 years, compared with just 21 years for the seven pre-war classes. For the classes of 1776 to 1783, the average age of the twelve future ministers whose ages are known was 24.5 years at graduation, a full year higher than the average for ministers in the classes of 1769-1775. The changes were not in any case so profound as to have made Nassau Hall unusual among American colleges for the age of its students, since graduation at or around 21 years was becoming the rule throughout the country.

For all the disruptions occasioned by the war, the College of New Jersey had one notable advantage over most of the other colleges in that Witherspoon retained the presidency and was thus able to maintain a relatively stable administration in firm hands for the duration of the crisis. Only President Manning of Rhode Island College likewise began and survived the war in office. Further, Witherspoon at first had the almost constant assistance of Professor Houston, who in 1779 also became treasurer of the College. And in the winter of that year, Samuel Stanhope Smith joined the faculty as Professor of Moral Philosophy and his father-in-law's right hand. This continuity and

Witherspoon's energetic leadership were crucial to the survival of the institution in the face of many dangers.

Threatened by mutinous militiamen in Philadelphia in June 1783, the Continental Congress sought refuge in Princeton, ultimately making Nassau Hall the temporary capital of the United States. At a time when most members were considering a permanent site for the seat of government, some delegates were impressed by the little college town, the "Montpelier of America,"[28] with a climate considered to be much more healthy than that of Philadelphia.[29] Benjamin Rush wryly expected that the air in Princeton, which "used to be famed *only* for curing consumption," might actually be "efficacious in curing a species of *madness* called congro-mania."[30] But some members were not at all happy with their new location. James Madison (A.B. 1771), future first president of the College's alumni association, waived loyalty to alma mater to complain of the "scanty accommodations," the overcrowding, and the impossibility of getting any work done.[31] By autumn the Congress had decided to turn elsewhere, but before leaving, the members adjourned to attend the commencement exercises of 1783, where they were joined by General Washington and the representatives of two European governments.

That distinguished company was something of a symbol, both of the College's gradual recovery and of the significance of the institution and its president for their time. Witherspoon was no longer in Congress, but he continued to serve the public and the church even as he conducted classes at Tusculum, Smith having taken up residence in the president's house. Among the 157 young men educated under Witherspoon's direction in the classes of 1776-1783, 52 saw some form of military service in support of the American cause, a much higher proportion than that among contemporary Harvard men or Yale men.[32] Three Princetonians from the classes of 1776-1783 were professed Loyalists, to make a total of only thirteen self-proclaimed Tories among the 673 Princetonians in the classes since 1748.

After leaving the College, members of the classes of 1776-1783 established their primary residences in at least fifteen states or territories and in Great Britain. This represented a somewhat less extensive distribution than that for the classes of 1769 to 1775, whose members resided in nineteen states or territories, the District of Columbia, the British Isles, and the West Indies. It nevertheless continued the tend-

---

28 *LMCC*, VIII, 841. 29 Ibid., VII, 235.
30 Ibid., 217n. 31 Ibid., 229, 282, 302-303.
32 Morison, *Three Centuries of Harvard*, 148. Morison explains that "Harvard rendered her proper service to the country in council." See also Kelley, *Yale*, 97.

ency among Princetonians to be a much more peripatetic group than the alumni of other colleges. Eleven of these men later served in the United States Senate, fourteen in the House of Representatives, four in the Continental Congress, and three in the Constitutional Convention of 1787. Among them they held five positions in the federal cabinet and filled at least 120 major state or national offices.

In spite of the ordeal of war, Nassau Hall, its faculty, and its president had upheld the standards of excellence and public service established with the College in 1746. By 1783 the four-story fieldstone building would bear the scars of the Revolution for years to come; the treasury would continue seriously diminished. But as enrollments grew and donations slowly increased, the efforts of Witherspoon and the trustees to restore the institution gradually succeeded. Over the next several years the management of the College incrasingly would devolve upon Professor Smith, as the aging and ailing president retired to Tusculum. But the transition was smooth, and the record of the sons of Nassau Hall would continue as one of high distinction in the new nation.

In the commencement exercises of 1780, three graduates joined in a rhetorical exercise of their own composition that proclaimed the unshaken confidence of students, alumni, and friends in the College of New Jersey. Boasting of the achievements, past and future, of Princetonians, Samuel W. Venable as "Cleander" predicted that the "highest merit" of the "greatest scholars" of Nassau Hall would be to *write well what we have acted.*

ABBREVIATIONS AND SHORT TITLES
FREQUENTLY USED

AASP Proceedings of American Antiquarian Society

A/C Annals of Congress

Adams Papers L. Butterfield et al., eds., *Diary and Autobiography of John Adams*

AHR American Historical Review

Alexander, *Princeton* S. D. Alexander, *Princeton College during the Eighteenth Century*

als autographed letter signed

APS Proc. American Philosophical Society Proceedings

APS Trans. American Philosophical Society Transactions

BDAC Biographical Directory of the American Congress

Beam, *Whig Soc.* J. N. Beam, *The American Whig Society*

Bentley, *Diaries Diary of William Bentley*

Bradford Journal Ms Journal of William Bradford (A.B. 1772) PHi

Butterfield, *Rush Letters* L. H. Butterfield, ed., *Letters of Benjamin Rush*

Calhoun Papers Robert L. Meriwether et al., ed., *The Papers of John C. Calhoun*, 2 vols. (1959-)

Cal. Va. St. Papers Calendar of Virginia State Papers

Clay Papers James P. Hopkins et al., ed., *Papers of Henry Clay*, 2 vols. (1959-1961)

Clinton Papers H. Hastings and J. A. Holden, eds., *Public Papers of George Clinton*

CNJ College of New Jersey

Col. Rec. Ga. Colonial Records of Georgia

Col. Rec. N.C. W. N. Saunders, ed., *Colonial Records of North Carolina*

Col. Rec. Pa. Colonial Records of Pennsylvania

CSmH Huntington Library, San Marino, California

CtHi Connecticut Historical Society

CtY Yale University Library

DAB A. Johnson and D. Malone, eds., *Dictionary of American Biography*

Davis, *Essays* J. S. Davis, *Essays on the Earlier History of American Corporation* (1917)

Del. Arch. Delaware Archives

Dexter, *Yale Biographies* F. B. Dexter, *Biographical Sketches of the Graduates of Yale College*

DLC Library of Congress

DN United States Department of the Navy Archives

DNA National Archives, Washington, D.C.

Doc. Hist. Fed. Elec. M. Jensen and R. A. Becker, *The Documentary History of the First Federal Elections, 1788-1790*

Doc. Hist. First Fed. Cong. L. G. DePauw et al., *Documentary History of the First Federal Congress of the United States of America*

DS United States Department of State Archives

Elliot's Debates Jonathan Elliot, *Debates in the Several State Conventions on the Adoption of the Federal Constitution*

First Census North, *Heads of Families . . . 1790*

Fithian Journal, I J. R. Williams, ed., *Philip Vickers Fithian, Journal and Letters, 1767-1774*

Fithian Journal, II   R. G. Albion and L. Dodson, eds., *Philip Vickers Fithian: Journal, 1775-1776*

Foote, *Sketches, N.C.*   W. H. Foote, *Sketches of North Carolina, Historical and Biographical*

Foote, *Sketches, Va.*   W. H. Foote, *Sketches of Virginia, Historical and Biographical*

Force, *Am. Arch.*   P. Force, ed., *American Archives . . . a Documentary History*

Franklin Papers   L. W. Labaree et al., eds., *The Papers of Benjamin Franklin*

GEU   Emory University Library

GHQ   Georgia Historical Quarterly

Giger, Memoirs   G. M. Giger, MS Memoirs of the College of New Jersey, PUA

GMNJ   Genealogical Magazine of New Jersey

GU   University of Georgia Library

Hageman, *History*   J. F. Hageman, *History of Princeton and Its Institutions*

Hamilton Papers   H. C. Syrett and J. E. Cooke, eds., *Papers of Alexander Hamilton*

Heitman   F. B. Heitman, *Historical Register of Officers of the Continental Army* . . . (1893) (1914)

Hening, *Statutes*   W. W. Hening, ed., *The Statutes at Large . . . of Virginia*

InHi   Indiana Historical Society

Jay Papers   R. B. Morris et al., eds., *John Jay: The Making of a Revolutionary . . . Unpublished Papers, 1745-1780*

JCC   W. C. Ford et al., eds., *Journals of the Continental Congress, 1774-1789*

Jefferson MSS   Microfilm collection, Papers of Thomas Jefferson (issuing authority)

Jefferson Papers   J. P. Boyd et al., eds., *Papers of Thomas Jefferson*

JPHS   Journal of Presbyterian Historical Society

Kegley, *Va. Frontier*   F. B. Kegley, *Kegley's Virginia Frontier*

KSHS Reg.... Register of the Kentucky State Historical Society

KyU   University of Kentucky Library

LCHSPA   Lancaster County (Pa.) Historical Society Papers and Addresses

LMCC   E. C. Burnett, ed., *Letters of Members of the Continental Congress*

LN   New Orleans Public Library

LU   University of Louisiana Library

Maclean, *History*   J. Maclean, *History of the College of New Jersey*

Madison MSS   Microfilm collection, Papers of James Madison (issuing authority)

Madison Papers   W. T. Hutchinson and W.M.E. Rachal et al., eds., *Papers of James Madison*

Md. Arch.   *Archives of Maryland*

Md. Wills   A. W. Burns, comp., Abstracts of Maryland Wills

MCCCNY   Minutes of the Common Council of the City of New York

MCCCNY, 1675-1776   Minutes of the Common Council of the City of New York, 1675-1776

MdHi   Maryland Historical Society

Md. Leg. Hist. Proj.   Maryland Legislative Historical Project, E. C. Papenfuse and D. W. Jordan, Principal Investigators, Hall of Records, Annapolis, Md.

MHi   Massachusetts Historical Society

MHM   Maryland Historical Magazine

MHS Coll.   *Massachusetts Historical Society Collections*

MHSP   Massachusetts Historical Society Publications

MiD   Detroit Public Library

Min. Gen. Assem., 1789-1820   Minutes of the General Assembly of the Presbyterian Church in the U.S.A., 1789-1820 (1847)

ERROR

Min. Gen. Assem., 1821-1835 Minutes of the General Assembly of the Presbyterian Church in the U.S.A. 1821-1835 (1847)

MiU University of Michigan Library

MiU-C William L. Clements Library, University of Michigan

MoHi Missouri Historical Society

MWA American Antiquarian Society

N New York State Library, Albany

Nc North Carolina State Library/Archives

NCHGR North Carolina Historical and Genealogical Records

NCHR North Carolina Historical Review

NcD Duke University Library

NcSal Rowan Public Library, Salisbury, North Carolina

NcU University of North Carolina Library

NEHGR New England Historical and Genealogical Register

NEQ New England Quarterly

NhD Dartmouth College Library

NHi New York Historical Society

N.H. St. Pap. New Hampshire State Papers

N.H. Town Pap. New Hampshire Town Papers

NIC Cornell University Library

Nj New Jersey Library/Archives

NJA New Jersey Archives

NjHi New Jersey Historical Society

NJHSP New Jersey Historical Society Proceedings

NjP Princeton University Library

NjPT Princeton Theological Seminary Library

NjR Rutgers Library, State University, New Brunswick, New Jersey

N.J. Wills NJA, Vols. XXIII-XLI

NN New York Public Library

NNC Columbia University Library

NNG General Theological Seminary, New York City

N.Y. Arch. B. Fernow, ed., *New York Archives*

NYGBR New York Genealogical and Biographical Record

NYHS Coll. New York Historical Society Collections

N.Y. Wills Abstracts of Wills, NYHS Coll., 1892-1906

OCHP Historical and Philosophical Society of Ohio, Cincinnati

OAHSQ Ohio Archaeological and Historical Society Quarterly

Pa. Arch. Pennsylvania Archives

Patterson Acct. Bk. Thomas Patterson, Account Book, 1774-1776, AM 77-98. Gen. MSS [bound], NjP

PCC Microfilm Papers of the Continental Congress (issuing authority)

PGM Pennsylvania Genealogical Magazine

PHC Haverford College Library

PHi Historical Society of Pennsylvania

PMHB Pennsylvania Magazine of History and Biography

PPAmP American Philosophical Society Library

PPiU University of Pittsburgh Library

PPL Library Company of Philadelphia

PPPrHi Presbyterian Historical Society

Princetonians, 1748-1768 J. McLachlan, *Princetonians, 1748-1768: A Biographical Dictionary*

PSQ Political Science Quarterly

PUA Princeton University Archives

Rec. Pres. Church Records of the Presbyterian Church . . . 1706-1788

Rec. St. Conn. C. J. Hoadly and L. W. Labaree, eds., *Public Records of the State of Connecticut*

Rev. Rec. Ga. Revolutionary Records of Georgia

Rush, *Autobiography* G. W. Corner, ed., *Autobiography of Benjamin Rush*

Sabin J. Sabin, *Bibliotheca Americana*

Sabine, *Loyalists* L. Sabine, *Biographical Sketches of the Loyalists of the American Revolution*

ScCleU Clemson University, Clemson, South Carolina

SCHGM South Carolina Historical and Genealogical Magazine

SCHM South Carolina Historical Magazine

ScU University of South Carolina Library

Sh-C R. Shoemaker and M. Francis Cooper, comps., *American Bibliography . . . Imprints, 1820-1829*

Sh-Sh R. R. Shaw and R. H. Shoemaker, comps., *American Bibliography . . . Imprints, 1801-1829*

Sibley's Harvard Graduates J. L. Sibley and C. K. Shipton, *Biographical Sketches of Those Who Attended Harvard College*

Som. Cnty. Hist. Quart. Somerset County Historical Quarterly (N.J.)

Sprague, *Annals* W. B. Sprague, *Annals of the American Pulpit*

St. Rec. N.C. W. Clark, ed., *State Records of North Carolina, 1777-1790*

STE C. K. Shipton and J. E. Mooney, *National Index of American Imprints Through 1800: The Short Title Evans*

Stiles, *Itineraries* F. B. Dexter, *Extracts from the Itineraries . . . of Ezra Stiles*

Stiles, *Literary Diary* F. B. Dexter, ed., *The Literary Diary of Ezra Stiles*

Ms Steward's accounts Ms Records of the CNJ Steward, 1773-1776, PUA

Stryker, *Off. Reg.* William S. Stryker, *Official Register of the Officers and Men of New Jersey in the Revolutionary War* (1911) (1967)

Susquehanna Papers J. P. Boyd and R. J. Taylor, eds., *Susquehanna Company Papers*

T Tennessee State Library and Archives

THi Tennessee Historical Society

THM Tennessee Historical Magazine

Thorp, *Eighteen from Princeton* W. Thorp, ed., *Lives of Eighteen from Princeton*

Tyler's Quart. Tyler's Quarterly Historical and Genealogical Magazine

Van Buren MSS Microfilm Papers of Martin Van Buren

VHi Virginia Historical Society

VHM Vineland Historical Magazine

ViU University of Virginia Library

VMHB Virginia Magazine of History and Biography

Washington Diaries (Jackson) D. Jackson, ed., *Washington Diaries, 1749-1770*

Washington Diaries J. C. Fitzpatrick, ed., *The Diaries of George Washington, 1748-1799*

Washington MSS Microfilm Collection, Papers of George Washington (issuing authority)

Washington Writings J. C. Fitzpatrick, ed., *Writings of George Washington . . . 1745-1799*

Webster, MS Brief Sketches R. Webster, Brief Sketches of Early Presbyterian Ministers, PPPrHi

Wertenbaker, *Princeton* T. J. Wertenbaker, *Princeton, 1746-1896*

Wharton, *Dip. Corresp.* F. Wharton, ed., *Revolutionary Diplomatic Correspondence*

WHi Wisconsin Historical Society

Wickes, *Hist. of Medicine N.J.* S.
  Wickes, *History of Medicine in
  New Jersey and the Medical
  Men from the Settlement of the
  Province to A.D. 1800*
Williams, *Academic Honors* John

Rogers Williams, ed., *Academic
  Honors in Princeton University,
  1748-1902*
WMQ William and Mary Quarterly
*WPHM Western Pennsylvania His-
  torical Magazine*

CLASS OF 1776

Nathaniel Alexander, A.B.

John Armstrong, Jr.

James Beekman, Jr.

Bartholomew Scott Calvin
  Shawuskukhkung
  or Wilted Grass

Lardner Clark

William Coates

William Richardson Davie, A.B.

Jonathan Dayton, A.B.

Nicholas Dean

Benjamin Erwin, A.B.

George Faitoute, A.B.

John Evans Finley, A.B.

Joseph Washington
  Henderson, A.B.

Robert Jenkins Henry

Robert Rosbrough Henry, A.B.

David Hyslop

William Johnes

Andrew Johnston

Samuel King

John Wilkes Kittera, A.B.

Joseph Flavius Lane, A.B.

John Leake, A.B.

Charles Lewis

Henry Philip Livingston, A.B.

John McAllister

Moses McCandless

Samuel McConkey, A.B.

Robert McCrea

Samuel McGee (MacGee)

Robert Martin (Marton,
  Marten)

Richard Mount, A.B.

Elisha Neil

Benjamin Olden

Thomas Parker

Eliphaz Perkins

Cyrus Pierson, A.B.

John Pintard, A.B.

William Ramsay

James Ramsey (Ramsay), A.B.

Archibald Campbell Read, A.B.

Aaron Rhea, A.B.

Joseph Rue, A.B.

John Rutherford, A.B.	Benjamin Brearley Stockton
Nathaniel Welshard Semple, A.B.	William H. Vernon, A.B.
Samuel Shannon, A.B.	Nehemiah Wade, Jr., A.B.
Benjamin Parker Snowden, A.B.	James Lewis Wilson, A.B.

Nathaniel Alexander

NATHANIEL ALEXANDER, A.B., physician and public official, was born on March 5, 1756, probably in that part of Anson County, North Carolina that became Mecklenburg County in 1762, the son of Moses Alexander and his wife, Sarah Taylor Alexander. The father is believed to have migrated from Cecil County, Maryland about 1750 and is known later to have served as sheriff of Mecklenburg County and as lieutenant colonel in its militia against the Regulators. Where the son prepared for college cannot be said, but Queen's Museum in Charlotte is a likely choice. In the incomplete records of the College, Nathaniel is first named in the steward's accounts as a member of the junior class in November 1774. His name does not appear among the members of either of the literary societies.

After leaving the College in the fall of 1776, Alexander presumably studied medicine, though just when, where, and with whom have not been established. A historian of his county has identified him as a physician but suggests that he may never have practiced. He did, however, see military service in a medical capacity. The dates given by several authorities are 1778-1782. Confirmation, at least for a part of this time, is found in the record of action by the North Carolina Assembly on a petition of doctors Robert Brownfield and Nathaniel Alexander presented in April 1784 by Benjamin Hawkins (Class of 1777). The House finally resolved to allot to each of them 1,000 acres "in consideration of their steady and faithful service rendered the militia of this State while acting as Surgeons in the Continental Hospitals in the Southern Department, such lands to be alloted within the bounds of the land laid off for the Continental Officers and Soldiers." The commissioners settling accounts for the North Carolina Line in the following winter allowed each of them £547 17s 10d.

After the war Alexander is said to have moved to High Hills on the Santee in South Carolina and subsequently to have returned to Charlotte for practice, but the available records are none too helpful on this question. In any case, he was certainly in North Carolina in 1797 when he sat for Mecklenburg County in the House of Commons. By then he had already married Margaret Polk, the daughter of Colonel Thomas Polk. In 1801 and 1802 Alexander was a member of the state senate. He next was elected to the United States House of Representatives, where he served from March 4, 1803 to November 1805. He left his seat in the Congress then to accept the governorship of North Carolina, which became vacant with the election of James Turner to the United States Senate.

Turner, an intensely partisan Republican, had been a controversial governor. By selecting Alexander, apparently in a party caucus, the Republicans went far toward restoring the governorship to bipartisan esteem. Elected by the legislature against a Federalist contestant in 1805, he was reelected without opposition in 1806. And in 1807 the Federalist Fayetteville *Minerva* conceded that he was "an ornament to the predominant party, and, like few of them, a scholar and a true patriot."

Alexander's administrations were not particularly memorable. He has been credited with support for education and with advocacy of internal improvements. But the high praise he received from Federalists may, in part, have been due to his disagreement with his own party over the hotly debated Court Law of 1806. A Republican measure, it created superior courts in all of the state's counties and thereby reduced the influence of six district towns where the Federalist-dominated legal profession was concentrated. Alexander argued that the new system would stifle the growth of important cities and drive lawyers from the state. In the election of 1807, therefore, he had the support of many Federalists. But he lost the election because his Federalist opponent was supported by the Republican majority in the legislature.

Alexander died on March 7, 1808. Since 1797 he had been an active Mason. He was buried beside his wife, who had died without issue in 1806, in the "Old Cemetery" in Charlotte.

SOURCES: R. W. Ramsey, *Carolina Cradle* (1964), 51, 55, 159; A. M. Stafford, *Index to Alexander Family of Md.* (n.d.); C. C. Alexander and V. W. Alexander, *Alexander Kin* (n.d.,), 15, 18, 19; *Col. Rec. N.C.*, VII, 821, 842; VIII, 535, 674; IX, 574; alumni file, MS Steward's accounts, PUA; J. B. Alexander, *Hist. of Mecklenburg Cnty.* (1902) 98; *St. Rec. N.C.*, XIX, 517, 533-34 ("steady and faithful service"), 536; XVII, 190, 191; J. M. Toner, *Med. Men of the Amer. Rev.* (1970), 322, 380; *First Census, S.C.*, 18; A. K. Gregorie, *Hist. of Sumter Cnty.* (1954), 60; D. H. Gilpatrick, *Jeffersonian Democracy in N.C.* (1931), 133-34 ("an ornament"), 149; J. H. Wheeler, *Hist. Sketches of N.C.* (1851), II, 267; S. A. Ashe, *Hist. of N.C.* (1908), II, 427; G. G. Johnson, *Ante-Bellum N.C.* (1937), 644; E. W. Bridges, *Masonic Governors of N.C.* (1937), 131-33; A. Henderson, *North Carolina* (1941), I, 534; *NCHR*, 2 (1925), 427; *BDAC*; H. T. Lefler and A. R. Newsome, *North Carolina* (1953), 286, 666. See William H. Vernon (A.B. 1776) for commencement of 1776.

WFC

John Armstrong, Jr.

JOHN ARMSTRONG, JR., soldier, public official, author, was born on November 25, 1758, in Carlisle, Cumberland County, Pennsylvania, the son of John and Rebecca Lyon Armstrong, Irish immigrants. John

John Armstrong, Jr., Class of 1776
ATTRIBUTED TO JOHN WESLEY JARVIS

Armstrong, Sr., a trained civil engineer and surveyor and one of Pennsylvania's heroes in the French and Indian War, was a general officer in the Continental Army, a member of the Continental Congress, and a trustee of Dickinson College.

John Armstrong, Jr. was prepared for college at the Latin school opened in Carlisle by Henry Makinly in 1770. He was a member of the junior class at Nassau Hall from 1774 to 1775, but he abandoned his studies to pursue a military career. After returning to Pennsylvania from the ill-fated expedition against Quebec late in 1775, Armstrong enlisted in a company of Associators. As a captain, he then joined the staff of Colonel James Potter of the state militia, serving in that capacity until the end of 1776, when one of his father's former subordinates, General Hugh Mercer, promoted him to major and took him on as an aide-de-camp.

In January 1777 Armstrong was with Mercer at the battle of Princeton. Both men were wounded, but Armstrong was able to carry his mortally injured commander to a nearby house and nurse him until

British troops approached. Mercer then ordered him to rejoin the army. The general, taken prisoner, died two days later, attended by George Lewis (Class of 1775).

General Washington expected Armstrong's father to find a place in his own command for the young major, but another influential Pennsylvanian, General Arthur St. Clair, interceded. With his help, Armstrong was named aide-de-camp to General Horatio Gates, with whom he remained a lifelong friend and with whom he went to Fort Ticonderoga and participated in the northern campaign. When Gates removed Benedict Arnold from his command in October 1777, Armstrong was assigned to guard the dismissed general. During the crucial battle of Freeman's Farm at Saratoga on October 7, Armstrong could do no more than try to catch Arnold, who had slipped his arrest and was heroically leading the American forces. Ordered by Gates to bring the escaped officer back to camp, he chased Arnold into almost every hazard of the battlefield but was unable to recapture him until the general's horse was killed and Arnold himself was wounded in the leg.

At the battle of Monmouth in June 1778, Armstrong was presumably able to devote more attention to the enemy. He remained with Gates until 1780, when the general headed south and Armstrong left his staff to become adjutant of the army in the southern department. While Gates was suffering a disastrous defeat at Camden, South Carolina, Armstrong was seriously ill nearby. When he recovered, he resumed his place as Gates's aide in the Hudson Valley of New York, where he remained for the rest of the war.

In October 1782, when Armstrong applied for appointment as secretary of the Pennsylvania Supreme Executive Council, politics in the state were particularly stormy. The conservative Republican Party, trying to elect John Dickinson president of the council, was busy attacking former president Joseph Reed (A.B. 1757), leader of the Constitutional Party. Armstrong initially took Reed's part and helped to write the tracts against Dickinson that were signed by "Valerius." Yet in letters to his father, he disingenuously wondered who "Valerius" might be. Anonymous political writing was one of Armstrong's primary occupations for as long as he lived, and a tendency to deny its authorship was one of his salient characteristics.

"Valerius" notwithstanding, Dickinson was elected and Armstrong pondered his own career. "Law," he conceded, "has its promises, but not without extreme labor—drudgery . . . to succeed you must be a Student for life." That prospect had little appeal. As to trade, he believed that he was unsuited because "I want ye love of wealth." For the time being, in February 1783, he was ready to take his father's advice and be a farmer. But he was diverted by a crisis in the army.

Alarmed at the prospect that provisions to pay their rightful pensions might not be made, a group of young Continental officers gathered around Gates, including Armstrong and William Barber (Class of 1777), decided that neither the polite appeals to Congress of previous months nor the efforts of Washington in their behalf were adequate. In an anonymous letter to their colleagues, they called for a meeting at the headquarters in Newburgh, New York on March 10.

Written by Armstrong, this first "Newburgh Letter" demanded an end to the "milk and water style" of earlier memorials. Brilliantly venomous, it implied that if Congress did not satisfy legitimate demands, the officers might refuse to fight if the war continued or, even more ominous, might refuse to lay down their arms if the war ended. When he learned of the letter, Washington moved quickly to prevent any irrevocable action. His own call for a meeting brought a second anonymous letter, also written by Armstrong, that was milder in tone and subtly designed to force the commander in chief into the circle of dissidents. The general refused to be trapped, however, and his masterful handling allowed the situation to cool.

Fourteen years later Washington generously assured Armstrong that he had not known at the time who wrote the "Newburgh Letters" and that he had come to believe that, whoever he was, the author's intentions had been noble even if his methods had been subject to misinterpretation. But in March 1783 Armstrong's part in the affair at Newburgh was common knowledge at headquarters, and there was no doubt in the general's own mind that the new nation had narrowly missed a crisis of the first magnitude. In fact, Armstrong's authorship was so well known that the implicit threat of a military coup, whether it had been serious or meant only to prod Congress into action, haunted his political career ever afterward.

Whatever the true import of the "Newburgh Letters," Armstrong's contempt for the Continental Congress was unquestionable. From Philadelphia in the spring of 1783, he wrote of the foibles of the "grand Sanhedrin of the Nation" with scorn, and Washington, "the Illustrissimo of the age," did not escape his derision. Meanwhile, he switched his political allegiances to the incumbent party in Pennsylvania and thereby obtained the post of secretary of the council as a Republican.

When the "Second Pennamite-Yankee War," violent clashes between settlers from Pennsylvania and Connecticut in the Wyoming Valley, erupted in the summer of 1784, the Pennsylvania Executive

Council appointed Armstrong a colonel of militia and sent him with four hundred men and a council member to quell the disorder. President Dickinson had opposed Armstrong's selection, warning that the secretary would not be as impartial an officer as the mission required, and Armstrong fulfilled Dickinson's expectations by tricking the Connecticut settlers into surrendering and then marching them off in chains to the strains of "Yankee Doodle." The violence ceased temporarily, but Armstrong was back with more men by September as the adjutant general of the state, an appointment that was also made against Dickinson's better judgment. Opposing all leniency toward the Yankees, Armstrong secured the area around Forty Fort until November. When he left, the Yankees rose once more and destroyed his fortifications in a last burst of violence before the "war" ended quietly. Among the settlers from Connecticut, Armstrong's name was an epithet for several years.

Armstrong was selected to represent Pennsylvania in the Annapolis Convention of September 1786, which, like all but one of his fellow delegates, he failed to attend. He lost a bid for a seat in Congress that year, but he was elected in the next contest, on March 24, 1787. He was considered but not chosen to sit in the Federal Convention of 1787. Of the Constitution it produced he generally approved, although he believed that some modifications were needed, as he confided to Gates, to reduce the government's tendency toward "foolish and feeble" popular democracy.

On October 16, 1787, soon after Armstrong vacated the office of secretary of the state council, Congress chose him as one of the three original judges for the Northwest Territory. He never served in that capacity, however, and resigned the appointment in January 1788, explaining privately that "a little in society is much more desirable than a great deal in a desert." He had been reelected to Congress in November, and his party then briefly promoted him as a candidate for the first United States Senate, until his obvious unpopularity, especially among farmers, led to the withdrawal of his name. He was then mentioned as a candidate for the House of Representatives, but doubts about his Federalist orthodoxy and his ability to win votes soon ended that project as well. Had he been chosen, he later said, he would have refused to serve in that body of "cormorants." Instead, he was reelected to the final Continental Congress on November 14, 1788.

On January 19, 1789, Armstrong married Alida Livingston, the daughter of Judge Robert Livingston of Clermont, New York, sister of Chancellor Robert R. Livingston and Edward Livingston (A.B.

1781), and sister-in-law of Morgan Lewis (A.B. 1773). He then moved to Dutchess County, New York, where he concentrated on cultivating his farm and was content merely to observe public affairs. He sneered at the pomp that surrounded Washington's first inaugural and expressed his conviction that New York society would gain immeasurably by the anticipated removal of Congress to another city. Yet he remained a Federalist longer than his Livingston in-laws. After their merger with the anti-Federalist Clintons in 1792, Armstrong adopted the name "Timothy Tickler" to publish attacks on Robert R. Livingston, and then convinced his suspicious victim that the true author had been John Jay.

Armstrong invested in some business ventures, such as William Duer's Connecticut Manufacturing Society, in which he bought fifty shares of stock for $5,000 in 1792. He declined Washington's offer of the post of Surveyor of the Revenue in New York in 1793, and the commission went instead to Nicholas Fish (Class of 1777). Two and one-half years later, Armstrong was among the men considered by Washington to replace Timothy Pickering as Secretary of War; but the office eventually went to James McHenry. In 1798 Armstrong and his close friend Ambrose Spencer, one of the most powerful men in New York politics, finally followed the Livingstons into the Republican ranks. That conversion, which he formalized with anonymous newspaper critiques of the Alien and Sedition Laws, signaled Armstrong's emergence from political retirement. With Spencer's help he was elected to the United States Senate from New York in 1800, a beneficiary of the Clinton-Livingston alliance and the Republican triumph.

For the three remaining years of Clinton-Livingston harmony, Armstrong worked faithfully to diminish the influence of Vice President Aaron Burr (A.B. 1772). In January 1802, claiming ill health, he even resigned from the Senate to make room for DeWitt Clinton, a maneuver that was roundly condemned by Burr's friends. When Clinton himself resigned in 1803, Armstrong was appointed to complete the term, but not before his enemies had made sure that his role in the "Newburgh Letters" was fresh in the public mind.

Although Armstrong tended to side with the Clintonians against the Livingstons, that tendency was not sufficiently pronounced by 1804 to prevent Robert R. Livingston from having Armstrong made his successor as minister to France. The Senate's consent to the appointment was grudgingly given, for some members, including John Quincy Adams, considered Armstrong one of the "most unprincipled public men" in the nation. Armstrong had long had reservations about American ties to any foreign nation, especially France, and his behavior as minister in no way concealed his personal opinions.

Two issues dominated Armstrong's diplomatic career. The first was the American effort to obtain clear title to West Florida and to add East Florida to the national domain. The Jefferson administration hoped that France would support American ambitions against Spain in that area. Armstrong took a hard line from the beginning, refusing to pay for French help and advising the administration to be as belli-cose as necessary to compel Spanish concessions. He even suggested that the United States seize Texas as a bargaining chip. He and James Bowdoin (Harvard 1771), the minister to Spain, were supposed to work in tandem, but Bowdoin disliked Armstrong and suspected him of conniving with French officials to obtain land in the Floridas for him-self. Their feud did nothing to help negotiations.

To the chagrin of those in Washington who were less willing to use threats than Armstrong, Jefferson named the minister one of his special commisisoners to treat with Spain in February 1806. The Sen-ate voted 15-15 on the nomination, which passed only because Vice President George Clinton broke the tie. John Quincy Adams found the appointment "one of the most disgraceful acts of Mr. Jefferson's administration." No progress whatsoever was made in the Spanish-American talks until Jefferson adopted a less belligerent position and the war in Europe forced Madrid to be more conciliatory.

The French had proven unhelpful to the Americans throughout these machinations, and Armstrong was therefore doubly rigid in dealing with Napoleon's government over the second issue, the Con-tinental System and its pernicious effects on American trade. Officials in Paris found the American minister "morose, captious, and petu-lant," for he would neither socialize at court nor deal face to face with the foreign office. Moreover, Armstrong resented what he considered the weakness of the administration's posture, as defined by Secretary of State James Madison (A.B. 1771), and was eager to force France to remove its restrictions on American commerce. His cold and stern protests brought some relief to captured ships but no change in policy. In fact, as relations deteriorated, Armstrong's enemies found reasons, most of them unfair, to blame him.

In July 1808 Madison instructed Armstrong to make what amounted to a threat of war unless offending French decrees were rescinded. But the minister did not believe that such a threat was credible in the light of previous policy and he refused to deliver the message. In the spring of 1809, Madison, as president, ordered Armstrong and his counter-part in London to advise both governments informally that the

United States might declare war against whichever of them was the last to lift its anti-American regulations. Armstrong not only delivered that message, he made it a formal, written promise, thus going far beyond what Madison had intended.

In August 1810 Napoleon and his foreign minister, the Duc de Cadore, responded to the passage of Macon's Bill No. 2 (named for Nathaniel Macon, Class of 1778) by insinuating that France would void its Rambouillet Decree, which authorized the seizure of American ships in French harbors. The emperor's plan was designed to persuade the United States to reimpose its nonintercourse policy against Britain unless London agreed to lift the Orders in Council that interfered with neutral trade and thus to provoke an Anglo-American war. Eager to leave Paris, Armstrong reported that Cadore's letter was proof that his mission was accomplished, and he returned to the United States as a hero. His failure to explain the motives of the French government and his precipitate acceptance of Napoleon's demarche as a firm promise contributed to the myth that France had met American demands while England had not and thus helped foster the Anglophobia that led to war in 1812.

His reputation enhanced by the supposed victory of the Cadore letter, Armstrong moved to secure his political future. From such well-informed sources as Morgan Lewis, Madison learned that Armstrong was plotting with the Clintons and with Samuel and Robert Smith (A.B. 1781) to unseat the president in 1812 and to run for vice-president with George Clinton, or even for president himself. Certainly, Armstrong was involved in an attempt to depose the "Virginia Dynasty," but when the Clintons supported rechartering the Bank of the United States in 1811 and then opposed war with England in 1812, he returned to the fold of Madison's supporters.

On July 6, 1812, Armstrong was appointed a brigadier general in the United States Army and given command of the defense of New York City. His diligence and success in that post led to his candidacy for secretary of war at the end of the year. Madison tried hard to fill the office with someone else, preferably Secretary of State James Monroe. But when Monroe and several others declined, the president reluctantly decided to strengthen his cabinet by including a pro-war, anti-Clinton New Yorker with military experience. That left Armstrong.

It was not a popular appointment, however. Armstrong's abrasive personality and reputation for intrigue and cynicism made him many enemies. The nomination "rubed hard in the Senate," but it passed by a vote of 18-15. Armstrong was installed at the War Department in

February 1813. His ability to recognize talented officers was a great asset to the nation. Through his personal attention, such men as Andrew Jackson, Winfield Scott, and Jacob Brown were promoted to important commands. Further, he did his best to protect the army supply system against favoritism and corruption and he supported efforts to recruit black soldiers over the powerful objections of southern congressmen. But Armstrong's political ambitions were not ended, and it was his attempt to maneuver himself into position to succeed Madison in 1816 that dominated his conduct in office.

From the first, that meant a bitter personal contest for power with Secretary of State Monroe. It also directly affected the course of the war, for Armstrong hoped to become a lieutenant general and to achieve the kind of battlefield victory that would catapult him to the White House. He therefore did his best to undermine the chances for advancement of possible competitors for supreme command, including William Henry Harrison and eventually even Jackson. He meddled in the making of strategy and in tactical decisions. In 1813 he assumed personal command in the north and then left his ill-conceived plan to take Montreal to the execution of two incompetent generals who also hated one another. Reprimanded by Madison for violating the chain of command, he sullenly refused to take any initiative without explicit orders; and that attitude, combined with his obstinate refusal to believe that the British would attack Washington, meant that he failed completely to prepare the capital's defense. The burning of the city in August 1814 was, in many quarters, blamed entirely on the secretary of war, and he resigned from the Cabinet in bitter disgrace in September.

His chances for the presidency ruined, Armstrong returned to Dutchess County, to his farm at Red Hook, which he called "La Bergerie" and which was later known as "Rokeby." There he raised merino sheep and fumed over his lost chances. Ambrose Spencer tried to arrange for his election to the Senate again in 1815, but such hopes were totally unrealistic. After 1816 Armstrong vented his political energies in forceful anonymous attacks on President Monroe. In 1819 his purpose was to belittle Monroe's part in the Louisiana Purchase and to scuttle ongoing negotiations with Spain. His attacks did not cease even after Monroe's death in 1833, when he excoriated John Quincy Adams's eulogy of the late president in more anonymous articles.

He also did what he could to salvage his reputation for history by publishing his *Notes on the War of 1812* and a review of a life of Nathanael Greene that purported to give the true account of events at Newburgh in 1783. Using the anagrammatic pseudonym John Montgars, Armstrong prepared a history of the Revolution. He corresponded with such other veterans as Timothy Pickering in 1820 to obtain their recollections, but Pickering at least discovered his true identity and made their exchange of letters more of a debate than a research project. The manuscript history, not quite finished, was destroyed when fire consumed part of "La Bergerie."

In the spring of 1842, Ambrose Spencer adopted a deeply religious attitude and urged Armstrong to look to the welfare of his own soul. With Spencer's encouragement Armstrong joined the Protestant Episcopal Church that spring. His concern was timely, for on April 1, 1843, Armstrong died at his home in Red Hook. He was survived by five sons and one daughter, the wife of William B. Astor, and was buried in the Armstrong mausoleum at Red Hook.

SOURCES: *DAB*; alumni file, MS Steward's accounts, PUA; *BDAC*; *WPHM*, 10 (1927), 129-45; C. C. Sellers, *Dickinson College* (1973), 35-36; Heitman; W. B. Reed, *Life and Correspondence of Joseph Reed* (1847), I, 290-91; W. S. Stryker, *Battles of Princeton and Trenton* (1887), 292n, 296-97; *Washington Writings*, VII, 250; XXXV, 397; S. W. Patterson, *Horatio Gates* (1941), 120, 363-64, 367; J. T. Flexner, *Traitor and Spy* (1953), 181-84; W. M. Wallace, *Traitorous Hero* (1954), 155, 157; *Jay Papers*, I, 485; *Pa. Arch.* (1 ser.), IX, 650; X, 658, 676-77, 686-87; J. F. Roche, *Joseph Reed* (1957), 204-209; *Pa. Hist.*, 28 (1961), 259; *PMHB*, 5 (1881), 108 "Law has its promises"); 22 (1898), 379; 100 (1976), 336-55; *WMQ* (3 ser.), 27 (1970), 187-220, 206 ("milk and water style"); 29 (1972), 143-58, 155 ("grand Sanhedrin"); 31 (1974), 273-98; 33 (1976), 567-72, 580, 584; *Hamilton Papers*, III, 286-88; XIV, 269-71 & n, 440 & n; *LMCC*, VII, 155n, 160n, 175n ("Illustrissimo"), 180-83n; VIII, xciv, 612, 635n, 659n, 742-43 ("foolish and feeble"); R. L. Brunhouse, *Counter-Rev. in Pa.* (1942), passim; W. L. Stone, *Poetry and Hist. of Wyoming* (1864), 336-43; *Susquehanna Papers*, VIII, xvi-xxii, 93, 132; IX, 43; *Wyoming Hist. and Geol. Soc., Procs. and Coll.*, 13 (1914), 95, 98; D. M. Arnold, "Political Ideology and the Internal Rev. in Pa.," Ph.D. dissert., Princeton Univ. (1976), 237; F. B. Tolles, *George Logan of Phila.* (1953), 84, 256-57, 272; *Franklin Cal.*, III, 362; *Doc. Hist. Fed. Elec.* I (1976), 238 ("a little in society," "cormorants"), 293, 295, 313, 348-49, 365, 369n ("Morris Junto"); E. B. Livingston, *Livingstons of Livingston Manor* (1910), 556; G. Dangerfield, *Chancellor Robert R. Livingston of N.Y.* (1960), 257-59, 305; M. Jensen, ed., *Doc. Hist. of Ratification of the Constitution*, II (1976), 33-35, 173, 228; Davis, *Essays*, 274n; *Memorial of Ambrose Spenser* (1849), 97-103; J. D. Hammond, *Hist. of Pol. Parties in the St. of N.Y.* (1842), I, 153-54; N. E. Cunningham, Jr., *Jeffersonian Republicans in Power* (1963), 39, 206-207; H. Adams, ed., *Writings of Albert Gallatin* (1879), I, 52, 538-39; O. Pickering, *Life of Timothy Pickering* (1867), I, 406-410, 426; C. F. Adams, ed., *Memoirs of John Quincy Adams* (1874-76), VI, 68 ("most unprincipled"); I, 421 ("most disagreeable acts"); II, 149-50 ("morose, captious, and petulant"), 167-68; IV, 219-20; V, 432-34; VIII, 552; M. Smelser, *Democratic Republic* (1968), 105, 172, 195-97, 256, 270; C. E. Hill, "James Madison," 58, 63-65, 139-40, and J. W. Pratt, "James Monroe," 263-64, in S. F. Bemis, ed., *Amer. Secretaries of State and Their Diplomacy*, III (1927); I. Brant, *James Madison, Secretary of State* (1953), 260-61, 285, 361-62, 366; Brant, *James Madison, the President* (1956), passim; Brant, *James Madison, Commander-in-Chief* (1961), passim; *Sibley's Harvard Graduates*, XVII, 495-97; C. R. King, ed., *Life and Correspondence of Rufus King*, IV (1897), 502;

v (1898), 365, 473; M. L. Mann, ed., *Yankee Jeffersonian* (1958), 93, 112, 114, 140; *VMHB*, 74 (1966), 57, 62; J.C.A. Stagg, "Revolt against Va.," Ph.D. dissert., Princeton Univ. (1973), 20-23, 31, 72; als M. Lewis to J. Madison, 8 Apr, 12 May 1811, Madison MSS, DLC; D. R. Fox, *Decline of Aristocracy in Politics of N.Y.* (1965), 166; C. E. Skeen, "John Armstrong and the Role of the Secretary of War in the War of 1812," Ph.D. dissert., Ohio State Univ. (1966); H. Ammon, *James Monroe* (1971), 318-36; *Hist. Mag. . . . of Amer.* (2 ser.), 4 (1868), 60-63; *Journal of Exec. Proc. of the [U.S.] Senate*, II, 315-16; B. C. Steiner, *Life and Correspondence of James McHenry* (1907), 396 ("rubed hard"), 602; G. Hunt, ed., *Writings of James Madison*, VIII (1909), 37; H. Adams, *Life of Albert Gallatin* (1943), 530; F. Hasbrouck, *Hist. of Dutchess Cnty., N.Y.* (1909), 430-31.

MANUSCRIPTS: DLC; ViU; ICHi; MiU-C; NcCU; NN; MdHi; THi; InHi

PUBLICATIONS: Sh-Sh #s 3689, 24629, 47013

James Beekman, Jr.

JAMES BEEKMAN, JR., merchant, was the son of merchant James Beekman and his wife, Jane Keteltas Beekman of New York City. Born in 1758, he was the younger brother of William (A.B. 1773) and Abraham Keteltas Beekman (Class of 1774). In the portraits of the Beekman children done by John Durand in 1766, young James was posed with a fat squirrel on his shoulder. After 1764 he and his family lived at "Mount Pleasant," a large estate on the East River.

Although younger than his brothers, Beekman was educated with them in local schools and by private tutors, notably Thomas Johnson, Isaac Skillman (A.B. 1766), and Elias Jones (A.B. 1767). All three boys went to Princeton in 1769, with James entering the grammar school. After one year, however, he had to return to New York, and while his brothers took dancing lessons, he was home receiving further academic training from Skillman. His own instruction in dance came in 1772, when his father hired a Mr. Hullett to teach him.

Beekman was back in Princeton as a freshman in the College by May 1773. Home on vacation at the time of Lexington and Concord, however, he agreed with his father that he should not return to Nassau Hall after completing his junior year. Instead, he moved with his family to Kingston, New York in September 1776. In October 1777 his father hired substitutes to fight in the army for his three oldest sons and soon thereafter took the family to Sharon, Connecticut. The James Beekman in Kingston who was a private in the Ulster County Militia in August 1778, therefore, may not have been the merchant's third son. Like his brothers, Beekman assisted his father and uncles in their businesses during the war. He and Abraham were

James Beekman, Jr., Class of 1776
BY JOHN DURAND

in New Jersey and Philadelphia in November 1778, for example, to deliver horses to some relatives.

At the end of the war, the Beekmans regained possession of "Mount Pleasant." James, Sr. rented the house for six months to Sir Guy Carleton, who was in charge of the final evacuation of English troops and Loyalists from New York. In November 1783, when General Henry Knox led the American army back into the city, James, Jr. rode in the parade of citizens that welcomed him. "Mount Pleasant," which had been British headquarters in the Revolution, soon became a favorite gathering place for American officers, including Washington.

The Beekman business interests had suffered during the war and James, Sr. enlisted his sons in his efforts to restore them. He bought stock in the Bank of New York and purchased some of the forfeited Loyalist estates in the city. In 1787 James, Jr. became a full partner in the family's firm.

By October 1786 young Beekman was a lieutenant in the New York County Militia. He was promoted to captain, effective March

1788, and in March 1796 was the first major of the Fifth Regiment. Beekman's primary interest was in business, however. In 1794 and 1795 he was the family's chief investigator in a complicated transaction that involved a loan from four Dutch bankers to the United States government. A man in London hired the Beekmans to collect interest on the loan in his behalf, claiming that the debt had been transferred to him. Beekman, working with his distant cousin, attorney Henry Brockholst Livingston (A.B. 1774), found evidence that the Londoner's claim was invalid and managed to untangle the difficult history of the loan.

Like the rest of his family, Beekman owned many pieces of property in New York City, but he made his residence in Harlem. Unlike his brothers, he apparently owned no slaves. During the war of 1812, he allowed the officers and men of the New York Militia to stay in his house and barn.

Beekman died on April 8, 1837. Sources disagree as to whether or whom he married, but the most likely version is that he married Lydia Drew, perhaps a widow, in Trinity Church in New York on June 17, 1800. In any case, he had no children. His estate went to a nephew.

SOURCES: P. L. White, *Beekmans of N.Y.* (1956), passim; J. G. Wilson, ed., *Memorial Hist. of N.Y.* (1893), III, 152; MS Steward's accounts, PUA; Patterson Acct. Bk.; *Clinton Papers*, III, 612; F. G. Mather, *Refugees of 1776 from Long Island to Conn.* (1913), 661-62; P. L. White, *Beekman Mercantile Papers* (1956), III, 1286, 1,073-75; E. T. Delaney, *N.Y.'s Turtle Bay Old and New* (1965), 4-9; R. A. East, *Business Enterprise in the Amer. Rev. Era* (1938), 327; A. C. Flick, *Loyalism in N.Y. During the Amer. Rev.* (1901), 246, 255, 256; *Mil. Min., Council of Appointment, St. of N.Y.*, VII, 220, 241; X, 23; H. S. Mott, *N.Y. of Yesterday* (1908), 69, 344-45; *NYGBR*, 77 (1946), 109.

MANUSCRIPTS: NHi

Bartholomew Scott Calvin

BARTHOLOMEW SCOTT CALVIN or SHAWUSKUKHKUNG (WILTED GRASS), American Indian teacher and Delaware chief or head man, is said to have been born at or near the Indian village at Crossweeksung (Crosswicks), Burlington County, New Jersey. The date of his birth is uncertain, but it was probably about 1756 to 1758. He was the son of Stephen Calvin, interpreter, teacher, and spokesman for the Delaware Indians of New Jersey. The name of his mother is unknown, but his daughter asserted in 1864 that her paternal grandmother was the orphaned daughter of a Delaware "king" named We-queh-a-lak. She also maintained that Stephen Calvin interpreted for David Brainerd, the noted missionary to the New England and New Jersey Indians. Bartholomew Calvin himself recalled in 1832 that "the preaching of David B[rainerd] was the means of awakening & converting my poor mother." Crossweeksung had, in fact, been the scene of a remarkable revival among the Delaware in 1745 and 1746 during Brainerd's ministry.

In 1758 Stephen Calvin was among the leaders of the New Jersey Delaware south of the Raritan who were granted power of attorney to treat with commissioners of the colony about land still claimed by the Indians. Described as "the Indian schoolmaster in West-Jersey," Stephen Calvin participated as interpreter at two conferences preliminary to the settlement; and he was one of the signatories to articles that assigned the Delaware a tract of land in Burlington County in lieu of all their other claims except for their hunting and fishing rights. In pursuance of this agreement, Calvin moved with his Delaware people to Brotherton or Edgepillock (now Indian Mills), a few miles south of Crossweeksung. Bartholomew Calvin grew up there, probably taught by his father, who continued as schoolmaster, as well as by David Brainerd's brother John Brainerd (Yale 1746), a trustee of the College of New Jersey from 1754 to 1780 and the resident minister.

Even before the move to Brotherton, Bartholomew's older brother Hezekiah had come to John Brainerd's attention as a talented boy who might profit greatly from the instruction available at Moor's Indian Charity School conducted at Lebanon, Connecticut by Eleazar Wheelock (Yale 1733). Enrolled in Wheelock's school in 1757, Hezekiah returned to Brotherton in 1768—confused, prone to drink, and uncertain of his future after an unsuccessful teaching mission to the Mohawks at Fort Hunter, New York. "Hezekiah Calvin is capable enough," Brainerd informed Wheelock in 1772, "but he will not be any thing: he seems to choose to be a useless creature after all the encouragements I can give him." Hezekiah was last heard of in jail after forging a pass for a black man, and Brainerd transferred his expectations to young Bartholomew.

Hezekiah's downfall probably left an impression on Bartholomew Calvin that stayed with him after his matriculation at the College of New Jersey. Unlike Hezekiah, who had enjoyed the support and comradeship of Indian classmates in Connecticut, Bartholomew was now isolated from all vestiges of his own society. Even though he had been reared as a Christian in a Delaware community strongly affected by European ways, he no doubt found the environment of a colonial college alien and perhaps intimidating. Furthermore, as Bartholomew probably knew, his only known Indian predecessor at Princeton, another Delaware named Jacob Woolley (Class of 1762), who had also been at Wheelock's school, had fared no better than had Hezekiah. Bartholomew did at least have the company of Nathan Calvin, probably another brother, who is believed to have been a grammar school student.

The date of Calvin's enrollment and the years of his residence at Nassau Hall are not entirely certain, but an entry in Princeton storekeeper Thomas Patterson's account book is helpful in fixing the dates of his attendance at the College. Bartholomew and Nathan had an account with Patterson that was marked as paid in full on September 30, 1774. Calvin's studies were sponsored by the Society in Scotland for the Propagation of Christian Knowledge; and in his old age Calvin informed a missionary of that society that "in his second year in college, the funds failed in consequence of the revolutionary war and he was obliged to abandon his studies." There are also two entries in the College steward's accounts of tuition and room payments that appear to refer to Calvin. The first of these is on an undated list of payments, which reads "Calvin . Scot," with the amount paid completing the entry. "Scot" is believed to be the steward's notation to himself that the account was being paid by the society in Scotland mentioned above. The steward may also have been using the word "scot" in its meaning of "money assessed or paid." Whatever the explanation for the entry on this list, the name "Calvin Scott" appears on another list for the period May 25, 1773 to September 25, 1774. No person of this name is known to have been a student at the College at this time, however, thus the second entry is also thought to refer to Calvin. The discrepancy between the two entries may be simply a copying mistake by the steward, who seems not to have been familiar with the Indian student's full name.

Calvin spent the rest of his life with his Brotherton kinsmen and compatriots, first in New Jersey, then in New York, and finally in Michigan Territory (later Wisconsin). His career can be followed through his public activities as a spokesman for the Delaware of New Jersey. Some details of his personal life have been learned as well, but very little is known about the community life and internal organization of the precarious Indian society of which he was a leader.

After leaving the College, Calvin returned to Brotherton, where he succeeded his father as schoolmaster and left a reputation for being "an excellent teacher." He is said to have had as many white as Delaware students, and his school was supported by collections from white neighbors. The Delaware of New Jersey did not prosper at Brotherton, however. As early as 1775, John Brainerd had complained that both the mission house and parsonage were in intolerable condition. In 1796 the lands of the Brotherton Indians were placed under the care of white trustees, and in 1801 Calvin and twenty-one others asked the New Jersey Assembly to assist them in relocating to a community near Oneida Lake, New York. In a petition that Calvin is thought to have written and that was signed by four other persons bearing his surname, the Brotherton Indians assured the assembly that they did not intend to "leave you entirely, but . . . were only removing out of one of your doors into another." The assembly authorized the sale of the Brotherton tract, and in 1802 Calvin and seventy or eighty of his Delaware brethren moved with the proceeds to New Stockbridge, an Indian settlement in Oneida and Madison counties, New York. There they were welcomed by a kindred people, the Stockbridges, originally from Massachusetts. They were close neighbors of the Oneidas and of several New England Indian remnants who had banded together and also assumed the name Brotherton.

Although they were now part of a much larger, though heterogeneous community, neither Calvin nor his tribesmen flourished in their new home. All the Indians near Lake Oneida had been introduced to Christianity, and the Stockbridges and Brothertons in particular had found a spiritual leader in the renowned Indian preacher Reverend Samson Occom. Nevertheless, the assimilation of Protestantism and the accelerating infringement of European civilization on their own cultures were difficult and disorienting experiences for these displaced peoples. Calvin shared in the general malaise. He may have continued to teach school, and he was associated with a Baptist church. But as he admitted to the Reverend Cutting Marsh (Dartmouth 1826, Andover 1829), the missionary friend of his old age, he "became intemporate & at times drank execessively, still from time to time the upbraidings of his conscience were very severe & sometimes he would resolve on reformation, yet so strong was the habit, that he as often broke his resolutions & ruin seemed inevitable." Calvin was not among the members of a new Indian congregation organized at New Stockbridge in 1818.

Despite his advancing age and his drinking problem, Calvin remained a leader among his people. In 1823 he and a Stephen Calvin, described as "chiefs and head men" of the New Jersey Brothertons, were among the signers to an agreement with the Stockbridges to share lands near Green Bay that had recently been purchased from Indian tribes in that region. Shortly thereafter, Calvin moved again with some forty Delaware and a larger number of Stockbridges to these new lands in Michigan Territory, a relocation that was desired both by the federal government and by the New York land companies. Their first settlement was at Statesburg (South Kaukauna), twenty miles up the Fox River from Green Bay, and they were joined there in 1827 by a Congregational minister. The following year there was a revival at the settlement, and Calvin was one of several persons who now became members of the Stockbridge congregation organized in New York a decade earlier. The conversion experience that preceded Calvin's admission to the church seems finally to have released him from his dependence on alcohol.

The first missionary to Statesburg, who died shortly after the 1828 revival, was replaced in 1830 by Cutting Marsh, whose annual reports through 1848 provide a fascinating commentary on the life of this transplanted Indian community. Marsh was partially supported by the Scottish missionary society that had aided Calvin at Princeton and that had for some time financially assisted the Stockbridge congregation. In his first report to the society, he told with some amazement of his discovery of an old Indian man who had enjoyed the society's patronage almost sixty years earlier. Describing Calvin after his recent renewal of faith and rescue from the plague of liquor, Marsh informed the society: "Seldom have I seen one who appears to possess more of the grace of humility, this is manifest in all his deportment, but especially in prayer, here he seems a suppliant indeed. His humility seems to arise from a deep sense of the sinfulness & depravity of his heart by nature and of the greatness & holiness of God."

In 1832 Calvin returned to New Jersey as the delegate of his people to request a legislative appropriation of $2,000 in return for relinquishment of the hunting and fishing rights still retained by them under the 1758 treaty to which Calvin's father had been a party. The aged Indian addressed the assembly by letter after both houses voted to accept this proposal. Calvin said in part:

> The final act of official intercourse between the State of New-Jersey and the Delaware Indians, who once owned near the whole of its territory, has now been consummated; and in a manner which must redound to the honor of this growing State, and in all human probability to the prolongation of the existence of a wasted, yet grateful people. . . .
>
> Not a drop of our blood have you spilled in battle, not an acre of our land have you taken but by our consent. These facts speak

for themselves and need no comment. They place the character of New Jersey in bold relief and bright example to those States within whose territorial limits, our brethren still remain. Nought save benisons can fall upon her from the lips of a Lenni Lenappi.

There may be some who would despise an Indian Benediction; but when I return to my people, and make known the result of my mission, the ears of the Great Sovereign of the Universe, which are still graciously open to our cry, will be penetrated with our invocation of blessings upon the generous sons of New Jersey.

Returning to Michigan Territory, Calvin made a final move in 1834 with the Stockbridge and Brotherton Delaware to a new settlement on the east short of Lake Winnebago. His family at that time consisted of at least two daughters, one of whom was also a member of the Stockbridge church, and an only son, described as "but a lad" in 1831. He revered the memory of the Brainerds and found spiritual guidance in David Brainerd's memoirs, but he was troubled by occasional anxiety over the certainty of his salvation as well as by a serious illness in 1833. In June 1840 Cutting Marsh reported to the Scottish society that Calvin had died in the interval since his last yearly report, saying:

It is perhaps sufficient to say that he held out firm to the last, and gave most satisfactory evidence of being a child of God. He devoted much time so long as he was able to reading, but his Bible and Hymn Book were his most constant companions, and in conversation shoed that he was familiar with them. He possessed naturally a strong mind and a retentive memory, and so long as strength held out was a constant attendant upon public worship and other religious meetings; and in the house of God seemed to receive with great "meekness the ingrafted word."

SOURCES: WHi, *Coll.*, xv, 6-8, 52, 53 ("funds failed," "became intemperate," "the grace of humility"), 54 ("but a lad"), 69 ("my poor mother"), 77, 86-88, 158-67, 168 ("firm to the last"), 169; IV, 291-98; C. A. Weslager, *Del. Indians, A Hist.* (1972), 265f.; *NJHSP* (2 ser.), 4 (1875-1877), 33-50; *GMNJ*, 5 (1929), 1-8; J. W. Alexander, *Forty Years' Familiar Letters* (1860), I, 184; T. Brainerd, *Life of John Brainerd* (1865) 304f., 373, 378, 382-83, 395 ("useless creature"), 415-16 & n, 460, 461; J. M. Sherwood, ed., *Memoirs of Rev. David Brainerd* (1891), 153f.; S. Smith, *Hist. of the Colony of Nova-Caesaria* (1877), 446f.; J. D. McCallum, *Letters of Eleazar Wheelock's Indians* (1932), 47-67; *Princetonians, 1748-1768*, 414-16; Patterson Acct. Bk.; MS Steward's accounts, PUA; W. Nelson, *Indians of N.J.* (1894), 143; copy of 1801 Petition, PUA; H. Blodgett, *Samson Occum* (1935), passim; J. N. Davidson, *Muh-he-ka-ne-ok: A Hist. of the Stockbridge Nation* (1893), 17f.; *Wisc. Mag. of Hist.*, 30 (1946), 14; *Votes and Proc. of the Fifty-sixth Gen. Assem. of . . . N.J.* (1932), 319-20 ("final act of official intercourse").
                                                                    GSD

Lardner Clark

LARDNER CLARK, merchant and public official, was born in Little Egg Harbor, Gloucester County, New Jersey. His mother was Jane Lardner Clark, a member of a wealthy and influential Philadelphia family. His father, Elijah Clark, was a prosperous merchant, miller, and farmer in Gloucester County who served in the New Jersey Provincial Congress and state assembly and as a lieutenant colonel in the militia in 1776 and 1777. When Philip Fithian (A.B. 1772) was preaching as an itinerant in southern New Jersey in February 1775, he stayed with the Clarks, and found them wealthy, hospitable, and admirably pious.

Clark entered the College as a freshman and in 1774, at the end of his sophomore year, took second prize in the undergraduate competition for "Latin Grammar and extempore exercises." On December 9, 1772, he joined the Cliosophic Society, using the name of the East Indian hero of the battle of Hydraspes, "Porus."

Clark finished his junior year in college but apparently left after that to join his father in business. At the end of 1778, his father sold his property in Little Egg Harbor and moved to an estate in Haddonfield, New Jersey, nearer to Philadelphia. Lardner retained some land in Gloucester County, but by 1780 he owned property worth £40,000 in Philadelphia as well, undoubtedly due to the largesse of his father and his mother's family. He shared some mercantile interests with the Stockton family of Princeton and received several bonds for letters of marque for privateers from the Continental Congress.

By May 1782 Clark's fortunes had suffered a decline so serious that he had to ask his father to send his personal slave to Philadelphia so that the servant could be sold. The elder Clark was not altogether willing to cooperate with that plan and suggested that his son might lease one of his brigantines instead. Apparently, Clark was trying to raise capital to support his partnership with William Wyckoff of Monmouth County, New Jersey, with whom in 1782 he went west to open a store at Kaskaskia in the Illinois country.

Kaskaskia was the trading center for much of the west, including the new settlement at Nashborough in the Washington District of North Carolina. In 1782 that state's legislature offered land in the district to veterans of the Revolution, and Clark seized the opportunity to increase his business. Leaving Wyckoff in Kaskaskia, he joined the expedition that was to survey and apportion the lands around Nashborough. In 1783 he moved there permanently. He bought 320 acres in the French Lick area in January 1784 and shortly afterward owned considerably more land in the neighborhood. That May, North Carolina incorporated the town, changing its name to Nashville, and Clark paid £4 for one of the original lots. He quickly became one of the new town's leading citizens.

Clark was Nashville's first merchant. His supplies came from Philadelphia and Baltimore at first, and later from Detroit and New Orleans as well. Much of his business was done on credit, and from their inception, the courts of Davidson County were kept busy with his suits to collect bad debts. He owned the largest of Nashville's few true houses and in it kept his general store and "ordinary" house, or tavern. On July 22, 1784, Clark obtained a license to marry Elizabeth Bowen, whose family had come to Davidson County from Augusta County, Virginia. In the residential section of their home they maintained a large private library, and Nashville's earliest religious services, conducted by Thomas Craighead (A.B. 1775), may also have been held there.

In December 1785 North Carolina's legislature provided for the relief of veterans and appointed Clark one of the commissioners for such relief in the Washington District. At the same time, it incorporated a town at the forks of the Cumberland and Red Rivers, and Clark was named a commissioner of that venture as well. The new settlement later became Clarksville. On December 29 the legislature also incorporated Davidson Academy, of which Craighead and Clark were original trustees, and which was the forerunner of the University of Nashville. The first meeting of the trustees of the academy occurred in August 1786, but Clark was absent. He was probably in Philadelphia at the time on the school's business and his own, for when he returned at the head of a train of pack horses, he brought books as well as drygoods. For the next nine years, Clark was the academy's business executive. He took charge of leasing its land and ferry for revenue, and his house was frequently the site of board meetings.

When North Carolina moved to encourage the production of salt in Davidson County in November 1787, Clark was selected as one of the officials who would lease the rights to the several salt licks in the area. Within a year Clark had formed a partnership with James Cole Montflorence and taken the lease on the "Sulphur Spring" in Nashville. They built an elaborate system of kettles and furnaces to extract the salt, but the venture was only marginally profitable, and they had frequently to seek relief from their obligations to the state.

In the spring of 1790 Congress accepted the territory south of the Ohio River from North Carolina and appointed William Blount its governor. On December 15 Blount issued commissions to the new officers of the courts of Davidson County; Clark received his as a justice of the peace. He was also responsible for such tasks as inspecting paper currency. At about the same time, he ended his partnership with Wyckoff. Their last years in business together must have been less than friendly, for their accounts had to be settled by an arbitrator. The store in Kaskaskia had proven a commercial failure, which added to Clark's financial embarrassment since he was increasingly unable to collect money due him in Nashville and to pay his own debts. Between 1791 and 1794 he was forced to sell most of his property in Davidson County, and by 1796 he was back in Kaskaskia, possibly trying to revive his business there. In that year he was a prothonotary of Randolph County, Illinois.

Clark traveled throughout the west to find an appropriate place to settle his family and his business interests. He died without finding it on February 18, 1801 in New Tennessee in upper Louisiana. He was buried in the local Catholic churchyard at St. Genevieve in the area that would later be part of southeastern Missouri.

Clark was survived by his widow and four daughters, who sold the remainder of his estate at an auction in Nashville on August 16, 1802. The decline of the family fortunes may be measured by the fact that while Clark had several expensive slaves in the 1780s, only "one old negro man" worth five dollars remained with his widow.

SOURCES: *THM*, 3 (1917), 28-50, 115-33, 127 ("one old negro man"); A. W. Putnam, *Hist. of Middle Tenn.* (1917), 174, 211-12n, 639, 641; *NJHSP* (n.s.), XII, 340-41; X, 389; J. W. Jordan, *Col. Families of Phila.* (1911), II, 925-28; *Fithian Journal*, II, 250-52 & n; MS Steward's accounts, MS Clio. Soc. membership list, PUA; *Pa. Journal and Weekly Advertiser*, 12 Oct 1774 ("Latin Grammar"); *Pa. Arch.* (3 ser.), XV, 321; Index, PCC; *PMHB*, 28 (1904), 107-108; H. McRaven, *Nashville* (1949), 17, 255; S. C. Williams, *Early Travels in the Tenn. Country* (1928), 285n; F. S. Frank, *Five Families and Eight Young Men* (1962), 53; East Tenn. Hist. Soc., *Pubs.*, 23 (1951), 15, 18; *St. Rec. N.C.*, XXIV, 736, 751, 780, 915.

William Coates

WILLIAM COATES was probably the farmer born in Warminster, Bucks County, Pennsylvania in 1758, the son of Benjamin and Ann Longstreth Coates and a descendant of an Irish Quaker family. His own religious inclinations may have been affected by the proximity of the Presbyterian church at Neshaminy to which the lives of so many men influential in the history of the College were linked.

Coates spent his freshman and sophomore years at Nassau Hall, but there is no record of his attendance beyond September 1774. After returning to Pennsylvania to live near his father's new home in West Bradford, Chester County, he married Rebecca Stalker, with whom he ultimately had at least five children. On October 18, 1834, Coates died, having been a widower for nearly five years. Four of his children survived him.

SOURCES: T. Coates, *Geneal. of Moses and Susanna Coates* (1906), 251-52; *First Census, Pa.*, 73; MS Steward's accounts, PUA.

William Richardson Davie

WILLIAM RICHARDSON DAVIE, A.B., soldier, lawyer, and public official, was born on June 22, 1756, at Egremont, County Cumberland, England, the oldest child of Archibald Davie and his wife, Mary Richardson. He bore the name of a maternal uncle, William Richardson, who had been educated at the University of Glasgow, migrated to America, and by 1755 was studying for the ministry with Samuel Davies, fourth president of the College, at Hanover, Virginia. Ordained in 1758, Richardson eventually settled as pastor of the Presbyterian church in the Waxhaw settlements of South Carolina, where he was joined by his sister and her family in 1764. The Davie farm, acquired in 1766, adjoined Richardson's property. The traditional assumption that young Davie was adopted by his childless uncle and inherited the entire estate on the latter's death in 1771 is unfounded, but he did share in a substantial inheritance and received most of a well-stocked library. Evidently his promise as a student was already established.

Davie's education began under the tutelage of his uncle, and he may have completed his preparation for college at nearby Queen's College in Charlotte, North Carolina, an academy of which his uncle was a founding trustee. Evidence establishing the time of Davie's arrival at Princeton, unusually specific for this period in the history of the College, is provided by a certificate from President Witherspoon, dated October 20, 1776, testifying that Davie had completed the requirements for his degree after studying "in this College for two years preceding this Date." Because of wartime disturbances, the trustees had lacked a quorum for the scheduled commencement of September 25, and the members of the Class of 1776 did not formally receive their degrees until a meeting of the trustees on May 24, 1777. The certificate, issued in lieu of a diploma, carries no suggestion that Davie was graduated with special distinction. There appears to be no way of confirming Alexander Garden's report that while a student Davie

William Richardson Davie, A.B. 1776
ATTRIBUTED TO ELIZA LEZINKA MIRBEL

led a group of undergraduates to Elizabeth, New Jersey for the purpose of joining the army. Indeed, Garden's statement that Davie was one of two who "remained with the army" when the others quickly returned to their studies casts doubt upon the whole story. Davie is listed among the members of the American Whig Society.

After leaving the College, Davie apparently began to read law in Salisbury, North Carolina. The tradition that he read with so recent a graduate as Spruce Macay (A.B. 1775) is open to some question, even though an implied confirmation is found in the urgent invitation that Davie extended to Macay in 1793 for attendance at the laying of the cornerstone of the first building of the University of North Carolina; Davie called himself, "one who once sat at the feet of Gamaliel in the intermissions between tours in the field." In any case, Davie's reading was interspersed among periods of active military service. Late in 1777 he joined a militia force sent south under the command of Brigadier General Allen Jones for the assistance of Charleston. The troops turned back near Camden, however, upon hearing that a threatened attack by the British had not developed. In the spring of 1779, Davie helped to recruit a company of dragoons in which he was commissioned a lieutenant by Governor Richard Caswell, and he soon succeeded to the command. Promoted to major after the unit had been assigned to Pulaski's Legion in South Carolina, Davie was seriously wounded at Stono, below Charleston, on June 20, 1779. It was after a period of hospitalization in that city that Davie received his license to practice law from the Rowan Court on November 2, 1779. On March 24, 1780, he secured a second and broader license admitting him to the practice of law before the courts of the state.

Prior to establishing his reputation as a lawyer, Davie was to win fame as one of the more aggressive and effective partisan leaders in campaigns made famous by such other guerrilla warriors as Marion, Sumter, and Pickens. Just when Davie raised the second troop of horsemen he commanded seems uncertain, but it was in time for him to participate in the action against a strong force of Tories at Ramsour's Mill on June 20 and to cover Gates's retreat from his disastrous defeat by Cornwallis at Camden on August 16, 1780. In the following September, Davie was promoted to colonel, with the command of "all militia Horse acting in the Western District" of North Carolina. Cornwallis took Charlotte on September 26, after Davie had contested its possession in the very streets of the village. The place having been abandoned by the British after Ferguson's defeat at King's Mountain on October 7, Davie followed the enemy into the Waxhaws, where he was thoroughly at home and where his father still lived. He sought to punish the British regulars in all ways short of full-scale engagement with superior forces, and where American Tories were involved, there might be no quarter given. His unit acquired the name of the "bloody corps," and Cornwallis early in December 1780 reported to Clinton that "Davie and other irregular Corps" had committed "the most shocking cruelties and the most horrid Murders on those suspected of being our friends."

Davie's days of active campaigning ended when General Nathanael Greene persuaded him to assume the post of commissary general for the Southern Army, an assignment accompanied by appointment to comparable responsibilities for the state of North Carolina by its board of war on January 16, 1781. He took the office on a promise that he would soon be released, a promise made good by June of 1781, but the onerous duties imposed by his commitment to the state continued.

Davie's reputation as a soldier brought calls for military service through many years after the war, as major general of the state militia in 1794, and as a brigadier general in the provisional army planned in 1798 for Washington's command in the event of war with France.

As late as 1813, during the second war with Britain, he declined President Madison's offer of a major general's commission. That Davie retained a deep interest in military affairs is evidenced by the publication in May 1799 of his *Instructions To Be Observed for the Formation and Movements of the Cavalry*, a training and tactical manual prepared at the instance of the state legislature for the guidance of militia units. The manual went far beyond what the legislature had in mind, according to its author, who also described it as having been "carefully compiled from the latest European publications." No one can peruse its 180 pages of text, with supplementary drawings of formations and movements, without sensing Davie's intention to bring militia units to an awareness of the highest professional standards. Writing at a time when war seemed imminent, Davie undoubtedly hoped the manual's influence would extend beyond the state. Washington's autographed copy has survived. Later, Davie began to record his recollections of the campaigns of the War of Independence in which he had participated. Although unfinished, they throw light on the role of guerrilla tactics in the southern war, seek to correct mistakes in existing histories of that war (especially those of Gordon), and extol the effectiveness of the American militiaman whose commander has explained to him the objective and the tactics to be employed for its achievement.

In 1782 Davie had settled in Halifax to begin to practice law in what was then one of the principal towns of North Carolina. His marriage on April 11 of that year to Sarah Jones, daughter of his former commander and niece of Willie Jones, brought him property as well as connection with one of the state's more prominent families. The prosperity indicated by his ownership of twenty-five slaves in 1787, and thirty-six according to the census of 1790, is hardly to be attributed solely to the returns from his law practice. Over the years he speculated in landed properties involving thousands of acres in different parts of the state, including some 4,800 acres in what became Tennessee, which he secured for his war services. Even so, there can be no question of his rapid rise at the bar. Tall, erect, eloquent, and possessed of a commanding presence, he was described in 1791 by James Iredell, then on the United States Supreme Court, as one of the two best lawyers in the state.

He also became one of the more important of the state's political leaders. From 1784 to 1798 he served nine terms in the legislature as a member of the House of Commons. He became an early advocate of a stronger national government and sat for the state in the Constitutional Convention of 1787. William Pierce, the Georgia delegate who left useful sketches of his colleagues, spoke of Davie as one who was "silent in the Convention" but whose "opinion was always respected." His chief contribution seems to have been his influence in swinging the vote of North Carolina, normally cast with the larger states, to the aid of the smaller states in the decision in favor of equal representation in the Senate. He served as North Carolina's delegate on the Grand Committee selected on July 2 to propose a settlement of this critical issue. He left the convention on August 13, explaining that the main questions had been settled and pleading urgent business at home.

Davie joined James Iredell as a leading advocate of the new Constitution in North Carolina and sat in the convention meeting at Hillsborough in July 1788 that failed to ratify it. Iredell and Davie continued their efforts to persuade the people, in part by publishing the debates of the Hillsborough convention, and ultimately they succeeded in bringing North Carolina into the union by action of a second ratifying convention meeting at Fayetteville in November 1789.

It was also in 1789 that Davie established his chief claim to remembrance in the history of the state by sponsoring the legislative measure conferring a charter upon the University of North Carolina. The constitution of 1776 had committed the state to the support of such an institution, but as yet no effective action had been taken to implement the provision. Davie's own commitment to education had been demonstrated by his leadership in securing a charter in 1786 for the Warrenton Academy, of which he became a trustee, and his role in the establishment of the state university was by no means limited to securing its charter. Over the following years, he was tireless in his efforts, in and out of the legislature, to raise the needed funds. As Grand Master of Masons in North Carolina, he presided at the laying of the cornerstone for the university's first building in 1793. He also helped to shape its program of studies, and for years after its formal opening in January 1795, he remained a steadfast friend, serving as a trustee until 1807. In 1811 the university conferred upon him its first honorary doctorate of laws as "the Founder of our Institution, and principal supporter, when in its infant state." The citation for the degree credited him with a "Master of Arts at Nassau Hall Princeton," but this lacks confirmation in the extant records of the College.

While the trend of political sentiment in North Carolina after 1789 had been toward Jeffersonian Republicanism, Davie remained a stout Federalist. In 1798 the Federalists mustered enough strength in the legislature, with some aid from Republicans, to elect Davie governor.

He resigned that post in 1799 to accept membership in the special commission headed by Chief Justice Oliver Ellsworth (A.B. 1766) sent by President Adams to France in the hope of averting open warfare with that country. After an arduous trip, Ellsworth and Davie reached Paris early in March 1800 and negotiated the convention of September 30 that marked a turning point in the relations of the United States with the government of Napoleon and helped prepare the way for the Louisiana Purchase.

For all practical purposes Davie's public career was over. Jefferson, whom he deeply distrusted, would soon win the disputed election from Aaron Burr (A.B. 1772), whom Davie apparently distrusted even more. At home he found himself ill equipped by temperament to make his way in the partisan politics of the time. Though agreeing to stand for Congress in 1803, he publicly advised that no man should "vote for me, who is not willing to leave me free to pursue the good of my country according to the best of my judgment, without respect either to party men or party views." He was defeated.

His wife died in 1802, having borne him three sons and three daughters, all of whom survived him. By 1805 he had decided to dispose of most of his extensive properties in North Carolina and transfer his residence to "Tivoli," his plantation on the Catawba River in South Carolina. He supervised the work of the plantation and took an active interest in the South Carolina Agricultural Society, of which he served as president in 1818, until his death on November 5, 1820. He left an estate valued at almost $47,000, including 116 slaves valued at $32,000 and a library appraised at $2,500. Although there are indications that Davie in his maturity became skeptical in his view of the traditional Christian faith, he was buried in the churchyard of the Waxhaw Presbyterian Church over which his uncle had once presided.

Sources: B. P. Robinson, *William R. Davie* (1957); F. M. Hubbard, *Life of William R. Davie* (1848); J. G. de R. Hamilton, *Memoir of William R. Davie* (1907); *DAB*; *St. Rec. N.C.*, XXII, 156; XIV, 291, 490-92, 760; XV, 306 (Cornwallis quotation); *Col. Rec. N.C.*, VIII, 487; X, 870 (Witherspoon certificate); Maclean, *History*, I, 320-21; A. Garden, *Anecdotes of the Rev. War* (1822), 37-38; B. P. Robinson, ed., *Rev. War Sketches of William R. Davie* (1796), esp. 13, 17, 25, 39; R.D.W. Connor, *Doc. Hist. of Univ. of N.C.* (1953), 1, 21, 504-505 ("at the feet of Gamaliel"); H. Lee, *Memoirs of the War*, 103-106; D. Higginbotham, *War of Amer. Independence* (1971), 363; *Hamilton Papers*, XXII, 32, 343, 387, 485-86, 504; *Washington Writings*, XXXVI, 515-17; XXXVII, 352; W. H. Hoyt, ed., *Papers of Archibald D. Murphey* (1914), II, 349-51; M. Farrand, *Rec. of Fed. Conv.* (1911–1937), I, 487-88, 509; III, 31, 74-75, 95-96 ("silent in the Convention"); Farrand, *Framing of the Constitution* (1913), 23, 97-99; *Elliot's Debates*, IV, 4-252 passim; A. DeConde, *Quasi-War* (1966), 223-58; K. P. Battle, *Hist. of Univ. of N.C.* (1912), I, passim; D. H. Fischer, *Rev. of Amer. Con-*

servatism (1965), 151 ("vote for me"). See William H. Vernon (A.B. 1776) for commencement.

MANUSCRIPTS: NcU; Nc

PUBLICATIONS: see text and *An Address Delivered before the S.C. Agricultural Soc. . . . 8th of Dec. 1818* (1819)

WFC

Jonathan Dayton

JONATHAN DAYTON, A.B., A.M. 1783, LL.D. 1798, soldier, lawyer, public official, farmer, merchant, and entrepreneur, was born in Elizabethtown, Essex County, New Jersey, on October 16, 1760. He was the eldest son of Elias Dayton, a wealthy merchant who was one of New Jersey's leading public officials and soldiers, and his wife, whose maiden name was Rolfe. Dayton probably received his earliest education in the grammar school at Elizabethtown and enrolled in the College no later than November 1774. On March 26, 1775, he joined the Cliosophic Society, adopting the pseudonym "Burke," after the distinguished British parliamentarian.

Like many members of his class, Dayton did not stay in Princeton for the truncated commencement of 1776, described by his classmate William Vernon in a letter home. On February 9 of that year he enlisted as an ensign in the Third Battalion of New Jersey Continentals, of which his father was commanding officer. On August 26 Congress appointed him battalion paymaster, a promotion that elicited loud but ineffective complaints from his father's political enemies.

Dayton served with the Third New Jersey in the Mohawk Valley of New York until May 1779, when, as a captain, he became aide-de-camp to General John Sullivan on that officer's expedition against the Indians in New York and Pennsylvania. By the next March, Dayton was back under his father's command as a captain in the Third New Jersey Regiment based at Elizabethtown. He carried intelligence from his father to General Washington; and when the commander in chief found it necessary to withdraw the regiment to a safer distance from the town in July, he made sure that young Dayton would still be available to bring him news of enemy activity.

In early November 1780 Dayton and Colonel Matthias Ogden were seized in their sleep by a party of Loyalists at Herd's Tavern in Connecticut Farms, New Jersey. They were taken to Staten Island for a brief incarceration and then exchanged. Washington knew why

Jonathan Dayton, A.B. 1776
BY CHARLES B. J. FEVRET DE SAINT MEMIN

Ogden was in the area, but he could not understand Dayton's presence. The general ordered that in future all officers captured out of
the line of duty and "by their own imprudence" should be arrested
when exchanged and held until their capture was investigated.

Dayton had his revenge for his captivity when in 1781 he led am-
bushes against loyalist bands who were raiding northern New Jersey
from Staten Island. He was then a member of the Second New Jersey
Regiment, into which he had again followed his father. By the spring
of 1782, he had resumed his reports to Washington, and in June he
was virtually in charge of inspecting the traffic between Elizabethtown
and New York to insure that neither contraband nor unauthorized
persons passed deeper into New Jersey. He was, however, too lenient
in granting passes for Washington's taste. Rumors of illegal trade between Americans and occupied New York were rife, and the general
wanted to put an end to such smuggling. When Dayton, who was
mentioned in some of those rumors, permitted two men to pass
through town without sufficient identification, Washington ordered
him relieved of his responsibilities at Elizabethtown.

The Second New Jersey served in New York in late 1782 and by the
next spring was at army headquarters around New Windsor. In April

1783 Dayton was retained in service as part of the consolidated New Jersey Regiment. He and his friend and neighbor Aaron Ogden (A.B. 1773) then took leave to return to Elizabethtown to settle their accounts as paymasters. Apparently, they never had to return to camp.

On June 11, 1783, Dayton participated in the establishment of the New Jersey chapter of the Society of the Cincinnati. He was also a Freemason and a member of the First Presbyterian Church in Elizabethtown. Within a few years of the war's end, he was serving on the church's board of trustees and that of the Elizabethtown Academy and was a subscriber to the Library Association. His family connections enhanced his social standing, especially after his sister married Matthias Ogden and he married Susannah Williamson, the daughter of Mattias Williamson and sister of Matthias Williamson (A.B. 1770). This gave him a strong base for the political career that he launched after studying law and being admitted to the bar, sometime before October 1786 when he was first elected to the state's general assembly.

When the legislative session ended in May 1787, Dayton was already known as New Jersey's most industrious speculator in public debts and securities. His position in the assembly provided him with information to which other speculators were not privy, and he prospered. He also showed an interest in the settlement of the American west as early as November 1786, when he chaired a committee in the legislature that instructed New Jersey's congressional delegates to insist upon the country's right to navigate the Mississippi.

When Abraham Clark, signer of the Declaration of Independence and longtime political ally of Elias Dayton, declined the state's appointment to the Constitutional Convention in May 1787, the senior Dayton himself was the alternative choice. But he, too, declined in favor of his son, and at the age of twenty-six, Dayton was the youngest man to sit in that body. He did not accept the assignment enthusiastically, for his financial dealings kept him busy enough at home. Indeed, he had to be called to Philadelphia by a colleague on June 5, when the state was underrepresented during some important debates. He arrived sixteen days later.

In the convention, Dayton argued against the payment of congressmen by the states and in favor of a controlled, but not impotent, military establishment. His primary interest, however, was the protection of the rights of small states, and he therefore fought for equal representation in the Senate, against a joint ballot by Congress to elect the president, and against the enumeration of slaves as part of the represented population. He declared that he "would in no event yield the security of [states'] rights." In later years he told friends that he had been the spokesman for the small states when they threatened to withdraw from the convention over the issue of Senate membership. In the end, he was a firm supporter of the compromises achieved at Philadelphia. His view of the Constitution was always colored by his conviction that every article was "founded on the presumption of a clashing of interests," by which he meant the competition among such political entities as states and branches of government. He resisted any alterations that would free those "interests" from the checks imposed on them by the convention.

Dayton signed the Constitution on September 17, 1787 and returned to his seat in the New Jersey Assembly in October. At that time, he was already working with John Cleves Symmes in the creation of the South Jersey Company, with the intention of buying 2,000,000 acres of land in the Ohio Territory. Throughout his service in the Constitutional Convention, the state assembly, and the last session of the Continental Congress, to which he was elected on November 7, 1787, Dayton worked diligently to protect his and Symmes's plans for the west. Less romantic than Symmes, he was the company's business manager and primary agent. He used his political connections to facilitate speculation in land warrants, military certificates, and government securities with which he intended to pay for the land, and in the spring of 1788, Congress agreed to transfer the Miami reserve to the company for $82,198, almost all of it payable in the certificates Dayton had been manipulating. Dayton's personal profit in military certificates alone was enough to finance his purchase of 15,000 acres in 1800. Part of his own share of the Miami tracts later became Dayton, Ohio, but it was among the few parcels of land from which he never realized a profit.

In New Jersey's first elections for the federal Congress, a caucus of the state legislature, which was dominated by the so-called West Jersey interests, proposed its own slate of candidates led by Elias Boudinot. The East Jersey faction in the state's ancient sectional rivalry was unable to produce a single opposition slate, but the several lists endorsed by East Jerseyites all included Dayton and Abraham Clark. During a scurrilous campaign, the West Jersey "Junto" villified Clark as an opponent of the Constitution, and the mud splattered freely on Dayton as well. Rumors of his private speculations were expanded into charges of cupidity. To persuade the Quakers in southern New Jersey, the "Junto" called Clark and Dayton "bloodthirsty Presbyterians" who would persecute dissenters. Dayton's supporters included Joseph Bloomfield, Andrew Hunter (A.B. 1772), Aaron Ogden, and John Noble Cumming (A.B. 1774), but they could not overcome the opposition of men such as Franklin Davenport (Class of 1773), who said that while the East Jersey people would take "anybody with Dayton," he would insist on "anybody *but* Clark."

For weeks each side waited for the other to report its final tallies, but on March 18 the West Jerseymen managed to persuade the governor's council to declare winners without the votes from Essex County, which certainly would have gone to their opponents. The result was a sweep for the "Junto" slate. Advised by Alexander Hamilton that any appeal to Congress would fail—as it did in September— Dayton returned to the state legislature and to the clerkship of the circuit and district courts to wait for another chance. He never again associated politically with Abraham Clark.

Dayton was considered by Washington for a federal appointment in 1789, but no post was offered him. In June 1790 he applied unsuccessfully for the position of New Jersey commissioner for funding the national debt. It was a job that would have fit perfectly into his private financial adventures, for in the same year he subscribed £11,000 in state securities toward that debt. He bought up military and state loan certificates voraciously. In February and March of 1791 alone, he obtained more than $50,000 worth of New York securities. At the same time, he and his father and Matthias Ogden owned ten shares of stock in the Society for establishing useful Manufactures, a creation of William Duer.

His speculations were an issue again when Dayton ran for Congress in 1791, but the East Jerseyites won that contest. Of the incumbents, only Elias Boudinot was returned. Dayton was elected with a reputation as a defender of states' rights. In the House of Representatives he supported efforts to create a strong army and to call cabinet members before Congress to report. He also took every opportunity to advance personal causes such as his family's drygoods business and his own speculations. As the holder of a great many military certificates, Dayton opposed James Madison's (A.B. 1771) plan to discriminate in favor of veterans while funding the national debt, and with other members of the Society of the Cincinnati, he was castigated as a traitor to his former comrades in arms.

The forum for those charges was Philip Freneau's (A.B. 1771) *National Gazette*, and by the summer of 1792 that paper was at the center of the momentous conflict between Hamilton and Thomas Jefferson. Seeking to prove collusion between Jefferson and Freneau, Hamilton asked Dayton for evidence that the secretary of state had brought the editor to Philadelphia to defame the government. Dayton's knowledge of the affair had come from Freneau's publisher,

Francis Childs, and he regretted that he could not embarrass Childs by citing his story in public. He did, however, tell Hamilton all that he knew.

Although generally regarded as a Federalist, Dayton was enough of a maverick to trouble Hamiltonians. For instance, in March 1794 he proposed the sequestration of British debts in the United States in reprisal for violations of the Treaty of Paris. The idea was roundly condemned by Hamilton and ultimately died in committee, but it left Dayton with a sufficiently nonpartisan reputation to keep him in Congress. To maintain his balance in 1794, he attacked the Democratic societies in Pennsylvania, which he blamed for the Whiskey Rebellion. He also participated in the legislative-executive meetings that produced a plan for a navy. By November 1795 he was among the men Washington was considering for the post of secretary of war.

The Federalist leader in the House was Theodore Sedgwick of Massachusetts. But in late 1795, with the Federalists in the minority, the party had to support someone other than Sedgwick for Speaker of the House or lose that office. Dayton was the choice. He was elected with Sedgwick's support in December 1795. In the only such election that saw members of the majority vote with the minority, Dayton's nonpartisan pose had been useful.

Dayton expected that Jay's Treaty would cause "agitations, collisions, and oppositions" in the House, and he was right. Personally, he disapproved of the pact, but he was convinced by Sedgwick to support it. The Massachusetts Federalist understood that Dayton was doing no more than protecting his chances for reelection in New Jersey and regretted that the fate of important questions rode on "the weakness and wickedness of unprincipled men," but Dayton's great popularity among his colleagues was of immense value in passing legislation to implement the treaty. Before the House, Dayton declared that he found more wrong than right with what Jay had done, but he cast two tie-breaking votes to prevent the addition of a preamble to the enabling laws that would have declared the pact "highly objectionable" or "objectionable."

His lukewarm attitude on that issue made Dayton a questionable factor in the election of 1796. Hamilton urged fellow Federalists to work with him anyway rather than risk a party split that could give the presidency to Jefferson. Predictably, however, Dayton tried to steer a middle course. Rather than John Adams or Jefferson, he supported Aaron Burr (A.B. 1772), to whom he had recently loaned at least £2,250. The Speaker tried to convince Sedgwick that Adams could not win and that the Federalists would be better served by a man they could trust, by whom he meant Burr. Sedgwick rejected the argument and sent Dayton's letters to Hamilton, who scornfully dismissed the "intrigue."

On May 15, 1797, Dayton was reelected Speaker of the House. The Fifth Congress, concerned largely with military preparations for the Quasi-War with France, was a crucible for political parties. Acrimonious as were debates in the House, partisan newspapers were even more venomous. Willingly or not, Dayton assumed a more rigidly Federalist posture, as when he barred Benjamin Bache, editor of the Republican Philadelphia *Aurora*, from the House chamber. In May 1798 the Speaker warned that troops then massing in France were not bound for England, as everyone believed, but were embarking for an invasion of the United States. That contributed to the hysterical atmosphere in which the administration's proposals for alien and sedition laws were debated. Dayton was called upon as a veteran of the Constitutional Convention to defend those bills against Republican claims that the vaguely worded constitutional provision for ending the slave trade by 1808 could be construed to mean that no ban on immigration might be imposed until then. The framers, he explained, had used the euphemism "persons as any of the States . . . shall think proper to admit" because they did not wish to "stain the constitutional code" with the word "slave."

In planning the provisional army in 1798, Washington, Hamilton, and Secretary of War James McHenry proposed Dayton for a general officer's commission. He was confirmed as a brigadier general by the Senate on July 19, but he was not eager to accept. That autumn, after receiving an honorary doctorate of laws from the College, he was elected by the state assembly to the United States Senate. Not until the end of the year did he officially decline his military commission. He did not, though, refrain from offering his advice to Hamilton on which officers to select and how best to run the army.

Dayton entered the Senate on March 4, 1799, ostensibly as a firm Federalist. His influence was significant enough for Hamilton to plan a legislative program with him to insure that "men of information and property" were not displaced from positions of national leadership. Hamilton's basic idea was to increase the power of the federal government, particularly in the areas of internal improvements and law enforcement, but he also made a special point of the desirability of silencing dissident newspapers. Dayton's experience with Bache made him a natural leader of that effort, and in February 1800 he sponsored and then chaired a standing committee in the Senate on privileges, which was responsible for the ultimate indictment of James Duane, new editor of the *Aurora*, under the Sedition Law.

Dayton was rumored to be associated with Hamilton's scheme to dump John Adams and elect Charles Cotesworth Pinckney president in 1800, but he had troubles of his own that would impair his influence with voters that year. In 1796 Dayton had formed a commercial partnership with Francis Childs and William Denning, Jr., but he soon regretted doing so. In 1800, having for three years been unable to collect on his partners' promissory notes, he resorted to suing them for fraud. In retaliation, Childs and Denning made public letters from Dayton that revealed beyond question the extent of his speculation in public lands and securities. At the same time, two Republican clerks in the Treasury Department gave documents to Duane that proved Dayton's guilt, at least of a conflict of interests, and possibly of embezzlement. The letters and charges were collected in a pamphlet called *Public Speculations Unfolded*, published in Philadelphia in 1800. As soon as he learned of its preparation, Dayton withdrew his suit. That, according to the publisher of the pamphlet, amounted to an admission of guilt.

After Adams's defeat in the election of 1800, Dayton played a loyally partisan role in the Senate for a time. His friends in the upper house included Jonathan Mason, Jr. (A.B. 1774), a pillar of New England Federalism, and he corresponded with such notable conservatives as Samuel Stanhope Smith (A.B. 1769), who urged him and other "patricians" to save the nation from the "tribunes" who would destroy it. Although he had hoped that William Paterson (A.B. 1763) would receive Adams's nomination to be Chief Justice of the Supreme Court, and even tried to delay confirmation of John Marshall to give the lame duck President time to change his mind, Dayton dropped that campaign rather than risk leaving the office for Jefferson to fill. He also fought vigorously against the repeal of the Judiciary Act of 1801, a losing battle in which he had the support of John Ewing Colhoun (A.B. 1774) and, in at least one critical vote, Vice President Burr. He also led the Federalist attempt to defeat what became the Twelfth Amendment to the Constitution.

But Dayton avoided binding himself irrevocably to the Federalist Party. As a longtime advocate of national expansion, he supported the Louisiana Purchase and thus won applause from his Republican constituents. He also endorsed the Jefferson administration's pressure on Spain and France to force additional concessions in the west. Of course, his financial interests in frontier lands stood to benefit greatly from such concessions.

Dayton had visited parts of the west occasionally, but after the end of his Senate term in March 1805, he regarded his land investments as a full-time occupation. He, Burr, senators John Smith of Ohio and John Brown of Kentucky (Class of 1778), and General James Wilkinson formed a company to build a canal in Indiana after the Senate refused to give a federal patent to the proposal. That company provided a base for more dramatic schemes.

In April 1805 Burr met Dayton in Cincinnati, Ohio, purportedly to discuss the canal. But Burr had just come from other meetings and was on his way to more, the subject of which has been a source of controversy among historians for many years but which allegedly involved at least a plan to conquer parts of the Spanish Empire in America. After his conversations with Burr and then Wilkinson, Dayton returned to Philadelphia. He met there in December with the Spanish minister, the Marquis de Caso Yrujo. Burr had just learned from Jefferson that the Spanish-American war upon which he had premised his scheme would not occur, and Dayton's mission was to obtain Spanish support for a filibuster against Spain herself.

As the minister reported their conversations, Dayton told Yrujo that Burr planned to lead the western states in secession to form a new republic, a prospect that should have appealed to Madrid. He said first that the plot was backed by English money but then changed his story to impress Yrujo with the urgency of his request for funds. As proof of his sincerity, Dayton told the Spaniard of a simultaneous expedition by Francisco de Miranda to liberate parts of Latin America, thereby insuring the defeat of a plot that competed with Burr's for support. It was for that information, Yrujo later claimed, that Spain gave Burr $2,500. Yrujo seemed disinterested in the enterprise until Dayton revealed to him a fantastic plan for a coup d'état in Washington that would spark the secessionist movement. However extravagant his own dreams, and although the government's least reliable witness in his later trial related a similar plot, it would have been uncharacteristically reckless of Burr to have envisioned such a plan except for use as Dayton probably used it with Yrujo—to get his listener's attention.

In July 1806, when he thought that Wilkinson might be wavering, Dayton tried to spur the general on with reports that Jefferson would soon remove him from his western command. Apparently, that had precisely the opposite effect from the one Dayton had expected, for during the summer of 1806, while stories of the plot and Dayton's role in it began to circulate, Wilkinson moved to prove his fidelity to the Union by betraying Burr and his associates. To accentuate the importance of his patriotic service, the general corroborated the most extreme version of the conspiracy. When Burr was indicted for treason in the spring of 1807, Dayton was charged with the same crime.

Protesting his absolute ignorance of any plot, Dayton personally pleaded with Jefferson and Madison to intercede for him with the prosecutors. Neither would do so. He went to Richmond, Virginia for trial, prepared to prove that he could not have attended the meeting in Ohio in which Burr allegedly hatched his scheme. But the charges against Burr were dismissed, and those against Dayton were dropped in September.

Although he was free, the trial had been disastrous for Dayton's reputation. He returned to his home, Boxwood Hall, in Elizabethtown to farm, apparently having resigned from public life. But he was not a man to live like a recluse. Beginning in 1808 he wrote a series of anonymous or pseudonymous letters to James Madison, urging him to run for president, warning him of the danger of war with England, and ultimately advising him of a conspiracy in New England to secede from the nation if such a war should start. The handwriting and the postmark identified the writer of those letters, the last few of which Dayton actually signed. By 1812, however, when the crisis had come and Madison wanted specific information on the secessionists in New England, Dayton tried at first to deny that he was the author of the earlier letters. Although the president dropped the matter, Dayton continued the correspondence in order, first, to advise the government on how to fight the war and, second, to volunteer his personal services in the nation's defense. The latter offer was politely refused.

Dayton then organized a local militia among his older neighbors. At the end of 1814, he was elected as a Republican to represent Essex County in the state assembly, an achievement that upset ardent Federalists and Republicans alike. In March 1815 he wrote to Secretary of State James Monroe to congratulate him on the end of hostilities and to be sure that the frontrunner for the presidency knew that Jonathan Dayton had done all he could to keep New Jersey in the lead of the war effort.

At the turn of the century, Dayton and his old friend Aaron Ogden had been partners in a ferryboat line between Elizabethtown and New York City. But Dayton had long since sold his interest to Thomas Gibbons, whose son married Dayton's only child. Gibbons and Ogden became bitter enemies, and before their quarrel eventually produced a landmark decision by the Supreme Court, Dayton was caught between his daughter's father-in-law and one of his own best friends.

In 1824, Dayton organized meetings in Elizabethtown to collect money for the Greek rebellion against the Ottoman Empire. Shortly afterward, he played host to Lafayette while the French general stayed at Boxwood Hall. Those efforts taxed him greatly, and on October 9, 1824, one week after Lafayette left his home, Dayton died. His widow and daughter inherited an estate worth slightly more than $3,000, including three slaves. In his lifetime, Dayton had made and spent several fortunes. His death, apparently, occurred during a trough.

SOURCES: *DAB; BDAC*; MS Steward's accounts, MS Clio. Soc. membership list, PUA; Heitman; Force, *Am. Arch.* (5 ser.), I, 1,618; L. Lunden, *Cockpit of the Rev.* (1940), 279-80; T. Thayer, *As We Were* (1964), esp. 117, 146, 149, 154, 204, 232; L. W. Murray, ed., *Notes on Sullivan Expedition of 1779* (1929), 1; *Washington Writings*, XVIII, 486 & n; XIX, 245; XXIV, 173, 270-71, 376, 427-28 & n; XXX, 413; XXXV, 12n ("highly objectionable"); XXXVI, 331, 356n, 425, 433, 463n; XXXVII, 60; *NJA* (2 ser.), V, 92, 101-102, 104, 109; E. F. Hatfield, *Hist. of Elizabeth, N.J.* (1868), esp. 216n, 268n, 230-31, 259 & n; *Cal. of Correspondence of George Washington* (1915), 1,599, 2,394-95; *PMHB*, 20 (1896), 463 ("by their own imprudence"); 63 (1939), 131 & nn; 77 (1953), 137 & n, 143, 155; als G. Washington to JD, 11 Jul 1782, and JD to G. Washington, 13 May, 18 May 1782, Washington MSS; JD to T. Jefferson, 27 Dec 1803 and 6 Aug 1807, and T. Jefferson to JD, 17 Aug 1807, Jefferson MSS; J. Madison to JD, 18 Aug 1807, 7 Mar 1812, 5 Apr 1813, Madison MSS; JD to J. Monroe, 1 Mar 1815, Monroe MSS, DLC; *Soc. of Cincinnati in . . . N.J.* (1960), 19, 49; R. P. McCormick, *Experiment in Independence* (1950), 113, 228-29, 259n, 291; *Votes and Proceedings, Gen. Assem. of N.J.* (11th Assem.), passim; C. Rossiter, *1787: the Grand Convention* (1966), 100-101, 143, 164, 251; J. Madison, *Journals of the Fed. Convention* (1894), 348 ("security of [states'] rights"), and passim; M. Farrand, *Rec. of Fed. Conv.* (1937), I, 428, 445, 490; II, passim; III, 37, 90, 467-73; IV, 72; *A/C*, XIII, 100-101 ("clashing of interests"), 21, 47-49, 109, 193-94; V, 1,273-80; VII, 248, 250, 252; VIII, 1,192-94 ("stain the . . . code"); XI, 148-49, 155-56; XII, 136-39, 237-40; *LMCC*, VIII, XC; C. A. Beard, *Economic Interpretation of the Constitution* (1913), 85-86; G. A. Boyd, *Elias Boudinot* (1952), passim; B. W. Bond, Jr., ed., *Correspondence of John Cleves Symmes* (1926), passim; *Hamilton Papers*, XVI, 153n1; V, 309-10 & n; XI, 253 & nn; XII, 196, 275 & n; XIII, 58, 521-24; XVI, 272-73 & n, 308n; XVIII, 115-17; XIX, 438; XX, 39 ("agitations"), 248-49n, 403-407 ("intrigue"); XXI, 462-63n; XXIII, 599-604 ("information and property"); W. R. Fee, *Transition from Aristocracy to Democracy in N.J.* (1933), 15 ("anybody *but* Clark"), 12-16, 47, 50, 64-65, 135, 234; *WMQ* (3 ser.), 6 (1949), 243 ("bloodthirsty Presbyterians"), 240-50; 12 (1955), 604-605 ("weakness and wickedness"); 24 (1967), 433; 7 (1950), 92-93; 17 (1960), 158-61; G. Hunt, *Cal. of Applications and Recommendations for Office during the Presidency of George Washington* (1901), 34; Davis, *Essays*, 370, 391, 405 & n; C. E. Prince, *N.J.'s Jeffersonian Republicans* (1967), 12, 32-33, 55-56, 186 & n; J. C. Miller, *Federalist Era* (1960), 151; H. B. Fuller, *Speakers of the House* (1909), 26-27; H. S. Parmet and M. B. Hecht, *Aaron Burr* (1967), 108-109, 237-38, 266, 294, 296, 303; A. DeConde, *Quasi-War* (1966), 84-86; *N.Y. Daily Advertiser*, 4 Oct 1798; *Pa. Gazette*, 8 Oct 1783; S. E. Morison, *Harrison Gray Otis* (1913), 1, 185 & n; D. H. Fischer, *Rev. of Amer. Conservatism* (1967), 327; *Public Speculation Unfolded* (1800); als JD to E. Dayton, 26 Nov 1797; J. Mason to JD, 17 Jun 1801; S. S. Smith to JD, 22 Dec 1801 ("patricians . . . tribunes"); A. Ogden to JD, 13 Aug 1805; M. Lewis to JD, 14 Feb 1813; JD to A. Ogden, 14 Mar and 26 Dec 1803; JD to J. Madison, 5 Aug 1807, 25 Mar 1812, 29 Mar and 9 Apr 1813; anon. to J. Madison,

Oct. 1808; "One of Seventy-Six" to J. Madison, 29 May 1809, NjP; T. P. Abernathy, *Burr Conspiracy* (1954), passim; W. F. McCaleb, *Aaron Burr Conspiracy* (1966), 53-58; T. R. Hay and M. R. Werner, *Admirable Trumpeter* (1941), 110, 128-29, 220-21, 241; *N. J. Wills*, XI, 376; *Princeton Univ. Library Chronicle*, 3 (1942), 150-51; *MCCCNY*, II, 224-26, 647; will #11641G, Nj.

MANUSCRIPTS: NjHi; DLC; PHi; NjR; NjP; OCHP

Nicholas Dean

NICHOLAS DEAN has been identified by his family connections as being the son of Lechevalier and Rebecca Bryant Dean. His father, an Anglican of Huguenot descent, was a busy and prosperous merchant and sea captain of New York City and Charleston, South Carolina. His mother was the sister of Ebenezer, Joshua, and William Bryant, all respected citizens of New Jersey. The Bryant family was related by birth or marriage to many people who figured prominently in the history of the College, including William Peartree Smith, Elias Boudinot, Benjamin Woodruff (A.B. 1753), and the Duffield family of Philadelphia. When he died in July 1760, attorney Ebenezer Bryant left £50 to the Presbyterian church in Elizabethtown, New Jersey and £50 to Nassau Hall.

Nicholas Dean was baptized in Trinity Church, New York City, on November 11, 1759, when his parents lived on Wall Street. He may have been raised for some years at least in Elizabethtown, where his widowed mother lived in 1774. Her brother Joshua died in that year, leaving her his real and personal property for the "better support and education of her 3 children."

Dean probably enrolled in the College as a freshman before September 1773, when he joined the Cliosophic Society. He stayed at least until April 1775, after which the College's records are almost nonexistent. He was probably the Nicholas Dean who joined the Elizabethtown militia in January 1776 and participated in the capture of a beached English ship that month. He may also have been the private Nicholas Dean in the second company of Colonel Elias Dayton's Third Battalion of New Jersey Continentals between February and November 1776.

No further trace of Nicholas Dean has been found. A Loyalist merchant of that name was sent from New York to Nova Scotia after the war, but Dean's youth argues against his being that man. When his uncle William Bryant made his will in October 1785, he mentioned Rebecca Dean, her daughter Mary, and her "second son" William.

Since she had only three children, it appears that her son Nicholas was dead by that time.

SOURCES: *NYGBR*, 10 (1879), 96-97; 68 (1937), 76; *N.J. Wills*, IV, 67-68; V, 71-72 ("better support and education"); *N.Y. Wills*, XIV, 134-36 ("second son"); MS Clio. Soc. membership list; MS Steward's accounts, PUA; E. F. Hatfield, *Hist. of Elizabeth, N.J.* (1868), 423-24; Stryker, *Off. Reg.*, 181; Sabine, *Loyalists*, II, 504.

Benjamin Erwin

BENJAMIN ERWIN, A.B., Presbyterian clergyman, probably was born in Augusta County, Virginia, about 1755 or 1756, the son of one of the several and evidently related Erwins who settled in that county at mid-century. The varying spelling of the surname and the continuing use of such baptismal names as Edward, Andrew, and Benjamin make a positive identification difficult. If he was prepared for college in his native county, it may have been by or under the general supervision of Reverend John Brown (A.B. 1749). Surviving accounts kept by the steward leave no room for doubt that he first enrolled in the College in the fall of 1774 as a member of the junior class. There is no indication that he belonged to either of the literary societies or that he won any special honors as a student.

Erwin seems to have returned at once to Augusta County after graduation and he may have begun his theological studies with William Graham (A.B. 1773), who in May 1776 had become the rector of Liberty Hall, forerunner of Washington College and the later Washington and Lee University. In any case, when illness prevented Erwin's attendance at a meeting of the Hanover Presbytery, it was Graham who assigned to him "pieces of trial," which brought his acceptance as a candidate for the ministry on April 30, 1778. A little over two years later, on June 20, 1780, he was ordained as the pastor of the Mossy Creek and Cook's Creek congregations. In May 1782 he and Archibald Scott (A.B. 1775) were two of the four Presbyterian ministers in the county licensed to "celebrate matrimony." In that same year he was chosen by the Hanover Presbytery as one of the trustees of Liberty Hall, but his name was omitted for some reason in the subsequent act of incorporation by the state legislature.

Erwin seems quickly to have settled into the quiet routine of a country parson, his activity leaving little in the way of a historical record, aside from the marriage ceremonies he continued to perform. He is credited with the organization of a third congregation in nearby Rockingham County to which he had devoted a third of his preaching before its formal establishment in 1789. Thereafter, he tends to slip from view, so much so that historians of the College and of his denomination have been inclined to assume that he ended his life in the same pastoral charge in which he began his career. Actually, by 1798 the Lexington Presbytery reported him to the Synod of Virginia as a member without a pulpit, and the same report was made again in 1804. Whether his health had failed, whether there had been a quarrel with his people, or whether he had turned to farming, perhaps preaching as a supply on the side, cannot be said. According to family tradition, he moved to Kentucky to become the pastor of the Paint Lick church in Madison County, and it can be noted that in Robert Davidson's *History of the Presbyterian Church* (1847) in that state, "Benj. Irvine" is listed among the members of the Kentucky Synod under the date of 1810. Even the record of his death is confused. In the *Minutes of the General Assembly* for May 1832 (p. 385), Benjamin Irvine of the Transylvania Presbytery is listed among the ministers of the church who had died "since the last annual report." The College's *Catalogue* had listed him as dead five years earlier, in 1827.

It is said that Erwin married on July 23, 1782, Sarah Brewster, daughter of James Brewster of Rockingham County, Virginia, and that of this marriage three children were born, two sons and a daughter.

SOURCES: L. Chalkley, *Rec. of Augusta Cnty. Va.* (1912), esp. I, 44, 365, 437, 505; II, 24, 30, 53-54, 299, 310, 359, 367, 508; III, 92, 245, 303, 348, 590; MS Steward's accounts, alumni file, PUA; Foote, *Sketches, Va.*, II, 107-8; I, 458; *Rec. Pres. Chh.*, 542; *Min. Gen. Assem., 1789-1820*, 19, 83, 165, 291; *WMQ* (1 ser.), 20 (1912), 109; (2 ser.), 3 (1923), 240; J. H. Harrison, *Settlers by the Long Grey Trail* (1935), 185, 321, 412; H. M. Wilson, *Tinkling Spring* (1954), 251; *KSHS Reg.*, 24 (1936), 349; typed notes, PPPrHi; Washington and Lee Univ., *Cat.* (1888), 35. Because there was more than one Benjamin Erwin, one hesitates to consider the marriage of Benjamin Erwin to Margaret Wallace in September 1793 (Chalkley, II, 310, 359) a second marriage. See William H. Vernon (A.B. 1776) for commencement of 1776.

WFC

George Faitoute

GEORGE FAITOUTE, A.B., A.M. 1792, Presbyterian clergyman and educator, was born in 1750. On December 15, 1772, while a freshman at the College, he joined the Cliosophic Society, in which he used the name of the Roman emperor "Trajan." After graduating he remained at Nassau Hall as a tutor while he studied theology. On October 4, 1777, he was accepted as a candidate for the ministry by the Presbytery of New Brunswick. He was licensed six months later and immediately assigned to supply the church in Allentown, New Jersey for four sabbaths.

When the presbytery met on October 20, 1778, it approved a request from the congregations of Allentown and neighboring Nottingham that Faitoute be their stated supply for the course of the winter. Both churches called him to be their permanent pastor on April 29, 1779, and he was ordained and installed the following August.

With a secure position, a parsonage, and 150 acres of farmland, Faitoute was able to begin his own family. On November 4, 1779, he married Euphamia Titus of Monmouth County, but they remained in Allentown less than two years. He and his congregations mutually agreed upon his dismission on July 25, 1781. Within a month he was supplying the church at Greenwich, Cumberland County, New Jersey, and on April 8, 1782, he was installed as its regular minister by the Presbytery of Philadelphia. His decision to leave Allentown was probably due to a better offer from Greenwich rather than to some failure on his part, for he occasionally visited the Allentown church and preached from his former pulpit until at least 1799.

Certainly, he was successful enough at Greenwich, where the congregation expanded greatly during his tenure. In 1783 he delivered the sermon at the funeral of Catharine Tennent, the widow of College trustee William Tennent, Jr., in Pittstown, Salem County. In May 1789 Faitoute received a call from the church in Jamaica, Queens County, Long Island. It took him less than a month, until the next meeting of the Philadelphia Presbytery, to decide that he wanted to accept. By July he and his family had moved into the parsonage near the old stone church in Jamaica. After the settlement of a jurisdictional dispute finally established that the church was part of the Presbytery of New York, Faitoute was installed on December 15. John Rodgers, trustee of the College, and John McKnight (A.B. 1773) officiated at the ceremony.

Faitoute wrote an unpublished history of the Jamaica church in 1793 in which he noted that the congregation had 96 families comprised of 539 people, of whom 58 were communicants. His own family in 1790 included him and his wife, their two sons and four daughters, and five slaves. By 1793 Faitoute counted twelve in his household.

Faitoute was a conscientious member of church governing bodies and was frequently the sole representative from Long Island to attend their sessions. In October 1793 he served as moderator of the Synod of New York and New Jersey, and in 1794 and 1795 he delivered the opening sermons at its annual meetings. His salary at Jamaica was $300 per year, but it was supplemented by "spinning parties" in which the members of the congregation delivered foodstuffs, household goods, and farm tools to the parsonage. Faitoute also augmented his income by teaching school at his home. He was, in addition, one of the original trustees of Union Hall Academy in Queens County and in 1797 was principal of the institution. One of the cardinal precepts of his life was that "the increase of Knowledge among People may be justly considered as a distinguished blessing."

Lame throughout his adulthood, Faitoute took no active part in either military or political affairs. But his Thanksgiving sermon of 1797 paid special tribute to an "excellent civil Constitution . . . the best in the known world," and in 1800 he composed two odes to be sung at the town's celebration of Washington's birthday. He was a vigorous performer in the pulpit, often weeping to make his point, a histrionic device which he may have used to disguise the fact that he repeated verbatim his sermons for special occasions every third year.

On Sunday, August 21, 1815, Faitoute preached his usual morning service in Jamaica and was preparing for the afternoon meeting when he died. He was buried in the churchyard there.

SOURCES: J. A. Macdonald, *Two Centuries in the Hist. of the Pres. Chh., Jamaica, Long Island* (1862), 200-205; B. F. Thompson, *Hist. of Long Island* (1918), II, 610; Webster, MS Brief Sketches. Thompson and Macdonald give N.Y. City as probable birthplace. Another possible birthplace is Elizabethtown, N.J., and he may have been the son or a relative of Aaron Faitoute, who lived there and was a member of the Anglican chh. in Perth Amboy. Faitoute was a member of an Anglican family (see Macdonald), his wife was a resident of the same general area of northeastern N.J., and the name was common in Elizabethtown at a time when many young men from that borough were attending the College. *N.J. Wills*, IV, 427; W. A. Whitehead, *Early Hist. of Perth Amboy* (1856), 222; *GMNJ*, 3 (1928), 84; *N.J. Journal*, 10 Oct 1792 (A.M.); MS Clio. Soc. membership list, PUA; F. D. Storms, *Hist. of Allentown Pres. Chh.* (1970), 35, 50, 51, 52; *NJA* (1 ser.), XXII, 136; MS "Brief Hist. of . . . Pres. Chh. at Greenwich," (n.d.), PPPrHi; *PMHB*, 6 (1882), 498; *First Census, N.Y.*, 150; G. Faitoute, MS "Thanksgiving Sermon," 7 Dec 1797, PPPrHi ("increase of knowledge"); H. Onderdonk, Jr., *Antiquities of the Parish Chh., Jamaica, Long Island* (1880), 88. See William H. Vernon (A.B. 1776) for commencement of 1776.

MANUSCRIPTS: PPPrHi

PUBLICATIONS: see Macdonald, above

John Evans Finley

JOHN EVANS FINLEY, A.B., Presbyterian clergyman, was born on July 26, 1753, in East Nottingham, Chester County, Pennsylvania. He was one of the nine children of Hannah Evans Finley and James Finley, the local Presbyterian minister and brother of College president Samuel Finley. John Evans Finley was thus the cousin of Samuel Finley, Jr. and Joseph Finley (both A.B. 1765) and Ebenezer Finley (A.B. 1772). Joseph Lewis Finley (A.B. 1775) was the son of James and Samuel Finley's brother Michael.

According to the records of steward Elias Woodruff, Finley enrolled in the College no later than April 1774. He joined the American Whig Society and returned to East Nottingham after completing his academic work to study theology with his father. In January 1779 he was licensed to preach by the Presbytery of New Castle.

On August 21, 1781, Finley was ordained and installed at the church in Fagg's Manor, Chester County. He was the first regular minister there since the death of John Blair. One of the members of his congregation, Job Ruston, was the father of Thomas Ruston (A.B. 1762); Finley married his daughter Elizabeth. They lived in West Fallowfield Township, where Finley apparently conducted a Latin grammar school. As a clergyman, Finley was the equal of neither his uncle nor his predecessor, and his ministry at Fagg's Manor was more troubled than successful. Moreover, he was involved in a chronic, nasty family feud with his wife's brother Thomas regarding the disposition of Job Ruston's estate. In 1785 Finley's father moved west, and two years later Finley himself bought 800 acres of land in Washington County, Virginia. In October 1793 he resigned his pulpit, gave his power of attorney to a local official, and headed for the frontier, arriving in Mason County, Kentucky where he bought another 100 acres in July 1794. He inherited £100 worth of land and £30 in cash when his father died in 1795. On February 11 of that year he joined the Transylvania Presbytery as pastor of the church in Bracken, Mason County.

In 1797 Finley undertook a missionary tour among the Indians in the Illinois Territory. He was the first Presbyterian minister to preach at Kaskaskia, Illinois, but the local tribes proved hostile and he prudently returned to Kentucky soon afterward. In March 1797 he was among the seven original members of the Presbytery of Washington, and he was active during the religious revival that swept Kentucky in 1800. He continued to acquire land, served occasionally as the local surveyor, and was involved in the establishment of the Bracken Academy early in the nineteenth century.

Finley may have left his pulpit soon after December 1805, when he purchased 200 acres in Adams County, Ohio. He was listed as a member of the presbytery without a charge in 1809, but by 1810 he was certainly a resident of Adams County. In March 1817 Brown County was created from the section of Adams in which Finley lived, and he remained there as pastor of the Red Oak Church in the town of Ripley until his death on January 7, 1818. He and his wife had had seven children, six of whom survived him.

SOURCES: Giger, Memoirs, II; Webster, MS Brief Sketches, II; Mrs. J. H. Gorley, "Clan Finley" (typescript in PPPrHi), 13-14; R. Davidson, *Hist. of the Pres. Chh. Ky.* (1847), 128-29, 369; Sprague, *Annals*, III, 101; J. S. Futhey and G. Cope, *Hist. of Chester Cnty., Pa.* (1881), 251; MS Steward's accounts, PUA; *Chh. at Home and Abroad*, 19 (1896), 111; Biographical data file, PPPrHi; MS Diary, Draper MSS, WHi; E. W. Powell, *Early Ohio Tax Recs.* (1971), 3; R. M. Torrence, *Torrence and Allied Families* (1937), 208. See William H. Vernon (A.B. 1776) for the commencement of 1776.

MANUSCRIPTS: WHi

Joseph Washington Henderson

JOSEPH WASHINGTON HENDERSON, A.B., Presbyterian clergyman, according to tradition acquired the middle name "Washington" while a student in the College "on account of some peculiar excellence which he possessed." It is true that the christening of a child with two names was not yet common, and further support for the tradition may be found in President Witherspoon's use of his full name, Joseph Washington Henderson, in the certificate, dated September 26, 1776, testifying that Henderson had been "examined for admission to the Degree of Bachelor of Arts and approved, and is entitled to that standing from this time." The certificate was given in lieu of a diploma because the trustees assembling for the scheduled commencement of September 25 failed to muster the quorum required for the award of degrees. The actual award would not come for the members of this class until May 24, 1777. At the truncated commencement exercises of September 1776, the president had advised that each member of the class might secure such a certificate, but evidence of only one other, that given to William R. Davie on October 20, has been found.

In the statement that Henderson had been resident in the College for two years prior to his graduation, the certificate adds a welcome detail to an otherwise sparse record of his early life. It is known that he was a native of that part of Cumberland County, Pennsylvania that became Franklin County in 1784, and from the date of his death on September 9, 1836, in the eighty-fourth year of his life it can be concluded that he was born about 1752. As for his parentage and preparation for college, no evidence has been found. The steward's account for November 1774 to the following April confirms his presence as a member of the junior class. He is not listed among the members of either of the literary societies.

After finishing his studies in Nassau Hall, Henderson presumably was reading theology, for he was licensed to preach on June 16, 1779, by the Donegal Presbytery. Probably for a time he served as itinerant or supply minister. In June 1780 he received a call from the Great Conewago congregation of York County, Pennsylvania, and, having entered into an agreement for a salary of 697 bushels of wheat per year, he was installed and ordained as pastor of that church on June 20, 1781. His ministry for a time seems to have been successful. In 1787 the old wooden church gave way to a more impressive building constructed of stone. But in 1795 he sought and received permission from the Carlisle Presbytery, of which he had been an original member since 1786, to resign the pulpit because of nonpayment of salary. His obituary described him as a strong advocate of temperance, even to the extent of preaching total abstinence "long before a temperance society was formed," but it cannot be said that this was a main cause for the break.

The minutes of the General Assembly for 1797 and 1798 show him as still being a member of the Carlisle Presbytery, but without a charge. Perhaps as early as 1796 he had gone westward to Kentucky, whence he returned, reportedly planning to settle in that state. Instead, he accepted a call in April 1799 to the joint pastorate of Bethel and Ebenezer congregations in Westmoreland County, Pennsylvania. And there he lived out his life, inactive after 1823 because of a loss of his voice. He was said to have excelled in the pulpit, with sermons that were compared to those of John Witherspoon, and to have been a "friend of all the benevolent operations of the day," especially the missionary work of his own denomination to which he left $50.

No information has been found regarding marriage or descendants.

SOURCES: D. Elliott, *Life of Rev. Elisha Macurdy* (1848), 261-66 (college certificate, "temperance society"); A. Alexander and J. Carnahan, MS "Notices of Distinguished Graduates," NjP; *Centennial Memorial of Presbytery of Carlisle* (1889), I, 100, 105, 106, 108, 110, 215, 424, 438-39; *Hist. of Cumberland and Adams Counties, Pa.* (1886) (Adams), 335, 337-338; *Hist. of Presbytery of Redstone* (1889), 186; *Rec. Pres. Chh.*, passim. See William H. Vernon (A.B. 1776) for commencement of 1776.

MANUSCRIPTS:PHi   WFC

Robert Jenkins Henry

ROBERT JENKINS HENRY, planter, was born about 1755, the son of Robert Jenkins Henry of Somerset County, Maryland, and his wife,

Gertrude Rousby. The father was a son of Reverend John Henry, a native of Ireland who in 1710 succeeded Francis Makemie as pastor of the Presbyterian church at Rehoboth in the southern part of the county, and his wife, Mary King Jenkins, through whom the older Robert inherited extensive properties, including his main seat on the Pocomoke River. Before his death in 1766, the father served many years as a member of the lower house of the provincial assembly and of the governor's council. Gertrude Rousby belonged to a family of property and influence in St. Mary's County.

The younger Robert Jenkins Henry, a first cousin of John Henry (A.B. 1769), is listed in the steward's account for the period November 6, 1774 to April 10, 1775 as a member of the junior class. Next in an alphabetical arrangement of the roll for the junior class comes the name Robert Henry, who only could have been Robert Rosbrough Henry (A.B. 1776). No doubt, it was the presence of two Roberts with the same family name in the same class that caused the steward to include the full name of Robert Jenkins Henry. Which of the two was the Robert Henry whose name appears on the steward's account for May 25, 1773 through September 25, 1774 cannot be said with certainty. The two entries for a Robert Henry in the ledger of the local merchant Thomas Patterson, under the dates of September 15, 1774 and March 22, 1775, provide no assistance. No evidence has been found of Robert Jenkins Henry's residence at the College of later date than April 1775.

Presumably Henry returned to the Eastern Shore of Maryland to assume the management of his properties there. Tax returns for 1783 show that he held property in both Somerset and Worcester counties. In the former, he owned more than 2,000 acres graced by a dwelling described as "Midling large" and other improvements that were "midling Good." The some 530 acres he held in Worcester seem chiefly to have been meadowland. Henry is not listed among the inhabitants of Maryland in the census of 1790. Perhaps he died at some time between 1783 and 1790.

Sources: W. H. Eldridge, *Henry Geneal.* (1915), 193-95; C. Torrence, *Old Somerset* (1935), 175, 268, 368-71; H. D. Richardson, *Side-Lights on Md. Hist.*, ii (1913), 127-29; *MHM*, 15 (1920), 302; 26 (1931), 247, 254-55, 348, 351; E. C. Papenfuse et al., *Directory of Md. Legislators* (1974), 24, 40; ms Steward's accounts, PUA; Patterson Acct. Bk.; Assessments of 1783, Somerset Cnty., Pocomoke Dist. #4, 134-35; Worcester Cnty., Pitts Creek, 1-2, Hall of Records, Annapolis.

WFC

Robert Rosbrough Henry

ROBERT ROSBROUGH HENRY, A.B., physician and farmer, was the son of David Henry and Mary Rosbrough Henry of Lamington, Somerset County, New Jersey. He was born there on May 27, 1753. His mother was the maternal aunt of his classmate Robert McCrea, and his father was a prosperous farmer who kept at least one slave. When David Henry died in 1783, he left an estate worth £1,780. After debts were deducted, the balance was divided among his eight children, including one daughter who was the wife of John Cleves Symmes, Revolutionary soldier, member of Congress, and one of the founders of Ohio.

Henry was probably prepared for college at the school run in Lamington by John Hanna (A.B. 1755). He apparently entered Nassau Hall as a junior in November 1774, when he also joined the Cliosophic Society. It is possible that he matriculated earlier, for the name "Robert Henry" appears on a steward's list of students for May 1773 to September 1774. That reference may, however, have been to Robert Jenkins Henry, a non-graduate of the same class. Similar entries in the accounts of merchant Thomas Patterson are of no assistance in clarifying which Robert Henry came first to Princeton. By 1774 the names of American Whigs had been included in the pantheon of heroes from which Cliosophic Society pseudonyms were drawn, and Henry was known to his fellow members as "Adams."

After graduation, Henry studied medicine, possibly in Philadelphia. On March 17, 1777, before completing his formal training, he joined the Continental Army as a surgeon's mate in the general hospital at Morristown, New Jersey. In that capacity, he assisted the Surgeon General of the Middle Department, John Cochran, and saw action at the battle of Brandywine in October.

Henry also worked closely with Benjamin Rush (A.B. 1760), whom he supported in opposition to the director of the Medical Department, William Shippen, Jr. (A.B. 1754). In February 1778, after being forced to resign from the department, Rush sent a long complaint against Shippen to George Washington. Enclosed in the letter was a statement by four young medical officers, including Henry and Samuel Finley, Jr. (A.B. 1765), in which the deplorable conditions at the hospital were enumerated and blamed, at least implicitly, on Shippen.

In the summer of 1779, Henry accompanied General John Sullivan's expedition against the Six Nations as surgeon to the Third New Jersey Regiment. That autumn he became surgeon of Colonel George Reid's Second New Hampshire Regiment of Continentals, part of General Enoch Poor's Brigade. On the New York-Connecticut border in 1780, Henry was wounded in the arm and held briefly as a prisoner of war after a skirmish on the Croton River. In April 1780 he married Mary Hilliard, the daughter of Isaac and Sarah White Hilliard of Redding, Connecticut. The wedding took place at the army headquarters in Danbury, Connecticut, where Henry was stationed with the hospital.

Early in 1781 Henry transferred to the First New Hampshire Regiment. His salary as regimental surgeon was $60 per month, and in 1779 he had also received $127 in depreciation pay. He was unsatisfied with the state's settlement of his account in May 1783, however. Then a member of the single New Hampshire Regiment of the Continental Line, he believed that he was due at least $25 more than the £195 given him.

Henry returned to New Jersey after the war, settling first on a farm of 200 acres at the "Cross Roads" in Somerset County, where he was a trustee of the Lamington Presbyterian Church. He later moved to another farm at Flanders in Morris County. He continued to practice medicine while he farmed, and on November 1, 1792, he and John A. Scudder (A.B. 1775) were admitted to the New Jersey Medical Society after a proper examination.

Henry died at Flanders on December 27, 1805, survived by his wife and nine of their ten children. His estate was worth an estimated $2,489.56 and included one slave, an "18 Day Clock," a "Dockter book," and a "medicine shop." He had received a pension for his military service in September 1789. Henry was buried first at his farm in Flanders. His widow moved to Penn Yan, Yates County, New York, where in 1836 she received a federal pension. After her death and interment there in 1843, Henry's remains were moved to be buried beside her.

SOURCES: *Som. Cnty. Hist. Quart.*, 7 (1918), 104-108; J. P. Snell, *Hist. of Hunterdon and Somerset Counties, N.J.* (1881), 599; Wickes, *Hist. of Medicine N.J.* (1879), 284-85; W. H. Eldridge, *Henry Geneal.* (1915), 154-55; *N.J. Wills*, VI, 188; IX, 168; MS Clio. Soc. membership list, PUA; Butterfield, *Rush Letters*, 201-202; L. W. Murray, ed., *Notes on Sullivan Expedition of 1779* (1929), 23; *N.H. St. Pap.*, XV, 719; XVI, 4, 203; 271; XVII, 450; Med. Soc. of N.J., *Rise, Minutes, and Proceedings* (1875), 46; will #1283N, Inv. 1806, Nj; *Index, Rev. War Pension Applications* (1966).

David Hyslop

DAVID HYSLOP was born on December 28, 1755, in Boston, Massachusetts. His mother, Mehetable Stoddard Hyslop, was a cousin of College president Jonathan Edwards. His father, William Hyslop, a native of Scotland who had come to America in the 1740s as a peddler, had quickly acquired one of the great fortunes in the city through shrewd investments and a lucrative importing business. In 1766 he purchased the Boylston family home on Fish's or White's Hill in Brookline, the childhood residence of the mother of John Adams.

William Hyslop was an ardent Presbyterian who worshiped in the congregational Brattle Street Church in Boston until that meeting house purchased an organ; then, in spite of the pleas from his own minister and those of Reverend Joseph Eckley (A.B. 1772) of Boston's Second Church, he refused to enter the Brattle Street Church again. Thenceforth he attended the church in Brookline, although the use of a bass viol by the choir there often stirred his ire. His departure was a blow to his former congregation, for Hyslop was an extremely generous donor and famous philanthropist. He was a close friend of President Witherspoon, with whom he was associated in supporting missionary work, and in 1787 made the largest donation—$2,754.67— to the founding of the Society for Propagating the Gospel among the Indians and Others in North America.

David Hyslop was always something of a family pet, for a childhood fall had left him with a permanently damaged leg and he also suffered a severe speech impediment. Those handicaps may well have explained his very brief enrollment in the College, which he entered in the autumn of 1772 and left by March 1773. Because his relatives always expected to have to care for him, Hyslop may not have undertaken any profession at all when he returned to Brookline. His father had been active in the boycott of British goods in 1767 and served on the Brookline Committee of Correspondence in December 1772, but business affairs took him and one of his two sons, possibly the erstwhile student, David, to England before hostilities began. They were stranded in London for four years during the Revolution, able to communicate with their family, which had fled to Medfield, Massachusetts during the siege of Boston, only indirectly, and carefully, using third person correspondence to seek the advice of John Adams, who politely declined to give any. The Hyslops returned to Boston in 1779, probably in time to attend the wedding of David's sister Elizabeth to Increase Sumner (Harvard 1767), a future governor of Massachusetts. The town government was satisfied with William Hyslop's explanation for his residence in enemy territory, although it was not entirely happy with his attitude toward its official inquiries.

When Hyslop's mother died in 1792 he inherited a one-sixth part of Noddle's Island in East Boston. But because no one expected him to marry, the fees from that land went to his sister and a cousin who were to see that he received his share of the income. Other bequests from other relatives had already made him wealthy, but they, too, may have been made with stipulations that assumed his dependency.

It must, therefore, have come as a shock to the family when Hyslop married Elizabeth Stone of Concord in September 1793. She was a devoted wife to a man who already had a reputation for eccentricity. He had inherited his father's orthodoxy and taken it even further. His detestation for music applied not only in church, but everywhere. He made a point of attending every religious ceremony within his reach, from ordinations to clerical conventions, and for years he faithfully attended the Thursday lectures in Boston. His wife accompanied him to the city but would visit the library while he listened to the lecture.

The death of his father in August 1796 left Hyslop and his sister as the two surviving children and sole heirs to an estate rumored to be worth £80,000. Because he had no children of his own, Hyslop made a will in which his nephew William Hyslop Sumner was the beneficiary. He visited Sumner's law office almost weekly, after the lecture, to amend or confirm portions of the document. After his wife died on June 6, 1808, in York, Maine, Hyslop was persuaded by Joseph Woodward, an uncle's former servant, to marry Woodward's beautiful twenty-five-year-old daughter Jane. Against the advice of friends and relations, the wedding took place on October 19, 1809, in Boston's First Church; and Hyslop changed his will to provide for his new wife and, eventually, for their four children. When one of those births caused Hyslop's wife to suffer a nervous collapse, he committed her to the temporary care of a Cambridge physician who influenced him to alter his will again, giving the doctor himself the lucrative status of trustee.

After years of sending invitations, Hyslop managed in 1821 to persuade John Adams to come to dinner in the old Boylston family mansion. It was a gala affair, the major social event of Hyslop's life. He died on August 16, 1822, leaving a healthy widow and his surviving son and daughter to share his substantial estate. Both children died shortly thereafter and Hyslop's widow remarried.

Sources: E. W. Stoddard, *Anthony Stoddard . . . and his Descendants* (1873), 124-26; W. H. Sumner, *Hist. of East Boston* (1858), 307-312, 274-78, and passim; MS Steward's accounts, PUA (in which the name is spelled "Haslop"); J. G. Curtis, *Hist. of the Town of Brookline, Mass.* (1933), 122-23, 135-36, 151; C. K. Bolton, *Brookline* (1897, 28-29; *NEHGR*, 7 (1853), 146, 149; 8 (1854), 110, 128n; 34 (1880), 290; *Pub. Col. Soc. Mass.*, XLI, 1,075; *Adams Papers*, III, 256n; IV, 103 & n; *Sibley's Harvard Graduates*, XVI, 532, 535; *MHSP* (3 ser.), LIX, 117 & n; LXVI, 117-19; *Essex Inst. Hist. Coll.*, LXV, (1929), 199.

William Johnes

WILLIAM JOHNES, farmer, was born on May 19, 1755, in Morristown, Morris County, New Jersey, where his father, Timothy Johnes (Yale 1737), was pastor of the Presbyterian church. He was the son of the Reverend Johnes's second wife, Keziah Ludlow.

Timothy Johnes was a trustee of the College from 1748 until 1788, a tenure second only to that of William Peartree Smith among the trustees of the 1748 charter. His son William entered Nassau Hall as a freshman and remained at least until May 1775, late in his junior year. In or before November 1774, he must have experienced a religious conversion, for he was accepted into full communion at his father's church on November 4. Unlike so many of his fellow students for whom a religious experience was the beginning of intense study toward a career in the ministry, however, Johnes soon left the College. In June 1776 he was among the freeholders of Morris County and joined the county militia to fight in the Revolution.

Although some sources list Johnes as a militia captain, it is as likely that he was a "captain and conductor of a team brigade," or ranking wagonmaster, for that was duty more closely related to his devotion to farming than commanding an infantry company would have been. In February 1777 he returned from a supply run to his farm in Morristown to find that the village had been converted to an army headquarters. The rails and posts of his fences and the lumber he had intended for a new house had all been appropriated for firewood, and his animals had been driven from their stalls so that the mounts of officers would have shelter. Johnes demanded that his barn, at least, be returned to him. A sword-wielding young officer who may have forgotten the determination of "embattled farmers" challenged him, and found himself disarmed and knocked senseless. Johnes protested his situation to General Washington, who had accepted the hospitality of the Johnes family, and the commander in chief ordered that the farm animals be returned to their stalls.

When his father died in 1794, Johnes inherited a small farm near Hanover, New Jersey and the homestead with seventy-four more acres in Morristown. He also obtained all of the family's "implements of husbandry" and one slave. He was responsible for the care of his ailing mother, but she died only two months later, leaving Johnes with her share of his father's estate.

On February 9, 1783, Johnes had married Anna Brewster. She died on January 21, 1785. In 1787 he married Esther Dubois. She died on July 24, 1789. His third marriage, in 1794, was to Charlotte Pierson.

She was the mother of all twelve of his children, and when Johnes
died on December 8, 1836, she and at least ten of those children survived him. *Johnes was followed at the College by several*

SOURCES: E. R. Johnes, *Johnes Family of Southampton, Long Island* (1886), 29-31;
Hist. of First Pres. Chh., Morristown, N.J. (n.d.), II, 117-18; Dexter, *Yale Biographies*, I, 577-79; MS Steward's Accounts, PUA; Patterson Acct. Bk.; A. M. Sherman,
Hist. of Morristown, N.J. (1905), 194; *DAR Patriot Index*; Stryker, *Off. Reg.*, 849,
852; *N.J. Wills*, VIII, 202 ("implements of husbandry").

*nephews: Timothy Ford (A.B. 1783), Gabriel Ford (A.B., 1784),
Jacob Ford (A.B., 1792), + Stevens Johnes Lewis (A.B., 1791).*

Andrew Johnston

ANDREW JOHNSTON, student and soldier, was the son of Lewis and
Laleah Peyton Johnston of Savannah, Georgia, and a distant cousin
of John (A.B. 1758) and Philip Johnston (A.B. 1759). Lewis Johnston had come to America from his native Scotland in 1752 as a
surgeon in the Royal Navy. He stopped first in St. Kitts, where he met
and married his wife, then in 1753 he settled in Savannah, bringing
with him a substantial amount of property and several slaves, which
may have been part of her dowry. Dr. Johnston established a prosperous medical practice, from which he ultimately realized an annual
income of £800, and lived on a plantation called "Annandale" on the
outskirts of the city. It was there that his many children were born.
The family attended Savannah's Independent Presbyterian Church,
whose pastor, John J. Zubly, was the father of David Zubly (A.B.
1769).

Almost as soon as he settled in Georgia, Lewis Johnston was active
in provincial politics. He was a member and then Speaker of the
House of Commons and later served on the governor's council. Loyalty
to the royal government was the paramount factor in his life and in
those of his sons, including Andrew.

Johnston may have entered Nassau Hall as a freshman in the fall
of 1772, for his name first appeared on the College steward's accounts
in an undated list that seems to have begun with that academic year.
He continued to be enrolled through the semester that began in November 1774, although in that term his was one of three names set
apart as "Resendentors" by the steward. At the time, his brother
William Martin Johnston was in Philadelphia studying medicine with
Benjamin Rush (A.B. 1760), who apparently defrayed some of the
expenses of both young men.

Undoubtedly, Andrew Johnston left Princeton during the spring
recess of 1775 to be with his family during the mounting political

crisis. That autumn his father was named treasurer of the colonial government, and his absolute adherence to the established authority marked the entire family for observation by the Whigs. In June 1776 the Georgia Committee of Safety declared an "Andrew Johnson" a threat to the "liberties of America." Barely two months later, that same committee conferred a captaincy on "Andrew Johnson." If it was the former student who accepted that commission, he did so merely as a way to avoid persecution. By early 1779 he was still a captain, but he was then serving in the King's Rangers, the scarlet-and-green-uniformed regiment of Loyalists commanded by Lieutenant Colonel Thomas Brown. His brother had also abandoned his studies to join the New York Volunteers, another Loyalist unit.

When Savannah was besieged by French and American forces in the late summer of 1779, both Johnston brothers manned the city's defenses. The siege was broken in October, but most of the rest of Georgia remained in rebel hands. After Benjamin Lincoln's defeat by the British in May 1780, Brown's Loyalists were sent to capture Augusta. They did so without a fight on June 8, thereby securing the west flank of a line of British forts that stretched into South Carolina and commanded the Savannah River. For reasons of economy, however, Brown was denied permission to fortify Augusta properly, and through the summer his 200-300 men and their Indian allies were garrisoned in mere field works. The rebel counterattack, which came in September, was therefore difficult to repel.

For security, Johnston's company had been posted at a house one mile from Augusta, but when the three-pronged rebel assault began on September 14, that house quickly became the stronghold of Brown's entire command. All of the Loyalists and their wounded colonel were surrounded there, completely cut off from food and water. The desperation of their situation lends credence to the tradition that Johnston volunteered to lead an extremely dangerous foraging expedition. Whether he did so or not, the Rangers were rescued by a regiment of South Carolina Loyalists on September 18. When the shooting had ended, Johnston was dead, possibly, as tradition holds, having been shot in the back while making a heroic return to the house with food and water. He had never married.

SOURCES: E. S. Johnston, *Recollection of a Ga. Loyalist* (1901), passim; MS Steward's accounts, PUA (in which the name is spelled "Jonson"); Butterfield, *Rush Letters*, I, 87n; *NYGBR*, 33 (1902), 246-49; H. E. Egerton, ed., *Royal Commission on the Losses and Services of American Loyalists* (1971), 247; *Rev. Rec. of Ga.*, I, 146-47 ("liberties of America"), 186; *GHQ*, 58 (1974), 424-33; W. B. Stevens, *Hist. of Ga.* (1859), II, 246-51; B. Fleming, ed., *Autobiography of a Colony* (1957), 141; H. E. Davis, *Fledgling Province* (1976), 93, 203, 204.

Samuel King

SAMUEL KING first appears in the incomplete surviving records of the
College's steward among the students who, under the date of September
29, 1772, were in arrears on their payments for tuition, room, and
board. Presumably, he had enrolled at some time earlier, possibly as
early as the fall of 1771. Although the record is confusing, even contra-
dictory, he may again have been in arrears on March 29, 1773. Another
list for the period from May 25 of that year to September 25, 1774, this
one not of arrears, groups him together with a number of students belonging to the Class of 1775, to which he should have belonged if admitted as a freshman in 1771. Still another list for the months from
November 6, 1774, to April 10, 1775, has Samuel King specifically assigned to the junior class—that is, to the Class of 1776. No answer to
the problems posed by this part of the record has been found, but his
name appears here among the members of the later class on the simple
assumption that the steward is to be followed on the most specific of his
entries.

Little help is to be found elsewhere. In January 1773 Israel Evans
(A.B. 1772) reported to his classmate Philip Fithian that there had
been a flurry of turkey stealings by the students, including some who
had been converted in an earlier religious revival, and listed a King
among those fined by a local magistrate. Perhaps it was Samuel; perhaps not, for Andrew King (A.B. 1773) was in the College at the time.
The King mentioned in letters of early 1772 by Andrew Hunter and
Moses Allen, both of whom graduated that year, seems probably to
have been Andrew. One additional source, the ledger of local merchant
Thomas Patterson, reveals that Samuel King kept an active account at
the store from the fall of 1774 to May 10, 1775, when his guardian apparently closed the account by a substantial payment. No subsequent
purchases are recorded in this source, so it can be assumed that he
dropped out of the College after the spring vacation of that year.

Unfortunately, it has been impossible to provide the clarification
that might be had through identification of Samuel King in terms of
his place of birth, parentage, and later career. In most, if not all, of the
colonies there were families bearing the name of King, and Samuel was
still among the more popular choices for a given name.

SOURCES: MS Steward's accounts, PUA; Patterson Acct. Bk.; *Fithian Journal*, I, 22, 30;
als M. Allen to A. Burr, Jan 1772, Gratz Coll., PHi. Among the possibilities was the
Samuel King who in 1804 at a relatively advanced age became member of the Kentucky Synod, and who in 1805 was apparently dropped by the Cumberland Presbytery as one of a group of trouble-making revivalists [R. Davidson, *Hist. of the Pres.
Chh. in ... Ky.* (1847), 224-25, 234, 239, 252-53]. Samuel was a favored name among

the King family of Southold, Long Island, but as the editor of the town Records, J. W. Case, has observed "many important links are missing" (II, 533). A check of Ezra Stiles' *Literary Diary* quickly disposes of the possibility that the student could have been the Newport painter of that name. In Pa. there were at least three Samuel Kings, and possibly four, all listed as privates in the militia. Among the three commissioned officers that have been found at the time of the Revolution, including Captain Samuel King of Mass. (killed at Guilford Courthouse in 1781), no identification with the College has been established. The reference in Patterson's Acct. Bk. to a settlement of King's account by a guardian invites attention to the record found in the Trustees Minutes for Sep 1773 of a bequest to the College, the sum not stated, by Mr. James King of Del., but efforts to follow this promising lead have been unsuccessful. There was a James King, "yeoman," of Kent Cnty. who died intestate earlier in 1773, and on March 3 administration of the estate was assigned to his widow Mariam and John Furchas [L. de Valinger, *Cal. of Kent Cnty . . . Probate Records* (1944), 274].

WFC

John Wilkes Kittera

JOHN WILKES KITTERA, A.B., A.M. 1780, lawyer and public official, was the son of Hannah and Thomas Kittera. He was born in November 1752 in the large sandstone house on his father's plantation at Blue Ball, in East Earl Township, Lancaster County, Pennsylvania.

Kittera's name first appeared on the lists of the College steward in November 1774, but he may have entered Nassau Hall as a freshman in the fall of 1772, when his father endowed two prizes "of considerable value" for competitions among freshmen in Latin grammar and English grammar. Kittera won neither prize. It is likely that he adopted Wilkes as his middle name while a student, for although the steward's list identifies him only as John, Princeton merchant Thomas Patterson knew him as John W. Kittera. After graduation he studied law, either in Philadelphia or in Lancaster County. He was at home in December 1779 when he witnessed a deed by which a relative conveyed title to a slave. In August 1780 he was an ensign in Lieutenant Colonel James Ross's Eighth Battalion of Lancaster County Militia, and in September he returned to Princeton to receive his second degree. He also took part in the commencement exercises that year, delivering an oration on "the power of the people to constitute their own governments, and to alter and reform them for their own advantage."

Kittera was admitted to the bar in both Philadelphia and Lancaster County in 1782 and in Chester County in 1783, but he established his law practice near his family home. In 1791 he was elected to represent his district in the United States House of Representatives, and two years later he was chosen for membership in the American Philosophical Society.

John Wilkes Kittera, A.B. 1776
BY ROBERT FULTON

During his five terms in Congress, Kittera became a loyal Federalist. He was an outspoken defender of Jay's Treaty when legislation to execute its provisions came before the House in 1796 and suggested that opposition to the pact was due to excessive sympathy for France, resentment against Britain, and the desire of a few members to destroy the Constitution. Kittera never hesitated to attack Francophiles in Congress, and his best opportunities came during the Quasi-War of 1797-1798 as he moved steadily to the right wing of the Federalist Party.

Kittera regularly voted for military and naval appropriations and fought efforts to impose congressional restrictions on how the armed forces might be deployed. He sponsored legislation to compel the French to compensate Americans whose neutral rights were violated by French privateers and he argued in favor of quick retaliation against such abuses in the future. He was, meanwhile, careful to guard against strains in Anglo-American relations and was privy to the machinations of the British minister.

Kittera was one of those Federalists most active in support of the Alien and Sedition laws in June 1798. He rejected the arguments of those who claimed that the measures might be unconstitutional, for he claimed that "the Constitution . . . in the hands of politicians, was like polemics in the hands of divines: it was made to prove everything or nothing." With the sarcasm that was a fixture of his political rhetoric, he pointed out that even in *"that land of liberty,"* France, aliens could be deported. And he argued that the danger in the United States was a government with too little power, rather than too much.

During the "XYZ Affair," when the French Directory peremptorily refused to treat with three American envoys but hinted that it might be willing to negotiate with one of them, Elbridge Gerry, some members of Congress proposed a new set of instructions for Gerry's use. To emphasize his contempt for that idea, Kittera sarcastically proposed that the instructions be addressed to Gerry or to whomever else the *French* selected after they expelled or imprisoned Gerry. His point made, he withdrew the amendment before the instructions were defeated in the House. By the end of July, Kittera was arguing for the abrogation of the Franco-American treaty. It was a measure of how his political philosophy had evolved since his speech at Nassau Hall in 1780 that when he published an address "To the Electors of Lancaster County" in August 1800, he stated that "obedience and submission to the powers that be is the duty of all" and that "resistance to lawfully elected officials is 'treason against society.' "

Kittera was not a candidate for reelection in 1800, probably because he had already been promised the appointment as United States Attorney for the eastern district of Pennsylvania. He moved to Philadelphia in anticipation of his new duties, but when Thomas Jefferson was elected president, Kittera's appointment went aglimmering. By March 9, 1801, Jefferson had decided to name Alexander James Dallas to the post Kittera had expected.

Kittera's tenure as federal attorney would not have been long in any case. He died at Lancaster on June 6, 1801 and was buried in the yard of the First Presbytrian Church. A memorial chapel was later built over that section of the cemetery, but Kittera's grave was not disturbed. On November 8, 1785, Kittera had married Anne Moore, a descendant of one of Lancaster County's earliest settlers. They had two sons and three daughters. One son, Thomas, later served in the House of Representatives. A daughter, Mary Louise, was the daughter-in-law of Pennsylvania governor Simon Snyder.

SOURCES: Arch., PPAmP; *BDAC* (which has Kittera as Jefferson's appointee to be U.S. Attorney); A. Harris, *Biog. Hist. of Lancaster Cnty., Pa.* (1872), 345; *LCHSPA*, 35 (1931), 164; 15 (1911), 47; 47 (1943), 99; 55 (1951), 40; 31 (1927), 40; 25 (1921), 141; 45 (1941), 137; 1 (1896), 168; 36 (1932), 114-15; *Pa. Gazette*, 14 Oct 1772 ("considerable value"); MS Steward's accounts, PUA; Patterson Acct. Bk.; *N.J. Gazette*, 11

Oct 1780 (A.M.); J. I. Mombert, *Authentic Hist. of Lancaster Cnty., Pa.* (1869), 430; J. H. Martin, *Bench and Bar of Phila.* (1883), 242, 284; *Benton's Abridgement of Debates in Congress,* I, 729-30; II, 101, 105; *A/C,* VII, 217, 229; VIII, 1,820, 2,016 ("polemics in the hands of divines"), 2,085, 2,122; als JWK to J. Yeates, 12 Mar 1798, NjP; (Baltimore) *Fed. Gazette,* 18 Aug 1800 ("submission to the powers that be"); *First Census, Pa.,* 136.

PUBLICATIONS: see text

MANUSCRIPTS: NjP, PHi

Joseph Flavius Lane

JOSEPH FLAVIUS LANE, A.B., A.M. 1780, Virginia planter, possible lawyer, and public official, probably was born about 1754, the son of James Lane, sheriff of Loudoun County in 1770 and Whig committeeman at the beginning of the Revolution, and his wife, Lydia Hardage. Certainly the Princeton graduate belonged to the numerous and generally prosperous family of Lanes whose members were scattered along the lower side of the Potomac River from Westmoreland County in the east, upstream to Loudoun County. Westmoreland seems to have been the chief and perhaps original seat of the family, and at the time of the Revolution, Colonel Joseph Lane of that county its leading member, but it would be easier to provide a more certain identification of the Princeton student were it not for the family's inclination through succeeding generations to perpetuate in the naming of its children the names James, Joseph, and William. In the 1780s there were no less than nine taxpaying Lanes in Loudoun County alone, three of them bearing the name of James.

Indeed, there may have been two Joseph Lanes attending school at Princeton during or about 1770. In the alumni file of Joseph Flavius Lane in the University Archives is found a letter of inquiry in 1965 from a postgraduate student of Indiana University, quoting from the court records at Leesburg regarding a suit by Joseph Lane against William Lane, administrator of the estate of James Lane, deceased, which affirmed that Joseph's father had sent him to "Prince Town in the Jerseys" in or about 1770. The case was before the court off and on from February 1791 to April 1802, when it was "abated" by the death of the complainant, who of course was Joseph Lane. Because the subject of this essay seems clearly not to have died until some time much closer to an inventory of his estate in 1804, perhaps the plaintiff in this case was the Joseph Lane, native of Virginia, who after military service in the Revolution died in Georgia in 1801.

Joseph Flavius Lane, A.B. 1776

Whatever may be the facts regarding this possibility, there can be little doubt that Joseph Flavius Lane first was in attendance at Princeton about 1770 or soon thereafter, probably as a student in the grammar school. In 1774 Philip Fithian (A.B. 1772), serving then as tutor in the family of Robert Carter of Nomini Hall in Westmoreland County recorded in his journal under the date of March 1 a visit by "Mr Lane a young gentleman, formerly my acquaintance at Princeton." Lane spent two nights with Fithian, who on March 2 noted in his journal that Joseph lived in Loudoun about 20 miles from Dumfries and that he was "to return to Princeton towards the close of this month." That he did so is indicated by Fithian's notation on March 20 that he wrote Lane, who had advised that he was about to depart for Jersey, "desiring him to remember me to my acquaintances in Pennsylvania, & New Jersey, as he will probably soon see many of them."

An undated list of students compiled by the College steward suggests that he probably became a freshman in the College during the fall of 1772, a date consistent with his graduation in 1776. Another of the surviving accounts of the steward, dated May 25, 1773 to September 25,

1774, indicates that Lane was present for at least a part of that period. A third list, for the months extending from November 6, 1774 to April 10, 1775, presents a problem. All save three students, one being Lane, are listed by their class, but these three are found in a space below the sophomores under the heading of "Resedentors." Although no explanation for this separate listing has been found, in Lane's case it seems reasonable to conclude that he was out of phase with the class to which he otherwise would have belonged. Perhaps there had been some interruption of his studies, through illness or other cause; Fithian's journal probably provides the clue. It places him in Virginia on the first of March 1774, too early for an assumption that he was merely at home for the spring vacation, which apparently came normally at some time in April. A likely supposition is that he had missed the winter term of 1773-1774, or some significant part of it, and so had fallen behind with his studies. It should be added that of the three "Resedentors," Lane was the only one who ultimately qualified for his degree. No steward's account has been found that extends beyond April 10, 1775, but it is probable that Lane was in continuing residence until he graduated, having come into full phase with his class at some time along the way. The ledger of a local merchant carries evidence of transactions arguing that he was in residence throughout the academic year 1774-1775 and that in November 1775 he was on hand for the beginning of what was to be his senior year.

Fortunately, Fithian's journal reveals more than a little about Lane and his background. When Lane left Nomini Hall after breakfast on March 3, 1774, Fithian was so impressed by his clothes that he recorded in his journal that "He was drest in black superfine broadcloth; Gold-laced hat; laced Ruffles; black Silk Stockings; & to his Broach on his Bosom he wore a Majors Badge inscrib'd 'Virtute and Silentio' cut in a Golden Medal!" To this the New Jersey farmer's son and later Presbyterian minister added: "Certainly he was fine!" There is interest too in Fithian's recollection on the following Sunday that "Mr. Lane the other Day informed me that the *Anabaptists* in Loudoun County are growing very numerous, & seem to be increasing in afluence; and as he thinks quite destroying pleasure in the Country; for they encourage ardent Pray'r; strong & constant faith, & an entire Banishment of *Gaming*, Dancing, & Sabbath-Day Diversions." Clearly, Lane's identification was with the Virginia establishment, and obviously, by much more than the formal requirement provided by his membership in a family that over the years had included more than one vestryman of the established church.

What Lane was doing immediately after leaving the College has not been discovered. The award of the A.M. degree often indicates that the recipient had been studying for one of the professions, but available evidence provides neither confirmation nor refutation for such an assumption. The time lag of four years between degrees would allow for some military service, but again the standard authority on Virginians credited with military service during the Revolution fails to provide firm confirmation for such service, possibly because there was more than one Joseph Lane living then in Virginia. That he acquired, and perhaps at an early date, the normal identification of one of his station with the militia is suggested by the fact that he held the rank of colonel at the time of the Whiskey Rebellion in 1794 and commanded Virginia troops who marched with him as far as Winchester, Virginia, before his own sickness forced him to halt. Meanwhile his earlier stay at Princeton apparently helped to find him a wife. According to family tradition, which seems to be confirmed by public record, he was married to Catherine Priest, daughter of Robert Priest of Windsor, Middlesex County, New Jersey on November 8, 1781, a little more than a year after he may have come to Princeton to receive his A.M. degree. The couple evidently had three surviving children, two boys and a daughter.

The Lanes made their home in Loudoun County, which he represented in the state assembly in 1792 and 1793. It perhaps was no mere chance that in the first term of his service the legislature passed an act for the incorporation of a new town, known as Centerville. It was a form of real estate promotion or speculation modern historians have paid less attention to than the subject deserves. Lane was one of the trustees to which the grant was made, which is to say one of the promoters of the settlement which was to be developed by selling off lots subject to the condition of building within a year on any lot purchased a house at least 16 feet square with a brick or stone chimney. Associated with him was one Leven Powell, a key figure in the founding under an act of 1787 of the town of Middleburg, near which Lane had begun to acquire property as early as 1791 and subsequently built a house of sufficient architectural merit to be preserved today as a national landmark. His property included a "Pot House," advertised for sale in 1796 as fully equipped with kiln and other equipment needed for the then profitable business of pottery manufacture. He named his home "Farmer's Delight" and there he died, without having made a will, at some time before the inventory of his estate was recorded under the date of January 4, 1804. The inventory reveals that he was a man of not insubstantial possessions.

He must too have been the Colonel Joseph Lane of Leesburg, Virginia to whom Reverend Joseph Clark (A.B. 1781) referred in the diary he kept of an especially successful mission through Virginia for the purpose of collecting funds for the reconstruction of Nassau Hall after its destruction by fire in March 1802. Clark went by way of Pennsylvania and Maryland, in the company of Judge John Bryan, a native of Virginia then living in New Jersey. The two reached Leesburg, county seat of Loudoun, where Lane possibly practiced some law, on November 25, 1802. Being ill on that day, Clark himself was unable to solicit, but Judge Bryan secured the promise of $70, of which Clark notes $30 was paid to Bryan and the remaining $40 was to be paid in time to Colonel Joseph Lane. Moreover, Lane apparently already had procured subscriptions for a total of $105, of which he already had in hand $52.50. Every circumstance argues that this Colonel Joseph Lane was the alumnus of 1776, who thus can be credited with a significant contribution to the revival of his alma mater as one of the last acts of his life.

SOURCES: The author is heavily indebted to the Honorable George C. McGhee of Washington, D.C., through the courtesy of Barksdale Penick of the Class of 1925, for information regarding Lane's service in the Whiskey Rebellion, the house built by Lane outside Middleburg that is now owned by Mr. McGhee, and other useful information, including the following transcription from Lane's tombstone: "COL. JO'S LANE, Who parted this life in the, 50th year of his age, It was my will this place to fill, These stones may testify, Observe the spot and till it not, But all prepare to die." The alumni file contains, in addition to other information, an abstract of the court case relative to the Joseph Lane sent to Princeton in or about 1770 mentioned in a letter of inquiry of 1965 from Henry A. Hawkins, then candidate for the Ph.D. at Indiana University. In PUA will be found also the MS Steward's accounts. See also J. Clark, MS Diary, NjP; Fithian Journal, I, 112-13 (1 Mar), 114, 117-18 (3 Mar), 121, 133 (20 Mar); Patterson Acct. Bk.; N.J. Gazette, 11 Oct 1780; N.J. Marriages, 236; N.J. Wills, VI, 35; J. W. Head, Hist. Loudoun Cnty., Va. (1968), 130; J. H. Gwathmey, Hist. Reg. of Virginians in Rev. (1938); A. B. Fothergill and J. M. Naugle, Va. Tax Payers (1966), 73; C. Torrence, Va. Wills . . . Index (1965), 252; E. G. Swem and J. W. Williams, Reg. of Gen. Assem. of Va. (1918), 37, 39; Cal. Va. St. Papers, VI, 209; Hening, Statutes, XII, 605-6; XIII, 580; DAR Patriot Index, 400; KSHS Reg., 47 (1949), 34-35; WMQ (2 ser.), 3 (1923), 104. A Major Joseph Lane (1740-1801) has been identified as dying in Ga. [DAR Patriot Index; D. F. Wulfeck, Marriages of Some Va. Residents, IV (1964), 119]. M. DeL. Haywood, Joel Lane, Pioneer and Patriot (1900), refers to the descendants of a Joseph Lane of Halifax, N.C., who died about 1774 and had a son Joseph who died in Wake Cnty. in 1798. Descendants in this line lived later in Ky., Ind., and other western states.

WFC

John Leake

JOHN LEAKE, A.B., was almost certainly a cousin of Samuel Leake (A.B. 1774) and so a member of one of the prominent families of the

Cohansie section of Cumberland County, New Jersey. When Philip
Fithian (A.B. 1772), also of Cohansie, returned from Virginia for a visit
in the spring of 1774, he recorded in his journal under the date of April
18 that John Leake was one of seven students then attending the
school conducted at Deerfield by Reverend Enoch Green (A.B. 1760).
Leake entered the College in the following fall as a member of the
junior class. In a letter dated February 11, 1775 from Nassau Hall,
Leake reported to his "Honoured Benefactor," Enoch Green, that he
had been sustained in the entrance examination "on the usual authors." He considered the test "very fair, as well as very strict," although he was later advised that his examiners had forgotten to question him "on the *Roman antiquities*." Since then he had been studying
"euclid, xenophon, and arithmetic . . . ; and besides these how I should
get clear of the *fever and ague*." It was his hope that "the *barks* will
free me of my last mentioned study in a short time," and so permit
pursuit of "those before mentioned with more pleasure and success."
But all this was preliminary to notifying his former master, with par-
donable pride and an appropriate apology, that he had recently successfully passed the quarterly examination.

With this letter, the known record of his identification with the
College ends, except for two additional items. He is listed among the
members of the American Whig Society as Reverend John Leake. He
is also listed in successively published catalogues of the College from
1789–1804, with credit for the A.B. degree and with his name italicized
to indicate that he was a clergyman, until the catalogue of 1804 for
the first time took note of his death. Actually, he probably had died
much earlier, possibly as early as October 25, 1776, when Enoch Green
recorded the burial at Deerfield of John Leake, Jr., but the identification in this instance is not certain. If the published catalogues of the
College are correct in listing him as a minister, he must have lived long
enough after graduation to have secured a license to preach, but the
records of the church for this troubled period are often incomplete.
The *Index of Presbyterian Ministers* compiled by W. J. Beecher and
published in 1883 does not carry Leake's names, and R. Webster, historian of the church, in his "Brief Sketches of Early Presbyterian
Ministers" seems to have come no closer than uncertain entries under
the names of Jacob Leake and John Lake, the one imposed over the
other. Perhaps the tradition recorded by Reverend A. H. Brown in his
History of the Presbyterian Church in West and South Jersey (1864)
provides a clue. After describing the deaths of Enoch Green and
Philip Fithian "of camp fever or dysentery" in 1776, he speaks of two
sons of Recompence Leake, "deacon of Deerfield church," who were

studying for the ministry in Princeton and who "also died of camp fever." This obviously overlooks the fact that Samuel, the other Leake at the College during this period, became a lawyer instead of a minister, was the son of Samuel Leake, and lived until 1820. But Recompence Leake, whose will was proved in 1801, and who left his property to a widow, two daughters, and a grandson named Recompense Leake, is a likely choice for the father of John Leake. No date has been found for his birth, nor evidence of a marriage by which he may have become the father of a son.

SOURCES: The John Leake in *DAR Patriot Index*, 405 was another and older person [see NJA (1 ser.), XXII, 239], as probably was the Capt. John Leak of Burlington in Stryker, *Off. Reg.*, 398. See *N.J. Wills*, V, 304-305, for a John Leek who died in 1777, with a son and grandson both named John, the latter described as under age; and *N.J. Wills*, X, 271, for the will of Recompence Leek, who seems to have been one of the four sons of Recompence Leek of Deerfield who died in 1749 [*N.J. Wills*, II, 296-97], the others being John, Nathan, Samuel (father of the Samuel [A.B. 1774]). See F. D. Andrews, *Biographical Sketch of Enoch Green* (1933), 18, for burial of John Leake, Jr., who could have been a son of John, son of the Recompence who died in 1749, though the use of "Jr." at this time tells nothing more than that the community found it helpful in distinguishing between the younger and the older of two persons bearing the same name. See also *VHM*, 42 (1959), 370-82; als JL to E. Green, 11 Feb 1775, NjP ("Honoured Benefactor," etc.); *Fithian Journal*, I, 157; MS Steward's accounts, NjP.

WFC

Charles Lewis

CHARLES LEWIS was born on October 3, 1760, in Spotsylvania County, Virginia, the fifth son of Colonel Fielding Lewis and his wife, Elizabeth (Betty) Washington Lewis, and the younger brother of George Lewis (Class of 1775). His mother was the only sister of George Washington, and his father was a prosperous planter, merchant, and political leader of county and province whose interests were centered around the town of Fredericksburg.

Both Charles and his brother George are listed among the students of the College who on September 29, 1772 owed the steward the relatively small sums of £1 and £1 1s 2d, respectively, which strongly suggests that they had been in residence for some time before that date, possibly as early as November 1771. Because Charles then would have just passed his eleventh birthday, it seems likely that he was first enrolled in the grammar school, but there is little room for doubt that by September 1772 he had been admitted to the freshman class in the College. It was an early age, but in the eighteenth century admission to college at about the age of twelve was by no means so exceptional as might be assumed. The fact that his brother George was more than three years older may argue only that Charles was the more apt student.

Little more is known of Charles. It was the custom of his Uncle George to stop over at Kenmore, Colonel Lewis's impressive residence, on the way to Willamsburg, and in October 1771, the month preceding the opening of the school year at Princeton, Washington was delayed for a couple of days because his horses had strayed. A gift of £1 6s to Charles and George before he departed suggests that it was they who found the horses. A letter from the father requesting that Washington visit the boys on a trip north in May 1773, and the record in his diary showing that he stopped at Princeton when going and coming, indicates that they were then still in residence. All indications are that they were not in residence after the academic year 1772-1773.

Charles and his brother George visited Mount Vernon on April 21, 1775, two days after the Battle of Lexington, and five days later Washington recorded that he had given them a guinea each. No evidence has been found in standard sources that Charles rendered military service during the Revolutionary War, and indeed at its beginning he was still quite young for that. Certainly, he died before its end. His father's will, dated October 19, 1781, and proved after his death in the following December, mentions six surviving sons, but not Charles.

SOURCES: *WMQ* (1 ser.), 10 (1901) 49, 51; MS Steward's accounts, PUA; S. M. Hamilton, *Letters to Washington*, IV (1901), 197; *Washington Diaries*, II, (1925), 39 & n, 112, 113, 192 & n.

WFC

Henry Philip Livingston

HENRY PHILIP LIVINGSTON, A.B., soldier, was the youngest son of Philip Livingston (Yale 1737), merchant, member of Congress, and signer of the Declaration of Independence. He was baptized in the Dutch Reformed Church in New York City on March 26, 1760. His mother, Christina Ten Broeck Livingston, was the sister of Dirck Ten Broeck Livingston (Class of 1758). Two of his brothers were Philip Philip (A.B. 1758), and Peter Van Brugh (A.B. 1766) Livingston, Jr.

Henry Philip Livingston entered the College as a freshman before May 1773. He joined the Cliosophic Society on June 3, 1774, using as his pseudonym the name of the seventeenth century English Whig, "Hampden."

On June 2, 1777, Livingston was commissioned a lieutenant, second in command of George Washington's Guard in the Continental Army. The guard was a small, carefully chosen unit that was created by Washington in March 1776 and reorganized in April 1777. Its members were selected from various regiments for their physiques, neatness, and soldierly conduct. After the discovery of the so-called Hickey plot, in which some guardsmen had conspired to assassinate Washington in June 1776, the general insisted that members of the guard be native Americans and men of property. In this reconstituted form, the infantry guard included two officers and fifty-six men.

Livingston joined the guard at Middlebrook, New Jersey and was responsible for much of the unit's administrative work, including ordering supplies and keeping accounts. On September 11, 1777, Livingston and the guard participated in the battle of Brandywine. Three days later, he sent an account of the fight to his father in which he maintained that, while the outcome seemed to be an American defeat, in fact it had been "the most unlucky affair that general [Sir William] Howe has ever encountered on this continent." He estimated that American losses were no more than half of the enemy's and said that he was confident that the British army would have been crushed had Washington only received better and more timely intelligence. The engagement convinced him that "our men can fight them on equal terms." The letter was intercepted by the English and published in such Loyalist newspapers as the *Pennsylvania Ledger*, which prefaced it with sarcastic deprecations of the author's optimism and then proceeded to identify both him and his father incorrectly.

Livingston spent the winter of 1777-1778 at Valley Forge, where the arrival of Baron von Steuben in February marked a new stage in the history of the guard. Steuben persuaded Washington to make the unit an elite corps, a model for the rest of the army. In March one hundred new guardsmen were enlisted, and on May 12 the officers of the guard took the oath of allegiance before the commander in chief. Six days later, Livingston and the infantry guard joined General Lafayette and his 2,400 men as they marched toward Philadelphia. They were surrounded by the British at Barren Hill on May 19, but Lafayette managed to escape from the trap while suffering fewer casualties than he inflicted.

After returning to Valley Forge, Livingston went to York, Pennsylvania to visit his father, whom he found ill with "palpitation of the Stomach and oppression of the bowels." On June 12, 1778, Philip Livingston died at York. His son was the only member of the family to be with him and bore the responsibility for sending the sad news to his relatives. Young Livingston inherited £700 sterling and a full share of his father's considerable estate.

Livingston's plans to visit his family after his father's death were probably thwarted by the British evacuation of Philadelphia at the end of May. After following the enemy into New Jersey, Washington's troops met and fought them at Monmouth on June 28. By autumn the guard was in Fredericksburg, near Fishkill, Dutchess County, New York. On October 5 a local citizen, one Noah Cook, filed a complaint against Livingston with the commander in chief. Cook's grievance is unclear, but it may have arisen from either of two circumstances. Discipline in the guard was shattered at Fishkill. Some guardsmen became marauders, and others took to vendettas against fellow soldiers. As second in command, Livingston might have been blamed for such episodes. Alternatively, he might have been identified in the complaints of local Quakers whose meeting house was commandeered as a hospital over their vigorous objections. In any case, Cook withdrew his complaint on October 28.

On November 5, 1778, Livingston asked Washington for permission to resign, explaining that his private affairs needed his attention but allowing that he would stay in the army were it not for the reduced opportunities for promotion in the guard. On November 11 Washington entrusted Livingston with a long and important message to the Congress, which the lieutenant "obligingly" agreed to deliver. Experience had taught Washington that the bearers of important messages were often rewarded by Congress, and it may have been his intention to speed Livingston's promotion by sending him. If that was the plan, it worked. Congress promoted Livingston to captain on December 4, 1778.

He then went on furlough until March 1779, when he rejoined Washington at Middlebrook, New Jersey. He transcribed some of the general's letters to other officers, until March 26 when he resigned his commission. No further record of his life has been found. According to the College's published catalogues, he died between 1786 and 1789. He never married.

SOURCES: E. B. Livingston, *Livingstons of Livingston Manor* (1910), 228, 286, 287, 288, 474, 524, 525, 552; *NYGBR*, 28 (1897), 138; MS Steward's accounts, MS Clio. Soc. membership list, PUA; C. E. Godfrey, *Commander-in-Chief's Guard* (1904), passim; *Washington Writings*, VIII, 172; XIII, 173n, 244 ("obligingly"); XIV, 171, 172n, 283n, 319n; *PMHB*, 38 (1914), 83, 84; *NJA* (2 ser.), I, 482 ("most unlucky affair"); *Clinton Papers*, III, 352; J. Sanderson, *Biography of the Signers to the Declaration of Independence* (1828), II, 134-35; *N.J. Wills*, V, 314; F. Hasbrouck, *Hist. of Dutchess Cnty., N.Y.* (1909), 173-74; *Cal. of Correspondence of George Washington . . . with the officers* (1915), 777, 818; *JCC*, XII, 1,188; *CNJ Cat.*, *1786* and *1789*.

MANUSCRIPTS: PHi

John McAllister

JOHN MCALLISTER, felon, was, except for one notable episode in his life, too obscure to be identified among the many men of that name. And given what little is known of him, it is not surprising that there has been no competition among McAllister families to claim him as their own.

Although it is likely that he was a member of the McAllister clan that was plentiful in Cumberland and York counties in Pennsylvania, it is also possible that he was the son of Edward and Mary "McAllester," born in New York City on December 4, 1756. Certainly he entered the College during the 1772-1773 academic year and remained there until at least the fall of 1774. Then or soon afterward he was expelled.

No record of the reason for his expulusion has been found, but it was probably not the first, and certainly not the last time that McAllister ran afoul of rules and laws. In March 1775 William Bradford, Jr. (A.B. 1772) wrote to James Madison (A.B. 1771) from Philadelphia to report that McAllister and one Andrew Stewart were about to be tried in the Pennsylvania Supreme Court. The charge was counterfeiting. The crime had been discovered earlier that month, when the province warned its citizens that counterfeit 50 shilling bills were in circulation. There were some discrepancies in design between the true and bogus bills, but the most glaring error in the counterfeits may have been the direct result of McAllister's having had at least two years of college education. The word "Pennsilvania" on the genuine scrip was spelled "Pennsylvania" on the false.

Bradford told Madison that Daniel Clymer (A.B. 1766), an attorney in Chester County with whom McAllister had been studying law, would defend him at the trial. But Bradford believed that the "fact [was] so plain, that the Eloquence of Gabriel could not prevent . . . conviction." He thought that McAllister's only hope of avoiding the required sentence of hanging without benefit of clergy lay in a pardon from Governor John Penn.

On April 10, 1775, McAllister and Stewart were convicted, as Bradford had predicted, and on May 18 the provincial council decided that they should be hanged. If Governor Penn had been inclined to issue a pardon, however, he never had the chance. On May 27 the colony's secretary, John Shippen, Jr. (A.B. 1753), placed a notice in the newspapers offering a reward of £200 for the capture and return to Philadelphia of John McAllister, who had escaped from the city jail. Stewart also escaped a few days later, and the jailer was then

arrested for conniving in their flight. Shippen's notice described Mc-
Allister as between eighteen and nineteen years of age, five feet eight
or nine inches in height, "round shouldered, bow legged, a little
pitted with small pox, and wears his own hair." The detail was to no
avail, for McAllister was never recaptured. And it is as a fugitive that
he vanishes into obscurity.

Several John McAllisters took part in the Revolution as members
of Pennsylvania and Maryland units. One of them may have been the
escaped convict. The most tempting possibility among them was the
commissary at York, Pennsylvania, who in June 1779 was accused by
almost everyone of maladministration and peculation. Among the
most flagrant of his alleged crimes was his watering the whiskey he
distributed to local workmen. So high was the feeling in York that
agents of the state found it impossible to take orderly depositions of
the charges. Too many people were too angry. But in the confusion,
the agents obtained one piece of information that might link the
beleaguered commissary with the counterfeiter. They learned that two
men from Philadelphia, a relative of a prominent merchant and a
hairdresser, were "acquainted with some misbehaviour of Mr. Mc-
Calister" in that city.

Although indicted, commissary McAllister was never tried, thanks
first to uncertainty about which courts had jurisdiction and then to
the efforts of some officials to delay the process as long as possible.
Evidently McAllister had friends in high places who agreed with his
defense of his conduct. It may be worth noting that Daniel Clymer's
cousin George Clymer was then between terms as a member of the
Continental Congress. Further, the officer under whom McAllister
had served as quartermaster before obtaining his post at York, Colonel
Thomas Hartley of the Eleventh Pennsylvania Regiment, was then a
member of the state legislature.

SOURCES: M. C. McAllister, *Descendants of Archibald McAllister* (1898); *NYGBR*, 4
(1873), 143; MS Steward's accounts, PUA; *Pa. Gazette*, 8 Mar 1775 ("Pennsilvania"),
27 May 1775 ("wears his own hair"); *Madison Papers*, I, 143 ("Eloquence of Gabriel"), 150; *Numismatic Notes and Monographs*, No. 132 (1955), 141, 155; *Col. Rec.
Pa.*, XII, 27, 41, 198; *Pa. Arch.* (1 ser.), VII, 490-91 ("acquaintance with some misbe-
havior"), 513, 529-30, 653; (5 ser.), III, 746; W. C. Carter and A. J. Glossbrenner,
Hist. of York Cnty. (1834), 72, App. 3-5.

Moses McCandless

MOSES McCANDLESS appears twice by name in the College records,
first in a steward's account that may cover the period from the fall of

1772 to the spring of 1773, and again on a list of tuition and room-rent payments from November 1774 to April 1775, where he is included among the junior class. Beyond this, he has not been identified. The surname, or some variation of it, occurs most frequently in Pennsylvania at this period, but can also be found in Virginia and North Carolina. In the 1790 census for Pennsylvania, eleven McCandlesses are recorded, scattered throughout the state, but none can be linked positively with the student. His name is sufficiently unusual, however, for it to be likely that he was related to the Moses McCandless who served as a private in the Pennsylvania militia in 1814.

SOURCES: Ms Steward's accounts PUA; *First Census, Pa.; Pa. Arch.* (6 ser.), x, 126; *DAR Patriot Index* (1966), 448 (for McCandlesses who fought in the Rev.).

JMR

Samuel McConkey

SAMUEL MCCONKEY, A.B., was the son of Samuel McConkey of Freehold, Monmouth County, New Jersey and was born sometime before October 9, 1760. On that day, his cousin William McConkey, yeoman, made out a will, noteworthy for its generosity to the Old Scots Church in Freehold, to the College of New Jersey, and to Samuel McConkey. William McConkey left £100 for the support of a Presbyterian minister at the Freehold church. But if the money could not be put to that use, he directed that it be used for the support of poor scholars at the College. "Likewise," McConkey added, "I do give and bequeath the sum of one hundred pounds to my cousin Samuel McConkey, son of Samuel, for the use of college learning: and if not put to the use, to return likewise for the support of poor scholars at the College of New Jersey. I do likewise give and bequeath the sum of one hundred pounds for the support of poor scholars at the College of New Jersey." The date of William McConkey's death is uncertain. If it occurred after Samuel McConkey's studies at Nassau Hall, the younger cousin may not have benefited fully from the will's provisions. By 1785 another William McConkey, who was unaware of the existence of the will, had been granted letters of administration; and it was he who was contacted by the College's trustees in that year when they became aware of the £100 legacy for poor scholars.

With or without his £100 legacy, Samuel McConkey first appeared in the College steward's accounts for the period of May 1773 to September 1774. He was admitted to the Cliosophic Society in 1774 and assumed the name "Waller," after either the English poet or the parliamentary general of that name. He completed his course of study in 1776. But like others in his class, McConkey may have been unable to participate in the irregular commencement of that turbulent autumn. He is not known to have been active in the Revolutionary military struggle, and information about his career is obscure and unhelpful.

When William McConkey's will was finally proved in 1787, a Samuel McConkey, who was perhaps the graduate and who was described as "near of kin," renounced his claim to any part of the estate and served as a fellowbondsman of the administrator. In 1793 a Samuel McConkey of Freehold was awarded letters of administration for another Samuel McConkey, "late of Franklin County, Pennsylvania" who died intestate. Either man may have been the graduate, and the dead man was probably the Samuel McConkey listed among the 1781 freemen of Guilford township in the section of Cumberland County that became Franklin County in 1784. Finally, a Samuel McConkey was appointed postmaster of Freehold on April 1, 1795. But nothing further has been learned of any Freehold man of that name after the appointment of another postmaster on April 1, 1798. The graduate's death was not noted in the College's triennial catalogues until 1851.

SOURCES: The spelling of the name adopted here follows that in two of the MS Steward's accounts, PUA. Trustee's Minutes, I, 248 (William McConkey's will); F. R. Symmes, *Hist. of the Old Tennent Chh.* (1904), 35; *N.J. Wills*, 1, 259; MS Clio. Soc. membership list, PUA. For the possibilities mentioned above, and others, see *N.J. Wills*, VIII, 242; *GMNJ*, 16 (1941), 86; Bucks Cnty. Hist. Soc., *Papers*, 5 (1926), 381; *Pa. Arch.* (3 ser.), XX, 431; *Hist. of Franklin Cnty., Pa.* (1887), 596; *First Census, Pa.* 119; F. Ellis, *Hist. of Monmouth Cnty., N.J.* (1885), 390, 460. See William H. Vernon (A.B. 1776) for commencement.

GSD

Robert McCrea

ROBERT McCREA, soldier, was born on November 2, 1754, at Lamington, Somerset County, New Jersey, the son of Reverend James McCrea and his second wife, Catherine Rosbrugh, an aunt of Robert's classmate, Robert Rosbrough Henry. The father, a Presbyterian clergyman, had attended the Log College at Neshaminy, Pennsylvania. McCrea's elder half brother John was a 1762 graduate of the College of New Jersey. An older half sister Mary was the wife of John Hanna (A.B. 1755) and the mother of James (A.B. 1777), John A. (A.B. 1782), and William Hanna (A.B. 1790).

Young Robert McCrea received £250 of the £3,000 in legacies left by his father, who died in 1769. He appears as an occasional customer in the account book of Princeton storekeeper Thomas Patterson between May and November 1775, evidence that supports the traditional story that he was a student at the College at the beginning of the Revolution. Unlike five of his brothers who advocated the American cause, Robert McCrea fought for George III in the Loyalist volunteer regiment known as the Queen's Rangers. He was wounded three times, losing an arm at Brandywine in September 1777. For the remainder of the war, he is said to have continued in military service as a noncombatant, and he may well have been the "Capt. M'Rae" of the Queen's Rangers who was active in Virginia in 1781.

McCrea regarded the Revolution as a time of "unparalleled misfortunes" for his politically divided family. In addition to his own injuries, he lost a brother who was an American officer; and the murder of his half sister Jane McCrea by a band of Britain's Indian allies was to become one of the most celebrated legends of the military struggle for independence. Moreover, McCrea and a younger brother who also fought in the Queen's Rangers went into exile at the war's end and were deprived of their New Jersey property, including an expected inheritance from a wealthy grandfather. In compensation, McCrea received an award of £1,000 from the Royal Commissioners charged with the relief of Loyalists, an annuity of £60, and a grant of land in New Brunswick, Canada.

On Christmas Day, 1782, McCrea was appointed captain in the regular British army, and three years later he was assigned to one of six independent companies of invalids stationed at Guernsey. He remained in the Channel Islands for the remainder of his life, except for the years from 1789 to 1791 when he was transferred to Chester. In 1802 he was promoted to major, serving in the Fourth Royal Veteran Battalion at Guernsey and subsequently in the Fifth Royal Veterans as major commandant. Few other details of McCrea's career at Guernsey have been discovered. After the death of his first wife, Jane Coutart of Guernsey in 1796, he married Sophia Le Mesurier, on June 12, 1804. Her family possessed the heredity governorship of Alderney, another of the Channel Islands. In 1830 he subscribed to a volume of Guernsey annals. McCrea died in Paris on July 2, 1835 and was buried at Père-Lachaise cemetery. He had at least five children, among whom were two British officers who died in action and Admiral Robert Coutart McCrea.

SOURCES: E. A. Jones, *Loyalists of N.J.* (1927), 136-38 ("unparalleled misfortunes"); *Som. Cnty. Hist. Quart.*, 7 (1918), 81-97; *Princetonians, 1748-1768*, 387-89; *N.J. Wills*, IV, 266; Patterson Acct. Bk.; J. G. Simcoe, *Simcoe's Military Journal* (1844), 233

("Capt. M'Rae"); E. C. Wright, *Loyalists of New Brunswick* (1955), 310; British *Army Lists* (var. dates). J. Jacob, *Annals of Guernsey*, 1 (1830), xiii. McCrea's assignment to Chester is apparently the basis of Jones's suggestion that he was governor of Chester Castle, Guernsey. Guernsey dos not have a Chester Castle, and whether Mc-Crea was Governor of Chester Castle in England has not been discovered.

GSD

Samuel McGee (MacGee)

SAMUEL McGEE (MACGEE) has not been identified. In the steward's account for November 6, 1774 to April 10, 1775, he is listed as a member of the junior class, which suggests that he may have been enrolled in an earlier academic year, a suggestion finding confirmation in the steward's account for the period from May 1773 to September 1774. The absence of his name from still another account, undated but possibly for November 1772 to the spring of 1773, argues that he perhaps was first enrolled in the fall of 1773 as a sophomore. How long he remained a student at Princeton cannot be said. According to the ledger of local merchant Thomas Patterson, McGee made a substantial purchase of materials apparently intended for clothing on November 5, 1774, the day before the opening of a new academic year; an entry for February 20, 1775 shows that he settled the resulting charge in full on that date. No further entry has been found in a ledger recording transactions as late as December 1775, and the steward's account ending with April 10 of that year is the latest known to have survived. McGee probably dropped out of college at some time during 1775.

SOURCES: Ms Steward's accounts, PUA; Patterson Acct. Bk. The name of McGee, with such additional variants as McGhee, Maghee, and Magie, was found in a number of the colonies, and Samuel was equally common. Among the possibilities explored is Samuel, son of John McGee of Guilford Cnty., N.C., whose will was dated 22 Nov 1773 and probated on 28 Jan 1774 [J. B. Grimes, *Abstract of N.C. Wills* (1910), 230], and whose brother Andrew McGee of Dorchester Cnty., Md., earlier in 1773 by will left properties there to his nephews Samuel and John, sons of John McGee of Guilford Cnty., N.C. [E. C. Papenfuse et al., *Dir. of Md. Legislators* (1974), 13; Md. Leg. Hist. Proj.]. *St. Recs. N.C.* indicates that John McGee settled in North Carolina at mid-century, held important county offices, and, as his will also confirms, accumulated considerable properties that were left to six surviving children. Whether Samuel was one of the older or younger of four sons is not clear, but he could have been of an age to have been attending college at the time of his father's death and to have studied by way of preparation with David Caldwell (A.B. 1761), Pres. minister in Guilford Cnty. who over the years after his installation in 1768 conducted a famous school. The father probably was a Presbyterian, and in a codicil to his will provided for a burying ground and meeting house. But no identification with CNJ has been established, and his career after 1780 remains uncertain.

Another and inviting possibility was Samuel, son of Robert and Hannah McGee of Philadelphia, who received a £100 bequest in the will of Capt. John Little of Princeton in 1794, and a further bequest from Little's widow in 1812 [*N.J. Wills,* VIII, 231; XII, 237]. Directories for Philadelphia provide identification of Robert as a lumber merchant from 1785 through 1797, and of Hannah as a widow from 1799, but the census of 1790 indicates that this Samuel was under sixteen years of age at that time [*First Census, Pa.,* 215].

WFC

Robert Martin (Marton, Marten)

ROBERT MARTIN (MARTON, MARTEN) probably entered the College in the fall of 1772 as a member of the freshman class, for he is found in the steward's accounts for the period extending from May 25, 1773 to September 25, 1774 and is included again, as a member of the junior class, on the steward's list of students enrolled from November 1774 to April 10, 1775. The ledger kept by local merchant Thomas Patterson, indicates that he (Marten) was in town as late as the following June 28. This would have been well into the summer term, so it can be assumed that he probably completed his junior year. But no evidence has been found that he returned for his senior year. Perhaps the consideration was financial, for the last mentioned of the steward's accounts suggests that he was at the time seriously in arrears in the payment of his charges.

No positive identification of Martin can be offered, but he probably was a younger, perhaps the youngest, son of Hugh Martin of Lebanon, Hunterdon County, New Jersey, whose will, proved on May 12, 1761, included among the beneficiaries a Robert as the last named of five sons. Among the others were two graduates of the College: Alexander Martin (A.B. 1756), later Revolutionary soldier, governor of North Carolina, member of the Constitutional Convention of 1787, and United States Senator; and Thomas Martin (A.B. 1762), who became an Anglican minister in Virginia and the tutor of James Madison (A.B. 1771). There may have been a third son who had attended the College, without graduating, for the will refers to two sons "who are at college," one of them of course being Thomas, and the other, either Samuel or James. The mother was Jane or Jean Hunter, who died in 1807, at the age of 90, at the home of her unmarried son Alexander in Rockingham County, North Carolina. Given a birth date falling somewhere in 1717, she may well have been the mother of a member of the Class of 1776.

Tradition holds that all five of Hugh Martin's sons eventually found their way south, and certainly two of them followed Alexander to North Carolina. Samuel Martin seems to have been the first. He served with North Carolina troops during the Revolutionary War and sustained a slight wound late in the war. James Madison, writing from Princeton to his father on October 9, 1771, reported that "Mr. James Martin was here at Commencement & had an opportunity of hearing from his Brothers & friends in Carolina by a young man lately come from thence to this College [possibly Spruce Macay (A.B. 1775) of Rowan County]." James, who was born in May 1742, moved to Carolina in the spring of 1774 and eventually settled in that part of Surry County, formed in 1770 from Rowan, that became Stokes County in 1789. He represented Stokes in the state assembly in 1791 and 1792, having formerly sat for Surry from 1783 to 1786. His son, also named James, graduated from the University of North Carolina in 1806 and later became a well-known judge. No positive proof that Robert migrated to Carolina has been found, but one notes with interest that a Robert Martin in 1788 was clerk of the Superior Court at Salisbury, county seat of Rowan and the place at which Alexander had had his start as merchant and king's attorney. Robert Martin, son of Hugh, has been said to have had a son also named Robert, and it is certain that the Robert Martin whose daughter Martha became in 1847 the first wife of Stephen A. Douglas, congressman and later senator from Illinois, was a nephew of Alexander Martin. Whether the son of Samuel, James, or Robert, this Robert Martin became a director of the Bank of North Carolina and possessor of an estate of some 800 acres in Rockingham County. Even more impressive was the plantation, manned by some 150 slaves, he owned on the Pearl River in the state of Mississippi. It was offered as a wedding gift to Douglas, who declined to accept it, but even so he suffered some political embarrassment thereafter from the extent of his family's slave-holding property.

The Martin family in New Jersey had connections in Pennsylvania as well as North Carolina. Notice has to be taken of the Robert Martin of Northumberland County, Pennsylvania who was visited more than once during the summer of 1775 by Philip Fithian (A.B. 1772), who described him as "a Gentleman who came lately from Jersey." This Robert, who apparently became one of the largest landholders in the county and one of its leading officials, seems to have settled there about or before 1768, but he may have been the father of one of the several Robert Martins that tax and other records show to have been resident in western Pennsylvania thereafter. If this Martin had a son at Princeton at the time of Fithian's visits, it is strange that the latter did not say so, for he was much inclined to comment upon any connection with the College. Among the New Jersey Martins was a Robert Martin of Middlesex County, who became a Loyalist, had his property confiscated, and settled after the war at Shelburne in Nova Scotia, but no identification with the College has been established.

SOURCES: Martin Family File, PUA; *Princetonians, 1748-68*, 157-60; *N.J. Wills*, IV, 273; W. H. Hoyt, ed., *Papers of Archibald Murphey* (1914), I, 129, 190, 388; II, 284n; *St. Rec. N.C.*, XX, 550; XXI, 100-101, 824-25; *Madison Papers*, I, 68-69 ("lately come from thence"); *Manual of N.C.* (1913), 448, 785-86, 792, 813; J. G. deR. Hamilton, ed., *Papers of Thomas Ruffin* (1918), I, 24, 133n, 216, 291, 422; II, 37; R. W. Johannsen, *Stephen A. Douglas* (1908), 145-49; *Journal Ill. St. Hist. Soc.*, 16 (1923-24), 363, 641-46; J. H. Wheeler, *Hist. Sketches of N.C.* (1851), I, 81, 181-82; II, 384, 405; Wheeler, *Reminiscences and Memoirs of N.C.* (1884), 413-15; *First Census, N.C.*, 160, 169, 180; D. C. Corbitt, *Formation of N.C. Counties* (1950); MS Steward's accounts, PUA. H. J. Martin, *Notices Geneal. and Hist. of the Martin Family* (1880), 320-21, records a Robert Martin, born 10 Apr 1755 near Lancaster, Pa., who moved at an early age to Rowan and thence to Mecklenburg Cnty., N.C., lived in the latter county until 1800, when he moved to Tenn., where he died 20 July 1840. See *NCHR*, XIV, 178, for a letter of July 1812 from Robert Martin of Caswell Cnty. to President Madison regarding a land transaction involving his grandfather, also named Robert. For the Pa. Robert Martins see *Fithian Journal*, II, 45, 47, 59, 61, 66; *Pa. Arch.* (3 ser.), esp. XIX and XXV, *passim*; *First Census, Pa.*, 184, 188; later volumes of *Susquehannah Papers*; for the Loyalist, see E. A. Jones, *Loyalists of N.J.* (1927); *NJHS Col.*, X, 293; *NJA* (2 ser.), II, 401-2, 557-58; III, 61-62, 63, 435-36; Sabine, *Loyalists*, II, 550; M. Gilroy, *Loyalists and Land Settlement in Nova Scotia* (1937), 94.

WFC

Richard Mount

RICHARD MOUNT, A.B., possibly a Loyalist, has not been positively identified, but a manuscript list of early members of the Cliosophic Society identifies him as a resident of New Jersey, and there is little if any room for doubt that he belonged to the numerous and generally prosperous family of farmers who were descended from George Mount, one of the original settlers in the 1660s of the Monmouth tract on the upper coast of New Jersey. Although their holdings in the eighteenth century were concentrated in Monmouth and Middlesex counties, they were also found in other counties. In the several branches of the family, succeeding generations were inclined to perpetuate the names of Richard, Mathias, Humphrey, John, and William, with the result that it can be difficult to identify all bearers of a given name.

In this case, it is possible to speak with reasonable certainty only of Mount as a student in the College. His name is found on three of the four surviving accounts of the steward for this period of time, all save the one that records students who at various dates were in arrears in their payments of fees. These accounts indicate that he was probably in continuous residence from the fall of 1772 through the months extending from November 6, 1774 to April 10, 1775, when the steward listed him as a member of the junior class. The ledger of a local merchant carries a transaction on the following May 15, which suggests that he continued in residence for the remainder of the academic year 1774-1775. His graduation with his class on schedule suggests further that he belonged to the minority of students whose residence in the College covered four full years. No record has been found to show what part he may have taken in the truncated commencement exercises of September 1776.

In the absence of a positive identification, it becomes all the more difficult to determine what his later career may have been. It seems unlikely that he was the private Richard Mount of the Middlesex militia who is the only Richard Mount found in the standard authority on New Jerseymen who saw military service during the Revolutionary War, and probably one and the same with the taxpayer of that name in Windsor Township between 1778-1780. Perhaps the graduate migrated to another state, but confirmation of such an assumption is lacking. Perhaps he died at an early age. Perhaps he was the Richard Mount of New Jersey who "at the peace, accompanied by his family of four persons, . . . went from New York to Shelburne, Nova Scotia, where the Crown granted him one town lot."

SOURCES: See William H. Vernon (A.B. 1776) for commencement of 1776. Richard Mount, son of Thomas (d. 1777) and grandson of Richard Mount (d. 1777) of Upper Freehold Township in Monmouth Cnty. might be considered a possibility, except for evidence that he died in 1825 at the age of 84 and had a child born as early as 1769. [See N.J. Wills, v, 360-61, for abstracts of wills of Richard Mount (22 Jul 1777) and Thomas Mount (17 Apr 1777). See also F. R. Symmes, Hist. of the Old Tennent Chh. (1904), 443-44; and will in Nj of Richard Mount dated 16 Oct 1824, proved 1825, signed by his mark, and disposing of substantial properties.] Richard Mount (d. 1777) had a second grandson named Richard (the son of Samuel Mount), who was to inherit by the grandfather's will the property bequeathed as a lifetime interest to Samuel upon the latter's death. Samuel Mount of Upper Freehold died in 1801 with a will [N.J. Wills, x, 323] that mentions a son Michael but not a Richard. Richard Mount of Nottingham Township, Burlington, Cnty., died intestate in 1787 with a son Michael, who was old enough to serve as an administrator, and four other children who were minors. The Index of N.J. wills refers to no other will for a Richard Mount who might have been the graduate.

For the graduate see MS Clio. Soc. membership list (which dates his membership from 9 Dec 1772), MS Steward's accounts, PUA; Patterson Acct. Bk.; Pa. Gazette, 14 Oct 1772. The College's catalogues list Mount as dead for the first time in 1827 and credit him with an A.M. degree from 1797 forward, but a check of the Trustee Minutes shows that it was not awarded by the College. See also Stryker, Off. Reg., 698; Heitman (for an ensign Richard Mount of the 2nd N.Y. in 1778); K. Stryker-Rodda, Rev. Census of N.J. (1972), 149; Sabine, Loyalists (1864), II, 559 (quotation); E. A. Jones, Loyalists of N.J. (1927), 296. If Mount was the Loyalist settling in Nova Scotia, he must have declared his allegiance promptly, for the Min. of the Council of

Safety . . . of N.J. (1872) record no proceedings against him, nor is there evidence of such in other sources that record actions against other members of the family [*NJA* (2 ser.), II, 386; III 94, 368.] No evidence that he served in the king's military forces has been found. See J. A. Mount, *Hist. and Geneal. Rec. of Mount and Flippin Families* (1954), 28-30, for a Richard, son of Matthias and Annie Disbrow Mount of Cranbury, N.J., who was born in 1741 and would have been 35 years old at the time of graduation.

WFC

Elisha Neil

ELISHA NEIL, the only record of whose attendance at the College is that of the Cliosophic Society, which dates his membership from November 1773, has not been identified. The search has been complicated by the many possible spellings of the name, but it may be noted that an Elijah Neil resided in Stonington, Hartford County, Connecticut, and that men named Elisha Niles lived in Chatham, Middlesex County and in New London County, Connecticut in 1790. Neil, Neal, Neale, and Niles families were numerous in the young United States and were especially concentrated in New England, the Carolinas, and New Jersey, any one of which might have been the home of this student.

SOURCES: Ms Clio. Soc. membership list, PUA; *First Census, Conn., Mass., N.Y., N.H., N.C., S.C., Va.*

Benjamin Olden

BENJAMIN OLDEN was a member of a large Quaker family, the first of whom had settled on Stony Creek near Princeton at the end of the seventeenh century, and many of whom had since joined the Presbyterian church. By 1776 there were several men of that name in New Jersey and Pennsylvania, but the most likely of them to have studied at Nassau Hall was the son of Joseph and Anne Gardner Olden, who owned a farm close by the Friends Meeting House at Stony Creek. Benjamin Olden was born, according to he family bible, on the "thirtyeth of the fifth month," 1760. That his parents were fairly well-to-do is evidenced by his father's will, made in 1789 and proved in 1790, which provided for an estate worth £617.

Olden enrolled in the College as a freshman and remained at least until the end of his junior year in 1775. In "the ninth month" of 1776 he died at home, a victim of "the Bloody flux."

SOURCES: Ms Joseph Olden's Bible, NjP (dates and death); MS Steward's accounts, PUA; *N.J. Wills*, VII, 171; Hageman, *History*, 28-29; M. S. and A. O. Wright, *Our Family Ties* (1900), 80-81.

Thomas Parker

THOMAS PARKER, merchant and tavern owner, according to the steward's list of students enrolled in the College between November 1774 and April 10, 1775, was at that time a member of the junior class. Because his name appears on neither the steward's list for the period immediately preceding this one, May 25, 1773, to September 25, 1774, nor on either of the other two surviving accounts of the steward for this general period, it can be assumed that he was first enrolled, with advanced standing, at the beginning of the winter term early in November 1774. That he remained in residence through the following spring and summer terms is indicated by the account book of a local merchant, where one finds more than ten entries for "Thos. Parker, std.," the last falling on July 30, 1775. The ledger continues past the opening of a new term in the following November with no further evidence of transactions by Parker, whose account had been a rather active one. It appears that he was a student at Princeton through the single academic year of 1774-1775.

There were many Thomas Parkers in colonial America, but fortunately John Pintard (A.B. 1776) in 1817 recalled having seen his former classmate as a prisoner of war on Long Island at some time after the Battle of Germantown and described him as "Tom Parker of Virginia." This recollection serves to provide a reasonably firm identification of the Princeton student as the Thomas Parker who was born on January 8, 1757, the son of George and Ada Bagwell Parker of Accomack County on the Eastern Shore of Virginia. He was descended from a long line of Parkers who had resided in the county since the seventeenth century and who held there substanial properties. Where he had been prepared for college is not known, but his admission to Nassau Hall with advanced standing reminds one that there had been a grammar school at Onancock, not far removed from his home, in which David Ramsay (A.B. 1765) and Luther Martin (A.B. 1766) formerly had taught.

On the question of what Parker was doing immediately after leaving the College nothing has been found. The earliest evidence of his subsequent activities comes with his commission on July 4, 1776, as a first lieutenant in the Ninth Virginia Regiment of the Continental

Line that was commanded by Lieutenant Colonel George Mathews. By May 1777 the unit had joined Washington's army in New Jersey in time to participate in the unsuccessful effort to bar General Howe's advance from the upper Chesapeake to Philadelphia. In the action that followed at Germantown in October, Parker became a prisoner of the British, as did Mathews and a large part of his command. Indeed, an early report mainained that the regiment had been "taken to a man" after it had conducted itself in a manner bringing to its members "much honour." Just when the prisoners were transferred to Long Island cannot be said, nor just when it was that John Pintard, as assistant to his uncle, the deputy commissary general of prisoners, visited him there. The only additional detail given in Pintard's recollection was that he had shared with Parker "the only 3 Guineas I had in the world." That Parker was still a prisoner on Long Island on May 24, 1780, is shown by a memorial of that date from the prisoners to Governor Thomas Jefferson seeking from him and the state assembly relief from "the calamities of indigency and want." Colonel Mathews was exchanged on December 5, 1781. Parker seems to have secured his release at an earlier date, for there is reason to believe that he was the Captain Parker reported late in August 1781 to Colonel William Davies (A.B. 1765), then head of Virginia's Board of War, as being in command of "a small company of regulars" on Virginia's Eastern Shore. A communication earlier in that month from the lieutenant of Accomack County to Governor Thomas Nelson advised that forces raised for "protection of the county" had been placed under the command of "Capt. Thomas Parker of the Army, a young gentleman of good character." Parker continued to exercise some such authority well into 1782, and in December of that year he was involved in the so-called Battle of the Barges off Onancock, which resulted in a number of casualties on both sides.

After the war, Parker settled permanently in his native county, where he rose ultimately to the rank of colonel in the militia. It was apparently not long after his return to Accomack that he married Elizabeth Andrews, daughter of William Andrews, who lived near Pungoteague. In that section of the county, he bought in 1786 a property from his brother-in-law Robert Andrews, which became his residence, and which he named Poplar Grove after the ancestral home of his father, who had died in 1784. Parker conducted a mercantile business in Pungoteague and eventually became the owner of a tavern known as "Last Shift," perhaps because southbound stagecoaches made their last change of horses there. There is no evidence that he ever lived at the tavern. He seems to have prospered. Tax records for the

1780s show that of the two Thomas Parkers then paying taxes in Accomack County one owned seven and the other seventeen slaves. Perhaps the smaller number belonged to the former Princeton student. If so, it still suggests a prosperous beginning toward the accumulation of an estate that in time included the rights to several thousand acres awarded for military service.

Parker died on December 18, 1819, survived by his wife Elizabeth and five of their ten children.

SOURCES: There were two Thomas Parkers of Va. who served as officers in the Continental Army, and their records seem to have been seriously confused by both Heitman and J. H. Gwathmey, *Hist. Reg. of Virginians in the Rev.* (1938). One became an ensign in the 2nd Va. Regiment on 4 Jan 1777, was promoted to lieutenant in the following October, taken prisoner at Savannah in Oct 1779, exchanged 22 Dec 1780, and breveted as a captain on 30 Sep 1783. This must have been the Parker who on 14 Nov 1782 sought from Col. Davies assistance for a drummer boy who had served with him "in the South" [*Cal. Va. St. Papers*, III, 371], and who in the War of 1812 became a brigadier general. The other Parker, from Accomack, apparently opposed that war, for Col. Thomas Parker served as clerk at "a meeting of the Freeholders and Citizens of Accomack County," which on 31 Aug 1812 adopted a lengthy protest of the recently declared war against Great Britain [R. T. Whitelaw, *Va.'s Eastern Shore*, (1951), II, 1408-13]. It is noticeable too that the newspaper notice on 20 Jan 1820 of his death assigned to him no higher rank than that of Colonel [*Bull. Va. St. Lib.* (1923), p. 208]. Capt. Thomas Parker is listed as an original member of the Society of the Cincinnati [*VMHB*, 6 (1898-1899), 27].

For the CNJ student's career, see *NYHS Coll.*, LXX, 53 ("Tom Parker of Virginia," "3 guineas"); MS Steward's accounts, PUA; Patterson Acct. Bk.; Whitelaw, *Eastern Shore*, I, 668, 698, 700, 712; II, 793-94, 922-25, 952, 966; C. H. Lesser, *Sinews of Independence* (1976), 46; H. E. Hayden, *Va. Genealogies* (1931), 707 ("much honour"); *Jefferson Papers*, III, 388-91 ("indigency of want"); *Cal. Va. St. Papers*, II, 305-6, 361 ("gentleman of good character"), 369 ("small company"), 595-96, 616; III, 14, 161, 201, 242, 391-92; *DAR Patriot Index*, 516; *Index, Rev. War Pension Applications* (1966), 863; A. B. Fothergill and J. M. Naugle, *Va. Tax Payers* (1966), 95; *VMHB*, 10 (1903), 318-19, 44 (1936), 261-64; *WMQ* (2 ser.), 8 (1928), 38.

WFC

Eliphaz Perkins

ELIPHAZ PERKINS, A.B. Yale 1776, A.M. Yale 1781, merchant, physician, public official, was born in Norwich, Connecticut, on August 21, 1753. He was the son of John Perkins, whose physique earned him the nickname "the great," and his second wife, Lydia Tracy Perkins. The family were members of the Newent Congregational Church in what is now Lisbon, Connecticut.

Perkins followed his cousin Nathan Perkins (A.B. 1770) to the College, where, according to the steward's accounts, he enrolled between May 1773 and September 1774, probably as a sophomore. But he went back to Connecticut to earn his degree at Yale, the alma mater of his uncle, Dr. Joseph Perkins (Yale 1727). Soon after he graduated, Perkins married Lydia Fitch, the daughter of Dr. Jabez Fitch of Canterbury, Connecticut. He then took up residence in Canterbury, where he earned his living as a merchant. He moved to New Haven in search of better prospects, but within a few years he had decided to pursue a career in medicine. He was trained by his father-in-law. His turn to a profession enabled him to take an A.M. degree from Yale in 1781, an honor for which he paid twenty-four shillings. He then moved to Volountown, Connecticut to begin his new vocation.

Suffering from a small practice and a large family, Perkins went west in 1789 to explore the opportunities in the Ohio Territory. While his wife and children stayed in Connecticut, he journeyed to the Marietta settlement. There he encountered a party of roadbuilders from Clarksburg, Virginia. He accompanied them back to Virginia and stayed for several months.

In the fall of 1790, Perkins apparently felt able once more to cope with the trials of civilization and parenthood and went back to New England and to the family with which he had not even communicated for more than a year. He tried again to build a successful practice, this time in Leicester, Addison County, Vermont. But on June 3, 1799, after years of frustration, he, his wife, and their seven children left to settle permanently in Ohio. Their journey took them through Vermont, Massachusetts, and Connecticut before they reached Reading, Pennsylvania, where Lydia Perkins gave birth to twins. After three weeks of rest, the family arrived in McKeesport, Pennsylvania to find that the Monongahela River was too low to navigate. They therefore walked from Pittsburgh to Wheeling, and reached Marietta in mid-November. The journey and the fever that swept Marietta that winter were too much for Lydia Perkins. She died on January 21, 1800.

Within a few months Perkins was invited to settle as the only physician in Athens, Ohio. It was a poor but growing town and he soon became one of its leading citizens. In 1803 he married Catherine Greene; and on November 5, 1804, he paid $131 for two prime lots of land in the town.

Perkins was active in the creation of common schools in Athens and had a hand in the establishment of Ohio University, which was chartered by the state in February 1804. The university's board of trustees held its first meeting in Perkins's home in Athens on June 5, 1804, when they elected their host treasurer of the institution. That the development of the university was slower than expected is indicated by Perkins's first financial report in April 1806. The school's account had in it at that time, he said, "not one cent."

Nevertheless, the trustees proceeded in December to make plans to build the "college edifice," designed by Jacob Lindly (A.B. 1800) to resemble Nassau Hall. Perkins was by then a member of the board. In March 1808 he was part of the committee of trustees that organized Athens Academy as a grammar school for the university. Lindly was the academy's first preceptor. Although he resigned as treasurer in 1807, Perkins remained one of the university's most active trustees until 1823.

He was also busy in community affairs. In 1813 he served as treasurer of Athens County, and in 1815 he subscribed to the building of a county court house. He was postmaster of Athens and county recorder for many years. When the Athens Presbyterian Society was created in 1809, with Lindly as its first pastor, Perkins was one of the founding parishioners. And in January 1811 he was among the three original members of the board of censors in Ohio's third medical district, charged with examining and licensing physicians to practice in the state.

Widowed a second time, Perkins married Mrs. Anna Catron in 1821. She and all nine of his children were alive when he died on April 29, 1828.

SOURCES: G. A. Perkins, *Family of John Perkins of Ipswich, Mass.* (1889), III, 34-36; C. M. Walker, *Hist. of Athens Cnty., Ohio* (1869), 215-58 passim, 329-30, 335, 341-43, 347-48; S. P. Hildreth, *Bio. and Hist. Memoirs of Early Pioneer Settlers of Ohio* (1852), 413; Dexter, *Yale Biographies*, III, 626-28; *NEHGR*, 14 (1860), 114, 117; *Vital Records of Norwich* (1913), I, 318; MS Steward's accounts, PUA; Stiles, *Literary Diary*, II, 555; *First Census, Vt.*, 12; T. N. Hoover, *Hist. of Ohio Univ.* (1954), 22, 25, 32, 33, 45; C. W. Super, *Pioneer College and its Background* (1924), 34-35; *OAHSQ*, 50 (1941), 253 ("not one cent"); 49 (1940), 369.

Cyrus Pierson

CYRUS PIERSON, A.B., physician and farmer, was the second son of Bethuel Pierson and his first wife, Elizabeth Riggs Pierson. He was born on his father's farm in South Orange, New Jersey, then called Newark Mountain, in August 1756. His early education was in the school at South Orange that had been founded in 1757 by Caleb Smith (Yale 1743), the College's first tutor.

Pierson joined the Cliosophic Society on January 3, 1774, in the middle of his sophomore year. His pseudonym in the society was "Nestor," after the garrulous king of Pylos in Homer's *Iliad*. After graduation Pierson went to Parsippanny, Morris County, New Jersey to study medicine with the minister and physician John Darby. He then returned to South Orange to open his practice.

Pierson's father was an active member of the Mountain Society, or First Presbyterian Church, in which he was both an elder and a deacon, and a leader in political affairs. He served on the Newark Committee of Observation and in the New Jersey Provincial Congress at the beginning of the Revolution. Pierson himself was far less politically active. A lifelong pulmonary disability precluded his participation in the war and also required him to move frequently in search of a better climate. In South Orange he divided his time between medicine and farming on his family's 100 acres. It was also during his years there that he married his distant cousin Nancy Pierson, the sister of Isaac Pierson (A.B. 1789). They were to have seven children. On May 6, 1788, Pierson was admitted to the New Jersey Medical Society.

By 1789 Pierson had moved to Caldwell, Essex County, New Jersey. He was a member of the committee that founded the village library and in 1792 he contributed to the construction of a new Presbyterian church. Soon afterward, he moved to Woodbridge, Middlesex County. There he established a large and lucrative practice. When Dr. John Gale Wall of Woodbridge died in January 1798, Pierson bought his house and took on most of his patients. Wall's practice extended all the way to Perth Amboy, however, and the burden of so large a circuit proved too much for Pierson's frail constitution. By 1800 he had moved again.

Pierson's final residence was in Newark, where he formed a partnership with Dr. Samuel Hays. He shared the current interest in vaccination and while in Newark decided to perform an experiment to test the procedure. He vaccinated two children of the local minister against smallpox and then infected one of his own offspring with the disease. When the children were later brought together, he found that the vaccinated youngsters did not contract smallpox from the diseased child. Presumably, he was able to cure his own son.

Pierson died in Newark on October 7, 1804. His estate, valued at $1,120, included a female slave and her two children, one-half of a "Medicine shop," and a large library in which religious, medical, and political volumes were plentiful. He was buried in the churchyard at South Orange, but his remains were later moved to Rosedale Cemetery there. Pierson was survived by his wife and family.

SOURCES: W. H. Shaw, *Hist. of Essex and Hudson Counties, N.J.* (1884), I, 305; II, 720, 783; L. B. Pierson, *Pierson Geneal. Rec.* (1878), 36; Wickes, *Hist. of Medicine*

N.J. (1879), 361-62; and *Hist. of the Oranges* (1892), 131-229 passim; MS Clio. Soc. membership list, PUA; J. Hoyt, "*Mountain Soc.*" (1860), 275, 277; *Med. Soc. of N.J., Rise, Minutes and Proceedings* (1875), 61-62; *N.J. Wills,* x, 352; will #10294G, Nj.

John Pintard

JOHN PINTARD, A.B., LL.D. Allegheny College 1822, soldier, merchant, stockbroker, philanthropist, banker, public official, was born in New York City on May 18, 1759. His parents, Mary Cannon Pintard and John Pintard, who was a merchant in the city, both died before their son was a year old. The boy was raised by his uncle Louis Pintard, also a merchant in New York, and his wife Susanna, the sister of Richard Stockton (A.B. 1748) and sister-in-law of Elias Boudinot. The Pintards were members of the French Protestant Church in New York until 1765, when Louis Pintard joined the Anglican Church because he disagreed with the choice of a new minister by his former congregation.

Pintard's earliest schooling was supervised in New York by James Lesley (A.B. 1759). He then boarded for three years in Hempstead, Long Island with Reverend Leonard Cutting, who had attended Eton and Cambridge in England and who prepared Pintard for college with solid classical training. Only late in his life did Pintard regret the "superficial" education he received at that early age. In retrospect, he realized that he had not possessed sufficient maturity of judgment when he entered the College as a freshman in 1772. That summer he joined the Cliosophic Society, in which his pseudonym was "Pliny," after one of the two Roman notables. His recollection in later years was that he paid one dollar per week for room and board and that he appreciated the low cost even though it meant that he had to eat baked mutton almost every night. It was, he thought, an improvement over the clam broth and Indian dumplings he had faced five times per week in Long Island. One hundred dollars paid his yearly tuition, board, and laundry costs, and left five dollars for pocket money. His roommate in his freshman year was Richard Platt (A.B. 1773), who remained his lifelong friend. Other close "chums" included another roommate, Andrew Kirkpatrick, and John R. B. Rodgers (both A.B. 1775).

Pintard enjoyed and excelled in courses in mathematics and algebra, but he found that learning by rote caused him some difficulty in more analytical subjects, such as moral philosophy. In his junior year he and other students rebelled against the college discipline by declaring that

John Pintard, A.B. 1776
BY JOHN RAMAGE

they would no longer study mathematics. Pintard later attributed this rejection of authority, which not even President Witherspoon's warning that the rebels would lose their standing could quell, to the political turmoil of 1775. He and his associates took to playing cards and drinking eggnog in violation of the College rules but were soon discovered by tutor John Duffield (A.B. 1773). Called to account before Witherspoon, the boys chose Pintard to speak their denial of all charges. But one of the culprits, George Blewer (Class of 1777), had confessed to Duffield; and the president, after warning Pintard not to compound his guilt with a lie, sentenced all nine boys to a public reprimand. For all except Blewer, the incident was closed. The tearful stool pigeon was "sent to Coventry" by his mates, and after spring vacation he never returned to the College.

By dint of intense studying to catch up with his class, Pintard entered his senior year on schedule. Yet he still chafed at rules. His respect for Witherspoon contrasted sharply with his contempt for the tutors. During the early part of 1776, he rose before dawn to help train militia units and then attended morning prayers in Nassau Hall. Against the explicit wishes of his uncle, he ran away from Princeton in August as a member of a company of students who were off to fight the British in New York. He saw no combat but did walk tours of guard duty and serve as company cook at Elizabethtown, New Jersey for six weeks before his family's entreaties and his lack of funds persuaded him to return to college just in time to take his final examinations.

Richard Stockton, who had sponsored Pintard's application to the College, offered to obtain an ensign's commission in the army for him after he graduated, but Pintard's uncle would not hear of it. He wanted the young man to go to Philadelphia to be apprenticed to Benjamin Rush (A.B. 1760) for the study of medicine. It was probably the war that changed those plans, and Pintard went instead to his uncle's country home in New Rochelle, New York, where he again served briefly in the local militia. When the British overran Westchester County late in 1776, he went to the house of his maternal uncle, John Cannon, in Norwalk, Connecticut. At the end of the year, when Louis Pintard was named deputy commissary general of prisoners assigned to the care of Americans being held in New York City, he immediately hired his nephew as his assistant.

From 1777 to 1780 Pintard aided his uncle in a heroic effort to improve the conditions under which American prisoners of war were confined. Not only was he offended by the brutality of their situation and the contempt with which the British treated all Americans, but his bookish nature was outraged by such atrocities as the pillaging of the King's College library. Enemy troops bartered the volumes for drink. Among the prisoners he met was George Blewer, his erstwhile college friend, who had been captured at Germantown. Blewer begged Pintard's forgiveness for his betrayal at Nassau Hall.

In 1780 Pintard left New York for Paramus, New Jersey, where he tended to his uncle Louis's interests in Madeira wine and flaxseed trade, living with his uncle's family at Basking Ridge. He volunteered to join the New Jersey Continentals but, probably at his uncle's insistence, did not march with them when they went south toward Yorktown. Instead, like his uncle, he accepted a position with the congressional finance department. The job, located at Morristown, New Jersey, had been offered by Elias Boudinot, whom Pintard regarded as yet another uncle and who secured for him the post of assistant paymaster for the army at Newburgh, New York on the eve of demobilization.

By the beginning of 1784, Pintard had had all he could stand of his uncle's overbearing authority. He dreamed of long, romantic sea voyages while he was bound to a desk in the family counting house. He sought advice and money from Boudinot's brother Elisha so that he could declare his independence and become "a useful and honorable member of society." In 1784, when he inherited a substantial legacy from his maternal grandfather, he finally had his chance. On November 12 he married his distant cousin Elizabeth Brasher, the daughter of Colonel Abraham Brasher, in the Dutch Reformed Church in Hempstead, Long Island. He then left his uncle's employ to form a partnership with James Searle, a cousin and an agent for a wine importer. Pintard had little to do except collect his share of the profits. In 1785 he purchased a mill in Wallkill, Dutchess County, New York and considered leaving the city to enjoy a more bucolic existence.

He abandoned that plan in 1786 when, on Elisha Boudinot's recommendation, he was appointed to the post of translator for the national department of foreign affairs and when he entered into a new business venture involving trade with China and the East Indies, with an office on Wall Street. He prospered. In 1787 he helped to found the Mutual Fire Assurance Company and in April was elected its first secretary. At the same time, he served as secretary of the Whig Society, an organization devoted to removing former Loyalists from positions of influence, which he had helped create in 1784. It was typical of Pintard that he would assume a secondary role in organizations whose establishment had been largely his own achievement. Almost deafened by an Independence Day explosion soon after the war, he was reluctant to take positions that required him to represent the groups before the public.

In May 1789 Pintard led some of his fellow members of the now-deceased Whig Society in reviving the moribund St. Tammany Society. He had helped establish the Sons of St. Tammany in New Jersey in 1782, and now, as one of the few wealthy men who took an interest in the organization in New York, he conceived of giving it the additional name "Columbian Society" as a token of patriotic respectability. He helped design the group's elaborate rituals as well. And in addition to serving as sachem of the society, he was its first sagamore, or curator of property.

Pintard was a "sagamore" by nature. What he called his "passion for American history" was the motivating factor in many of his most important enterprises. In August 1789 he visited Boston and met with Jeremy Belknap (Harvard 1762) to discuss with him a scheme for the creation of a "Society of Antiquarians." Belknap was impressed by Pintard's enthusiasm but asked his friend Ebenezer Hazard (A.B. 1762) for more information about the "loquacious and unreserved" New Yorker. He learned that Pintard was a "lively, chearful man" who was a "mixture of heterogeneous particles"—not solid, but with potential. Pintard and Belknap corresponded about their progress toward the sort of organization they had discussed, and on January 24, 1791, Belknap presided over the first meeting of the Massachusetts Historical Society. Six months earlier, under Pintard's guidance, the Tammany Society had established the American Museum in New York as a repository for material relating to the natural and political history of the United States. Pintard frequently contributed articles on historical subjects to local publications.

On September 29, 1789, Pintard was elected an assistant alderman for the East Ward of New York and joined the city's Common Council. He was reelected in 1790 and 1792 and also served as fire inspector of the East Ward.

Nominated by the city's mechanics, he served one term in the state legislature in 1791. Meanwhile, he had participated in the establishment of the New York Manufacturing Society, joined the trustees of the New York Society Library, and been licensed, on November 25, 1790, as a broker in United States bonds. His appointment as translator, for which his fluency in French qualified him highly, continued after the foreign affairs office became the Department of State, but he resigned that post when the government moved to Philadelphia in August 1790. His successor was Philip Freneau (A.B. 1771). In his letter of resignation to Secretary of State Thomas Jefferson, Pintard pleaded on behalf of the American Museum for the donation of any "supernumerary" departmental papers. Although his correspondence with Belknap was full of "republican" phrases and he touted the antiaristocratic purposes of the Tammany Society, Pintard was never really a Jeffersonian. Basically uncommitted in these years to any political party, he found his friends among the wealthy Federalists with whom he did business. Many of them were his fellows in the Holland Lodge of Free and Accepted Masons, of which Pintard was master in December 1790.

Among Pintard's commercial ventures was the Society for establishing Useful Manufactures, founded in New Jersey in the spring of 1791 by friends of Alexander Hamilton who were inspired by the Treasury secretary's "Report on Manufactures." Pintard himself owned 100 shares of stock at $100 each. The corporation was over-subscribed by at least $125,000, but after a brief panic in the late summer, stock prices soared. As agent for the society's governor, William Duer, Pintard collected a huge profit in stocks and certificates.

In December 1791 Pintard suddenly encountered several of Duer's creditors who demanded to be paid. Duer was out of the city, but after receiving his assurances that the money was available Pintard countersigned his notes. He also joined in Duer's abortive scheme for a Connecticut Manufacturing Society and in his speculative attempt to gain control of new banks that were being organized in New York in early 1792 as competitors to the Bank of the United States and the Bank of New York. But Duer's circle had to contend with others in the bank war of 1792, and it lost. In March the winners called in all of Duer's notes, ruining him entirely and sending him to debtor's prison. As Duer's agent and the guarantor of his debts, Pintard was ruined as well.

By the end of March, Pintard had fled to Newark, New Jersey, protesting his innocence of charges—some of them from Duer—that he had absconded with hundreds of thousands of investors' dollars. In June he lost his seat on the Common Council. Jeremy Belknap regretted Pintard's ill fortune, but mostly because it required Belknap to find another salesman for his *History of New Hampshire*.

Bonds posted by friends kept Pintard from debtor's prison in New Jersey, while Elias Boudinot worked in Congress to secure passage of a uniform bankruptcy law. Hounded by creditors, Pintard occasionally had to go into hiding in Newark; and when he was not hiding, he was petitioning the New York courts for relief. Gradually, he entered social life in Newark, attending Masonic rites, joining the militia and helping to organize the Newark Fire Association and the Newark Patriotic Society. For all of his organizations he was a successful fund raiser. In his free time, he tended a vegetable garden and, his tribulations having turned his mind to theology, supervised the religious education of his children. In 1797 he briefly joined the *Institutio legalis*, a moot court society at Newark in which aspiring lawyers were trained for the bar, in the hope of beginning a new career and possibly with an eye to solving his own legal problems. But on July 15 of that year, he was finally committed to debtor's prison in Newark, and for the next thirteen months he occupied himself with reading, especially the works of Dr. Johnson, which he quoted almost constantly thereafter. He also papered and painted his prison rooms and installed a Franklin stove before his wife and son joined him there in October 1797. In February 1798 he began to publish from prison the *Rural Magazine*, featuring excerpts from his current reading and some book reviews, which he continued for a full year.

Pintard was released on a technicality in August 1798. Unable to return to New York, where he was still subject to arrest for debt, he applied to President John Adams for a position as a government clerk. That job was filled, so Pintard joined his brother-in-law in Medford, Massachusetts to work on a new process for distilling liquor. He resumed the study of law in Medford but soon decided that it was "too slow a profession" for a man of his age. In November 1799, with the assurances of Luther Martin (A.B. 1766) that he would not be arrested there, he went to Baltimore, and in January 1800 he spent some time in Princeton. After the first national bankruptcy law was enacted in April, he returned to New York, was declared bankrupt, and began to rebuild his life.

At first, Pintard supported his family by working as a bookseller and auctioneer, but he had hopes of making a new fortune in the west. In November 1800 he went to Washington, D.C. to obtain information about the Louisiana Territory and on January 12, 1801, sailed for New Orleans. He found that city "a very sink of pollution" and hurried back to New York by way of Havana, arriving on July 6, 1801. With him, he brought a detailed statistical account of the region with which he hoped to convince President Jefferson to name him consul at New Orleans, his low opinion of the port city notwithstanding. Vice President Aaron Burr (A.B. 1772) endorsed his application, and Jefferson considered it seriously, until Chancellor Robert R. Livingston of New York advised the president to find someone else.

In January 1802 Pintard paid $15,000 for a one-quarter interest in the *New York Daily Advertiser*, which was owned by his cousin Samuel Bayard (A.B. 1784). As editor of the newspaper, Pintard published several articles based on his own travels and a few rather tepid defenses of Burr, who was increasingly under attack by political foes. Before embarking on a mission to France that eventually produced the Louisiana Purchase, James Monroe consulted Pintard for expert advice about New Orleans. And once the purchase, of which Pintard whole-heartedly approved, had been made, Secretary of the Treasury Albert Gallatin asked him for a full report and for his suggestions on how to govern the new territory.

In February 1803 Pintard's fortunes took another plunge. He resigned from the newspaper to find a more satisfying career but had no success in doing so. Then his only living son was lost at sea. In January

1804, when he was almost desperate, Pintard applied for help to Mayor DeWitt Clinton of New York. Although they were fellow Masons, the two men had never been close until that meeting. Afterward they were bosom friends. With Clinton's support, Pintard received the post of City Inspector when it was created in 1804. He held that difficult and lonely job for four years, and during the yellow fever epidemic of 1805, as a member of the Board of Health, he was one of the few municipal officials to stay in the city to do what he could for the victims.

At a salary that never exceeded $1,300 per year, Pintard amassed a voluminous statistical portrait of New York. His innovations in records-keeping were dramatic, and his suggestions for future procedures were far in advance of current practices. His data enabled him to make a remarkably accurate prediction of the city's population growth for the next century. On May 4, 1807, he was given the additional position of clerk of the council. He held both jobs until January 8, 1808, and later compiled an exhaustive index to the minutes of the Common Council's proceedings.

In November 1804 one of Pintard's greatest dreams was realized with the creation of the New York Historical Society, which he considered his "own brat," and which was his preoccupation for the next twenty years. He was its first recording secretary and later its librarian and treasurer. Under his leadership, several of its members established the Public School Society of New York in February 1805. And with the historical society as a base, Pintard was active in or a founder of such philanthropic enterprises as the American Academy of the Arts, the Society for the Prevention of Pauperism, the American Bible Society, Sailor's Snug Harbor, the House of Refuge, the Mercantile Library, and the General Theological Seminary.

After resigning his municipal offices, Pintard was hired as secretary of the Mutual Insurance Company, successor to the fire assurance company he had created twenty years earlier. It was a salaried position that he would hold for another twenty years, and which finally allowed him to live with a modicum of luxury. In 1822 he was taxed on $12,000 worth of real estate and $1,000 in personal property. His other business interests included the Merchant's Bank, founded with his help in 1810, the Brooklyn Steamship Company, and the first savings bank in New York. The deaths of his uncle Louis and Elisha Boudinot in 1818 and 1819 brought Pintard inheritances of additional stocks and land. From 1817 to 1827 he was secretary of the New York Chamber of Commerce, and after resigning as secretary of Mutual

Insurance in 1828, he served as one of its directors and as president of the New York Savings Bank. Only as his hearing and eyesight declined in the late 1820s did he gradually withdraw from some of his business and philanthropic activities.

The historical society remained the most important of all to him. He sold his library to it at cost in 1809 and then invested thousands of dollars of his own money to build the collection. With DeWitt Clinton's help, he obtained state endowments for the society; partly in return for his friend's faithful support, he campaigned vigorously for Clinton's election to the presidency in 1812. By then he was considered a loyal Federalist, and like the rest of that party, he opposed the War of 1812, especially as it was conducted by the Republicans.

From 1812 to 1816 Pintard fought to obtain Bridewell, the former city almshouse, as a rent-free headquarters for several philanthropic organizations, including the historical society. Even Clinton, to whose son Pintard was by then a devoted godfather, considered the idea "impudent" at first, but by 1816 the New York Institution, comprised of all the groups Pintard had mobilized to support his appeal, was installed at Bridewell for a rent of one peppercorn per year. Pintard believed that the institution would be a "monument to [his] useful existence." It disappeared by 1832, but the historical society was his true monument.

In 1814, when specie was so scarce as a result of the war that there were no small coins to be had, the city authorized Pintard to sign more than $245,000 worth of scrip in denominations of less than one dollar. He worked for eight to twelve hours every day for six months to complete the task, after which he made sure that all of the documents relating to it, including the scrip, were delivered to the historical society. He was paid three dollars for every 1,200 pieces he signed.

Pintard's genius was as a promoter, as in 1815 when he helped organize support for construction of the Erie Canal, a project which he vigorously sought to keep in state rather than federal hands. Determined to use his wealth and influence for the public good, he almost never failed to achieve his goals. There were two notable exceptions to that success, however. In 1818, when Governor Clinton's foes in the legislature blocked a state endowment for the Academy of the Arts, Pintard resigned as the academy's treasurer in disappointment. And between 1816 and 1823 he engaged in a dispute with the Episcopal bishop of New York, John Henry Hobart (A.B. 1793), regarding the propriety of Pintard's American Bible Society and control of the fund raising for the General Theological Seminary. The two men began as respectful adversaries and ended as enemies; and when Hobart's assertion of his authority prevailed, Pintard severed his own formal connections with the seminary.

In 1825 Pintard experienced a much more painful disappointment when the new leaders of the historical society accused him of peculation and threatened to sell some of the society's library to pay debts for which they blamed him. Pintard, who regarded the new officers as usurpers, never attended another meeting, although he continued as treasurer of the organization until 1827. As it happened, the state provided $5,000 to rescue the society and the books were never sold. The society owed Pintard $3,000 for books he had purchased, but when the state's grant was spent, less than half of that amount went to the founder and treasurer, and what was paid was accompanied by bitter recriminations. The balance of his claim was disallowed because Pintard, that sagamore of sagamores, had failed to keep his receipts. When he died, the society pronounced its official regrets and resolved to cherish his memory. It did not offer to repay his estate.

In the late 1820s Pintard was a director of the Greek Fund in New York, which sent money to European revolutionaries. He had little confidence in the administration of John Quincy Adams and none whatever in that of Andrew Jackson, except only when that president took a strong stand against the doctrine of nullification. Martin Van Buren he considered "an intrigant, much such another as Burr." Among national politicians, his favorite seems to have been Henry Clay, although he detested the Missouri Compromise of 1820 because he believed that "Free men never can submit to the extension of the rights of Slavery."

Pintard spent his last years in semiretirement, continuing, however, to be a very active bank president. During a cholera epidemic in the summer of 1832, he insisted on going to the bank daily to be certain that panic-stricken customers and their families would be able to withdraw whatever money they needed for the emergency. Much of what free time he had was spent in funeral corteges. His letters of the period read like a necrology of New York's elite. He died on June 21, 1844, survived by his two daughters. In all, three sons had died before 1817. Pintard was buried beside his wife in a family vault under St. Clement's Church in New York. When that building was demolished, his remains were moved to St. Michael's Cemetery in Queens County.

SOURCES: *NYHS Coll.*, LXX-LXXIII, passim, esp. LXX, ix-xxii, 121 ("sink of pollution"), 347 ("superficial" education), 119 ("my own brat"), 275 ("Free men"), LXXII, 204-205 ("an intrigant"); *DAB*; *NYHS Quart.*, 43 (1959), 453-62; 45 (1961), 346-62; 55 (1971), 156; 59 (1975), 116-17; D. L. Sterling, "New York Patriarch," Ph.D. dissert., N.Y. Univ.

(1958), esp. 74 ("useful and honorable"), 217 ("too slow a profession"); J. G. Wilson, *John Pintard* (1902); and *Memorial Hist. of N.Y.* (1893), III, 16, 28, 64-65, 71-72; IV, 115; J. Pintard, MS "Recollections" and "Autobiography," NHi; J. A. Scoville, *Old Merchants of N.Y. City* (1864), 217-45; R. H. Kelby, *N.Y. Hist. Soc.* (1905), 13-15, 24-25 ("impudent"); MS Clio. Soc. membership list, PUA; Butterfield, *Rush Letters*, 106; *WMQ* (3 ser.), 13 (1956), 382-83; 30 (1970), 384, 390; G. A. Boyd, *Elias Boudinot* (1952), 100 & n, 122, 194-96; *NYGBR*, 68 (1937), 47; 51 (1920), 136; E. V. Blake, *Hist. of Tammany Soc.* (1901), 35-36; N.Y. Cnty. Democratic Committee, *Tammany* (1924), 24-25, 66; *MHS Coll.* (5 ser.), III (1877), 157 ("loquacious and unreserved"), 162 ("lively, chearful"), 165, 231 & n, 290, 292, 295; (6 ser.), IV (1891), 470, 489 ("passion for Amer. hist."), 505-506; L. W. Dunlap, *Amer. Hist. Societies, 1760-1860* (1944), 7; *MCCCNY*, I, III, IV, V, passim; VI, 770; VII, 613, 738; VIII, 51, 104, 113, 124, 132, 176; XIV, 765; *N.Y. Red Book* (1895), 371; *Journal of the [N.Y.] House of Assembly, 14th Session*, passim; *Jefferson Papers*, XVII, 352-53 ("supernumerary" papers); A. F. Young, *Democratic Republicans of N.Y.* (1967), 220-23, 298; *Hamilton Papers*, XI, 126, 127n; XX, 195-99; Davis, *Essays*, 274n, 278, 284-85, 296, 370, 392, 394; *MHM*, 5 (1910), 71; R.W.B. Vail, *Knickerbocker Birthday* (1954), 23, 30, 34, 48-49, 55 ("useful existence"), 120n, 66, 68; C. C. Robbins, *David Hosack* (1964), 124, 162; D. Bobbé, *DeWitt Clinton* (1933), 179, 185-86, 200, 203, 225, 258, 267; H. W. Lanier, *Century of Banking in N.Y.* (1922), 126; M. J. Lamb and Mrs. B. Harrison, *Hist. of City of N.Y.* (1896), III, 648, 696-97; R. A. Mohl, *Poverty in N.Y.* (1971), 108-109, 211, 242-43, 250-52, 258; *N.J. Hist.*, 97 (1979), 127n8 (with thanks to the author of this article on the *Institutio legalis*, Don C. Skemer). See William H. Vernon (A.B. 1776) for commencement of 1776.

MANUSCRIPTS: NHi, NjR (Boudinot MSS); NNG

William Ramsay

WILLIAM RAMSAY, physician, who was the son of William Ramsay and his wife, Ann McCarty, of Alexandria, Virginia, had the distinction of having his education at Princeton paid for, at least in substantial part, by George Washington. The father was a leading merchant of Alexandria, one of its founders, and its first mayor, and at the time of his death in 1785, he was described by Washington, who participated in the Masonic funeral, as the oldest of Alexandria's inhabitants. The elder Ramsay had served as commissary for Washington's troops during the French and Indian War, and through the years that followed, he and members of his family were frequent visitors at Mount Vernon, as Washington in turn was in their home. In 1782 the senior Ramsay paid taxes for ten white polls and twenty blacks, who were only a part of the property he held.

Why Washington should have assumed any part of the cost for educating the son of such a family is an interesting question. It can be noted that Washington was a relative of the mother, and the ties with the father formed through past military associations were undoubtedly strong. That Washington had been favorably impressed by the studious habits of the young man, and that the father was experiencing some financial need, as any man of property may from time to time, is indicated by the letter of January 29, 1769, in which the offer of support for young Ramsay's education is made to William Ramsay, Sr. The opening paragraph explains Washington's inability to advance the money Ramsay had requested. It then proceeds:

> Having once or twice of late hear [sic] you Speak highly in praise of the Jersey College, as if you had a desire of sending your Son William there (who I am told is a youth fond of study and instruction, and disposed to a sedentary studious life; in following of which he may not only promote his own happiness, but the future welfare of others) I shou'd be glad, if you have no other objection to it than what may arise from the expence, if you wou'd send him there as soon as it is convenient and depend on me for Twenty five pounds this Currency a year for his support so long as it may be necessary for the completion of his Education.

The letter continues, stipulating that it is to be taken as evidence of an obligation binding his heirs or executors in the case of his death, that Mr. Ramsay is not to consider that he in any way is placed under obligation to Washington, and "that from me it will never be known."

Young Ramsay came to Princeton in the fall of 1771, according to the following entry, under the name of his father and the date of February 24, 1772, in Washington's ledger: "By my promise to allow towards the Support of his Son at the Jersey College £25 pr. Ann. to commence from the time of his going there which was in Oct. last." Ramsay must have been enrolled first in the grammar school and was probably among the ten members of its senior class who, on September 28, 1772, after examination, were admitted to the freshman class in the College. His name is found on the steward's account of payments for tuition, rent, and board for the period from May 25, 1773 to September 25, 1774, and a newspaper report of the commencement exercises of September 1774 reveals that he then was a member of the sophomore class. These reports show too that he had excelled in his studies, for he took three prizes in competition with other undergraduates: third prize in reading Latin and Greek, first prize in Latin grammar, and first prize in "Latin Version." The steward's account for the period of November 1774 to April 10, 1775 shows that at the time Ramsay was a member of the junior class. Moreover, the ledger of local merchant Thomas Patterson indicates that Ramsay was in residence throughout the academic year of 1774-1775, which ended in September of the latter year.

Indeed, two transactions recorded by Patterson for the 19th and 26th of October, and another under the date of November 24, 1775, suggest that Ramsay was on hand for the beginning of his senior year. It must be noted that in this last instance the payment of a relatively large sum was made by President Witherspoon, but this was not unusual. Such a payment had been made for Ramsay on two earlier occasions during the year, one in June and another in late September, and the entry of the name under October 26, 1775 as "William Wash. Ramsay" may indicate that the payment was made by the president from funds Patterson knew about, unless perchance Ramsay had adopted the name of a benefactor who as commander of the Continental Army already was on the way to becoming a national hero. Parents on occasion seem to have placed money on deposit with the president for the use of their sons, perhaps to assure prudent expenditures, and Washington had recorded a payment of June 1773 to President "Weatherspoon" of "Princeton College." Happily, independent evidence of Ramsay's presence in Princeton toward the end of November is provided by a letter of Martha Washington to Ramsay's sister Betty, written from Cambridge, Massachusetts, on December 30, 1775. It reports her trip up from Virginia to join General Washington at his Cambridge headquarters, and near the end of the letter she wrote: "I see your Brother at princeton he was very well but did not talk of comeing home soon."

One would like to know what he did talk of on that occasion, for it might help to explain a failure to complete his course of study at the College. Just when he left the College is not known. It has been suggested that he studied medicine with Benjamin Rush (A.B. 1760). This is possible, for a list of his students compiled by Rush late in his life, while not including Ramsay, has a gap for the period in which Ramsay would have been most likely to have been apprenticed to him. Ramsay apparently served during the war as a surgeon's mate and surgeon, and there is reason for believing that he was the Doctor Ramsay who in later years was on occasion a guest at Mount Vernon. Actually, little has been found regarding his later life. He seems to have lived quietly in Alexandria, possessed of the considerable properties he inherited from his father and presumably practicing medicine. He apparently remained a bachelor and probably died at some time before September 21, 1795, when the will of a William Ramsay, made in September 1787, was proved in the local court. The will made provision for a William Tucker alias Ramsay, who could have been an adopted or illegitimate son and was probably the William Ramsay who was an occasional visitor at Mount Vernon in the later years of Washington's life.

SOURCES: M. G. Powell, *Old Alexandria* (1928), esp. 26-34; G. M. Moore, *Seaport in Va.* (1949), 52-61, 58-59 ("I see your brother"); S. M. Hamilton, *Letters to Washington* (1898-1902), II, 218-21; esp. III, passim; *Washington Writings*, I, 130, 345, 509; II, 233, 261, 499-500 ("Having once or twice of late"); IV, 133-34, 165n, 200-202; XXVIII, 341n; XXXVII, 135n; *Washington Diaries*, II, 95, 342, 356, 414; IV, 280, 299; *First Census, Va.* 16; MS Washington Ledger A, 356f., Ledger B, 3, 47f. ("By my promise"), 90, 105 (which suggests that the last payment on Ramsay's behalf was in Dec 1774), Washington MSS; MS Steward's accounts, PUA; *Pa. Journal and Weekly Advertiser*, 12 Oct 1774 (undergraduate prizes); Patterson Acct. Bk.; J. H. Gwathmey, *Hist. Reg. of Virginians in the Rev.* (1938), 648; W. B. Blanton, *Medicine in Va. in Eighteenth Century* (1931), 362, 406; H. E. Hayden, *Va. Genealogies* (1931), 88; College of Physicians of Phila., *Transactions and Studies* (4 ser.), 14 (1946), 127-32; *Cal. Va. St. Papers*, v, 617-19. The author is indebted to W. W. Abbot of The University of Virginia for information regarding the will of William Ramsay proved in 1795.

WFC

James Ramsey (Ramsay)

JAMES RAMSEY (RAMSAY), A.B., physician, finds specific identification through a manuscript sketch of Archibald Scott (A.B. 1775) housed in the Princeton University Library, which explains Scott's presence in Augusta County, Virginia through a lifelong ministry as the end result of a friendship he formed while in the College with a fellow student "by the name of Ramsay." There were two Ramsays, or Ramseys, in the College during the time of Scott's residence: William Ramsay of Alexandria, Virginia, a nongraduate in the Class of 1776; and James Ramsey who graduated with that class. Statements in the sketch that indicate that Ramsey was from Rockbridge County (formed in 1778 partly from Augusta) and that Scott married Ramsey's sister, for which there is confirming evidence, clarify the identification. Further comments on Ramsay have a special interest here, for it is said that he was "a serious young man, . . . who at that time had the ministry in view" but that afterward he "studied medicine, and settled in the Cow-Pastures, in Augusta County."

James Ramsey, probably born about 1754, was the son of William Ramsey, who held extensive property in Augusta County, Virginia and who probably was the oldest son and heir of an earlier James Ramsey. No specific information regarding young Ramsey's preparation for college has been found, although it may have involved the school that was later known as Augusta Academy, in whose somewhat

shadowy history the Reverend John Brown (A.B. 1749) figured significantly. Ramsey probably entered the College in November 1774,
for his name appears on a list of the junior class in the steward's
account for the term that began in that month, and does not appear
on any surviving account of earlier date. He did not belong to either
of the literary societies. No evidence has been found as to where or
with whom he subsequently studied medicine. It is unlikely that he
was the James Ramsay found at the University of Edinburgh in 1786,
for it was on February 16 of that year that Ramsey married Jane
Lyle, daughter of a locally prominent family in Augusta County.

Ramsey may have had some military service during the Revolution,
but the number of James Ramseys or Ramsays who did so make it
difficult to be certain. The one James Ramsey linked with his wife's
name in a standard source is listed as a private, but this rank seems
unlikely for a college graduate and person of property. It is more
likely that he was the captain listed for an Augusta militia company.
His later career was that of a practicing physician and a large land-
holder, his place of residence being on a tract along the Big Calf
Pasture River on both sides of the line between Rockbridge and
Augusta counties. He may have been the tax commissioner named in
1787 and the justice of the county court named in 1792. As early as
1784 he had become a trustee of Liberty Hall, later Washington College, forerunner of Washington and Lee University. Beginning in
1797, the triennial *Catalogues* of the College of New Jersey credited
him with the A.M. degree, but with no indication of its source; they
did not list him as dead until after 1842. A more likely indication of
the time of his death is the termination in 1807 of his service as trustee
of Washington College, after some twenty-two years. One source indicates that he died in 1815. Ramsey seems to have been survived by
two daughters.

Sources: A. Alexander and J. Carnahan, ms "Notices of Distinguished Graduates,"
NjP ("serious young man"); Washington and Lee Univ., *Historical Papers*, 3 (1892),
157-59, and *Catalogue* (1888), 37; D. F. Wulfeck, *Marriages of Some Va. Residents*, vi
(1967), 7; O. F. Morton, *Hist. of Rockbridge Cnty., Va.* (1920), 500, 523; *DAR Patriot
Index*; L. Chalkley, *Records of Augusta Cnty., Va.* (1912), iii, 178, 457, 461; A. B.
Fothergill and J. M. Naugle, *Va. Tax Payers* (1966), 102; ms Steward's accounts, PUA;
W. B. Blanton, *Medicine in Va. in Eighteenth Century* (1931), 118-19 (for Edinburgh);
Cal. Va. St. Papers, vi, 51; J. H. Gwathmey, *Hist. Reg. of Virginians in the Rev.*
(1938), 648. See Archibald Scott (A.B. 1775), and William H. Vernon (A.B. 1776) for
commencement of 1776. As in the case of Scott, Ramsey's attendance at CNJ seems to
have been forgotten in Va. sources.

WFC

Archibald Campbell Read

ARCHIBALD CAMPBELL READ, A.B., A.M. 1780, soldier, public official, and probably farmer, was almost certainly born in Pennsylvania. There were several branches of the Read or Reed family in the neighborhood of Philadelphia in the eighteenth century, but Archibald Read's date and place of birth and parentage are unknown. He joined the Cliosophic Society at the beginning of his junior year in the fall of 1774, the time at which his name first appeared on the records of the College steward. As a Cliosophian, he used the pseudonym "Randolph," probably after Peyton Randolph of Virginia, one of the several American Whigs who were so honored by the society at that time.

Whether Read remained in Princeton for the unusual commencement exercises of 1776 and what he did during the year after his graduation have not been established. On December 13, 1777, he was appointed paymaster of the Eighth Pennsylvania Regiment of the Continental Army, then stationed near Valley Forge under the command of Colonel Daniel Brodhead. With the rank of first lieutenant, Read also assumed the duties of regimental clothier in 1778, the year in which the unit went west to reinforce Fort Pitt.

Read remained under Brodhead's command in Fort Pitt even after the Eighth Pennsylvania was broken up in January 1781. He therefore was not present at the College to receive his A.M. degree in September 1780. In the spring and summer of 1781, Brodhead's rivals for rank and authority, working with the army's auditor for the Western Department, brought charges of misconduct against the colonel and several of his officers. Read stood accused of defrauding the soldiers of his regiment and of embezzling their pay, but he was acquitted in a court-martial of July 1781. The charges against Brodhead, which also involved the misuse of regimental funds, were even more serious, and in August Read and some of his brother officers addressed a letter to the colonel in which they regretfully informed him that they could not obey his orders until he was exonerated by a military court. The situation at Fort Pitt exasperated General Washington, who complained that "the parties make it a point to thwart each other as much as possible." Brodhead was finally acquitted in early 1782, but the ill feeling among the garrison at Fort Pitt nevertheless required Washington to remove him permanently from his command. Read probably resigned from the army at the same time.

Read then settled in the region of Pitts Town. At least in 1786, he was a clerk to John Story, one of the commissioners of accounts for

Pennsylvania; between April and June of that year, Read earned $125 for his services in that capacity. In February 1787 he signed a petition to the state assembly to create Allegheny County. Four years later, as a resident of Pitts Town, Read paid three pence in Allegheny County taxes.

The record of his life thereafter is meager. In 1800 he was the head of a household in Pitts Town that included one adult woman, a girl between the ages of ten and sixteen, and two boys between ten and twenty. Read's name does not appear in the local census records for 1810 or 1820, but the state's record of his military service notes his death in Allegheny County in 1823.

Sources: See William H. Vernon (A.B. 1776) for commencement of 1776; *Pa. Arch.* (5 ser.), III, 316, 317, 313; (3 ser.), XXII, 694; *Washington Writings*, X, 152; XXIII, 90-92, 396 ("thwart each other"); XXIV, 29, 30; *PMHB*, 35 (1911), 298; als officers at Ft. Pitt to D. Brodhead, 19 Aug 1781; MS Proceedings of court-martial, 9-17 Jul 1781, Washington MSS; Continental Congress Board of Treas., Expenditures re: Civil List, Apr-Jun 1786, Jul-Sep 1786, PCC; *WPHM*, 4 (1921), 93; Arch. of Hist. Soc. of Western Pa. (courtesy of Ruth Salisbury, Archivist); *PGM*, 7 (1918), 144; *Index, Rev. War Pension Applications* (1966).

Aaron Rhea

AARON RHEA, A.B., soldier and probably a farmer, was the son of Jonathan Rhea, a farmer, and Lydia Forman Rhea. He was baptized in the Presbyterian church in Freehold, New Jersey on May 8, 1757, by trustee of the College William Tennent, Jr. When his father died in June 1767, Rhea and each of his two brothers, one of whom was probably John Rhea (A.B. 1780), inherited £100.

Rhea probably enrolled in the College as a sophomore in November 1774. He did not rush to join the army after his degree was conferred, but waited until September 1778 before enlisting as an ensign in the First Battalion of New Jersey Militia. That winter his unit was stationed in and near Elizabethtown, New Jersey. In May 1779, as the First New Jersey Regiment, it joined General John Sullivan's expedition against the Six Nations. After returning to New Jersey in October, Rhea resigned his commission.

Also attached to Sullivan's expedition had been Colonel Elisha Sheldon's Second Regiment of Continental Light Dragoons. In August 1781, as a lieutenant, Rhea joined that unit, then designated as the Second Legionary Corps and assigned to Connecticut's quota. On June 9, 1783, the corps was furloughed for fourteen months, during which the army was demobilized. Sheldon's unit never mustered again.

Rhea returned to Monmouth County and probably took up farming. He died intestate in May or June 1795. Apparently, he had never married, for when he was granted a pension a few weeks after his death, it went to his administrators. The pension records include no reference to a wife.

SOURCES: F. R. Symmes, *Hist. of the Old Tennent Chh.* (1904), 400-401; *N.J. Wills*, IV, 352; VIII, 295; MS Steward's accounts, PUA; Heitman; Stryker, *Off. Reg.*, 42-43, 106; F. A. Berg, *Encyclopedia of Cont. Army Units* (1972), 30; *Index, Rev. War Pension Applications* (1966).

Joseph Rue

JOSEPH RUE, A.B., A.M. 1783, Presbyterian clergyman, was born on June 19, 1751, near Shrewsbury, Monmouth County, New Jersey. His parents, Joseph and Sarah Rue, owned at least two substantial farms. Before he died in 1765, Joseph Rue, Sr. settled his family on 200 acres "southward of Perth Amboy" in Middlesex County, near the Monmouth County line. His will provided that the "Grape Vine Neck" plantation along the Manalapan be sold, the proceeds to be divided like the rest of the estate among his children.

After losing his right arm in an accident, Rue had to abandon the shoemaker's trade and decided to pursue a career in the ministry. With financial support from the Presbytery of New Brunswick, which accepted him as a prospective candidate on October 12, 1773, he entered the College between May of that year and September 1774. After graduation he returned to Monmouth County to study theology with trustee William Tennent, Jr. of Freehold, who had supplied the church at Shrewsbury in which Rue worshiped as a child.

After Tennent died in 1777, Rue completed his theological training with the new minister at Freehold, John Woodhull (A.B. 1766). He then joined the New Brunswick Presbytery as a candidate on October 17, 1780 and was licensed to preach on July 25, 1781. He served an itineracy of almost two years before April 1783, when the Shrewsbury church asked him to be its stated supply. One year later, that church and its sister congregation at Shark River invited him to settle as their permanent pastor. Rue was ordained as an evangelist after preaching a trial sermon at Pennington, New Jersey on June 15, 1784. At the same time, he declined the call from the churches in Monmouth County. In April 1785 he accepted an invitation to settle at the Pennington church and was installed there in October.

With his bride, the former Elizabeth Liscomb of New York City, whom he had married on February 9, 1785, Rue moved into the parsonage farm of the "church of Hopewell at Pennington." He was to remain the resident minister there for forty-one years. In April 1789, at the request of the church in Trenton, the presbytery assigned Rue to devote one-fourth of his time to that congregation for one year, when the regular pastor, James F. Armstrong (A.B. 1773), was preaching at Maidenhead. The arrangement was renewed for three years in 1791, extended to include one-third of Rue's time in 1800, and continued until 1821, when Rue's request to be excused from his responsibilities at Trenton was granted.

From the beginning of his service at Pennington, Rue delivered very rosy reports to the presbytery about the state of religion in his community. In 1801 he noted that the number of communicants in Trenton and Pennington had gone from 68 to 168 in the previous year. Revivals occurred in both churches in 1803; and after 1821, when he was able to concentrate his full attention on the Pennington congregation, there was another sharp increase in the number of communicants there. Between 1801 and 1826 Rue claimed to have added 255 souls to full membership in the church. Yet he was remembered when he died as having "labored long without seeing much fruit." He was selected to represent the presbytery in the Presbyterian General Assembly in 1793, 1801, and 1802.

Rue was performing a baptism in 1823 or 1824 when he suddenly forgot the words to the ceremony and had to leave the pulpit. It was his last appearance as minister in Pennington. For two years he was too disabled to perform his duties, and the Presbytery paid the salaries of several ministers who supplied the church during his absence. In March 1826 Rue's final illness began. He died on April 15 of that year, leaving his widow and their two sons and two daughters.

SOURCES: G. Hale, *Hist of the Old Pres. Congregation . . . at Pennington, N.J.* (1876), 66-71, 70 ("labored long"); *GMNJ*, 45 (1970), 102; Webster, MS Brief Sketches, I; *N.J. Wills*, IV, 367; MS Steward's accounts, PUA; *Pa. Gazette*, 8 Oct 1783 (A.M.); J. Hall, *Hist. of Pres. Chh. in Trenton, N.J.* (1912), 28. See William H. Vernon (A.B. 1776) for commencement of 1776.

John Rutherford

JOHN RUTHERFORD, A.B., gentleman farmer, lawyer, and public official, was born in New York City on September 20, 1760, the son of Walter Rutherford and his wife, Catherine Rutherford. The father was one of the many Scottish officers who served in North America

John Rutherford, A.B. 1776
BY REMBRANDT PEALE

with the British army during the French and Indian War. Walter's
brother, Major John Rutherford of the Royal American Regiment,
was killed at Ticonderoga in 1758; and Walter, a captain in the same
regiment, resigned his commission at the end of hostilities to settle
permanently in America. In December 1758 he had married the widow
of Elisha Parker of Perth Amboy, New Jersey, a daughter of James
Alexander, who before his death in 1756 had been a leading attorney,
officeholder, and landowner of New York and New Jersey. Her brother
was William Alexander, later major general in the Continental Army
and commonly known as Lord Stirling because of the claim he made
to a Scottish earldom. Among the students attending the College before the Revolution, John Rutherford enjoyed unusual advantages of
wealth and station.

It is difficult to determine just when Rutherford entered the College, where he was a member of the Whig Society. The fragmentary
surviving records of the steward suggest that it may have been as early
as the fall of 1772. He certainly was in residence during the academic
year 1773-1774, and in the following year he was listed as a member
of the junior class. A clue may be found in the regret he expressed

ten years after graduation that students did not "stay longer at [their] Colledges, where they might have some Assistance, but they generally hurry thro', and the greater Part think no more of the Classics or the Sciences." In the same document he expressed pride in the fact that New Jersey boasted two colleges, "of which Princeton brings many Students from distant Parts, is very flourishing, and has bred many eminent men." One has to leave to conjecture the question of how far a further comment reflects the attitude he took toward his fellow students while still in college. Said he: "It must be owned that the Farmers, and middle Class of People run too much on sending their Sons to Colledges, which unfits them for their own Employments, greatly overstocks the learned Professions, gives other Ideas beyond their Circumstances, makes too many Candidates for public offices and Employments, and greatly contributes to prolonging the annual Elections, which sometimes throws the Country idle for ten days or more, and occasions Animosities even among near Relations, that the rest of the year hardly make up." One can be certain only that Rutherford emerged from the Revolution with no great satisfaction in the drift it brought toward a more democratic society.

There is little room for doubt that the coming of the Revolution had presented Rutherford with a difficult problem, though hardly so difficult as that faced by his father. A former officer of some twenty years' service in the regular military establishment who recently had been rewarded by a grant of 5,000 acres in New York, Walter Rutherford was unwilling to abjure his allegiance to the king. Having moved his residence from New York to New Jersey, where the family held extensive properties, he obviously hoped to sit out the war without active participation on either side, but the Council of Safety refused to make it easy for him. Twice in the latter half of 1777 he was required, and refused, to take the oath of abjuration and allegiance, and over the course of several months he either was severely restricted in his movements or was in prison. His relief from these restrictions in February 1778 was largely due to a not altogether unsuccessful attempt to use him and his stepson James Parker, against whom the council simultaneously instituted proceedings, for the purpose of bargaining for the release of prisoners held by the British in New York. The ultimate success that attended Walter Rutherford's effort to sit out the war undoubtedly owed much to the close personal and social ties linking him with leading figures on the American side of the struggle.

As with the father, so it seems to have been with the son. No evidence of military service on either side has been discovered. The best testimony as to his activity during the war is that he was reading law, at first with Richard Stockton (A.B. 1748), signer of the Declaration of Independence, and later with William Paterson (A.B. 1763), first attorney general of the state of New Jersey. He was licensed to practice in 1782, and in that same year, a New York newspaper carried the announcement of his marriage on October 30 "at Society Hall, near Princeton" to Helena Morris, daughter of Lewis Morris III of "Morrisania" in New York's Westchester County, another signer of the Declaration, and sister of Colonel Lewis Morris IV (A.B. 1774), who then was still on duty in South Carolina as a valued aide to General Nathanael Greene. The couple soon took up residence in New York City, where Rutherford's father also returned and lived until his death in 1804. There is some question as to how active a practitioner of the law Rutherford ever became, although he was listed in 1786 among the lawyers of the city with an address at 50 Broadway. But there is no question that he quickly assumed positions of leadership in New York, as vestryman of Trinity Parish and regent of the University of the State of New York 1784-1787, and as trustee of Columbia College in the last of these years.

About 1787 or not long thereafter, he moved his residence back to New Jersey, to property the family owned in Sussex County, which he represented in the General Assembly elected in October 1789. He belonged to a family long active in the affairs of both provinces, but he was not counted in the census of 1790 among the inhabitants of New York City, as was his father, whose household included five slaves. Over the preceding years, he had been notably active in promoting the commercial and industrial development of New Jersey, and especially the interests of the reestablished Board of Proprietors of East Jersey, of which by 1785 he became surveyor general and of which he would be president from 1804. In January 1789 he was appointed one of the state's presidential electors for the first election under the new federal constitution. He obviously found easy identification with the political leaders who had brought the state into the new union with a minimum of controversy, and in 1791, when barely past the age of thirty required by the Constitution, he took his seat as a member of the United States Senate. He served, with one reelection, until November 1798, when he resigned, perhaps because of ill health, perhaps, as has been suggested, because he preferred the private to the public stage. Although clearly defined party alignments had been slow to develop within the state, his natural affiliation was with the Federalists.

Thereafter, he followed chiefly the life of a country gentleman who took an active interest in the improvement of agriculture. For a time he lived along the banks of the Delaware near Trenton, but he settled finally a few miles above Newark on the east side of the Passaic River, where the town of Rutherford perpetuates his name today. He owned large properties in the upper parts of the state and had a jealous view of proprietary prerogatives. Apocryphal or not, there is a story that he once in Sussex County came across a group engaged in raising a log structure, and, having inquired as to its purpose and the source of the logs, he was told that it was to be a church and that the logs came from his own land. He is said then to have agreed that the church might be completed, but only on the condition "that your preacher preaches a sermon once every year on the sin of timber stealing."

From time to time he responded to calls for return to public service, for a few years after 1807 as a member of the legislative council. He gained more prominence from his service on a number of special commissions. The first of these was the commission of which Gouverneur Morris was also a member, appointed by the New York legislature for the purpose of drafting a plan for the expansion of New York City above the present Washington Square Park. Appointed in 1807, the commissioners submitted their plan in 1811. It extended so far beyond the then existing bounds of the city (all the way to 155th street) as to invite ridicule. But whatever one may think of its gridiron pattern of broad avenues frequently intersected by lesser streets, providing ready access to the waterways on either side of Manhattan Island, the plan has to be viewed as a farsighted one, even if not farsighted enough to have anticipated the automobile. The Common Council of the City of New York on October 26, 1812 recorded its gratitude to Rutherford and Morris for the performance of "arduous duties" without compensation by providing that each of them should receive a "handsomely colored and mounted" copy of the officially adopted map.

Rutherford acquired an active interest in the development of turnpikes and canals and in 1816 headed a commission established by act of the New Jersey legislature for determining the best route and possible cost of a canal connecting the Delaware and Raritan Rivers. The report showed his inclination to favor a national program of internal improvements, but the legislature failed to act, and a private corporation chartered in 1820 failed to recruit adequate funds. In 1827 he served on a commission, which included Richard Stockton (A.B. 1779), that attempted unsuccessfully to reach an agreement with New York for settlement of a longstanding and at times dangerous dispute over the water boundary between the two states.

Rutherford died at his home on the Passaic on February 23, 1840, survived by one son, Robert Walter Rutherford (A.B. 1806) and five daughters. It is said that his grandson, also named John Rutherford (1810-1871), was intended for schooling at Princeton, but that on a visit to the College he was so offended by the table manners of the students in the dining hall that he enrolled instead at Rutgers. However that may be, it is believed that thereafter each generation of Rutherford's descendants, beginning with Livingston Rutherford (LL.B. 1882), has been represented by at least one graduate of Princeton.

SOURCES: Alumni file, MS Steward's accounts, PUA; Giger, Memoirs; L. Rutherford, *Family Record and Events* (1894); K. Scott, *Geneal. Data from N.Y. Post-Boy* (1970), 67, 70, 73; A. Valentine, *Lord Stirling* (1969), esp. 55-56, 199, 111-12; *NJHSP* (2 ser.), 1 (1867-1869), 89 ("stay longer at . . . Colledges"); 2 (1870-1872), 197-204; 3 (1873-1875), 181-90; *NJA* (2 ser.), I, 454n, 455n; *Min. of . . . Council of Safety of N.J.* (1872), passim; *NJHS Coll.*, IX, 186-87; X, 303; VII, 456-59; *NYGBR*, 106 (1976), 149; 85 (1954), 237-39; J. Whitehead, *Judicial and Civil Hist. of N.J.*, II (1897), 381; W. Roome, *Early Days and . . . Surveys of East N.J.* (1897), 42-60; *Manuscripts*, 2 (1959), no. 3, 42-46; L. Lundin, *Cockpit of the Rev.* (1940), 446-48; R. P. McCormick, *Experiment in Independence* (1950), 29-30, 111-12, 132, 137-41, 151-57; M. Dix, ed., *Hist. of Parish of Trinity Chh.*, II (1901), 16, 17, 21, 85, 88-90, 96, 147, 245, 255; IV (1906), 578; M. H. Thomas, *Columbia Univ., Officers and Alumni* (1936), 9, 11, 13, 82; *First Census, N.Y.*, 135; *A/C*, VIII (indicates his absence from most of the Second Session, 5th Cong.); *Adams Papers*, III, 225, 237-38; J. W. Reps, *Making of Urban Amer.* (1965), 296-99; *MCCCNY*, IV, 368; VII, 287; W. R. Fee, *Transition from Aristocracy to Democracy in N.J.* (1933), 125; W. J. Lane, *From Indian Trail to Iron Horse* (1939), 230, 253-55; C. C. Madeira, Jr., *Del. and Raritan Canal* (1941), 11-21; *Report of Commissioners* (1817). See William H. Vernon (A.B. 1776) for commencement of 1776.

MANUSCRIPTS: NHi, NjR, NjHi

WFC

Nathaniel Welshard Semple

NATHANIEL WELSHARD SEMPLE, A.B., Presbyterian clergyman and educator, was born at Peachbottom, York County, Pennsylvania on April 10, 1752. There were several branches of the Semple or Sample family in central Pennsylvania at the time, and Semple's precise parentage has not been discovered, although his middle name may indicate the name of his mother's family. It is certain, however, that he was educated at Robert Smith's academy in Pequea, Lancaster County, which sent several of its students to Nassau Hall. Semple may also have been influenced to go to Princeton to complete his education by John Strain (A.B. 1757), who from 1760 to 1774 was the minister of the Presbyterian church that served Peachbottom.

On November 30, 1774, Semple joined the Cliosophic Society. To

Nathaniel Welshard Semple, A.B. 1776

his fellow members he was known as "Woolsey," after the prelate-statesman of Tudor England. From Princeton he went back to Lancaster County to study theology with William Foster (A.B. 1764), pastor of the Upper Octorara church.

Semple was licensed to preach by the Presbytery of New Castle in 1779 and then sent to supply the congregation in St. George's Hundred, Delaware for six months. He declined a call to settle there and again came back to Lancaster County where John Woodhull (A.B. 1766) had recently resigned from the pulpit of the Leacock church. Semple apparently supplied that congregation for a few months, since he was in the area when his former tutor Foster died in September 1780. By then the Leacock church had combined with the neighboring congregations of Lancaster and Middle Octorara, and on October 30, 1780, Semple was invited to settle as minister of all three. He accepted the call in August 1781 and was ordained at Leacock the following December. It was probably at about that time that he married Elizabeth Cowan of Chester County, Pennsylvania.

Semple and his family lived on East Main Street in Strasburg, a village approximately equidistant from his three pulpits. Corpulent and with a strong voice, Semple was a popular preacher who tried to entertain his audiences as well as enlighten them. His churches prospered during his long tenure, but the details of his ministry are obscure because he kept no records. He was a trustee of the Leacock church when it was incorporated in 1787, and of the Lancaster church when it was incorporated in 1804.

Semple was active in community affairs, as in 1815 when he helped to found the Lancaster Auxiliary Bible Society and served on its board of managers. Little can be said with certainty about his political opinions, but he may have been the "Rev. Mr. Semple" who was rumored to have condemned James Ross, a Federalist candidate for governor in 1799, 1802, 1805, and 1808, because Ross had allegedly named his twelve dogs for the apostles. The rumor, current many years after Semple's death, asserted that the minister in question was dismissed from his pulpit for making that condemnation. Ross did carry Lancaster County, but Semple was not dismissed until 1821. Whether politics was at issue then is unknown.

It is more likely that Semple simply withdrew from the ministry to concentrate on his second vocation as a teacher. As early as 1790 he had opened the parlor of his home to students of theology, thus establishing the first school in Strasburg. In October 1802 a new classical academy was advertised there. Founded by Robert Elliott, it was to open on January 1, 1803, but any children sent to the town before that date would be cared for by Semple, who was obviously a patron of the school. Elliott moved to Washington, D.C. in 1815 to become chaplain to Congress, and in 1823 Semple himself opened an academy in Strasburg. Like the first, his was coeducational, and as superintendent, he provided board for some of the students in his own home.

Semple died in Strasburg on July 23, 1834. He was survived by his widow and eight children. Among his sons was Nathaniel W. Semple, Jr., a prominent physician and abolitionist.

SOURCES: P. J. Timlow, *Hist. of Leacock Pres. Chh.* (1892), 21-23; Webster, MS Brief Sketches, 1; G. S. Klett, *Presbyterianism in Colonial Pa.* (1937), 205; MS Clio. Soc. membership list, PUA; J. S. Futhey, *Hist. Discourse . . . on the . . . One Hundred and Fiftieth Anniv. of the Upper Octorara Pres. Chh.* (1870), 81; A. Harris, *Biog. Hist. of Lancaster Cnty., Pa.* (1872), 510; J. I. Mombert, *Authentic Hist. of Lancaster Cnty., Pa.* (1869), 458; *LCHSPA*, 9 (1905), 217; 19 (1915), 37, 39; 11 (1907), 404; 32 (1928), 14-17. See William H. Vernon (A.B. 1776) for commencement of 1776.

Samuel Shannon

SAMUEL SHANNON, A.B., soldier and Presbyterian clergyman, was born in 1746, probably in the region of what was then York County, Pennsylvania, served by the Lower Marsh Creek Presbyterian Church. There were several Samuel Shannons of his generation in Pennsylvania, and his specific parentage has not been identified.

Shannon probably entered the College as a junior, and he graduated, it seems, without having decided on a career. Early in the Revolution, he joined Captain David Wilson's company of York County Militia as a first lieutenant. No later than 1779 he began to study theology under the general supervision of the Presbytery of Donegal. But in October of that year he moved to Virginia, where, with Donegal's recommendation, he was accepted into the Presbytery of Hanover. His sponsor was James Waddell, pastor of the church at Tinkling Spring in Augusta County; Shannon may have completed his theological training with Waddell.

On October 24, 1780, Shannon presented himself for examination by the presbytery. He did well enough in Greek and Latin and in reading and preaching, but his responses to questions on divinity and moral philosophy were not satisfactory. The presbytery advised him to find another line of work. Shannon came back in October 1781, however, and received his license on the second attempt. After three years of itineracy he was ordained in the Cowpasture region of Augusta County, Virginia and installed at the Windy Cove church on November 25, 1784. He also served the nearby congregation at Blue Spring. He was licensed to perform marriages in the county on December 20, 1785.

A member of the Presbytery of Lexington when it was created out of Hanover in 1786, Shannon did not remain in that body very long. In April 1787 he was dismissed from his charges in Virginia and moved to Kentucky, where he was received by the Presbytery of Transylvania on April 22, 1788. After a few months as the stated supply at the churches of Bethel and Hopewell, he accepted the call of the Bethel and Sinking Spring congregations and settled as their pastor. He was chosen moderator of the presbytery in October 1789 and February 1795, and of the second meeting of the Synod of Kentucky in September 1803.

Shannon had come to Kentucky in the midst of a furor precipitated by Adam Rankin, pastor of the congregation at New Providence. Rankin was fanatically opposed to the use of Watts's *Psalms* and accused anyone who used them of heresy. The complaints of some members of Rankin's own church brought the matter to the attention of the presbytery, where Shannon served on an investigating committee. Rankin's wrath was soon aimed specifically at his new colleague, whom he charged with harboring "Errorious principles," and the affair degenerated for a time into a personal feud.

A neighbor of the New Providence church, Shannon welcomed almost one-half of Rankin's flock into his congregation. Angrily, Rankin left the country to spend two years in England, hoping that the quarrel would be forgotten in his absence. But when he returned in 1791 he was put on trial by the presbytery. Along with Shannon, James Crawford (A.B. 1777) was one of the judges. Ultimately, Rankin resigned from the presbytery and took more than 100 of his followers with him into a separate body.

Shannon's militia service had whetted his appetite for military affairs, an area in which his competence was well respected. In 1790 or 1791 he joined the troops of General Charles Scott as a chaplain in campaigns against the Indians in Ohio and Indiana. He may have been present at the battle of Fallen Timbers, but his military exploits were less notable than his behavior when he returned to Kentucky. He had, apparently, taken to drinking while on the march, and one of his later parishioners recalled that the minister was sometimes so drunk that he could not stay on a horse.

Shannon did not have a shining reputation as a preacher, in any case. A large man of immense physical strength, he was careless to the point of slovenliness about his dress. His habits, moreover, were coarse if not crude, and he spoke haltingly and with a slight impediment. His sermons, full of "zeal without warmth," tended to repel rather than inspire his audience. It is not likely that he enhanced his appeal by taking a plug of scarce chewing tobacco out of his mouth before starting to speak and storing it in a crevice in the pulpit from which he could retrieve it occasionally in mid-sermon. That he was an acceptable pastor at all was probably due to his exceptionally genial disposition. He enjoyed music in church and would have a violinist play hymns until he tired of their sobriety, stepped from the pulpit, and joined in some merrier music-making.

In 1792 Shannon left his posts at Bethel and Sinking Spring to go to Woodford County, Kentucky. There he gathered another congregation, including Caleb Baker Wallace (A.B. 1770). He also traveled occasionally to Frankfort County, where he preached to the unorganized congregation at Upper Benson. He founded a church there in the spring of 1795 and served it along with his church in Woodford for eleven years. In 1802 he established a second congregation in Frankfort, at Lower Benson, and added it to his circuit.

When the state legislature chartered the Kentucky Academy in Woodford County in 1794, Shannon, Wallace, Crawford, and David Rice (A.B. 1761) were all original trustees. From 1796 to 1798 they worked to unite the institution with Transylvania Seminary, and their ultimate success produced Transylvania University. When the Presbytery of Transylvania divided in 1799, Shannon was assigned to the new West Lexington Presbytery.

In 1806 Shannon resigned from his church in Woodford and moved to the area served by his Lower Benson church in Franklin County. He established his permanent residence there and served as a sort of unofficial legal adviser to the members of his two congregations. In 1812 he bought 35.5 acres of land in the area. Shortly thereafter, he joined the Kentucky troops who were headed north to fight the British. In October he preached to the army at Fort Defiance, Virginia and then accompanied it to Lake Erie. He returned in 1814 to find his own churches declining in the midst of a religious revival that involved much of the west.

Shannon then undertook missionary tours to the areas of Ohio and Indiana he had first seen in the Indian wars of the 1790s. In February 1816 he founded the Bethel Church, later called the Livonia Church, in Washington County, Indiana. Seventeen months later he established a church at Salem in Washington County. In the summer of 1822, while he was visiting those churches, he was stricken with a fever. He tried to ride the 100 miles back to his home in Kentucky but had to stop at a house on the way. There he died on August 10, 1822. He was buried at the Upper Benson church. No record of a wife or children has been found.

SOURCES: Alumni file, PUA (which includes one notation that his "family" reached him before he died); A. Nevin, *Churches of the Valley* (1852), 186; Sprague, *Annals*, III, 235-37 (Waddell); Foote, *Sketches, Va.*, II, 110; W. M. Gewehr, *Great Awakening in Va., 1740-1790* (1930), 220; L. Chalkley, *Chronicles of the Scotch-Irish Settlement in Va.* (1912), I, 244; L. Collins, *Hist. of Ky.* (1878), I, 458; *KSHS Reg.*, 29 (1931), 10-12; 54 (1956), 48; R. Davidson, *Hist. of the Pres. Chh. . . . in Ky.* (1847), 90-91; 83 ("zeal without warmth"), 178; Draper MSS #S 16CC247, 16CC302, 13CC133, 16CC304, 14CC147, WHi; W. R. Jillson, *Hist. of First Pres. Chh. of Frankfort, Ky.* (1965), 25-28; R. Peter, *Transylvania Univ.* (1896), 63, 69-71; *Hist. of Lawrence, Orange and Washington Counties, Ind.* (1889), 825-26. See William H. Vernon (A.B. 1776) for commencement of 1776.

Benjamin Parker Snowden

BENJAMIN PARKER SNOWDEN, A.B., physician, was born on February 3, 1760, in Philadelphia, Pennsylvania. He was the only child of Isaac and Mary Parker Snowden, and his mother died soon after he was born. In 1763 his father married a widow, Mary Cox McCall. They had five sons, including Gilbert Tennent Snowden (A.B. 1783), Isaac Snowden (Class of 1785), Samuel Finley Snowden (A.B. 1786), Nathaniel Randolph Snowden (A.B. 1787), and Charles Jeffry Snowden (A.B. 1789). Their father was an elder of the Second Presbyterian Church and a prosperous merchant who had risen from being a tanner to treasurer of the city and county of Philadelphia and to trustee and treasurer of the College.

Snowden joined the Cliosophic Society at Nassau Hall on January 3, 1774. His pseudonym was "Hallam," after the fourteenth-century English scholar, prelate, and church statesman. As a sophomore Snowden took third prize in the annual undergraduate competition in "Pronouncing English Orations."

Snowden was back home in the "Dock Ward" of Philadelphia in December 1776. He was studying medicine at the time but was on the list of the Second Battalion of the city militia in July 1777. Sometime between then and December 1779, he joined the hospital department of the Continental Army, probably as a surgeon's mate. His active service until at least February 1780, is certain.

Snowden was in Philadelphia in March 1784 when his brother Gilbert, who was pursuing postgraduate work at Princeton, sought his advice about finishing in Philadelphia. It is unclear, however, how far Snowden's own medical education had progressed. His prewar training had been too brief to be thorough and there is no evidence that he completed it while on active duty. He decided to continue his professional studies in Europe, but the ship on which he sailed in or before 1784 was lost at sea. His will was proved on March 23, 1784.

SOURCES: Alumni file, MS Clio. Soc. membership list, PUA; *PGM*, 22 (1961), 16; *Col. Rec. Pa.*, XII, 636; *Pa. Arch.* (2 ser.), VIII, 239; (6 ser.), I, 138, 142; *PMHB*, 18 (1894), 127; *Princeton Univ. Libr. Chron.*, 14 (1953), 73n, 82; *Pa. Journal and Weekly Advertiser*, 12 Oct 1774 ("English Orations"); Index, PCC; MS abstracts of Phila. wills, Ph2A: 4, Geneal. Soc. of Pa.; CNJ, *Catalogue*, 1786. See William H. Vernon (A.B. 1776) for commencement of 1776.

Benjamin Brearley Stockton

BENJAMIN BREARLEY STOCKTON, physician, was born on August 14, 1754, in Princeton, New Jersey; where his father, Thomas Stockton, was the leading merchant. His mother was Sarah Brearley Stockton. He was prepared for college in Princeton, possibly at the College's grammar school, and probably entered Nassau Hall as a freshman in the fall of 1772. He apparently remained a student there at least until the end of his sophomore year.

Stockton left college to study medicine, but he had not finished that project before June 21, 1776, when the New Jersey Provincial Congress appointed him surgeon's mate to a battalion of Middlesex and Monmouth County Militia in "Heard's Brigade." He and his unit were at the battle of Long Island in the summer of 1776.

In December Stockton joined the hospital department of the Continental Army, and in June 1777 he was appointed a junior surgeon with a regiment of New York Continentals by William Shippen (A.B. 1754). That commission expired in February 1778. Four months later, Stockton was a full-fledged regimental surgeon in the New York Line and participated in the battle of Monmouth.

Stockton left the army in 1781. That November, he applied for membership in the revived Medical Society of New Jersey and after a proper examination was admitted at the society's first meeting in Princeton. It was probably at that time that he married Sarah Howell Arnett, the daughter of Isaac Arnett of Elizabethtown, New Jersey. The marriage produced four sons and eight daughters.

Stockton was not a particularly devoted member of the medical society and attended only three meetings between 1782 and 1786. The sessions were held in Princeton and New Brunswick, and although he practiced for a time near his birthplace, he apparently lived in Burlington County by 1793. In or around 1800 Stockton moved his family to the frontier of New York where he practiced medicine in Cohocton, Steuben County and in Vernon, Oneida County. He was a surgeon in the hospital in Buffalo, New York that was destroyed by fire in 1813. He then moved to Caledonia in Genesee County and remained there until he died, on June 9, 1829.

SOURCES: Wickes, *Hist. of Medicine N.J.*, 408-409; E. F. Cooley, *Geneal. of Early Settlers of Trenton and Ewing* (1883), 13; *DAR Patriot Index*, 651; A. H. Bill, *House Called Morven* (1954), 55; MS Steward's accounts, PUA; Force, *Amer. Arch.* (4 ser.), VI, 1,627; Stryker, *Off. Reg.*, 335, 378; *Fithian Journal*, II, 192 & n; Heitman; L. C. Duncan, *Med. Men in the Amer. Rev.* (1970), 410; *NYGBR*, 90 (1959), 240; *Med. Soc. of N.J., Rise, Minutes and Proceedings* (1875), 40, 41, 97; J. S. Norton,

N.J. in 1793 (1973), 32; G. H. McMaster, *Hist. of Settlement of Steuben Cnty.,* *N.Y.* (1853), 37.

William H. Vernon

WILLIAM H. VERNON, A.B., merchant, was born at Newport, Rhode Island, on March 6, 1759, the son of William Vernon and his wife, Judith Harwood. The mother died when Vernon was three years of age, and he grew up under the care of a maiden aunt. The father was a prosperous Newport merchant, engaged in the many-sided trade of the Atlantic basin. Beginning in the spring of 1777, the elder Vernon was to assume the heavy responsibilities of chairmanship of the Navy Board of the Eastern Department, established by the Congress for "the Superintendence of all Naval and Marine Affairs of the United States" within New England. At the time of young Vernon's enrollment in the College, both he and his father were members of the Congregational church in Newport of which Ezra Stiles was the minister. The record Stiles kept of his pastoral calls indicates that he had a more intimate relationship with the elder Vernon than with most of the members of his congregation. This perhaps was because Vernon had intellectual interests. He had collaborated with Stiles in June 1769 for observation of the transit of Venus, and later he would serve as the second president of the Redwood Library in succession to its founder. The style in which he lived is suggested by the fact that the Compte de Rochambeau, arriving at Newport in 1780 at the head of a French army, established his headquarters in Vernon's home, a house purchased at about the time the son entered Nassau Hall.

It has been said that young Vernon was enrolled in the College as early as 1772, but confirmation is lacking. A letter to his father from Nassau Hall, dated August 23, 1773, suggests that he had been in residence for a while, but that he was not yet fully settled. It advised that the bed and bedding the father had agreed he might buy had been sold to another, asked that "English Books" be sent for reading "in my leisure hours," and protested that it would be better to have "a Black gown made here" than at home because "Miss Nancy Reed, and my Aunts, and as many Old Maids as you can consult, know but little about the fashion and the mode in which they make them here." Two accounts of the steward, one for the period May 25, 1773 to September 1774, the other for November 1774 to April 10, 1775, confirm his continuing residence as a student, in the latter, as a member of the junior class.

Especially interesting is the letter he addressed from Nassau Hall to his "Honor'd Papa" on September 26, 1776, for it fills a longstanding gap in the history of the College. Commencement that year had been scheduled for September 25, but for reasons undoubtedly reflecting the military disasters experienced by the American army, the trustees failed to muster the quorum required for the award of degrees. Not until May 24, 1777, would the trustees assembled at Cooper's Ferry formally award degrees to the 27 members of the Class of 1776. The surviving record has been so incomplete as to leave a question whether any commencement exercises had been conducted in the preceding September. Historians have tended to follow the suggestion of President John Maclean, in his informative *History of the College,* that since "the exercises for the day had been assigned some time before, it is highly probable that these exercises were attended to in the usual manner." But no supporting evidence has been found.

Vernon's report of what actually occurred is worth quoting in full:

I now take up the pen to inform you of the proceedings of the Senior Class at once before Commencement; two days before we met, and Considering the public disturbances, and the back preparations we ourselves had made, one half of the class being unprepared and absent, in expectation of a private Commencement, having deliberately and maturely considered these on the one side and the disappointment of the people on the other, We determined on a private one, therefore all future preparations were laid aside, untill the day came, when the Doct. sent to the class desiring as many of us as were prepared, to speak that the People might not be entirely disappointed; accordingly having met seven appeared willing, perhaps you will be surprized when I inform you, I was not one of the number, because I had not practiced on my Oration, which was on Heroism, occasioned by our predetermination that there should be no speaking, however I was persuaded by some of the Speakers to appear on the stage with an Oration on Standing Armies, which I had spoken the last winter; as for the manner in which it was delivered, you must get information from a person who was not the deliverer, as he certainly could not be a judge of his own speaking. A sufficient number of Trustees not appearing to constitute a board, we could not have our Degrees confer'd, but the President signified to the Audience that we had gone our Course through College with honor and were admitted to the Degree of Bachelor of Arts; the Audience being dismissed, we were told there would be a fall meeting of

the Trustees on the first Wednesday of November; that then Each
one might have his Degree sent to him if he could not be present,
and in the meantime might have a Certificate signed by the
President purporting his having gone through College with
honor, and on Examination thought worthy of a Degree.

Copies of two such certificates have been found, one given to Joseph
W. Henderson on September 26, the other to William R. Davie on
October 20. Needless to say, hopes for degrees in November proved to
be illusory.

Vernon, on the advice of his father and with encouragement from
President Witherspoon, had decided to remain in Princeton for study
of the French language. He apparently fled the place late in November, when Witherspoon dismissed the students because of the approach of British forces in pursuit of Washington's retreating army,
and for a time thereafter he seems to have been in Philadelphia. A
letter of January 20, 1777, to Vernon's father from William Ellery,
friend and member of Congress, reported that Vernon was back in
Princeton. The source of this information was President Witherspoon,
who advised that Princeton had advantages over Philadelphia for purposes of study and that although Vernon's studies would be subject
to interruption by the enemy, it would not be difficult for a person
without family to make his escape. Vernon apparently remained in
Princeton until the following June, when he was advised to return to
Rhode Island.

In February 1778 Vernon sailed from Boston for France under the
shepherding care of John Adams, then departing on his first diplomatic mission. The elder Vernon, undoubtedly anticipating an expanding trade with France, wished his son to perfect his command of
the language and to gain the advantage of experience with some
French firm "of Protestant Principles" and "of general and extensive
Business." He was prepared to pay £100 sterling to the merchant who
might take his son on for two or three years, and perhaps in addition
to pay his yearly board. At the beginning of April, the voyage ended
at Bordeaux. Vernon's conduct had been such that Adams offered
him appointment as his private secretary, but he undoubtedly followed his father's intent, which Adams described as "commercial
rather than political," by electing to remain in Bordeaux. For a time
he moved inland to Montauban in Guyenne, apparently for the purpose of strengthening his command of the language by living in an
area where English was not spoken, but later he returned to Bordeaux.
There John Adams visited him in February 1780 and reported to the

elder Vernon that he found his son in good health and speaking French very well.

Almost two decades were to elapse before Vernon's return to America, and more than a little mystery surrounds his activity during that period of time. From Bordeaux in May 1779, he wrote to Benjamin Franklin, to whom the father had written in behalf of his son in the preceding December, asking for a recommendation that might assist him in getting a connection for a year or two with some French commercial house. Presumably, he remained in Bordeaux until April 1782, when he went to Paris carrying a letter of introduction to Franklin from Jonathan Williams, Franklin's nephew, who then was American agent at Nantes. This was about the time Vernon's father had expected him to return home, but instead, in November of the following year the young man visited England in the company of Lewis Littlepage. If Vernon returned to France from London when Littlepage did, it was a short visit ending late in December 1783.

By September 1784 Vernon was in financial difficulties. He then advised Franklin that he had been disappointed in the expectation of a bill of exchange from London and asked for assistance in getting an order of John Bondfield, American agent at Bordeaux, honored by a Paris banker. When the banker continued his refusal to honor the order, even with Franklin's voucher of the signature, the latter advanced a loan to Vernon. Unable to repay, he received another loan from Franklin in February 1785. Not long thereafter, William Temple Franklin, Benjamin's grandson, was told by a masked lady at a ball that Vernon was in trouble serious enough for him to consider going into the Dutch army. Franklin sent word of his willingness to provide further financial assistance if Vernon would agree to go home. The answer was that he would have no trouble in meeting his debts when he sold a carriage he had brought from England, and that he expected to leave for home in May. Soon Vernon's landlord called on Franklin to complain that Vernon was behind in payments for rent to the extent of 1,500 livres. Hearing at about the same time of other debts, and being on the point of departure from the country, Franklin proposed that the debt to him be settled by a bill drawn on Vernon's father; this was done on April 15 by an order for 840 livres. Franklin then wrote a strong letter of advice to Vernon, urging him to return home and promising additional assistance in clearing his debts if he would do so immediately. There was no answer, but the landlord called again to report that the carriage had been "clandestinely remov'd from his Stables" without payment of the rent.

All of the above was reported to Vernon's father in a letter of Oc-

tober 14, 1785, from Franklin, by then in Philadelphia. It was written
in response to a letter of October 1 from the elder Vernon asking for
news of a son from whom he had had no letter for four years past.
Franklin's advice was that the father go to Paris "to reclaim & bring
him home with you." He was not certain as to the cause of the trouble;
"if a Lady is in the Case," there was no reason for surprise, and Vernon
himself could "best judge whether there is any thing at home, that
gives him an Aversion to Returning." Franklin estimated that 8,000-
10,000 livres, possibly less, would discharge the son's full indebtedness,
for he had "never gam'd, nor liv'd . . . extravagantly," but he also
warned that the young man would "inevitably be lost" if he continued in Paris.

There is no reason for assuming that the father, who may have been
suffering the effects of an earlier inclination to watch too closely his
motherless son, followed this advice. A report late in 1788 advised
that young William was still in Paris and that probably his creditors
prevented his departure from the city. By the spring of 1789, he had
been imprisoned for his debts. This imprisonment certainly was terminated before July 10, 1790, when he appeared before the National
Assembly to speak for a delegation of American citizens in Paris to
request that they be permitted to participate in the forthcoming celebration on July 14 of the fall of the Bastille in the preceding year.
His speech is said to have been written by Joel Barlow, a member of
the delegation, as also was John Paul Jones; presumably Vernon's selection as spokesman is attributable to the superior command he had
acquired of the language. In that same summer, the father renewed
his efforts to secure the return of his son by appeals to Lafayette and
to Secretary of State Thomas Jefferson. On Jefferson's advice he wrote
to William Short, chargé d'affaires in France and Joseph Fenwick,
United States consul at Bordeaux for assistance. He was in a mood,
as he explained to Jefferson, to compel the son's return, even at the
cost of humiliating him. To Short he sent a bill of exchange for £50
sterling to cover the cost of getting young Vernon out of Paris. Short,
on the advice of a friend of the son, advanced a part of the sum to
Vernon, and sent the other part to Bordeaux. This stratagem served
at least to get young Vernon as far on the way home as Bordeaux,
where in the first half of 1791 the captains of three vessels sailing for
America offered him passage, only to be refused.

The remainder of the story leaves a continuing puzzle. Perhaps
there was a lady "in the Case," as is suggested by an unaddressed letter
from Vernon of August 14, 1791, written in French. Whatever the fact,
the next item in the known record finds Vernon once more in prison.

The news came to Newport in a letter from Bordeaux by a J. C. Johnson that was dated December 12, 1793; Johnson did not hesitate to suggest that the imprisonment could be blamed on the father's determination to force the son's return, or that it was a particularly dangerous time to be in a French prison. Perhaps Fenwick had interpreted his instructions from the father too literally. Perhaps the son stubbornly refused to give bond for his return home as a condition for his release from prison. A postscript indicated that Vernon's friends, disturbed that an American citizen could be imprisoned without trial, had no success in their efforts in his behalf. It is not possible to say when Vernon was released from prison. Instead, it has to be reported that William Vernon, Sr., in an emotional letter dated at Newport on September 12, 1795, disinherited and disowned his son William as a "miserable ingrate, unworthy of the affections of a Parent—Adieu, for ever Adieu."

Even so, the story was to have a happy ending. On July 21, 1797, William H. Vernon wrote from Philadelphia to his father that he had left Bordeaux on May 27, had just landed in America, and hastened to transmit "the joyful idea that the wide Atlantic no longer separates us." There was no explanation of how the reconciliation had been achieved, only expressions of filial affection, the news that he would proceed immediately to Newport, and a list of the baggage he was forwarding: two trunks, three cases of pictures, one card table, two wash basins, a fowling piece, and "a Canary Bird."

Vernon returned to a Newport suffering a serious decline from the eminence it had enjoyed as a leading commercial center of colonial America. He went into business with his father, who lived until 1806, neither of them joining the exodus of merchants in quest of expanding opportunities in other cities. The firm continued in trade, often in loose association with friends or relatives in New York and Boston, but the eventful part of William's life was behind him. He died in 1833, having never married and leaving an estate in which a number of paintings brought by him from France seem to have been the principal asset. He left too a legend of having once enjoyed high favor at the court of Marie Antoinette, and the memory of a man known about town as "Count Vernon" because of the French manners and dress he affected.

SOURCES: The author owes a heavy debt to Mrs. John R. Bennet, formerly of Princeton, for calling his attention to the Vernon Papers in the Newport Historical Society and for her generosity in making her notes available for his use, which greatly facilitated his own checking of the collection in Newport. The society's permission to quote from these Papers is much appreciated. Other sources include: *R.I. Hist. Tracts*, no. 13 (1881), 119-40; M. L. Stevens, *Hist. of the Vernon House* (1915); Stiles,

Literary Diary, I, 13, 82, 141, 328, 332, 430, 506, 532, 538, 565; *DAB* (father); Maclean, *History*, I, 320-21; R.I. Hist. Soc., *Pubs.* (n.s.), VIII, 204-205, 206, 221-22, 258, 262; *Adams Papers*, II, 269, 271, 272-73, 281, 433; IV, 9-10, 96-97; *Franklin Cal.* (1906), I, 542-43; II, 76, 466, III, 252, 278, 551; IV, 111, 137; C. Van Doren, *Franklin's Autobiographical Writings* (1945), 658-62 ("if a Lady"); C. C. Davis, *The King's Chevalier* (1961), 85-87; *Discours à l'Assemblée Nationale, prononcé par M. William Henry Vernon, Au nom des Citoyens unis de L'Amérique*, 10 July 1790, *Procès-verbal*, no. 345; *Princeton Univ. Libr. Chron.*, 17 (1956), 200; *Jefferson Papers*, XVII, 483-84, 655, 631-32; G. C. Mason, *Reminiscenses of Newport* (1884), 165-73. There is some question about the middle name "Henry" that is found in the literature, apparently drawn from the French source cited above. In college he used William Vernon, Jr. It seems probable that local tradition, which holds that the "H" in his later signature stood for his mother's maiden name, is correct.

MANUSCRIPTS: RNHi, where the letter of 26 Sept. 1776 from the son to his father appears to be a later transcription from the original

PUBLICATIONS: *A methodical treatise on the cultivation of the mulberry tree, on the raising of silk worms, and on winding the silk from the cocoons. United to an accurate description of the winding mill. With plates. Abridged from the French of M. de la Brousse; with notes and an appendix* (1828); see A. Field, *State of Rhode Island and Providence Plantations*, III (1902), 366-67

WFC

Nehemiah Wade, Jr.

NEHEMIAH WADE, JR., A.B., A.M. 1786, lawyer and public official, was born in 1760 in Connecticut Farms (now Union), Essex County, New Jersey. His parents, Abigail Mulford Wade and Nehemiah Wade, Sr., were active members of James Caldwell's (A.B. 1759) congregation in the Presbyterian church in nearby Elizabethtown. Nehemiah Wade, Sr. was commissary general of stores for the state militia from 1771 to 1773, and when the Revolution began, he was commissioned a major.

Young Wade was almost certainly prepared for college at the academy in Elizabethtown, where he probably stayed until he entered the junior class at Nassau Hall in the fall of 1774. It is unlikely that he was among the few members of his class who remained in Princeton for the unusual commencement exercises of 1776 that his classmate William H. Vernon described in a letter home, for Wade's father was fatally ill in Elizabethtown at the time. Major Wade died on October 20, 1776, leaving £200 to his eldest son and namesake, including enough money to pay for the boy's education. The rest of the estate was divided among the widow and all six children.

Apparently, Wade did not assume a military role during the Revolution. Only sixteen years of age, he was suddenly the head of a large family. At some point, however, he began to study law and after his mother died in 1783 he moved to New Barbadoes Township, Bergen County. There he was admitted to the bar in 1784 and he established a lucrative practice.

On July 3, 1786, Wade deeded some of his own land in neighboring Hackensack to the county to be used for the county clerk's office. A few weeks later he returned to Princeton to receive both his A.M. and the diploma he had not been able to collect ten years before.

Wade's business interests extended beyond the practice of law. When the Ohio Company advertised its land in the Miami District for sale in January 1788, Wade was one of the agents from whom warrants could be purchased. In that enterprise, he worked with his classmate Jonathan Dayton, who was the legal representative in New Jersey for the administrator of the Miami lands, John Cleves Symmes. In 1790 Wade bought a substantial number of tracts in Ohio as a personal investment.

From 1789 until 1804 Wade served as clerk of Bergen County. He was also an officer in the state militia and commonly used the title "Colonel." The county Board of Justices and Freeholders paid him £2 2s in May 1790 for calling a special session of the court of oyer and terminer and for buying some blank ledger books. One month earlier Wade had married Phebe Hendricks, another native of Elizabethtown, in St. John's Episcopal Church there. Also in 1790 he was one of the original trustees of Washington Academy in Hackensack.

Among Wade's business interests was the building of a bridge across the Hackensack River and Meadowlands. With thirteen others, he signed a £1,000 bond to the county board in August 1793 for permission to pursue the project. He was at the peak of his career when he died on July 29, 1805. The public demonstration of affection for him during his military funeral in Hackensack was testimony to the esteem in which he was held.

SOURCES: The Wade family was numerous in northern N.J., and there were at least two Nehemiah Wades in the area in 1793. One lived in Elizabethtown and one in Hackensack [J. S. Norton, *N.J. in 1793* (1973), 131, 353]. Identification of the CNJ graduate is based partly on his legal career [Alexander, *Princeton*, 199], but that source asserts that Wade lived and died in Elizabethtown. Records of Elizabethtown are silent on Nehemiah Wade, but the NjHi files include notice of a marriage to Jane Smith on 19 Sep 1784 that produced at least one son. Jane Smith Wade died in 1822. The coincidence of two men with the same name who both were attorneys and both born in the same year is dubious, and the absence of additional information on Wade in Elizabethtown tends to indicate that Alexander and other sources confused two individuals. Other possible explanations are that the same Nehemiah Wade maintained a domicile in both Elizabethtown, where the graduate had property from his father's estate, and in Hackensack, and that the Smith marriage is in error. It is also possible, of course, that Wade was a bigamist. See also *Hist. of Bergen and Passaic Counties, N.J.* (1882), 84, 99, 100, 101; E. H. Hatfield, *Hist. of*

Elizabeth, N.J. (1868), 520, 522; *DAR Patriot Index*; Stryker, *Oc. Reg.*, 370, 379; *N.J. Wills*, v, 561; MS Steward's accounts, Trustees Minutes, PUA; *NEHGR*, 44 (1890), 260; 45 (1891), 44; B. W. Bond, Jr., ed., *Correspondence of John Cleves Symmes* (1926), 265, 281-84; *Min. of the Justices and Freemen of Bergen Cnty., N.J.* (1924); *GMNJ*, 9 (1933), 5; J. M. Van Valen, *Hist. of Bergen Cnty., N.J.* (1900), 99.

James Lewis Wilson

JAMES LEWIS WILSON, A.B., probably was the physician and Episcopalian clergyman of that name who lived during the last decade of the century in the section of North Carolina embraced by Edgecombe, Halifax, and Martin counties. He was perhaps the son of one of the several Wilsons inhabiting the northeastern part of the province before the Revolution, his mother possibly belonging to the no less numerous Lewis family of the same area. No date or place of birth has been discovered, nor is it possible to say who may have prepared him for college, although the possibilities include Henry Patillo, Presbyterian minister who conducted a school in Granville County, and his former student Charles Pettigrew, who before his ordination as an Anglican clergyman in 1775, had taught in Bute (Warren) County, Benjamin Hawkins and Joseph Hawkins (both Class of 1777), and Nathaniel Macon (Class of 1778). Wilson evidently entered the College in November 1774 as a member of the junior class, for the steward's account for the period running from that month to April 10, 1775 so lists him by his full name, and his name is not found on the account for the period immediately preceding that one. As with other members of his class, he was awarded his degree, as of September 1776, at a special meeting of the trustees in May 1777, the trustees having failed to muster the required quorum in the preceding September.

Wilson left his mark in history chiefly through the part he took in efforts to revive the former Anglican church within North Carolina in identification with the emerging organization of the Protestant Episcopal Church in the United States. He was ordained for the priesthood of the new denomination by Bishop William White at Philadelphia in 1789, and it is probable that his family had been parishioners in the "Old Church" before the Revolution. The extraordinary disruption and decline that the church suffered as a result of the Revolution make it difficult to speak with certainty, but evidently Wilson's first choice of a career was medicine. Writing to Charles Pettigrew in 1792, he stated that he had studied "physics" a dozen years before, which was to say toward the close of the Revolutionary War, in which, incidentally, he seems not to have served in a military capacity. Perhaps not long after leaving Princeton he began to study with some established physician. Perhaps, as was true of other professional men at the time, his livelihood came principally from land he owned and cultivated, for in the same letter to Pettigrew mentioned above he professed a disinclination to preach "for money." It is apparent that he well understood the limited income any rural Episcopalian parish at the time could provide for its minister.

He seems to have settled first in Halifax County, but the census of 1790 shows James Lewis Wilson as a resident of the adjoining Martin County and the head of a family of one free white male over 16 years of age, one under 16, and two free white females. He may have owned property in both counties, and apparently he served his coreligionists as best he could in Edgecombe County as well. In 1795 he advertised in a newspaper published in the town of Halifax the opening of a Latin school "in this county near Conoconary Church under the direction of Rev. Mr. Wilson." In 1797 he bought a town lot in Williamston, county seat of Martin, and was described as of Halifax County. His activity as an ordained clergyman of the Episcopal faith finds its chief focus in the town of Tarboro, county seat of Edgecombe.

It was in Tarboro in June 1790 that the first convention of Episcopalians in North Carolina met, at the suggestion of Bishop White and the call of Charles Pettigrew, for the purpose of reviving the old colonial church and giving it an organization appropriate to membership in the new denomination. A second convention, like the first very small in the number present, followed in the fall, and a third meeting in October 1791 appointed Wilson a delegate to the next General Convention of the church to be held in Philadelphia in 1792. Wilson made the trip but, delayed by contrary weather at sea, he arrived in September 1792 after the convention had adjourned. A fourth convention met at Tarboro in 1793, and the next, meeting in 1794, took the important step of electing Pettigrew to the office of bishop, an office he never actually filled for the want of a formal consecration. Pettigrew suffered from uncertain health, and Wilson seems to have been the only ordained clergyman in the state to have attended all of the conventions intended to breathe new life into an old church. Sadly for him, no doubt, the effort failed to achieve its purpose. Many years were to pass before the Episcopalians of North Carolina became a fully organized unit of the Protestant Episcopal Church.

These were years too in which Wilson seems to have been lost to history. He is reported to have preached a funeral sermon at Scotland Neck in southeastern Halifax in 1801. No reference to him of later date has been found. Perhaps he died not long thereafter.

SOURCES: See William H. Vernon (A.B. 1776) for commencement of 1776. See also *Journals of Gen. Conventions . . . 1785-1835*, I (1874); MS Steward's accounts, PUA; W. S. Perry, *Hist. of Amer. Episcopal Chh.* (1885), II, 145-46; W. White, *Memoirs of Protestant Episcopal Chh.* (1836), 172; *NCHR*, 28 (1951), 15-46; S. M. Lemmon, *Parson Pettigrew of the "Old Church,"* J. Sprunt Studies, no. 52 (1970), 63-78, 111; and *Pettigrew Papers*, I (1971), 75, 77, 85, 87, 105-6 ("for money"); J. K. Turner and J. L. Bridges, *Hist. of Edgecombe Cnty., N.C.* (1920), 432-48; S. H. and C. T. Smith, *Hist. of Trinity Parish . . . Halifax Cnty., N.C.* (1955), 25-29 ("in this county"); *First Census, N.C.*, 67. The College seems to have lost track of Wilson; at no time did its general catalogues italicize his name to indicate that he was a clergyman, and they for the first time listed him as dead in 1851, when it seems to have been assumed that all five members of his class carried in 1848 without such a notation must have been dead.

WFC

CLASS OF 1777

Theodorus Bailey

Abraham Bancker

William Barber

James Ashton Bayard, A.B.

Richard Bibb

George Blewer

John Brownfield, A.B.

Jacob Conant

James Crawford, A.B.

Nicholas Fish

Alexander Graham

John Graham

Samuel Reading Hackett

Luther Halsey

James Hanna, A.B.

Benjamin Hawkins

Joseph Hawkins

George W. Hazard

Adam Hoops, Jr.

Levi Hopkins

Daniel Jenifer

John Jordan

Richard Longstreet

Tristrim Lowther

Thomas Harrison McCalla, A.B.

John Young Noel, A.B.

Matthew Perkins

Lewis Allaire Scott

Abraham Smith

Gilbert Tennent, Jr.

Samuel Thane

Samuel Vickers, A.B.

John White

Theodorus Bailey

THEODORUS BAILEY, A.M. 1780, soldier, lawyer, public official, was born on October 12, 1758, the son of John and Altie Van Wyck Bailey of Dutchess County, New York. He was baptized in the Presbyterian Church at Rumbout. His father, the son of a noted jurist, was a respected and fairly prosperous farmer and later a militia officer. Bailey's maternal grandfather was a delegate to the first Provincial Congress in New York. In 1766 Bailey's father was an elder in the Dutch Reformed Church in Fishkill, but the family moved to Poughkeepsie before 1775, when the first liberty pole in that town was raised at the Bailey house.

Bailey was listed by the steward as a sophomore in the fall of 1774, when he probably first enrolled in the College. How long he remained at Nassau Hall is not known. Because of the confusion in the record of degrees granted in 1777, it is possible that he should be included among the graduates of that year, and a newspaper report that he received the A.M. degree in 1780 reinforces that possibility. That report lists him as one of five recipients of the second degree who are all described as "alumni of this College." Since men who had merely attended the College but did not graduate might also be identified as alumni, however, the question of whether Bailey completed his course of study for the first degree must be left unanswered. In those unusual times, the A.M. may well have been honorary, given perhaps in recognition of Bailey's study for the profession of law. In the latest general catalogue of Princeton University, not even that degree is mentioned.

At some time, Bailey returned to Poughkeepsie, which would remain his permanent home, to study law and serve in the Dutchess County Militia. By May 1778 he was adjutant of the Fourth Regiment of local forces, and on October 10, 1779, with the grade of major, he became adjutant of Colonel Morris Graham's First Regiment. His legal studies continued until at least September 1781, when he witnessed a codicil to the will of Peter Jay, father of John Jay, identifying himself as a "student." His teacher may have been Egbert Benson, whose other apprentices included Bailey's close friend and his sister's future husband, James Kent (Yale 1781), who was later Chancellor of the State of New York. In 1786 Bailey and Kent borrowed money from Peter Jay's widow to buy a substantial tract of land in Poughkeepsie.

On June 10, 1783, Bailey married Elizabeth Hoffman in the First Reformed Church in Poughkeepsie. By then he was almost certainly practicing law, occasionally tending to some legal matters for Alexander Hamilton. He was also active in the congregation of Christ

Theodorus Bailey, Class of 1777
BY JAMES SHARPLES

Church, mostly as a contributor to building funds. In addition to his law practice, Bailey served in the county militia, rising from major to lieutenant colonel between 1786 and 1797, when he resigned temporarily. Active again between 1798 and 1805, he had command first of a regiment and then of a brigade; he used his title of brigadier general even after resigning for the last time.

Bailey's practice prospered and, with his contacts as the brother-in-law of Gilbert Livingston, a leading anti-Federalist in New York, provided a base for his political career. In 1789 he joined the Livingstons as they moved toward a coalition with the Clintonians. That year he stood against Federalist Egbert Benson for election to the Second United States Congress. His defeat by ten votes was a surprise and a blow to the Livingstons. But more than family connections made Bailey an anti-Federalist. He was, from the outset, suspicious of the national government. That principle greatly complicated his political loyalties, for in the Byzantine maneuvers of New York politicians, allegiance to more than family or faction only confused matters.

In 1791 Bailey supported Aaron Burr (A.B. 1772) for the United States Senate. In April of that year, he lost a contest with Clintonian Thomas Tillotson for a seat in the state senate in a race that proved both the fragility and immaturity of the Clinton-Livingston alliance. But in 1793, when he ran against his Federalist brother-in-law James Kent for the House of Representatives, Bailey was successful. It was not defeat that Kent resented, since he had not sought the office, but he never forgave Bailey and his own law partner Gilbert Livingston for what he considered the scurrilousness of their campaign against him.

Bailey served in the Third and Fourth congresses. Although he was never a party leader, he was always regarded as a dependable member of the anti-Federalist, and then Democratic-Republican faction. Yet he occasionally voted against that coalition when the demands of his constituents required it. In the spring of 1794, for example, the Republicans split over renewal of a temporary embargo against England. Bailey, with most of his colleagues from New York, voted against renewal. In April 1796 Bailey joined the minority of Republicans who voted with the Federalists to pass legislation enabling Jay's Treaty to go into effect. That issue cost the Republicans the elections of 1796 in New York, and even though Bailey had supported the treaty he was defeated for reelection.

During the next two years, Bailey tended to his law practice and other personal affairs, such as his share of a tract of land in Herkimer County, New York that he and his cousin John B. Van Wyck had purchased from James Madison (A.B. 1771). On February 16, 1798, his first wife having died, Bailey married Rebecca Talmadge in Poughkeepsie. The three slaves he owned in 1790 were no longer in the family by 1800.

Bailey was elected to the Sixth and Seventh United States congresses and voted the straight Republican line. When the presidential election went to the House in February 1801, he was among the six New Yorkers whose votes put the state in Thomas Jefferson's column. Nevertheless, Vice President Aaron Burr sponsored Bailey for the post of supervisor of the revenue in New York.

Indeed, it was not Burr but Jefferson who kept Bailey from a federal appointment. With the advice of DeWitt Clinton, who was eager to supplant Burr as the arbiter of patronage in New York, the president juggled Burr's list of candidates and then rejected them in favor of Clintonians. Clearly, the Republican coalition in New York was ready to shatter, and Bailey, who sat in the state assembly as well as Congress in 1802, chose to cast his lot with the president's friends.

Although he had had Burr's support when he was elected to the United States Senate in 1803, Bailey turned against the vice president in 1804 and exulted in Burr's defeat in the gubernatorial race that year. He also did his best to ingratiate himself with Jefferson, in tones so deferential that they approached sycophancy. For example, he assisted the president in obtaining several hundred bottles of champagne in 1804. By then, his efforts had already been rewarded with a presidential appointment to the office of postmaster of New York City. Bailey resigned from the Senate in January 1804, thereby opening the way for the return to the upper house of John Armstrong (Class of 1776).

Bailey's correspondence with Jefferson continued even after the president had retired to Monticello, but it was largely confined to unofficial and nonpolitical affairs. In fact, Bailey made only one more foray into politics. That was in 1805 and 1806, when as an ally of DeWitt Clinton he tried to reunite the Clintonian and Burrite groups against the Livingstonian governor Morgan Lewis (A.B. 1773). He arranged meetings between leaders of the two factions and on February 20, 1806 sponsored a dinner at Dyde's Hotel in which the Clintonians promised to restore Burr and his friends to the party. But Clinton himself was not present at that dinner and he quickly disavowed any promises made in his name. The intraparty schism only widened, and Bailey had played his last role in the theater of high politics.

He spent the rest of his life as postmaster of New York and continued to buy land, much of it in the city itself. On December 18, 1808, in his final wedding, he married Martha McWhorter in Essex County, New Jersey. He had fathered seven children in his first two marriages, and his third wife bore him one more. Bailey died in New York on September 6, 1828 and was interred in the Dutch Burying Ground in New York until 1864, when his body was moved to the Rural Cemetery in Poughkeepsie.

SOURCES: See James Ashton Bayard (A.B. 1777) for awarding of degrees to Class of 1777. See also C. M. James, Biog. Sketches of the Bailey-Meyers-Mason Families (1908), 123-24; BDAC; NYGBR, 68 (1937), 295; 73 (1942), 245; 75 (1944), 75; 66 (1935), 159; F. M. Kip, Discourse . . . on the . . . First Reformed Dutch Chh., Fishkill, N.Y. (1866), 52; W.P.A., Dutchess Cnty. (1937), 31; MS Steward's accounts, Trustees' Minutes, 27 Sep 1780, PUA; N.J. Gazette, 11 Oct 1780; I. Huntting, Hist. of Little Nine Partners, . . . N.Y. (1974), 55, 66, 68; N.Y. Wills, IX, 263; F. Hasbrouck, Hist. of Dutchess Cnty., N.Y. (1909), 214; J. T. Horton, James Kent (1939), 35-36, 43, 52n; Hamilton Papers, III, 635, 647; H. W. Reynolds, Recs. of Christ Chh., Poughkeepsie, N.Y. (1911), 69, 93-94, 101, 357; Mil. Min., Council of Appointment, St. of N.Y., I, 87, 373, 440, 505, 563, 711, 799; A. F. Young, Democratic Republicans of N.Y. (1967), 133, 135, 185, 193, 388 & n, 465-67, 552, 561, 193; W. Kent, Memoirs *and Letters of James Kent* (1898), 39, 49-50; MS agreement, 5 Jan 1796, Madison MSS; *First Census, N.Y.*, 90; *A/C*, x, 1032; X-XII, passim; H. S. Parmet and M. B. Hecht, *Aaron Burr* (1967), 170, 174-76, 248; D. S. Alexander, *Political Hist. of the St. of N.Y.* (1906), I, 121, 156; N. E. Cunningham, Jr., *Jeffersonian Republicans in Power* (1963), 38, 40; *N.Y. Red Book* (1895), 376; *Journal of [N.Y.] House of Assembly, 25th Session*, passim; als TB to T. Jefferson, 9, 16, 17, 26 Jun 1804, and T. Jefferson to TB, 10, 21 Jun 1804, Jefferson MSS; D. Bobbé, *DeWitt Clinton* (1933), 118-19; *MCCCNY*, IV, V, VII, IX, XI, XIII, XIV, XV, XVII, passim; *GMNJ*, 10 (1935), 67; *SCHGM*, 39 (1938), 45.

MANUSCRIPTS: James Kent Papers, DLC

PUBLICATIONS: see Sh-Sh 7905, 7906

Abraham Bancker

ABRAHAM BANCKER, honorary A.B. 1786, A.M. 1789, espionage agent and public official, of Staten Island, Richmond County, New York, according to family tradition was educated at King's College (Columbia), but he actually seems to have been at Princeton. The College steward's account for the period extending from November 6, 1774 to April 10, 1775 lists Abraham Bancker as a member of the sophomore class. The name is that of a family identified with the Dutch Reformed Church, and a preference for Princeton over King's, where the influence of the Anglican Church was strong, is understandable. There appears to be no reason for doubting that this Abraham was the son, baptized May 15, 1760, of Adrian and Anna Boelen Bancker.

There was another Abraham Bancker, a first cousin on the maternal side, the son of Elizabeth Boelen and her husband Evert Bancker, a New York merchant who also was active in public affairs. Baptized September 25, 1754, this Abraham was of an age that makes it much less likely that he would have been a sophomore at Nassau Hall in 1774. Moreover, he seems rather consistently to have been known as Abraham B. Bancker, a fact which is of assistance in maintaining a distinction between his career, ending with death and burial in 1806 at Kingston, New York, and that of the other Abraham. A final and clinching piece of evidence that supports the identification of the first Abraham as the Princeton student is found in a letter of November 26, 1816, from Abraham Bancker to Anthony Rutgers, then a student at Nassau Hall, which recalls Bancker's own days as a student there.

The letter adds to and clarifies what has to be viewed as an extraordinary record of Bancker's identification with Princeton, though, unhappily, it fails to resolve all questions. Because his name does not appear on the steward's account for the period immediately preceding November 1774, it would be assumed that he first was admitted at that time. But a manuscript list of early members of the Cliosophic Society gives March 7, 1773 as the date of his admission to that society, his pseudonym being "Leander," after the amative swimmer of Greek mythology. There is some question, however, regarding the accuracy of a list that was compiled some time after the original records were destroyed by fire or other cause. Bancker resolves the discrepancy by closing his letter with a request that his "best respects" be presented to the Cliosophic Society, "of which I became a Member in the month of December 1774 and was their Clerk in the year 1776."

Bancker's recollection is specific enough to confirm that he began his studies at Princeton in November 1774 with the advanced standing of a sophomore, that he was promptly admitted to the Cliosophic Society, and that he continued in residence at the College probably until November 1776, when at the beginning of his senior year the students were dismissed because of the approaching British army. The question that remains, whether or not he completed his undergraduate study at Princeton, is not resolved by the action of the College's trustees on September 27, 1786, awarding him an honorary A.B. degree. No explanation is given in the minutes of the trustees. When three years later he received the A.M. degree, he was merely listed among the other "alumni" of the College who were so honored.

The trustees, in conferring these degrees, may have been influenced by knowledge of Bancker's wartime service from his home on Staten Island, after July 1776 within the British lines, as an agent for the transmission of intelligence to General Washington regarding enemy movements. On September 10, 1789, Bancker wrote from Castleton, Staten Island to President Washington applying for a federal appointment, evidently without specifying a particular office. In this application, he identified himself as the person who during the war had communicated with Washington under the name "Amicus Reipublicae." The application was transmitted together with supporting testimonials from Brigadier General Elias Dayton, father of Jonathan Dayton (A.B. 1776), of Elizabethtown, New Jersey, dated November 3, 1783; from Captain Asher F. Randolph of the "State troops of New Jersey," dated November 29, 1783 at Woodbridge; from John Vanderhooven at Woodbridge, dated November 14, 1788; and finally from John and Joshua Mercereau under the dates November 22 and December 1, 1788, respectively. General Dayton certified that Bancker "resided in the enemy's lines during the war and was zealous in transmitting information at the risk of his life." John Mercereau undertook to remind the president that General Washington had placed a special confidence in Bancker's reports.

Espionage is a branch of military activity that leaves an inadequate record for the historian, but in this case, several points are well enough established. Staten Island, lying across from Long Island at the entrance to New York's harbor and separated by narrow reaches of water from Elizabethtown, Perth Amboy, and other points in New Jersey, became a main center of intelligence activity for the Americans. Washington wrote to the President of the Congress on July 5, 1777: "I keep people constantly upon Staten Island, who give me daily information of the operations of the Enemy." Elias Boudinot, trustee of the College since 1772 and resident of Elizabethtown, had been responsible for army intelligence as an extra duty following his appointment as commissary general of prisoners in the spring of 1777. Elias Dayton had a role at critical points in the history of the war in the collection and transmission of intelligence. It is known that Randolph, Vanderhooven, and the two Mercereaus, all supporters of Bancker's application of 1789, at one time or another served as secret agents.

Perhaps in awarding the degrees the trustees were also prompted by Bancker's elevation in 1784 to membership in the original Board of Regents of the University of the State of New York, a position he held until 1787. His father was a leading resident of Richmond County, supervisor of the town of Westfield, representative of the county in the Second Provincial Congress of 1775, and sometime member of the state assembly. Abraham, in his turn, became county clerk in 1781, sheriff in 1784, member of the state assembly 1788-1790, and surrogate in 1792, and he had represented the county in the ratifying convention of 1788, casting an affirmative vote in its final action in favor of ratification of the new national constitution. His cousin Abraham B. Bancker had served the convention as a secretary. He himself was a presidential elector in 1804 and reportedly voted for Jefferson.

It is evident that Bancker continued to reside in Richmond County until May 1809, when another succeeded him as surrogate, but at some time thereafter he transferred his residence to New Jersey. His letter of 1816 was written from Belleville (Second River), Essex County, which obviously then was his residence. He probably remained there until his death in 1832. His will, dated June 19, 1822, was proved in Essex County on February 6, 1832. No evidence has been found that he ever held a federal office, and he probably was never married.

SOURCES: *NYGBR*, 72 (1940), 286-88; H. J. Banker, *Partial Hist. and Geneal. Rec. of the Bancker or Banker Families* (1909), 254-55; MS Steward's accounts, MS Clio.

Soc. membership list, Trustee Minutes, PUA; als AB to A. Rutgers, 26 Nov 1816, NjP; G. Hunt, *Cal. of Applications and Recommendations for Office during the Presidency of George Washington* (1901), 6 ("resided in the enemy lines"); *Washington Writings*, VIII, 353 ("people constantly on Staten Island"); VII, 343; XIX, 161-62; G. A. Boyd, *Elias Boudinot* (1952), 33-35, 39, 46-47; B. L. Clark, *Story of Elias Boudinot* (1977), 73f.; E. Boudinot, *Journal of Elias Boudinot* (1894), 50; J. Bakeless, *Turncoats, Traitors and Heroes* (1959), 165-83; M. H. Thomas, *Columbia Univ., Officers and Alumni* (1936), 10, 48 (the government of the newly named Columbia College was entrusted to the board in 1784, and this connection is probably responsible for the tradition that Bancker studied there); I. K. Morris, *Mem. Hist. of Staten Island*, I (1898), 124-28; R. M. Bayles, *Hist. of Richmond Cnty.* (1887), 327-32; Hist. Rec. Survey, *Staten Island Recs., 1678-1813* (1942), 54, 84; *Elliot's Debates*, II, 207, 412, 413; L. G. DePauw, *Eleventh Pillar* (1966), 188; *Index of N.J. Wills*, I (1912), 336. A Clio. Soc. catalogue published in 1876 lists Bancker under the year 1774.

WFC

William Barber

WILLIAM BARBER, soldier, public official, gentleman farmer, was the son of Patrick and Jane Fraser (Frasher, Frazer) Barber, who owned a small farm in Princeton, where he was born on April 15, 1755. He was the brother of Francis Barber (A.B. 1767). In 1764 the family, members of the Presbyterian church, moved to a 200-acre farm in what was then Ulster County, New York, where Barber's father later became a judge of the court of common pleas and, during the Revolution, a commissioner for disposing of confiscated Loyalist property. It is possible that Barber remained with his brother in Princeton at that time and received his early education in the grammar school while Francis attended the College.

Apparently, William Barber was admitted to the Cliosophic Society on January 1, 1777, taking the name "Lelius," a Romanized form of the name of the first king of Laconia in Greek legend. His brother had joined the society as a postgraduate member in September 1773. But Barber had already left the College before he became a Cliosophian. On October 29, 1776, he joined Colonel Elias Dayton's Third New Jersey Battalion of Continentals as an ensign. His brother was a major in the same unit. Dayton found him a worthy officer, but when the New Jersey Line was reorganized in November, Barber resigned from the battalion's third company to seek a better assignment.

On the same day that he was inducted into Clio, Barber was appointed aide-de-camp to General William Maxwell, with the grade of lieutenant. Four months later he was promoted to captain. With Maxwell he served in Pennsylvania and New Jersey throughout 1777,

William Barber, Class of 1777
ATTRIBUTED TO JOHN RAMAGE

and he was with the army in its winter quarters at Valley Forge, where
he spent part of the time in a hospital bed.

Early in 1778 Barber was assigned to one of the additional continental regiments as an adjutant, an office that had little promise of
advancement since the regiments were destined to be disbanded. At
the urging of his brother, he resigned and went to his father's home
to await a better position. His brother and father appealed to their
neighbor and relative, Governor George Clinton of New York, to take
him on as an aide, and Clinton agreed that William deserved a worth-
while assignment. The governor and General Thomas Conway, for
whom Barber had acted as brigade major occasionally at Valley Forge,
arranged for a majority in the regiment of Colonel Oliver Spencer,
Francis Barber's brother-in-law. Barber received the promotion but
he may never actually have joined Spencer, for on May 7, 1778, at
Valley Forge, Washington appointed him aide-de-camp to General
William Alexander, Lord Stirling.

Barber retained that office for almost three years, but with dimin-
ishing enthusiasm. By February 1781 his brother was again seeking a
better assignment for him, perhaps in the New Jersey Line. Washing-

ton blocked the transfer, however, because it would have violated accepted seniority procedures, so Barber finally took matters into his own hands. Without orders, he attached himself to the troops of General Lafayette as they marched south through New Jersey at the end of February. On March 14, 1781, he found time to write to Lord Stirling from Annapolis, Maryland, explaining his absence and re-signing as aid-de-camp. He served as a deputy adjutant with Lafayette until September 29, when Washington appointed him inspector of the division.

In November 1781 Patrick Barber learned that both of his sons had been wounded at Yorktown, but he did not know how seriously they might be hurt. Governor Clinton put the worried father's mind at ease on November 9 by passing along Alexander Hamilton's account of the battle. Francis Barber had been cut in the lip by a bayonet. William Barber had been grazed by a ball that passed through his coat. For William it had been perilously close, but his wound was not serious, and he refused to leave the field.

Back in Philadelphia after the Yorktown campaign, Barber had once again to seek an assignment that would keep him in the army. In March 1782 he thought that he had arranged for one when he con-vinced a New Jersey officer to resign in his favor. He was confident that he could obtain the approval of all other officers who might be affected by the change, and on the basis of that promise, Washington approved of the scheme to retain "a very meritorious Officer" in serv-ice. The commander in chief urged Governor William Livingston to use his influence with the New Jersey legislature to facilitate Barber's commission. The refusal of one officer, John Noble Cumming (A.B. 1774), to accept the departure from the seniority system ended the venture.

Barber remained, therefore, a member of Baron von Steuben's de-partment, one of the few assistant inspectors still on duty at the end of 1782, when he was stationed at headquarters in Newburgh, New York. He was badly overworked, and to help him, Washington recalled Colonel Walter Stewart to active duty.

February and March of 1783 were tense times for the army. Officers were disturbed that the pensions they had been promised might be paid late or not at all. When Stewart returned to Newburgh from Philadelphia, he brought word that Congress was already planning to disband the army and that no arrangements for officers' pensions had been made. As far as some of the officers were concerned, Wash-ington was not representing their interests forcefully enough before the Congress. Some of them turned to Horatio Gates for leadership, and nationalists in Congress itself wanted to exploit their demand for commutation of the pensions in order to increase the power of the central government. Stewart, whom those nationalists had used to communicate with the most disgruntled officers, was a close friend of Barber and of John Armstrong (Class of 1776). All were in Gates's circle.

In March Armstrong wrote an anonymous letter calling all officers to a meeting. The inflammatory document included a threat, barely veiled, that unless their demands were met the officers would refuse to surrender their arms when peace came and would refuse to fight if the war continued. Barber took copies of this first "Newburgh letter" to the adjutant's office and distributed them among the officers who assembled there daily. When Washington denounced the plan, Armstrong penned a second, and somewhat less incendiary letter to proclaim that the commander in chief agreed with his subordinates and would speak for them. Again, Barber distributed the letter among his colleagues. Only by exerting his immense personal prestige was Washington able to calm the situation.

By April Barber was concerned about less earth-shaking matters, such as helping his friend Matthias Ogden obtain leave to go to Europe on business. He also persuaded Steuben to write letters of introduction for Ogden to use on the continent. On June 17 Barber petitioned Congress for a land grant in Ohio. His appeal was granted in August 1791, when he received title to 400 acres. He was eligible for membership in the New Jersey chapter of the Society of the Cincinnati at the end of the war, and although he was not an original member, he apparently joined the organization later. In October 1786 his interest in the problem of army pensions cooled when he accepted a commutation from half-pay for life to five years' full pay.

After leaving the army, Barber became the continental commissioner in New York, assigned to settle the accounts between the state and the nation. He opened an office in Goshen, Orange County on February 20, 1784, but his permanent residence was in New York City until at least the summer of 1786. On April 17 of that year he married Ann Crooke. Her deceased father, Charles Crooke, had been a wealthy merchant and had left a substantial estate that included a farm known as Krom Elbow, near Hyde Park in Dutchess County. Sometime after his marriage, and probably after the establishment of the federal government ended his service as commissioner, Barber moved to Krom Elbow. He may have shared the house with some of his wife's family, for while the household in 1790 included fourteen members, eight of whom were slaves, Barber and his wife had only two children.

Thereafter, Barber apparently was content to live the life of a country squire. He had taken an interest in paleontology during his last months in the army when some mastodon bones were discovered on his father's farm, and in 1792 he found a few more fossils at Krom Elbow. He died at that estate on June 17, 1798, survived by his wife and daughter. His son had died at the age of three. Barber's remains were moved to the Crooke burying ground at Bellfield in Hyde Park in 1871.

Sources: *NYGBR*, 62 (1931), 3-22, 122-25; MS Clio. Soc. membership list, PUA; *PMHB*, 34 (1910), 465, 471, 475; 35 (1911), 183, 295; Stryker, *Off. Reg.*, 18-22, 35, 36, 67; *Valley Forge Orderly Book of Gen. George Weedon* (1902), 47, 55, 151, 311; *VMHB*, 53 (1945), 191; *Clinton Papers*, III, 67, 75, 101, 114; VI, 640; VII, 459; *Washington Writings*, XI, 360; XXI, 196; XXIII, 152; XXIV, 62 & n ("very meritorious Officer"), 80; XXV, 400, 492-93; XXVI, 93-94, 143, 305; D. S. Freeman, *George Washington*, V (1957), 432-36, 436-37n; *WMQ* (3 ser.), 27 (1970), 206; 29 (1972), 144-49; als WB to M. Ogden, 21 [Apr] 1783, NjP; *JCC*, XXV, 786; *Hamilton Papers*, VI, 122; XI, 269, 270n3, 570n; *N.Y. Wills*, XIV, 18; *N.Y. Directory, 1786*; *First Census, N.Y.*, 76.

Manuscripts: NjHi; NjP

James Ashton Bayard

JAMES ASHTON BAYARD, A.B., A.M. 1781, merchant, was born in Philadelphia on May 5, 1760, the eldest son of Colonel John Bayard and his wife, Margaret Hodge, and brother of Andrew Bayard (A.B. 1779), Samuel Bayard (A.B. 1784), Nicholas Bayard (A.B. 1792), and Jane Bayard, wife of New Jersey Chief Justice Andrew Kirkpatrick (A.B. 1775). He should not be confused with his first cousin, also named James Ashton Bayard (A.B. 1784), who was the son of Colonel Bayard's twin brother Doctor James Ashton Bayard. Colonel Bayard won his military title during the revolutionary war. He had moved from his birthplace in Cecil County, Maryland to Philadelphia in 1756 and became a prominent merchant and leading political figure among the city's Whigs as the Revolution approached. In addition to active campaigning with the Second Regiment of the Philadelphia Militia, he served in the state assembly, on the state's executive council, and represented the state in the Continental Congress in 1785. In 1778 he became a trustee of the College, and through the years before his death in 1807, he was one of the more faithful among them. After 1788 he resided in New Brunswick, New Jersey. Margaret Hodge Bayard, James's mother, was a sister of Andrew Hodge (A.B. 1772) and Hugh Hodge (A.B. 1773), and an aunt of Reverend Charles Hodge (A.B. 1815).

James Ashton Bayard of this class completed his preparation for college in Nassau Hall's grammar school, from which he apparently was admitted to the freshman class after examination on September 27, 1773. That evening he was one of three of the grammar school students who delivered orations in the Prayer Room of Nassau Hall, he speaking in Latin. There is reason for believing that he returned to the College for his sophomore year and that he was in Princeton at the beginning of his junior year. It seems likely that after three years of residence he was among the students dismissed by President Witherspoon on November 29, 1776 because of the approach of the British army. Perhaps he continued his studies at home during the following winter and spring. In any case, he probably was one of the small number of students who returned to Princeton for pursuit of their studies after the College reopened in the summer of 1777.

The evidence of his presence in Princeton for at least a part of that summer, whether for study or merely for the final examination that qualified him for his degree, is found in the misadventure he suffered on the way home in September. The story was told many years later by Mrs. Kirkpatrick, his sister. Their father had purchased a farm some eighteen miles up the Schuylkill near Plymouth Meeting, in part with the thought that it might provide a refuge for his family in the event of a British attack on Philadelphia. James was on his way home at some time between Washington's defeat at Brandywine on September 11 and Sir William Howe's occupation of Philadelphia on September 27 and had the bad luck of being apprehended by British soldiers. When asked his name, he gave it; and when it was recognized, he was accused of being a spy. The story may have grown with the passage of time to include Mrs. Kirkpatrick's recollection of later having been shown the very spot on which James had stood with a noose about his neck as he waited to be hanged. But one does not have to doubt that his mother went into the city, as reported, to plead with General Howe for the release of her son, and it is certain that George Washington intervened in his behalf. To Howe on January 20, 1778 he wrote:

> Mr. James Bayard was taken prisoner near Swedes Ford, the day your Army crossed the Schuylkill. He had just returned from College, and had no rank in, or connection with the Army. He is not to be considered as a prisoner of War, but as a Citizen, and as such his Friends will propose an exchange for him.

Just when James regained his freedom is not known.

It is not easy to determine just when Bayard formally received his degree. The only recorded meeting of the trustees during 1777 assembled on May 24 at Cooper's Ferry. A principal item on the agenda was the conferring of degrees upon members of the Class of 1776, who had not received them at the truncated commencement of 1776 because the trustees had failed to muster a quorum. On the remedy provided, the minutes read: "Resolved that the last senior class, who were approved by the faculty, but had not their degrees conferred at the commencement, because the board failed to meet, be admitted to their degree of Batchelor of Arts; & that they receive their diplomas, so soon as the confusions of the war will admit of it." The next paragraph in the minutes begins, "The class consisted of," and then lists in alphabetical order the names of James Ashton Bayard and the six other members of the Class of 1777. This is an obvious error, attributable no doubt to the confusion of the clerk who later, perhaps much later, undertook to fill in the gaps he found in the minutes for this troubled period of time. More dependable is the published report by President Witherspoon, under date of August 21, 1778, and in the *New Jersey Gazette* for the following September 16. In this the president announced that members of the Class of 1776 had been "formally admitted to their Bachelors degree of the standing of September 1776, and may have their diplomas when they please to call for them." Secondly, the president announced that the "senior scholars of the year 1777" had been "examined and approved in August that year" and that, while there had been "no public Commencement," the members of this class had been admitted to their degrees at the next meeting of the trustees "and may have their diplomas, bearing the proper date, when they apply for them." The reference here apparently was to the meeting of the trustees on April 16, 1778—according to the minutes, the next meeting to be held after that of May 1777. Doubtless the president's recollection in August 1778 of what had occurred at the meeting was more accurate than that of the clerk who later wrote up the minutes, which record no action whatsoever regarding degrees for the Class of 1777.

The confusion in the official minutes probably explains the further confusion of the record arising from subsequent actions by the trustees. There seems to be little room for doubt that all seven qualified members of the Class of 1777, as listed in the minutes for the meeting of May 1777, were awarded their degrees by the trustees in their meeting of April 1778. And yet the minutes for September 25, 1782 carry a resolution that "John Noel, Samuel Vickers, and James Hanna, alumni of the College, who on account of the confusions of the war have not received their degree of B.A. at the regular time, be now admitted to it." One evident result was that the published catalogues of the College for a while thereafter carried only these three men as members of the Class of 1777. On September 28, 1790, the trustees sought correction of the four omissions by ordering that the names of James Bayard, Thomas H. McCalla, James Crawford, and James [*sic*] Brownfield "be now inserted in their proper place" as members of the Class of 1777. For some reason, the catalogue of 1794 added only Bayard's name, and not until the catalogue of 1797 was the full list included. But even the catalogue of 1908 assumes that the degrees for this class were awarded either in 1782 or 1790, and because Bayard died in 1788, it lists his degree as "*post. obit.*" The truth seems to be that he sustained the examination for the degree in August 1777 and that he was formally awarded the A.B. in April 1778. His receiving the A.M. degree in 1781 tends to confirm this assumption.

Little has been found in the usual sources regarding the remaining years of his short life. A tax list for 1782 shows him to have been resident then in Philadelphia. Because of his age, one hesitates to assume that he was the James Bayard who on March 18, 1783 was commissioned as a member of the High Court of Errors and Appeals. But he may have been, for under the statute, its membership was to include three who had no more specific qualification than that they be men of "known integrity and ability," and his father had political influence. It is known that James was married to Eliza Rodgers, the daughter of Doctor John Rodgers, trustee of the College from 1765 to 1807, but the date of the marriage has not been found.

Fortunately, his sister Jane Kirkpatrick liked to write, and a selection of her essays was posthumously published in 1856 under the title of *The Light of Other Days: Sketches of the Past*. The characters portrayed in these moralistic pieces are not named but the more important of them are easily identified by their initials and by the details of their lives, which conform for the most part to the known record. One may follow with only one reservation the tragic story of James, oldest son of "Col. B.," as it unfolds in these pages.

James was "handsome, gay, witty, with a touch of sarcasm in his nature." He was impetuous and ardent by temperament. He had been taken into the "counting-house" of his father, a Philadelphia merchant. He fell in love with Eliza, who had come to the city on a visit, with no more polish than was afforded by the opportunities of a rural parish, but with a quick eye for the main chance. Because of their ages, they were persuaded to postpone marriage for a year, after which James was taken into his father's business. For a time, all went well, but Eliza was self-indulgent, and her young husband all too indulgent of her love of luxury. He soon found himself in financial difficulties, from which he was rescued at considerable cost by his father. Finally, on a trip to South Carolina (its purpose is not explained), he contracted a disease from which he died aboard ship on the return voyage. He was buried at sea. The reservation one feels as the story is read is an obvious one. Mrs. Kirkpatrick did not like Eliza, and the bad end Eliza ultimately reached, the details of which need not be elaborated here, served to point up a hopefully useful moral.

It needs to be added only, from other sources, that Bayard, in fact, "died at sea on his return from South Carolina" in June 1788. He left two sons, James Ashton and Anthony Walton Bayard.

SOURCES: The evidence of Bayard's attendance at the College is open to some questions of interpretation. A newspaper account of the examination and admission to the freshman class in September 1773 [*NJA* (1 ser.) XXIX, 50] does not specifically state that James Bayard was among those admitted, but the implication that he was finds confirmation in the steward's account for 25 May 1773 to 25 Sep 1774, which lists James Bayard among the College's students and places his name immediately after that of Theodorus Bailey (all such accounts in PUA). In a list of members of the sophomore class for the period Nov 1774 to 10 Apr 1775, the name of Theodore Bailey is followed immediately by that of a James Biard or Beard, depending upon how one deciphers the steward's hand. This list is more or less alphabetized, but the same order of names—Bailey and Biard or Beard—is followed in a third and unalphabetized list of the steward, which carries no date but belongs somewhere between 1773 and 1776. Efforts to identify a James Biard or Beard who may have attended the College at this time have been so unsuccessful as to invite the assumption that James Bayard and James Biard or Beard were one and the same person. Knowledge that the steward was inclined to spell names phonetically, and that Bayard and Beard were at times used interchangeably, as also were the letters y and i, has led to the conclusion stated in the text above. Bayard's presence at the beginning of what would have been his junior year is established by the ledger of a local merchant, in which a transaction by James Bayard is entered on 9 Nov 1775 [Patterson Acct. Bk.]. A final consideration is the fact that it becomes difficult to explain Bayard's graduation on schedule without assuming that he had been in residence for much, or most, of the preceding four years, in which his name as James Bayard is found on only one of three surviving accounts of the steward.

NYGBR, 16 (1885), 49-72; 23 (1892), 1-14; *NJHSP* (2 ser.), 5 (1878), 139-60; Hist. Soc. Del., *Papers*, VII (1888), 46-73; *DAB*; *LMCC*, VIII, xciv; S. Miller, *Memoirs of the Rev. John Rodgers* (1813), 93-94, 112-15; A. A. Hodge, *Life of Charles Hodge* (1880), 3-9; *Washington Writings*, X, 324 ("a citizen"); Trustee Minutes and College *Catalogues*, PUA; Maclean, *History*, I, 320-23; *NJA* (2 ser.), II, 435-37 ("examined and approved" in Aug 1777). At least two members of the senior class in 1776, and one in 1777, received certificates from Witherspoon testifying that they had completed requirements for their degrees; see William R. Davie and Joseph W. Henderson (both A.B. 1776), and James Crawford (A.B. 1777). See also *Pa. Arch.* (3 ser.), XVI, 486; XXV, 68; J. H. Martin, *Bench and Bar of Phila.* (1883), 64. Mrs. J. E. Cogswell was responsible for selection and publication of Kirkpatrick, *Light of Other Days*; 26 ("handsome, gay, witty").

WFC

Richard Bibb

RICHARD BIBB, planter, businessman, public official, and Methodist preacher, was born on April 15, 1752, in Prince Edward County, Virginia, the son of John Bibb and his wife, Susanna. His father died in 1769 and his mother late in 1786. Judging by the thirty slaves Richard owned in 1783, the family was prosperous. It was probably also identified with Virginia's established church, for family tradition holds that Richard was once prepared for the Episcopalian ministry, which suggests that the impulse to preach came after the Revolution rather than before it. This assumption is reinforced by the further tradition that Bibb read theology with Reverend John Blair Smith (A.B. 1773), presumably during the period of Smith's presidency of Prince Edward Academy, later Hampden-Sidney College (1779-1789). Bibb's decision to become a Methodist preacher came much later in his life.

Even so, the traditional view that he earlier had prepared for the Episcopal ministry adds complexity to the problem of explaining his presence at Princeton as a student during the winter term of 1774-1775. The steward's list of students then enrolled arranged them by the classes to which they belonged, except for three, including Bibb, who were listed in the space below the sophomore class under the heading of "Resedentors." The other two are known to have been previously enrolled in the College, and one of them, Joseph Flavius Lane (A.B. 1776), later qualified for his degree. It is assumed that in these two cases the students were in some way out of phase with their regular classes, perhaps because of interruptions occasioned by illness or some other difficulty. But there is no evidence that Bibb had attended the College before November 6, 1774, when the term began— or for that matter, that he was in attendance after April 10, 1775, when evidently the term ended. Perhaps Bibb's assignment to the category of "Resedentors" means no more than that for the time being he was regarded, in modern parlance, as a special student.

What ever may be the explanation for Bibb's attendance, there is little difficulty in explaining his early departure. On September 28, 1775, he was married to Lucy Booker, member of another Prince Edward family. The couple's first child, George M. Bibb (A.B. 1792), was born October 30, 1776. It may be, as tradition suggests, that Richard continued his studies at Prince Edward, but it is evident enough that he quickly began to assume the responsibilities of a man of property. He served as captain of militia between 1776 and 1778. From 1783 to 1787 he sat for the county in the lower house of the assembly through four successive sessions, during which he cast a vote in favor of Jefferson's Statute of Religious Liberty. The management of his extensive properties, which he seems to have enlarged both by acquiring additional land and by engaging in commercial activities, undoubtedly required much of his attention. In 1784 he was elected a trustee of the recently chartered Hampden-Sidney College. In 1785 he became a justice of the county court. And in 1794 he was the purchaser of a mill. By that time, his interests may have reached into Kentucky. He is said to have gone there as early as 1789, but any assumption that he became then a permanent resident of the territory is refuted by the record he entered into a family bible showing no less than three children born after that year in Virginia, the youngest on April 3, 1800. It appears that he did not move his family to Kentucky until some time after his son George migrated there in 1798 to practice law and to begin a career that would take him twice to the United States Senate.

Having acquired a salt works in Bullitt County, Richard represented the county in the Kentucky legislature in 1803. But he ultimately settled at Russellville in Logan County, where his son Richard, Jr. became a merchant and president of the local branch of the Bank of Kentucky. It was in Kentucky that Richard, Sr. became a Methodist preacher. The date of 1815 for the beginning of his ministry is deduced from the inscription on his tombstone, which notes his death on January 25, 1839, after he had been for "twenty four years a minister of the Methodist Church." Another of Bibb's sons inherited the family bible in which his father in 1813 had begun to record births, marriages, and deaths in the family and is assumed to have been the person who added the comment that Richard had been a successful farmer, businessman, and "local preacher in the Methodist Church." The sequence followed in this description of Bibb's career is helpful in defining the office of a "local preacher." Essentially a layman licensed to preach, he by 1815 might also be ordained for an office that locally supplemented the services of the itinerant "circuit-rider" upon whom the church continued chiefly to depend. In brief, he was a part-time preacher.

The most notable act of Bibb's later years was the freeing of his slaves. There are two possibly conflicting stories. One maintains that in 1833 he responded to the effort of the American Colonization Society to settle emancipated slaves in Liberia by freeing fifty-one slaves and helping to send the thirty-two who were willing to migrate in the first group of former slaves to leave Kentucky for Liberia. The other is that he freed fifty-one slaves by his will, with provision that they should have land of their own. The conflict, if that it be, matters less than does the evidence that a man once heavily committed to the institution of slavery came in time to question it.

Bibb was twice married. Lucy Booker Bibb died on August 21, 1815, close to the time when her husband became a minister. On December 25, 1817, he married Mary Ann Jackson, who predeceased him on March 20, 1831. There were nine children, all by the first marriage, six boys and three girls. Three sons and a daughter survived their father.

SOURCES: *KSHS Reg.*, 26 (1928), 158-61; 39 (1941), 3; 40 (1942), 145; 45 (1947), 314, 319; 59 (1961), 332 ("minister of the Methodist Church"); 70 (1972), 300; C. W. Bibb, *Bibb Family in Amer.* (1941), 66-67; MS Steward's accounts, alumni file of G. M. Bibb (A.B. 1792), PUA; H. C. Bradshaw, *Hist. of Prince Edward Cnty., Va.* (1955), passim; Bradshaw, *Hist. of Hampden-Sidney College*, I (1976), 68, 77; J. T. Main, *Pol. Parties before the Constitution* (1973), 445; J. H. Gwathmey, *Hist. Reg. of Virginians in Rev.* (1938), 63; *First Census, Va.*, 59, 101; E. G. Swem and J. W. Williams, *Reg. of Gen. Assem. of Va.* (1918), 347; L. Collins, *Hist. of Ky.* (1878), II, 772; W. W. Sweet, *Religion on the Amer. Frontier*, IV (1946), 47-48, 572n.

Bibb's attendance at Princeton was possibly related to the fact that Samuel Stanhope Smith (A.B. 1769), former tutor in the College, later Professor of Moral Philosophy, and still later its president, had gone in 1773 to Prince Edward Cnty., where he became by 1775 the leading spirit in formulating plans for the academy that eventually became Hampden-Sidney College. Perhaps Smith found in Bibb an apt and relatively advanced student and so encouraged him to go to Princeton for further study. Perhaps Bibb arrived not quite prepared to assume full standing either in the freshman class or one of the more advanced classes. His age, then 22, would have argued against grouping him with the younger boys of the grammar school, if the question was admission to the freshman class. The decision may have been to classify him for the time as a special student. Obviously, the College was attempting to establish a regular four-year progression to the degree, but as the careers of many students show, the program of study still had a marked degree of flexibility. Here Bibb has been somewhat arbitrarily assigned to the Class of 1777, on the assumption that, even if not quite qualified for the freshman class in 1774, his maturity might have permitted him to attain the degree in something less than four years, as did many others.

WFC

George Blewer

GEORGE BLEWER, soldier, had a very short stay as a student in Nassau Hall, one apparently limited to a single term, and one that ended for him tragically. In the steward's account for the period of November 1774 to April 10, 1775, Blewer is listed as a member of the sophomore class. His name appears on none of the other surviving lists of students kept by the steward, including that extending from May 25, 1773 through September 25, 1774. Presumably, Blewer was first en-

rolled with the standing of a sophomore at the beginning of a new
academic year in November 1774.

The circumstances of Blewer's departure from the College were
recorded many years later in a letter of January 28, 1817 from John
Pintard (A.B. 1776) to his oldest daughter. A report of recent riotous
conduct by the students at Princeton prompted Pintard to observe
that there was "something fundamentally wrong in the discipline" of
the College and to suggest "that the professors & tutors are too rigid &
inexperienced in life" and "know not how to enforce the laws or to
relax with discretion." He went on to boast that there had been
trouble even "in my day" but said that "Doctor Witherspoon understood human nature & we never had such dreadful explosions." He
recalled that in his junior year he and Blewer were members of a
group of nine students who "wasted the winter in frolicking, playing
all hours & drinking Eggnog" and who eventually were betrayed into
the hands of the tutors by their "obstreperous mirth at late hours."
Called finally to account, the group agreed that Pintard should "make
our defence," one "founded on the principle of sturdy denial & the
presumption of no proof against us." The president opened the hearing by warning the young men that they should not compound their
offences "by telling a lee" and that sufficient proof of their guilt was
in hand, whereupon Pintard, having noticed the "downcast counte-
nance & suffused face" of Blewer, suggested that the party who may
have made a confession might "explain for us all." Then Blewer, at a
call from the president, "bursting into tears, disclosed the truth."
Eight of the culprits for not "telling *lees*" were given the relatively
light penalty of a public reprimand "after prayers in the College."
Blewer went free of punishment but "lost his character, no one spoke
to him or w^d associate with him and after spring vacation, a high
spirited youth he came no more to College."

To this sad story Pintard added a sequel. At some time after the
Battle of Germantown on October 4, 1777—just when was not said—
Pintard had occasion to visit the quarters of American prisoners of
war on Long Island. There he found among the prisoners his classmate "Tom Parker of Virginia" and poor Blewer, who "burst into
tears & hung round my neck & asked pardon for having betrayed us;"
Blewer blamed John Duffield (A.B. 1773), a tutor at the time, "for
having excited him to this conduct & breach of faith." Pintard continued: "Here we see the generous conduct of Doct^r Witherspoon who
saved us from ignominy, by not suffering us to be entrapped as the
Tutors left to themselves w^d undoubtedly have done."

George Blewer was a son of Captain Joseph Blewer of Philadelphia, shipmaster and man of property in and around the city, who for a number of years before the Revolution was engaged in traffic along the coast as far south as Florida and to the West Indies. At the end of November 1775, Captain Blewer was the carrier of a dispatch from General Washington at Cambridge to John Hancock in Philadelphia, and during the following year he was one of those charged by the Pennsylvania Council of Safety, of which he was a member, with heavy responsibilities for preparing the defenses of that city for an attack by water. On February 13, 1777, he was second in a list of six men constituting a navy board in charge of all "Vessels of War, Armed Boats, fire-ships, fire-Rafts, &ca." available for the defense of the city. The name of his wife, George's mother, was Sarah.

George apparently had no inclination to follow his father to sea, for on December 4, 1776, he was commissioned a second lieutenant in the Fourth Regiment of the Pennsylvania Continental Line. On the following October 4, he was taken a prisoner at Germantown, and at some time thereafter, was transferred to Long Island. It is to be hoped that his mother was successful in her purpose to visit him there, for which, on September 8, 1778, she received a pass from the Pennsylvania Executive Council on petition from her husband. Blewer was exchanged on January 29, 1781, having meanwhile been pro-moted to a first lieutenancy. The next indication of his service finds him among the troops engaged in the siege at Yorktown, Virginia, where on the night of September 23, 1781 he seems unwisely to have sought an amicable settlement to a quarrel between two other officers, only to have one of them seize his pistol and "snap" it at him. That officer went before a court-martial on October 2 and was discharged from the service. The court seems not to have been able to decide whether the pistol was loaded, but in any case, Blewer was fortunate and no blame was attached to his own conduct. After the surrender of Cornwallis on October 19, Blewer seems to have been among those dispatched by Washington for reinforcement of General Nathanael Greene's Southern Army. He was at Halifax, North Carolina, on March 20, 1782, when he was described by a fellow officer as being of the Fourth Pennsylvania, serving as an officer with the Maryland Line. Presumably, he subsequently joined General Greene in South Carolina. On January 1, 1783, he was a lieutenant in the Pennsylvania First Regiment, but a return for that unit on the following September 23 does not list him among its officers. His service thus probably had ended during the preceding summer.

Little can be added beyond the evidence provided in support of an application by one George Ord, as an heir to George Blewer, to the federal government in the fall of 1825 for a pension or land warrant. The supporting documents included a statement "affirmed" on September 29 of that year before a justice of the peace in Philadelphia by two women, described as credible and disinterested, that they had been acquainted with Blewer, "late of the said City Deceased." It was further affirmed that Blewer had "died single and without having Children or Brother or Sister and that his mother" was heir to him as the "next of kin." She had died in 1801. George Ord is described as a nephew, so "one of the Heirs at Law" to "the said George Blewer both in his right and that of his mother." Just when Blewer died has not been determined, but he is not mentioned in the will of his father, proved on August 25, 1789.

SOURCES: MS Steward's accounts, PUA; *NYHS Coll.*, LXX, 50-54; II, 26 (Pintard letter); *Pa. Arch.* (3 ser.), XIV, 143, 434, 582, 711; XV, 21, 153, 353, 366, 392, 489, 687, 765; XVI, 366, 520, 663 (2 ser.), X, 328, 330; *PMHB*, 3 (1879), 195; *PGM*, 26 (1969-1970), 170, *Col. Rec. Pa.*, XI, 571; XXIX, 210; *Va. Gazette*, 27 Nov 1766, 14 Apr 1768, 24 Nov 1768, 16 Sep 1773, (D & N) 12 Jun 1779; *Va. Hist. Reg.*, II (1849), 140; *SCHGM*, 24 (1923), 68, 69; W. B. Clark, *Naval Documents of the Amer. Rev.* (1966-1976), II, 1,199; III, 11; IV, 1,336; V, 81, 698, 715; VI, 326, 823, 915, 966, 1,131, 1,223, 1,355, 1,408; VII, 108, 130, 224, 1,195; J. W. Jackson, *Pa. Navy* (1974), 85-86, 128, 435; Heitman; F. A. Berg, *Encyc. of Continental Army Units* (1972), 94-96; *Washington Writings*, XXIII, 206-207; *PMHB*, 19 (1895), 61; 21 (1897), 387, 390; J. H. Gwathmey, *Hist. Reg. of Virginians in Rev.*, 71; *Index of Rev. War Pension Applications* (1966), 113; MS abstracts of Phila. wills, Ph 2A:5,6, Geneal. Soc. of Pa.

WFC

John Brownfield

JOHN BROWNFIELD, A.B., has not been positively identified, and there is no record of his study at the College aside from the degree he was awarded as a member of the Class of 1777. Moreover, the record of that award is full of faults. Possibly he was among the small group of students who assembled in the town during the summer of 1777. And certainly he must have been one of those who, according to a published announcement by President Witherspoon in August 1778, sustained the examination for their degrees in August 1777. There having been "no public Commencement" in the following September, when evidently for a second year the trustees were unable to muster a quorum, the members of this class were awarded their degrees formally at a meeting of the trustees on April 16, 1778. The minutes of the board covering that action are almost hopelessly confused, with the result that Brownfield's name was omitted from the published catalogues of the College until that for the year 1797. Thereafter, it was regularly included in each catalogue, until in 1851 he was for the first time listed as dead. Quite evidently, the College lost track of some of its former students, and it is difficult to avoid the conclusion that Brownfield was one of that group. The A.M. degree appended to his name beginning with the catalogue for 1808 was not awarded by the College. The notation in the *General Catalogue* of 1908 that Brownfield had his A.B. conferred in 1790 is also mistaken. Rather, it was in 1790 that the trustees ordered that his name, together with the names of three of his classmates, be included in the College's catalogues thereafter as members of the Class of 1777, which for a time was not done. To add to the confusion, when the clerk recorded the trustees' order in 1790, he rendered the name "James" Brownfield.

SOURCES: See James Ashton Bayard (A.B. 1777) for awarding of degrees to Class of 1777. Brownfield may have been the son of John Brownfield, a native of Greenwich, England, who accompanied James Oglethorpe to Ga. in the winter of 1735-1736, moved to Bethlehem, Pa. in 1745 (where he was ordained for itinerant missions by the Moravians in 1749), and died there in 1752 at the age of 38, five years after he married Catherine Kearney, a convert from N.J. or N.Y., who lived until 1798. No evidence has been found that the couple had any other child than a daughter, however, and the relatively advanced age of 24 or more for a graduate in 1777 raises additional, although not insurmountable, questions.

It is much more likely that the graduate belonged to the Brownfield family or families of western Pa., whose members were found in Cumberland, Bedford, Westmoreland, and Fayette counties, to name them in the order of their creation. He may have been the John Brownfield of Hopewell Township, Cumberland Cnty., who in a tax list for 1778 was recorded as the owner of one horse and two cattle; who in 1779 owned 100 acres, three horses, three cattle, and one slave; who in 1780 had 200 acres and no slaves; and who five years later held 180 acres, four horses, and four cattle—i.e., a substantial. but not wealthy farmer. A John Brownfield was listed in the Seventh Class of Cumberland Cnty. Militia as of 11 Sep 1777. Brownfields were also found in the nearby parts of Va., including the John Brownfield who on 14 Jul 1792 was married in Augusta Cnty. to Kitty Fauver or Fauner. There were persons of that name in S.C., but no John has been discovered.

F. L. Weis, *Col. Clergy of Middle Colonies* (1957), 189; Moravian Hist. Soc., *Transactions*, 5 (1895-1899), 122, 163, 176; J. M. Levering, *Hist. of Bethlehem, Pa.* (1903), 41, 42n, 183, 261, 263; L. F. Church, *Oglethorpe* (1932), 198, 233, 257; *PMHB*, 12 (1888), 450; 22 (1898), 505; *Pa. Arch.* (3 ser.), xx, 40, 58, 171, 306, 634, 723; xxii, passim; xxiii, 614; xxv, 455; xxvi, 32, 40, 393, 401; J. A. Searight, *Reg. of Searight Family* (1893), 108-19; *PGM*, 9 (1924-1926), 302; J. Hadden, *Hist. of Uniontown* (1913), 87, 146-49; L. Chalkley, *Rec. of Augusta Cnty., Va.* (1912), ii, 293, 353; *NJA* (2 ser.), ii, 435-37 ("no public commencement").

WFC

Jacob Conant

JACOB CONANT, A.B. Harvard 1777, was the son of Samuel and Rebecca Coffin Conant of Charlestown, Massachusetts. He was born there on September 1, 1758 and baptized two days later in the Congrega-tional church. His father was a baker by profession but also owned a substantial amount of property in Charlestown. After the town was burned by the British in June 1775, Samuel Conant estimated his losses to be £965 14s, of which £800 covered his buildings.

Jacob Conant entered the College as a freshman and on February 28, 1774 joined the Cliosophic Society. Probably because he was needed at home during the Revolution, he transferred to Harvard College. He applied for admission there on December 6, 1775, and on February 17, 1776, after passing the entrance examinations, he joined the junior class.

Concerning Conant's subsequent career no record has been found. He signed the oath of allegiance in Boston on April 1, 1778 but ap-parently took no active part in the war. It is likely that he died fairly young and unmarried. The will of Samuel Conant, drawn in 1794 and proved in 1802, mentions only Conant's mother, one brother, one sister, and the brother's two children. There is no reference to Jacob Conant or to five of his brothers and sisters, all of whom must be presumed to have died earlier.

SOURCES: F. O. Conant, *Hist. and Geneal. of the Conant Family* (1887), 239-40, 303; J. F. Hunnewell, *Century of Town Life* (1888), 129, 165; MS Steward's accounts, MS Clio. Soc. membership list, PUA; Harvard Univ. Arch.; Index, PCC.

James Crawford

JAMES CRAWFORD, A.B., Presbyterian clergyman, was one of the eleven children of Alexander and Mary McPheeters Crawford of Augusta County, Virginia. He was born on the family farm in the northern part of the county in 1752. When Crawford was twelve years old, his parents were reportedly killed by Indians. All of the children survived and were undoubtedly accepted into the homes of their many rela-tives in the area. James may have joined the family of his mother's brother John McPheeters, whose daughter Rebecca he married some-time before 1784. Like his brother Edward (A.B. 1775), Crawford was probably educated under the direction of John Brown (A.B. 1749), the supervisor of Liberty Hall Academy and pastor of the Timber Ridge and New Providence Presbyterian churches. Almost as soon as Edward Crawford entered the College, his younger brother besieged him with requests for books and advice on how he, too, might com-plete his education at Nassau Hall.

Crawford was apparently well enough trained at home to be considered for a teaching post of his own in 1773, but for some reason he was unable to accept the job. In August 1774, he was at Red Creek, Virginia and received specific instructions from his brother on what to study in order to pass the examination for admission into the junior class at the College. Edward thought that two years of higher education, the minimum permitted by President Witherspoon, would be quite adequate.

Crawford entered Nassau Hall as a junior in the fall of 1775, but he was not to have the two years he expected. The College closed in November 1776 and did not resume its regular sessions until the next summer. During the war-imposed recess, most of the students went home. But Crawford must have come back to Princeton to take his final examinations, for on September 23, 1777 a time when commencement exercises normally would have been held, Witherspoon presented him with a certificate in lieu of the diploma, certifying that he had completed all of the requirements for a bachelor's degree and would receive his diploma when affairs at the College were settled enough for it to be granted. It is likely that in 1777, as in 1776, the trustees had failed to muster the quorum needed to award degrees in course. Their formal approval of the degrees for the graduates in the Class of 1777 came in their meeting of April 16, 1778, although confusion regarding Crawford's A.B. and those of three of his classmates persisted for many years thereafter due to a variety of clerical errors.

From Princeton, Crawford returned to Virginia to begin his theological studies, but not, it seems, near his home. His pastor gave him a letter of recommendation to another church in which he noted that Crawford was "well affected towards American liberty." On October 26, 1779, he was licensed by the Presbytery of Hanover in a ceremony at Hampden-Sidney. An abscess in his side prevented him from preaching regularly, and even after the condition healed, it left him with a permanently fragile constitution. By 1783 he was strong enough to take a missionary tour of Kentucky, however, and he returned to settle there with his family in 1784, leaving a homestead and some cattle in Augusta County.

In Fayette County Crawford organized a congregation at Walnut Hill, six miles from Lexington. In March 1785 he bought a tract of land there from General Levi Todd with the stipulation that some of it would be used for a Presbyterian meeting house. The log church was built, and in November the Presbytery of Hanover sent Charles Cumming and Crawford's brother Edward to join David Rice (A.B.

1761) as a committee empowered to ordain Crawford in a ceremony at Danville, the first Presbyterian ordination in Kentucky.

Crawford founded another congregation in the Jessamine settlement, also near Lexington, before 1788. He was a member of the Presbytery of Transylvania. In 1789 he and Samuel Shannon (A.B. 1776) were on that body's commission to investigate the conduct of Adam Rankin, pastor of the New Providence Church. Rankin, who was also married to a McPheeters, claimed that his perfervid opposition to the use of Watts's *Psalms* was divinely inspired. At his trial in April 1792, Crawford testified to having heard Rankin assert that God communicated directly with him through dreams. It was a damning deposition.

In 1792 Crawford represented Fayette County in the Kentucky Constitutional Convention. With several other ministers, he argued for a constitutional ban on slavery in the new state, but that provision was defeated by a vote of 26 to 16. Crawford remained a firm abolitionist until he died.

Like most of his fellow alumni who went to Kentucky, Crawford was deeply involved in fostering education there. He and Caleb Baker Wallace (A.B. 1770) were trustees of the Transylvania Seminary. In October 1793 Crawford was one of the members of the board who elected James Moore president of the school. Their choice was immediately challenged by absent members, since the statutory requirements for choosing a president were ambiguous and the trustees who supported Moore had obviously tried to take advantage of the uncertainty. In February 1794, with more members present, the board appointed Henry Toulmin to the presidency. Toulmin's Unitarian leanings were totally unacceptable to the Presbyterian minority of trustees and they, including Crawford and Wallace, angrily resigned their seats.

When the presbytery established its own school, Kentucky Academy in Woodford County, Crawford, Wallace, Shannon, and Rice were all original trustees. The academy and the seminary finally merged to form Transylvania University in December 1798, and Wallace and Crawford sat on that institution's board as well. Crawford was also a commissioner in Kentucky for the Synod of Virginia's project of establishing an Indian school at the head of the Mad River. He was an original member of the West Lexington Presbytery in 1799 and of the Synod of Kentucky in 1802.

Crawford was a party to the massive religious revival that swept Kentucky in and after the summer of 1801. Normally a somber man, he was not a particularly popular preacher. But his zeal was never questioned. He was present at the great Cane Ridge meeting in Bourbon County in August 1801 and counted three thousand people who were so overcome by emotion that they collapsed on the spot. Whether he took the heat of the day into account in that calculation is unknown. Although he discussed with Rice and others ways in which the excesses of revivalist hysteria might be curbed, Crawford was known to sympathize with some of the most frenetic proselytizers, including Robert Marshall, before their enthusiasm led to a schism in the church in 1803.

In March 1803 Crawford preached to a large revival meeting at Paint Lick in Garrard County. The effort drained him, but he spoke again the next day and then rode nearly twenty miles to reach his home. Exhausted, he was unable to leave his bed for two weeks. He died on the night of April 11, 1803 and was buried in the yard of the new stone church at Walnut Hill. A memorial service in June featured a eulogy by Samuel Shannon.

Crawford's epitaph credits him with an A.M., which may have been granted by Transylvania University. It also includes a poem that ends:

> Then some vain hireling void of Special Grace
> Be brought to fill this faithful Pastor's Place.

The verse was not meant as an insult to Crawford's successor. James Welsh, pastor of the church in Lexington, had selected the poem for his friend's gravestone. He had seen it on the grave of his father-in-law, Joseph Smith, at Upper Buffalo Creek, Pennsylvania. Smith's friend Thaddeus Dod (A.B. 1773), who never hesitated to be blunt in expressing his opinions, had written the poem for Smith, and Welsh simply plagiarized it without any apparent concern for the feelings of the new minister at Walnut Hill.

Crawford was survived by his wife and at least one daughter.

SOURCES: See James Ashton Bayard (A.B. 1777) for awarding of degrees to this class. R. H. Bishop, *Outline of the Hist. of the Chh. . . . in Ky.* (1824), 159-62; R. Davidson, *Hist. of the Pres. Chh. . . . in Ky.* (1847), 79, 80, 90-92, 107, 128, 369; *KSHS Reg.*, 54 (1956), 113-15, 117, 120, 121 ("well affected towards American liberty" and epitaph), 227; 34 (1936), 281-82; 42 (1944), 103; 39 (1941), 61; Edward Crawford Papers, PPPrHi; G. W. Ranck, *Hist. of Lexington, Ky.* (1872), 108-109; A. Rankin, *A Process in the Transilvania Presbytery* (1793), 46-50; L. Collins, *Hist. of Ky.* (1878), I, 355; *Journals of the Convention, July 1788-April 1792: Minutes of 1792*, 22; N. H. Sonne, *Liberal Ky.* (1968), 54-56; R. Peter, *Transylvania Univ.* (1896), 63 & n, 72; R. McNemar, *Ky. Revival* (1846), 17.

MANUSCRIPTS: PPPrHi

Nicholas Fish

NICHOLAS FISH, soldier, speculator, banker, public official, was the son of Jonathan and Elizabeth Sackett Fish. He was born on August 28, 1758 in New York City, where his father was a wealthy merchant and customs officer. The family had a country residence at Newtown, Long Island, and it was there that Fish received his primary education from Benjamin Moore (King's 1768).

Possibly as early as 1772, Fish entered the New York City law office of John Morin Scott as an apprentice. Scott's political activities were too Whiggish for Jonathan Fish's tastes, however, and he sent his son to the College to remove him from the radical atmosphere. In 1774 Jonathan Fish resigned his position at the customs house and retreated permanently to Newtown. At about the same time, after less than a year at the College, Nicholas Fish returned to Scott's employ. In spite of his family's Loyalism, he was thereafter an enthusiastic Whig.

Fish's closest friends were his fellow apprentice Richard Varick and two King's College students, Robert Troup and Alexander Hamilton. All four belonged to a debating club at King's and by early 1775 all were members of the Hearts of Oak, a volunteer militia company whose motto was "Liberty or Death!" In April, Fish was a lieutenant in Colonel William Malcolm's New York Regiment, soon part of Colonel John Lasher's First Battalion of New York Independents. On January 31, 1776, he voted with the majority of officers in favor of joining the Continental Army, and with William Willcocks (A.B. 1769), reported that decision to the New York Provincial Congress.

Fish retained his position as Scott's legal clerk, tending to the city's records until May 1776, when business was so slow that he advised Scott, then a general officer, to close the office. New York became a garrison town in 1776, and Fish regretted most of all the absence of women. "I find from the want of females," he told Varick, "the necessity of them."

As brigade major to Scott's First New York Regiment, Fish fought in the battle of Long Island and, while the Americans were making their hasty retreat, was personally responsible for warning a Delaware regiment that had been forgotten in the confusion. He then took part in the action at Harlem Heights, where he blamed the American rout on the "dastardly sons of Cowardice" from Connecticut, and then saw action at White Plains.

When the enlistment of the New York militia expired late in 1776, Scott urged the state government to give his young clerk a commission in the new establishment, declaring that there was "not a better

Nicholas Fish, Class of 1777
BY EDWARD G. MALBONE

Brigade-Major in the Army." The Continental Congress appointed Fish a major in the Second Regiment of New York Continentals on November 21, 1776, and while he awaited that commission, he lived at Scott's home in Kingston. In December he was given command of a sloop under a flag of truce to bring the families of some prominent Loyalists to New York City. He visited the H.M.S. *Asia* in the harbor and there learned that his mother was seriously ill. His request to be allowed to see her was refused by the British, and for the rest of his life, he believed that the enemy had thereby tried to force him to change sides in the war. He would not do so, and he never saw his mother again.

In February 1777 Fish had temporary command of Scott's regiment while the general attended the New York Convention at Kingston. By April he had joined the Second New York, with which he served throughout the Saratoga campaign. At Valley Forge in March 1778, he was named a deputy inspector general of the army under Baron von Steuben. That June, at the battle of Monmouth, Fish had command of a light infantry unit. He was with the Second New York in its winter quarters at Wawasink, New Jersey at the end of the year.

Washington was so pleased with Fish's performance as brigade inspector that he assigned him to the same post with General George

Clinton's brigade in General John Sullivan's expedition against the Six Nations in May 1779. Fish was ill when he received his orders and for a time considered leaving the army. But Washington hoped that he would accept, for he found the major an "officer of merit." His health recovered, Fish joined Sullivan before the end of May.

Back in New Jersey that winter, Fish led raids against Loyalists on Staten Island. Washington then sent him to West Point, New York. In September 1780 he was one of three New York officers who appealed to the state to do something for the relief of soldiers whose pay had depreciated. And in January 1781 he returned to his regiment at Albany in time to help relieve Fort Schuyler and then to inspect the returns of militia units around Schenectady. He was deputized by Governor Clinton to persuade Lieutenant Colonel Jacobus S. Bruyn (Class of 1775) to remain in the army, but Fish knew as well as anyone that that would be a difficult assignment against the "force of female entreaty," for since the winter of 1779 he too had been contemplating matrimony.

Any such personal plans were postponed in the spring of 1781, while the Second New York marched south. On October 14, as second in command to his friend Hamilton, Fish led the assault against the British redoubts at Yorktown, Virginia and then secured the positions as soon as they were captured. In December he was at Pompton, Morris County, New Jersey, where he received some urgent personal advice from Hamilton. Fish had decided not to marry after all, leaving his erstwhile fiancée "in great distress." He already had a reputation as a womanizer, and Hamilton advised him to act honorably, since rumors were rife that this was not his "first infidelity." The girl's father, a "Mr. G.," was on his way to see Fish. Forewarned, Hamilton thought, was forearmed.

That interview with an enraged father may have been Fish's last brush with combat. His military duties thereafter were entirely administrative. He was stationed at Newburgh, New York in March, 1783 and, according to a much later account by John Armstrong, Jr. (Class of 1776), was one of the young officers there who subscribed to the Newburgh Letters with their implied threat of violence unless Congress acted to insure the payment of their rightful pensions. Fish's own recollection was that he had been out of camp when Armstrong wrote the Newburgh Letters and that he had had nothing to do with them. At the end of the war, Fish was breveted to the rank of lieutenant colonel. He was among the original members of the New York Society of the Cincinnati, serving as its first assistant treasurer and, from 1797 to 1803 and in 1805, as its president.

Fish's plans for his life were uncertain. He told Governor Clinton in April 1783, while applying for the post of naval officer of the port of New York, that he had forgotten what law he knew and had lost "all relish for the profession." He did not receive that appointment, but in the spring of 1784, Clinton sent him on a special mission to Governor Frederick Haldimand of Canada to discuss the transfer of the frontier forts, as stipulated in the Treaty of Paris. Haldimand, however, had no intention of discussing the issue with the agent of a single state.

In November 1784 Hamilton recommended Fish to Francisco de Miranda, who was in the United States hoping to raise an army of 5,000 men to liberate Venezuela from Spain. Nothing came of that scheme, and Fish spent most of his time dabbling in stock and land speculation. He bought up confiscated Loyalist property in New York City and upstate, eventually accumulating many thousands of acres, some of which he later sold at a profit. But with no alternative employment, Fish rejoined the army in April 1785 as a major in the First (and only) United States Regiment, organized at West Point to defend the frontier against Indian attacks. After several months as commander of Fort McIntosh and other posts along the Ohio River, he resigned his commission in August 1786 to accept Clinton's appointment as the first adjutant general of New York. Among his duties was the welcome of George Washington for the presidential inauguration in April 1789.

Fish lived at Mrs. Mary Daubeney's boarding house on Wall Street in New York and was a member of the clique that met at the Belvedere House tavern and called itself the "Belvedere Club." In 1792 he bought one of the original shares in the Tontine Coffee House. A year earlier he had applied for the federal post of inspector of the revenue in New York but had failed to obtain it. Washington proposed him for adjutant general of the army with the rank of lieutenant colonel in August 1792, but Fish respectfully declined the offer, because he was simply no longer interested in military life.

The office of revenue supervisor for New York fell open in 1792 when William Stephens Smith (A.B. 1774) resigned. It went briefly to John Armstrong, Jr. and then on December 30, 1793 to Fish. During the Whiskey Rebellion, Fish was responsible for provisioning the army in western Pennsylvania. Whether he liked military affairs or not, he could not, it seems, escape them. At late as 1799 he and William Stephens Smith worked together to design a new uniform for the army, and he was a member of a municipal committee that bought cannon to defend New York.

Both personally and politically, Fish was very close to Alexander Hamilton. In July 1795 he acted as his friend's second in an affair of honor with Commodore James Nicholson. Fish and Rufus King worked with Nicholson's seconds, Brockholst Livingston (A.B. 1774) and DeWitt Clinton to achieve a peaceful settlement of the quarrel. In April 1797 Hamilton urged Treasury Secretary Oliver Wolcott, Jr. to consider Fish for the post of collector of the port of New York. Again, however, the job was already filled. Claiming a conscientious objection to dueling, and probably aware that another nonviolent settlement was not likely, Fish declined to serve as Hamilton's second when his friend went to meet Aaron Burr (A.B. 1772) at Weehauken in 1804. He was, however, an executor of Hamilton's will and a constant protector and benefactor to Hamilton's widow and children.

During the Quasi-War, Fish took a prominent role in mobilizing anti-French sentiment in New York. He chaired a meeting of the "Youths" of the city who volunteered to fight against France. When Brockholst Livingston satirized the gathering in a newspaper article, Fish took the sarcasm quietly. Another participant, James Jones, took it more seriously and died in a duel with Livingston.

An adamant Federalist, Fish was exasperated by the election of Thomas Jefferson in 1800. He opposed the new administration's plan to reduce the army and called the Jeffersonians "Demagogues" when they moved to repeal the Judiciary Act of 1801. He feared that the demise of the Alien Act would open the nation to an invasion of "Foreigners of every description."

On April 30, 1803, Fish married Elizabeth Stuyvesant, the daughter of Petrus Stuyvesant. It was not an altogether happy occasion, however, for Fish's reputation as a ladies' man was still intact. During the fifteen years he lived at Mrs. Daubeney's, he had professed to be in love with her daughter Charlotte, and their relationship was obviously understood by his friends. After she was jilted for Elizabeth Stuyvesant, Charlotte Daubeney drowned herself in the North River.

Once married, Fish took a more active interest in politics than he had before. His house on Stuyvesant Street, a gift from his father-in-law, was a favorite stop for some of the great names in the Federalist Party. In 1804 and 1805 he was an election inspector for the city's ninth ward, and on February 24, 1806, he was appointed by the city to assess taxes for an extension of Broadway. He served frequently as an assessor after being elected an alderman in November 1806. On the Common Council until 1817, he was the senior member of the committee on defense, taking charge of preparations to protect the city in the War of 1812. That responsibility sent him to Washington and

Albany during a conflict that he, like most Federalists, vigorously opposed. He lost two elections for lieutenant governor of the state in
1810 and 1811 and one for Congress before the war, and in August
1812 he chaired a meeting in New York that characterized the dispute
with Britain as a reckless and unwarranted risk of American independence. His last try for public office, again unsuccessful, was in
1821, when he sought a place in the state constitutional convention.

In 1817 Fish became a trustee of Columbia College. In 1823 he was
treasurer of the board and from 1824 to 1832 served as its chairman.
He was also a vestryman of St. Mark's Episcopal Church in the Bowery
from 1805 to 1821 and then served fourteen years as a warden of that
congregation. During some of those years, he was also a member of the
Standing Committee of the Diocese of New York. His income, derived
from his real estate, was substantial and in 1815 and 1820 he was taxed
on $7,500 in personal property alone. With other owners of vast tracts
of upstate land, he called for the construction of a canal between Lake
Champlain and the St. Lawrence in 1824, a project that would have
multiplied the value of his land holdings.

In 1824 Fish entertained Lafayette at his home and then went with
his former comrade to Albany and Yorktown, where the Marquis insisted that a commemorative laurel wreath be presented to Fish rather
than to himself. In his subsequent correspondence with Lafayette, Fish
enunciated more clearly than anywhere else his thoughts about public
affairs. He refused to support either Jackson or Adams in the election
of 1828, for both candidates disgusted him. But he could not remain
neutral during the nullification controversy of 1830-1833. "The idea
of any one State withdrawing from the Union whenever she may judge
it expedient," he wrote, "is I think subversive of the principles upon
which the Union and government were formed and altogether inad-
missible." In December 1830 he congratulated Lafayette on the recent
revolution in France, which he contrasted favorably with the excesses
of the first French Revolution. By then Fish had sufficiently recon-
ciled himself to some of the older Republicans to visit former President James Monroe, who had moved to New York and who sent his
regards to Lafayette through Fish.

Fish had held stock in New York banks since at least 1803. In 1831,
at the age of seventy-three, he became president of the Butchers' and
Drovers' Bank. He was, meanwhile, actively promoting the Mohawk
and Hudson Railroad between Albany and Schenectady. In 1832 Fish
became too ill to continue his duties at the bank, the church, and the
college. Infirm for more than a year, he died on June 20, 1833, and was
buried at St. Mark's. His wife and five children, including Hamilton

Fish (Columbia 1827), later governor of New York and Secretary of State of the United States, shared his estate. A man who believed in discipline, order, and propriety, at least after he was married, Fish had been the personification of authority and respectability to his children. His friends, including John Pintard (A.B. 1776), remembered him as "one of the best bred politest men" of New York.

Sources: *DAB*; S. Fish, *Ancestors of Hamilton Fish* (1929), 42-43; A. Nevins, *Hamilton Fish* (1957), I, 5-9, 17; S. Fish, *1600-1914* (1942), 30 ("want of females"), 81 ("Demagogues," "foreigners"), 106 ("any state withdrawing"), 23-112, passim; F. G. Mather, *Refugees of 1776 from Long Island to Conn.* (1913), 669; als NF to T. Pickering, 26 Dec 1823, Pickering MSS, MHi; NF to H. Knox, 7 Sep 1792, Washington MSS; *N.Y. Arch.*, I, 51, 65; W.H.W. Sabine, ed., *Hist. Memoirs of William Smith*, II (1958), 72; Force, *Am. Arch.* (4 ser.), VI, 1,423; (5 ser), I, 913, 982; III, 301 ("not a better Brigade-Major"), 834, 1,351, 1,464; *Narratives of the Rev. in N.Y.* (1975), 99 ("dastardly sons of Cowardice"); *Washington Writings*, XI, 174; XV, 129 ("officer of merit"), 173, 258; XIX, 466; XX, 13; XXV, 41; XXVI, 278, 366; XXXII, 105, 117, 152n; L. W. Murray, ed., *Notes on Sullivan Expedition of 1779* (1929), 6, 79; *Clinton Papers*, VI, 216-17, 588 ("female entreaty"), 716; VIII, 137-38 ("all relish"), 217; *Hamilton Papers*, II, 680, 684 ("first infidelity"); III, 585-87 & n; XIV, 269-71 & nn; XVII, 297, 470-71; XXIII, 294; XXIV, 126n; XVIII, 471, 490, 501-503; XXI, 54-55 & n; E. W. Spaulding, *N.Y. in the Critical Period* (1932), 135; W. C. Ford, ed., *Correspondence and Journals of Samuel Blachley Webb* (1894), III, 40-41; H. B. Yoshpe, *Disposition of Loyalist Estates in the Southern District of . . . N.Y.* (1939), 32, 63-64, 68; A. C. Flick, *Loyalism in N.Y. during the Amer. Rev.* (1901), 230, 235; *NYGBR*, 30 (1899), 139, 242; 32 (1901), 29; 72 (1941), 83; 84 (1953), 14; *WMQ* (3 ser.), 31 (1974), 276; O. Pickering, *Life of Timothy Pickering* (1867), I, 435; H. Fish, *N.Y. State: Battlefield of the Rev. War* (1976), 167-69, 183, 226-28; *JCC*, XXI, 488; *PMHB*, 19 (1895), 334-35; 78 (1954), 342-53; G. Hunt, *Cal. of Applications and Recommendations for Office during the Presidency of George Washington* (1901), 43; *NYHS Coll.*, LXII, 254; LXXIII, 164 ("best bred politest"); J. A. Scoville, *Old Merchants of N.Y. City* (1865), III, 67; *MCCCNY*, III-VIII, passim; *Mil. Min., Council of Appointment, St. of N.Y.*, II, 1,171-72; D. R. Fox, *Decline of Aristocracy in Politics of N.Y.* (1965), 156-57, 170 & n, 237; P. G. Hubert, Jr., *Merchants Bank of . . . N.Y.* (1903), 28.

Manuscripts: PHi, NNC

Alexander Graham

Alexander Graham was the son of Ennis Graham, prosperous New York City merchant, and so a brother of John Graham, also of the Class of 1777, and of Edward Graham (A.B. 1786). In making his will on September 15, 1777, Ennis Graham described himself as a native of North Britain and a merchant lately of New York City then residing in Middlesex County, New Jersey. His new home was at Bound Brook, and the witnesses to his will, proved on September 24, 1777, included Israel Read (A.B. 1748), longtime Presbyterian minister of that place. The inventory of his estate carried an evaluation of more than £25,000 and showed that he possessed substantial real properties in New York City, Brooklyn, and at Bound Brook, and, in addition, some 7,000 acres in "Cumberland County," which was in the disputed area between New York and New Hampshire that already was in the process of becoming Vermont. His wife Elizabeth and two New York merchants were charged with the execution of the will. Her advertisement in 1778 of an extensive list of items for sale—broadcloths, serges, velvets, silks, stockings, garters, gloves, buttons, and so on— indicates that his primary business was in drygoods, much of the stock no doubt imported from Scotland. Graham, who politically was a Whig, probably had been living in New Jersey since the British occupation of New York City in the fall of 1776.

He had married Elizabeth Wilcox as recently as the summer of 1763, so she can hardly be viewed as the mother of either Alexander or John Graham, who apparently entered Nassau Hall together in 1773. Surviving records of the College's steward strongly suggest that they were first enrolled at the beginning of the academic year in November 1773. In the steward's account for November 6, 1774 to April 10, 1775, the two Grahams are listed as members of the sophomore class. An account book kept by a local merchant shows that Alexander Graham, described as a student, was in residence through the summer of 1775. A cash settlement of his account for £4 15s on the following November 9 suggests that he had returned for the beginning of his junior year. The merchant carried no account in the name of John Graham, but the purchase by Alexander in August 1775 of two felt hats, each at a price of 7s 6d, raises a question of whether the father may have entrusted the funds to him, either as the older or the more responsible of the two. John Graham was certainly present when President Witherspoon dismissed the College late in November 1776, and it is possible, though perhaps unlikely, that both of them were on hand at that time for the beginning of their senior year.

It has been very difficult to determine with any degree of certainty the subsequent career of Alexander Graham. He could have been the Alexander Graham who served during the Revolution with the Eighth Pennsylvania Regiment of the Continental Line, rising from the rank of ensign to that of second lieutenant on August 9, 1777, and to first lieutenant on April 1, 1779. He is said to have resigned in that year. That a native of New York and a resident of New Jersey should have joined a Pennsylvania unit may seem surprising, but it is not impossible. It might be expected that after his military service Alexander would either settle in Pennsylvania or return to New York, but it has not been established that he followed either of these alternatives, and it can only be said that the census returns of 1790 show no Alexander Graham living a that time either in New York or Pennsylvania.

Whatever may have been his residence, he and his sister Sarah, together with her husband Charles Tomkins, entered a suit in chancery in New York against Elizabeth Graham and the other executors of Ennis Graham's estate in 1785, a case in which Aaron Burr (A.B. 1772) appeared as attorney for the defendants and Morgan Lewis (A.B. 1773) represented the complainants. The proceedings, which were not fully terminated until several years had passed, provide eloquent testimony to the complexity and extent of the estate.

SOURCES: See John Graham (Class of 1777); *N.Y. Wills*, XII, 220-21; *N.J. Wills*, V, 209; *NJA* (2 ser.), II, 140; IV, 259; *Cal. N.Y. . . . Land Papers* (1864), 321-22, 439, 459, 558; *Marriage Licenses . . . Province of N.Y.* (1860), 157; *MCCCNY, 1675-1776*, VI, 33, 36; *MCCCNY, 1784-1831*, I, 230, 245-46; III, 6; M. H. Thomas, *Columbia Univ., Officers and Alumni* (1936), 107. Alexander and John Graham are listed on two other steward's accounts: 25 May 1773 to 25 Sep 1774; and an undated list that raises the possibility that they were enrolled earlier than the date given above. Ms Steward's accounts, PUA; Patterson Acct. Bk; Heitman; *Pa. Arch.* (5 serv.), III, 316, 328, 329, 333, 335, 341, 368. The only Alexander Graham found in *DAR Patriot Index* was from N.C. with inclusive dates 1738-1794. If Heitman is followed, Alexander Graham was first enrolled in the Fifth Pa. Battalion as an ensign on 9 Aug 1776, and two different dates in 1779 are given for his resignation by the original and revised editions. See also microfilm of Papers of Aaron Burr, Reel 18, frames 496-558.

WFC

John Graham

JOHN GRAHAM was one of the seven sons of Ennis Graham, wealthy New York City merchant, and so a brother of Alexander Graham, another member of the Class of 1777, and of Edward Graham (A.B. 1786). Ennis Graham was a native of Scotland whose chief stock in trade seems to have been drygoods imported from that country. His will, dated September 15, 1777 and probated on the following September 24, disposed of properties inventoried at a value above £25,000. Included were substantial holdings of real estate in New York City, Brooklyn, New Jersey, and in the area then in the process of becoming Vermont. The will was probated in Middlesex County, New Jersey, where Ennis lived at Bound Brook, having apparently taken up a New Jersey residence at the time of the British occupation of New York in late 1776. His exile carries its own testimony to the political identification he previously had established with the city's Whigs. He had married Elizabeth Wilcox after obtaining a license on July 21, 1763, and she, together with two New York merchants, was charged as executors of the will. It can hardly be assumed that Elizabeth Wilcox was the mother of either of the two Grahams who apparently entered the College in the fall of 1773.

Surviving steward's accounts of payments for tuition and board indicate that the Grahams were in continuous residence until at least the spring of 1775, and these records show them to have been members of the sophomore class during the academic year 1774-1775. There is firm evidence that Alexander was in residence through the summer of 1775, and that John returned to the College in November 1776 for the beginning of his senior year is indicated by President Witherspoon's report of his family's flight from the village as the British army approached late in that month. The report is found in the president's letter of January 8, 1777 to his youngest son David Witherspoon (A.B. 1774). "We carried nothing away of all our effects," Witherspoon wrote, "but what could be carried upon one team. Benjamin Hawkins drove your mother in the old chair, and I rode the sorrel mare, and made John Graham drive the four young colts."

John Graham became one of the large majority of his classmates who never returned to the College for the completion of their education, and even a broad outline of his later career has to be left here uncertain. There were many Grahams in America at the time of the Revolution, and all too many of them were named John. In New York City alone, the census of 1790 shows no fewer than five John Grahams. Those did not, however, include the College's alumnus. The proceedings in a suit in chancery instituted in New York in 1785 by Alexander Graham, his sister Sarah, and her husband Charles Tomkins against Elizabeth Graham and the other executors of the estate of Ennis Graham reveal that John Graham died at some time between April 1786 and the spring of 1790. The evidence is found in a schedule of advances by Elizabeth Graham in account with John Graham, deceased, which shows periodic advances made between October 1, 1777 and April 1, 1786. The accounting specified chiefly payments for items of clothing and one was for board, a possible indication that John continued to be some kind of a student although the period seems unduly long for preparation for one of the professions.

SOURCES: See Alexander Graham (Class of 1777); P. L. White, *Beekmans of N.Y.* (1956), 435n; *Christian Advocate*, 2 (1824), 443 ("four young colts"); Microfilm of Papers of Aaron Burr, Reel 18, frames 552-54. *NYGBR*, 55 (1924), 32, identifies a John Graham, merchant of N.Y. City, as the son of James Graham of Westchester Cnty. The likeliest candidate in N.C., where the family was prominent and had associations with CNJ graduates, is eliminated by a certificate from Liberty Hall

Academy of Charlotte, dated 22 Nov 1778, specifying that John Graham had been a student there for "the space of four years preceding the date hereof" (Foote, *Sketches, N.C.*, 516; photo copy, NjP). The Princeton student is not to be confused with the well-known John Graham (Columbia A.B. 1790). The will of Theodorus Van Wyck of Dutchess Cnty., dated 1 Oct 1775 and proved 14 Aug 1782, (*N.Y. Wills*, IX, 281) carries a bothersome reference to his grandson John Graham, son of his deceased daughter Elizabeth, specifying that the "said John Graham is to be carryed through Colledge," but this lead has not been productive.

WFC

Samuel Reading Hackett

SAMUEL READING HACKETT, soldier and man of property, was born about 1757, the son of John Hackett and his wife, Elizabeth Reading Hackett, probably in Sussex County, New Jersey, where the father owned substantial properties, served as a county justice, and may have given his name to Hackettstown, now in Warren County. His mother was the daughter of John Reading, who as senior member of the council served for a time as acting governor of the province after the death of Governor Jonathan Belcher in 1757. She was a sister of Anne Reading, who married Reverend Charles Beatty, trustee of the College from 1763 to 1772, thus her son was a first cousin of John Beatty (A.B. 1769) and Charles Clinton Beatty (A.B. 1775). Another connection with Princeton had been established through the marriage of Samuel's aunt Mary Reading to Reverend William Mills (A.B. 1756).

John Hackett died intestate at the age of thirty-eight in September 1766. His widow and two others were charged with the administration of the estate, to which Samuel seems to have been the sole heir. In August 1767 he became a ward of his uncle George Reading, on petition from his grandfather and his mother, who planned to accompany her sister, Mrs. Charles Beatty, to Britain in search of medical care for a serious illness. Mrs. Beatty died there, and Elizabeth Hackett and her brother-in-law remained in England for the better part of two years, from 1767 until their return to New York in July 1769. In the following October, Elizabeth Hackett once more assumed responsibilities as guardian for her son.

Where and by whom young Hackett was prepared for college have not been discovered, but there is little room for doubt that he was first enrolled in the College in November 1773. Not only does his name appear on the steward's account for the period May 25, 1773 to September 25, 1774 but a further account for the period of November 1774 to April 10, 1775 shows him in that academic year as a member of the sophomore class. Records of the Cliosophic Society indicate that he was admitted to membership on January 25, 1774 and that his pseudonym was "Orpheus," after the musician of Greek mythology. Correspondence of the Beatty family places cousin "Sammy" Hackett in Princeton during the summer of 1775, and an account book of a local merchant shows him to have been a customer at various times through that year, the last entry on November 23 arguing that he may have returned from the fall vacation for the beginning of his junior year. No evidence of his presence in Princeton thereafter has been found, but it seems likely enough that he may have continued at the College through at least a part of the academic year 1775-1776.

It is unlikely, however, that he returned for his senior year. Instead, on November 29, 1776, the day on which President Witherspoon dismissed the College because of the approach of the British army, Samuel Hackett was commissioned an ensign in the Fourth Company of New Jersey's Third Batallion, in the so-called "second establishment" of the Continental Army. He was promoted to the rank of second lieutenant in the following January. According to one source, he resigned in October 1777. Another indicates that he served until September 26, 1780.

Thereafter, the surviving record is skimpy. Reading Beatty, in a letter of August 12, 1783 to his sister Elizabeth, widow of Philip Vickers Fithian (A.B. 1772) and then wife of Philip's cousin Joel Fithian, reported having recently seen "Sam" Hackett at Amwell in Hunterdon County. The next item is Hackett's will, dated January 11, 1790 and proved January 29, 1790. He described himself as of Hacketts Town. His first bequest was to his "kinswoman" Mary Halsted, the daughter of William Mills and Mary Reading who had married Dr. Robert Halsted (A.B. 1765), for her care of his mother, who seems to have died that same month. Among other bequests was a silver bowl to his cousin Doctor Reading Beatty. To the Presbyterian church of Independence, the township in which Hackettstown lay, he left £40, and to Sarah Young, £6, "if she nurses me until my death." The bulk of his "fortune" was described as being in the hands of his uncle Augustine Reid, who had married his mother's younger sister Sarah Reading. The cause of Hackett's death is unknown. He apparently had never married.

SOURCES: J. G. Leach, Memorials of the Reading, Howell, Yerkes, Watts, Latham, and Elkins Families (1898), 48, 51; N.J. Wills, IV, 168; VII, 94; G. S. Klett, ed., Journals of Charles Beatty, 1762-1769 (1962), 79, 80, 84, 86, 91, 98; MS Steward's accounts, MS Clio. Soc. membership list, PUA; NJHSP, 81 (1963), 36n., 38; Patterson Acct. Bk.; Heitman; Stryker, Off. Reg., 36, 37, 100; VHM, 16 (1931), 70 ("Sam"); J. P. Snell, Hist. of Sussex and Warren Counties, N.J. (1881), 581, 584.

WFC

Luther Halsey

LUTHER HALSEY, soldier and schoolmaster, a native of Morristown, Morris County, New Jersey, was born on May 10, 1758. His father, Silas Halsey, was a prosperous hatter and member of the Morristown Presbyterian Church. Halsey's mother, Abigail Howell Halsey, was his father's second wife. By his first marriage, Silas Halsey was also the father of Jeremiah Halsey (A.B. 1752).

Halsey probably entered the College as a sophomore, while his half-brother was clerk to the board of trustees. On March 26, 1775, he joined the Cliosophic Society, using the name of the ancient Numidian kings, "Juba," as a pseudonym. In that same year he enlisted in the Morris County Militia, and in November he entered the Second Battalion of New Jersey Continentals as a sergeant. On November 28, 1776, he became adjutant of the reorganized Second Battalion. One year later, as a lieutenant, he was adjutant of the Second Regiment of the New Jersey Line. Under Colonel Elias Dayton, the unit took part in the Yorktown campaign of 1781.

Halsey received no further promotions until he was discharged in November 1783. Then, in accordance with an act of Congress, all officers who had remained in one grade for seven years were breveted to the next higher rank. It was as a brevet captain, therefore, that he became an original member of the New Jersey Society of the Cincinnati and petitioned Congress for a pension, which was awarded on June 11, 1789.

After the war, Halsey settled in Elizabethtown, New Jersey. Even before he left the army, he had married Sarah Foster of that town. They had three children before she died in August 1787. Their youngest son died only weeks afterward. Halsey may have supported his family by tutoring youngsters, for in June 1789, when the Elizabethtown Academy opened, he was given charge of English instruction there. He had by then married his first wife's sister, Demaris Foster. She died on September 12, 1789, before they had any children.

In 1790 John Taylor (A.B. 1770) became principal and Latin teacher at Elizabethtown Academy. Halsey continued on the faculty at least until July 1791, when a second of his sons died in Elizabethtown. At some point, he moved with his third wife Abigail, another of the Foster sisters, and his surviving daughter to Schenectady, New York. The date of that move is uncertain, but it was probably in 1792 or 1793, when Taylor went to Schenectady to become director of the Union Academy there. Certainly, Halsey was on the faculty at Union

Luther Halsey, Class of 1777

by January 1794, when the first of the thirteen children of his third marriage was born in Schenectady.

However devout a Presbyterian Halsey may have been before, his zealous religiosity did not sit well with his neighbors in New York. His work in circulating tracts and copies of the Bible caused no trouble, but when he decided that serving liquor at funerals was a sin, he made a few enemies. And when he physically tried to stop the carting of produce to market on Sundays, the people of Schenectady had had enough. Halsey was prosecuted for causing a riot. Undoubtedly, the community's attitude contributed to the peripatetic life Halsey led after 1798.

He moved first to Whitesboro in Oneida County, New York, where at least one of his children was born. He was back in Schenectady in 1800, but by 1802 he had settled in Newburgh, Orange County. Another child was born in Schenectady in 1804, after which the family apparently went back to Newburgh. Halsey was principal of the local academy there sometime after 1809. Orange County may have been his permanent home for the rest of his life. Halsey died on February 28, 1830, while visiting one of his married daughters in Cincinnati, Ohio, and was buried there.

Halsey was survived by his third wife and at least seven of his children. Their careers reflected the religious and intellectual training they had received at home. The Reverend Doctor Luther Halsey, Jr. (Union 1812) was professor of chemistry and natural sciences at Nassau Hall from 1824 to 1829. The Reverend Doctor Abraham O. Halsey (Union 1822) and his brother the Reverend Job Foster Halsey (Union 1819) both studied divinity at the theological seminary in Princeton. Another son was the Reverend John Taylor Halsey (Union 1816). Halsey's eldest daughter, Abigail, married the Reverend Isaac Van Doren (A.B. 1793).

SOURCES: J. L. and E. D. Halsey, *Thomas Halsey of Hertfordshire* (1895), 61-62, 97-102; *NEHGR*, 45 (1891), 45-47; *N.J. Wills*, v, 220; MS Clio. Soc. membership list, PUA; *Soc. of the Cincinnati in . . . N.J.* (1960), 92-93; *Index, Rev. War Pension Applications* (1966); E. F. Hatfield, *Hist. of Elizabeth, N.J.* (1868), 560; E. M. Ruttenber and L. H. Clark, *Hist. of Orange Cnty., N.Y.* (1881), 324; *NJHSP* (n.s.), 2 (1917), 97.

James Hanna

JAMES HANNA, A.B., A.M. 1784, probably a farmer, was the son of John Hanna (A.B. 1755), a Presbyterian clergyman and physician in Hunterdon County, New Jersey, and his wife, Mary McCrea Hanna. Hanna's mother was the sister of John McCrea (A.B. 1762) and half-sister of Robert McCrea (Class of 1776). Hanna's parents were married in approximately 1759, and he was the first of their thirteen children. His two brothers who survived infancy were John Andre (A.B. 1782) and William R. Hanna (A.B. 1790).

It is likely that Hanna prepared for college under his father's supervision and that he entered Nassau Hall as a junior in the fall of 1775. He was probably among the few students who returned to Princeton in the summer of 1777, when the College was again in session after a hiatus imposed by the war in the previous November. According to President Witherspoon's public announcement in August 1778, the qualified seniors were examined for their degrees in August 1777. But there were no public commencement exercises that year, presumably because, for the second year in a row, too few trustees had been able to meet to authorize the awarding of degrees. That was remedied in April 1778, and Witherspoon's announcement in the summer of that year was to advise the graduates of 1777 that they might collect their diplomas whenever they wished. Hanna and his classmates John Young Noel and Samuel Vickers must not have applied for their diplomas at once, for in 1782 a confused board of trustees admitted them again to the A.B. degree.

Two years later, Hanna received his second degree. That was usually the mark of a man who had entered one of the professions, but in Hanna's case no evidence of a professional career has been found. He resided at Newtown, Sussex County, New Jersey, the home of his wife Mary Stewart, daughter of John Stewart. Sussex County was the most sparsely settled region in the state, and it may be surmised that Hanna kept a farm there. Sometime after 1793 he moved to Frankfort, Franklin County, Kentucky, the residence of another branch of the Hanna family to whom he was probably a second cousin. He was alive in December 1801, when as a "resident of another state" he renounced his share of his father's estate. After that, no record of his life has been found.

SOURCES: See James Ashton Bayard (A.B. 1777) for granting of degrees to Class of 1777. *Som. Cnty. Hist. Quart.*, 7 (1918), 92; MS Steward's accounts, PUA; *N.J. Gazette*, 16 Sep 1778, 9 Oct 1782, 7 Oct 1784 (A.M.); J. S. Norton, *N.J. in 1793* (1973), 280; *N.J. Wills*, x, 197 ("resident of another state"); *KSHS Reg.*, 44 (1946), 234-35.

Benjamin Hawkins

BENJAMIN HAWKINS, congressman, senator, and Indian agent extraordinary, was born August 15, 1754, in what became Bute and after 1779 Warren County, North Carolina, the third son of Colonel Philemon Hawkins and his wife, Delia Martin, natives of Virginia. The father was a chief aide of Governor Tryon when the Regulators were defeated in 1771 and a member of the Provincial Congress in the spring and fall of 1776. Benjamin was trained for college by Charles Pettigrew, later bishop-elect of the Protestant Episcopal Church, who conducted a school in Bute County at some time before 1774. Benjamin's younger brother Joseph (Class of 1777) and their neighbor Nathaniel Macon (Class of 1778) also attended this school. Just when Benjamin entered the College is unknown, but he was a member of the senior class when in November of 1776 President Witherspoon announced to the students a suspension of studies at the College because of the war.

Of Hawkins's experience at Princeton the surviving record tells nothing until a letter from President Witherspoon of January 8, 1777

Benjamin Hawkins, Class of 1777

to his son David (A.B. 1774) regarding the family's flight from the town suggests that Benjamin had won a reputation for responsibility. "We carried nothing away of all our effects," the president wrote, "but what could be carried upon one team. Benjamin Hawkins drove your mother in the old chair, and I rode the sorrel mare, and made John Graham drive the four young colts." There is uncertainty too regarding Hawkins's career immediately thereafter. He may or he may not have joined General Washington, as tradition would have it. Whatever the fact, he was back in his native state by the spring of 1778, when on April 14 he took his seat as representative of Bute County in the state assembly. This apparently disposes of the further tradition that he was with the army at the Battle of Monmouth in the following June.

From the latter half of 1778 to the end of the war, Hawkins carried heavy administrative responsibilities in support of the state's war effort. In February 1779 he was appointed Commercial Agent for North Carolina with instructions to purchase 200 hogsheads of tobacco for shipment abroad and to go himself to France, Spain, Holland, or elsewhere in quest of military supplies and other necessities. Late in that year, or possibly early in the next, he went to St. Eustatius, the

Dutch Caribbean island that served as a principal entrepôt for trade between Europe and the rebellious colonies. Back in North Carolina by February 14, 1780, he reported a generally successful mission despite difficulties experienced in the marketing of tobacco in the West Indies. During the critical last year of the war, he may have served as aide-de-camp to the governor, thereby possibly acquiring the title of colonel by which he was known to the end of his life.

In July 1781 Hawkins was elected to membership in the Continental Congress. He was reelected in each of the two following years and was among the members who sat in Nassau Hall during the summer and fall of 1783. He returned to the Congress for the last time in 1787. Having served in three sessions of the state assembly in 1778 and 1779, he was again in the House of Commons in 1784 as a representative of Warren County. In 1787 he favored ratification of the new national Constitution and was a member of the second ratifying convention, which in 1789 finally brought North Carolina into the Union. He then was elected as one of the two men who first represented the state in the United States Senate, and by lot he drew the term lasting until 1795. He was not reelected, and after 1795 he held no elective office, either state or national. In 1786 he had been one of the founding trustees of the Warrenton Academy and in 1789 of the University of North Carolina. In 1790 he owned 19 slaves and something like 4,000 acres of land.

Efforts to identify Hawkins during his service in the Senate with one or the other of the political parties then emerging have been none too successful. For example, he opposed the Bank of the United States, favored the excise duties, refused to admit Albert Gallatin to a seat in the Senate, and voted against confirmation of John Jay's appointment for a famous mission to Great Britain. In the later years of his career, he was to be chiefly identified with an Indian policy that never really became a cause for partisan conflict.

How early his concern for the fate of the Indian, a concern that would lead to one of the more unique careers in the history of the new nation, may have developed cannot be said. It is noticeable that while serving in the Continental Congress Hawkins more than once was assigned to committees dealing with the related issues of western lands and the Indians. In 1785 he was one of the commissioners who, under the provisions of an act of Congress, negotiated the Treaty of Hopewell with the Cherokees, and in January 1786 he negotiated treaties with the Choctaws and the Chickasaws.

Efforts to reach a settlement with the Creeks at this time failed, partly through a refusal of all but a few of the Creeks to meet the commissioners and partly through the recalcitrant attitude of the state of Georgia. Hawkins had refused an invitation to serve as a representative of Georgia in negotiation with the Creeks and thus early identified himself with the view adopted by Congress that it held an exclusive jurisdiction in all such negotiations. It is significant that Washington early in 1790 turned to Hawkins, then in the Senate and described as "a correspondent" of Alexander McGillivray, famed leader of the Creeks, for assistance in preparing the way for the Treaty of New York signed in August of that year.

Upon the completion of his term in the Senate, Hawkins was appointed by Washington as one of three commissioners to reopen negotiations with the Creeks, with whom relations had badly deteriorated since 1790. He seems to have been chiefly responsible for negotiating the important Treaty of Coleraine of June 1796, which introduced a sixteen-year period of peace with the Creek Nation. In 1796 Washington appointed him "Principal Temporary Agent for Indian Affairs South of the Ohio River." President Adams continued the appointment, as also did President Jefferson, who removed "Temporary" from the title, and President James Madison (A.B. 1771), for whom Hawkins named his only son.

After 1796 Hawkins dedicated his full energies to implementing a policy based upon a hope that the Indian's economy and society might be so far converted to "civilized" standards as to permit him to make do with less land and so to be incorporated on a mutually advantageous basis into an expanding United States. Jefferson in a letter to Hawkins in February 1803 provided this succinct summary: "While they are learning to do better on less land, our increasing numbers will be calling for more land, and thus a coincidence of interests will be produced between those who have lands to spare, and want other necessaries, and those who have such necessaries to spare, and want lands." However naive may have been the hope upon which the policy depended, no other person more earnestly sought to prove its validity than did Hawkins.

Despite the broad responsibilities implied and at times imposed by his official title, Hawkins's chief mission was to the Creek Nation, with whose people he lived, quite literally, through many years. On November 24, 1796, he departed from Hopewell in western South Carolina for a journey through the Cherokee and Creek country that would take three months to complete. This was but the first of many such tours in which he meticulously recorded his observations regarding the people and the land in which they lived. One result was the compilation of "A Sketch of the Creek Country in the years 1798 and

1799," of which Jefferson possessed a copy in manuscript that he considered worthy of deposit with the American Philosophical Society in 1816.

It was early in Jefferson's presidency that Hawkins established a permanent residence for himself on the Flint River, across from the site of the modern city of Macon. There he developed a model farm, cultivated in part by slaves brought down from his plantation in North Carolina, and experimented with a wide variety of vegetables, fruits, and other crops, thus setting for the Indian, as one author has aptly said, "a high example of how to do by doing."

To speak of his establishment as a farm can be misleading, for Hawkins sought to demonstrate the full range of economic opportunities the Indian might borrow from the white man. As he toured the countryside, he showed an alert eye for mill sites. He encouraged the introduction of cotton culture, and among the women, the domestic industries of spinning and weaving. In August 1808 he could write:

> The plan of civilization is progressive. We are clothing and feeding ourselves. The tin ware we use; and hats; shoes and boots, and the saddle I ride on, are made in the Agency; and all the leather we use or want is tanned at the Agency. My family of eighty persons are all clothed in homespun.

Hawkins quickly won the confidence of the Indians. In 1799 he persuaded the Creeks to seek a more effective "national Government" through an annual meeting of a council representing all of the towns, on an understanding that any agreement reached became the "will of the nation." Through this agency, Hawkins was able to gain an important influence over the internal affairs of the Creek nation and in effect to become its chief spokesman in dealing with others. Indeed, President Jefferson, writing to Andrew Jackson in February 1803 regarding a complaint against Hawkins, observed that it was "essential that our agent acquire that sort of influence over the Indians which rests on confidence," and added, "in this respect, I suppose that no man has ever obtained more influence than Colonel Hawkins." But the president continued to admit that Hawkins had gained his influence at the cost of "doubts entertained by some whether he is not more attached to the interests of the Indians than of the United States."

Of Hawkins's sympathy with the Indians there can be no doubt, despite occasional outbursts such as the following in February 1798: "I cannot express to you the difficulty I have with this proud, haughty, lying, spoiled, untoward race." In the same paragraph, he reported to

Secretary of War McHenry that he had made "considerable progress
in learning their language; this I find is flattering to them, and it
amuses me during my leisure hours, which are but few." He became a
recognized authority on the history, religion, economy, society, and
language of the southern Indians. Jefferson turned to him, for example, for assistance in acquiring vocabularies for the Creek, Choc-
taw, and Chickasaw languages needed for the purposes of a comparative study of the North American Indians through their languages.
Hawkins in his search for knowledge of Indian ways included observation of the women, of whom he wrote to his friend Mrs. Eliza Trist
in 1797: "They have a great propensity to be obscene in conversation,
and they call every thing by its name, and if the concurrent testimony
of the white husbands may be relied on, the women have much of the
temper of the mule, except when they are amorous, and then they
exhibit all the amiable and gentle qualities of the cat."

Hawkins seems to have held himself aloof from too close an identification with the native, male or female, perhaps because he felt that
the agent of the United States government would lose standing
through closer ties. In his surviving papers, there are references to
"Mrs. Hawkins" as early as 1798, and there seems to have been only
one such person, Lavinia Downs, about whom the closest student of his
career has found no firm information other than that Hawkins lived
with her as a common law wife until they were married on January
9, 1812, by which time they had six children. On this same day Hawkins, whose health seems never to have been robust, made his will.
Whatever premonitions may have prompted his actions that day, he
lived on until his death at his plantation on June 6, 1816, having
meanwhile fathered another child for a total of six daughters and one
son. The property was divided in equal shares among his wife, his
children, and William Hawkins, a nephew who had spent some time
in Georgia with his uncle and who was governor of North Carolina
from 1811 to 1814. The estate was substantial. It included seventy-two
slaves and a library of more than 500 volumes, among them Gibbons
on Rome, Blackstone on the Common Law, Adam Smith's *The Wealth
of Nations*, Jefferson's *Notes on Virginia*, and Adair on the Indians.
To his daughters, Hawkins had been inclined to give geographical
placenames, as with Virginia, Carolina, Georgia, and Muscogee, but
one was named Jeffersonia.

The later years of Hawkins's life were difficult. The influence of
Tecumseh and his brother "The Prophet" extended into the Creek
country with resulting incidents that complicated Hawkins's never
exactly cordial relations with the state of Georgia. A second war with

Britain encouraged many Creeks, especially the Upper Creeks, to take the warpath against the Americans. Defeat at the hands of General Jackson and the Tennessee militia brought a forced surrender in the peace of August 9, 1814 of approximately half of the lands theretofore belonging to the Creeks. There could have been little satisfaction for Hawkins in knowing that not all of the Creeks had turned against the United States, for the course of history had outrun the vision to which he had dedicated the mature years of his life.

SOURCES: M. B. Pound, *Benjamin Hawkins* (1951), the fullest study, esp. 147 ("plan of civilization"); and see also *GHQ*, 13 (1929), 392-409; *NCHR*, 19 (1942), 1-21, 168-86, 455; *DAB; Letters of Benjamin Hawkins*; Ga. Hist. Soc., *Coll.,* IX, esp. 5-12, 10 ("how to do by doing"), 256 ("obscene in conversation"), 293 ("untoward race"), 345; III, 19-85 (Hawkins's "Sketch of the Creek Country"); B. W. Sheehan, *Seeds of Extinction* (1973); R. Horsman, *Expansion and Amer. Indian Policy, 1783-1812* (1967); W. E. Dodd, *Nathaniel Macon* (1908), 4-5; S. M. Lemmon, *Pettigrew Papers* (1971), I, 295-96; *Christian Advocate*, 2 (1824), 443 (Witherspoon quotation); *St. Rec. N.C.,* esp. XII, 655; XIII, 605-606, 625, 889; XV, 337-39; XIX, 376, 379, 489; XXII, 910; XXIV, 184; *LMCC,* VI-VIII, passim; *Washington Diaries*, IV, 90, 95-96; P. L. Ford, ed., *Writings of Thomas Jefferson* (1903), X, 161, 358 ("more attached to the interests of the Indians"), 362 ("better on less land"); XIX, 231-32; I. Brant, *James Madison, the President* (1956), 273.

MANUSCRIPTS: DLC, PPAmP, GEU, T, GU, ViHi

WFC

Joseph Hawkins

JOSEPH HAWKINS, soldier and public official, was one of the four sons of Colonel Philemon and Delia Martin Hawkins, who migrated from Virginia to North Carolina, possibly as early as 1737, and settled in the area later embraced by Bute County and still later Warren County. The date of his birth has not been found, but he was the younger brother of Benjamin Hawkins, also of the Class of 1777, so was born at some time after 1754. Having been trained by Charles Pettigrew, the two brothers presumably entered the College together at some time after 1773 and probably were both members of the senior class when President Witherspoon dismissed the students in November 1776.

The tradition that Joseph then joined the Continental forces is open to question. He probably returned to his home in North Carolina, where in May 1779 he took a seat in the state House of Commons that thereafter can almost be described as the family seat. His immediate predecessor was his brother Benjamin, and Joseph continued to be one of the two representatives from Warren County until the spring of 1783. Benjamin succeeded him in 1784, and for nearly a decade more, their nephew Wyat Hawkins usually sat for the county. The mother has been credited in part with the political influence of the sons, and certainly membership in one of the more prominent families in the county helps to explain the opportunities and responsibilities public office brought to them. The father was by no means the largest slaveholder in the county, but the fifty-four held at the time of the 1790 census put him well up on the list. At this time Benjamin held 1,290 acres inherited from Joseph and nineteen slaves.

In the more familiar records of the state, Joseph's name disappears after the spring of 1783, the year in which he is supposed to have died. The journals of the House of Commons present the fullest surviving record of his brief career, and these show him to have been faithful in attendance, except for a period of military leave during the latter half of 1781. Indeed, he more than once proposed penalties for members less faithful in this regard than was he, and the committee assignments he received indicate that he was both responsible and influential. On July 7, 1781, he was given a leave of absence from the House, on July 11 he was nominated for "Major of the Horse" for troops to be raised from the state militia, and on July 14 he was appointed Lieutenant Colonel pro tempore for Warren County. Actually, he seems already to have been in the field, for on June 17, 1781, he reported to Governor Abner Nash that he had been at the head of Black River, in the southeastern part of the state, operating against local Tories upon receiving orders to report to Camp Smithfield, from which he wrote. He complained of the conflicting orders he had been receiving, of the exhaustion of his men and their horses, and of the impossibility of attending "the assembly and the Campaign at the same time." The report constitutes a very brief record of his military service, the most interesting item being perhaps his statement that most of six prisoners taken had enlisted in his own troop, but there is good reason for believing that this tour of duty and the subsequent appointment in the Warren County Militia, rather than an assumed service at some time with the Continental forces, explains references thereafter to him as Colonel Hawkins. On December 5, 1781, he was acting secretary to a new governor, Alexander Martin (A.B. 1756).

SOURCES: See Benjamin Hawkins (Class of 1777); M. W. Wellman, Cnty. of Warren, N.C. (1959), W. C. Watson, Men and Times of the Rev. (1856, 1968), 286-88; St. Rec. N.C., XIII, 785, 913; XVI, 2; XVII, 715, 716, 858, 868, 1,050; XIX, 234, 381-397; NCHR, 27 (1938), 455; 15 (1926), 487-88; First Census, N.C., 77. The Carolinian is not to be confused with the Joseph Hawkins accused of misconduct in office in Va. during the spring of 1781. Index, Rev. War Pension Applications (1966), 515, shows an application by a survivor for a Joseph Hawkins of N.C.

WFC

George W. Hazard

GEORGE W. HAZARD, probably a merchant, was born in Newport, Rhode Island on March 30, 1758. His parents were George and Martha Wanton Hazard. The father, who had been born a Quaker but had joined the Congregational church in Newport in 1750, was a prominent merchant, jurist, and public official, mayor of Newport under the fist city charter, and a delegate to the Rhode Island ratifying convention in 1790. He was also one of the original incorporators and then a trustee of the College of Rhode Island, later Brown University. At least three of his five sons studied there.

Why George W. Hazard did not also enter the Rhode Island college is unclear, but it is possible that he chose to go south because his friend William H. Vernon (A.B. 1776) was a student at Nassau Hall. Hazard was in the sophomore class in 1774–1775 and probably completed most of his junior year as well. Then, without permission from his father or from President Witherspoon, he ran away to join the army.

For Hazard, military life was singularly unrewarding. On Long Island in the summer of 1776 he contracted dysentery, and his already slight body grew dangerously thin. He was evacuated to Newark just before the American withdrawal from Long Island, but his trunk with all of his clothes and money remained behind. After being treated in Newark he learned that the trunk had been recovered but that its contents were gone. Left penniless and with only the clothes he wore, he headed for Philadelphia. There he met Vernon, who had accompanied Witherspoon to the city and who found Hazard "Emaciated almost to a skeleton." The two young men dined with Rhode Island's congressional delegate William Ellery in late September. Ellery too found Hazard in "a most miserable plight."

Thoroughly chastised, Hazard was also in a "most humble repenting situation." He hoped that the College and his father would forgive his impetuosity and allow him to resume his studies. Ellery assured him that he could do so, but in November 1776 the College was closed and Hazard never earned his degree. He went back to Rhode Island. Apparently and predictably, he did not take any further military role in the Revolution. He may have entered the family business. In any case, he definitely acquired a reputation for eccentricity. It was customary in the Hazard family to use nicknames to distinguish the many Hazards with the same names from one another. George W. Hazard was known as "Crazy George." He bragged that while his father was a "money-getting man" he could spend much more than his father could earn, and quickly. He seems to have made that his goal in life.

Hazard married Martha Babcock, the daughter of Christopher and Martha Babcock of Bristol, Rhode Island. Together they had four children, the first of whom was born in June 1780. According to local tradition, "Crazy George" called on a cobbler in 1834 to order a pair of boots in which he planned to be buried. He insisted that they be delivered on a specific date in November, which he said would be the day of his funeral. The boots were delivered on time, and in time, for Hazard died on November 6, 1834.

SOURCES: C. E. Robinson, *Hazard Family of R.I.* (1895), 53, 97-98 ("Crazy George," "a money-getting man"); MS Steward's accounts, PUA; als W. H. Vernon to W. Vernon, 26 Sep 1776, Vernon MSS, RNHi ("almost to a skeleton"); R.I. Hist. Soc., *Pubs.* (n.s.), 8 (1900), 201 ("miserable plight," "repenting situation").

Adam Hoops, Jr.

ADAM HOOPS, JR., soldier, merchant, surveyor, landowner, the youngest son of Adam and Elizabeth Hoops, was born in Carlisle, Cumberland County, Pennsylvania on January 9, 1760. His father, a justice and coroner of the county, was also a merchant and had served in 1755 as a commissioner to build a road west from Shippensburg. He was a friend and associate of College trustee Edward Shippen. After one of his daughters married the half-brother of Patrick Henry and moved to Virginia, Adam Hoops, Sr. extended his business activities to include the affairs of such southern families as that of James Madison (A.B. 1771). He died at his home in Falls Township, Bucks County, in June 1771.

Two years later Adam Hoops, Jr. entered the College. He probably remained there until Nassau Hall was closed in November 1776, after which he sought a military commission. On December 9, 1776, he was appointed by Congress to be a second lieutenant in Colonel Moses Hazen's Second Canadian Regiment, "Congress's Own," and with it for the next two years remained under Washington's direct command.

Having been a first lieutenant since October 1777, Hoops joined General John Sullivan's expedition against the Six Nations in May 1779, serving as one of Sullivan's aides-de-camp. The other was Jonathan Dayton (A.B. 1776). From Easton, Pennsylvania Hoops rode with the ineffectual foray into northern Pennsylvania and western New York, returning to Hazen's regiment near Philadelphia by October. He then received a promotion to captain, but before it took effect, he arranged to change places with an officer of the Fourth Maryland Continentals. After the exchange took place on December 15, 1779, Hoops remained on the Maryland rolls for the rest of the war.

Although the transfer delayed his promotion, Hoops refused to accept the role of a subaltern in the Fourth Maryland. He thereby offended some of his fellow officers who, in April 1780, brought him to court-martial. The charges were that he had falsely reported himself ill to escape duty after having bragged that he would do so and then attended a dance in Morristown, New Jersey while he was on the sick list. He admitted to reporting that he was ill and going to the officers' "Morristown Ball" dancing society near headquarters, but he was acquitted of doing anything improper.

It was as a captain lieutenant, something of a compromise, that Hoops went south with the regiment that spring and was captured when the British defeated General Horatio Gates at Camden, South Carolina on August 16. His full captaincy came while he was a prisoner in March 1781, by which time he had been transferred to the Second Maryland Regiment. On October 4 of that year he was released on parole, the status he held until the war ended. He was able, therefore, to resume his personal career, which he apparently decided would be in his late father's mercantile business. He may have been the Mr. Hoops who visited John Adams in Paris in December 1782, for he was definitely in Europe on some business for two years before the spring of 1785. He was an original member of the Maryland Society of the Cincinnati.

Hoops was apparently back in the United States by May 1784, when he applied to Congress for an appointment as surveyor of one district of western lands. On May 18, 1784, the provost and the professor of mathematics at the University of Pennsylvania certified Hoop's qualifications for the surveyor's post, and while Congress considered his application, Hoops unsuccessfully sought a place on a commission for treaties with the Indians.

On May 27, 1785, Hoops was appointed surveyor of the western lands for Pennsylvania. He spent at least two years along the Ohio River, in northern Pennsylvania, and in the Genesee country of western New York. In May 1789 his brother Robert submitted Hoops's name for the position of geographer of the United States. In spite of reports that the late incumbent had hoped Hoops would succeed him, the post went to another candidate.

Back in Philadelphia, Hoops attached himself to the circle of financier Robert Morris as the resident expert on western lands. Another of his friends was Oliver Phelps of Massachusetts, and it was Hoops who interested both Morris and Phelps in land investments in the Genesee country. First Phelps and Nathaniel Gorham joined to purchase several million acres, and then Morris paid them for a 1,000,000-acre package of his own. Morris hired Hoops to survey his property, some of which he sold to English investors through the agency of William Temple Franklin and William Stephens Smith (A.B. 1774). Hoops continued his surveys in 1791 and 1792, and in August 1793 he went to find the best location for a settlement of French royalist refugees. When the Asylum Company was established for that enterprise in April 1794, Hoops was paid a salary of $1,000 to act as one of its agents.

Title to the Genesee lands was a subject of hot dispute between New York and Massachusetts as well as among the several speculators involved. By 1797 the Holland Land Company, with its headquarters in the Netherlands, was one of the most interested parties. Its claims conflicted with some of Morris's, who in that year had bought up as many Indian land titles as he could in the area where he had previously purchased the preemptive rights from Massachusetts. That effort to protect his original investment had put Morris deeply in debt. He hoped to recoup by selling some of his land, and so in the fall of 1797 he sent Hoops to work with the Holland Company's surveyor, Joseph Ellicott, in order to define the respective titles.

Morris's creditors meanwhile tried to seize his land as payment. They included even his own attorney, Edward Livingston (A.B. 1781), one of the galaxy of legal experts such as Alexander Hamilton, Aaron Burr (A.B. 1772), and Brockholst Livingston (A.B. 1774), involved in the case. After two court decisions were returned against Morris, the Holland Company hoped that one of his prospective sales would be completed so that it could be challenged in court. When no sale occurred, the company blamed its bad luck on the mismanagement of Morris's affairs by Hoops. With the judicial question still unanswered, Hoops and Ellicott managed to complete a preliminary survey on the shores of Lakes Erie and Ontario and along the Niagara River.

Ellicott and Hoops prepared for a more extensive survey in the spring of 1798. They met in Canandaigua, New York in June, but in spite of Ellicott's determination to get on with the work, they could not agree on what lands were to be examined or which titles were in doubt. They talked for weeks, but each discussion had the same result. Hoops would not accept any of the company's terms. He and his party had not even brought provisions for an extended expedition. After Ellicott finally agreed to allow the Morris surveyors to use the company's camp and supplies, Hoops accepted a few very basic principles and deputized one of his assistants to execute the survey. He then went to New York City.

Since 1794 Hoops had pestered the federal government for a military appointment. His chance finally came with the Quasi-War in 1798; and on June 1, just before he met with Ellicott, he had been commissioned a major in the Corps of Artillerists and Engineers. He at once requested the command of a regiment, and he had the Morris family's support. But in October he was named commandant of New York Harbor instead. It was a thankless job in which he continually encountered problems with supplies and logistics. In December 1798 Alexander Hamilton and Secretary of War James McHenry agreed that Hoops would be a good choice for inspector of artillery or command of the Second Artillery Regiment, because, as Hamilton put it, he was "very *intelligent* industrious and persevering." Both men recognized that Hoops's great failing was a tendency to be "importunate," but Hamilton ascribed that to "zeal." Neither appointment eventuated, however.

With the end of his military service, Hoops returned to the Genesee country, where Joseph Ellicott was still the agent for the Holland Land Company. In 1802 Hoops applied to buy 20,000 acres of the company's land. He had no money to make the purchase, but as Hamilton had noted, Hoops was nothing if not persistent. It took him two years to wear Ellicott down, but in 1804 Hoops had his land and established a settlement at the head of the Allegheny River. It was first called Ischua, then Hamilton, and finally Olean. But under any name, it was doomed by Hoops's bizarre business sense and was the single most exasperating problem with which Ellicott had to contend.

The key to the trouble was Hoops's refusal to accept reasonable offers for his land. He demanded exorbitant prices, which discouraged rather than promoted settlement. Hoops never had the money to pay even the interest he owed the Holland Company, and Ellicott's annual reports were studies in frustration. He loaned Hoops additional capital to get the town started, and he never saw a penny of the money again. The agent had to admit that it was Hoops's importunity that had led the state legislature to finance an important road into the area, but even that improvement did nothing to increase the population.

Hoops blamed the company for his woes. He complained that the land was too hilly, that the road was badly placed. By 1807 he had to sell one-half of his 20,000 acres, but the proceeds from the sale never reached Ellicott. The agent extended to Hoops the most liberal terms possible, forgiving missed payments and waiving deadlines as well. In 1809, when Ellicott had no more to give, Hoops decided that the company had a vendetta against him because he was a Federalist. As Ellicott explained to his principals, the company's men cooperated with whatever party was in power in New York in order to promote their business affairs. In 1809 that was the badly divided Republican party. But there was no political vendetta against Hoops. The disgruntled Federalist threatened to go to Holland to complain. He never did. Instead, he took the company's foreclosure notice of 1816 through every court in New York for four years. Only when Chancellor James Kent found against him was he forced to accept defeat.

Hoops then went back to Pennsylvania, where he lived, apparently in retirement, for the rest of his life. He also grew more bitterly partisan as the Federalist party died. In 1822 he related to Timothy Pickering some anecdotes of the Revolution that Pickering later used in his attack against Washington's memory. Hoops died in West Chester, Pennsylvania on June 9, 1846. No record that he ever married has been found.

Sources: *PMHB*, 35 (1911), 512; 27 (1903), 52; 68 (1944), 186; *Hist. of Cumberland and Adams Counties, Pa.* (1886) [Cumberland], 27, 75, 132; W. Brewster, *Pa. and N.Y. Frontier* (1954), 62; *Madison Papers*, I, 48-50 & n; *LCHSPA*, 11 (1907), 5; MS Steward's accounts, PUA; Force, *Am. Arch.* (5 ser.), III, 1,603; L. W. Murray, *Notes on Sullivan Expedition of 1779* (1929), 1; *Clinton Papers*, v, 230; *Washington Writings*, XVIII, 261-62 & n; XXXVI, 448; Heitman (which is in error); *Md. Arch.*, XVIII, 123, 363, 379, 479; *St. Rec. N.C.*, XVI, 673; XVII, 459; *Adams Papers*, III, 91; *Franklin Cal.*, v, 165; *MHM*, 41 (1946), 335; *JCC*, XXVII, 490; G. Hunt, *Cal. of Applications and Recommendations for Office during the Presidency of George Washington* (1901), 61, 62; *LMCC*, VIII, 854; Index, PCC; O. Turner, *Hist. of . . . Phelps and Gorham's Purchase* (1851), 135; W. Ketchum, *Hist. of Buffalo* (1865), II, 50; W. G. Sumner, *Financier and Finances of the Amer. Rev.* (1892), II, 254; E. P. Oberholtzer, *Robert Morris* (1903), 302; *Buffalo Hist. Soc. Pub.*, VII, 296, 315-16 & n; XXVI, 51 & n, 58-60; XXVIII, 181, 196, 257-59; XXXI, 147; XXXII, 57-63, 112, 115, 120, 300-301, 342, 350-58, 381-84; XXXIII, 86, 87, 142; W. Chazanoff, *Joseph Ellicott and the Holland Land Co.* (1970), 26; *Hamilton Papers*, XXII, 129, 203, 224-25 & n, 378-79 & nn ("intelligent . . . persevering," "importunate," "zeal"), 397, 548, 554; B. C. Steiner, *Life and Correspondence of James McHenry* (1907), 402, 404, 433; K. E. Bradley, *Hist. Sketches* (1920), 23; *Tyler's Quart.*, 7 (1926), 38.

Manuscripts: NHi

Levi Hopkins

Levi Hopkins, soldier and farmer, was born in Great Barrington, Berkshire County, Massachusetts on March 31, 1753. His mother was Susanna Ingersoll Hopkins, and he was the third of her eight children. His father, Samuel Hopkins (Yale 1741), then the Congregational clergyman in Great Barrington, was a colleague and friend of College President Jonathan Edwards and was to become one of the seminal forces in American religious thought, the father of Hopkinsian theology.

Hopkins entered the College as a freshman in 1773 and stayed through his sophomore year, until his health began to fail and he went home to recuperate. He never returned, but remained in Berkshire County with relatives. His father had left Massachusetts in 1769 and settled in Newport, Rhode Island.

In 1776 and 1777 Hopkins served periodically as a private under various officers in the Great Barrington companies of the First Regiment of Berkshire County Militia. According to his own recollection, he saw action at White Plains, New York and Bennington, Vermont. Like most militiamen, his periods of service ranged from a few days to a few months, depending upon the imminence of an enemy attack. But Hopkins apparently had fulfilled his obligation by the end of 1777. He stayed in Great Barrington for the duration of the war.

In 1784 Hopkins moved to Baltimore, Maryland, the residence of his oldest brother David. During his ten years in Maryland, he married Abigail Stevens of Bladensburg. They moved west in 1794 and settled in the region that later became Preston County (West) Virginia. On November 5, 1798, in a letter to a college mate who had been one of his bitter critics thirty years earlier, and with whom he had not communicated since then, Samuel Hopkins reported on the whereabouts of his children. His third son Levi, he said, lived in northwest Virginia, near the Appalachian Mountains, with his wife and six children. Another daughter, "a promising young woman," had recently died. Although he rendered portraits of his other sons that were touched with unmistakable parental pride in their careers and accomplishments, the aging minister had no more to say about Levi.

Within a few years Hopkins lost his wife. His second marriage, on September 10, 1811, was to Elizabeth Looper of Allegheny County, Maryland. In 1833 he received a pension for his service in the Revolution. It was discontinued after his death on September 1, 1835, but twenty years later his widow obtained a land bounty of 160 acres.

SOURCES: *W. Va. Hist.*, 4 (1943), 123-24; *DAB*; Dexter, *Yale Biographies*, I, 670-73; L. D. Avery, *Geneal. of the Ingersoll Family in Amer.* (1926), 138-39; MS Steward's accounts, PUA; S. West, *Life of Rev. Dr. Samuel Hopkins* (1805), 82; *Mass. Soldiers and Sailors of the Rev. War* (1901), VIII, 241; *NEHGR*, 5 (1851), 44 ("promising young woman"); *DAR Patriot Index*.

Daniel Jenifer

DANIEL JENIFER, physician, of Port Tobacco, Charles County, Maryland, was born in 1756, the son of Daniel Jenifer and his wife, Elizabeth Hanson Jenifer. The father was a brother of Daniel of St. Thomas Jenifer, best remembered as a Maryland delegate to the Constitutional Convention of 1787. He was himself politically active within the county and state, as a member of the extralegal conventions of 1774-1776, and thereafter, of the state legislature, as a justice of the county court, and during the later years of the war, as procurement officer for supply of army forces. Young Daniel's older brother, who bore the name of his uncle, was enrolled at the College in the Class of 1775 but died at the end of his junior year.

Jenifer completed his preparation for admission to the College in the grammar school conducted under its auspices at Princeton. The *New York Gazette and Weekly Mercury* for October 11, 1773, carried a report of the graduation from the school of a class of seven members, including Jenifer, all of whom, upon sustaining their examinations on September 27 in the "Presence of the President and Officers of College, and several other Gentlemen of Letters," were admitted to the freshman class in the College. That evening "the Ladies and Gentlemen in the Neighborhood, and Strangers who came to Commencement" were entertained in the Prayer Hall of the College by three orations: two of them delivered in Latin by "DANIEL [J]ENIFER, of Port Tobacco, in Maryland, and JAMES BAYARD, of Philadelphia," the third in English by John Jordan, also of Port Tobacco. The only other record of Daniel's identification with the College is found in two surviving accounts of the steward, which suggest that he was at least for a brief time enrolled as one of its students. There is, however, no complete file of such accounts, and it can be said with certainty only that he did not graduate.

This in itself is not extraordinary, for in the later years of the eighteenth century, a growing number of young gentlemen were enrolled for a time without taking the degree, as often was the case in the English universities. Perhaps at an early date, Daniel decided that he had enough Latin to meet his needs as a practicing physician, which he became. It was a profession that claimed two other members of his immediate family: his grandfather Dr. Daniel Jenifer and his brother Dr. Walter Hanson Jenifer, who is known to have trained students apprenticed to him in medicine, and who may have trained his younger brother. His medical studies must have predated his entry into military service in August 1776 as a surgeon's mate. He was promoted in October 1781 to the status of hospital physician and surgeon and served until October 1782.

Thereafter, he returned to Charles County, where he took up the life of a planter and physician and was described on occasion as Dr. Daniel Jenifer, Jr. On January 25, 1785, he married Sarah Craik, daughter of Dr. James Craik of Alexandria, Virginia. According to the census of 1790, Jenifer owned thirty-eight slaves, a considerably larger number than the twenty-two possessed at that time by his father. He had become an original member of the Maryland Society of the Cincinnati, and in 1799 he was one of the founding members of the Medical and Chirurgical Faculty of Maryland. He died in 1809, predeceased by his wife in 1800. They were parents of seven children, four daughters and three sons, one of whom, named Daniel, served later in Congress and after that as United States minister to Austria. One daughter died in infancy.

SOURCES: G. A. Hanson, *Old Kent* (1876, 1967), 124; J. B. Kremer, *John Hanson* (1938), chart after p. 40; *DAB* (Daniel of St. Thomas Jenifer); E. C. Papenfuse et al., *Directory of Md. Legislators* (1974), 11, 42; R. Barnes, *Marriages and Deaths from Md. Gazette* (1973), 101; A. W. Burns, *Md. Wills, Charles Cnty.*, bk. IX, 10-11; bk. XI, 40-41; *Md. Arch.*, XVI, 184; XLIII, 352; XLV, 184; XLIII, 352; XLV, 53; XLVII, 517-18 (identification of Dr. Wm. H. Jenifer seems to be an editorial slip); *Cal. Md. St. Papers*, no. 4, *Red Books*, passim; *NJA* (1 ser.), XXIX, 50; MS Steward's accounts; Heitman; *Washington Writings*, XX, 19; XXIII, 176; *MHM*, 41 (1946), 335; *First Census, Md.*, 51, 55; E. F. Cordell, *Med. Annuals of Md.* (1903), 24, 453. *Washington Diaries*, II, 161, 187, 337, 343, 359, 364, 420; III, 242.

WFC

John Jordan

JOHN JORDAN, soldier, a native of Charles County, Maryland, was the son of John and Eleanor Dent Jordan. The date of Jordan's birth has not been found, but it was probably after October 1756, when Jordan's grandfather William Dent included legacies for Jordan's older brother and sister in his will but made no mention of a grandson named John. John Jordan, Sr. was a Maryland legislator who served in the Lower House from Charles County from 1754 to 1757. His son's name appears in the College steward's records for March 1773, but young John Jordan was only a schoolboy at the time. An account of the September 1773 grammar school exercises describes both Jordan and Daniel Jenifer (Class of 1777) as being from Port Tobacco, Maryland. After presenting an English oration for this occasion, Jordan and six others who had completed their preparatory course were admitted to the freshman class of the College. That Jordan's name does not appear in the steward's accounts for November 1774 to April 1775, suggests that he may have left Nassau Hall after his first year.

After the outbreak of the Revolutionary War, Jordan returned to his home state and entered upon a military career. Commissioned an ensign in January 1776, he was appointed a first lieutenant in the First Maryland Regiment on December 10, 1776 and was promoted to captain one year later. In June 1779 he was one of a group of Maryland officers who petitioned the state's governor and assembly for an increase in their subsistence as compensation for the depreciation of American currency and for their personal wartime losses. Maryland documents record a payment to Jordan and other officers of a welcome $1,900 and £3 10s specie each in September 1780. In July 1781, now in the Second Maryland Regiment, Jordan received £20 from the state as one of the "officers going to the Southward," which suggests that he may have been involved in the southern campaign of 1781. A week after the surrender of Cornwallis at Yorktown in October 1781, Captain Jordan was on the move again with a Maryland warrant authorizing him "to impress such Boats and hands as are necessary to transport his Men and Horses across any of the Rivers in the State of Maryland in his route to Virginia." In the same month, Jordan is reported to have been appointed a cornet in the legion commanded by and named for Henry Lee (A.B. 1773). He remained in the military until 1783.

Returning to civilian life, Jordan probably derived some benefit from the estate of his father, who died sometime before 1784 with property worth £819 11s 1d, debt free. Title to forty-four acres of land in Charles County also passed to Jordan after the deaths of his father and brother, and he received additional acreage as the gift of an aunt. On December 27, 1787, he married Sarah Harrison, daughter of Robert Hanson Harrison, former aide to George Washington and Chief Judge of the General Court of Maryland. The couple's only child, Maria, was born on October 21, 1788. But John Jordan died less than three weeks later on November 8, and his daughter died in 1792. Sarah Jordan remarried in 1796, and after the death of her second husband in 1835, she successfully applied to the state of Maryland and to the federal government for pensions as a survivor of the revolutionary captain.

SOURCES: Sarah (Jordan) Easton's federal pension application, Rev. War pension file W24098, DNA; Md. Leg. Hist. Proj.; MS Steward's accounts, PUA; *N.Y. Gazette and Weekly Mercury*, 11 Oct 1773; Heitman; *Md. Arch.*, XVIII, 125, 363, 379; XLV, 97, 503, 653; *Cal. of Md. St. Papers*, no. 4, pt. 3 (1955), 67; *MHM*, 35 (1940), 335.
                                                                                          GSD

Richard Longstreet

RICHARD LONGSTREET was the son of Richard (Derrick) Longstreet, a landed gentleman who resided near Princeton, New Jersey and was a trustee of the Princeton Presbyterian Church after its incorporation in 1786. The senior Longstreet is believed to have been the man of that name who married Mrs. Margaret Schenck Cowenhoven in 1749. If this assumption is correct, she was the mother of the Richard Longstreet who first appears in the College steward's tuition and room accounts for May 1773 to September 1774. He is listed as a member of the sophomore class in the steward's accounts for November 1774 to April 1775, and he also appears in the account book of Princeton storekeeper Thomas Patterson from November 1774 to September 1775. He may have continued as a student at the College until the British descent on Princeton in the autumn of 1776.

What little else is known of Longstreet comes from John F. Hageman, the usually reliable nineteenth-century historian of Princeton, who wrote:

> Richard Longstreet was a private in Capt. McMakin's company in the Revolution, and was killed near Morristown when retreating, and while saying, "Hold on, don't let us retreat any further." A ball struck him in the head and killed him. He was buried there.

It has not been possible to verify Hageman's story from other sources or to determine the date of Longstreet's death. The young soldier's sister was the wife of John Beatty (A.B. 1769).

SOURCES: Hageman, *History*, 194 ("Hold on"); E. F. Cooley, *Geneal. of Early Settlers of Trenton and Ewing* (1883), 251n; A. S. Link, *First Pres. Chh. of Princeton* (1967), 15; A. L. Holman, *Reg. of the Ancestors of Dorr Eugene Felt* (1921), 72; MS Steward's accounts, PUA; Patterson Acct. Bk.

GSD

Tristrim Lowther

TRISTRIM LOWTHER, probably a merchant, was the son of William and Barbara Gregory Lowther. He may have been born in New York or in Chowan County, North Carolina, for his father migrated southward from the former province after June 1754, when he became executor of the estate of his brother Tristrim in Northampton County, North Carolina. The family was certainly residing in Chowan County in

1766, when William Lowther was named by the provincial assembly to be a commissioner for the town of Edenton.

Lowther entered the College between May 1773 and September 1774. Possibly because of his Anglican background, he left after only one year to enroll at King's College in New York City in 1774. But the war closed King's, and Lowther never received a degree. He was probably the "Mr. Louther" who went from army headquarters to Philadelphia in May 1776 and into whose care Joseph Hewes of the Continental Congress entrusted a letter to James Iredell in North Carolina. That, however, was his only service for the American side in the Revolution.

The Lowther family may have been Loyalists during the war, after which Tristrim Lowther renewed his contacts with Iredell, then the leading opponent of the confiscation of loyalist property in North Carolina. By 1782 Lowther had married Penelope Eden Dawson, a cousin of Iredell's favorite niece, and established his residence in Bertie County. Three years later, with letters of introduction from Iredell, he traveled to Halifax County, North Carolina, apparently to renew business contacts broken during the Revolution. He reported to Iredell on July 4 that the "prejudices against me are narrowly confined" to a smaller group than he had expected. In August he bore a letter from Iredell to Dr. Samuel Cutler, the former Loyalist and Anglican clergyman in Hartford, Connecticut.

In May 1789 Lowther sailed to New York, hoping to see the first presidential inauguration, but a rough voyage delayed his arrival until one day after the ceremony. He then spent several weeks observing the sessions of the new Congress. He was impressed by the freedom of debate in the House of Representatives, where he expected great things from James Madison (A.B. 1771) of Virginia. He was, however, disappointed to note that when Madison spoke he did so in a voice too low to be heard in the gallery.

Lowther and his wife had one son and one daughter before his death early in 1790. In his will, which was probated on February 18, he named Iredell as one of the executors of his estate.

SOURCES: The most common alternate spelling is "Tristram Louther." *WMQ* (1 ser.), 22 (1913), 50-51; J. B. Grimes, *Abstract of N.C. Wills* (1910), 224; *St. Rec. N.C.*, xxv, 505; MS Steward's accounts, PUA; M. H. Thomas, *Columbia Univ., Officers and Alumni* (1936), 104; *Col. Rec. N.C.*, x, 458; *NCHGR*, 2 (1901), 8; G. J. McRee, *Life and Correspondence of James Iredell* (1858), I, 429-30; II, 124-25 ("prejudices against me"), 127, 258-59, 260; R. E. Demond, *Loyalists in N.C. during the Rev.* (1940), 172, 174-75.

Thomas Harrison McCalla

THOMAS HARRISON MCCALLA, A.B., soldier, physician, and public official, was the son of John and Jane Harrison McCalla of Philadelphia, Pennsylvania. He was born several years prior to the birth of a younger brother in 1763. The large McCalla family was distributed throughout southeastern Pennsylvania and southern New Jersey, and Thomas H. McCalla was almost certainly related to Daniel McCalla (A.B. 1766) and to the McCalla clan that was part of the congregation of the Presbyterian church in Greenwich, Cumberland County, New Jersey.

McCalla's name does not appear on the records of the steward through April 1775, thus it is likely that he enrolled in the College with some advanced standing after that date. When President Witherspoon dismissed the students in November 1776 because of the approach of the British army, McCalla must have returned to Philadelphia. He was a lieutenant of the city militia in early 1777. On June 23 the unit was reorganized as the First Battalion of Philadelphia Militia, with McCalla as a second lieutenant in its fifth company. He may also have begun the study of medicine during these months, yet he found time if not to return to Princeton when the College resumed its sessions in the summer of 1777, at least to go back to Nassau Hall in August for his final examinations.

The diplomas for the graduates of 1777 were not granted until April 1778, which apparently was the first time that a sufficient number of trustees could be gathered to authorize the degrees. When or whether McCalla applied for his diploma, as President Witherspoon invited him and his fellow graduates to do in August 1778, is unclear, for earlier in the year he had joined Colonel Stephen Moylan's Fourth Regiment of Continental Light Dragoons as a lieutenant. On May 1 he became the regimental surgeon's mate while the unit was assigned to the upper reaches of the Susquehanna River in Pennsylvania. After two years of service in his home state, he was promoted to surgeon and may have accompanied that part of the regiment that went south in 1780. There the dragoons faced their first real combat and after suffering heavy casualties withdrew to Pennsylvania. In 1781, as the Fourth Legionary Corps, the regiment was assigned to the Pennsylvania quota.

In June 1781 McCalla was definitely in Lancaster, Pennsylvania and in contact with Reading Beatty, brother of John (A.B. 1769) and Charles Clinton Beatty (A.B. 1775). Beatty instructed his sister Elizabeth, the widow of Philip Fithian (A.B. 1772) to send her letters from Cumberland County to McCalla's brother in Philadelphia. Clearly, the two families were well acquainted. Beatty also mentioned that McCalla was thinking about paying a visit to the Cohansie region of New Jersey that summer.

After the war McCalla practiced for a time in Cumberland County, New Jersey. By 1789, however, he had moved to Charleston, South Carolina, the home of Daniel McCalla since 1788. A member of the Medical Society of South Carolina, McCalla also served as vice-president of the Vigilant Fire Company at its inception in Charleston in 1789, and as a director of the Reciprocal Insurance Company in 1791. In both of the latter enterprises, he was a colleague of David Ramsay (A.B. 1765). He was also active in the South Carolina Society of the Cincinnati, which he represented to the third triennial meeting of the national society in May 1799.

In Charleston, where he served for several years as the city's physician for the poor, alderman, and intendant, McCalla married Sarah Barksdale. They had one daughter, Sarah Barksdale McCalla, born in late 1789 and baptized in the Independent Congregational Church. The girl died at the age of nineteen, only weeks after she was married. Her death was a blow from which McCalla, already a widower, never recovered. He died in his house on Anson Street in Charleston in January 1813.

SOURCES: See James Ashton Bayard (A.B. 1777) for awarding of degrees to Class of 1777. *Transactions of Med. Soc. of N.J., 1871*, 116; *VHM*, 27 (1942), 392; 38 (1953), 81-82; 16 (1931), 27; *N.J. Gazette*, 16 Sep 1778; MS Steward's accounts, PUA; *Pa. Arch.* (6 ser.), I, 18, 20; (5 ser.), III, 836-37; J. M. Toner, *Contributions to Annals of Med. Progress* (1970), 83; F. A. Berg, *Encyc. of Continental Army Units* (1972), 31; J. I. Waring, *Hist. of Med. in S.C.* (1964), 347; *SCHGM*, 32 (1931), 79, 80, 287; 33 (1932), 159; 38 (1937), 67; 55 (1954), 103; J. C. Daves, ed., *Proc. of Gen. Soc. of the Cincinnati*, I (1925), 53-56.

John Young Noel

JOHN YOUNG NOEL, A.B., lawyer and public official, was born in New York City on June 18, 1762, the son of Garrat Noel and his wife, Experience Young Noel, a relative of Benjamin Youngs Prime (A.B. 1751). The father, a native of England, was a prosperous bookseller and stationer who, according to historian Isaiah Thomas, "dealt largely . . . in imported books and stationery." Ebenezer Hazard (A.B. 1762) in 1765 became his apprentice and by 1770 was a partner in the firm of Noel and Hazard. At the time of his death on September 22,

1776, Garrat Noel resided in Elizabethtown, New Jersey, where his widow in May 1778 advertised for sale a variety of household furnishings, including a "handsome mahogany desk and book-case, mahogany chairs and tables, China Bowls, looking-glasses, pictures; a large copper kettle, brass andirons, shovels and tongs," together "with a large assortment of new books in history, divinity, law, physic and miscellany, with stationary, &c." Also offered for sale was "an exceeding good PHAETON, almost new." She seems still to have been residing in Elizabethtown at the end of the war. According to tradition, when James Caldwell (A.B. 1759) was murdered on November 24, 1781, his body was brought to her home.

The earliest evidence of John Noel's enrollment among the students of the College is found in a record indicating that he used the Roman name "Cassius" when he joined the Cliosophic Society in November 1776. This would have been close to the time, November 29, when President Witherspoon disbanded the College because of the approach of the British army. Noel probably was among the small number of students who reassembled in the following summer and undoubtedly was one of the seniors who in August 1777 sustained the examination for the A.B. degree. There was no public commencement that year, and evidently the degrees for the Class of 1777 were formally awarded at a meeting of the trustees in April 1778.

What Noel did immediately after graduation has not been determined, but in time he studied law with William Paterson (A.B. 1763) and was licensed to practice as an attorney in April 1783. On the following February 13, according to Paterson, he was married "to the widow Stites," who seems to have been Sarah, the daughter of John Dennis of North Brunswick, Middlesex County, New Jersey. In July 1784 Noel was described in a court record as a resident of New Brunswick. Presumably he still lived there in May 1786, when he qualified as a counselor-at-law. But at some time before June 19, 1788, he seems to have moved to Augusta, Georgia, where he appears as a witness to a deed for a lot on Broad Street. On November 21, 1789, court records show him to have been a justice of the peace for Richmond County, of which Augusta was the county seat.

Early in the 1790s Noel moved to Savannah, where he served as mayor in 1796-1797 and again through three successive terms extending from July 9, 1804 to September 14, 1807. He also was an alderman of the city in 1798-1799 and 1801-1802. Governor John Milledge in February 1805 complimented Mayor Noel and other city authorities on the precautions they had taken "for preventing the introduction of the small pox within that place."

Perhaps the most celebrated case in which Noel appeared as an attorney occurred in the spring of 1804. A judge of the superior court, apparently a recent immigrant from one of the northern states, delivered a charge to the grand jury that was mainly a vigorous attack upon the institution of slavery. The jury's presentment on the next day was a hardly less vigorous indictment of the judge for "disseminating principles that may tend to involve the community in the horrors of domestic insurrection." The twenty-two jurors having been committed to jail, Noel was one of the attorneys who secured their release on a writ of *habeas corpus* by the judges of the inferior court. The offending judge found himself in jail for a couple of weeks on a warrant issued by a local justice of the peace. He soon left the state.

Noel was an investor in the Georgia Company, among whose original stockholders was Matthew McAllister (A.B. 1779), and which in 1795 was largely responsible for the famous Yazoo land fraud. Otherwise, Noel's life and practice seem to have been quiet and uneventful. He has not been remembered among the great lawyers of the Georgia bar, but he is credited with the training of a number of young men for the law, including George McIntosh Troup (A.B. 1797), the Federalist governor of the state after previous service in the national House of Representatives and the Senate; and John Forsyth, congressman, senator, minister to Spain, and United States secretary of state as well as governor of Georgia. Noel died in Savannah on November 1, 1817. The son of his wife by her earlier marriage, Richard M. Stites, apparently accompanied the family to Georgia, where early in 1813 his will named as his mother Sarah C. Noel, the name she used when serving jointly with her husband as a witness to legal documents. Whether there were children by her marriage to Noel has not been determined. She seems to have survived him.

SOURCES: See James Ashton Bayard (A.B. 1777) for awarding of degrees to Class of 1777. Alumni file, MS Clio. Soc. membership list, PUA; I. Thomas, *Hist. of Printing in Amer.*, AAS *Transactions*, VI (1874), 235 ("imported books"); *NJA* (2 ser.), II, 193, 209 ("mahogany desk"), 251; (1 ser.), XXXV, 86, 91; XXXVI, 243; XL, 101-102; E. F. Hatfield, *Hist. of Elizabeth, N.J.* (1868), 445, 530-34; Alexander, *Princeton*, 201; *WMQ* (3 ser.), 7 (1950), 35; *Som. Cnty. Hist. Quart.*, 2 (1913), 182 ("widow Stites"); *Hist. Coll. . . . DAR: Rec. of Richmond Cnty.*, II (1929), 127, 231, 252, 304; C. C. Jones, Jr., *Hist. of Savannah* (1890), 423-25; H. M. Salley, *Correspondence of John Milledge* (1949), 71, 125 ("small pox"), 134; M. F. LaFar and C. P. Wilson, *Abstracts of Wills, Chatham Cnty.* (1963), 72, 76, 95, 143-44; C. P. Wilson, *Annals of Ga.*, III (1933), 128; *Hist. Coll. . . . Habersham Chapt., DAR*, III (1910), 35; S. F. Miller, *Bench and Bar of Ga.*, II (1858), 13; E. J. Harden, *Life of George M. Troup* (1859), 10; A. L. Duckett, *John Forsyth* (1962), 5. Beginning in 1797 the College's triennial catalogues credit Noel with an A.M. degree, but no evidence has been found to indicate its source. The *Catalogue* of 1815 incorrectly lists him as dead.

WFC

Matthew Perkins

MATTHEW PERKINS was the son of Matthew and Hannah Bishop Perkins, members of the Hanover Congregational Society in the Lisbon section of Norwich, Connecticut. He was probably born in 1756, the year after his brother of the same name died at the age of ten. Another brother was Nathan Perkins (A.B. 1770), and like him, Perkins may have received his earliest education from Joseph Lathrop (Yale 1752) in Springfield, Connecticut.

On May 3, 1773, Matthew Perkins, Sr., a man of unusually robust health and physique, died of tetanus, the result of being bitten on the thumb by a young slave whom he was punishing. His son Matthew entered the College between that time and February 14, 1774, when he joined the Cliosophic Society. A cousin, Eliphaz Perkins (Class of 1776) was a student in Nassau Hall as well. On March 26, 1775, in the middle of his sophomore year according to the College steward's accounts, Perkins died in Princeton.

SOURCES: *NEHGR*, 14 (1860), 113-15 (which confuses the order of the two brothers named Matthew); *Vital Recs. of Norwich, Conn.* (1913), I, 191, 357; MS Steward's accounts, MS Clio. Soc. membership list, PUA.

Lewis Allaire Scott

LEWIS ALLAIRE SCOTT, lawyer and public official, was born on February 11, 1759, the son of the New York City lawyer, revolutionary general, and politician John Morin Scott (Yale 1746) and his wife, Helena Rutgers Scott. An alderman at the time of his son's birth, the elder Scott had already established his reputation as a persuasive controversialist in the literary and sectarian hostilities that accompanied the establishment of King's College in 1754. John Adams was impressed by the Scotts' lavish manner of living when he visited them in 1774, but Lewis Scott undoubtedly adopted a more austere style when he came down from New York City to the College of New Jersey. He probably entered the College in the fall of 1773, and he joined the Cliosophic Society in February 1774 under the rather curious name of "Cynthia."

Like many of his classmates of the revolutionary period, Scott did not complete his degree. That he left Princeton by November 1776 when the approach of British troops required the closing of Nassau Hall is likely, but his whereabouts and activities during the remainder of the war have not been fully determined. In June 1777 he was with his father, then a state senator, in Hurley, New York, a village in Ulster County near Kingston, the state's wartime seat of government. In that month Scott was sent by his father to Livingston Manor with a letter and a verbal message for William Smith (Yale 1745), a longtime friend of the father and a former member of the colonial Council whose loyalty to the new state regime was then under suspicion. Lewis Scott's friendship with the Livingstons is mentioned in his father's letter to William Smith. Smith recorded another visit to the manor by the younger Scott in January 1778, this time in the company of Brockholst Livingston (A.B. 1774). Scott apparently did not take any part in the military struggle. He may have studied law during the war, perhaps with his father, since he is described as an attorney in the 1789 New-York Directory.

After the conclusion of hostilities and the British evacuation of New York City, Scott and his father returned to Manhattan. The elder Scott had been appointed the first secretary of the state of New York in 1778. After his death in 1784, Lewis Scott succeeded him in office. In this capacity, Scott also became ex officio a regent of the University of the State of New York and in 1787 a trustee of Columbia College. By an act of the legislature of 1784, the expropriated mansion of a colonial councilor became Scott's official home and the depository for state documents in his care. On January 18, 1785, he married Juliana Sitgreaves, the daughter of a merchant of Philadelphia and Easton, Pennsylvania and the sister of Samuel Sitgreaves, later a Pennsylvania congressman. The couple took up residence in the secretary's house at 2 George Street (subsequently renumbered 221 Broadway). They were recorded there in the first federal census in a household that included six other persons.

The secretary of state of New York was also a commissioner of the land office, and in 1791 the legislature granted Scott and the other land commissioners, who included Governor George Clinton and Attorney General Aaron Burr (A.B. 1772), discretionary authority to dispose of vast amounts of land still in the public domain. Within a matter of months they distributed over 5.5 million acres in large grants, much to the dismay of New York Federalists who pointed to many instances of political favoritism in the awards. Lewis Scott's part in this affair was probably a minor one since his colleagues among the commissioners were far more influential than he. He did not gain a political reputation himself, and references to his career are so infrequent as to suggest that his life may have been that of a reclusive functionary. With the exception of his membership in the Saint Andrew's Society, Scott does not appear to have been active in the many New York fraternal, charitable, or political organizations of his day.

Lewis Allaire Scott made out his will in September 1793. He died on March 17, 1798, leaving his estate to his wife, his son John Morin Scott (A.B. 1805), and his daughter Maria Litchfield Scott. Scott was buried in Trinity churchyard near his father and his brother-in-law Charles McKnight, Jr. (A.B. 1774). Although the elder John Morin Scott is known to have been a Presbyterian before the Revolution, the location of the family burial plot and the Episcopal affiliation of the 1805 graduate suggest that the family embraced the Episcopal communion during Lewis A. Scott's lifetime.

SOURCES: W. M. MacBean, *Bio. Reg. of St. Andrew's Soc. of N.Y.,* I (1922), 186-87, 25-26; *DAB* (father); *Adams Papers,* II, 105; MS Clio. Soc. membership list, MS Steward's accounts, PUA; W.H.W. Sabine, ed., *Hist. Memoirs of William Smith,* II (1958), 152-53, 293; *N.Y. Directory, 1789,* 77; *N.Y. Red Book* (editions before 1942 which give Scott's tenure as secretary of state as 23 Oct 1789 to 24 Mar 1793 repeat early mistakes or misprints); C. Z. Lincoln, *Constitutional Hist. of N.Y.,* II (1906), 524-25; M. H. Thomas, *Columbia Univ., Officers and Alumni* (1936), 13, 83; J. A. Scoville, *Old Merchants of N.Y. City* (1866), 232; *PMHB,* 13 (1889), 255; *First Census, N.Y.,* 135; A. F. Young, *Democratic Republicans of N.Y.* (1967), 232-39; *N.Y. Wills,* xv, 86; M.S.B. Chance and M.A.E. Smith, *Scott Family Letters* (1930), 8-9.

MANUSCRIPTS: PHi

GSD

Abraham Smith

ABRAHAM SMITH, lawyer, was the oldest son of Thomas Smith (A.B. 1754) and his wife, Elizabeth Lynsen Smith. No date of birth has been found, but his parents were married on November 22, 1756, which suggests a birthdate of 1757 or 1758, though there is an indication that it may have been 1760. Any one of these dates fits well enough with Abraham's appearance in the College steward's list of students for the period of May 25, 1773 to September 25, 1774. His appearance again, as a member of the sophomore class, in the steward's list for November 1774 to April 10, 1775 strongly suggests that he had been enrolled since November 1773, and this assumption finds some confirmation in a manuscript list of members of the Cliosophic Society, which indicates that he was admitted to that society on February 7, 1774, with the pseudonym "Cliophel."

Smith's New York family was an especially prominent one and had close ties to Princeton. His grandfather William Smith (Yale 1719) was a founding trustee of the College of New Jersey and served it as a trustee until his death in 1769. One of his uncles was Doctor James Smith (A.B. 1757). Another uncle was William Smith (Yale 1745), who became chief justice of New York, member of the governor's council, historian of the province, and a Loyalist at the time of the American Revolution who subsequently served as chief justice of Quebec. Abraham's father was a leading lawyer of New York City, who later would include among his students Aaron Burr (A.B. 1772) and who through 1775 was active in the Whig cause as a member of the Committee of One Hundred and of the Provincial Congress. The family owned extensive properties outside the city, including the country home that Thomas built on Haverstraw Bay, some thirty miles up the Hudson, to which he withdrew when the British moved toward New York in 1776.

How long Abraham may have remained a student at Nassau Hall cannot be said. There are no known accounts of the steward that extended beyond April 1775, and the ledger of a local merchant covering the period from the summer of 1774 to the end of 1775 carries no entry for Abraham Smith, as it does for many other students. At some time prior to June 1779, he had joined his family at Haverstraw, for at that time, according to his father's later report to Governor George Clinton, Abraham had "imprudently" left to join his Uncle William in New York City, where he arrived on July 1.

Suffering from "intermittent fever" as late as June 1780, Abraham became anxious to return home, and his father, who kept in touch with his brother William, advised that Abraham "retire to Long Island and prosicute [sic] his studies until I could consult my Friends." This, at any rate, was the substance of a letter of September 15, 1780, from Thomas Smith to Governor Clinton, which sought permission to cross the lines and bring his son home under a flag of truce that General Benedict Arnold had promised to give him provided the governor gave his consent. The governor in an otherwise friendly letter of September 18 refused his permission, and it is impossible here to say just when Abraham was reunited with his parents. It can be noted, however, that his father had expressed to Clinton his concern on hearing from his brother William that the son "inclines to none of the learned Professions but to the life of a Soldier," which the father insisted did not "arise from Inclination but from Dispair of ever being Restored to us again." This passage from the letter of September 15 lends added interest to the will of Thomas C. Williams made aboard the ship *Tarter* on the following December 17, and witnessed by Abraham L. Smith, the signature later employed by the son of

Thomas, and Robert Rollo, "Captain in His Majesties American Legion."

If Abraham had committed the further indiscretion of joining the king's armed forces, as appears to be a strong possibility, he undoubtedly was saved from the full cost of his misstep by his father's discretion. Although Thomas Smith was often a source of intelligence for the Americans regarding British movements along the Hudson, his own loyalty was open to suspicion, if only because he was a brother of Chief Justice William Smith. His position became the more embarrassing when another brother, Joshua Hett Smith, became a principal agent in bringing Major John André and Benedict Arnold together in September 1780, in of all places Thomas's Haverstraw home, to plot the surrender of West Point to the British. Joshua was acquitted of charges of treasonous conduct by a military court, but he was imprisoned by civil authorities, escaped, and took refuge in New York City and later in England. His brother Thomas was never formally accused of involvement. Indeed, he survived the Revolution with sufficient reputation as a supporter of the American cause to make it possible for him to hold on to his own property and even with time to protect no small part of the property of Chief Justice William Smith.

For a time after the war, there is uncertainty as to where Thomas and his son Abraham were located, but a broadside published by the latter on October 7, 1785 establishes their presence in New York City and, more important, makes clear that the son had come to use the signature Abraham L., the middle initial presumably drawn from his mother's family name. He had become involved in some kind of controversy with Brockholst Livingston (A.B. 1774), who apparently had attacked Abraham in the public press on October 3, and who on the evening of October 5 was so violently assaulted as to persuade the Common Council of the city that he was the victim of an attempted assassination and that a reward of $125 should be offered for discovery of the would-be assassin. Obviously, the finger of suspicion had pointed toward Smith, and his broadside was published to deny that he had any part in so "horrid an act" and to offer an additional $125 for discvovery of the real culprit. Appended was a deposition that Abraham was at home on the evening of the fifth, "preparing his vindication for the press, until eleven o'clock." Signed by Thomas Smith, Esq., his wife Elizabeth, and his sons Thomas Smith, Jr., James Scott Smith, and William Smith, the deposition stated that all of the family was at home that evening, but it was noted that William Smith was then living in New Jersey.

Little can be added beyond the fact that Abraham ultimately ful-filled his father's hope that he might enter one of the learned pro-fessions. How early he began the study of law has not been discovered, but he probably was the Abraham Smith who in the New York di-rectory for 1792 is described as an attorney at law with a Beaver Street address. He may have been the Abraham Smith of Beaver Street who in the directory for the preceding year was identified as a schoolmaster. There seems to be no room for doubt that he was the Abraham L. Smith, attorney at law of 5 Beaver Street, who was listed in the directory for 1794, which was the year in which he was ad-mitted to the bar in Orange County, New York. Abraham L. Smith continued to be listed at varying addresses as an attorney and/or counselor-at-law through *Longworth's Directory* for 1826-1827. His name is not found in the directory for 1827-1828, so presumably he died, or moved from the city, about 1827. Through later years he evidently had experienced adversity, for he must have been the Abraham L. Smith who in 1820 petitioned the Common Council for relief from the payment of his taxes. On the ground that the peti-tioner was then confined to the limits of the city "and in needy cir-cumstances," the petition was granted and the collector instructed to "return the same in the list of errors and insolvencies of the second ward." Whether the embarrassment was anything more than tempo-rary must be left to conjecture for no further information about his career or his personal life has been discovered.

SOURCES: *NYGBR*, 85 (1954), 20; R. J. Koke, *Accomplice in Treason: Joshua Hett Smith and the Arnold Conspiracy* (1973), passim (gives Abraham's age in 1779 as 19, and indexes all references to him under the full name of Abraham Lynsen Smith); *Princetonians, 1748-1768*, 122-25, 209-13; L.F.S. Upton, *The Loyal Whig: William Smith of New York and Quebec* (1969); *N.Y. Hist.*, 16 (1935), 392-404; P. M. Hamlin, *Legal Education in Colonial N.Y.* (1939) 80-82, 164, 201-3; MS Steward's accounts, MS Clio. Soc. membership list, PUA; Patterson Acct. Bk., W.H.W. Sabine, ed., *Hist. Memoirs of William Smith*, III (1971), 123, 153, 172, 236, 331-32 ("retire to Long Island"); *N.Y. Wills*, x, 274 ("American Legion"); XIII, 232-33; *STE*, 44793 ("So horrid an act"); *MCCCNY*, I, 175-76; XI, 86, 234; XII, 480 ("needy circumstances"); XIII, 793; XIV, 3, 28, 29; *Clinton Papers*, VIII, 395-96; E. M. Ruttenber and L. H. Clark, *Hist. of Orange Cnty.* (1881), 143.

WFC

Gilbert Tennent, Jr.

GILBERT TENNENT, JR., military physician, was the son of Gilbert Ten-nent, Sr., an original trustee of the College and one of the most influ-ential clergymen in America, and his third wife, Sarah Spofford Tennent. He was born in Philadelphia, where his father was pastor of the Second Presbyterian Church. Although his exact birthdate is unknown, it was obivously before 1760 since he was the oldest of three minor children who were alive in October 1763 when their father made his will providing for the care and education of the youngsters. The senior Tennent was especially hopeful that his namesake would follow him into the ministry, and to encourage the boy in that direction, he left him £300 and his personal library.

Young Gilbert Tennent was a sophomore at Nassau Hall from November 1774 to at least April 1775, according to the steward's accounts. But he did not feel the call to join the clergy and so left college to study medicine with Benjamin Rush (A.B. 1760) in Philadelphia. On April 22, 1777, he joined the army as a surgeon's mate, and while the main force ended its winter at Valley Forge, Tennent served in the nearby hospital at French Creek. He was there at least until October 1778.

Tennent was included on a return of the medical department at the end of 1779, and he signed memorials from the military doctors at Philadelphia to Congress in February 1780. He then apparently left the army, for late in 1780 he was aboard the *General Sinclair* when that ship was lost at sea.

In November 1791 one of Tennent's colleagues at French Creek, William W. Smith, who was also Tennent's executor, appealed to Congress for depreciation pay for himself and for his friend's estate. After more than two years of investigation, Secretary of the Treasury Alexander Hamilton was unable to prove Tennent's membership in the army beyond December 10, 1779. Hamilton admitted that the records were incomplete, and he reported that Tennent's estate should receive any depreciation pay due it if evidence of the doctor's extended service could be had. On March 21, 1794, however, the House of Representatives closed the matter.

SOURCES: Sprague, *Annals*, III, 35-38; M. A. Tennent, *Light in Darkness* (1971), 95-96; MS Steward's accounts, PUA; College of Physicians of Phila., *Transactions and Studies* (4 ser.), 14 (1946), 128, 130; *PMHB*, 27 (1903), 442, 445; Index, PCC; *Hamilton Papers*, XVI, 91-92.

Samuel Thane

SAMUEL THANE, possibly a medical man, may have been the son of the Reverend Daniel Thane (A.B. 1748) and Mary Clowes Thane. The elder Thane's marriage in 1749 and the rarity of this Scottish surname in America make this a strong possibility. Samuel Thane was a member of the Cliosophic Society and assumed the secret name "Martius" at the time of his admission to the society. Perhaps this alias was taken from the Roman word for "March" or after the god Mars, who gave his name to the season of winter's end and the beginning of the Roman new year. Whether Thane's temperament reminded his fellows either of that fierce month or of that fierce god is uncertain.

Indeed, little about Samuel Thane's life is at all certain. He was unable to complete his college course after the evacuation of Nassau Hall and the dispersal of its residents just ahead of advancing British units in November 1776. No record of military service has been found for him. The only subsequent reference that has been discovered to a man of this name is found in a will dated August 7, 1784, at Pompton Plains, Morris County, New Jersey, in which Samuel Thane is listed as a witness. The will was proved there by Joseph Lewis of Morristown on October 2, 1784. Lewis recorded in his diary the following day that he had dined with a Doctor Thane, who was probably the Samuel Thane of the will, and who was perhaps the Samuel Thane who attended the College of New Jersey. Nothing further has been learned about this man's career, however.

SOURCES: *Princetonians, 1748-1768*, 11-12. If Samuel Thane was Daniel Thane's son and was born in the 1750s, he was most likely born either at Connecticut Farms (now part of Elizabeth), N.J. or in New Castle Cnty., Del. Daniel Thane definitely had other offspring in addition to his daughter Catherine, mentioned in his biography as an only child. Another daughter of Daniel and Mary Thane was included in the 1780 will of Mary Thane's sister, but the will makes no mention of a Samuel Thane. Catherine died in 1771 in Elizabeth, where Mary Thane had returned with her children after Daniel Thane's death in 1763. [*N.Y. Wills*, XIII, 10; *NEHGR*, 44 (1890), 265-66; W. O. Wheeler and E. D. Halsey, *Inscriptions on Tombstones . . . at Elizabeth, N.J.* (1892), 77.] Despite the obscurity that surrounds Samuel Thane, he came from a family with other ties to collegiate education. Daniel Thane of CNJ may earlier have matriculated at a college of the Univ. of Aberdeen, and Samuel Thane was a contemporary of Alexander Thain, who was at the Univ. of St. Andrews, 1776-1777. [P. J. Anderson, *Fasti Academiae Mariscallanae aberdonensis*, II (1898), 313 & n; J. M. Anderson, ed., *Matriculation Roll of of the Univ. of St. Andrews, 1747-1897* (1905), 26. MS Clio. Soc. membership list, PUA, (but Thane could not have been admitted at a regular society meeting in December 1776, as the list suggests, because the College had been dismissed at the end of November). See also *N.J. Wills*, VI, 410; *NJHSP* (n.s.), 59 (1941), 279.] Dr. Thane does not appear in the *Rise, Minutes, and Proceedings* (1875) of the N.J. Med. Soc. He has not been found in lists of N.J. inhabitants for this period, nor has he been located in any other state in the 1790 census.

GSD

Samuel Vickers

SAMUEL VICKERS, A.B., A.M. 1785, military physician and surgeon, was born in New Brunswick, Middlesex County, New Jersey, in 1755, the oldest son of Joseph Vickers and his wife, Sarah Walker Vickers. The father may have been the Joseph Vickers who in January 1779 advertised for sale the farm of about 150 acres on which he then lived, located about five miles from Cranbury, also in Middlesex County.

Samuel may first have attended Queen's College (Rutgers) in New Brunswick. A newspaper account of that institution's first commencement, held on October 12, 1774, after reporting that "high applause" greeted orations in three different languages delivered by the single graduate of the day, lists Samuel Vickers among the five members "of the present senior class," who in the afternoon "spoke with gracefulness and propriety on various subjects." This presumably should be read to mean that Vickers and his fellow orators had been admitted to the senior class at Queen's. At Princeton the steward's account for the period extending from November 1774 to April 10, 1775, shows Samuel Vickers as a member of the senior class there, however. Either there were two Samuel Vickers of approximately the same age or the student at Queen's for some reason had elected to transfer to Nassau Hall. The latter is the likelier of the two possibilities. In either case, a question remains. There was no Samuel Vickers among the seniors graduating from Nassau Hall in September 1775, and no clue has been found that might help to determine what Vickers was doing before the members of the Class of 1777, according to President Witherspoon's public announcement, sustained the examination for their degrees in August of that year. The degrees, including that of Vickers, were formally awarded at a meeting of the trustees on April 16, 1778.

A standard source indicates that in January 1778 Vickers had become a surgeon's mate with the General Hospital of the Continental Army and that on June 30, 1779 he was promoted to the rank of surgeon. Whether, when, where, or with whom he may have studied medicine has not been determined. Conceivably, he could have done so between April 1775 and August 1777, the two dates at which his presence in Princeton is reasonably well established.

At some time, probably with the Continentals who were detached from Washington's force for reinforcement of the Southern Department after the fall of Charleston in May 1780, Vickers was transferred for duty in the Carolinas. As Senior Surgeon of the Flying Hospital at Cheraw, South Carolina, he signed a return for the period December 30, 1780 to February 1, 1781. A letter from Vickers, dated at Ashley Ford on October 12, 1782, reported that Secretary of War Benjamin Lincoln had recently offered him a promotion to Surgeon of the Hospitals and that he had accepted. In this letter, which was written to "Dr. [John] Cochran," Vickers said that he was then hopefully awaiting the British evacuation of nearby Charleston. He complained of the "amazingly unhealthy" state of the hospitals in that quarter and noted that he himself was suffering from the effects of the malaria that generally infected the area. "By repeated attacks of the ague," he observed, "I am now completely reduced to the So. Carolina standard of animal proportion—Nox et praeteria nihil."

This letter argues against an assumption that he, along with his classmates James Hanna and John Young Noel, was in Princeton on the preceding September 25, when for the second time he was formally awarded the A.B. degree by a board of trustees, who obviously lacked an adequate record even of their own transactions since 1776. Perhaps Vickers, Hanna, and Noel had missed President Witherspoon's announcement in the summer of 1778 that the graduates of the previous year might "have their diplomas, bearing the proper date, when they apply for them." Perhaps the three did not apply until 1782.

Whatever distaste he may have developed for the climate of the Charleston area, Vickers may have gambled on the possibility that Savannah enjoyed a better one. Perhaps the attraction that drew him there was something quite different. Certainly the end was tragic. The *Georgia Gazette* of October 20, 1785 carried the following report:

> Last Saturday forenoon Dr. Samuel Vickers shot himself with a pistol, in the garden of Sharon Plantation near this town, and immediately expired. The coroner having held an inquest on his body, the jury found that he had been for some time before insane and not of sound memory and perfect understanding.

The date of his death was October 15, a little over two weeks after he had been awarded the A.M. degree at the Princeton commencement on September 28.

His younger brother Thomas Leonard Vickers apparently went to Georgia to settle his affairs and had erected over the grave in the Old Colonial Cemetery in Savannah a tombstone inscribed as follows:

> Here lies interr'd the / Body of Doct. Samuel / Vickers, who departed / this Life, Octor. the 15th / Anno Domini 1785 In / the XXX, Year of His Age / He / Was born in New Brunswick / and / Received the honours of the / College at Princeton in N.

Jersey / This Monument is erected to his Me / mory by his affectionate brother TLV.

Apparently, Samuel Vickers had not married.

SOURCES: See James Ashton Bayard (A.B. 1777) for awarding of degrees to Class of 1777. Alumni File, PUA (includes photograph of tombstone, typed copy of letter of 12 Oct 1782, photographic copy of return for hospital at Cheraw, copy of newspaper report of death supplied by Ga. Hist. Soc., and geneal. data drawn from Bibles in NjR); *GMNJ*, 34 (1959), 93, 95, *NJA*, (2 ser.), II, 435-37 ("diplomas, bearing the proper date"); III, 55-56; (1 ser.), XXXVII, 266, 381; XXIX, 506; W.H.S. Demarest, *Hist. of Rutgers College* (1924), 89-90, 132; Rutgers College, *Gen. Cat.* (1909), 42; MS Steward's accounts, PUA; Trustee Minutes, 25 Sep 1782; *N.J. Gazette*, 9 Oct 1782, 10 Oct 1785; Stryker, *Off. Reg.*, 74; Heitman.

                                                        WFC

John White

JOHN WHITE, soldier, merchant, and apothecary-physician, was born in New York City on June 25, 1759, the son of Townshend White, Philadelphia merchant and sometime business associate of the Beekman family in New York. The mother was Ann Ellsworth, sister of Elizabeth, the widow of John Beekman (1720-1774). Elizabeth Beekman's will, which was drawn and proved in 1790, directed that her estate be divided into four equal parts and given one-fourth each to a brother, her sisters Jane Osborn and Mary Chevalier, both widows living in Philadelphia, and "the children and grandchildren of my late sister, Ann White." One-sixth of this last portion was to go to "my nephew, John White, merchant of Philadelphia," and another sixth was to be divided among "the children of my late nephew, Townshend White, Jr.," provisions that seem to establish the paternity of John White the Princeton undergraduate.

It has been said that White was prepared for college by Peter Wilson in a school at Hackensack, New Jersey, before Wilson became professor of the classical languages at Columbia College in New York. Two of the surviving accounts kept by the steward of students enrolled at Nassau Hall carry White's name, the earliest of them dated May 25, 1773 to September 25, 1774. The name comes close to the end of the list, as though added perhaps at a late date, and so suggests that he was first enrolled at some time during the academic year 1773-1774. Confirmation of such an assumption is indicated by a manuscript list of early members of the Cliosophic Society, which dates his membership from February 21, 1774, and by the steward's account for November 6, 1774 to April 10, 1775, which lists him as a member of the sophomore class. No additional evidence of his presence in Princeton has been found, so the tradition that he abandoned his studies not long after the Lexington and Concord engagements may be true.

According to an excerpt from what appears to have been a funeral sermon preached in the Second Presbyterian Church of Philadelphia on July 16, 1838, White proceeded from Princeton to Philadelphia for the study of medicine. Perhaps he did, but the statement may simply reflect a tradition attributable in part to the courtesy title of doctor that seems to have been extended to him much later in life. The sermon also credits him with service as a militiaman in the Pennsylvania component of the Flying Camp established in New Jersey during the latter half of 1776, an assertion that is supported with a detailed narrative of his service from January 1777 to August 1779 as a surgeon's mate in a number of military hospitals. Thereafter, it was said, White served as surgeon aboard a privateer, was captured by the British, experienced four months of imprisonment at Charleston, South Carolina, and another seven at New York. Because of the number of John Whites who served during the Revolution, it is difficult to confirm any part of the story. Members of his family, and perhaps he himself, seem to have been part owners of ships engaged in privateering, however, and the name John White appears on a list of prisoners of war incarcerated on the famous *Jersey* prison ship. Further, a John White was among those who took an oath of allegiance and as late as October 11, 1784 was described as mate of the "General Military Hospital."

The published directories for the city of Philadelphia, beginning with Macpherson's directory of 1785, list a John White at 352 Fifth Street, but it is impossible to know whether he was the former Princeton student. His name is not found in another directory for that year that carried a list of physicians and surgeons. Indeed, not until 1809 is the name given with M.D. appended, and even then it continues to be omitted from separate listings of physicians. His aunt's will establishes that by 1790 John White was engaged in some kind of mercantile business at Philadelphia, but a directory for 1793 was the first to identify him as a druggist, as he would be known through many years. In 1794 the description was chemist and druggist, and this in the next year was enlarged by the additional designation "apothecary." With occasional variations of identification, he continued at 163 High Street until 1808. In the next year, the address became 309 North Third, and there in 1810 a James White, possibly a relative, was listed as an M.D. and chemist, and was also given place, in contrast with John, in the separate listing of physicians. The scale of John White's business is suggested by the three listings given him in 1820: for a laboratory at 163 St. John, where it had been so listed in 1814, and a drugstore at 82 North Front in addition to what was apparently his residence. In the sermon previously cited, White was described as "a prominent manufacturer of chemicals" and as a member and trustee of the Second Presbyterian Church. From 1831 through 1834 he served as a city commissioner, a post filled by appointment of the mayor. During the later years of his life, he apparently became less active in the management of his business. For more than three years before his death, he even disappears from the city directories.

Described as "kind hearted, benevolent, liberal and affectionate," he died on July 8, 1838. He had been married to Elizabeth Standley, who died in 1806. Information regarding the children who may have been born to the marriage is lacking, but at the time of the census of 1790 White apparently headed a household that consisted of himself and four free white females.

SOURCES: *PMHB*, 38 (1914), 248-49 (funeral sermon); *N.Y. Wills*, VIII, 183; XIV, 178-79; W. B. Aitken, *Distinguished Families in Amer. Descended From Wilhelmus Beekman and Jon Thomasse Van Dyke* (1912), 153; *DAR Patriot Index*, 736; P. L. White, *Beekmans of N.Y.* (1956), 243, 299; P. L. White, *Beekman Mercantile Papers*, I, passim; M. H. Thomas, *Columbia Univ., Officers and Alumni* (1936), 92; MS Steward's accounts, MS Clio. Soc. membership list, PUA; C. H. Lincoln, *Naval Records of Amer. Rev.* (1906), 281, 350, 371; D. Dandridge, *Amer. Prisoners of the Rev.* (1911), 490; T. Wescott, *Names of Persons Who Took Oath of Allegiance to Pa.* (1965), 29, 50.

                                                              WFC

CLASS OF 1778

William Boyd, A.B.

John Brown

John Brown

Benjamin Dunlap

John Ellet (Ellit, Elett)

William Halkerston

James McDonald

Nathaniel Macon

Jacob Morton, A.B.

Andrew Pettit

William Ross

Joseph Scudder, A.B.

Jesse (Jessy, Jesles) Smith

John Smith

William Smith

William Stephens (Stevens)

Daniel Thatcher (Thacher)

John Trotman

Robert Wharry (Wherry)

Peter Wilson, A.B.

Matthew Woods, A.B.

William Boyd

WILLIAM BOYD, A.B., A.M. 1782, Presbyterian clergyman, was born in 1758 in that part of Cumberland County which later became Franklin County, Pennsylvania, the son of John Boyd. The father had migrated from Northern Ireland to Pennsylvania about the middle of the century and had married in America a woman whose name has not been found. He seems to have been a farmer and is said to have died when his son William was about fifteen years of age. Tradition holds that Boyd's own perseverance in the desire to become a minister explains his achievement of a college education. But nothing definite seems to be known regarding his early education and preparation for college. Even the question of when he was admitted to the College cannot be answered, and it is impossible to determine how much time he may have spent in residence at the College before his graduation, with four other young men, in September 1778.

The very fragmentary records of the steward for the 1770s suggest that Boyd could not have been enrolled before the fall of 1775 and that the fall of 1776 is a more likely choice for the time of his matriculation. That would have been just before President Witherspoon dismissed the students on November 29 because of the approach of the British army. A few students were assembled at Princeton in the following July, most of them probably members of the senior class who in August sustained the examination for their degrees. Through the following year Nassau Hall served as a hospital for American troops, and the small number of students in attendance found such accommodations as they could in the village and recited their lessons in the president's house. In August 1778 President Witherspoon publicly announced that there would be a commencement "on the last Wednesday of September, when not only those who have attended constantly or occasionally, but those who have studied at home, provided they will submit to examination, shall be admitted, if qualified, to degrees according to their standing." It can be said with certainty only that Boyd was one of five who that year qualified for the first degree. He had become a member of the American Whig Society, and at commencement he spoke on "the Strength of human passions."

After graduation Boyd taught school, first at an academy in or near Annapolis, Maryland, and then as a private tutor for a family living close to Baltimore. His teaching evidently was combined with continued preparation for the ministry, and on October 17, 1782 he was licensed to preach by the Carlisle Presbytery. For a time he supplied a number of congregations in the middle state area, and on October 20, 1784, he was ordained and installed as pastor of the Lamington congregation of Somerset County, New Jersey, having been previously dismissed by the Donegal Presbytery for affiliation with the New Brunswick Presbytery. He continued in this pastorate until his death, occasionally serving the nearby Bedminster church as well. His friends credited him with scholarly and other professional qualifications that might have brought him a more prestigious pulpit had he not preferred the quieter life of a rural community.

The terms of his settlement at Lamington included a 100-acre farm, to which in 1802 he acquired a personal title by purchase from the congregation. He built quite a reputation as a pulpit orator in that section of New Jersey, and his standing outside the area was such as to bring him election in 1800 as a trustee of the College. His manner in the pulpit was characterized as one of "remarkable gravity and dignity," but outside the pulpit he was known as a man of wit who "abounded in anecdotes and historical narratives of families, of persons and events." Thoroughly orthodox in his beliefs, he showed little patience with "innovations," but was not much given to controversy. Through many years he suffered a "delicate state of health" that was described as "consumptive" and attributed to overzealous study. On May 17, 1807, he died after an illness brought on, it was believed, by exposure to inclement weather while supplying a nearby congregation.

In 1784 he had been married to Catherine Ker Taylor, daughter of Colonel John Taylor, who predeceased her husband. The couple had six children, two of whom died in infancy. Four survived their father, one daughter and three sons, including John T. Boyd (A.B. 1807). The other two sons were named James and William, and there is a high degree of probability that they were College graduates James Boyd (A.B. 1810) and William Boyd (A.B. 1815), but positive identification is lacking.

Sources: *The Evangelical Intelligencer*, 2 (1808), 201-208 ("anecdotes," "consumptive"); I. V. Brown, *Memoirs of the Rev. Robert Finley* (1819), 289-96; *Som. Cnty. Hist. Quart.*, 7 (1918), 139, 280-84; Sprague, *Annals*, III, 444-46 ("gravity and dignity," "innovations"); Giger, Memoirs; Alexander, *Princeton*, 61-64; *Rec. Pres. Chh.*, 498, 503, 507; *Min. Gen. Assem., 1789-1820*, 15, 136, 169, 289; *Centennial Memorial of the Presbytery of Carlisle*, I, 422.

WFC

John Brown

JOHN BROWN, lawyer, congressman, and United States senator from Kentucky, was born September 12, 1757, in Augusta (later Rockbridge) County, Virginia, the oldest surviving son of Reverend John Brown (A.B. 1749) and his wife, Margaret Preston Brown, and the brother of William Brown (Class of 1780). The father was one of the pioneer Presbyterian ministers in western Virginia and a schoolmaster who carried major responsibilities for the academy in Augusta County that in 1776 became Liberty Hall, later Washington College, and still later Washington and Lee University. No doubt, the son's preparation for college began under the tutelage of his father. The mother was a sister of Colonel William Preston, prominent political and military leader in that section of the province and state, and was herself a woman of forceful personality and "uncommon understanding." Such was the description of her given by Philip Fithian (A.B. 1772), who visited the family in December 1775. Fithian added that she "was at no loss in talking of any trifling incident which has taken place at Princeton since my first acquaintance at College." The circle of Princeton graduates in the community at the time included Samuel Doak (A.B. 1775), John Montgomery (A.B. 1775), and William Graham (A.B. 1773).

The younger Brown's enrollment in the College is established by his own statement late in life that he "was a student at Princeton College, when that institution was broken up by the British." This places him among the students President Witherspoon sadly dismissed on November 29, 1776, shortly after the opening of a new academic year, because of the approach of the British army. At first glance, the question of the length of his stay in Nassau Hall seems to be immediately solved by the steward's listing of a John Brown at the head of the freshman class in November 1774, and confirmation seemingly is found in a letter of February 18, 1774, from the father to William Preston, which advised that he was thinking of sending "Jony" to college in the following fall. Instead, however, John was sent east to the Northern Neck, where the Reverend James Waddel was opening a new school in which apparently he would assist in instruction while pursuing his own further studies. In a letter of the following August 22, his father explained to Preston that John would "be yong enough next year." In the spring of 1775 Preston was advised that Waddel was insisting that John continue with him for another year and that he had been given "his liberty to stay longer" on the condition that he come home during "Ague time." This he did in the following summer, and late in August his father reported that he recently had left for the

John Brown, Class of 1778
BY JOHN TRUMBULL

Northern Neck. The father's expression of continued concern for the
son's health in that part of Virginia suggests that the son had agreed
to stay with Waddel for another year, or at least for a part of it. It is
possible that John Brown may have been enrolled in the College during some part of the academic year 1775-1776, but it must be left here
as no more than a possibility.

As with others who left the College in November 1776, tradition
holds that Brown joined Washington's army. Perhaps he did, for there
is evidence that at some time during the war he saw service in the rank
of a private. Confirmation of the further tradition that he served as
aide to Lafayette has not been found, but the tradition suggests that
he may have been among the militiamen who served with Lafayette on
the Virginia peninsula beginning with the spring of 1781. Brown enrolled at the College of William and Mary at some time prior to December 4, 1778 when he was initiated into the Phi Beta Kappa Society
there. Through the better part of the ensuing two years, he remained
a student at Williamsburg, until in the fall of 1780 he fell victim to a
serious and prolonged illness.

A revealing record of his student days at William and Mary has been
preserved in a series of letters he wrote to William Preston, who as-

sisted his nephew in meeting the cost of his education and who may have been partly responsible for John's decision to go to Williamsburg rather than return to Princeton. These letters reveal that initially Brown was debating a choice between law and medicine for a career, with some preference for the latter, but by the fall of 1779 the decision favored the law. On October 20 he advised his uncle that he had reached an agreement for study with Virginia's Attorney General Edmund Randolph, who in return for assistance "in writing" would charge no fee. The decision to move the state capital to Richmond soon called this arrangement into question, and Brown on Randolph's advice elected to remain in Williamsburg for attendance upon the lectures of George Wythe, newly appointed professor of law and police. In the summer of 1780 John was reporting his participation in the proceedings of a moot court and mock legislature that Wythe had set up for his students. But as the year approached its end, not only was he ill but the British invasion of Virginia was bringing for the college prospects he reported in dismal terms, its students "all turnd Soldiers." His activity during 1781 has not been established, but on January 20, 1782, he wrote from Albemarle County to Preston that he was living "as happily as I could wish," within easy reach of "Colonel Jefferson" who "supplies me with all necessary Books & proper Instructions & when any difficulty in reading arises I can attend him for assistance." Possibly Wythe, Thomas Jefferson's former mentor, had interceded in Brown's behalf. Brown reported that he was thinking of settling permanently in Albemarle for practice in it and neighboring counties.

Actually, Brown settled not long thereafter in Kentucky. He had shown an interest in that section of Virginia while still in college. Then in 1780 he applied for, and sought his uncle's advice regarding, appointment as surveyor in one of the three counties into which Kentucky was divided before the year was out. He settled first in Danville, seat of the superior court established in 1783, and later moved to Frankfort. Connected with more than one of the leading families of Kentucky and possessed of winning personal qualities, Brown quickly emerged as one of the more influential political leaders of the district. He was sent as senator to the Virginia legislature as early as 1784, and in October 1787 he was chosen by the legislature for membership in the Virginia delegation to the Continental Congress for the specific purpose of giving Kentucky representation. Contrary to what often has been said, Brown was not a member of the Virginia ratifying convention of 1788. During the June deliberations in Richmond, which brought a critically important decision in favor of the new constitution, Brown was in New York anxiously seeking a decision by the Congress in favor of statehood for Kentucky. Apparently, it is not correct to assume, as often it has been, that Brown was opposed to ratification of the Constitution. Letters from him to James Madison (A.B. 1771) on the eve and during the Richmond convention indicate the opposite.

For Brown, the summer of 1788 was one of extreme frustration. Since January he had been hoping for action that would implement an enabling act of the Virginia Assembly that had conceded statehood to Kentucky on the condition that Congress agree to its admission into the union by July 4, 1788. After months during which Congress repeatedly was unable to act on any question because it lacked the required quorum of state delegations, it agreed on June 2 to admit Kentucky and appointed a committee to draft an act for that purpose that would be "conformable to the Articles of Confederation." Before the month was out, the committee had decided that the Congress lacked the requisite power and that an amendment of the Articles would be necessary. When the committee was discharged on July 2, Brown moved ratification of the compact between Virginia and Kentucky, but on that day news arrived that New Hampshire had become the ninth, and so the deciding state to ratify the Constitution. On the next day, Congress adopted a motion to refer the decision on Kentucky's admission to the new Congress. Brown concluded that the "Eastern" states were in a conspiracy to prevent Kentucky from joining the union, in part through fear of strengthening the southern states in Congress. On the advice of colleagues at home, he believed that sentiment in Kentucky favored independence, with or without the consent of Virginia, and that another application for admission to the United States might not be made, partly because of a general distrust of the Constitution. This he set forth in a letter of August 10 to Jefferson that expressed the hope "that it may still be in the power of Congress to conciliate their minds and to secure their attachment to the Confederacy."

Before leaving New York for Kentucky, Brown conferred with the Spanish ambassador, apparently on the latter's initiative. There was no legal or other reason why he should not have done so. He was keenly aware of the critical importance of the Mississippi River for Kentucky and of the extent to which residents there feared that the United States might not give full backing to the need for free navigation of the river. Even so, as events proved, his consultation with the ambassador was politically indiscreet, or perhaps his real indiscretion was in several letters he wrote about the meeting. A letter of July 9, 1788 to his fellow Virginian John Smith, for example, enigmatically reported: "I have engaged in foreign negotiations which, if successful will be of great consequence to Kentucky. Am not at liberty to inform you of particulars at present." Another letter to a political ally who subsequently switched sides was made available for publication in support of charges brought by James M. Marshall, son of Thomas Marshall and brother of the later chief justice, in a heated political campaign of 1790 for election to Congress. Brown won the election and with it the Marshall family's enduring animosity, which found expression, among other places, in Humphrey Marshall's *History of Kentucky*, first published in 1812. It marked the beginning of an unparalleled feud continuing through the century among historians of Kentucky, in which one side declared Brown a traitor and an instigator of a plot to separate Kentucky from the United States and join it to the Spanish Empire in exchange for a Spanish guarantee of the coveted right to navigate the Mississippi.

Although the questions raised by the alleged "Spanish Conspiracy" involving Brown and General James Wilkinson have continued to divide historians, one point is above debate: throughout an especially troubled period in the history of Kentucky, Brown retained the confidence of most of its voters. He was elected to both the first and the second United States congresses, and after Kentucky was admitted to the union in 1792, he became one of its first senators. Twice reelected, he served in the Senate until 1805. Brown's friendship with both Jefferson and Madison continued, and he found natural affiliation with the emerging Republican party. His acquaintances included, of course, Aaron Burr (A.B. 1772), himself a senator from 1791 to 1797, and through Brown's last years in the Senate, its presiding officer. Brown's entertainment of Burr during the latter's famous western journey in 1805 was perfectly consistent with their amicable relationship and may have reflected no further association between them than a common interest in a speculative canal scheme.

After his failure to win reelection to the Senate in 1805, Brown held no elective office, either state or national. Through the years that followed, he practiced law, became a director of the Bank of Kentucky, and engaged in extensive land speculations. Apparently wearied by public life, he was nonetheless cognizant of his responsibilities as a leading citizen of town, county, and state. Twice he served as a commissioner for the replacement of statehouses destroyed by fire.

Brown did not marry until February 19, 1799. His home in Frankfort, commemoratively named "Liberty Hall," seems to have been begun in 1796, probably with a thought chiefly for its use by his aging parents, who moved to Kentucky about 1798. The house was still uncompleted when Brown's wife, Margaretta Mason, daughter of Reverend John Mason of New York, trustee of the College from 1779 to 1785 and holder of its honorary D.D., first came to Kentucky in 1801. The tradition that Jefferson planned the house seems to be mistaken, although his advice was sought after construction had begun. Margaretta Mason Brown lived there with her husband until his death on August 29, 1837. She died in the following May. They were survived by two of their four sons, Mason Brown, a Yale graduate, and Orlando Brown (A.B. 1820). A daughter had died young.

SOURCES: O. Brown, *Memoranda of the Preston Family* (1842), 5-6 ("a student at Princeton"); photocopy of orig. MS in PUA through courtesy of Prof. Stuart Sprague; S. Sprague, "Sen. John Brown of Ky.," Ph.D. dissert., N.Y. Univ. (1972); J. M. Brown, *Pol. Beginnings of Ky.* (1889), 111 (which states that Brown went from CNJ "at the age of nineteen, upon John Witherspoon's certificate of leave and approbation, to serve as a volunteer *aide* to Lafayette"). Brown has been included in the Class of 1778 because his additional study with Waddel after his father considered him ready for college probably gave him the advanced standing assigned to many other students. If he was enrolled during the academic year 1775-1776, he probably belonged to the Class of 1777. An entry in Patterson Acct. Bk. for a John Brown on 28 Aug 1775 could indicate that he had come to CNJ after calling briefly on Waddel, but a more probable assumption is that this was the John Brown listed as a freshman by the steward in Nov 1774.

R. K. Pruett, *The Browns of Liberty Hall* (1966); *John P. Branch Hist. Papers of Randolph-Macon College*, 4 (1915), 257-88; *Filson Club Hist. Quart.*, 16 (1942), 75-87; 19 (1945), 3-5; 44 (1970), 19-37; J. A. Waddell, *Annals of Augusta Cnty, Va.* (1902), 90-91; *Fithian Journal*, II, 141 ("uncommon understanding"); *DAB*; L. Collins, *Hist. of Ky.* (1878), 252-53; *BDAC*; *KSHS Reg.*, 36 (1938), 61-65; 70 (1972), 108-20; 71 (1973), 69-86; 69 (1971), 313-18; Washington and Lee Univ., *Cat. of Alumni* (1888), 47; als JB to W. Preston, 30 Jan 1782, Draper MSS, 5QQ103, WHi; for pertinent correspondence of J. Brown, Sr. with Preston, see ibid., 3QQ8, -81, 4QQ12, -15, -26, -28, -31, WHi; *WMQ* (1 ser.), 4 (1896), 213-54; 9 (1900-1901), 18-23, 75-83; *Jefferson Papers*, I, 42-43 (for explanation of Jefferson's colonelcy); *DAR Patriot Index*; P. Watlington, *Partisan Spirit* (1972), 79n; *LMCC*, VIII, xcvii, 715, 733, 749-50 (which expresses to Madison the hope for a "decided majority" for ratification of the Constitution by Va. even without the votes of the Ky. delegates, so "that the ninth pillar may be raised in Virga."), 775-77 ("attachment to the Confederacy"); *Doc. Hist. Fed. Elec.*, I, 33-34 ("foreign negotiations"). *Elliot's Debates*, III; and H. B. Grigsby, *Hist. of Va. Fed. Convention* (1890), I, 7n, establish that Brown was not a member of the ratifying convention. See also E. C. Burnett, *Continental Congress* (1941), 707-10.

Considerations of space forbid inclusion here of the full bibliography for the "Spanish Conspiracy." Informed guidance is found in Watlington, *Partisan Spirit*, 253-60; and *Jefferson Papers*, XIX, 471n124. The continued diversity of historical judgments on the subject is also represented by Watlington and Julian A. Boyd, ed. of the *Jefferson Papers*. The former tends to credit some of the charges against Brown, even to the extent of suggesting, mainly through the boastful testimony of Wilkinson's "Memorials" to the Spanish governor of La., that Brown may have served as a Spanish agent while sitting in the U.S. Congress. Boyd, on the other hand (in XIX, xxxiv, 429-518), finds the evidence supporting charges of treasonable actions by Brown insubstantial. He argues that "despite the obliquy cast upon him . . . [Brown] was one of the most formidable obstacles to Western separatism . . . [and] deserves to be known as the principal architect of [Ky.'s] admission to the Union."

MANUSCRIPTS: Filson Club, Louisville, Ky.; ViU, DLC   WFC

John Brown

JOHN BROWN has not been identified. His name appears at the head of the steward's account of payments for tuition and board for the period of November 1774 to April 10, 1775. There is an entry also for a John Brown in the ledger of a local merchant under the date of August 28, 1775, which suggests that the John Brown listed as a freshman in November 1774 may have been in residence for the full academic year 1774-1775. There is persuasive evidence that this John Brown and the John Brown of Augusta County, Virginia, another member of the Class of 1778, were two distinct persons. Brown was a very common family name throughout the colonies, and from the historian's point of view, an unforgivable number of the Browns bore the name John.

SOURCES: Ms Steward's accounts, PUA; Patterson Acct. Bk. See John Brown of Augusta Cnty. (Class of 1778). In view of the lack of information regarding procedures for matriculation at this time, it is possible that Brown's name at the head of the steward's list represents some prearrangement for the enrollment of the student from Augusta County which was not followed up, but this seems to be unlikely.

WFC

Benjamin Dunlap

BENJAMIN DUNLAP, hapless scholar and organist, was born in Pennsylvania, probably after the birth of his brother Francis Franklin Dunlap in 1755. His father was William Dunlap, a printer at Lancaster from 1754 to 1757, and his mother was Deborah Croker, a niece of Benjamin Franklin's wife. This family connection brought the elder Dunlap to Franklin's attention as "a sober young Man" in 1754, and Franklin appointed him postmaster of Philadelphia in 1757, a position he held until 1764 when he was removed after falling seriously behind in his accounts. In hopes of recovering the means to support his family, Dunlap traveled first to Barbados, where he had an interest in a printing business, and then to England, where he was ordained a priest in 1766. A few years after his return to Philadelphia, he became the rector of Stratton Major parish, King and Queen County, Virginia, the site of a new church edifice said to have been the costliest and largest in the colony.

Benjamin Dunlap began his college preparatory studies in Virginia as early as 1771. In that year William Dunlap announced in the *Virginia Gazette* that he had employed a tutor for his sons and offered to board other boys and grant them access to his personal library "of several thousand volumes in most arts and sciences." Benjamin Dunlap was also organist for his father's congregation, and in January 1772 Benjamin Franklin's advice was solicited by a sea captain who had been commissioned by the rector to procure "a good armonica" in England for the boy's use. A year later the church's organ was advertised for sale at £200. The Stratton Major vestry minutes suggest that the parson's interests in Barbados and elsewhere kept him away from the parish for much of 1773 and 1774. Perhaps because of his absence from Virginia, he placed Benjamin in the grammar school at Princeton.

Benjamin Dunlap "of Virginia" is mentioned in a newspaper account of the grammar school's September 1774 commencement, but he does not appear either as a freshman or as a schoolboy in the steward's tuition and room accounts for November 1774 to April 1775. This by itself is insufficient to prove that he left Princeton after the grammar school commencement; it is possible that he matriculated in the College as early as the winter of 1774-1775. His improvident clerical father was, however, no longer able to support Dunlap's education, and his further studies were made possible by an anonymous English benefactor. On July 15, 1775, President John Witherspoon made minor purchases for Dunlap at Thomas Patterson's Princeton store. This is the first clear indication of Dunlap's presence at Princeton after September 1774. It suggests both that Witherspoon was administering the benefaction that made Dunlap's studies possible and that Dunlap had entered the freshman class during or before the session beginning in spring 1775. Witherspoon made extensive purchases of cloth and apparel for him in late September 1775, which may indicate that Dunlap returned to Virginia during the autumn vacation. Such a visit would have been fitting on the occasion of his mother's death, noticed in the *Virginia Gazette* earlier in the month.

Dunlap was required by his benefactor to "bend his Profession to Divinity," but he was released from this obligation before August 1776 on Witherspoon's advice that "the Exigencies of the Times" made it impossible for the English patron to continue his support. On August 10, 1776, his father addressed an appeal to Benjamin Franklin to assume the cost of his namesake's education. The *Virginia Gazette* for July 26, 1776 had reported the rector's marriage to Mrs. Johanna Reeve. But William Dunlap lamented to Franklin that "the Lady in Question," worth upwards of £2,000 and without children of her own, had "secur'd every Farthing of the Income of her Estate for the Maintenance of herself and the Family." At her death, the rector was to have the disposal of half her property for his children, but until that unhappy event he could do little to advance his son. Though

Benjamin Dunlap now had prospects of a modest inheritance, his debt-encumbered father was thus still unable to provide for him. The printer turned preacher may also have been disillusioned with his new calling, for he and Benjamin agreed that medicine would be a more suitable profession for the boy than divinity.

Franklin's response to the parson's request has not been found, and his attitude toward his wife's distant relative at Nassau Hall is uncertain. Dunlap's studies at the College must have ceased in any case with the suspension of classes in November 1776. He is said to have died in military service during the Revolution, as did his brother. The Reverend Mr. William Dunlop died in 1779.

SOURCES: *Franklin Papers,* esp. v, 199 ("sober young Man"); vi, 73n; vii, 158-59; xi, 418-22; xiii, 84-87; xix, 38 ("armonica"); als W. Dunlap to B. Franklin, 10 Aug 1776, PPAmP ("Lady in Question"); *WMQ* (2 ser.), 23 (1943), 445-47; (1 ser.), 6 (1897), 6 ("several thousand volumes"); C. G. Chamberlayne, *Vestry Bk. of Stratton Major Parish* (1931), 196-99; *Pa. Journal and Weekly Advertiser,* 12 Oct 1774; MS Steward's accts., PUA; Patterson Acct. Bk.; *VMHB,* 41 (1933), 137; but Dunlap's military service is not recorded in J. H. Gwathmey, *Hist. Reg. of Virginians in the Rev.* (1938).

GSD

John Ellet (Ellit, Elett)

JOHN ELLET (ELLIT, ELETT) is named on three of the surviving lists of students kept by the College steward, on the latest of which he is identified as a member of the freshman class during the term that extended from November 1774 to April 1775. There is no record of his presence as a student in Nassau Hall thereafter.

The ledgers of Princeton merchant Thomas Patterson include records of several purchases made by John Elliot between November 1774 and March 17, 1775. Patterson identified "Elliot" as a student, and since the steward's lists include no name closer to Elliot than Ellet, it is likely that they were the same person.

Ellet's identity has proved elusive. He may have been a member of the Quaker Ellet family of Salem County, New Jersey. But the general disinclination of Friends at that time to send their sons to College and the purchases by John from Patterson of items obviously intended for fashionable clothing not at all in keeping with the "plain way" tend to argue against that possibility. It is more likely that he was a member of the Ellet family in and around King William County, Virginia, although the name was also found in Pennsylvania, North Carolina, and elsewhere. If Patterson's spelling was more accurate than the steward's and the name was a form of the extremely common "Elliot," positive identification of the student is even more difficult.

SOURCES: Ms Steward's accounts, PUA; Patterson Acct. Bk.; *N.J. Wills*, V-IX, passim; Bucks Cnty. Hist. Soc., *Papers*, VIII, 276n; K. Stryker-Rodda, *Rev. Census of N.J.* (1972), 36; T. Cushing and C. E. Sheppard, *Hist. of Gloucester, Salem, and Cumberland Counties, N.J.* (1883), 372, 436; P. N. Clarke, *Old King William Homes and Families* (1897), 47-51; C. G. Chamberlayne, *Vestry Bk. of St. Paul's Parish, Hanover Cnty., Va.* (1940), 282, 298-99; J. W. Wayland, *Va. Valley Recs.* (1930), 46, 111, 156; L. Chalkley, *Rec. of Augusta Cnty., Va.* (1912), II, 125, 144, 436; *Pa. Arch.* (3 ser.), XI, 131, 190; (5 ser.), II, 538; V, 326; *Col. Rec. N.C.*, IV, 950; F. A. Olds, *Abstract of N.C. Wills* (1968), 219. John Ellets (or a variation on the name) also appear in the 1790 census records of N.Y., Vt., and Md.

JMR

William Halkerston

WILLIAM HALKERSTON, tobacco planter, is believed to have been the son of Robert Halkerston, a physician of Fredericksburg, Virginia and Port Tobacco, Charles County, Maryland. Dr. Halkerston, the bearer of a rare Scottish surname, was an acquaintance of George Washington, who had an account with him in 1754. The doctor relocated to Port Tobacco sometime before April 19, 1760, when Washington unexpectedly spent the night with him on a roundabout trip to Williamsburg, Virginia. William Halkerston, who was probably born about then, was later sent to the grammar school at Princeton for his early education. He took part in the school's public exercises on September 26, 1774, and may have been admitted to the freshman class of the College at that time.

The evidence bearing on Halkerston's possible enrollment in the College is, however, so unsatisfactory as to leave his designation as a student of the College of New Jersey open to question. The newspaper account of the 1774 grammar school commencement, which lists "William Halkenter of Portobacco," is itself ambiguous in this respect. The story notes that the members of the "highest class" in the grammar school were admitted to the freshman class in the College, and it names "Halkenter" as one of the schoolboys who gave English and Latin orations for the occasion. But it does not say explicitly that the schoolboys who gave orations were all among the grammar school graduates. Of the eight boys whose names are given by the newspaper as speakers, only George Merchant and Richard Stockton graduated from the College, both in 1779. Merchant and James McDonald (Class of 1778) are the only two of the group whose names appear on the list of freshmen in the College steward's tuition and room accounts

for November 1774 to April 1775. Four of the remaining five have
been regarded as College students, two of them on the basis of additional evidence and one (Richard Bland Lee, Class of 1779) on the
basis of a strong presumption. The fourth, John Coburn, may also
have attended Nassau Hall, but not even circumstantial evidence to
support his inclusion among the College students has been found. William Halkerston completes the group. In his case, there is also additional evidence, but it merely adds to the confusion.

Halkerston was one of the best student customers of Princeton storekeeper Thomas Patterson between August and December 1774. His
frequent purchases recorded in Patterson's account book for October
and November of that year suggest that he remained in or near
Princeton during the autumn vacation period. Though he may not
have visited his Maryland home during the holiday, his widowed
mother did receive a visit from a recent Nassau Hall graduate. Philip
Fithian (A.B. 1772) lodged with Mrs. Halkerston in Port Tobacco on
October 21, 1774. Fithian discovered that the people of the town and
neighboring region had suffered greatly from dysentery in recent
months, and the Halkerston family had not escaped the scourge. He
recounted in his journal:

> M[rs] Halkinson my Land Lady, a poor aged, distress'd Widow,
> when she found that I was acquainted with her little son at
> Princeton, seemed a little to revive; she beg'd me to encourage
> her Son to be diligent & industrious, to caution & admonish him
> from her against bad company and wicked practices—She told me
> of her great & sore loss of an only Daughter, a young woman of
> 15 this Summer, since which, she told me in tears, that She had
> been a stranger to health & Quiet.

The widow Halkerston's concern about her son's company at Princeton suggests that she expected him to stay there for some time, presumably as a student at the College. He abruptly disappears from the
Patterson account book after December 8, 1774, however, the final
entry reading: "Cash 20/ to Philad[a]." The list of Halkerston's purchases over the previous months indicates that he was carefully
equipping himself with a complete new wardrobe, suitable either for
a college student or for a young gentleman planter. His purchase of
"14 yd. Mourning Crape" on October 29 and Patterson's entry of December 8 may indicate that Halkerston decided during the vacation
to return to Port Tobacco to help or to support his mother following
his sister's death. It is not possible to say whether he ever returned to
Nassau Hall or even if he intended to return, nor is it possible to say

whether he attended either grammar school or College classes in the term beginning in November 1774.

In fact, little else can be said about William Halkerston. His brother Robert Halkerston and another Halkerston performed military service in the Revolution in Maryland, but no record of service has been found for William. His name appears in the 1790 census returns for Charles County in a household that included one woman over sixteen, nine slaves, and no children. He appears in Charles County wills dated 1795 and 1797 and died intestate sometime before March 1799 with an inventory totaling £534 19s 6d. His chief assets at his death were six slaves, a horse, forty barrels of corn, and a tobacco crop "Estimated at 2000$^{w.g.t}$ Unstript." Halkerston was probably survived by children, because his administrator swore to inform the Charles County orphans' court of any changes in the inventory. And Halkerston's wife probably predeceased him, for his brother Robert is described in the inventory as "nearest of Kin." His church affiliation was probably Episcopal like that of the Reverend John Weems, who preached his funeral sermon for $10. William Halkerston's estate was not finally settled until March 1824, less than a year before the death of his brother.

SOURCES: S. J. Quinn, *Hist. of the City of Fredericksburg, Va.* (1908), 220; *Washington Diaries*, I, 156; *Washington Diaries* (Jackson), I, 156; *Washington Writings*, I, 426; D. S. Freeman, *George Washington*, II (1948), 4n (the spelling "Halkerston" used by Freeman and the eds. of *Washington's Diaries* has been adopted here); W. B. Blanton, *Med. in Va. in the Eighteenth Century* (1931), 361; *Pa. Journal and Weekly Advertiser*, 12 Oct 1774; Patterson Acct. Bk.; *Fithian Journal*, I, 272 ("my Land Lady"); Heitman, 267; *First Census, Md.*, 50; A. W. Burns, *Md. Wills: Charles Cnty; Bk. XI*, 42, 56; Charles Cnty. Inventories 1797-1802, 117-18, Charles Cnty. Inventories and Accounts 1822-24, 475-78, Hall of Records, Annapolis, Md.

GSD

James McDonald

JAMES McDONALD, possibly a percussionist, was the son of Alexander and Amy McDonald of Princeton. His father, probably a gentleman farmer and Scottish immigrant, came to Princeton sometime before September 1771 when Richard Stockton (A.B. 1748) conveyed 301.25 acres to him. Prepared for College at the grammar school, James McDonald was admitted to the freshman class in the autumn of 1774. His name appears in the steward's tuition and room accounts for November 1774 to April 1775.

Little is known about McDonald or his immediate family, but he was clearly connected with the Highlands Scottish clan whose name he bore. His father was a good friend, and probably a close relative, of another Alexander McDonald of Staten Island, who acted as the nominal family chief in the colonies. This second Alexander Mc-Donald was a captain and later a lieutenant colonel of the Royal Highland Emigrants, a Loyalist regiment that spent most of the revolutionary war at Halifax, Nova Scotia.

Captain McDonald had business of his own with the College. In a letter written from Halifax on January 15, 1776, he asked his wife, who was still living on his Staten Island farm, "Pray Let me know whether Mr Weatherspoon refuse to keep the boy in the College or whether it were your own Choice that he should remain at home and whether or not you have paid Mr Weatherspoon any Money Agreeable to my former Orders." The passage is intriguing and certainly open to different interpretations. On whose account, precisely, was Captain McDonald paying Witherspoon? There is no reason to believe that the captain was supporting James McDonald at Nassau Hall. The letter seems rather to suggest that another McDonald, probably the captain's own "boy," was being schooled in Princeton or that the captain and his wife were considering assigning a boy to Witherspoon's care. Captain McDonald's oldest sons, subsequently sent to Edinburgh for their education, were too young to be admitted to the College at the time of the letter, however. Perhaps the captain meant to have the boy enrolled in the College's preparatory school and used the term "College" loosely to refer to both College and school.

James, the McDonald who did study at Nassau Hall, was unable to take his bachelor's degree. His education was interrupted by the outbreak of the Revolution and the forced closing of the College in November 1776. In spite of Captain McDonald's best efforts to retain the services of as many of his family as possible for the British Crown, James McDonald took the side of the American patriots. His father Alexander remained in Princeton, probably hoping to be left undisturbed by rebels and redcoats alike. In the first year of independence, however, James's father suffered property losses at the hands of the King's soldiers. Learning of his friend's misfortunes, Captain McDonald wrote on October 16, 1777:

I am sorry for poor Sandy McDonald of Princeton & Yet I think he might have acted better than he did. People that will endeavor to keep in wth both parties in a Controversy like this betwixt Great Britain & the Collonies allways runs in risque of being despised by both parties in the End, I am mad with him for Suffering his Boy to go as a drumr. in the Rebell Service after giving him a College Education.

Suggestive as this information is, service as a drummer seems rather lowly for a college student, unless he was extremely young. It has not been possible to identify the Princeton James McDonald with the New Jersey private of that name or with any of the James McDonalds among the troops of neighboring states.

James McDonald's father retained his Princeton property until April 1782 when he sold it for £2,000 sterling, having advertised it as early as July 1780. A few months later, Captain McDonald placed a notice in *Rivington's New York Gazette* warning that Alexander McDonald of Princeton was not authorized to sell the captain's Staten Island farm. James McDonald and his father may have remained in Princeton after the war, or they may have relocated elsewhere. The task of finding them is complicated by the frequency of their given names within the family. The McDonald clan's ties to the College of New Jersey were emphasized in 1785 when Captain McDonald's brother, the Reverend John McDonald of Edinburgh, was admitted *ad eundem* to the degree of Master of Arts.

SOURCES: Ms deeds, Pyne-Henry Coll., NjP; *Pa. Journal and Weekly Advertiser*, 12 Oct 1774; MS Steward's accounts, PUA; *NYHS Coll.*, xv, 240 ("Pray let me know"), 375 ("drumr in the Rebell Service"), 438-39; W. M. MacBean, *Biog. Reg. of St. Andrew's Soc. of St. of N.Y.*, 1 (1922), 121-23; K. Scott, *Rivington's N.Y. Newspaper* (1973), 299; *N.J. Gazette*, 10 Oct 1785.

GSD

Nathaniel Macon

NATHANIEL MACON, LL.D. University of North Carolina 1825, planter and United States congressman and senator, was born December 17, 1758, in Granville County (after 1764 Bute, in 1779 Warren County), North Carolina, the son of Gideon and Priscilla Jones Macon. The father, who is said to have been of a Huguenot family, had migrated in the 1730s from Virginia to North Carolina, where in 1756 he was a justice of the peace for Granville County. He died in 1763 possessed of enough property to leave for Nathaniel, a sixth child and younger son, 500 acres of land and three slaves. Macon's formal education apparently had its beginning under the tutelage of Charles Pettigrew, later bishop-elect of the Protestant Episcopal Church, who for some time before 1774 conducted a school in Bute County of which Macon's mother and the neighboring Hawkins family were the chief patrons. His schoolmates included Benjamin and Joseph Hawkins of the Class of 1777.

Nathaniel Macon, Class of 1778

Although the surviving and incomplete records of the College for this period in its history provide no confirmation that Macon attended Nassau Hall, the assumption is supported by a strong tradition that has been accepted both by those who knew him in life and by historians. That he was at Princeton in 1776 is attested in his own handwriting on the back of the letter he wrote on November 14, 1828, to the North Carolina legislature resigning his seat in the senate. "While at Princeton New Jersey in 1776 I served a short tour of militia duty," begins a statement that continues by saying that he subsequently served without pay in the militia from the fall of Charleston in May 1780 to late November in 1782, that as senator he had not received "double pay for travelling," that he had never sought any man's vote for public office, that he twice had been offered the office of postmaster general, and that he had served as Speaker of the House of Representatives from 1801 to 1807. This is a succinct and characteristic summary of his career, but it unfortunately leaves more than one question remaining, regarding his presence at Princeton. An informed and responsible North Carolina historian has stated that Macon entered the College in 1774 and remained for two years. This is possible, for he would have been 18 years of age in December 1776, an age not unusual among students in the College at that time, but it is also possible that for at least a part of his stay in Princeton he was completing his preparatory studies in the grammar school. The uncertainties are such that even his assignment here to the Class of 1778 must be viewed as tentative. As for his militia service in 1776, there seems to be no official evidence that he served with the New Jersey militia. Perhaps the venture fell in the long fall vacation. Whatever the fact, there is no reason for assuming that he remained in Princeton beyond President Witherspoon's dismissal of the students shortly after the beginning of a new academic term in November.

Macon probably returned immediately to North Carolina, where he seems to have been studying law until 1780, though apparently he was never to practice it. In 1781 he was elected to represent Warren County in the state senate. He took his seat on June 23, it is said, only after General Nathanael Greene had persuaded him that he could do more for the army in the legislature than on active duty. He was returned to the upper house in 1782 and again in 1784. In 1790 he sat in the lower house. He was elected a delegate to the Continental Congress in December 1785 but did not attend. When in the following December he was urged to proceed to New York, where the Congress then met, he promptly resigned. His explanation, that the provision made by the "General Assembly will not enable me to proceed to New York," was probably only one of the reasons for his refusal. His interests were local rather than national, and he shared many convictions with Willie Jones (apparently not related), who soon was to lead the successful opposition in the state to the new federal Constitution. Macon did not sit in the ratifying convention of 1788, as did his brother John, one of the decisive majority against ratification, but he was known to be in opposition.

Meanwhile, Macon was prospering as a tobacco planter on the land he had inherited from his father, to which he later added substantially. At the time it was somewhat remotely situated, about twelve miles from the county seat of Warrentown, but this hardly could have bothered one who has been quoted as saying that a man should not live near enough to a neighbor "to hear his dogs bark." In 1784 he owned seven slaves, and according to the census, in 1790 there were twenty. At his death in 1837 his estate included seventy-seven slaves. He had married Hannah Plummer on October 9, 1783, also of a family that had moved down from Virginia. Three children were born to the couple, two daughters and a son, before the mother's death on January

11, 1790. The son died less than two years later. Macon did not re-
marry.

Macon's career in national politics can be quickly summarized. He
was elected to Congress in 1791, and by successive reelections, he
served continuously in the House of Representatives from that year
until December 13, 1815, when he entered the Senate as the elected
replacement for Francis Locke. He continued as senator until November 14, 1828. On that date, just over a month before his seventieth
birthday and two days before the Senate was to reconvene, he wrote
as follows to the North Carolina Assembly: "Age and infirmity render
it proper for me to retire from public service, I therefore resign the
appointment of Senator to the Senate of the U.S., that of Trustee of
the University of the State, and that of Justice of the Peace for the
County of Warren." He had been a trustee of the University of North
Carolina since 1826. How long he had been a justice of the peace has
not been determined. After almost a decade in retirement on his
Warren County property, he died on June 29, 1837.

So brief a sketch, however, does much less than justice to one of the
more remarkable public figures in the early history of the nation.
From first to last, and above all, Macon was a republican in the nonpartisan sense, who with impressive consistency followed a political
creed deeply rooted in his own agrarian background and the ideology
of the American Revolution. For him, the government that governed
least governed best, and without being fully democratic in his political
philosophy, he trusted chiefly that part of government which was
closest to the people and so became a defender of the state governments against encroachment by the national government. Indeed, he
has come to be viewed by some historians as ultimately a conservative
who helped significantly to preserve doctrines that later would be
employed in support of nullification and secession in defense of the
peculiar interests of the south.

So complex a career carries grave risks of oversimplification by those
who seek to interpret it. In Congress, Macon opposed the economic
program sponsored by Alexander Hamilton, for whom he had a deep
distrust, the Jay Treaty, and the Alien and Sedition Acts. By 1800 he
had become in his own state the most influential leader of the emerging Republican party that was destined to enjoy dominance in the
state's politics through many years thereafter. Testimony to the position he had won on the national scene is found in his choice as Speaker
of the House following Jefferson's election to the presidency in 1801.
On each of the thirty-six ballots in the House, Macon had voted for
Jefferson, and as the new administration got underway, he enjoyed the

confidence not only of the president but also of two former colleagues in the House, Secretary of State James Madison (A.B. 1771) and Secretary of the Treasury Albert Gallatin. Although a strict construction of the Constitution was a cardinal principle with Macon, he welcomed the Louisiana Purchase of 1803, and in general agreed with the administration's foreign policy. His regard for Madison cooled, however, partly it seems through the influence of his friend, the erratic John Randolph (Class of 1791); and his close identification with Randolph helps to explain the refusal of the House in 1807 to return him to the speaker's chair.

Ever an independent rather than one willing to follow the party in all matters, Macon supported Jefferson's embargo but opposed measures for the strengthening of harbor defenses and for gunboats. Because of his membership in a special committee, his name has been given to the Macon Bills, nos. 1 and 2. The second, after the failure of the first to be enacted, was adopted on May 1, 1810, authorizing President Madison, in the event that either Britain or France recalled its restrictions on American commerce, to enforce a policy of nonintercourse against the other. Macon seems not to have been the author of either bill, and actually voted against the second. When the issue of war came in 1812, he voted for war, but on the other measures he was increasingly out of line with the administration. He was a part of the successful opposition to rechartering the Bank of the United States in 1811, and voted against the act providing a charter for the Second Bank of the United States in 1816. He also opposed the tariff of 1816, the provision for maintaining a regular army of 10,000 men, and measures for strengthening the navy. The new nationalism of his party had no more appeal for him than had the nationalism of Alexander Hamilton.

Identified with increasing justification as an "old Republican," Macon had no inclination to move with the times. He vigorously opposed proposals for internal improvements at federal expense, affirming that he was "in favor of improvements of every kind, but by individual enterprise, not by the United States." His opposition expressed his conviction that the Constitution provided no justification for such action by the national government and his continuing belief in frugality as one of the virtues of sound government. "In proportion as men live easily and comfortably," he declared in opposing the new army, "in proportion as they are free from the burdens of taxation, they will be attached to the government in which they live." His opposition to almost any expansion of federal power also expressed a growing fear that it would lead ultimately to interference with the

institution of slavery. That fear found confirmation in the great debate leading to the Missouri Compromise of 1820, which he opposed
and in which he vigorously defended slavery, a tactic most of his
fellow southerners avoided.

As factionalism overtook the Republican party, Macon chose to
back the ambition of William H. Crawford of Georgia for the presidency. When Crawford's health put an end to that ambition, Macon
found no other candidate, either in 1824 or 1828, who awakened in
him great enthusiasm. He welcomed his old friend John Randolph of
Roanoke into the Senate in 1825 and off the floor spent many agreeable hours with him. In retirement he looked with favor on the trend
of Jackson's policies, especially in his war with the Second Bank of
the United States. His attitude toward John C. Calhoun softened as
the latter took a lead in opposition to the tariff, but he opposed nullification in 1832 and at the same time criticized Jackson for threaten-
ing the use of force against a state.

Macon probably found some satisfaction in the decision of 1830 by
Methodist sponsors of Randolph-Macon College in Virginia to perpetuate the memory of an old alliance between two close friends,
though neither of them was a Methodist and Macon described himself
as of "the Baptist persuasion" while belonging to no church. There
must have been satisfaction too in his unanimous election to the presidency of a convention called in 1835 to revise the constitution of his
own state, but this was an empty honor due an elderly statesman no
longer able to exert the influence he once had enjoyed.

Macon has been alternately described as a radical and as a conservative. Perhaps an essential quality of the man was captured by the
contemporary who observed that should Macon be drowned, it would
be well to look for the body upstream.

SOURCES: W. E. Dodd, *Life of Nathaniel Macon* (1903), esp. 42 ("hear his dogs
bark"), 288 ("in favor of improvements"), 298 ("in proportion as men live easily"),
368 ("Age and Infirmity" and correction of error in *Branch Papers,* below); *DAB*
(the authority for attendance at CNJ); M. W. Wellman, *Cnty. of Warren, N.C.*
(1959), passim; *Col. Rec. N.C.,* v, 591; S. M. Lemmon, *Pettigrew Papers,* I (1971),
296; T. H. Benton, *Thirty Years' View* (1854), 115; E. R. Cotten, *Life of . . .
Macon* (1862); *U.S. Mag., and Democratic Review,* 1 (1838), 17; C. J. Ingersoll,
Hist. Sketch of Second War between U.S. . . . and Great Britain (1845), 209;
John P. Branch *Hist. Papers of Randolph-Macon College,* 3 (1909), 88-89 ("while
at Princeton"); MS Steward's accounts, PUA (do not list Macon); Stryker, *Off. Reg.*
(does not show Macon among N.J. militia); *St. Rec. N.C.,* XVII, 795; XVIII, 337; XX,
605 ("will not enable me to proceed"); *First Census, N.C.,* 78; *NCHR,* 32 (1955),
376-86; 38 (1961), 482-99; 46 (1969), 335-64; 47 (1970), 115-29; N. E. Cunningham,
Jr., *Jeffersonian Republicans, 1789-1801* (1957); Cunningham, *Jeffersonian Republicans in Power* (1963); N. K. Risjord, *The Old Republicans* (1965); D. H. Gilpatrick,
Jeffersonian Democracy in N.C. (1931); H. M. Wagstaff, *State Rights and Pol.*

Parties in N.C., 1776-1861 (1906); R. Irby, *Hist. of Randolph-Macon College* (n.d.), 16-19.

PUBLICATIONS: Sh-Sh #29027, Sh-C #2068

MANUSCRIPTS: Evidently Macon destroyed his own files of correspondence, but the number of persons who saved letters received from him is impressive. As a result, those letters are to be found in a wide variety of depositories, including NcD, NcU, Nc, and PHi, and not a few of them have been published.

WFC

Jacob Morton

JACOB MORTON, A.B., A.M. 1782, lawyer, soldier, public official, was born in New York City on July 8, 1761. His mother was Maria Sophia Kemper, the wife of John Morton, a prominent merchant and active Whig whose generous financial support of the Revolution earned him the sobriquet "the rebel banker" among Loyalists.

Morton may have been prepared for college at Elizabethtown, New Jersey. He entered the freshman class at Nassau Hall in the fall of 1774, although the fragmentary and reconstructed records of the Cliosophic Society cite March 1774 as the date of his induction, with the pseudonym "Hamlet." That he graduated with his original class would indicate that Morton was among the few students who were present in Nassau Hall during the difficult years of 1777 and 1778. At commencement he delivered an oration on *"the horrors of war."*

Two years before Morton graduated, his family had fled from New York to New Jersey, settling first in Elizabethtown where they joined the Presbyterian church of which James Caldwell (A.B. 1759) was pastor. When the British approached, they moved seven miles further inland to Springfield, and then finally to a farm at Basking Ridge in Somerset County. Morton joined them there after leaving Princeton and studied law with William Paterson (A.B. 1763) in nearby Raritan. He ended his training by the spring of 1782, when his father died suddenly and he became the administrator of the estate and head of a family that included three brothers: John (A.B. 1782), George Washington (A.B. 1792), and George Clark (A.B. 1795).

In September 1782 Morton was back at Nassau Hall to take his second degree. It was far from the last of Morton's visits to Princeton, for the family was always close to the College and was especially friendly in later years with President Samuel Stanhope Smith (A.B. 1769).

Morton had joined the New Jersey bar in September 1782, shortly

Jacob Morton, A.B. 1778

before he moved his family back to Elizabethtown. In December 1783 they returned to New York and to their former home on State Street. Morton then joined the bar in New York and opened a legal office at 215 Water Street. Much of his time was devoted to settling his father's affairs. In October 1785, for example, he and his mother appealed to the city government for some relief from the taxes levied on wharf property. He also had to decide what property to hold and what to sell, and whether to retain his father's sizable collection of wartime loan office certificates. His adroit management of the family finances left him and his relatives with a respectable fortune after the federal government assumed state debts.

On October 4, 1786, Morton began a militia career of remarkable longevity when he was commissioned a captain in one of the battalion companies of the New York County Militia. His membership in the Society of the Cincinnati in New York would seem to indicate that he had seen some Continental service during the war, but no evidence of such service has been found. His other memberships included the

Free and Associated Masons and, as an indication of his social standing, the exclusive Tontine Coffee House. That he shared his wealth is evinced by his participation in the Humane Society for the relief of debtors.

Morton's first political office was that of election inspector for the West Ward of the city, to which he was appointed by the city council on April 5, 1791. He held the post several more times during the next seventeen years. When the Saint Tammany Society, inspired by John Pintard (A.B. 1776), established the American Museum in May 1791, Morton was one of its original trustees. On June 25 of that year he married Catharine Ludlow, the daughter of merchant Carey Ludlow, in her father's home on Front Street. After a brief honeymoon on Long Island, he left his own family and their three slaves and moved with his bride to a house on Broadway, near the Battery, which had a value of approximately £3,000.

Morton was elected to the New York legislature in 1795 and served as a delegate in the nineteenth and twentieth assemblies. His votes reflected his Federalist leanings, as he opposed amendments to the Constitution and favored the gradual abolition of slavery without compensating slave owners. While in the assembly, he was promoted to the rank of first major in the militia. As a brevet major in 1789 he had been one of the military marshals of the day for the first presidential inauguration, and since then he had advanced to the grade of second major of the Third Regiment of state militia. In 1796, after being promoted to lieutenant colonel, he was given command of that regiment, and it was in that capacity that he attracted the attention of Alexander Hamilton, who considered him a worthy candidate for a majority in the United States Army during the Quasi-War of 1798. But Morton would take nothing less than a regimental command, and so no appointment was offered him.

He did not want for activity, however. He had served as a justice of the new city court that dealt with debts and debtors since February 1797. And in June 1799, when the Sixth Regiment of state militia was created, Morton transferred to it as commanding officer, taking with him his regimental surgeon, John R. B. Rodgers (A.B. 1775). At the end of the year, Colonel Morton was one of five members of a committee to plan New York's obsequies for George Washington.

In October 1801 Morton was considered by the Common Council of New York City for appointment as superintendent of the alms house. He failed by one vote to be confirmed, but he was sworn as a freeman of New York in November 1802. His growing reputation suffered a slight reversal seven months later, when militia troops under his command terrorized the city with their rowdiness. Morton was personally reprimanded by the local government. But before the end of the year, he had been elected alderman for the Eighth Ward, and after an unsuccessful Republican challenge, he joined the council. A loyal partisan, he participated in the unsuccessful move to have the city sell its stock in the Republican Manhattan Company, but he and his colleagues were able to turn back a Republican effort to have municipal funds transferred from the Federalist Bank of New York.

In March 1805, the state government created three brigades of New York Artillery, incorporated into one division. With a promotion to brigadier general, Morton took command of the First Brigade, of which his Sixth Regiment was part. Called "Morton's Brigade," the unit was the pride of the state militia, and it came to include the first military band in New York. The First Brigade had primary responsibility for the defense of the city during the War of 1812, and when no alarm existed it led almost all martial parades. As its commander, and after 1815 as the major general in command of the entire division, Morton was invariably in the reviewing stand for those parades or on the platform as the official host to such luminaries as Isaac Hull, captain of the U.S.S. *Constitution*, in 1814 and the Marquis de Lafayette in 1824.

Meanwhile, Morton's career in public life virtually precluded his private practice of law. In January 1807, after his term as alderman ended, the Common Council elected him city comptroller. Two years later he was selected to be clerk of the council and city inspector. While the Republicans managed to oust him from the latter post in May 1816, he continued as clerk for the rest of his life. His annual salary was $1,500.

Helped greatly by his wife's inheritance from her father in 1815, Morton and his family lived comfortably and socialized with his brother-in-law Josiah Quincy (Harvard 1790) and other distinguished personages in New York, Boston, and Princeton. Except for the election riots of 1834, when Morton had to call out the militia to quell disturbances that must have confirmed him in his opposition to Jacksonian Democracy, his military service was almost entirely ceremonial. Too infirm to command the troops in person in his last years, he was allowed to review them from his own balcony as they marched in the Battery. Morton died of an apoplectic stroke on December 3, 1836. He was survived by his wife, his daughter, and seven sons.

SOURCES: Giger, Memoirs, II; L. A. Keyes, *Lineage of the Ninth Reg. . . . N.Y.* (1953), 50-51; alumni file, MS Steward's accounts, MS Clio. Soc. membership list, PUA; J. G. Wilson, ed., *Mem. Hist. of N.Y.* (1893), III, passim; IV, 277-83; M. J.

Lamb, *Hist. of City of N.Y.*, II (1880), 445 & n.; *Memoir of the Life of Eliza[beth] S[usan] M[orton] Quincy* (1861), pt. 1, passim; *NEHGR*, 5 (1851), 103; *N.J. Wills*, VI, 284; *N.Y. Wills*, XII, 307-308; *N.J. Gazette*, 21 Oct 1778 (commencement), 9 Oct 1782 (A.M.); *Som. Cnty. Hist. Quart.*, I (1912), 241, 242, 249; *N.Y. Directory* (1786), 64; *MCCCNY*, I, 180-81, 635; V, 307, 514; IV, 332; VIII, 532; III, passim; *Mil. Min., Council of Appointment, St. of N.Y.*, I, passim; II, 1,404, 1,537; J. A. Scoville, *Old Merchants of N.Y. City*, III (1865), 225; I (1864), 174, 296; *NYGBR*, 75 (1944), 87; 50 (1919), 143n; 71 (1940), 257, 259; *First Census, N.Y.*, 134; *N.Y. Red Book* (1895), 373; *Journal of the Assem., St. of N.Y.* (1796-1797); *Hamilton Papers*, XXII, 89 & n.; 165; XXIV, 120; M. A. DeW. Howe, ed., *Articulate Sisters* (1946), 70-71; *N.Y. Times*, 5 Dec 1836.

PUBLICATIONS: Sabin #50999

MANUSCRIPTS: NHi

Andrew Pettit

ANDREW PETTIT, soldier, merchant, insurance underwriter, and public official, was born on February 22, 1762 in New Jersey. He was the son of Charles Pettit, who was then a provincial surrogate and probably lived near Burlington. A lawyer, Pettit's father later served as deputy secretary of the province and then joined the American cause during the Revolution, becoming an official of the state of New Jersey, deputy quartermaster general of the Continental Army, and, after the war, a member of the Continental Congress and a prominent merchant in Philadelphia. Pettit's mother, Sarah Pettit, was the daughter of Andrew Reed and the half-sister of Joseph Reed (A.B. 1757).

Pettit received at least part of his primary education in Nassau Hall's grammar school before enrolling in the College, probably in the fall of 1775. He apparently went to Philadelphia after leaving Princeton and by August 1780 he had completed a tour of duty as an aide-de-camp in the Philadelphia militia. He remained on the militia rolls until May 1787, when he was elected to membership in the elite City Troop, the First Troop of Philadelphia Cavalry. With it he served in the expedition against the Whiskey Rebellion from July to September 1794 and in the Northampton Expedition of March 1799. In 1803 his services were rewarded with honorary membership in the troop.

By the time he joined the cavalry, Pettit was a partner in his father's mercantile firm. Their home, warehouse, and wharf were in the city's middle district, on the waterfront. On December 8, 1791, he married Elizabeth McKean, the daughter of Thomas McKean, chief justice of Pennsylvania. The ceremony was performed in the First Presbyterian Church of Philadelphia, of which Pettit was a member until he died.

Andrew Pettit, Class of 1778
BY REMBRANDT PEALE

As a wedding gift, the chief justice gave the newlyweds a portrait of himself done by Charles Wilson Peale. By 1793 Pettit and his brother-in-law Andrew Bayard (A.B. 1779) were partners in their own business, investing heavily in government certificates and bank stocks and underwriting maritime insurance.

McKean's election as governor in 1799 added to Pettit's string of important family connections, which included the marriages of his sisters to Jared Ingersoll (Yale 1766) and Alexander Graydon. The new governor named his son-in-law flour inspector for the state, a post that brought an annual salary of $5,000. Later, when McKean's brand of Democratic-Republicanism became too conservative for Pennsylvania's radical wing of the party, the governor and his several relatives on the state payroll were vilified in the Philadelphia *Aurora* as the "Royal Family." But McKean was regularly reelected and Pettit went on inspecting flour as long as his father-in-law was in office, undoubtedly a moderate Republican like the rest of the governor's appointees. He also served for some time as an alderman of Philadelphia.

Among the insurance firms in the city was the Insurance Company of North America, of which Pettit's father was an original director and then president, and of which Ebenezer Hazard (A.B. 1762) was secretary. Both Pettit and Bayard later became directors of that company, although they continued their own underwriting activities at the same time. In 1801 one of their clients, Thomas Passmore, objected to their appeal from an insurance award. The case soon reached the state supreme court and degenerated into a political contest when Passmore was cited for contempt. With the support of radical politicians, Passmore sought legislative protection against arbitrary judicial power, and the quarrel led in December 1804 to the impeachment of the three Federalist members of the court. The fourth, Hugh Henry Brackenridge (A.B. 1771), asked to be included in the trial as a protest against legislative interference with the judiciary, a request that solidified his standing with McKean's circle of moderates and helped defeat the impeachment effort. In February 1805 Pettit received $150.50 from the state as compensation for being a witness in the judges' trial.

Soon after Pettit became a director of the Insurance Company of North America, in the summer of 1806, his father asked to be relieved temporarily of his presidential responsibilities. Pettit then served as president pro tempore of the firm until his father's death in September necessitated the election of a new chief executive. He returned to the board of directors, on which he sat until 1837.

Pettit's wife died on September 8, 1811, leaving him with four sons and four daughters, three of their eleven children having predeceased her. When Governor McKean died in 1814, he left 2,200 acres of land in Beaver County to these children. And after all specific bequests were made, the governor willed equal shares of the rest of his large estate to five of his forty-one grandchildren, including Pettit's oldest son Thomas McKean Pettit (Pennsylvania 1815). Pettit was an executor of the will.

Pettit himself died in Philadelphia on March 6, 1837. Three years later the last of the claims of Pettit and Bayard for French "spoliations" before 1800 were received by the House of Representatives.

SOURCES: The author is indebted to Roland M. Baumann, Chief of the Division of Archives and Manuscripts in the Pa. Hist. and Museum Commission, for his contribution to this sketch. R. Buchanan, *Geneal. of the McKean Family of Pa.* (1890), 96-97, 115-16, 120, 127-28; *DAB*; MS Steward's accounts, PUA; *Pa. Arch.* (6 ser.), I, 369; III, 959, 1,086, 1,288; (2 ser.), IX, 68; *First Troop of Phila. Cavalry* (1840), 13, 17, 58; *First Census, Pa.*, 217, 230; U.S. Treas., Card Index to "Old Loan" Ledgers, passim; *PMHB*, 52 (1928), 112; S. W. Higginbotham, *Keystone in the Democratic Arch.* (1952), 56-57, 77-78; L. B. Walker, *Burd Papers* (1899), 209; M. James, *Biog. of a Business* (1942), 76; J. H. Montgomery, *Hist. of the Insurance Co. of N. Amer.*

(1885), 132; U.S. House of Reps., *Private Claims . . . from the First to the Thirty-First Congress* (1853), III, 64 ("spoilations"); G. S. Rowe, *Thomas McKean* (1978), 266.

William Ross

WILLIAM ROSS is listed as a member of the freshman class in the steward's account of tuition, room, and board for the period of November 1774 to April 10, 1775, but that entry has to be left as the beginning and the end of what has been found regarding his identification with the College. The Ross family was almost ubiquitous in revolutionary America, and in its several branches the name William was obviously popular. In Virginia alone there were five men who bore the name that are credited with military service during the Revolution, and in other states there has been no difficulty in finding a William Ross who might have attended Princeton. There remains no positive identification of the Princeton student.

SOURCES: Among the possibilities, the most inviting is that Ross may have been the son of a West Indian planter sent to Princeton in response to President Witherspoon's "Address to the Inhabitants of Jamaica, and other West India Islands" of 1772 [*NJA* (1 ser.), XXVIII, 289-308]. It is unlikely that he was the William Ross of Jamaica who in June 1776 was captured while on his way to London by an American privateer and carried, together with his wife and a daughter, into Boston, where with the permission of the Mass. Council he purchased a vessel and sailed for Britain in the following fall with several dozen additional passengers who were allowed to join him [W. B. Clark and W. J. Morgan, *Naval Documents of Amer. Rev.*, V (1970), 110-11; VI (1972), 213, 249-50, 303, 675-76, 777, 881, 998-99, 1,000, 1,019-20; VII (1976), 4]. Evidence has not been found that would identify the former student as the William Ross who in 1803 was attorney general of Jamaica [als W. Hylton to W. Ross, 1 Mar 1803, Jefferson MSS] or as the William Ross, Esq., of Kingston, Jamaica (28 Apr 1753-10 Jul 1815), for whom his brothers erected an appropriate monument in a Jamaican cemetery [*Monumental Inscriptions of the British W. Indies*, x (1875), 149]. Among the Loyalists reaching Jamaica from Ga. about the end of the Rev. was a William Ross [*NEHGR*, 52 (1965-66), 301]. Another Loyalist was William Ross of Phila., who was attainted in 1778 and subsequently settled at Shelburne in Nova Scotia [Sabine, *Loyalists* (1847), 581 (1864), 573]. The student could have been related to the William Ross of York Cnty., Pa., who assumed a number of public responsibilities during the last quarter of the century [W. C. Carter and A. J. Glossbrenner, *Hist. of York Cnty., Pa.* (1975), 44, 94, 103, 109]. Two members of the Ross family or families in Pa., James Ross, U.S. Senator (1794-1803), and James Ross, pioneer member of the faculty of Dickinson College, on occasion have been credited with study at CNJ but evidence to confirm the assumption is lacking in both cases. Perhaps, however, such a tradition points toward an identification of William Ross that has not been established.

WFC

Joseph Scudder

JOSEPH SCUDDER, A.B., A.M. 1781, lawyer and public official, was born at seven o'clock in the morning on February 12, 1762, in Freehold, Monmouth County, New Jersey, the son of Isabella Anderson Scudder and Nathaniel Scudder (A.B. 1751), a physician, soldier, and public official. His older brother was John Anderson Scudder (A.B. 1775). Scudder may have received his early education from College trustee William Tennent, Jr.

On January 1, 1777, Scudder joined the Cliosophic Society, in which he was known as "Franklin." In his commencement exercises, he delivered an English oration on "contentment." In the same ceremony, his brother John gave the salutatory address on "civil discord." The latter's speech must have made quite an impression on his younger brother, for when Joseph took his second degree in 1781 he regaled the audience with a discourse on "discord."

After graduation Scudder went to Philadelphia, where his father and President Witherspoon were members of the Continental Congress. Those connections must have facilitated his appointment as a clerk of the "War Office," a post he held at least until the end of 1780. Aside from transcribing and filing documents, Scudder's preoccupation as clerk was to try to obtain some of the salary due him. Between November 1779 and February 1781, Congress authorized warrants in his favor amounting to more than $27,500, but little if any of that money actually reached Scudder. In May 1781 he asked that his warrant on the national treasury be cancelled and his account be transferred to the New Jersey loan office. By then, it seems, he had resigned his clerkship to serve as a lieutenant in the Monmouth County Militia. He held this post from December 1780 until June 1781. Although he apparently retained his commission, he then pursued the study of law.

On November 24, 1788, probably after having been admitted to the Monmouth County bar, Scudder married Maria Johnston, the daughter of Colonel Philip Johnston (Class of 1759) of New Brunswick, New Jersey. His wife became a communicant of the Old Tennent, or First Presbyterian Church of Freehold in 1793. Scudder himself was never a full member of the church, although he served on its board of trustees in 1803, and all nine of his children were baptized there.

A prominent attorney, Scudder was named surrogate of Monmouth County by Governor Richard Howell in 1794. His connection with Howell may have indicated that he was a Federalist, but his brother was a Republican and Scudder may have joined that party later in the decade. He served as surrogate until 1797, and in 1798 he was elected clerk of the county, a post he held for ten years.

When the Monmouth County Bible Society was founded in 1817, Scudder was an original member of its board of managers. It is possible that he later moved to New Brunswick, for in 1831 his wife was dismissed from the Old Tennent Church to the Presbyterian church there. Yet he seems to have retained his legal practice in Freehold, and it was in Freehold that he died on March 5, 1843. He was buried in the cemetery at Old Tennent.

Scudder's children included Eliza, the wife of William C. Schenck (A.B. 1805); Juliet, the second wife of Congressman Daniel B. Ryall; Philip Johnston (A.B. 1809); William Washington (A.B. 1821); and Joseph (A.B. 1822). Another son, John (A.B. 1811), wanted to enter the ministry but was prevented from doing so by his father's stubborn resistance. Instead, he studied medicine in New York City and carried on a very successful practice there until he decided to become a missionary, was ordained in the Reformed Dutch Church, and went with his wife to India.

SOURCES: *NJHSP* (3 ser.), 7 (1912-1913), 141; H. Cochrane, *Scudders in the Amer. Rev.* (1976), 87-88; *PMHB*, 15 (1891), 244; MS Clio. Soc. membership list, PUA; *N.J. Gazette*, 21 Oct 1778 (commencement), 3 Oct 1781 (A.M.); *JCC*, XV, 1,269; XVI, 53, 202, 343; XVII, 520; XVIII, 835; XIX, 123, 131-32; XX, 522-23; F. R. Symmes, *Hist. of Old Tennent Chh.* (1904), 177, 190, 231-43; Wickes, *Hist. of Medicine N.J.* (1879), 392; J. S. Applegate, *Early Courts and Lawyers of Monmouth Cnty., N.J.* (1911), 64; J. E. Stillwell, *Hist. and Geneal. Miscellany*, II (1970), 324; E. F. Cooley, *Geneal. of Early Settlers of Trenton and Ewing* (1883), 243; *DAB* (father and son).

Jesse (Jessy, Jesles) Smith

JESSE (JESSY, JESLES) SMITH is established as a student in the College by two separate accounts of the steward for the periods of May 25, 1773 to September 25, 1774 and November 1774 to April 10, 1775, where he is listed as a member of the freshman class. The apparent contradiction in Smith's identification as a freshman though he had been previously enrolled probably has its answer in a late admission at some time in the academic year of 1773-1774, perhaps in the summer term of 1774. That Smith was in Princeton during that term is indicated by the ledger of local merchant Thomas Patterson, which shows a purchase by him on August 27 of that year. The ledger begins in July 1774 and continues with evidence of Smith's presence in Princeton until early December 1775. It includes further purchases by

Smith under the dates of November 9, 1774 (an entry that shows that his classmate John Smith was his brother), January 8, 1775 and June 19, 1775. A final entry for Jesse on August 21, 1775 records that John Smith for himself and "Brother Jessy" paid an overdue bill of £3, for the period before the "last vacancy," which would have been the spring vacation. Jesse was perhaps a student for no more than the year extending from the summer of 1774 into the summer of 1775. In spite of the evidence that Jesse had a brother John, which presumably should be helpful in identifying the two, it has not been possible to find for either of them a positive identification.

SOURCES: Patterson Acct. Bk.; MS Steward's accounts, PUA. It seems likely that the two Smiths belonged to the very large Smith family, or families, of Suffolk Cnty., Long Island, many of whose members were Presbyterian and some of whom earlier had been identified with the College, including Jeffrey Smith (A.B. 1756), Caleb Smith (Yale 1743), first tutor and later trustee of the College, and Elizabeth Smith, mother of John Woodhull (A.B. 1766). According to the census of 1790, there were three Jesse Smiths in Suffolk Cnty., located severally in the towns of Brookhaven, Huntington, and Smithtown, and the census of 1800 shows a Jesse Smith then living in Brookhaven and another at Smithtown [First Census, N.Y., 161, 163, 166 (for Jesse Smiths in other parts of the state, see 18, 76, 83, 105, 144); NYGBR, 56 (1925), 13, 279]. If the latter was the former student, the seven slaves he owned suggest that he was among the more prosperous of the Smiths. The student may have been the Jesse Smith who on 10 Dec 1775 married Hannah Carll, but he also may have been the Jesse Smith, son-in-law of Job Smith, father of George Smith (A.B. 1770), who was executor in 1780 of the Job Smith's will. [NYGBR, 42 (1911), 131; N.Y. Wills, IX, 145]. A check of known genealogical and historical records has failed to find among the Suffolk Smiths a Jesse Smith who definitely had a brother John.

An inviting possibility is the Jesse Smith, said to have been born at Lexington, Mass. on 13 Apr 1756 and to have died at Salem, Mass. on 4 Jun 1844, who served during the Rev. in the commander in chief's Guard, and afterward settled in Salem, [C. E. Godfrey, Commander-in-Chief's Guard (1904), 248], but the place of birth is not confirmed by Lexington's Rec. of Births, Marriages and Deaths (1898), and no identification with CNJ or a brother John has been found. Jesse Smiths who apparently were of an age fitting the assumption that they could have been in college about 1775 have been found in N.J., Va., and Ky., but no identification with CNJ has been established.

WFC

John Smith

JOHN SMITH was a brother of his classmate Jesse Smith, and probably an older brother, for two entries in the ledger of Thomas Patterson, Princeton merchant, show that John made payments on Jesse's account, first on November 9, 1774, close to the beginning of a new academic year, and again on August 21, 1775, near the end of the summer term. This last entry was in payment of old accounts, one of them for six months' "wash," no doubt laundry, provided for both John and Jesse before the "last vacancy"—that is, the spring vacation. From July 1774 to August 21, 1775, John's account was among the more active recorded for students in the College, but there were no entries for either John or Jesse between August 21, 1775, and April 27, 1776. The ledger provides an apparently full record of transactions for the period ending early in December 1775, but two final pages in the book carry scattered entries of later dates, including a notation that John Smith paid "in Full" on April 27, 1776, the sum of £3 2s 8d. Whether this can be read to mean that John was in residence as a student at that time is doubtful. One can be sure only that he was in residence for the summer of 1774 through that of 1775. It is true that his name, together with his brother's, appears in the steward's account for the period of May 1773 to September 1774, which argues that he was a student in the College for at least a part of that time, but his listing in the steward's account for November 1774 to April 10, 1775 as a member of the freshman class suggests that he could have been in residence for no more than a part of the earlier period.

The number of John Smiths living in America at the time is staggering, and not even the knowledge that this one had a brother Jesse has served to provide a positive identification.

SOURCES: Patterson Acct. Bk.; MS Steward's accts., PUA. See Jesse Smith (Class of 1778). The census of 1790 shows no fewer than five John Smiths living in Suffolk Cnty., N.Y. No indication has been found that U.S. congressman and senator John Smith, who died on 12 August 1816, attended CNJ.

WFC

William Smith

WILLIAM SMITH, planter, born in 1761, was the second son of Thomas Smith (A.B. 1754) and his wife, Elizabeth Lynsen Smith, and so the younger brother of Abraham Smith (Class of 1777), a grandson of William Smith, one of the original trustees of the College, and a nephew of Doctor James Smith (A.B. 1757). The father, a leading lawyer of New York City, was identified with the Whigs as the Revolution approached but was also a brother of the Loyalist chief justice William Smith of New York and later of Quebec.

William, son of Thomas, was first enrolled in the College in November 1774 as a member of the freshman class, according to a steward's list of students for the term beginning that month, which also carried Abraham Smith's name and identified him as a member of the sophomore class. It is impossible to say how long either of the two boys may have remained in the College. The steward's list for the period of November 6, 1774 to April 10, 1775 is the latest for pre-Revolutionary years that has been found, and there appears to be no other evidence that places the two Smiths in Princeton after that time.

The family abandoned New York City in 1776 and took refuge on a property Thomas Smith owned on Haverstraw Bay up the Hudson River. William, who reached his fifteenth birthday in 1776, must have joined his family there, but nothing certain seems to be known of his activity before June 7, 1779. In the preceding year his uncle William had become a professed Loyalist and had taken up residence within British lines at New York City. In his memoirs the chief justice recorded under the date of June 8: "Nephew William Smith arrives from Haverstraw," which he had left on the preceding day. The uncle added that he "drew out" from "this Lad" information regarding the strength and disposition of Washington's forces that was sent to British headquarters. Shortly afterward, on July 1, William was joined by his brother Abraham on a similar visit to his uncle. How far these visits may be considered a significant indication of the young men's political leanings may be debatable, despite the fact that William eventually would wear the king's uniform, as Abraham may have also. Family ties were strong, and passage through the lines by noncombatants was not uncommon.

Even so, the open avowal of the king's cause by the most prominent member of the family brought suspicion of pro-British sentiment upon all of its members. Thomas Smith, while undertaking to demonstrate his continuing loyalty to the American cause, obviously felt a need for the caution demonstrated in a puzzling letter of September 15, 1780, to Governor George Clinton of New York. The letter is primarily concerned with the problem of his son Abraham. It confesses that the young man's going to New York in June of the preceding year had been imprudent, and seeks the governor's permission to secure a promised flag from General Benedict Arnold for a trip down the river that he hoped would enable him to bring Abraham home. Abraham is said to have been ill and in a state of depression owing partly to the captivity of his brother William. This was the only reference to William, and it was enigmatic, to say the least, and all the more so because there is evidence that shortly after the letter was written William, if not at home, was certainly not far from his home. It was on the night of September 21/22 that Major John André of the British Army met

Benedict Arnold in the house of Thomas Smith by arrangement with the latter's brother Joshua Hett Smith for the purpose of agreeing upon the conditions for the surrender of West Point to the British. After the capture of André on September 23, Joshua was arrested and charged as an accomplice in treason, a charge of which he subsequently was acquitted by a court-martial but for which he was nevertheless imprisoned by the civil authorities. William was present at the time of his uncle Joshua's arrest, during the night of September 25/26, and immediately became involved in efforts to assist him. This drew suspicion upon William, but no formal charges against him were made. Thomas too went free of formal charges of complicity, as seems to have been only just, but it is difficult to believe that he had been entirely frank in his earlier letter to Governor Clinton.

The further embarrassment brought to all members of the family, and perhaps anger over the treatment of his uncle, may help to explain William's decision to identify himself fully with the Loyalists. On June 21, 1781, he and a younger brother James Scott Smith joined their uncle William in New York City, evidently with a plan to enlist in the king's army. Justice Smith on the next day sent a note of the intelligence that his nephews had brought to Sir Henry Clinton, British commander, and recommended them "to his Patronage and Protection." At a conference on the morning of June 23, Sir Henry agreed to provide for them but advised that "it was his Course to take them up after they had joined such Corps as they chose." In the fall each received a commission as ensign in the Sixty-fourth Regiment, William's dating from October 22. They thus had declared their allegiance as the war approached its end, and its end brought them to England, as it did also their uncles William and Joshua, the latter having escaped from prison in May 1781 and found a refuge in New York City. Their uncle James had been resident in London during much of the war.

William's military career, apparently an uneventful one, was short. When he and his brother James appeared before the royal commission on Loyalist claims on November 1, 1784, in support of Joshua Smith's claim for compensation, they were described as "late Ensigns in his Majestys 64th or Staffordshire Regiment" who were "speedily about to depart to America." William's departure must have been indeed speedy, for he was back in New York City in time to marry there Sarah Frances Gordon on January 16, 1785. His bride was a sister of Elizabeth Gordon, recently deceased wife of Joshua Hett Smith. She was also the step-daughter of Joshua's sister Catherine, who had become the second wife of John Gordon, a leading merchant of Charleston, South Carolina. The newly wedded couple apparently lived first in New Jersey, but they soon moved south.

John Gordon had died in 1778, leaving a substantial inheritance for his daughters Elizabeth and Sarah below Charleston in Prince William Parish. Sarah also had inherited property in Charleston from a maternal aunt. William's decision to move south shortly after his marriage probably depended chiefly upon the consideration of his wife's properties in South Carolina, but he may have been influenced too by the knowledge he had of the opportunities the area might afford him through his family's connections there. In addition to those previously mentioned, there were the marriages of his aunt Elizabeth Smith to John Torrans, Charleston merchant, and his aunt Margaret Smith to Alexander Rose, another Charleston merchant. Torrans had died in 1780, and at the time of William's move, his aunt was living with a second husband, John Hatter.

Only the barest outline can be given of William's later life. At some time he acquired property in or near Savannah; the deed for land in Haverstraw he donated for a church building in 1806 describes him as "of the town of Savannah, in the State of Georgia." Subsequently, he lost the property, not long perhaps before 1811, when he seems to have moved to Charleston. That move apparently coincided with a second marriage to his first cousin Rosella Blanche Torrans, the daughter of his aunt Elizabeth, whose residence was 36 Queen Street. A city directory for 1819 places a William Smith, identified simply as "judge," at that address. Smith died in December 1822. An obituary notice in the *Charleston City Gazette and Commercial Daily Advertiser* of December 30 stated that he had been a resident of Charleston for eleven years past. His will, dated March 21, 1816 and proved January 9, 1823, blamed a "sett of Villains in Savannah" for the loss "of the Bulk of my property" and assigned full control of the "little" he possessed in New York and elsewhere to his wife for herself and an unspecified number of minor children.

SOURCES: R. J. Koke, *Accomplice in Treason* (1973), esp. 36, 105, 120, 209, 213, 223, 226, 243, 253, 261n12, 282nn15&19, 290-91n22, 301-302; *Princetonians, 1748-1768*, 122-25, 209-13; see Abraham Smith (Class of 1777); MS Steward's accts., PUA; W.H.W. Sabine, *Hist. Memoirs of William Smith*, III (1971), 115 ("arrives from Haverstraw"), 117 ("this Lad"), 332, 422 ("Patronage and Protection"), 423 ("such Corps as they choose"), 424, 501; *Washington Writings*, xx, 90; Charleston Cnty. Wills, Will Book F (1818-1826), 457.

WFC

William Stephens (Stevens)

WILLIAM STEPHENS (STEVENS) was carried on the steward's list of students enrolled in the College between November 6, 1774 and April 10, 1775, as a member of the freshman class. No other evidence of his presence as a student at Nassau Hall has been found, and it is possible that he was enrolled for no more than the academic year ending in September 1775, or even for only a part of that year. His name is not found in the accounts of a local merchant, Thomas Patterson, whose ledger for the period from the summer of 1774 to late 1775 records transactions by many other students. The family name was as common throughout the colonies as was the given name of William. Among those bearing the name of William Stephens (Stevens), it has been possible to establish some connection with Princeton in only one case, and in that case the connection is too tenuous to provide the basis for a positive identification.

SOURCES: Ms Steward's accounts, PUA; Patterson Acct. Bk. Early in 1779 Dr. David Ramsay (A.B. 1765) wrote from Charleston, S.C. to Dr. Benjamin Rush (A.B. 1760) that he had sent "two students from my own shop to Philada this last fall for lectures (Stevens & Waring)," who reportedly had been shipwrecked on the way up the coast. Ramsay sought Rush's aid for them, and assured his former mentor that "they are both possessed of fortunes & well able to repay any thing done for them." Stevens has been identified as the William Smith Stevens who served in the Revolution as a surgeon's mate, afterward opened an apothecary's shop in Charleston with Ramsay's nephew Joseph Hall Ramsay, the second son of William Ramsay (A.B. 1754), and ultimately became a practicing physician. [See R. L. Brunhouse in *APS Trans.* (new ser.), 55, pt. 4 (1965), 59, 62, 77; A. S. Salley, *Marriage Notices in S.C. Gazette* (1902), 73; L. C. Duncan, *Med. Men in Amer. Rev.* (1970), 326, 409; Charleston *Directories*, 1785-1824.] An inviting possibility is William Stephens of Savannah, Ga., grandson of Secretary Wm. Stephens during the early history of that colony, but with a birth date of c. 1752, he would have been old for a freshman in 1774 and there is further evidence that at about that time he may have been studying at the Inns of Court in London. [See *GHQ*, VII, 203-7; H. Chase et al., *Biog. Dict. of Federal Judiciary* (1976), 262. His claim to have studied at one of the Inns of Court is not confirmed by E. A. Jones, *Amer. Members of Inns of Court* (1924), or by J. G. deR. Hamilton in *NCHR*, x (1933), 280.]

WFC

Daniel Thatcher (Thacher)

DANIEL THATCHER (THACHER), Presbyterian clergyman, is identified as a student in the College by only one source, and it of a somewhat uncertain character. A manuscript list of members of the Cliosophic Society includes his name, without the usual indication of the state from which he came and with no other notation than that he was admitted in the year 1778. This information is repeated in a *Catalogue* of the society published in 1876. Standard histories of the society indicate that it was virtually moribund from the time of the dismissal of the students from the College in November 1776 until the time of the society's revival in 1781. Whatever may be the fact, it is believed that all original records of the literary societies were destroyed either through the severe damage done to Nassau Hall during the course of the Revolution or in the fire that destroyed the building in 1802, with the result that all such lists were compiled at a later date from such sources, including the recollections of surviving members, as may have been available. The list would seem to establish presumptive evidence that at some time Thatcher was enrolled as a student in the College, however, and it could have been in 1778, to which year he has been assigned here for want of more exact information.

His subsequent career fits well enough into the assumption that he had attended the College. The Orange Presbytery of the Carolinas reported to the Synod of New York and Philadelphia in May 1780 that a Mr. Thacher was a candidate for the ministry under its care, and two years later it reported that it had ordained Daniel Thatcher. George Howe in his *History of the Presbyterian Church in South Carolina* (I, 655-57) presented a somewhat jumbled account, which indicates that Thatcher while under the jurisdiction of Orange Presbytery was an early missionary to Georgia. Another authoritative account identifies him as one of the first missionaries to be active in that state after the Revolution. Howe also offers a clue to a molding influence in Thatcher's career by stating that he was a native of New Jersey whose "early studies were conducted under Dr. James Hall, at 'Clio's Nursery.' " This reference is to a school that Hall (A.B. 1774) conducted near Salisbury, North Carolina. It seems debatable that Thatcher studied in that particular school, which apparently was concerned with education at a level below that attained by a candidate for the ministry, but it is known that Hall had a lifelong interest in frontier missions and that he trained more than one candidate for the ministry. It would appear likely that somehow, and possibly through a Princeton connection, Thatcher went south to study with Hall, a member of the Orange Presbytery, and that he was ordained, despite the lack of a college degree, on the assumption that some compromise with what was becoming the standard would have to be made if the critical need for missionaries in frontier communities was to be met. Whether he was ordained *sine titulo*, as at times missionaries were, is unknown, but in 1784 he was listed by the clerk of Orange Presbytery as a minister without a stated charge, as he was again in 1789. In 1787 and 1788 he apparently sat with the Presbytery of South Carolina as a "corresponding member," and in April 1793 he was dismissed by Orange for membership in the South Carolina Presbytery. He remained a member of that presbytery until he was reported in May 1797 as having been dismissed to join the newly created Hudson Presbytery of New York. Thatcher had been appointed by the General Assembly of the Presbyterian Church in May 1795 to undertake a mission from the Wyoming Valley in Pennsylvania northward to Lake Seneca in New York. He reported in 1796 the results of a twelve-month mission that included the collection of better than £34 and was reappointed as missionary for the same general area, as he was again in May 1797. In the minutes of the General Assembly, there would be for him one more entry, a notation in the minutes for May 1798 that Thatcher had died in the preceding August, "in the discharge of his important trust, to the great loss of our Church."

The one other piece of firm information is the will he made on June 4, 1796, near the beginning of his second assignment from the General Assembly, that disposed of real property in the states of Georgia, New Jersey, and New York, in the last named, of 140 acres. Evidently, Thatcher on his missionary tours had not been exclusively concerned with preaching, baptisms, and the administration of the sacrament to the faithful. In addition, he bequeathed an unspecified number of slaves and unidentified personal property. He was described in the will as the Reverend Daniel Thatcher of Hunterdon County in New Jersey. He directed that his property be sold and the proceeds divided equally among five named sisters and a brother Edward's children. Their names have served to identify him as the son of Jeremiah Thatcher and his wife, Nancy, of Hunterdon County. His birth date has not been found, and evidently he had not married. The will was proved on November 17, 1797, and an inventory of his personal property in Georgia in the following fall showed a value of $483.01. An additional accounting as late as 1814 showed a balance of $441.75.

SOURCES: *Rec. Pres. Chh.*, 486, 494, 497, 502, 542; *Min. Gen. Assem., 1789-1820,* 19-139, passim; E. T. Thompson, *Presbyterians in the South* (1963), 123. It can be noted that the Gen. Assem. in 1795 (p. 98) authorized the Synods of Va. and the Carolinas to ordain "such candidates as they may judge necessary to appoint on missions," but with the condition that the permission be limited to "such candidates only as are engaged to be sent on missions." E. W. Caruthers, *Life and Character of the Rev. David Caldwell* (1842), 250; Foote, *Sketches, N.C.,* 281. *N.J. Wills,* IX, 367; MS Clio. Soc. membership list, PUA; G. M. Giger, *Hist. of the Clio. Soc.* (1865), 85; C. R. Williams, *The Clio. Soc.* (1916), 20-21. The author of this sketch is heavily indebted to Dr. James Thatcher Shaw of Logan, Utah, for information supplied on the Thatcher family.

WFC

John Trotman

JOHN TROTMAN, reluctant seaman, was born about 1759 in Barbados, the son of Henry Trotman, a merchant. He was sent to Philadelphia in April 1773 and assigned to the care of the prominent Quaker merchants Abel James and Henry Drinker with the understanding that they would see to his education. Shortly after his arrival, the youth was placed in the grammar school at Princeton. This may have been at his father's own suggestion, because the year before Trotman left home, President Witherspoon had penned an address to the inhabitants of the British Caribbean colonies in which he favorably compared the College with the British universities, where he feared young West Indians might become "only well acquainted with the Laws of the Turf or Gaming-table." The petition included a request for donations, and trustee Charles C. Beatty was sent to the West Indies to collect money and to publicize the College. Beatty died soon after reaching Barbados; and the West Indies venture produced no funds for the College, though it may have brought John Trotman to Princeton.

Trotman was one of several grammar school boys who presented English and Latin orations on the eve of the 1774 commencement. After completing his college preparation, he was admitted to Nassau Hall. But his student days were abruptly terminated in 1776 while he was spending his fall vacation with his guardians in Philadelphia. According to Trotman's own account, he and his school fellow George West (Class of 1779) were "walking out rather later than usual" one night in September 1776, when they were surprised on a wharf by a gang of sailors. The two students were forced aboard the *Andrea Doria*, a brig in the fledgling Continental navy, and pressed into service as crew members. Trotman sailed with the *Andrea Doria* in October when it was sent to St. Eustatius to pick up military supplies, and he witnessed one of the first foreign salutes to the American flag when the vessel arrived at the Dutch island.

Finding himself close to home, and having been severely beaten several times by the boatswain, Trotman took advantage of his earliest opportunity to flee the American navy. As soon as the ship dropped anchor, he and three other non-American crewmen made their escape in a small boat and rowed all night to nearby St. Christopher, a British possession. He swore a deposition concerning his adventure and the Dutch salute, which was sent to Whitehall by the acting governor of St. Christopher to demonstrate the Dutch governor's violation of neutrality. Trotman probably returned to Barbados, but no record of his life thereafter has been found.

SOURCES: W. B. Clark and W. J. Morgan, *Naval Documents of the Amer. Rev.*, VII (1976), 485-86; *N.J. Arch.* (1 ser.), XXVIII, 95-96 ("walking out"); Wertenbaker, *Princeton*, 54-55; *Pa. Journal and Weekly Advertiser*, 12 Oct 1774; *AHR*, 8 (1903), 691-92.

                                                 GSD

Robert Wharry (Wherry)

ROBERT WHARRY (WHERRY), physician and planter, may have been born in or near Hopewell Township, Cumberland County, Pennsylvania. Persons of his surname resided there and were active in the Middle Spring Presbyterian Church, which was served by Robert Cooper (A.B. 1763) at the time Wharry was a student at the College of New Jersey. Wharry may also have been related to David Wherry of East Nottingham, Chester County, Pennsylvania, who served on a committee of safety with Anthony Wayne, whose military abilities subsequently failed to impress the Princeton student.

He appears as a freshman in the College steward's accounts for room and tuition for the term from November 1774 to April 1775, and he is thought to have continued his studies until 1776. A member of the Cliosophic Society, Wharry assumed the name "Warren," after the medical hero of Bunker Hill, Dr. Joseph Warren. After leaving Nassau Hall, he pursued Warren's profession in the army medical service. He was appointed surgeon's mate of Malcolm's Additional Regiment in June 1778 and was transferred first to the Eleventh Pennsylvania in December 1778 and then to the Third Pennsylvania in January 1781.

In the course of his studies, Wharry became acquainted with Reading Beatty, surgeon of the Eleventh Pennsylvania from 1780 to 1781 and a brother of John Beatty (A.B. 1769) and Charles C. Beatty (A.B. 1775). When Wharry went south to Virginia and South Carolina with the Third Pennsylvania in 1781, he kept in touch with Beatty, and in four surviving letters, the surgeon's mate reveals himself to have been a good-humored man who missed "the Flesh Pots, the Onions and Garlick of Pennsylvania." Fearful that South Carolina would prove to be "a Country as hot as the Antichambers of Hell," he was instead "in Raptures" with the temperate southern winter and was even more enraptured with the "plenty of Ladies" he found there. Wharry was particularly interested in wealthy widows and planters' daughters, informing Beatty in July 1781: "I have a mind to pay my addresses to eight hundred acres of good Land and twenty or thirty *black* Negro's." By March 1782 Wharry had become more cautious with the ladies, "least I should receive a new wound, and perhaps a mortal one." He returned to Pennsylvania with his regiment and was transferred to the First Pennsylvania in January 1783, serving until the end of the war.

Believing that "the means of making mony very fast" were readily available in the southern states, Wharry probably took little comfort in his monthly salary as surgeon's mate of $42. He went back to South Carolina after his discharge. He acquired a plantation in St. Johns Parish, Charleston precinct, but whether his new property and lifestyle came to him as a result of a fortunate marriage is unknown. As a revolutionary veteran, Wharry received a three-hundred-acre grant of bounty land and became a member of the South Carolina Society of the Cincinnati. He probably had a medical practice in his new location because he was referred to as a doctor in a newspaper notice of his death, which occurred on August 6, 1790. Wharry was remembered as "a gentleman, who, for his excellent qualities, was greatly esteemed, and is much regretted."

SOURCES: B.M.H. Swope, *Middle Spring Pres. Chh.* (1900), passim; *Hist. of Cumberland and Adams Counties, Pa.* (1886) [Adams], 548; *Amer. Ancestry*, XI, 204; J. S. Futhey and G. Cope, *Hist. of Chester Cnty., Pa.* (1881), 68; MS Steward's accounts, MS Clio. Soc. membership list, PUA; Heitman (1893), 429; *PMHB*, 54 (1930), 160-63, 165-66 (quotations from correspondence); *Pa. Arch.* (2 ser.), II, 701; *Index, Rev. War Pension Applications* (1966); L. C. Duncan, *Med. Men in the Amer. Rev.* (1970), 412; J. I. Waring, *Hist. of Medicine in S.C., 1670-1825* (1964), 343; *SCHGM*, 51 (1950), 244-45 ("a gentleman").

GSD

Peter Wilson

PETER WILSON, A.B., A.M. 1783, Presbyterian clergyman, according to most accounts was born in 1750 in Amwell Township, Hunterdon County, New Jersey, the son of Peter Wilson and his wife, Hannah Vanoy Wilson. The father, undoubtedly a farmer, is said to have been of Scottish birth and to have migrated to New Jersey from Cecil County, Maryland. The date of birth given for the son would have made him considerably older than was the norm for other students, but it was not unusual for prospective candidates for the ministry to enroll in college at a significantly older age. One of his own children carried the middle name of Vanoy, which has also occasionally been attributed to him, although no direct evidence that he himself used it has been found.

As with other students at the time, it is impossible to say just when he was first enrolled in the College. Incomplete records of the steward, which happen to be fuller for the academic years between 1773 and 1775 than for any other years, indicate that he was not enrolled before the fall of 1775. Another question that must go unanswered is that of how much time he actually spent in residence at the College. All classes were suspended between November 29, 1776 and July 1777. Thereafter, a small number of students resided in the town, meeting their classes in the president's house while Nassau Hall served either as barracks or hospital, and it is reasonable to assume that the even smaller number of those who graduated in 1777 and 1778 were among them. Wilson must have been among those who responded to President Witherspoon's invitation of August 1778 to advanced students who had "attended constantly or occasionally, or had "studied at home," to appear for the examination that might qualify them for the degree. Wilson is listed among the members of the American Whig Society.

Whether he was present for commencement in September may be debatable, though it is likely that he was. The program that day was obviously a makeshift one. Despite the longstanding custom of having most, if not all, of the seniors speak in exercises that normally ran through the morning and afternoon, two of the five graduating seniors, Wilson and Matthew Woods, did not speak. Perhaps they had not had sufficient warning to permit preparation. John A. Scudder (A.B. 1775), on hand to receive the A.M. degree, delivered the salutatory address, an honor traditionally belonging to the ranking member of the senior class. Belcher Peartree Smith (A.B. 1773), who also was awarded his A.M. that day, spoke on "Eloquence," the subject on which he had spoken at his own commencement five years earlier.

Through the two years following graduation, Wilson presumably was studying theology. He was licensed to preach by the Presbytery of New Brunswick in 1780 or early 1781. Thereafter he probably was engaged in missionary work, for in May 1785 the New Brunswick Presbytery reported to the Synod that he had been ordained *sine titulo* "in order to go on a mission." In 1786 he was installed as pastor of the Independence (Hackettstown) and Mansfield congregations in what later became Warren County, New Jersey. He combined this joint pastorate with continued missionary activity that reached into Pennsylvania.

Wilson was twice married: first, to Ann Wikoff, daughter of Jacob Wikoff of Monmouth County, at some time before her death in 1787, and secondly, to Catherine Henry, daughter of David Henry and sister of Robert R. Henry (A.B. 1776). It probably is of greater importance to note that Catherine's sister Mary had been the second wife of John Cleves Symmes, pioneer settler in Ohio, and that her brother James was actively associated with Symmes in the original settlement of the so-called Miami or Symmes Purchase. Symmes was a visionary and none-too-businesslike leader of a group of speculators, drawn largely from New Jersey, which included Elias Boudinot, trustee of the College, and Jonathan Dayton (A.B. 1776). Wilson seems to have become interested in Ohio as early as 1795, when reportedly he purchased 640 acres there. He gave up his pulpits in New Jersey perhaps as early as 1796, but certainly by 1798 when the New Brunswick Presbytery reported to the General Assembly that he was a member without charge. The records of the General Assembly meeting in May 1799 show him then to have been a member of the Washington Presbytery, and at that time the New Brunswick Presbytery reported him as being in Cincinnati, Ohio.

It was there evidently that he died on July 24, 1799, as did his wife during the same summer. The couple had seven children, two of whom died in infancy. The five who survived their parents, two daughters and three sons, included Robert Henry Wilson (A.B. 1807).

SOURCES: Non-graduate file, MS Steward's accounts, PUA; *Som. Cnty. Hist. Quart.*, 6 (1917), 138; 7 (1918), 107-11; Giger, *Memoirs*, II; Alexander, *Princeton; N.J. Gazette*, 21 Oct 1778 (commencement); *Pa. Gazette*, 8 Oct 1783 (A.M.); *NJA* (2 ser.), II, 436 ("constantly or occasionally"); *Rec. Pres. Chh.*, 490, 507; *Min. Gen. Assem.*, 15, 136, 166, 169, 210; B. W. Bond, Jr., *Foundations of Ohio*, XIX (1941), 272, 290-301; and *Correspondence of John Cleves Symmes* (1926), passim; and *Intimate Letters of . . . Symmes* (1926), xvii, 35.

WFC

Matthew Woods

MATTHEW WOODS, A.B., Presbyterian clergyman, had a tragically short career. His parentage and date of birth have not been established, but a newspaper account of the commencement of 1778 describes him as of Pennsylvania, and it is likely that he belonged to the extensive family of Woods who were descended from some of the earlier settlers of Cumberland and Bedford counties and who were Presbyterian in their religious affiliation. It is possible that he was first enrolled in the College in November 1775, for his name does not appear in any of the surviving steward's accounts, which are relatively complete for the period extending from the spring of 1773 to the spring of 1775. After the suspension of studies at the College from November 1776 to July 1777, Woods probably was among the handful of students in attendance during the sessions ending with the examinations that preceded his graduation. At some time he became a member of the Whig Society. It may be significant that he, like his classmate Peter Wilson, evidently took no active part in the commencement ceremonies, probably because he was unprepared to speak his part. As one of five seniors who received their degrees that day, he belonged to the smallest class ever to graduate from the College. Perhaps the most hopeful thing about the occasion was that the exercises were held in Nassau Hall, which for more than a year had been serving as a military hospital.

After graduation Woods evidently continued his preparation for the ministry. He was licensed to preach by the Donegal Presbytery on October 20, 1780 and, after declining a call from the Lower Marsh Creek Church near modern Gettysburg, was ordained and installed as pastor of the Hanover Congregation in Northumberland County, Pennsylvania, on June 19, 1782. He attended the meeting of the Synod at Philadelphia in May 1784. He died on September 13, 1784. No evidence that he married has been found.

SOURCES: *Pa. Arch.* (3 ser), XII, 214; *Centennial Memorial of Presbytery of Carlisle* (1889), I, 300-302, 426; *Rec. Pres. Chh.*, 491, 501, 508; Giger, Memoirs, II; Alexander, *Princeton; Hist. of Cumberland and Adams Counties, Pa.* (1886), [Adams] 285; *N.J. Gazette*, 21 Oct 1778 (commencement).

WFC

CLASS OF 1779

Andrew Bayard, A.B.

Richard Bland Lee

Matthew McAllister, A.B.

George Merchant, A.B.

James Riddle, A.B.

Richard Stockton, A.B.

George West

Aaron Dickinson Woodruff, A.B.

Andrew Bayard

ANDREW BAYARD, A.B., A.M. 1783, merchant, banker, insurance under-writer, and civic leader, was born in Philadelphia on February 24, 1762, the second son of Colonel John Bayard and his first wife, Margaret Hodge Bayard, and a brother of James Ashton Bayard (A.B. 1777), Samuel Bayard (A.B. 1784), and Nicholas Bayard (A.B. 1792). He was also a first cousin of James Ashton Bayard (A.B. 1784), and nephew through his mother of Andrew Hodge (A.B. 1772) and Hugh Hodge (A.B. 1773). The father was a prominent Philadelphia merchant and political leader in revolutionary Pennsylvania, who saw combat service with state troops, served as speaker of the state assembly, sat on the executive council of the state, and after the war repre-sented it in Congress. He also was a trustee of the College from 1778 to his death in 1807.

It is impossible to say when Bayard was admitted to the College, or for how long he actually was in residence there. He may have been among the students dismissed by President Witherspoon on Novem-ber 29, 1776, three days before Washington's retreating army passed through the town. A few students had returned by the summer of 1777, finding accommodations as they could in the town and reciting their lessons in the President's House. During the next academic year, a small number had rooms in Nassau Hall, and in the summer of 1779, Bayard, as a senior, was probably counted among the ten stu-dents enrolled. At some time he became a member of the Whig So-ciety, and at commencement on September 29, he delivered an English oration "on the horrors of war."

After graduation Bayard seems to have returned to Philadelphia, and not long thereafter, to have entered into his father's counting house. His career was to be that of a merchant whose business moved by a natural progression into the fields of insurance and banking, but many details of its beginning are obscure. It has been said that he made several voyages abroad, presumably when still a young man. That he owed a great deal of his success to family connections is clear in any case. The first of these connections came through his father, who in 1788 moved to New Brunswick, New Jersey, where from 1791 to 1793 he was a director of the Society for establishing Useful Manu-factures, the none too successful ventures of which included some of the more influential men of that state and of New York. Bayard was involved as well as his father. He gained a second influential connec-tion by marrying Sarah Pettit, the daughter of Colonel Charles Pettit,

Andrew Bayard, A.B. 1779
BY THOMAS SULLY AFTER JACOB EICHHOLTZ

earlier a leading political figure in New Jersey and veteran of the Revolution, who after the war moved to Philadelphia and at the beginning of 1796 became the second president of The Insurance Company of North America. Andrew Bayard was a director of the company from 1798 to 1805. In 1804 he also became a director of the newly organized Delaware Insurance Company.

The closest family tie of importance for his business interests became that formed with his brother-in-law Andrew Pettit (Class of 1778). By the 1790s the firm of Pettit and Bayard was developing a significant import business, its activity including investment in government paper and the underwriting of marine insurance. Early in the 1800s the firm became involved in a celebrated case before the state's supreme court that led ultimately to an unsuccessful attempt to impeach its judges, with Hugh Brackenridge (A.B. 1771), a judge who had not participated in the case, unsuccessfully attempting to be included in the impeachment proceedings. The firm conducted its business from an address on Walnut Street.

It is possible that the most profitable family connection for Andrew Bayard, and his firm, was that provided by his first cousin, James Ashton Bayard of Wilmington, Delaware, a member of Congress from 1797 to 1803 and a United States senator from 1804 to 1813. James's surviving correspondence indicates that he and Andrew enjoyed close ties of friendship as well as kinship. He looked to Andrew for the supply of certain wants, especially it seems of good wine. It also appears that from time to time Andrew performed banking services for him and gave useful advice on investments. Thus, on June 11, 1812, James wrote: "I thank you for the information as to the stocks. The low price at which the Insurances stand, will induce me to hold what I possess at all hazards." In return, Andrew enjoyed remarkably full and current intelligence regarding prospective actions by the government, especially those that might affect a mercantile business.

There was nothing secretive about the correspondence. It included mainly estimates of the fate of pending bills in Congress, or such items as the membership of a committee that would receive applications for compensation of claims growing out of French spoliations at sea, or the prospect at varying times for renewal of the charter of the Bank of the United States. Foreign affairs through this uncertain time claimed much attention, with a focus on the question of whether there would be war or peace. Only in the days immediately preceding the War of 1812, when Congress was subject to special rules of secrecy, did James advise that his name not be identified with "any opinions you may form inferred from my letters." But there was no dependence on inference in the advice written on June 17, 1812 that Andrew "consider the War *as certain* and act accordingly." The next day two letters were written, the first reporting that Congress had passed a declaration of war, the second that the president had signed it.

Andrew Bayard in 1808 had become a trustee of the College. He served for several years after 1813 as a member of the Select Council of the City of Philadelphia. In 1814 he became president of the newly organized Commercial Bank of Pennsylvania, and in 1816 he accepted the presidency of the Philadelphia Saving Fund Society, which has been described as the first savings bank in the United States. In concept it was designed as a charitable institution intended to "promote economy and the practice of saving amongst the poor and laboring classes of the community." Bayard served it faithfully until the very eve of his death, and without compensation. He died on June 1, 1832, mourned in the public press as one of the city's most respected inhabitants. He was the father of six children, three sons and three daughters. He was said to be one of the last three gentlemen in Philadelphia "who continued the use of powder and who wore their hair behind the head tied in a cue."

SOURCES: See James Ashton Bayard (A.B. 1777); *NJA* (2 ser.), III, 324-25, 435-37, 671-72, 669-71; *N.J. Gazette*, 13 Oct 1779 (commencement); J. Kirkpatrick, *Light of Other Days* (1836), 33; Davis, *Essays*, 391, 395, 477-78; Index to "Old Loan" Ledgers of Bureau of the Public Debt, 1790-1836; J. H. Montgomery, *Hist. of Insurance Co. of North Amer.* (1885), 125, 127, 132; M. James, *Biog. of a Business* (1942), 69, 375, 380, 382; *Alphabetical Index of Private Claims . . . Presented to House of Rep.* (1853), 64; A. Ritter, *Phila. and Her Merchants* (1860), 68; S. W. Higginbotham, *Keystone in the Democratic Arch.* (1952), 55-58, 78-80; *PMHB*, 54 (1930), 335; 61 (1937), 119; E. Donnan, ed., *Papers of James A. Bayard*, AHA *Report* for 1913 (1915), passim, esp. 199 ("hold what I possess"), 200 ("opinions you may form"), 201 ("consider the War *as certain*"); J. M. Wilcox, *Hist. of Phila. Saving Fund Soc.* (1916), 24, 25 ("promote economy") 81, 101-103 ("tied in a cue").

WFC

Richard Bland Lee

RICHARD BLAND LEE, lawyer and public official, was born January 20, 1761, the third son of Henry and Lucy Grymes Lee of Prince William County, Virginia, and the brother of three graduates of the College: Henry Lee (A.B. 1773), Charles Lee (A.B. 1775), and Edmund Jennings Lee (A.B. 1792). Richard originally came to Princeton as a student in the grammar school, where his brother Charles previously had been prepared for college. Two newspaper accounts of the commencement exercises in September 1774 report that on September 26 the students in the grammar school were examined according to their standing and that the "highest class" was admitted to the freshman class of the College. In the evening of that day, continue the accounts, eight of the school's scholars delivered orations in Latin and Greek, among them "Richard Lee of Virginia." Richard Bland Lee was the only member of the Virginia family with the name of Richard who was of an age to be attending a grammar school at the time. Presumably, he had been in attendance for at least a year, and if so he would have been admitted to the school at the age of twelve as had been his brother Charles in 1770. Because the steward's list of members of the freshman class for the period of November 1774 to April 10, 1775 does not include Richard's name, it may be concluded that he did not graduate from the grammar school in September 1774. That he continued as a student in the school through at least a part of the academic year 1774-1775 is suggested by the fact that President Witherspoon on September 25, 1775, two days before Charles Lee would deliver the salutatory address at that year's commencement, made a payment on Richard's account which was recorded in the ledger of a local merchant. The ledger records further payments by the president on the accounts

Richard Bland Lee, Class of 1779
BY JAMES PEALE

of both Richard and Charles Lee on September 29. A payment of the following November 24 on Richard's account strongly suggests that he was on hand for the beginning of the academic year 1775-1776, probably as a member of the freshman class, for it is unlikely that at his age he would have continued in the grammar school through three full years. The surviving ledger for all practical purposes ends with the fall of 1775, and no proof has been found that would place Richard among the students dismissed by President Witherspoon on November 29, 1776 because of the deteriorating military situation, but it is quite possible that he was. That in the preceding May he was in the north rather than in Virginia is indicated by an entry in the journal of William Bradford (A.B. 1772) that records that on the tenth Bradford went from Philadelphia to Wilmington and fell into the company of "Masters" Shippen and Lee, the latter "a sprightly sensible lad, brother of my friend Charles." On May 10 Lee could have been visiting his Shippen cousins during the spring vacation. The evidence supporting the view that Richard was for a time enrolled in the College is not absolutely conclusive, but it is persuasive, especially in view of his parents' obvious preference for the education of their sons at the College of New Jersey.

Lee is listed among the students attending the College of William and Mary during the period from 1776 to 1781. A more specific reference records his admission into the Phi Beta Kappa Society on June 17, 1780 and his activity as a member until the end of that year. Unfortunately, however, this does not necessarily fix a time for his possible residence as an undergraduate at Williamsburg.

Lee was prompt to enter public life, becoming a member of the General Assembly for Loudoun County in 1784 to 1788 and in 1796. Having advocated ratification of the federal Constitution in 1788, he was elected to the House of Representatives in 1789 and served to 1795. As a congressman he is remembered chiefly as one of the two Virginia representatives who in 1789 agreed to support Hamilton's plan for assumption of state debts in return for the location of the national capital on the Potomac, which bordered Lee's district. Being, like his brothers, a Federalist, he failed of reelection in 1794 and retired to property in Loudoun he had inherited upon his father's death in 1787. He had been married on June 19, 1794 to Elizabeth Collins, the daughter of Stephen Collins, a wealthy Quaker merchant of Philadelphia. About twenty-seven miles above Alexandria, Lee built a house that was described by a visiting member of the Shippen family in 1797 as "lately furnished from Philada" and handsomely comparing with "the very best furnished houses in Philada."

Lee moved to Washington in 1815, where he served for a time as a commissioner for reconstruction of public buildings and as a member of another commission on claims for property destroyed during the recent war. By appointment of President Monroe in 1819, he became a judge of the Orphans' Court for the District of Columbia, a position held until his death on March 12, 1827. Married only once, he became the father of six children, four of them girls, two of whom died in infancy.

Sources: *DAB; BDAC*; E. J. Lee, *Lee of Va., 1642-1892* (1895), 370-72, 462, 466; *Pa. Journal and Weekly Advertiser*, 12 Oct 1774 ("highest class"); *N.Y. Gazette and Weekly Mercury*, 24 Oct 1774; *NJA* (1 ser.), xxix, 496; ms Steward's accounts, PUA; Patterson Acct. Bk.; College of William and Mary, *Gen. Cat.* (1874), 97; *WMQ* (1 ser.), 4 (1896), 213, 215, 237-39; (2 ser.), 2 (1922), 251-52; O. M. Voorhees, *Hist. of Phi Beta Kappa* (1945), 15-17; J. C. Ballagh, ed., *Letters of R. H. Lee*, ii (1914), 535; D. Malone, *Jefferson and the Rights of Man* (1951), 301; C. G. Lee, Jr., *Lee Chronicle* (1957), 244; W. B. Bryan, *Hist. of National Capital*, i (1914), 636; ii (1916), 34.

PUBLICATIONS: *An Oration Delivered at the Request of the Washington Society*, 22 Feb 1811, Alexandria, Va.; *An Oration Delivered July 5, 1819 in the House of Representatives*.

MANUSCRIPTS: VHi, PHi

WFC

Matthew McAllister

MATTHEW McALLISTER, A.B., A.M. 1794, lawyer, was born on May 4, 1758, in York County, Pennsylvania, the son of Colonel Richard McAllister and his wife, Mary Dill McAllister. The father held substantial properties, is credited with the founding of the town of Hanover, and as the Revolution approached, became a leader of the York County Whigs. A colonel in the Pennsylvania militia, he joined the force collected during the summer of 1776 in northern New Jersey as the Flying Camp under General Hugh Mercer and was given command of one of its battalions. After his military service ended in 1777, he returned to York County, where he became county lieutenant, a presiding justice, and a member of the state's executive council.

There are no records to indicate when the son entered the College, but it may have been in the fall of 1775. If so, he was just beginning his second year when President Witherspoon dismissed the students on November 29, 1776, as the British were about to overrun the village. Because McAllister was among the very few students who managed during the remaining war years to complete their course of study, it seems reasonable to conclude that he was one of the exceedingly small number (no more than ten in the summer of 1779) who were in residence at the College during the academic years 1777 to 1779 and only in the last of these with accommodations in Nassau Hall. McAllister became a member of the American Whig Society, and at his commencement on September 29, 1779, he spoke in Latin "de peregrinatione." The *New Jersey Gazette* reported the satisfaction that the audience found in the performance of the graduating scholars and its pleasure in seeing "this seminary beginning again to rise from its ruin, and to recover from the desolation it has suffered in the present unnatural war."

After graduation McAllister studied law in Lancaster, Pennsylvania, and in June 1782 he was admitted to the practice of law before the courts of the city and county of Philadelphia. Like other young lawyers before and after him, he quickly elected to try his fortune on one of the frontiers of settlement and about 1784 moved to Savannah, Georgia. At the end of the Revolution, Georgia was still little more than a string of settlements stretching along the lower side of the Savannah River, with rice plantations extending southward along the coast toward the Altamaha River. Savannah was its principal town and the entrepôt for its trade. The town's white population in 1784 probably was less than a thousand, but during the following decade, it more than doubled. Subsequently, an expanding cultivation of long staple cotton would bring continuing growth.

The war in Georgia had been extremely disturbing to property rights, both in land and in slaves, and at its end, the state must have been a lawyer's paradise. At the March term of the superior court in 1785, the grand jury presented "as a Grievance replete with distress the enormous Docquet of the Civil actions now before the Court, and it is much to be lamented that the Legislature did not adopt some mode to prevent the ruin of our citizens."

McAllister soon became one of the leading lawyers of the Georgia bar, winning as early perhaps as 1786 the office of the state's attorney general. Citing his previous service in this post, he applied to President Washington in 1789 for appointment as the federal attorney for the district of Georgia and became the first to hold that office. Neither of these offices imposed serious limits upon his private practice. Indeed, they were generally viewed at the time as helpful in the expansion of one's own practice. McAllister acquired other offices as well. He sat in the state assembly, had a part in framing a new constitution for Georgia in 1788, served as a judge of the superior court early in the following century, and in 1814 represented Chatham County in the state senate. For a number of years after 1790 he served as an alderman for Savannah and from time to time took his turn as mayor of the city, an office filled by vote of the aldermen from among their own number.

He seems to have invested a considerable part of the returns from his practice in Savannah real estate. According to family tradition, at the time of the great fire of 1820, the most destructive of the city's history, he owned a substantial part of the business district and in his determination to rebuild became seriously overextended. It is also a part of the tradition that he refused in the midst of the fire to leave his residence and had to be carried forcibly from the building seated in his chair.

There is nothing surprising in the fact that he succumbed to the fever of land speculation that swept through Georgia and other states in the 1790s in an especially virulent form. He became a key figure in the so-called "Yazoo fraud" of 1795 as a member of the Georgia Com-

pany, the most important of the four land companies to which the
state legislature that year sold the vast territory, or most of it at least,
lying above Florida to the west of the Coosa River and extending past
the Yazoo River to the Mississippi for $500,000, or a cent to a cent and
a half per acre, depending on the estimate of the total acreage involved. Amidst serious charges that the legislature had been grossly
corrupted, a newly elected legislature in 1796 and a new state constitution in 1798 repudiated the sale under the leadership of James Jackson, who resigned his seat in the United States Senate to conduct the
fight. It is difficult to determine the exact part played by McAllister,
partly perhaps because the act of repudiation required that all references to the transaction be expunged from the state records and that
the act of 1795 be publicly burned. Probably James Gunn, the other
senator from Georgia, was more influential, but there can be no question that in Jackson's view McAllister was a principal actor in the land
sale. Moreover, McAllister held one of the ten shares belonging to the
original seven members of the company, who raised the funds for the
payment due the state by selling rights to many others, including John
Young Noel (A.B. 1777) and Robert Goodloe Harper (A.B. 1785).

The political reverberations from the Yazoo adventure were far
reaching at both the state and national levels. They included in 1810
a landmark decision by the United States Supreme Court in the case
of *Fletcher* vs. *Peck*, upholding claims to title based upon the act of
1795 despite its subsequent repudiation. After Georgia ceded her
western lands to the nation in 1802, and after bitter controversies extending into 1814, the federal government assumed responsibility for
providing compensation for such claimants as might apply for it. Many
did, especially those outside Georgia, but many did not, preferring apparently to hold onto their claims in the expectation that they eventually might be converted into specific titles to land. How much Mc-
Allister may have gained or lost through his own speculations cannot
be said. Evidence has not been found, either, beyond Jackson's bitter
attacks upon him, to determine how active he may have been in the
subsequent politics of the state. It can only be said that he held thereafter more than one office of trust and that Jackson's charges are obviously open to some discounting. In party affiliation McAllister may
have leaned toward the Federalists, as did others among the "Yaz-
ooists," but no confirmation of this assumption has been found.

Whatever the fact, he was allied, in part by marriage, with the more
substantial segment of eastern Georgia's society. It apparently was in the
first half of the 1790s that he married Hannah Gibbons, daughter of
Joseph Gibbons of Chatham County and sister of Thomas Gibbons,

an especially prosperous lawyer and planter who subsequently acquired a handsome property in Elizabethtown, New Jersey and entered into commercial ventures that eventually brought him into conflict with Aaron Ogden (A.B. 1773) in the celebrated case of *Gibbons* vs. *Ogden*. Their son Matthew Hall McAllister (Class of 1819), who was the youngest of three children born of the marriage and who attended Nassau Hall without graduating, became a highly successful attorney and leader of the Whig party. In 1840 he switched to the Democratic party and ran unsuccessfully on their ticket for governor in 1845, before ending his career by appointment in 1855 as the first federal circuit judge in California. One of his sons was Ward McAllister, who later in the century was arbiter of New York and Newport society and who is credited with coining the phrase "the four hundred" for the purpose of defining the elite of New York City. Matthew McAllister, who died in Savannah on May 9, 1823, was predeceased by a son Richard, who was born in 1795 and died young, and by a daughter named Harriet Hannah, who was born in 1796 and died in 1819.

SOURCES: Alumni file, PUA; G. R. Prowell, *Continental Congress at York* (1914), 170, 180-81, 185-86, 245-48; *DAB* (son, grandson, and Thomas Gibbons); E. F. Hatfield, *Hist. of Elizabeth, N.J.* (1868), 565-568; H. Chase et al., eds., *Biog. Directory of Fed. Judiciary* (1976), 180; W. McAllister, *Society as I have Found It* (1890), 5-6, 19-25; Savannah Writers' Project, *Savannah River Plantations* (1947), 287, 292, 299-312; M. C. McAllister, *Descendants of Archibald McAllister* (1898), 13; *N.J. Gazette*, 13 Oct 1779 (commencement); *Dunlop and Claypoole's American Daily Advertiser*, 7 Oct 1794 (A.M.); J. H. Martin, *Bench and Bar of Phila.* (1883), 179, 289; C. C. Jones, Jr., *Hist. of Savannah* (1890), 311n, 336, 339 ("Grievance replete with distress"); *Ga.'s Official Reg., 1927*, 437; F. D. Lee and J. L. Agnew, *Hist. Record of . . . Savannah* (1869), 185; *GHQ*, 1 (1917), 127, 131, 132; 7 (1923), 187-91, 200-203; 51 (1967), 425-42; G. Hunt, *Cal. of Applications and Recommendations for Office During the Presidency of George Washington* (1901), 79; *Jefferson Papers*, XVII, 625-26, XVIII, 360-61; *Hamilton Papers*, XII, 207; XV, 504; S. G. McLendon, *Hist. of Public Domain of Ga.* (1924), esp. 100, 137-42, 150-63; C. P. Magrath, *Yazoo . . . the Case of Fletcher v. Peck* (1966), esp. 1-36; T.U.P. Charlton, *Life of Maj. Gen. James Jackson* (1809), esp. 157f.; *Papers AHA*, V (1891), 393-437; E. M. Coulter, *Short Hist. of Ga.* (1933), 187-92.

WFC

George Merchant

GEORGE MERCHANT, A.B., A.M. 1783, schoolmaster and public official, was born in the winter of 1756-1757 in Princeton, New Jersey, where his parents, Johannes and Wishulathe (or Ursula) Kauffman, are thought to have settled in 1745. Merchant's father, a native of Stuttgart, changed the German surname to its English equivalent after his arrival in America. At some time in the early 1770s, George Merchant entered the grammar school at Princeton, and after the school's September 1774 exercises, he was admitted to the freshman class of the College. A member of the American Whig Society, Merchant should have completed his studies in 1778; but the wartime suspension of classes from November 1776 until the following summer delayed his graduation for a year. At the 1779 commencement he delivered the Latin salutatory, "de conjunctione pietatis cum doctrina, sive scientia humana, ut sibi mutuo adjumento sint." He is said to have been placed immediately in charge of the "Princeton academy"; but it has not been possible to determine what, if any, responsibilities he had at the College's preparatory school at this time.

The following summer Merchant came to the attention of the Corporation of Albany, then searching for a man qualified to superintend an academy under the city's care. Merchant accepted the position of rector, and the school was opened on his arrival in November 1780. With the assistance of a master and an usher, the rector quickly prepared his young scholars for a public examination held on February 16, 1781.

By autumn 1781, when plans were being made for the erection of a new school building, the academy had grown to fifty students, and the rector was requested to report disciplinary problems to the corporation, especially the names of "such Students as shall be guilty wantonly of breaking any pains of Glass." Merchant also needed the assistance of another instructor for writing and mathematics, a position the board offered to former Queen's College tutor John Bogart (Queen's 1771) at £100 per annum, one half the sum Merchant was receiving. Bogart's friend Colonel John Taylor (A.B. 1770) cautioned him against accepting the offer because Merchant, who would be his superior, was a younger man and in Taylor's judgment not "eminent in the classick studies." This difficulty was resolved in April 1782 when Merchant left the Albany school. The rectorship was offered to Taylor, but both he and Bogart eventually declined to come, and the school was placed in the hands of Simeon Baldwin (Yale 1781) and John Lovett (Yale 1782). The Albany Board, however, understood that Merchant would "hold himself in readiness when called upon . . . to return again to resume the Rectorship."

Residing again near Nassau Hall after his departure from Albany, Merchant was contacted by Ashbel Green (A.B. 1783), future president of the College, who had agreed with several other undergraduates to reconstitute the American Whig Society. Both student literary societies suffered from disorganization during the confusion of the

Revolution. But the Cliosophic Society, which at least may have continued to induct new members in the war years, had been formally reestablished in 1781. Green and his friends were anxious to see the rival society resume its activities as well. That was made possible by the recovery of the society's constitution, which was found in Merchant's hands, and by a meeting of graduate members living in the vicinity to admit the new men, a meeting Merchant may have attended.

Already experienced in the opening of grammar schools, George Merchant was engaged in September 1782 to take charge of the new Trenton Academy. The trustees of this school, one of whom was William Churchill Houston (A.B. 1768), advertised Merchant's appointment in the local press, noting that he would teach "the English, Latin, and Greek languages grammatically; geography, practical mathematicks, the principles of natural philosophy and astronomy, public speaking, and the rudiments of any other branch of useful education, either to fit pupils to finish a course at college, or to go immediately into business." How long Merchant remained at the Trenton Academy has not been discovered. In 1783 the College awarded him a master's degree. And in 1785 he married Elizabeth Spencer, daughter of the recently deceased Reverend Elihu Spencer (Yale 1746), a longtime trustee of the College and pastor of the Trenton Presbyterian church.

Merchant is said to have returned to the academy in Albany in 1786 at the request of the corporation, and an observer of 1789 reported that the school was flourishing under his direction. He or others maintained the school at least until 1797, and Merchant himself made a lasting impression as a teacher and classicist. When Union College was organized in 1795 at nearby Schenectady, the Albany teacher became one of its original trustees; but he served for only one year, perhaps an indication that his interest in education was waning.

By the end of the century, Merchant had emerged as a substantial Albany citizen—so substantial as to be elected alderman for the city's first ward, an office to which he was annually returned, with the exception of one year, between 1799 and 1807. By 1805 Alderman Merchant and his large family were residing in a "spacious brick mansion" on State Street. The causes of the Latin schoolmaster's rise to such prominence are not readily apparent, although George Merchant's story is by no means unusual. He was remembered as "an energetic, self-made man," and his wife's inheritance of a part interest in three thousand acres of Vermont land was certainly a welcome addition to whatever he received from his own father.

A Republican in politics, Merchant was replaced as alderman by a Federalist at the Albany charter election of 1808, and in 1810, when a new Federalist state Council of Appointment purged six thousand local officeholders, he lost his place as one of the city's justices as well. The following year he was named a director in the law incorporating the Mechanics and Farmers' Bank, the city's third banking institution and one dominated by the Albany Republicans. Merchant and most of the bank's other directors were reelected in 1812, despite dissatisfaction on the part of some stockholders with their politics. At some time after the declaration of war with Great Britain in 1812, the Republican national administration rewarded Merchant with an appointment as district paymaster for the United States Army. He was still concerned with army business in 1818, though his accounts had by that time been closed. During the war he was also appointed clerk of the city and county of Albany, offices he held until 1822 or 1823. Merchant was active in local politics as late as August 1824, when he was a member of the Albany Democratic Republican committee that circulated a letter condemning the failure of a special session of the Bucktail-dominated legislature to pass an electoral reform bill.

In 1820 Merchant purchased "for a mere song" a five-acre estate and mansion at Arbor Hill on the northern edge of the city. (The property had been sold for $15,000 a few years earlier.) He died there on August 14, 1830, predeceased by his wife, an infant daughter, and a son named after Samuel Leake (A.B. 1774), and was buried in the cemetery of St. Peter's Episcopal Church, which he had served for several years as a warden. He was survived by six sons "remarkable for both their mental and *physical activity*, particularly the latter," among whom were a lawyer and two engravers.

SOURCES: J. Munsell, *Annals of Albany*, IX (1858), 214-15 ("energetic, self-made," "*physical activity*"); IV (1853), 293; V (1854), 33; *Pa. Journal and Weekly Advertiser*, 12 Oct 1774; *Pa. Packet*, 7 Oct 1779 (commencement); J. Munsell, *Coll. on the Hist. of Albany*, I (1865), 311, 313-15, 320, 335 ("pains of Glass"), 339, 341-42 ("hold himself in readiness"); II (1867), 16, 18 ("spacious brick mansion"); J. Bogart, *Bogart Letters* (1914), 21, 35-36 ("classick studies"); Beam, *Whig Soc.*, 62; C. R. Williams, *Clio. Soc.* (1916), 20; J. O. Raum, *Hist. of City of Trenton* (1871), 363 ("languages grammatically"); A. J. Weise, *Hist. of City of Albany* (1884), 405; A. V. Raymond, *Union Univ.* (1907), III, App., 3; C. Reynolds, *Albany Chronicles* (1906), 392-403; *N.J. Wills*, VI, 367; *The Balance, and N.Y. State Journal* (Albany), 6 Apr 1810; D. R. Fox, *Decline of Aristocracy in the Politics of N.Y.* (1965), 110-11; *Calhoun Papers*, II, 309, 311; *Annual Reg. and Albany Directory* (1815), 9, 63; R. H. Shoemaker, *Checklist of Amer. Imprints for 1824* (1969), 164; *N.Y. Hist.*, 34 (1953), 422-23 ("for a song").

GSD

James Riddle

JAMES RIDDLE, A.B., A.M. 1783, lawyer and jurist, was born in York, Pennsylvania on January 20, 1755, the son of James Riddle of Londonderry, Ireland, who is said to have settled in York County in the early 1750s. The elder James Riddle was probably the man whose warrant for 300 acres on Marsh Creek was recorded on January 16, 1767, and who was taxed in Cumberland township in 1779 and 1782 on 340 acres, three slaves, and livestock. James Riddle, Jr., slightly older than most of his classmates, was a member of the American Whig Society. He presented an English oration on the "source of true nobility" at the September 1779 commencement.

After receiving his degree Riddle may have seen military service as the lieutenant or as the ensign of that name active in the Cumberland County, Pennsylvania Militia in 1780. In September of that year he was back in Princeton. The reasons for his return and the length of his stay are uncertain, but the visit became newsworthy when he lost his horse and offered a $200 reward for its return to Captain James Moore of Princeton. In 1781 he again came back to Nassau Hall, this time as a tutor, and continued in that position until 1783, receiving his A.M. at the 1783 commencement.

After his final departure from the College, Riddle entered the office of York lawyer Robert McPherson. He was soon to marry McPherson's daughter Elizabeth, whose sister married Riddle's fellow student Alexander Russell (A.B. 1780). Admitted to the bar in York on January 25, 1785, Riddle moved shortly thereafter to Chambersburg in nearby Franklin County and is listed there in the first federal census with a household that included two slaves. On September 1, 1791, Riddle was appointed to the Pennsylvania High Court of Errors and Appeals. In 1794 he became president judge of the Fourth Pennsylvania Judicial District, then including the counties of Franklin, Cumberland, Bedford, Huntingdon, and Mifflin. A strong Federalist like his brother-in-law Russell, he remained president judge until 1804, when he resigned because of popular dislike for his politics.

Following the death of his first wife, Riddle married Ariana Kennedy in 1800, and after his return to private legal practice, he is said to have acquired a "large fortune." He owned at least 117 acres in Franklin County and may have been a part owner of land in Bedford County as well. According to one nineteenth-century account, "his legal abilities were very respectable, though he was not considered a great lawyer. He was well read in science, literature and the law; was a good advocate and very successful with the jury." Beginning in 1798, he served as a trustee of Dickinson College in Carlisle for thirty-five years. In September 1812, when Pennsylvania Federalists gathered at Carlisle to consider means for defeating President James Madison (A.B. 1771), Riddle was selected as chairman of the meeting.

Riddle died at Chambersburg on February 5, 1837. He was remembered as "a tall man, broad shouldered and lusty, with a noble face and profile and pleasing manner."

SOURCES: *Hist. of Cumberland and Adams Counties, Pa.* (1886) [Cumberland], 151 ("tall man") [Adams], 22, 98, 364; F. M. Eastman, *Courts and Lawyers of Pa.* (1922), III, 613 ("not considered a great lawyer," "large fortune"); F. A. Virkus, *Abridged Compendium of Amer. Geneal.*, I (1925), 172; VI (1937), 529; *Pa. Packet*, 7 Oct 1779 (commencement). Two other James Riddles recorded in Pa. tax returns for Cumberland Cnty., 1778-1785, may also have been the Cumberland militia officers [see *Pa. Arch.* (3 ser.), XX, 40, 157, 290, 515, 566, 715; XXIII, 290, 671, 672; XXV, 39, 609; (5 ser.), IV, 494, 637; V, 471, 473, 619; *N.J. Gazette*, 20 Sep 1780; W. C. Carter and A. J. Glossbrenner, *Hist. of York Cnty.* (1975), 59; *First Census, Pa.*, 119; J. H. Martin, *Bench and Bar of Phila.* (1883), 65; C. C. Sellers, *Dickinson College* (1973), 484; S. W. Higginbotham, *Keystone in the Democratic Arch* (1952), 262; R. Stover, *Abstracts from the Republican Compiler, Adams Cnty., Pa.*, II (1976), 113]. Joseph Riddle (A.B. 1783) may have been a brother of James Riddle, although this has not yet been conclusively established. James Riddle, Esq. is separated by only one name in the 1790 Pa. census returns for Franklin Cnty., from a Joseph Riddle, perhaps the 1783 graduate. James Riddle's relationship, if any, to a man of the same name who was an Allegheny Cnty., Pa. judge, 1818-1838, has not been discovered.

GSD

Richard Stockton

RICHARD STOCKTON, A.B., A.M. 1783, LL.D. Queen's 1815 and Union 1816, lawyer, public official, and gentleman farmer, was born on April 17, 1764, at Morven, the Princeton estate of the his father Richard Stockton (A.B. 1748), a signer of the Declaration of Independence and a trustee of the College for many years. The mother of John Richard Stockton (as the 1779 graduate was known as a youth) was Annis Boudinot Stockton, the sister of Elias Boudinot, another long-time trustee of the College. The younger Stockton, who was to be associated with the College in different capacities for most of his life, was prepared at the grammar school in Princeton and participated in its public exercises on September 26, 1774. He is believed to have been admitted to the College before its closing in November of 1776. According to family tradition, after his father's flight from Princeton, the lad was left behind with an old servant to protect Morven from injury at the hands of advancing British troops. He is presumed to have returned to his course of study when the College reopened in the sum-

Richard Stockton, A.B. 1779
BY CHRISTIAN GULLAGER

mer of 1777. A member of the American Whig Society, Stockton graduated in 1779, giving an English oration on the "principles of true
heroism" at his commencement.

After leaving Nassau Hall, Stockton probably studied law with his
uncle Elias Boudinot, a delegate to the Continental Congress and soon
to become its president. As the eldest son, Stockton assumed the management of Morven and other family properties after the death of his
father in 1781. Two years later he was awarded his A.M., and soon
thereafter, he was among the founders of the *Institutio legalis*, a moot
court society for the training of lawyers in New Jersey. On April 7,
1784, not quite twenty years old, he was recommended by the justices
of the state supreme court for admission to the bar. Immediately succeeding to his father's influential position in the political and legal
life of central New Jersey, Stockton intermittently served as Common
Pleas justice for Somerset County, as had his father. He married Mary
Field of Burlington County in 1788, and in 1792 he became a sergeant-
at-law. Stockton's skill in courtroom argument made him one of the
most sought after lawyers between New York and Philadelphia, while

his sharp wit and forceful personality quickly brought him to the attention of older political leaders. He frequently appeared before the New Jersey Supreme Court and later before the United States Supreme Court.

His substantial patrimony permitted Stockton to assume an active part in corporate and speculative ventures during the first decade of his career. Taking his place among the proprietors of West Jersey, he became a member in 1785 of the proprietary committee that prompted the group's interest in a boundary dispute with the East Jersey proprietors. He has been assigned the authorship of the West Jersey proprietors' pamphlet on the disagreement of that year. In 1788 Stockton was involved in two new land schemes. He acted with several other alumni of the College as warrant agents for John Cleves Symmes's Miami River land grant in Ohio, and he participated in the unsuccessful effort of the New Jersey Land Society to secure a two-million-acre western land grant from the Continental Congress. Stockton was also involved in the late 1780s in two companies organized to finance experiments with steamboats. In 1791 he acquired eighty-two shares in the Society for establishing Useful Manufactures, encouraged by Alexander Hamilton as the pioneer industrial corporation of New Jersey.

A supporter of the federal Constitution, Richard Stockton was one of the inner circle of the West Jersey "Junto," an elite faction that engineered the victory in 1789 of a congressional ticket of its choosing in the first election under the Constitution. Stockton was favored in the first federal appointments with the office of district attorney for the state of New Jersey. Like others involved in the "Junto," he was shortly to emerge as a leading Jersey Federalist. In 1792 he was chosen as one of the state's presidential electors. And in November 1796 the state legislature elected him to the United States Senate, where he served until 1799, completing the term of Frederick Frelinghuysen (A.B. 1770) who had resigned.

As senator, Stockton was occasionally out of sympathy with the policies of President John Adams. He supported the Alien and Sedition Acts as well as measures to strengthen the American military establishment. Although Adams considered the New Jersey senator for appointment in 1798 as envoy to Paris, he subsequently nominated William Vans Murray for that position without consulting his cabinet, a decision that aroused the opposition of Stockton and other Federalist senators who were skeptical of the Directory's good intentions. After leaving the Senate, Stockton was rumored to favor Oliver Ellsworth (A.B. 1766) as the Federalist candidate for chief executive in 1800. He eventually dropped his reservations, however, and as a presidential elector he supported Adams. In January 1801 the defeated president offered Stockton an appointment as circuit judge under the terms of the Judiciary Act then before Congress. Stockton declined the appointment, but he commended Adams for his nomination of John Marshall as chief justice of the Supreme Court.

Unhappy with the election of Thomas Jefferson, the former senator was unable to find any solace in the changing pattern of politics in New Jersey, where a 1798 statute for the election of congressmen by district, opposed by Stockton, had helped the Republicans. Although the state returned to a general congressional election in 1800, Stockton's organizing efforts in that contest failed to prevent the defeat of the five Federalist House candidates, among them Aaron Ogden (A.B. 1773) and Franklin Davenport (Class of 1773). Stockton himself was the Federalist candidate for governor for four consecutive years beginning in 1801, but he was three times defeated by Republican majorities in the joint legislative meetings whose responsibility it was to fill the office. The election of equal numbers of Federalists and Republicans to the legislature in 1802 led to a tie in the gubernatorial balloting between Stockton and incumbent Governor Joseph Bloomfield. Neither a Federalist proposal to divide the offices of governor and United States senator between the parties in order to break the deadlock nor the substitution of Aaron Ogden's name for Stockton's was acceptable to the New Jersey Republicans, who preferred to see the vice-president of the council assume the governorship until they could resecure their legislative majority.

Alarmed at what he perceived as the spread of "Jacobinism" and factional intrigue under the cloak of democracy in American politics, Richard Stockton was no less dismayed to discover the seeds of conspiracy, rebellion, and even incendiarism among the students of his alma mater. Briefly treasurer of the College, from 1787 to 1788, Stockton served as a trustee from 1791 until his death thirty-seven years later. His residence in Princeton and his political stature contributed to his influence on the board, and in 1802 and 1807 he was a key figure in two of the most famous events in the history of the College.

On the afternoon of March 6, 1802, Nassau Hall was completely gutted by a blaze of uncertain origin. Appointed by the trustees to investigate the matter, Stockton and John Beatty (A.B. 1769) determined that "the College was *intentionally set on fire*." President Samuel Stanhope Smith (A.B. 1769) joined Stockton and Beatty in further inquiries, leading to a recommendation for the expulsion of those most active in the "immoralities, disorders and combinations which prevailed among some of the students during the late session." Unable to discover either the names or the motives of the alleged arsonists, Stockton and his colleagues were perhaps too ready to assume a connection between unruly students and the disastrous fire. They were no less restrained in promulgating a harsh new code of College rules designed not only to deprive the students of many varieties of entertainment but also to reduce them to an impoverished equality by limiting their receipt of parental allowances.

The repressive measures that Stockton encouraged at Princeton were not dissimilar to new administrative and disciplinary procedures at other American colleges, but they were hardly calculated to satisfy a high-spirited student body that had assimilated the libertarian ideology of the eighteenth century. In March 1807, five years after the fire, three students were expelled for violations of the College rules, but the great majority of their fellows signed a petition of protest couched in the rhetoric of natural rights and due process. As the only resident trustee, Stockton was summoned by the faculty to bolster their authority, but uncompromising speeches to the students by Stockton and Smith served merely to provoke the indignant denizens of Nassau Hall. As recounted in the faculty minutes, Stockton addressed the students at "considerable length . . . explaining the illegality of their thus openly combining against the authority and proceedings of the College." Unconvinced, the students interrupted the speakers with foot scraping and showed "other signs of their disapprobation." When they were presented with an ultimatum to disavow the petition one by one, most refused, "occupied" Nassau Hall, and prepared for a siege. Stockton, Smith, and the faculty were supported by the other trustees who met shortly thereafter and expelled 125 of the College's 200 students.

In 1812 Stockton returned to active political life. Long an opponent of the foreign policy of Jefferson and the Republicans, he attended the "peace" convention of the New Jersey Federalists on July 4 of that year. He probably also attended the general meeting of Federalist party leaders in New York City in September. The declaration of war with Great Britain in 1812 provided the Federalists of New Jersey with the issue they needed for a successful comeback. Stockton and three other peace candidates were elected to the Thirteenth Congress (as were two Republicans), and Aaron Ogden was chosen governor by the new Federalist majority in the state legislature. In Washington, Stockton took his place on a committee of Federalist representatives charged with organizing opposition to the war policies of President James Madison (A.B. 1771). On the floor of the House, he opposed restrictions on maritime commerce, the expansion of the army, and the conscription of state militia into the federal military establishment and ridiculed the "idle doctrine of free trade and sailors' rights" as an unsuitable justification for the war.

Stockton declined to be renominated for Congress by the Federalist state convention he attended at Trenton on July 4, 1814 and announced on the House floor in October that he did not expect ever to be there for another session. He was probably missed by the Federalist barber who argued that Stockton, with his queue "as big as your wrist, and powdered every day," would make a much better president than "this little Jim Madison, with a queue no bigger than a pipe stem!"

One of Stockton's chief personal satisfactions as a congressman was his lasting friendship with a first-term member from New Hampshire, Daniel Webster. In 1821, when Stockton's son Robert Field Stockton (Class of 1813), then captain of a navy frigate, found himself in legal difficulties after seizing several French slave vessels, Richard Stockton wrote a letter of encouragement to Webster who had taken the case. Stockton believed that if Webster could vindicate the young officer's actions the case would have a greater effect in bringing the illegal slave trade to an end than all the abolition societies in the country. He feared, nevertheless, that the trade could never be ended "as long as the General Govt. is under absolute Southern influence." Stockton's attitude toward slavery itself was equivocal. He is believed to have owned several slaves; and in 1797 he won a case for the master of an enslaved Indian woman who had sued for her freedom on the grounds that only Africans could be made slaves under American law. In 1823 Stockton freed one slave.

Although Stockton received eight votes for Vice President from Massachusetts electors in 1820, he withdrew from politics after leaving the House of Representatives. Devoting himself to his law practice and to local affairs, he had by this time acquired the sobriquet, "the Old Duke," suggestive both of his intimidating courtroom presence and of his refined manners. As distressed as the Old Duke was with the rule of an "unprincipled faction" in Washington, he preferred in 1822 to see President James Monroe remain in office rather than suffer the uncertain policies of such "Pretenders" as John Quincy Adams and John C. Calhoun. The possibility of a reconciliation with the Adams administration was lost in 1826 when Stockton failed to receive an appointment as district judge, a decision that cost Adams the support of the Stockton family in the election of 1828. In 1827 Stockton and John Rutherford (A.B. 1776) were named to a New Jersey commission to settle the state's disputed water boundary with New York, a problem they were unable to resolve.

As Princeton's premier citizen, Stockton remained active in the affairs of both village and College until his death. Though not a communicant of the Presbyterian Church, he served as its trustee for over twenty years. He is said also to have helped defray construction expenses for the original structure of Princeton Theological Seminary. In 1823, when College President James Carnahan (A.B. 1800) was disturbed in his sleep by a firecracker on his doorstep, Stockton reacted in predictable fashion. He suggested that the students be coerced into proper behavior by a solemn judicial enquiry to be headed by no less a personage than the chief justice of the New Jersey Supreme Court. The outraged trustee maintained that unless the culprits were immediately punished, "we might as well close the College doors." A year later, the Old Duke was chosen to welcome the Marquis de Lafayette on his visit to Princeton. In 1825 Stockton's name was suggested as head of the projected Princeton law school (established for a few years two decades later). He was made one of the first vice presidents of the College's alumni association in 1826, the same year in which he was chosen a manager of an abortive canal company.

Stockton was the father of nine children, among them his eldest son Richard Stockton III (A.B. 1810), who was killed in a duel in 1827. The Old Duke himself suffered a stroke and died on April 7, 1828. On hearing the news, Stockton's acquaintance John Pintard (A.B. 1776) remarked that "he had grown exceedingly corpulent, of w^h he did not like to be told." Pintard further confided in his daughter, "Mr S. you know was exceedingly proud & haughty w^h rendered him very unpopular, tho' his high talents commanded respect, but not esteem. Very selfish & not benevolent." Stockton's three surviving sons inherited several Princeton properties including Morven and Tusculum (once the country estate of College President John Witherspoon), 5,000 acres in New York along the Erie Canal, 1,000 acres in Pennsylvania, and one-half interest in 60,000 acres in North Carolina. His daughters received as a trust the residue of the estate, estimated by Pintard as worth $60,000 to $80,000. Not until fifty years after his death were the intricacies of Stockton's will finally unraveled by the New Jersey courts.

SOURCES: A. H. Bill, *A House Called Morven* (1954), 69-87; *DAB*; Hageman, *History*, I, 214-19; D. D. Egbert, *Princeton Portraits* (1947), 189-90; L.Q.C. Elmer, *Constitution and Government of . . . N.J.* (1872), 409-415; *Princetonians, 1748-1768*, 7-11; *N.J. Wills*, VI, 375; *Pa. Journal and Weekly Advertiser*, 12 Oct 1774; *N.J. Gazette*, 13 Oct 1779 (commencement); als D. Brearley and J. C. Symmes to W. Livingston, 7 Apr

1784, Livingston MSS; RS to T. Pickering, 21 Feb 1822, Pickering MSS ("unprincipled faction," "Pretenders"), MHi; *N.J. Hist.*, 97 (1979), 123-34 (with thanks to Don C. Skemer, author of this article on the *Institutio legalis*); *Som. Cnty. Hist. Quart.*, 8 (1919), 121; 1 (1912), 279; R. P. McCormick, *Experiment in Independence* (1950), 154, 232, 263n, 294; B. W. Bond, Jr., *Correspondence of John Cleves Symmes (1926)*, 284; J. T. Flexner, *Steamboats Come True* (1944), 177; Davis, *Essays*, 392; *Jefferson Papers*, XVIII, 151-52; *A/C*, VIII, 544-46, 578, 599; XXVI, 988-90 ("idle doctrine of free trade"); XXVII, 2,034-42; XXVIII, 345-46, 834-50, 1,225-29; *NJHSP* (2 ser.), 3 (1874), 181-90; (3 ser.), 5 (1909), 79-80; S. G. Kurtz, *Presidency of John Adams* (1957), 342; R. E. Welch, Jr., *Theodore Sedgwick, Federalist* (1965), 185-86, 215; J. Adams, *Works*, IX (1954), 94; *WMQ* (3 ser.), 18 (1960), 162; W. R. Fee, *Transition from Aristocracy to Democracy in N.J.* (1933), 93, 120, 125, 130-32, 175n, 185-86; als RS to A. Ogden, 6 Nov 1800; RS to J. Carnham, n.d. ("close the College doors"); RS to G. D. Wall, 3 Feb 1826; MS Will (copy), NjP; F. B. Lee, *N.J. as a Colony and as a State* (1902), III, 155-56; Trustee Minutes, I, 264; II, 60-70 ("intentionally set on fire"); Faculty Minutes, 31 Mar 1807 ("authority and proceedings of the College"), PUA; H. Miller, *Revolutionary College* (1976), 259-71; S. J. Novak, *Rights of Youth* (1977), 31-37; Wertenbaker, *Princeton*, 126-28, 138-42; Maclean, *History*, II, 32-43, 75-79; D. H. Fisher, *Rev. of Amer. Conservatism* (1965), 88n, 217 ("queue no bigger than a pipe stem"), 328; C. M. Wiltse and H. D. Moser, eds., *Papers of Daniel Webster*, I (1974), 155, 278, 296 ("absolute Southern influence"); II (1976), 354-55; *Proc. and Address of the Second Convention of Delegates* (1814), 2-4; S. Livermore, Jr., *Twilight of Federalism* (1962), 87; C. F. Adams, ed., *Memoirs of John Quincy Adams*, VII (1875), 313-14; *NYHS Coll.*, LXXII, 16-17 ("proud & haughty," "corpulent").

PUBLICATIONS: Sh-Sh #s 32874-75. Also, probable author of *A Concise View of the Controversy between the Proprietors of East and West Jersey* (1785): attribution by McCormick, *Experiment*, 154n.

MANUSCRIPTS: NjP, NjHi, NN, NHi, PHi, MHi, DLC, CtY

GSD

George West

GEORGE WEST is identified as a student in the College by two items of record. The first is a deposition given by John Trotman of Barbados (Class of 1778) to authorities of the British isle of St. Christopher in the West Indies on December 14, 1776. He told there that in the preceding September he had been visiting his guardians in Philadelphia for the vacation period just then beginning; that he walked out rather late one evening "with George West, of Carolina, who was one of his Scool fellows"; and that they had the misfortune of meeting with a "gang of Men" who pressed the two into the crew of the *Andrea Doria*, a brigantine in the service of the Continental Congress. The vessel soon afterward sailed for St. Eustatius, a Dutch West Indian Island, in quest of military supplies. Trotman related his own escape, with two Englishmen and a Frenchman, to St. Christopher, and the implication is that West continued aboard the American ship as a crewman. The second item is found in the records of the Cliosophic Society, which indicate that West became a member of that society in 1778. Unless there were two George Wests enrolled at the College, and there seems to be no reason for assuming that there were, West had returned to North America, possibly aboard the *Andrea Doria*, and resumed his studies at Nassau Hall, presumably at some time after the reopening of the College in the summer of 1777.

Efforts to provide a fuller identification of George West have been unsuccessful. There were many Wests in Carolina, and in North Carolina more than one of them was named George, but the student's date of birth and parentage has not been established, nor has evidence been found as to his subsequent career.

SOURCES: W. J. Morgan, *Naval Documents of the Amer. Rev.*, VII (1976), 485-86 (Trotman's deposition); MS Clio. Soc. membership list, PUA; *AHR*, 8 (1902-1903), 691-94; *New England Mag.* (n.s.), 8 (1893), 576-85; F. A. Olds, *Abstract of N.C. Wills* (1925), 30, 98, 238; *American Ancestry*, VII (1892), 230; *First Census, N.C.*, 62, 127; *DAR Patriot Index*.

WFC

Aaron Dickinson Woodruff

AARON DICKINSON WOODRUFF, A.B., A.M. 1783, lawyer and public official, was born on September 12, 1762, at Elizabethtown, Essex County, New Jersey, the oldest son of Elias Woodruff and his wife, Mary Joline Woodruff, and the older brother of George Whitefield Woodruff (A.B. 1783) and Abner Woodruff (A.B. 1784). His mother was the sister of John Joline (A.B. 1775). The numerous Woodruff family was one of the older families in Elizabethtown, and it seems likely that Aaron was related to Benjamin and Joseph Woodruff (both A.B. 1753), and to Hunloke Woodruff (Class of 1772). His name probably was intended to perpetuate the memory of the first two presidents of the College, of which his father served three separate terms as steward, 1773-1776, 1782-1784, and 1786-1788. It can be noted that newspaper accounts of his commencement in 1779 described him as being "of Princeton." It is said that his father moved to Princeton in 1772, and it is possible that young Woodruff's final preparations for college were completed in Nassau Hall's grammar school. He may have been admitted to the College as a freshman as early as the fall of 1772, for his name is found in the steward's account of payments for tuition and board for the period from May 25, 1773 to September 25, 1774, which, of course, was kept by his father. In the account for

Aaron Dickinson Woodruff, A.B. 1779

the period from November 1774 to April 10, 1775, Woodruff is listed as a member of the sophomore class. If his studies continued unbroken, he should have been a senior just beginning his final year of study as a member of the Class of 1777 when President Witherspoon dismissed the students and closed the College on November 29, 1776.

No answer to the question of where he was or of what he was doing during the three years that elapsed before his graduation has been found, although it seems to be evident enough that he at some time had returned to his studies. The records of the Cliosophic Society list him with three others as having been admitted to membership on January 1, 1777. This seems unlikely in view of military developments in and around Princeton at that time, but it does suggest that he may have been among the small number of students who studied at the College during that year, beginning with a summer term. He could have been the Aaron Woodruff who is credited with service as a private in the Essex County Militia at some time during the war. His graduation with a class of six members on September 29, 1779 suggests that he was in residence for at least a part of the academic year 1778-1779, and his enjoyment that day of the honor of delivering the valedictory address indicates that he had been around long enough to establish his reputation as an orator. He spoke in English on the subject "of affability."

Having taken up the study of law, he was admitted to the bar in 1784 and was called as sergeant in 1792. In that year he also became attorney general of the state by election of the legislature, a position he held by annual reelection until his death, except for a single break occurring in 1811. His private practice prospered, and as did other lawyers of his day, he spent much of his time on circuit, moving from courthouse to courthouse according to the schedule of the courts. A resident of Trenton, then in Hunterdon County, he was from an early date active in its affairs. He has been credited with an important influence in its selection for the state capital, and sitting for Hunterdon County in the legislature in 1791, he presented bills for building legislative and other public buildings there. Under the town's charter of 1792, he served as its first recorder and later as mayor. He was a trustee of the Presbyterian Church from 1789 and became a proprietor or stockholder of the Trenton Library Company in 1797. Ten years earlier he had become a founder and master of the Masonic Lodge, fifth in the state, and he remained an active mason throughout his life. While in the legislature in 1791, he had supported the incorporation of the Society for establishing useful Manufactures, the earliest of New Jersey's business corporations, and he was one of the directors of the Trenton Banking Company on its opening in 1805. In politics, Woodruff, who served as a presidential elector in 1792, became a Federalist, disliked Jefferson's embargo, and was one of the delegates to a New Jersey convention assembled in Trenton on July 4, 1812 that directed to the public an address condemning the policies of Madison's administration that had led to a second war with Britain. His removal from the post of attorney general in 1811 was part of a short-lived purge of Federalists from state offices by the then-dominant Republican party.

Woodruff was married on September 14, 1786 to Grace Lowrey, daughter of Colonel Thomas Lowrey, who served during the Revolution with the Third Regiment of the Hunterdon County Militia. There were five children, two girls and three boys, including Elias Decou Woodruff (A.B. 1804) and Thomas L. Woodruff (A.B. 1806). The other son died in his youth. Aaron continued to have a close relationship with his brother George, who moved to Savannah, Georgia, where in 1798 he became federal attorney for the district of Georgia. Early in the nineteenth century, George sent his sons north to reside with Aaron while getting their schooling in Trenton, and in 1801 Aaron undertook a commission from George to acquire a property on the Delaware outside Trenton for the building of a summer home for his family. The building of "Oaklands," a fine residence that remained in the family until near the end of the century and later served the Trenton Country Club, was closely supervised by Aaron and completed in July of 1808. The correspondence between the brothers reveals an extraordinary mutual trust and also shows that Aaron's services went beyond mere supervision of the construction according to agreed upon plans. He helped to arrange for the financing and oversaw the landscaping, fencing, and planting of fruit trees, berries, and asparagus.

The correspondence also reveals that Aaron, certainly from 1799 forward, suffered acutely from the gout and that he managed to find relief only by repeated dosages of laudanum. To another correspondent in October 1806 he cried out: "Many Blessings on him who first discovered the balmy Properties of Opium, how oft hast it given rest to the poor gouty Wretch and permitted him to slumber in his torture." Whether he suffered from other ills is unknown, but it is said that his health was in rapid decline for several months before his death on June 24, 1817. He was remembered in Trenton and around the lawyers' circuit as an affable and sociable person.

SOURCES: Alumni File, PUA; C. N. Woodruff and M. R. Herod, *Woodruff Chronicles*, II (1971), 19, 48-50; E. M. Woodward and J. F. Hageman, *Hist. of Burlington and Mercer Counties, N.J.* (1883), 554-55; *The Jerseyman*, 1 (1891), 26; J. Whitehead, *Judicial and Civil Hist. of N.J.* (1897), II, 375; E. F. Cooley, *Early Settlers in Trenton and Ewing* (1883), 312-13; Trenton Hist. Soc., *A Hist. of Trenton, 1679-1929* (1929), I, 354; II, 561, 607, 758, 861, 867; MS Clio. Soc. membership list, PUA; *N.J. Gazette*, 13 Oct 1779 (commencement); "Votes and Proceedings, Gen. Assem., 17th session, 25 Oct 1791," 6, 19, 67, 70; Woodruff Family Papers, als ADW to T. P. Johnson, 27 Oct 1806, NjP ("balmy Properties of Opium"); *NJHSP*, 68 (1950), 83-92; Stryker, *Off. Reg.*, 343, 353, 827; W. R. Fee, *Transition from Aristocracy to Democracy in N.J.* (1933), 174-75; C. E. Prince, *N.J.'s Jeffersonian Republicans* (1964), 238; G. A. Boyd, *Elias Boudinot* (1952), 129n; J. Hall, *Hist. of Pres. Chh. in Trenton, N.J.* (1912), 242.

MANUSCRIPTS: NjP

                                                                    WFC

CLASS OF 1780

William Brown

Samuel Coles

John Rhea, A.B.

James Roosevelt, A.B.

Alexander Russell, A.B.

Ebenezer Stockton, A.B.

William Van Ingen

Abraham Bedford Venable, A.B.

Samuel Woodson Venable, A.B.

William Brown

WILLIAM BROWN, physician, was born on November 22, 1760, in Augusta (later Stockbridge) County, Virginia, the second surviving son of John Brown (A.B. 1749), a Presbyterian clergyman, and his wife, Margaret Preston Brown. The only known evidence of his attendance at Princeton is found in a memorandum of his older brother John Brown (Class of 1778), United States senator from Kentucky 1792-1805, who late in life, after recording his own presence as a student in the College in November 1776, added the following notation: "William Brown, was educated at Princeton, studied medicine, and commenced the practice in South Carolina, with prospects of success, but died shortly afterward, unmarried."

That Senator Brown specified in his own case that he attended the College, and did not in the case of his brother, raises a question of whether the latter may have been enrolled only in the grammar school. But the father's close identification with the Augusta Academy, which in 1776 was renamed Liberty Hall and later became Washington College and still later Washington and Lee University, makes it unlikely that he would have sent his son to Princeton for the kind of preparatory education that was readily available close at hand. Not only is William listed in the general *Catalogue* of Washington and Lee University, together with John and three other brothers, among the alumni attending the institution before its charter from the state was received in 1782, but his father, writing on February 18, 1774 to his brother-in-law William Preston, reported that his "little son Will" was in his own school and "doing very well." Later in the year, on August 22, he advised Preston that his son John would join Reverend James Waddel, who had opened a new school on the Northern Neck, and "if I am able to send Billy with him they will be company for one another, for I expect he will be ready." No further references to William have been found in later correspondence regarding John's stay with Waddel, which seems to have continued into a second year, but the evidence, slim as it is, suggests that William was making sufficient progress for him to have been enrolled in the College when he came to Princeton.

Just when he came cannot be said. Perhaps it was in the fall of 1776, when he turned sixteen, in the company of his older brother. On that assumption, and the further assumption that he was probably less advanced in his studies than was his brother, he is placed here somewhat arbitrarily in the Class of 1780. If indeed he entered in the fall of 1776, his stay may have been very brief.

Little can be added here. When, where, and with whom he studied medicine have not been found. His death probably occurred in 1783, for his father in writing to John Preston, son of Colonel William Preston, on February 26, 1784, bemoans William's death by murder. It is said that he was killed by highwaymen.

Sources: See John Brown (Class of 1778); O. Brown, *Memoranda of the Preston Family* (1842), 5-6 ("education at Princeton"), and photocopy of original MS, PUA; R. K. Pruett, *The Browns of Liberty Hall* (1966), 5, 8; *SCHGM*, 18 (1917), 89 (including announcement from S.C. *Weekly Gazette* for Saturday, 4 Oct 1783, of the death "on Sunday morning, in the bloom of life," of "Mr. William Brown, Merchant, a young gentleman whose amiable disposition causes his death to be sincerely lamented by all his friends and acquaintance"); als J. Brown, Sr. to W. Preston, 18 Feb 1774, Draper MSS 3QQ8 ("little son Will"); 22 Aug 1774, Draper MSS 3QQ81 ("to send Billy with him"); J. Brown, Sr. to J. Preston, 26 Feb 1784, Draper MSS 5QQ119, WHi.

WFC

Samuel Coles

SAMUEL COLES, perhaps a farmer, was born on March 3, 1759, probably the son of Kendall and Ann Budd Coles of Gloucester County, New Jersey. His attendance as a student in the College is established by his membership in the Cliosophic Society, and the date given for his admission to the society is 1778. While a surviving manuscript roster of early members lists the name "Solomon" Coles, two subsequently published catalogues of the society, one in 1845 and the other in 1876, give the name as Samuel Coles. There is little doubt that the later listings are the correct ones. No Solomon Coles has been located, and the name Samuel was common among the generally prosperous Coles family inhabiting Gloucester and neighboring counties. There is a further question of how exactly the date of his admission to the Cliosophic Society fixes the time of his enrollment as a student in the College. Not only have the original records of the society been lost but it is supposed to have been moribund for several years prior to its revival during the summer of 1781. Even so, it cannot be said that the society had been entirely inactive, and certainly the College was in session in 1778.

How long Coles may have remained in the College is unknown, and little can be said regarding his life thereafter. His father's will, dated February 23, 1798 but not proved until February 20, 1804, bequeathed the "plantation" on which he lived to his son Joseph, probably the oldest, and described it as "lying between lands heretofore conveyed to my sons, Job and Samuel Coles." That the father could divide his lands three ways several years before his death is suggestive of their extent. Suggestive too is the valuation $1,365 placed upon his personal property in 1804, a sum well below the £3,489 left by his older brother Samuel in 1772 but still respectable. The older Samuel in his will described himself as a yeoman, but he was the owner of several grist and saw mills and he received a not insignificant income from rental properties. Earlier in the century, members of the family had held a number of public offices, but later they seem to have been less active in this regard, although Kendall in 1774 was a member of the Gloucester County Committee of Observation for enforcement of the boycott of British imports decreed by the first Continental Congress. The original settler, whose name was Samuel, had been a Quaker, but some of the family seem to have followed the divisive George Keith into an early identification with the Anglican Church.

Thomas Coles, one of Kendall's older brothers, also had a son named Samuel who may have been the student at Princeton, but little has been discovered regarding him beyond the bequest to him of £20 by his Uncle Samuel in 1772. It has been assumed that he probably was of an age less likely for a college student in 1778 than was the son of Kendall and Ann Coles. The former may have been the Samuel Coles of Gloucester County who died in 1842. He is said to have been married twice, first to Rebecca Paul and then to Deborah Lathbury.

Sources: Ms. Clio. Soc. membership list, PUA; Pa. Geneal. Soc., T. C. Matlack Coll., box 2, notebook 59; N.J. Wills, IV, 84-85; V, 100-101; X, 88; Index to N.J. Wills, 533; J. Clement, Sketches of First Emigrant Settlers in Newton Township, Old Gloucester Cnty., N.J. (1877); W.P.A., Early Cnty. Records of N.J. (1940), 2, 3; F. H. Stewart, ed., Notes on Old Gloucester Cnty., N.J., I (1917), 106, 119, 130-31; T. Cushing and C. E. Sheppard, Hist. of Counties of Gloucester, Salem, and Cumberland, N.J. (1883, 1974), 122a, 137b, 139a.

WFC

John Rhea

JOHN RHEA, A.B., was probably a son of the Freehold, New Jersey yeoman Jonathan Rhea, who died in 1767 leaving three minor sons, among them Aaron (A.B. 1776) and John, who was baptized in 1762. Jonathan Rhea's wife was Lydia Forman Rhea, and she may have been the Lydia Rhea recorded among the Freehold ratables in 1779 and 1780. A newspaper account of the 1780 commencement, at which John

Rhea gave an English oration on "The Advantages of Civil Liberty to particular States," describes him as "of Pennsylvania," information that at first seems to challenge the identification proposed here. This apparent contradiction can possibly be accounted for by Jonathan Rhea's mention in his will of a brother named John Rhea, presumably the Philadelphia merchant of that name who owned a grist mill in Allentown, Upper Freehold Township in 1767. Young John Rhea of Freehold, who lost his father in that year, may have lived for awhile in the household of this mercantile uncle, a man well placed to advance him in life. And if this was the case, he might have been "of Pennsylvania" in 1780. Unfortunately, no other evidence to support this hypothesis has been discovered, and nothing else can be said with any confidence about the College's graduate.

When Varnum Lansing Collins compiled the *General Catalogue of Princeton University* (1908), he identified John Rhea as the Tennessee congressman of that name (1753-1832), a friend and supporter of President Andrew Jackson. Other circumstantial evidence, however, supports the identification of John Rhea made here, and it is discussed below together with the reasons for rejecting John Rhea of Tennessee.

SOURCES: *N.J. Wills*, IV, 352 (Jonathan Rhea's will); *GMNJ*, 49 (1974), 86; *N.J. Gazette*, 11 Oct 1780 (commencement); F. Ellis, *Hist. of Monmouth Cnty., N.J.* (1885), 620.

Jonathan Rhea was from an old Monmouth Scots family of Presbyterian background and was the last Rhea buried in a family plot near Freehold. The presumption that his brother John Rhea was the Philadelphia merchant of that name is strengthened by the fact that the Allentown mill was in the possession of Robert Rhea of Allentown in 1774; and this Robert Rhea was no doubt the brother of that name also mentioned in Jonathan Rhea's 1767 will. On the basis of these identifications of John Rhea, the graduate, and of Jonathan Rhea's two brothers, there emerges a strong connection between this family and CNJ. John, son of Jonathan Rhea of Freehold, appears to have been the brother of one graduate, the cousin of a second graduate, and the uncle of a third. Aaron Rhea (A.B. 1776) has been noted above and in the biography of him as the son of Jonathan Rhea of Freehold. Ebenezer Rhea (A.B. 1791) was the son of John Rhea, the Philadelphia merchant; he married a younger sister of College President Samuel Stanhope Smith (A.B. 1769). Nicholas G. R. Rhea (A.B. 1809) was the son of Jonathan Rhea of Trenton and a grandson of Robert Rhea of Allentown. [F. R. Symmes, *Hist. of the Old Tennent Chh.* (1904), 361, 400-401; *NJA* (1 ser.), XXXIV, 420; alumni folders of Ebenezer and Nicholas G. R. Rhea, PUA.]

What little else is known about John Rhea, the Philadelphia merchant, also points to the family's Presbyterian loyalties and business ties to other families interested in CNJ. This John Rhea was probably trading in Philadelphia as early as 1756 when "Wickoff & Rhea, Mrchts" were taxed in Chestnut Ward. He may have attended the Second Presbyterian Church of Philadelphia where his son Ebenezer was baptized. In 1765 he was involved in the Philadelphia Co., organized to promote the settlement of a grant of land in Nova Scotia and remarkable for the Princeton ties of several of its promoters. College President John Witherspoon, Richard Stockton (A.B. 1748), Rev. James Lyon (A.B. 1759), Andrew Hodge (father of two

Nassau Hall graduates), and Col. John Bayard (father of four graduates) were all associated in this venture with the Philadelphia John Rhea. Although these connections of John Rhea of Philadelphia do not prove that his nephew of the same name was the Princeton graduate, they do make such an identification very reasonable. [*PGM*, 22 (1961), 11; *PMHB*, 51 (1927), 280, 284. On the Philadelphia John Rhea and his wife, also see: *PGM*, 7 (1920), 208; *PMHB*, 16 (1892), 304; *Pa. Arch.* (3 ser.), XIV, 188; *Franklin Papers*, XVI, 116; H. L. Hodge, *Memoranda of Family Hist.* (1903), 27.]

Assuming that John Rhea has been correctly identified, it then becomes difficult to account for the total obscurity of the scion of a family with so many connections to the College and to prominent families associated with it. The difficulty in locating the graduate after 1780 has been complicated by the variety of spellings of his surname, which in addition to Rhea, include Rae, Ray, Rhe and Wray. The construction of a career for the graduate in N.J. or in Pa. has not been possible, although there were persons of the name (under different spellings) active in both states during and after the Revolution. No reason has been found to extend the search for John Rhea beyond these states, though his removal to another part of the country is a possible explanation for his seeming disappearance from the region of his birth and education. The graduate was probably too young to have been the Monmouth Cnty. sergeant of the name active in the Revolution. The only reference found to a John Rhea in Freehold after 1780 is in a 1783 will that was witnessed by a man of the name.

The College's triennial catalogues indicate that the 1780 graduate did not hold a high public office and that he died sometime between the 1827 and 1830 issues, but the catalogues are an imperfect guide to death dates. Rhea is credited with an A.M. beginning in the 1797 catalogue, but the Trustees' Minutes do not confirm this as a Princeton degree. [*Pa. Arch.* (2 ser.), IX, 99, and also see esp. various spellings in index to 3 ser.; Stryker, *Off. Reg.*, 470; *N.J. Wills*, VI, 71; VIII, 295.]

V. L. Collins was neither the first nor the last scholar to identify the College's John Rhea with Tenn. congressman John Rhea. The education of this man at Nassau Hall was also accepted by writers in *BDAC* and *DAB*, and these authorities have been followed by other students. Moreover, there is a tradition among the descendants of the Tenn. congressman that he and his brother Matthew Rhea came to CNJ in 1777. According to the family, both men left the College to enter military service, but John Rhea returned sometime before 1780 and was the man who received his A.B. in that year.

This story is not implausible because the father of these men was a Presbyterian minister from Ireland who was "of Pennsylvania" after his arrival in the colonies in 1769, later moving with his family to what is now eastern Tennessee. No evidence has been found to place Matthew Rhea at CNJ at any date, but much evidence suggests that the 1780 graduate was not the future congressman. Born in 1753, this John Rhea was somewhat older than the students in the Class of 1780. He was an ensign in a Va. unit for most of 1777, the year he is said to have come to Princeton. In April 1779 he was a staff officer to Col. Evan Shelby in the western campaign against the Chickamaugas. In 1780 he was not "of Pennsylvania" but a resident of newly-created Sullivan Cnty., N.C. (subsequently Tenn.), serving as the county's first clerk from February of that year. Also said to have been at the Battle of Kings Mountain in S.C. on 7 Oct 1780, this John Rhea is unlikely to have received a degree at Princeton, New Jersey on 27 Sep 1780. Finally, the Tenn. congressman was still alive in 1830 when the triennial catalogue of that year first indicated the death of the 1780 graduate; and the graduate's name was not capitalized in any catalogue between 1780 and 1830, although capitalization was the customary method of designating graduates who held important state and federal offices. [East Tenn. Hist. Soc., *Pubs.*, 4 (1932), 35; Heitman (1914), 464; S. C. Williams, *Tenn. During the Rev. War* (1944), 92, 126; J.G.M. Ramsey, *Annals of Tenn.* (1853), 189; K. K.

White, *The King's Mountain Men* (1924), 220; J. W. Caldwell, *Sketches of the Bench and Bar of Tenn.* (1898), 15; letters of John and Matthew Rhea descendants in John Rhea alumni folder, PUA.]

Another man investigated in the preparation of this biography was John Rae (1755-1829), a congressman from Chambersburg, Pa. He was "of Pennsylvania" in 1780, and he was a member of a Presbyterian congregation served by a Nassau Hall graduate. John Rae died between the publication of the 1827 and 1830 triennial catalogues, but this is the only evidence pointing to him as the 1780 graduate. [*BDAC; Hist. of Franklin Cnty., Pa.* (1887), 586-88.]

GSD

James Roosevelt

JAMES ROOSEVELT, A.B., merchant, public official, and landowner, was born in New York City on January 23, 1760 and baptized in the Dutch Reformed Church there as Jacobus Roosevelt. He used the anglicized "James" throughout his life. His father, Isaac Roosevelt, was a prominent merchant who had established a sugar refinery in his back yard and who was to serve in the New York Provincial Congress of 1775, the New York Constitutional Convention, and the state senate. James Roosevelt's mother was Cornelia Hoffman Roosevelt, a member of a wealthy family of Dutchess County, New York.

In 1772 the Roosevelts moved from their home on Wall Street to a larger house on Queen Street that was still contiguous to the sugar refinery. That was his permanent address when James Roosevelt left to enter the freshman class at the College in 1773. On February 1, 1774, he joined the Cliosophic Society, in which he was known by the name of the Roman historian "Livy." Roosevelt completed his sophomore year as a member of the Class of 1777, but he was probably unable to continue his studies thereafter. In 1775, while his father was in the Provincial Congress at Kingston, the family left the troubled city for the Hoffman estate near Rhinebeck. It was there that Roosevelt spent the first years of the Revolution while the College was closed and then commandeered as a barracks and military hospital.

Roosevelt returned to Nassau Hall, however, perhaps as early as 1778, to complete his education in the Class of 1780. He was the valedictorian of that small group of graduates and devoted his address to "the beauties and utilities of poetry." He also participated in a "dialogue on the present state of the college, the prospects of its restoration and the revival of letters throughout America, along with the return of peace and the Establishment of our independence"—an exercise in which he was joined by his classmate Abraham B. Venable and by Richard Venable (A.B. 1782). With its paean to "Harvard! Yale!

James Roosevelt, A.B. 1780
BY HENRY INMAN

and Nassau . . . the first upon the mighty stage," the dialogue might be credited with the original undergraduate identification of the later so-called "Big Three." In any case, it thoroughly entertained the audience. Roosevelt then rejoined his family in Dutchess County, where he studied law in the office of Egbert Benson. His younger brother Martin (Class of 1783) died while a student at the College in 1781.

The Roosevelts rode back to New York City after its evacuation by the British in 1783 to find that their house and refinery had escaped the ravages of the fire of 1776 and the occupation. Rather than become a member of the bar, Roosevelt used his legal training to help in the family's business, which he joined in 1784. When Isaac Roosevelt became a founder of the Bank of New York, and then the institution's president in 1785, the management of the refinery devolved almost completely on his son and junior partner.

On November 15, 1786, Roosevelt married Maria Eliza Walton, the daughter of loyalist merchant Abraham Walton, in Trinity Church,

New York. He and his wife then moved to 18 South Street, where by 1791 they had had three of their ten children. When his father died in 1796, Roosevelt inherited the refinery and its grounds, as well as several commercial and riverfront lots.

Already established as a leading merchant, Roosevelt made his first foray into politics in 1796, when he was elected to the state legislature. He served only one term. His true interests lay neither in politics nor in business, but in farming. And while he conscientiously performed both his civic and commercial duties, he sought solace in the countryside. He thought that he had found the perfect compromise when he bought 400 acres near Haarlem village on Manhattan, not as an investment, but as a working farm where he could engage in his favorite pastime, breeding fast horses. He visited the farm whenever he could, often commuting to the refinery.

In 1797 and again in 1800, while his brother-in-law Richard Varick was mayor of New York, Roosevelt served as an election inspector for the Fifth Ward. Like most of his family, he was a Federalist, and when the Republicans carried two wards in the municipal elections of 1800, he was as alarmed as the other members of his party. The election of 1801 was certain to be a test of strength, and Roosevelt was enlisted to run for the post of alderman.

To protect themselves, the Federalists on the city council had refused to expand the franchise. As a countermeasure, the Republicans created "tontines," associations of several persons who collectively bought a single piece of property in the various wards in order to claim the right to vote there. Seventy-four persons made up the cooperative in the Fourth Ward, which went Republican by thirty-five votes. Thirty-nine members of the tontine in the Fifth Ward decided that contest against Roosevelt by six votes.

There had been no attempt to keep these maneuvers secret, and as soon as the election results were known, the Federalists challenged them before the incumbent, Federalist-dominated city council. All but three of the thirty-nine "faggot" votes in the Fifth Ward were invalidated, and Roosevelt was duly sworn as an alderman on December 7, 1801. But the mayor, Republican Edward Livingston (A.B. 1781), would not surrender his party's triumph in the Fourth Ward. When a crucial vote to unseat the Republicans was carried by a margin of one, Livingston insisted on casting a vote himself to make, rather than break, a tie and thus defeat the motion. In protest, Roosevelt and the other Federalist members refused to attend any further sessions of the council until the Fourth Ward Republicans were removed and until

Livingston promised to abide by standard procedure. The city was effectively without a government until March 1802.

Roosevelt served only one year on the council but was elected again in 1809, this time as alderman from the Fourth Ward. In March 1810 the council adjourned to attend the funeral of the woman Roosevelt called the "most affectionate, best of wives, and most tender of mothers," Maria Walton Roosevelt, who was buried at the Dutch Church in the city. On September 7, 1812, Roosevelt married Catherine Eliza Barclay, the daughter of another Loyalist, James Barclay, at the Episcopal Church of St. John the Baptist. They had two children before she died in 1816.

By then Roosevelt was a director of the Bank of New York as well as owner of the refinery. In 1815 he was taxed on $50,000 worth of property in the city. More than half of that was his farm, which extended from modern Fifth Avenue to the East River, and from 110th to 125th Streets. In 1819 he unhappily decided that the land was too rocky to produce crops and, since he believed that the city's limits would never extend that far north, he sold the farm for $25,000. He reinvested the money in an estate near Poughkeepsie, Dutchess County, which he called Mount Hope. It was there that he spent his summers after 1819 and where he concentrated on his horses. His property in the city was assessed at $20,000 in 1820.

On January 29, 1821, Roosevelt married for the third time. His wife was Harriet Howland, the aunt of Mary Rebecca Aspinwall, who had married his oldest son Isaac (A.B. 1808). In 1823 the couple sold their house on South Street and moved to 64 Bleecker Street in Greenwich Village, and in that year Roosevelt paid taxes on $15,000 of real estate and $15,000 of personal property in New York. He contributed generously to several charities, including the New York Society Library, of which he was a frequent user. He was no longer involved in electoral politics, but he did serve as an umpire in a city assessment dispute in 1823. And as he made improvements on the streets around his new home he was paid $4,200 in awards by the municipal government.

On December 7, 1847, Roosevelt suffered a fatal stroke in New York. He was buried near Mount Hope. His son Isaac, although a practicing physician, moved his family to the estate and fulfilled his father's dream of living the life of a country gentleman. Isaac's son James married Sara Delano in 1880 and two years later they became the parents of Franklin Delano Roosevelt.

SOURCES: A. Churchill, *Roosevelts* (1965), 69-71, 76, 80, 96 ("most affectionate, best of wives"), 97-99, 102; K. Schriftgiesser, *Amazing Roosevelt Family* (1942), 101-21,

177-81; B. Partridge, *Roosevelt Family in Amer.* (1936), 30-31, 87, 281-82; Alumni File, MS Steward's accounts, MS Clio. Soc. membership list, PUA; *N.J. Gazette*, 11 Oct 1780 (commencement); *NJA* (2 ser.), V, 31-35 ("Harvard! Yale! and Nassau"); A. Nevins, ed., *Diary of Philip Hone* (1936), 788; *NYGBR*, 75 (1944), 33; 76 (1945), 69; *N.Y. Wills*, XIV, 274-78; *N.Y. Red Book* (1895), 373; *MCCCNY*, II, 333, 617, III, 59-61, 72, 83-85; V, 770; VI, 119; XIII, 63; XIV, 213; S. I. Pomerantz, *N.Y. an Amer. City* (1938), 134-37 ("tontines"); H. W. Lanier, *Century of Banking in N.Y.* (1922), 130.

Alexander Russell

ALEXANDER RUSSELL, A.B., soldier, merchant, public official, was the son of Hannah Blackburn Russell and James Russell, a prosperous farmer, military hero, and member of the Pennsylvania Convention of 1776. He was born on his parents' farm near Hamiltonban, York County, Pennsylvania, on February 25, 1758.

Sent to the College by his father so that he could be educated for the Presbyterian ministry, Russell was a student at Nassau Hall in 1775. He was eager to fight in the Revolution but remained at Princeton until he was able to convince his father to let him enter the military, probably sometime in 1776. He then joined a company of Pennsylvania militiamen in Carlisle. On January 20, 1777, Russell was commissioned a second lieutenant in the Seventh Pennsylvania Regiment of the Continental Line.

In September the Seventh Pennsylvania participated in the battle of Brandywine and then took the brunt of the fighting at the disastrous skirmish at Paoli. On the twentieth of that month Russell was promoted to first lieutenant, the grade in which he served in the engagements at Germantown and White Marsh. Presumably, he was with his regiment at Valley Forge during the winter, and he saw action again in the more successful fighting at Monmouth in June 1778.

In or after the summer of 1778 Russell was assigned to duty as a ranger on the frontier in Washington County, Pennsylvania. Between September 1778 and January 1779 he recruited a dozen men for the Seventh Pennsylvania, a service for which he was entitled to $1,188 in bounty for himself and subsistence for the new soldiers. The money was slow in coming, and Russell twice asked the state's supreme executive council to give him his due. By March 1779 his requests prompted an investigation, which revealed that the recruits had never been properly mustered or inspected. Russell might have corrected that oversight and collected his money, except that nine of his twelve recruits had deserted within two months of their enlistment, a fact that had somehow not been mentioned in his appeals. President

Joseph Reed (A.B. 1757) of Pennsylvania decided that the bounty should not, after all, be paid until someone retrieved the missing recruits. Apparently, Russell never did.

Instead, he resigned from the army on April 16, 1779. He may have gone back to York County for a time, for he was among the taxpayers in Hamiltonban in 1779. But his primary objective was to complete his education, so he returned to Nassau Hall at the beginning of the 1779-1780 academic year. He joined the Cliosophic Society, possibly as early as 1778 while he was in the army near Princeton. His resumption of his formal studies made him a rare exception among the students who had left college to fight, and, armed with a certificate from President Witherspoon testifying that he had completed the full course, he graduated with the Class of 1780. During his year at Princeton, he was listed as a resident of Hamiltonban, but he paid no taxes there.

Russell went from Princeton to Philadelphia and, having lost interest in the ministry, established himself as a merchant. In 1784 he moved back to York County and opened a store. On May 23, 1785, he married Mary McPherson, the daughter of Colonel Robert McPherson. They moved to a farm on Marsh Creek, close by the site of what became Gettysburg, and Russell began his career in public service.

In October 1786 he applied for the offices of register of wills and recorder of deeds in newly created Luzerne County. But Timothy Pickering, who was already prothonotary of Luzerne, was given these positions as well on November 7. Russell remained in York County, where by the early 1790s he held a lifetime appointment as justice of the peace. He also served as brigade inspector of the county militia. It was in that capacity that he levied fines of £9 each against militiamen who failed to march on the "Western Expedition" to put down the Whiskey Rebellion in 1794. Those fines left Russell in something of a quandary, as he reported to Governor Thomas Mifflin, for not all county inspectors had been equally harsh, and some of the men who had been derelict in their service did not have £9 to their names. Russell wanted to be fair, but he also insisted that unless the heavy fines were paid promptly, injustice would be done to those men who had done their duty and "it will be in vain ever to make another legal call of Militia in this County." However he resolved the problem, Russell continued as militia inspector at least until 1798, when he advised Alexander Hamilton on the qualifications of some local officers who sought commissions in the provisional army.

Russell prospered in the public service. In 1799, as a resident of Cumberland Township, he owned property worth $2,328, the third highest assessment in the area. Included in that evaluation was his one female slave, part of his household since at least 1790, who was assessed at $100. He retained a smaller holding in Hamiltonban as well.

Russell was one of Adams County's leading citizens from the time of its creation out of York in 1800. He subscribed to a private loan of $7,000 for the construction of public buildings in Gettysburg that helped make the town the county seat. He served on the county's first grand jury in August 1800. And, while still a justice of the peace, he was a leader in local politics.

A staunch Federalist, Russell was ineluctably drawn into the bitter partisan disputes that followed the election of Thomas Jefferson. In 1802 the Republicans investigated his conduct as brigade inspector in a purely political effort to harass him, but his books were in order and the episode had no effect on his career. When the county grand jury endorsed moderate Republican Thomas McKean for governor in 1805, a choice too conservative for radical Republicans and too radical for Federalists, Russell was among the signatories of a protest against the panel's meddling in politics. As Federalist power waned, Russell led the local party into its new identity as "Federal Republicans," and in 1808 he chaired a meeting that condemned nominations for office by Republican-dominated legislative caucuses.

On May 1, 1810, Russell was elected burgess, or mayor, of Gettysburg, where he and his family had lived after 1800. He owned two of the original lots in the town. In 1813 he was elected to the first of two one-year terms as a county commissioner. It was while he held that office, in July 1814, that he participated in the "Friends of Peace," an arch-Federalist society created to oppose the War of 1812.

Peace and the beginning of the "Era of Good Feeling" marked the end of uncompromising Federalism, and Russell's public service was thereafter confined to his duties as a justice of the peace. He was a leading member of the corporations that constructed turnpike roads in and around Gettysburg, but for the most part he lived quietly with his wife, nine children, and a dog named Pointer. He was a trustee of the Gettysburg Presbyterian Church for several years before his death, on April 15, 1836. His widow lived on in Gettysburg until she died on September 29, 1850.

SOURCES: Alumni file, PUA; *Hist. of Cumberland and Adams Counties, Pa.* (1886), [Adams], passim; Heitman; *Pa. Arch.* (5 ser.), III, 228, 246, 298-301; (3 ser.), XXIII, 520; XXI, 140, 286; (2 ser.), IV, 502-503 ("legal call of Militia"); G. R. Prowell, *Continental Congress at York* (1914), 192-96; *Susquehanna Papers*, VIII, 414 & n; *Hamilton Papers*, XXII, 142 & n; *First Census, Pa.*, 290; I. D. Rupp, *Hist. and Topography of Dauphin, . . . and Percy Counties, Pa.* (1846), 520; R. Stover, *Abstracts from the Republican Compiler*, II (1976), 410.

His brother Job was a nongraduating member
of the Class of 1792.

303

Ebenezer Stockton

EBENEZER STOCKTON, A.B., physician, was born in 1759 or 1760, the son of Major Robert Stockton, Esq., of Constitution Hill, Princeton, New Jersey, and his wife, Helen Macomb. His sister Nancy married Francis J. James (A.B. 1781), and another sister Elizabeth married Ashbel Green (A.B. 1783). A distant cousin of Philip Stockton (Class of 1773) and Richard Stockton (A.B. 1779), and also probably related to Benjamin B. Stockton (Class of 1776), Ebenezer Stockton matriculated at the College in autumn 1774. He appears as a freshman in the steward's tuition and room accounts for the term beginning in November of that year. Stockton became a member of the American Whig Society during his student years, but his studies were interrupted in November 1776 when the students and faculty evacuated Nassau Hall in the face of advancing British troops.

Stockton's father, who served the Continental Army as a quartermaster, is said to have billeted General Washington at his home during the American retreat through New Jersey in early December 1776. The following year Ebenezer himself entered military service and was commissioned a surgeon's mate of the army's general hospital. But he probably returned to the College before 1780 when he was awarded his A.B. In 1782 he was appointed a New Hampshire regimental surgeon on the recommendation of Benjamin Rush (A.B. 1760), with whom he may have studied, although his name does not appear on Rush's list of his apprentices. Remaining with the army until November 1783, Stockton was later admitted to the Society of the Cincinnati in New Jersey and was also issued a land bounty for his services during the war.

Dr. Stockton spent the remainder of his career in Princeton and its neighborhood, carrying on his practice for many years at "Bainbridge House," which still stands on Nassau Street. Among his four successive partners were John Maclean, subsequently a professor of chemistry and related disciplines at the College, and John Van Cleve (A.B. 1797). In 1803 Stockton and Maclean purchased Pleasant Valley plantation in Montgomery, New Jersey, for $3,100, and in 1807 Stockton was named a commissioner in the act of the state legislature incorporating the Princeton and Kingston branch of the Trenton and New Brunswick Turnpike. The Princeton doctor's account book for 1804 to 1810 records his treatments and fees for such patients as Richard Stockton, Andrew Hunter (A.B. 1772), and College President Samuel Stanhope Smith (A.B. 1769). In 1810 Stockton attended the annual meeting of the New Jersey Medical Society and probably advanced

Maclean's proposal of a fund for the survivors of deceased physicians. He was admitted to the medical society on this occasion, his delay in application due in part to a lengthy suspension of the society's meetings, and in 1811 he was appointed an examiner of medical candidates for the middle part of the state for the following two years. After the incorporation of the borough of Princeton, Stockton served as a common councilman. In 1817 he was an alderman.

Stockton was a trustee of the Presbyterian Church in Princeton from 1805 to 1835, and on April 20, 1814, he married the widowed Mrs. Elizabeth (Story) Duncan at the Kingston Presbyterian Church. In 1828 the elderly doctor made out a will naming Professor John Maclean (A.B. 1816), the son of his onetime partner and subsequently the College's tenth president, as executor and guardian of his three children. In 1830 Stockton freed a female slave; in 1832 he assigned his power of attorney to a friend; and on December 9, 1837, he died at the age of seventy-seven. A memorialist in the *Princeton Whig* recalled Dr. Stockton's "unimpeached and incorruptible integrity, . . . his liberal and extensive patronage of the poor, . . . and his conciliatory and unostentatious manners and deportment." He left an estate inventoried at $35,500 and an unvalued mill to his widow, a son, and two daughters. One of his daughters married Alexander R. Boteler (A.B. 1835), a United States and Confederate congressman from Virginia. His other daughter married Abner W. C. Terry (A.B. 1839).

SOURCES: Hageman, *History*, I, 223-24, 77-78; II, 4, 7; Wickes, *Hist. of Medicine N.J.*, 409; T. C. Stockton, *Stockton Family of N.J.* (1911), 72-73; MS Steward's accounts, PUA; Heitman (1914), 522; College of Physicians of Philadelphia, *Transactions and Studies* (4 ser.), 14 (1946), 127-32; *Soc. of the Cincinnati in . . . N.J.* (1960), 146; *Index, Rev. War Pension Applications*; D. S. to "Pleasant Valley," als J. Maclean to ES, 10 Jun 1810; MS abstract of will, power of attorney, inventory, NjP; *NJHSP* (n.s.), 62 (1944), 25; N.J. Med. Soc., *Rise, Minutes, and Proceedings* (1875), 133, 135; *GMNJ*, 29 (1954), 62; *Som. Cnty. Hist. Quart.*, 2 (1913), 48; *Princeton Whig*, 15 Dec 1837 ("incorruptible integrity").

MANUSCRIPTS: NjP

GSD

William Van Ingen

WILLIAM VAN INGEN, merchant skipper, was born on November 23, 1760, in Schenectady, New York, the son of Dirk Van Ingen and Margaret Van Syse (Sice, Seysen). A native of the Netherlands and once a surgeon for the Dutch West Indies Company, Dirk Van Ingen was a successful Schenectady physician, was active in the Revolution, and was later a justice of the peace and a New York assemblyman. As a professional man with public responsibilities, he had a strong interest in education. In 1779 he was among the trustees for the proposed Clinton College, to be located in Schenectady, and in 1791 he was involved in efforts to establish and endow an academy in his home town. He sent his oldest son to the College of New Jersey. Probably matriculating after the resumption of classes in the summer of 1777, William Van Ingen was admitted to the Cliosophic Society on January 1, 1778, according to a list of the society's early membership. He assumed the secret name "Schuyler" after the prominent Albany Dutch family of that name.

Van Ingen did not remain at Princeton long enough to take his degree. He probably returned to Schenectady, where he witnessed a will on September 10, 1781. Another witness to the will was Henry Glen, a deputy quartermaster general, whose clerk Van Ingen became about this time. In this capacity Van Ingen made a report to Lord Stirling on October 26, 1781 about a skirmish he had just witnessed between American and British units near the former seat of Sir William Johnson. Also from Schenectady, Henry Glen had been associated with Van Ingen's father in the Clinton College venture. The friendship between the two families was deepened by Van Ingen's marriage to Glen's daughter Elizabeth. This took place sometime before the birth of their son Henry Glen Van Ingen on June 19, 1784. By the time of the first federal census, the family, which still included only one child, was residing in the first ward of Albany. Van Ingen owned one slave in 1790; two of his brothers and his father-in-law were also slaveholders.

What little else is known about Van Ingen suggests that he was a man of some standing in Albany, but only a fragmentary account of his career can be given. He was a supporter of the federal Constitution, and in August 1788, when the city of Albany celebrated the ratification of the new compact, Van Ingen spread the banquet tables with "viands and American cheer." Concerned with public education like his father, he was a subscriber to the library company chartered in Albany in 1793, an organization of which his brother was first treasurer and librarian.

He appears in the minutes of the Common Council of New York City for June 1793 at the head of a petition from the "Masters & Owners of Vessels imployed in the North River and New Jersey Trade." As captain of the sloop *Cincinnati*, Van Ingen made a round trip on the Hudson from Albany to New York in December 1794 in remarkably good time. He may have made a regular business of transporting goods, but whether he was trading on his own account or for others is open to question. Despite the continuing prominence both of his father and of his father-in-law, a Congressman from 1793 to 1801, Van Ingen himself seems not to have held any local offices. He may have been a Federalist like Glen, and his name appears once on a list of those who made recommendations to Alexander Hamilton in 1798 for army appointments from New York.

Before his premature death on January 10, 1800, Van Ingen saw the realization of his father and father-in-law's dream of a college in Schenectady. Union College was established there in 1795 with John Blair Smith (A.B. 1773) as its first president. Among the new institution's first students were Van Ingen's son H. G. Van Ingen (Union class of 1802) and another William Van Ingen (Union class of 1801).

Sources: J. Sanders, *Early Hist. of Schenectady, N.Y.* (1879), 184; *Webster's Calendar, or the Albany . . . Almanack* (1788); *Clinton Papers*, vi, 536; vii, 443-44; J. Munsell, *Coll. on the Hist. of Albany*, i (1865), 297; G. R. Howell and J. Tenney, *Hist. of the Cnty. of Schenectady* (1886), 127; and *Hist. of the Cnty. of Albany* (1886), 486; ms Clio. Soc. membership list, PUA; *N.Y. Wills*, ix, 244; *BDAC* (father-in-law); A. F. Young, *Democratic Republicans of N.Y.* (1967), 337, 423; *First Census, N.Y.*, 12, 13, 42; C. Reynolds, *Albany Chronicles* (1906), 373 ("American cheer"); *Cat. of the . . . Albany Libr.* (1793), 2-3; *MCCCNY*, ii, 13 ("Masters and Owners"); *Hamilton Papers*, xxii, 101; A. V. Raymond, *Union Univ.* (1907), iii, App., 18.

GSD

Abraham Bedford Venable

ABRAHAM BEDFORD VENABLE, A.B., planter, lawyer, public official, and banker, was born in Prince Edward County, Virginia, on November 20, 1758, the second son of Nathaniel Venable and his wife, Elizabeth Woodson Venable. He was the younger brother of Samuel Woodson Venable (A.B. 1780) and the older brother of Richard N. Venable (A.B. 1782) and Nathaniel Venable (A.B. 1796). The father was one of the more substantial property holders of the county, sat more than once in the House of Burgesses, and later served in the state legislature. The mother was of a comparably well-established family.

According to family tradition, Abraham began his education, as did his brother Samuel, at the Hampden-Sidney Academy. Published records of that institution provide no confirmation, but there is every reason for believing that the tradition is correct. Not only was the academy located in Prince Edward County but their father was one of its founders and a trustee from 1775 until his death in 1804. There is a further tradition that maintains that the critically important meet-

Abraham Bedford Venable, A.B. 1780

ing of the Presbytery of Hanover in February 1775 at which the academy was founded was held at the Venable family residence, "Slate Hill." Samuel Stanhope Smith (A.B. 1769) was rector of the academy from 1775 until 1779, when late in the year he returned to Princeton as Professor of Moral Philosophy. Since Hampden-Sidney did not secure a charter authorizing it to award degrees before 1783, nothing could be more natural than that students seeking a bachelor of arts degree should move up to Princeton. Just when the two brothers did so cannot be said. It is possible that Smith sent them ahead of his departure from Prince Edward, as it also is possible that they came up with him, already sufficiently advanced in a program of study at Hampden-Sidney, which was modeled after that of Princeton, to permit them to qualify for their degrees after a year of residence.

Both of the brothers became members of the American Whig Society, whether while resident in the College or by admission after graduation is unclear. The one certain record of their residence at Princeton is of its ending with the commencement of September 27, 1780, in which each had a prominent part. Samuel delivered the salutatory oration, and Abraham closed the morning session of exercises with an oration on "The origin and advantages of civil society." In between, they collaborated with James Roosevelt to provide the main feature of the program, "A dialogue on the present state of the college, the prospect of its restoration and of the revival of letters throughout America, along with the return of peace, and the establishment of our independence." One of those present was so impressed by the performance that he sent a copy of a part of the exchange to the editor of the *New Jersey Gazette* for the attention of the public, and fortunately the editor printed it.

The young men obviously had spent a good deal of time in preparation, and equally obvious is the zest with which they spoke. Each spoke under an assumed name: Samuel as *Cleander*, Abraham as *Cleoron*, and Roosevelt as *Eugenius*. Cleoron's role was to express "within the walls of this dismantled college" the indignation all properly felt in contemplating the "tyranny of Britain." Eugenius shared with him lamentation for "the ruins of our *Alma Mater*," but looked forward to its restoration and "the growth of science, of the glory and improvement of human nature throughout America." Cleander advised dependence upon reason rather than passion and saw in the free institutions of a free people, subject only to "the laws of reason," the prospect that "America will yet nurse in her free bosom, Orators, Legislators and Generals, that shall more than rival the Greek and Roman fame," adding "Then Nassau! thou shalt flourish in the glory of thy country." When Eugenius declared, "I could weep that we were born so soon, just in the dawning of these mighty scenes!" Cleoron spoke for the special honor of coming on the stage for "the dawning of these mighty scenes!" And he added: "Harvard! Yale! and Nassau, are not your sons the first upon the mighty stage, giving an example to future ages of virtue, of the love of liberty, and of the glorious fruits of science?" Cleander joined in to affirm that when "the laurels of Parnassus shall fade, when compared with the boys of Nassau-Hall, the highest merit of her greatest scholars shall be to *write* well what we have *acted*."

After graduation Abraham apparently returned to Prince Edward County and began reading law. He was licensed to practice in 1784 and in 1789 was among the residents of the county who actively participated in the speculative attempt to purchase from Georgia several million acres of its claims to undeveloped western lands, a venture that ultimately miscarried. In 1790 he became a trustee of Hampden-Sidney College, a position he held until the end of his life. From 1800 to 1804 he represented the county in the lower house of the state legislature, where he was especially active as a member of the committee for the courts of justice. At some time before his father's will was drawn in 1803, he had received his portion of an obviously valuable estate.

Meanwhile, Venable had been elected to the national House of Representatives, where he served through the four terms extending from March 4, 1791 to March 3, 1799. It was in the first of these terms that he became involved in the celebrated Reynolds affair, perhaps because the speculations of James Reynolds in soldiers' claims had been conducted very largely in Virginia. Venable was one of the three public officials—the others being Senator James Monroe and Speaker of the House F.A.C. Muhlenberg of Pennsylvania—who on the evening of December 15, 1792 confronted Alexander Hamilton with evidence purporting to establish the complicity of the Department of the Treasury, perhaps even its head, in Reynold's operations, and who received Hamilton's confession of illicit relations with Reynold's wife as an explanation of the charges. Whether fully persuaded or not, the congressmen made no attempt to capitalize upon Hamilton's embarrassing confession and left him, according to their memo of the next day, "under an impression our suspicions were removed." When almost five years later the story was broken in the press, Venable wrote Hamilton, in response to a request by him, that he had had "nothing to do with the transaction since the interview" and that he did not possess and had not possessed any of the papers involved. To this he added his recollection at the end of the interview: "it was said I believe by us in general terms, that we were Satisfyed with the explanation and regretted the necessity of making the enquiry." He also expressed his resentment of Hamilton's recently published charge that he in any way had been guided by partisan motives. Venable's recollection of his own part in the affair probably was correct.

Venable's party alignment was with the Jeffersonian Republicans, in whose organization within the state of Virginia he would be active for a number of years after his departure from Congress. While in the House, he was critical of Hamilton's financial policies, opposed the Jay Treaty, and voted against the Alien and Sedition Acts. In 1798 he did not stand for reelection, and his service in the national legislature was finally terminated after a brief term in the Senate that began on December 13, 1803. He resigned in a letter of July 5, 1804 to the governor that explained that the time he had spent in the public service "has so far disabled me from attending to my private affairs as to make this measure rather a matter of necessity than of choice."

The occasion for this resignation seems clearly to have been the opportunity he had to become president of the Bank of Virginia, which had been chartered by act of the legislature on January 30, 1804. The commissioners designated for securing subscriptions to its stock reported their success in June, and in keeping with the provisions of the act, the state promptly added its $300,000 subscription to the capital stock of $1.5 million. The stockholders elected a board of directors that included Venable, and subsequently the directors elected him to the presidency at a salary of $2,500 a year. He was still in office on the evening of December 26, 1811 when he became one of the seventy-two persons who perished in the fire that destroyed the Richmond Theater on Broad Street. He had never married.

SOURCES: E. M. Venable, *Venables of Va.* (1925), esp. 29-36; W. G. Stanard and M. N. Stanard, *Colonial Va. Reg.* (1902), 173, 175, 177, 179; Hampden-Sidney College, *Gen. Cat.* (1908); A. J. Morrison, *College of Hampden-Sidney* (1912), passim; H. C. Bradshaw, *Hist. of Hampden-Sydney College*, I (1976), 56, 93; J. D. Eggleston, *Historic Slate Hill Plantation* (1945), 8-11, 17; C. E. Burrell, *Prince Edward Cnty.* (1922), 32; H. C. Bradshaw, *Prince Edward Cnty., Va.* (1955), passim; Beam, *Whig Soc.*, 59-65 (which indicates that the society was moribund in 1780); *N.J. Gazette*, 11 Oct 1780 (commencement); *NJA* (2 ser.), v, 31-35 ("dialogue"); *BDAC*; *VMHB*, 20 (1912), 313-15; 51 (1943), 297-99; *Tyler's Quart.*, 2 (1921), 137, 138; S. G. McLendon, *Hist. of Public Domain of Ga.* (1924), 35-39; *Journal of the House of Delegates*, 1800-1804; *Jefferson Papers*, XVIII, 611-88, 648 ("our suspicions were removed"); *Hamilton Papers*, XIII, 115-16; XXI, 121-44, 153-54, 159 ("satisfyed with the explanation"); *A/C*, v, 1,291; VIII, 2,029, 2,171; N. E. Cunningham, Jr., *Jeffersonian Republicans in Power* (1963), 183; *Cal. Va. St. Papers*, IX, 403-404, 410 ("a matter of necessity"), 422; W. L. Royall, *Hist. of Va. Banks and Banking Prior to the Civil War* (1907), 9-11; W. A. Christian, *Richmond . . . Past and Present* (1912), 59, 61; G. D. Fisher, *Hist. . . . of the Monumental Chh.* (1880).

WFC

and cousin of Henry Edward Watkins (D.B. 1801)

Samuel Woodson Venable

SAMUEL WOODSON VENABLE, A.B., planter, merchant, and public official, was born July 9, 1756, in Prince Edward County, Virginia, the oldest son of Nathaniel and Elizabeth Woodson Venable, elder brother of Abraham Bedford Venable (A.B. 1780), Richard N. Venable (A.B. 1782), and Nathaniel Venable (A.B. 1796). Both of his parents belonged to prominent families of the county. The father was one of the founders of the Prince Edward Academy, which in 1783 became Hampden-Sidney College, and served it as a trustee to the end of his life. There is no reason for doubting the family tradition that Samuel began his education at the academy, and in time for him to serve as ensign of a militia company of students who in the late summer of 1777, when Sir William Howe's army moving up the Chesapeake for its attack on Philadelphia raised fears for the safety of Vir-

Samuel Woodson Venable, A.B. 1780

ginia, marched to Williamsburg under the command of tutor John Blair Smith (A.B. 1774). Samuel Stanhope Smith (A.B. 1769) was the guiding spirit of the academy until his return to Princeton as Professor of Moral Philosophy toward the end of 1779. No doubt it was he who encouraged Samuel, and his brother Abraham, to transfer to Princeton for the purpose of securing the A.B. degree, which Hampden-Sidney was not yet qualified to award.

Samuel Venable's residence in Nassau Hall may have been limited to a single year, but whatever may have been the length of his stay, he distinguished himself as a student. Indeed, at the commencement of 1780 he enjoyed the highest distinction for a graduating senior of delivering the salutatory address. He also took part in a lively dialogue with his brother and James Roosevelt on "the present state of the college, the prospect of its restoration and of the revival of letters throughout America."

After graduation Samuel returned to Virginia, where he enlisted as cornet in Captain Thomas Watkins's troop of Virginia Dragoons. By the time of his participation in the Battle of Guilford Courthouse in March 1781, he had been promoted to lieutenant.

It has been said that after the war Samuel hoped to study law. Instead, he began almost immediately to assume the responsibilities that came with his birth. One of the first of these came with his acceptance of appointment by the Presbytery of Hanover on December 19, 1782 as trustee of Hampden-Sidney, in a move to assist in its recovery from the reversals brought on by the war. In the act elevating the institution to the rank of a college, he became with his father a charter trustee. From June 1788 to November 1806 he acted as clerk for the board. In the year of his death he gave a building and land to the college for a place of worship, and an additional eleven acres for the use of the congregation. With good reason the trustees noted his death with the following: "Hampden-Sidney College has lost one of her firmest supporters, and her board of Trustees one of its most efficient members." He had served also as a justice of the county court, and had been a sponsor of the Prince Edward Library Company.

He was married on August 15, 1781, to Mary S. Carrington of Charlotte County, who later was described by Archibald Alexander, president of Hampden-Sidney from 1797 to 1806 and for many years a professor in the Princeton Theological Seminary, as a "woman of uncommon vivacity, wit and power of sarcasm," and whose fame as a conversationalist brought her the description of "John Randolph in petticoats." Of her husband, Alexander observed that "he was a man of clear head and sound judgment," who "had made observations on the character of men as they passed before him" and reduced his observations "to maxims." Alexander continued: "He was confident in the opinions which he had formed, but not inclined to dispute with those who did not agree with him. He used to say that when a young man he was fond of disputation, and thought he could bring others to see as he did, but that after some experience he found it to be vain, and therefore suffered others undisturbedly to enjoy their own opinions." Alexander's son recorded that his father "was accustomed to speak of Col. Venable as the most remarkable instance of wisdom matured by experience and observation, that he had ever known." A correspondent of Bishop Meade of the Episcopalian Church described Venable as the "leading mind" in his section of Virginia and reported that his better known brothers, Abraham and Richard, "always veiled their pretensions in his presence, partly from affection, but more from deference to the ascendent intellect and acknowledged wisdom of their elder brother, which impressed all who approached him."

Samuel and Mary Venable became parents of twelve children, four sons and eight daughters, all of whom survived their father. Samuel died on September 7, 1821, at Sweet Springs, Virginia, where he probably had gone for his health. He had drawn his will on January 26 of that year, and it was proved in Prince Edward County on September 17. It made handsome provision of land and slaves for each of his children, and for his widow, who died at their home of Springfield in Prince Edward in 1837. The estate included hundreds of acres in Virginia or Kentucky, some "Georgia certificates," mills owned by the firm of Venable & Co., bank stock, and sixty-one slaves valued at $13,445. Each of his daughters received an additional bequest of £200-400 in money.

SOURCES: See Abraham B. Venable (A.B. 1780); E. M. Venable, *Venables of Va.* (1925), 41-54, 43 ("Randolph in Petticoats"); J. W. Alexander, *Life of Archibald Alexander* (1854), 128-30 ("woman of uncommon vivacity . . . man of clear head and sound judgment"); W. Meade, *Old Churches, Ministers, and Families of Va.*, II (1900), 31-32 ("leading mind"); Foote, *Sketches, Va.* (1850), 400-404; *VMHB*, 49 (1941), 165; J. H. Gwathmey, *Hist. Reg. of Virginians in Rev.* (1938), 794; *Cal. Va. St. Papers*, VIII, 258; H. C. Bradshaw, *Hist. of Hampden-Sydney College* (1976), esp. 48-49, 382-83; A. J. Morrison, *Hampden-Sidney College, Cal. of Board Minutes* (1912), 86 ("firmest supporters").

WFC

CLASS OF 1781

Joseph Clark, A.B.

William Crawford, A.B.

William Branch Giles, A.B.

Francis Jefferson James, A.B.

Edward Livingston, A.B.

Robert Smith, A.B.

Joseph Clark

JOSEPH CLARK, A.B., A.M. 1784, D.D. Jefferson College 1809, Presbyterian clergyman, was born near Elizabethtown, Essex County, New Jersey on October 21, 1751. The Clarks were among the older families inhabiting the area, but Joseph's parentage has not been established. At the age of seventeen, he was apprenticed to a carpenter, but after some three years in that trade he is said to have aspired to a higher calling and to have prepared himself for college. Just when he was admitted to Nassau Hall is unknown, but a journal he kept, which begins with a moving account of President Witherspoon's dismissal of the students on November 29, 1776 because of the approaching British army, argues for the disruption of an education already well under way.

The account of the closing of the College has been familiar to College historians, but heretofore they have failed to identify the author and have attributed it to some anonymous student. Since Clark's authorship is now unmistakable, it is appropriate here to repeat his description of that crisis in the College's history. It reads:

> On the 29th of November, 1776 New Jersey College long the peaceful seat of science and haunt of the Muses was visited with the melancholy tidings of the approach of the enemy.
>
> This alarmed our fears and gave us reason to believe we must soon bid adieu to our peaceful Departments and break off in the midst of our delightful studies; nor were we long held in suspense, our worthy President deeply affected at this solemn scene entered the Hall where the students were collected, and in a very affecting manner informed us of the improbability of continuing there longer in peace; and after giving us several suitable instructions and much good advice very affectionately bade us farewell. Solemnity and distress appeared almost in every countenance. Several students that had come 5 and 600 miles, and just got settled in College, were now obliged under every disadvantage to return with their effects or leave them behind, which several through the impossibility of getting a carriage at so confused a time were obliged to do, and lost their all.

Clark, hopeful that he might somehow continue his studies, agreed with a Mr. Johnson, who apparently lived not too far from the College, to tutor his son until the spring. But Washington's continued retreat

Joseph Clark, A.B. 1781

and the British advance as far as Kingston by December 6 put an end to this plan.

Before the month ended, Clark had enlisted in what he described as the "Amwell Battalion" of the New Jersey militia, the Third Regiment of Hunterdon County, which he served through better than four months as adjutant. Although more than once close to major scenes of military action, Clark's involvement in actual combat seemed to have been limited to a few minor skirmishes. On July 8, 1777, he became deputy quartermaster on the staff of Major General Adam Stephen of the Virginia Continental Line. After a delay imposed by illness, he followed Stephen's division to Pennsylvania but returned to New Jersey on August 14 and to Princeton two days later where he "made some preparations for pursuing my studies." On August 22 he was again in Princeton, this time waiting "to see the doctor," no doubt Doctor Witherspoon, on the subject of a possible return to the College, which that summer had managed to reopen with a handful of students. But he was not soon to resume his studies. Instead, he marched off with two New Jersey regiments "on their way to the grand army" and rejoined his own division some four miles below Wilmington, Delaware. He was in or near the action that followed at Brandywine and Germantown, and in December he went into winter quarters at Valley Forge.

During that famous winter, Clark seems to have been chiefly impressed by grumbling among the troops against the Congress. At one point he commented: "I plainly saw that those the cry of Liberty had called into the field, could now (when the same cause ceased to be a novelty) be held in it by no other tie than that of Interest." With the coming of spring, he was heartened by Baron von Steuben's efforts to improve the discipline of the army and by news of the French alliance. Early in May he left for a visit to New Jersey, which included two days at Princeton, where he "was very happy with my friends." Having bought a horse there, he rode to Elizabethtown, then to Morristown for a visit with his mother, and returned to Princeton for a stay from May 27 to 30. Back in camp on June 5, he found "all in expectation of a speedy and sudden move." Thereafter he accompanied the army as it followed the British across New Jersey to the battle at Monmouth Court House on June 28, 1778. By the end of July he was in camp near White Plains, New York. In September he again visited Princeton, but early in October he was back in camp "opposite West Point fort." His account of wartime experiences or such part of it as has survived, ends abruptly late in 1778, as the troops once more were moving into winter quarters.

Clark continued in military service through at least most of 1779. Just when he returned to his studies must remain uncertain, but it was in time for him to graduate as one of six in his class in September 1781, enjoying the highest honor of delivering the Latin salutatory address on the subject of "luxury." He was then just short of thirty years old.

Clark may have remained in Princeton for a time to begin his theological studies, but by April 1782 he was reading with John Woodhull (A.B. 1766), who advertised the reopening under his supervision of a Latin school at Freehold in Monmouth County. Included in the advertisement was a statement that "Mr. Clark, a very worthy and capable gentleman, late of New-Jersey college, is instructor, who gives the fullest satisfaction, so that the school is already in a flourishing state." Though suffering some disadvantage from a late start, Clark obviously was an apt student. He was licensed to preach on April 23, 1783 by the New Brunswick Presbytery. On October 26 of that year he was sent to supply the pulpit in Allentown, New Jersey, where he continued as a "stated supply" until his installation as pastor in June 1788. He had been ordained *sine titulo* in June 1784. At Allentown he found a wife in Margaret Imlay, sister of James H. Imlay (A.B. 1786).

The couple had four children, a daughter and three sons, including Reverend John Flavel Clark (A.B. 1807). In January 1796 Clark transferred to the Presbyterian church in New Brunswick, New Jersey. He remained there to the end of his life.

A man of medium height and slender build, firm convictions, and a sociable disposition, Clark apparently won attention through the quality of his sermons rather than through any special animation in their delivery. Certainly, the best known of them, delivered in 1806 on the death of William Paterson (A.B. 1763), shows skill in the development of the opportunity afforded by Paterson's deathbed acceptance of full communion with a church whose interests he more than once had served. Clark was considered to be a man of good judgment and persuasive effectiveness in the drafting of resolutions and reports. He rose quickly to offices of responsibility within his denomination, including his election in 1800 as moderator of the Presbyterian General Assembly.

Perhaps this election was a reward for the outstanding success he is reported to have had in raising funds for the support of missions on the nation's expanding frontiers. Perhaps too it was the reputation thus established that led the trustees of the College to call upon him for special assistance in raising funds for the reconstruction of Nassau Hall after its destruction by fire in 1802. At an emergency session in March, the trustees asked President Samuel Stanhope Smith (A.B. 1769) to undertake a fund-raising mission as far south as Washington, D.C., the elderly Alexander MacWhorter (A.B. 1757) to travel through New England for the same purpose, and Joseph Clark to undertake a similar mission to South Carolina and Georgia. Possibly, it was for the purpose of lending Clark additional authority as an agent of the College that he was elected as a trustee at the board's regular meeting in September 1802, although he did not take office until the following April. At the September meeting two additional agents were appointed: Reverend Robert Finley (A.B. 1787) for solicitation in four New Jersey counties, and Reverend William M. Tennent (A.B. 1763) for a mission through Delaware and the Eastern Shore of Maryland and Virginia.

Joseph Clark began his mission on November 2, 1802, not to South Carolina and Georgia, but with the ultimate destination of Virginia. He traveled in the company of Judge John Bryan, a native of Virginia who then lived in Peapack, New Jersey and was a justice of the Somerset County court. Apparently, Clark rode in a "coach" with a servant for whose wages $48 would later be allowed, and Judge Bryan rode on horseback. They reached Pequea, Pennsylvania on November 6 and reached Lancaster on the next day, where they stayed almost a full

week, the local court being then in session, and where they had their
first major success. Before moving on, they had collected or received
subscriptions for more than $800. They crossed the Susquehanna River
on November 13 and collected $17 "from house to house" before ar-
riving at York that afternoon. There on the next day, a Sunday, Clark
preached twice, and after "much hard begging" on the following days,
they collected $138.50. As they moved into Maryland, they adopted the
practice of having Clark work the town or village while Bryan rode
into the countryside. At Frederick, Clark preached on November 21,
and through the Monday and Tuesday that followed, they counted
the results of their combined efforts at better than $300. They crossed
the Potomac into Virginia on Wednesday, November 24.

They came to Leesburg on the next day, to Fauquier Court House
on November 29, collecting in and around that place $81. A journey
through Stafford County, which seems to have yielded no more than
$8, brought them to Fredericksburg. There they found a letter from
President Smith, advising them that he had worked that area and was
on his way to Richmond. They joined Smith in Richmond on December 3, and two days later Smith was robbed of $600. It was decided
that Bryan and Clark would split up, the former riding down the Virginia peninsula for calls at its plantation houses, while Clark gave his
attention to members of the state legislature, then in session. He found
much prejudice against the College among the legislators and managed to secure no more than $285 from them and a few local citizens.
In contrast, Bryan returned from his journey with subscriptions for
$714. A joint visit to Petersburg brought a gratifying total of $792.
Back in Richmond, they agreed that Bryan would go up the James
and through the Virginia Valley back to Pennsylvania, a journey he
failed to complete because of his death in December in Albemarle
County. Clark drew the assignment of visiting the "lower counties" of
Virginia and Maryland lying along the York, Rappahannock, and Potomac rivers. He left Richmond on January 8, 1803, visiting first King
and Queen, Gloucester, and Middlesex counties, and then above the
Rappahannock, Lancaster, Richmond, Northumberland, Westmoreland, and King George counties. In King George he reached the home
of Landon Carter of Cleve on February 12 in the midst of a winter
storm and coming down with a fever. He remained a guest of Carter's
for a month, while recovering from his illness and while his servant
struggled with a severe attack of the measles. Carter's hospitality,
and in addition a contribution of $50 for the College, possibly was
attributable in part to the fact that his sister had married William
Burnet Browne of the Class of 1760. But throughout his tour of east-

ern Virginia, Clark enjoyed the hospitality of more than one well-known planter.

Leaving Carter's on March 17, he went by way of Fredericksburg to Mount Vernon, Alexandria, and across the Potomac to Georgetown, Washington, Bladensburg, and Annapolis, which he found already had been canvassed. On February 19 he had written Ashbel Green that his "zig-zag tour" was nearly over, that he was "weary, really I am weary," and anxious to be at rest once more with his family and his people. He estimated that he had been collecting about $25 a day. From Annapolis he went through Baltimore to Philadelphia, not neglecting to solicit along the way. At Philadelphia on April 9 he turned over $3,300 to Elias Boudinot, trustee of the College and at the time director of the United States Mint. The diary ends on April 11, when Clark reached Maidenhead (Lawrenceville) on the way home. It is difficult to determine exactly how much he had raised for the College. The trustees in September 1803 received a report that his account had been settled, and the minutes confirm that the payment to Boudinot was in cash. Several hundred dollars of additional sums had been subscribed, some of them as yet unpaid, and it is clear enough that Clark and Bryan had handsomely exceeded the total costs for their mission of $625.24. It is clear too that this mission was long remembered as one of the more successful in the effort to restore Nassau Hall.

Clark was to raise still more money for Princeton. In September 1803 he was asked to accept responsibility for additional solicitation in the New Jersey counties of Middlesex, Somerset, and Essex, the last two formerly assigned to Robert Finley. In June 1810 he and justice Andrew Kirkpatrick (A.B. 1775) were requested to collect funds in their home town of New Brunswick for the support of a vice-president of the College. That Clark went beyond this limited commission is shown by a receipt, dated December 13, 1811, for $915 collected by him and trustee Joshua Wallace for this purpose in Philadelphia. The item has more than passing interest, for the decision to appoint a vice-president has been interpreted as a move preliminary to the ouster of President Smith in 1812. Clark thus apparently was numbered among the trustees whose dissatisfaction with the conduct of the College contributed to the establishment that same year of the separate Princeton Theological Seminary, of whose board of directors he became an original member.

Clark died, suddenly it seems, on October 19, 1813.

SOURCES: Two apparently separate journals of Clark's military service have survived in print: one covering the period from May 1777 to late 1778, in *NJHSP* (1855), 93-110; and another printed serially in the *Princeton Standard* for May 1, 8, and 15,

1863, that begins on November 29, 1776, with the quotation regarding Witherspoon's dismissal of the students, and continues to the end of June 1777. The latter, according to Hageman, *History*, I, 124-25, was printed from a manuscript belonging to Dr. John N. Woodhull of Princeton, a grandson of the John Woodhull with whom Clark studied and taught after leaving the College. The original manuscript of the text published in *NJHSP* is found in the society's manuscript collections. A comparison of the texts for the overlapping period of time, May and June 1777, serves to establish the common authorship; for fuller detail, see introduction to Clark's journal of 1802-1803 as published in *Princeton University Library Chronicle*, XLI (1979), 54-68. The NJHS at Newark has a number of other items of interest that are filed with the memorandum booklet containing the original manuscript of the 1855 printed text, the chief of them being a receipt for payment of tuition, suggesting that Clark may have been graduated still owing tuition for two terms. If this be true, it apparently is an unprecedented concession by the trustees of the College.

Sprague, *Annals*, III, 446-49; Alexander, *Princeton*, 208-9; Giger, Memoirs; als JC to J. Ward, 9 Sep 1779, MS 548.5, PPPrHi; Stryker, *Off. Reg.*, 71, 168, 540; *N.J. Gazette*, 3 Oct 1781 (commencement); *NJA* (2 ser.), V, 434; *Rec. Pres. Chh.*, 498, 507; *Min. Gen. Assem., 1789-1820*, 15, 136, 187; *DAR Patriot Index*, 134; Trustee Minutes, II, 65, 87, 89, 90, 91, 94, 97, 107-108, 111, 121, 293, PUA; als JC to A. Green, 19 Feb 1803 ("weary"), Moore Coll.; JC to J. Hopkins, 19 Mar 1803; MS "List of Delinquent Subscribers"; ads to JC, 13 Dec 1811 (filed under Samuel Bayard), NjP; Maclean, *History*, II, 47n (with error in date); *VMHB*, 31 (1923), 44, 58n; *NJHSP* (1 ser.), 6 (1853), 165; Wertenbaker, *Princeton*, 128-30, 147-51; I. V. Brown, Memoirs of the Rev. Robert Finley (1819), 213-27.

PUBLICATIONS: *Rules Established by the Presbytery of New Brunswick . . . with a Pastoral Letter . . .* [signed by Joseph Clark, Moderator], (1800); *A Sermon on the Death of the Hon. William Paterson . . .* (1806); *Sermon Delivered in the City of New Brunswick, . . . July 30, 1812, Being the Day Set Aside by the Gen. Assem. of the Pres. Chh. for Fasting, Humiliation, and Prayer* (1812); "The True and False Grounds of Religion," sermons XIV and XV in G. S. Woodhull and I. V. Brown, *The N.J. Preacher* (1813). There were other men by his name with whom the Princeton graduate has at times been confused.

WFC

William Crawford

WILLIAM CRAWFORD, A.B., is identified by a cryptic entry in the minutes of the board of trustees meeting on September 26, 1781. President Witherspoon having reported that five members of the senior class (all named) had passed the usual examinations and having recommended them in consequence for their "first degree in the Arts," there followed immediately this minute: "Mr. William Crawford, a young gentleman from the state of Virginia, who had completed his studies under the care of Professor Smith, was recommended for the same degree." The minutes continue: "Upon these recommendations, Resolved that Joseph Clarke, Francis James, William Giles, Robert Smith, Edward Livingston & William Crawford be admitted to the degree of Batchelor of Arts."

Professor Smith, of course, was Samuel Stanhope Smith (A.B. 1769), who had served as rector of the Prince Edward Academy in Virginia from 1775 to 1779, in which year he had assumed the office of Professor of Moral Philosophy at Princeton. The academy received its charter as Hampden-Sidney College in 1783 and was not authorized to grant the degree before that date. Young Crawford must have begun his studies with Smith there. Whether in Virginia Crawford had advanced so far and so well with his studies that Smith coveted for him the advantages of a degree, or whether he had followed Smith to Princeton for their completion must be left to conjecture. It seems certain only that he had not followed the usual course of study to the examination taken by other members of the class. A suggestion that Crawford was not even present for the commencement is found in the report of the exercises carried by the *New Jersey Gazette* of October 3, 1781. There all other graduating seniors are reported as speakers, together with two of the former graduates who received the A.M. degree, but Crawford is merely listed with those awarded the A.B. degree.

In the College's published catalogues through that for 1808, Crawford's name was carried at the bottom of the list for the Class of 1781 and so was out of alphabetical order. It was placed in alphabetical order for the first time in the catalogue of 1812 and was so carried thereafter until finally in the catalogue of 1848 he was for the first time listed as dead. No other member of his class was alive after 1836. Perhaps it was in 1848, or not very long thereafter, that in Princeton the Virginia graduate of 1781 was confused with Dr. William Crawford of Adams County, Pennsylvania, a native of Scotland who migrated to this country after receiving the M.D. degree from the University of Edinburgh in 1791, who represented his district in the United States Congress from 1809 to 1817, and who died in 1823. Unfortunately, efforts to determine Crawford's true identity have established only that he was still a resident of Virginia in 1796, when President Samuel Stanhope Smith addressed to him in Amherst County, Virginia a printed form letter requesting assistance in raising funds to provide the College with scientific equipment needed for instructional purposes. The copy surviving in the Princeton University Library is marked as having been received on March 9.

SOURCES: Giger, Memoirs; Alexander, *Princeton*; Clio. Soc. *Cat.* (1876); and *Gen. Cat.* (1908), all use the mistaken identification. See also als S. S. Smith to WC, 19 Jan 1796, NjP. Beginning with the catalogue of 1808, Crawford is credited with an A.M. degree, but a check of the Trustee Minutes indicates that it was not awarded by CNJ. In the catalogue of 1815 and thereafter, Crawford's name is printed in capital letters to indicate that he held public office. Whether this indicates that the mistaken identification goes back that far, or that there was knowledge at the time of a public office held by the graduate, is unknown. The Crawford family was established in Va. during the seventeenth century, was a prolific one, and many of its members carried the name William. The identification with Amherst Cnty. suggests that the graduate may have been related to William H. Crawford of Ga., who was born in that county in 1772. There is a possibility that the Princeton student was a son of David Crawford, a justice of the peace in Amherst during the 1760s and 1770s. [See J.E.D. Shipp, *Giant Days, or The Life and Times of William H. Crawford* (1909); *Bulletin Va. St. Libr.*, 14 (1921), 62, 70, 97; L. H. Sweeny, *Amherst Cnty.* . . . *in the Rev.* (1951), passim. For Dr. William Crawford of Pennsylvania, see *Hist. of Cumberland and Adams Counties* (1886) [Adams], 72; *BDAC.*] One additional possibility is that William Crawford was a relative of Edward (A.B. 1775) and James Crawford (A.B. 1777). Their older brother William had a son of that name, and their uncle Patrick Crawford, who married Sally Watson, also had a son William, born on 6 Aug 1767. On June 22, 1802, this William, son of Patrick, married a Nancy Smith in Rockingham Cnty., Va. [See J. A. Waddell, *Annals of Augusta Cnty., Va.* (1902), 205-208; J. W. Wayland, *Va. Valley Recs.* (1930), 14.]

WFC

William Branch Giles

WILLIAM BRANCH GILES, A.B., lawyer and public official, was born on August 12, 1762, in Amelia County, Virginia, the youngest son of William Giles and his wife, Ann Branch Giles. He was prepared for college in the Prince Edward Academy, of which Samuel Stanhope Smith (A.B. 1769) was head, and the tradition that he followed Smith to Princeton when the latter in 1779 assumed the position of Professor of Moral Philosophy in the College of New Jersey is probably correct. While at Nassau Hall, Giles became a member of the American Whig Society. On the occasion of his graduation he spoke twice, first delivering an oration on "the misapplication of talents," and later participating in a dialogue on "the origin and comparative merits of poetry and eloquence." Returning to Virginia after graduation, he studied law with the celebrated George Wythe of Williamsburg and the College of William and Mary. He received a license to practice law in 1786. Success as an attorney, his office located in Petersburg, seems to have come quickly and easily.

Giles's entry into politics was comparably prompt. Numbered among the advocates of the new federal Constitution, he was elected at the age of twenty-eight to fill the vacancy in Virginia's delegation to the first federal Congress that had been created by the death of Theodorick Bland; he took his seat on December 7, 1790. By three successive reelections, he served until October 2, 1798, when he resigned, giving ill health as the explanation. Whatever may have been the trouble, he promptly accepted election to the Virginia House of Delegates and was

William Branch Giles, A.B. 1781
ATTRIBUTED TO GILBERT STUART

reelected in 1799. After Jefferson's election as President of the United States, Giles returned in 1801 to Congress, where he served through March 3, 1803. Upon the resignation from the Senate in July 1804 of Abraham B. Venable (A.B. 1780), a close friend he probably had known when both were students in the College, Giles was appointed to fill the vacancy and took his seat on November 5. On December 17, 1804, he was sworn in again for a term ending in 1811 after his election to fill the vacancy created by the resignation of Wilson C. Nicholas. He remained in the Senate through March 3, 1815, when once more he resigned. Thus, for the better part of a quarter of a century he sat in one house or the other of the national legislature.

Aggressive by nature and facile in speech, Giles from his first entry into the Congress showed no inclination to sit quietly on a back seat. The acidulous William Maclay of Pennsylvania found occasion as early as January 20, 1791 to write the following comment in his journal:

Giles, the new member from Virginia, sat next to me but one. I saw a speech of his in the papers, which read very well, and they say he delivers himself handsomely. I was, therefore, very attentive to him. But the frothy manners of Virginia were ever uppermost. Canvas-back ducks, ham and chickens, old Madeira, the glories of the Ancient Dominion, all fine, were his constant themes. Boasted of personal prowess; *more manual exercise than any man in New England*; fast but fine living in his country, wine or cherry bounce from twelve o'clock to night every day. He seemed to practice on this principle, too, as often as the bottle passed him. . . . He is but a young man, and seems as if he always would be so.

However unfair this judgment may have been, the emphasis upon Giles's identification with Virginia was rightly placed.

In the House, Giles became a chief lieutenant of his fellow Virginian and alumnus James Madison (A.B. 1771). It was Giles who introduced five resolutions adopted on January 23, 1793 that, in sequence to earlier resolutions adopted in late December, called into question Alexander Hamilton's conduct of the Treasury Department. The secretary's prompt response with detailed reports that were completed by February 19 confirmed his supporters' suspicion that Giles's purpose had been to convict Hamilton of serious misuse of his office in order to drive him from public life, a view accepted by many later historians. This view found further confirmation when Giles on February 27 introduced an additional nine resolutions specifically charging misconduct, even violation of law. In the voting that preceded the adjournment of Congress on March 3, the House rejected these resolutions by decisive margins, and Hamilton and his supporters found in these votes a vindication of the secretary. A renewed inquiry on motion by Giles in the following December when Congress reassembled was actually invited by Hamilton, who sought to make his vindication complete; he found that vindication in the subsequent report of a special committee on which Giles served.

The survival of a draft of Giles's resolutions of the preceding February in Secretary of State Thomas Jefferson's hand, though with important differences, has invited the charge that Giles was a mere tool employed by Jefferson and/or Madison, but there are reasons for believing that his own convictions as much as any other consideration guided him. There is a consistency in his attitude toward public questions that runs throughout the earlier part of his career and lends logic to his identification with the emerging Republican Party. He was opposed to the Bank of the United States and was to become a bitter opponent of Jay's Treaty, which he regarded as a "sell-out" to the British. He remained friendly with the French and during the Quasi-War with France resisted measures designed to strengthen national defenses, especially those intended to rebuild the navy. After 1793, when Jefferson left the cabinet, Giles was one of the correspondents upon whom Jefferson depended for information regarding developments in

Congress. Among the Republicans there Giles may not have been the shrewdest tactician, for he had a major part in the Congressional demand on the executive branch that led to the publication of the "XYZ" Papers, which served to bring patriotic sentiment to the support of Giles's opponents, President Adams and his Federalist advisers. His resignation from Congress came at a moment of consternation and disarray in the Republican ranks. Giles took his seat in the state assembly in time to vote for the famous Virginia Resolutions of December 24, 1798, thereby putting himself on record as opposed to the Alien and Sedition Acts. He was a member of the Republican ticket of presidential electors circulated in behalf of Jefferson as the election of 1800 approached. Back in the House of Representatives and subsequently in the Senate, he followed Jefferson's leadership through the two terms he served as president.

In 1808, faced with a choice between Madison and James Monroe, Giles backed Madison, but President Madison was not to find him the faithful lieutenant he earlier had been. Instead, he became one of the senators who frequently was counted among the president's foes, and often in alliance with his own former Federalist foes. In the ultimate test, he voted for Madison's war with Britain and so maintained a certain consistency with the record he earlier had established, but there had been a marked inconsistency with that record through recent years in his repeated criticism of the administration for failing to adopt foreign policies based upon strength, including the strength of the navy.

Historians generally have shown little sympathy for Giles. Those who might be viewed as partial to the Jeffersonians have condemned him for his abandonment of Madison. Those who might be viewed as partial to Hamilton have almost gleefully pointed to his abandonment of Madison as proof that in 1793 he had been no more than a cat's-paw and an unworthy one at that. To these can be added Henry Adams, whose portrayal of Giles's career can be described, at some risk of understatement, as the most unflattering of all.

Perhaps here Giles is entitled to a more sympathetic view of his career, but there are difficulties. There can be no question as to the influence he was capable of exerting at critical points in the early history of the nation, as any number of histories for the period testify. Yet even the most sympathetic of those accounts concede that the man had serious faults. He tended occasionally to adopt the most extreme position his convictions might persuade him to take, with the result that his natural allies did not always agree with him. An example might be found in the attempted impeachment of Supreme Court justice Samuel Chase in 1805, when Giles took the lead in the Senate's discussion of questions of procedure and denied that impeachment proceedings necessarily were of a judicial character. Said he: "Impeachment is nothing more than an enquiry, by the two Houses of Congress, whether the office of any public man might not be better filled by another." At the time, many of his fellow Republicans felt a need to reduce the power that the judicial branch of the government seemed to be assuming under chief justice John Marshall, and it has been suspected that Giles's ultimate aim was to establish a principle that might permit the removal of Marshall. But Chase was acquitted in proceedings having some of the character of a trial at law.

Other questions also remain. What does Madison's failure in 1809 to give Giles special preferment in the new administration suggest as to the president's judgment of his longtime associate? Did Giles turn against Madison out of personal disappointment in not receiving the preferment he felt was his due? Is the explanation to be found in his growing dislike of Albert Gallatin, who was continued by Madison at the treasury, though denied the post of secretary of state that he desired, and which some suspected Giles wanted? Did Giles move too close to his classmate Robert Smith, who after serving as Jefferson's secretary of the navy, succeeded Madison at state, only to break with the president on questions of foreign policy and be dismissed finally in favor of James Monroe? Robert's brother, Senator Samuel Smith of Maryland, and Giles were often allied in opposition to the administration. How far, to mention one other example, did Giles's bitter opposition in 1811 to the proposed rechartering of the Bank of the United States reflect his attitude toward that institution from its beginning, and how far did it reflect the fact that the proposal was Gallatin's? Or was Giles perhaps one of those political leaders in the early history of the republic whose conduct is most charitably described as erratic? Certainly, there seems to have been on occasion, to recall the subject of his commencement oration, some "misapplication of talents."

After retirement from the Senate in 1815, Giles returned briefly in 1816 to the state assembly, and thereafter for the better part of a decade he was relatively inactive in politics. He reentered the field in 1824 with vigorous attacks in the public press upon John Quincy Adams, Henry Clay, the protective tariff, and internal improvements. In a bid to return to the Senate in 1825 he was defeated, but in 1827 he was elected governor of Virginia, an office he held until 1830, the year of his death on December 4. Given the conventional wisdom of his time and a renewed emphasis upon states' rights among southern political leaders, he probably viewed this office as an appropriate climax to his career.

Giles died at his home in Amelia County, a handsome twenty-eight-room house he had built not far from the Appomattox River and named "The Wigwam." He had built it after his first marriage in March 1797 to Martha Peyton Tabb. Following her death in 1808, he was married on February 22, 1810 to Frances Ann Gwynn, a cousin of his first wife who at the time of marriage was no more than seventeen years of age. Giles was survived by one son and two daughters, all apparently by the second marriage.

SOURCES: For so controversial a figure as Giles has become, there seems to be remarkably little controversy regarding the substantive facts of his political career—what he did and what he said. There appears to be, therefore, little point in appending here a lengthy bibliography of the many historical studies that at one point or another deal with Giles's activity, especially in view of the fact that D. R. Anderson, *William Branch Giles: A Biography* (1915) provides a carefully documented summary of Giles's public career from 1790 to 1815 [see esp. 95-96 ("impeachment")].
    DAB; R. A. Brock, *Va. and Virginians* (1888), 153-56; M. V. Smith, *Hist. of the Executives . . . of Va.* (1893), 338-39; *BDAC*; H. Adams, *Hist. of the U.S.* (1931 ed.), passim esp. I, 284; E. S. Maclay, *Journal of William Maclay* (1890), 374 ("new member from Virginia"); N. E. Cunningham, Jr., *Jeffersonian Republicans* (1957), 21, 78, 80, 86-87, 151-52; Cunningham, *Jeffersonian Republicans in Power* (1963), 13-14, 73, 93; *Hamilton Papers*, XIII, 532-41; B. Mitchell, *Alexander Hamilton*, II (1962), 245-75; P. L. Ford, *Works of Thomas Jefferson*, VII, 220-23; *WMQ* (3 ser.), 33 (1976), 557-85.
    PUBLICATIONS: see Anderson, above, 211-14

                                                                                    WFC

Francis Jefferson James

FRANCIS JEFFERSON JAMES, A.B., was a Virginian who probably lived out his life as an obscure planter, and may well have been the Francis James born in Goochland County on December 30, 1761, the son of Richard James and his wife, Mary Turpine James. The James family had been settled in Virginia since the seventeenth century, and through successive generations, many of its members had borne the names Richard and Francis. Because the College's graduate settled ultimately in Cumberland County, it is possible that he was the son of the Richard James, justice of the peace and prominent planter who served as a minuteman and on that county's committee of safety in 1776, and who almost certainly was related to him. That the middle name was not added at a later stage in life, as in some instances seems to have been the case, is indicated by the fact that the newspaper report of the commencement of 1781 lists the graduate's name as Francis Jefferson James. James's mother, therefore, may have come from a branch of the Jefferson family. No evidence has been found as to when James entered the College, unless it can be assumed that the mistaken listing of him as a member of the Class of 1779 in the 1876 catalogue of the Cliosophic Society provides some indication.

James was married to Nancy Stockton, daughter of Major Robert Stockton of Princeton and sister of Ebenezer Stockton (A.B. 1780), at a time probably not too far removed from his delivery on September 26, 1781 of a commencement oration on the subject of "Matrimony." His name appears among those residents of Cumberland County who in November 1789 signed a petition to the Virginia Assembly protesting the heavy taxes they had to pay. From Cartersville, in Cumberland, James wrote on March 31, 1806 to Thomas P. Johnson, who had married his wife's sister, acknowledging receipt of the news of Robert Stockton's death. He had delayed in telling Nancy because of her illness, and when he did the news brought on a relapse, but she was helped by the hope, perhaps through her father's bequest, that she might "visit once more her friends in your part of the World." In March of the following year a letter to Ebenezer Stockton, one of the executors of the father's estate, indicates that the bequest had not yet been received and reports that Nancy was then enjoying good health. The census of 1820 suggests the possibility that Francis James may still have been a resident of Cumberland County. The latest reference to him that has been found is in the standard genealogy of the Stockton family, which merely records that Nancy Stockton had married a "Mr. James."

SOURCES: W. M. Jones, *The Douglas Reg.* (1928, 1966), 223; *VMHB*, 17 (1900), 379; 35 (1927), 352, 354; *Bulletin Va. St. Libr.*, 14 (1921), 63, 90; J. H. Gwathmey, *Hist. Reg. of Virginians in the Rev.* (1938), 413; *N.J. Gazette*, 3 Oct 1781; G. E. Hopkins, *Cumberland Cnty: Petitions since 1776* (n.d.), 6, 31; als FJJ to T. P. Johnson, 31 Mar 1806; FJJ to E. Stockton, 21 Mar 1807, NjP; J. R. Felldin, *Index to 1820 Census of Va.* (1976); *N.J. Wills*, x, 427-28; T. C. Stockton, *Stockton Family of N.J.* (1911), 33.

WFC

Edward Livingston

EDWARD LIVINGSTON, A.B., LL.D. Columbia 1823, Transylvania 1824, Harvard 1834, lawyer, public official, entrepreneur, jurist, and penal reformer, was born on May 28, 1764, at Clermont, New York, the youngest of eleven children of Margaret Beekman and Robert R.

Edward Livingston, A.B. 1781
BY JOHN TRUMBULL

Livingston, Sr., judge of the supreme court of New York, landed mag-
nate, and a leading provincial Whig. Livingston followed several
cousins to the College, and his brothers-in-law included Morgan Lewis
(A.B. 1773), John Armstrong (Class of 1776), and Peter R. Livingston
(A.B. 1784). His older brother Robert R. Livingston, "the Chancellor,"
was the political leader of the Clermont branch of the Livingston
family during the formative years of the republic, and Edward, who
was some eighteen years younger, enjoyed a close father-son relationship with his brother after the death of Robert R. Livingston, Sr. in
1775. Prepared in schools at Albany and Esopus, Livingston accompanied his brother, a delegate to the Continental Congress, on a trip
to Philadelphia in the fall of 1779 and matriculated in the junior
class at Nassau Hall. While at Princeton he became a member of the
American Whig Society, and at his commencement in 1781, he delivered an oration on "The love of glory." Thirty-five years later Livingston remembered his student days with some regret, writing that he
had spent his "time rather idly at school, and still more so at college."
Livingston spent the winter following his graduation at the family

seat at Clermont and devoted his time to the French and German languages under the instruction of two resident tutors. In 1782 he began the study of law in Albany, completing his preparations in New York, where he was admitted to the bar and to practice as solicitor and counsel in the Chancery Court on April 24, 1786. An officer in the New York County Militia from 1786 to 1789, Livingston was also a member of a philological society and an original shareholder in the Tontine Coffee House. On April 10, 1788, he married Mary McEvers, the daughter of a merchant, and in 1790 their household included one slave. Livingston quickly impressed New York political society with his subtle mind, his talent for oratory, his intuitive seizure of opportunities for profit, and his penchant for flamboyance in dress and demeanor. Unlike several prominent Livingstons, "Beau Ned" was an innate democrat, and his first political base in New York City was not among the elite families of which his own was one, but rather among the immigrants and mechanics of the uptown wards.

Livingston's early emergence as a leader of the opposition to New York's Federalist establishment was facilitated by Chancellor Livingston's alignment of the family with the popular New York faction headed by Governor George Clinton. In 1791 Edward Livingston was nominated for the state assembly from New York City on a ticket supported by the Mechanics Society and opposed to a "merchants" ticket of Federalist candidates. He was defeated then, and was again defeated in 1792. Hoping for a state appointment, he exerted himself in the 1792 gubernatorial contest between Clinton and John Jay, but his services went unrewarded after Clinton's triumph. A warm advocate of the French Revolution, Livingston addressed the first meeting of the New York Democratic Society in 1794, and he consistently endorsed countermeasures against Britain for the seizure of American ships. His outspoken ideological radicalism secured him popular endorsements for the city's congressional seat in 1794, and he was elected as "the poor man's friend and the uniform assertor of the Rights of Man."

If Livingston's principles were extraordinary for a man of his lineage, his attention to financial opportunities and speculative enterprise was not. Like other members of the Clermont Livingstons, he held title to vast tracts of undeveloped land in New York, and shortly after the establishment of the federal government, he and his brother John bought almost $76,000 of the depreciated debt certificates of the southern states in anticipation of their assumption by the new national regime. In 1792 Livingston and several close relatives were among the most active promoters of a scheme to establish a state bank in New York City, but he escaped the worst effects of the panic that followed the New York speculative orgy of early 1792. He retained his ties to city financial figures after his election to the House of Representatives in 1794 and later in the decade became counsel for the insolvent Robert Morris, probably with an eye toward securing the financier's upstate lands for himself.

In Congress from 1795 to 1801, Livingston quickly earned a national reputation. On March 2, 1796, one day after Washington's proclamation of the Jay Treaty with Great Britain, Livingston offered a motion requesting the president to submit to the House all documents that might bear on the constitutionality of the pact. Even the leaders of the opposition to the treaty in the House, including James Madison (A.B. 1771), thought the resolution both premature and unduly provocative. Although Livingston modified the wording of his motion, his proposal became the focus of a vigorous constitutional debate. As he himself argued, the resolution raised the fundamental question of whether statutory law might be overridden by treaties. Several of his Republican colleagues maintained that the House had a discretionary authority in the implementation of treaties because of its control of appropriations, a claim that irate Federalists condemned as an attempt to encroach upon the constitutional authority of the chief executive and of the Senate. Livingston's resolution was adopted by a vote of sixty-two to thirty-seven, but Washington refused to submit the requested documents.

The "Aristocratical, Democratical, Jacobinical Edward Livingston" of Federalist rhetoric was reelected in 1796 and 1798. In the Fifth Congress he was one of the most outspoken opponents of the Alien Act, which he described as "a refinement upon despotism," and of the Sedition Act, which he feared would shackle not only the press but also congressional debate. He was accused in Federalist newspapers of seditious intentions after he advised popular disobedience to the Alien Act and called for a treaty with the detested French Directory. President John Adams long remembered Congressman "Neddy" Livingston as a "naughty lad as well as a saucy one."

Although he decided not to seek reelection in 1800, Livingston was still in Congress in February 1801 when the tie vote between Thomas Jefferson and Aaron Burr (A.B. 1772) threw the selection of a president into the House of Representatives. Livingston had been a friend of Burr's since his law student days in Albany, and this association fed rumors that Livingston was involved in intrigues to elect his fellow New Yorker as chief executive in place of the Virginian. But Livingston supported Jefferson through thirty-six ballots and was rewarded by the new Republican administration with an appointment as United States attorney for the New York district.

Livingston was also appointed mayor of New York City in 1801 by the state's Republican-dominated Council of Appointment. The position was worth $10,000 to $15,000 annually in salary and fees, and in accepting the office, Livingston became one of a dozen family members whose attachment to Governor Clinton put them on the public payroll. His mayoralty was noteworthy for his partisanship and for his proposals for the prevention of crime and the rehabilitation of the poor. He suggested the cooperative establishment by the city and the Mechanics Society of a city employment office and of public workshops for distressed immigrants, widows, orphans, and criminal offenders. During the yellow fever epidemic of 1803, he refused to leave the city and contracted the disease himself after accompanying the physicians and overseeing the city watch. But Livingston was already involved in a personal disaster that forced his resignation as mayor and as district attorney, interrupted his public career for almost two decades, blasted his reputation, and offended the national leadership of the Republican party.

As United States attorney, Livingston was entrusted with the federal revenues collected in the city. This responsibility he assigned to a political assistant, whose work he failed to superintend properly. When a Treasury Department audit of the books in June 1803 revealed a serious shortage, Livingston assumed responsibility both for the dishonesty of his agent and for the debt to the government. Confessing judgment in favor of the United States for $100,000, he assigned his estate to trustees for sale in payment of his debts. Although the sum due the government was eventually fixed at only $44,000, the value of Livingston's property was insufficient to reimburse the Treasury or to cover all his private indebtedness of almost $200,000. Determined to restore his name and credit as quickly as possible, Livingston left New York in December 1803 for the small Mississippi port town of New Orleans. He went alone and with a mere $100 in cash. His wife had died in 1801, as had a son in 1802. Another son and a daughter remained behind with relatives.

Although Livingston came to New Orleans more or less under duress, he was uniquely prepared for life and business there. His urbanity, intelligence, reputation, relative youth, and especially his sympathy for the laws, language, and customs of the French inhabitants recommended him initially to both the "ancient" Louisianians and to the new American territorial administration that was established after the

Louisiana Purchase. Moreover, the first American governor was Re-
publican William C.C. Claiborne of Tennessee, who had served with
Livingston in Congress and who welcomed him as a probable friend.
Livingston was an immediate success as an attorney in New Orleans.
He was also a leading promoter of a territorial bank, the successful
flotation of which violated the charter of the Bank of the United
States. Within weeks of his arrival, he secured a one-third interest in
the million-acre Spanish land grant of the Baron De Bastrop on the
Washita River, and by January 1805 Claiborne thought that Living-
ston had made a clear profit of $30,000 in one speculation alone. His
disclaimers of any intention to meddle in civil affairs notwithstanding,
Livingston quickly became a "warm advocate of the *Rights of Louisiana*," and he authored the popular remonstrance against the act of
March 1804 that created Orleans Territory in southern Louisiana.
This widely circulated petition demanded self-government and the
immediate admission of the new territory to the Union. It also condemned the congressional restriction on the importation of slaves, a
restriction that Livingston feared would handicap his exploitation of
the Washita lands.

Professional success, daring speculative ventures, and an outspoken
devotion to popular political principles were thus as characteristic of
the New Orleans émigré as they had been of the New York politician.
But in these same qualities were the seeds of the difficulties that would
keep Livingston in New Orleans for many years beyond the few he had
originally expected to regain his fortune and to pay his debts.

First came a break with Claiborne. The mutual distrust between the
governor and the leaders of the French-speaking community had po-
larized the politics of the Territory of Orleans around hostile camps of
"ancients" and Americans. Livingston's deep involvement in the 1804
remonstrance signaled his alignment with the Creole faction, and he
emerged as the leading opposition figure in 1807 following the ensnarl-
ing of territorial politics with the "Burr conspiracy." He was widely
suspected at the time of being privy to the former vice-president's
mysterious western designs and he is said to have been a leading member of a New Orleans association interested in the "liberation" of
Mexico. Burr stayed with Livingston on his visit to Louisiana in 1805,
and one of the declared intentions of his 1806 expedition was the
settlement of the same Washita tract with which Livingston was concerned. Nevertheless, Livingston escaped arrest in General James
Wilkinson's anti-Burrite "reign of terror" in New Orleans in 1806-
1807. Condemning Wilkinson as a "petty little tyrant" and Claiborne,

who cooperated with Wilkinson, as a "wretched cowardly civil magistrate," Livingston successfully argued in court that the general had violated the constitutional rights of the two principal arrested "conspirators."

Livingston's first four years in New Orleans were thus personally rewarding if somewhat unnerving politically. In 1805 he found a second bride in the widowed Louise Moreau de Lassy, a refugee from the revolution in French Santo Domingo and the sister of the future Jacksonian diplomat, Auguste D'Avezac. Livingston believed that he had finally secured the means to wipe out his outstanding debt to the federal government in 1807, when he gained an interest in an alluvial tract of land between the Mississippi River and the Faubourg Ste. Marie. Unfortunately for him, the land, known as the Batture, was also claimed by the corporation of New Orleans, which was completely unreconciled to a recent territorial superior court decision against the city's alleged title. Livingston's acquisition of the Batture and his attempt to exploit its great commercial potential for his own gain became the occasion for violent public disturbances and exceedingly complex and protracted litigation.

The dispute permitted Claiborne and hostile journalists to depict Livingston as an insidious land-hungry mogul with scant respect for the well-being of New Orleans or the interests of its inhabitants. Because the territorial court decision upon which Livingston's claim to the Batture rested seemed to French-speaking Louisianians to interfere with the customary privileges of the corporation of New Orleans, it was widely regarded as an attack upon Creole legal practices by unsympathetic alien judges. The isolation of Livingston as a public enemy as a result of the dispute was especially ironic because he was the foremost American champion of the civil law in the territory. Shortly after his arrival, he had been commissioned to work on a civil code and a code of superior court practice, and he authored the territorial practice act of 1805.

President Thomas Jefferson transformed Livingston's new problem from a petty local squabble into a national issue in November 1807 when he precipitously ordered the seizure of the property by the New Orleans marshal. Jefferson acted at the behest of Claiborne and of the corporation, which had decided that the best defense of the public right to the Batture could be obtained by turning over the city's claim to the federal government. The order had the desirable political consequence of placing the administration and the territorial government on the popular side of the dispute, and it also accorded with the slight information on the matter available to Jefferson at the time. Livingston, however, was convinced that he had been deprived of his rightful property by an unconstitutional executive order.

In May 1808 Livingston arrived in Washington to plead his interest only to discover an implacably hostile administration. Already fearful that the legal aspects of the Batture case might not be as clear-cut as he had originally thought, Jefferson advised secretary of the treasury Albert Gallatin: "if you can possibly have him [Livingston] arrested here for his public debt, the opportunity ought not to be lost." Although Livingston was not arrested, neither did he secure any relief from the administration or from the Congress, to which the matter was eventually referred. His *Address to the People of the United States* (1808) on the subject of the Batture was directed against Jefferson and was answered in 1812 by the latter's defense of *The Proceedings of the Government of the United States*. By the time of the publication of Jefferson's treatise, the controversy had reached a new stage with Livingston's 1810 suit against the former president for damages of $100,-000. This case was dismissed for technical reasons by the federal circuit court in Virginia. A decision of 1813 by the United States court of the Orleans district in favor of Livingston's Batture title and an agreement ironed out with the corporation in 1820 enabled Livingston to realize his initial intention of using the Batture to pay his still outstanding debt to the federal government. In 1830 Livingston's account with the Treasury Department was finally closed after further litigation, negotiation, and the public receipt of over $100,000 from the enforced sale of Batture lots.

In the meantime, Livingston's renewal of his friendship with Andrew Jackson, which had begun with their service together in Congress, contributed to his political comeback. The future president relied on Livingston as his civilian spokesman in New Orleans in 1814-1815, and Livingston aroused popular enthusiasm for Jackson's army as chairman of a committee of public defense and as a voluntary aide-de-camp to the general. The services of the brothers Lafitte and their rude followers were also secured by Livingston, who had previously been retained by the privateers for their defense against federal smuggling charges. His popularity somewhat improved as a consequence of his role in the defense of the city, Livingston attempted to revive his political career after the war. Previously defeated for the Louisiana constitutional convention in 1811 and for the Senate and the House of Representatives in 1812, he ran unsuccessfully for the state assembly in 1816 and again for Congress in 1818 and 1820. Finally, in 1820 he was elected to the assembly. In 1821 he was appointed to prepare a criminal code for the state, and the following year he was appointed to a commission to revise the state's civil code.

Livingston's work on the Louisiana codes is the basis of his enduring reputation as a legal philosopher and social reformer. His revised civil code and code of practice were promulgated by the state, but his influential penal codes were never accepted by the assembly. The formative assumption of Livingston's penology was that "crime is the effect principally of intemperance, idleness, ignorance, vicious associations, irreligion and poverty—not of any defective natural organization." Influenced by the writings of Beccaria, Diderot, Montesquieu, Voltaire, and Bentham, Livingston was an advocate of the social responsibility of the state for the relief of paupers and vagrants and for the rehabilitation of criminal offenders. His system of penal laws was designed to make punishment proportionate to specific offenses, to reform the criminal in order to reduce crime, and to clarify the criminal law through the simplification of its language. His proposal for an interlocking system of public workshops, a house of detention, a penitentiary, and a reform school was the most original feature of the system and was also an elaboration of the program he had advanced as mayor of New York City. Also noteworthy were Livingston's restrictions on the judicial interpretation of penal law and his unqualified opposition to capital punishment. His persistent writings and endeavors as an opponent of the gallows made him the most respected figure in the antebellum campaign against public executions. Inspired by the hope of providing the republic with a model of democratic criminology, Livingston's system of penal law was widely hailed by reformers on both sides of the Atlantic. But it was too advanced for most American legislators. Livingston's achievement was recognized by his election in 1825 to the American Philosophical Society and by his selection as the first American associate of the French Academy of Moral and Political Sciences.

In 1822 Livingston returned to national politics as a representative from Louisiana, and he remained in the House until his defeat in the election of 1828. A second generation of Republican leaders already wrestling with the complicated questions of sectionalism, slavery, and economic development welcomed him to their ranks. Both Livingston's friendship with Jackson, the hero of New Orleans, and his own public philosophy made him a Jacksonian spokesman. As one of only two congressmen serving in the House on both occasions when that body has been called upon to elect the nation's chief executive, Livingston voted for Jackson in 1824. He made extensive efforts on behalf of his friend's successful presidential candidacy four years later. On the

floor of the House, he supported internal improvements; he opposed
the tariff measures of 1824, 1827, and 1828; and he proposed a constitutional amendment for the direct election of the president. As a
champion of the rights of revolutionary war veterans, he was made an
honorary member of the Society of the Cincinnati in 1827.

After his unsuccessful bid for reelection in 1828, Livingston was
sent to the Senate by a Jacksonian-dominated state assembly in January 1829. The newly elected president immediately offered him the
ambassadorship to France, which Livingston desired but was unable
to accept because of the condition of his private affairs. He continued
in the Senate as a staunch supporter of internal improvements, and he
voted to override the presidential vetoes of such projects as the Maysville Road and the Washington Turnpike. He unsuccessfully urged
the adoption of his system of criminal law by the United States. Opposed to the states' rights philosophy of John C. Calhoun and of the
South Carolina nullification movement, Livingston was a speaker for
the administration in the 1830 Senate discussion on the nature of the
federal union. In the Webster-Hayne debate, he adopted a position
somewhere between the extreme particularism of the South Carolinian
and the extreme nationalism of the New Englander. His understanding
of federalism was incorporated into the Nullification Proclamation of
1832, which Livingston drafted for Jackson after his appointment as
secretary of state.

Livingston's removal from the Senate to the Cabinet in May 1831
was welcomed by Nicholas Biddle and the friends of the Second Bank
of the United States, the renewal of whose charter the new secretary
supported with reservations. As the head of the Jackson cabinet, Livingston became a target of the Antimasonic party in 1832 because of
his position as the General Grand High Priest of the General Royal
Arch Chapter of the United States, the highest Masonic office in the
country. As secretary his attention was directed to the northeast boundary question, the negotiation of commercial treaties with Russia and
Latin American states, and the settlement of spoliation claims against
France, Portugal, and the Kingdom of the Two Sicilies.

In 1833 Livingston left the Cabinet in order to realize a cherished
ambition of becoming minister to France, a position filled by his
brother, "the Chancellor," some three decades earlier. As ambassador
to the court of Louis-Philippe, his primary instruction from Jackson
was to secure compliance with the Franco-American convention of
1831, which required French payment of the outstanding claims of
American citizens. In spite of Livingston's solicitations, the French
Chamber of Deputies in April 1834 repeated its previous refusal to ap-

propriate the necessary funds. The minister counseled Jackson to adopt a "forceful attitude" after this setback, but he was stunned by the president's angry call for reprisals upon French property in the annual message of December 1834, which prompted the French government to recall its ambassador to the United States and to offer Livingston his passport. Livingston nevertheless remained at his post to continue lobbying for the appropriation, and his efforts were rewarded by the chamber's approval of the funds in April 1835. He then returned to the United States, leaving affairs in the hands of the secretary of the legation, his son-in-law, Thomas P. Barton. Although his conduct was approved at home, Livingston, who was then seventy-one, resigned shortly after his return.

At the finish of a public career that had spanned five decades and had twice thrust him into the foreground of American politics, Livingston retired to Montgomery Place, near Red Hook, New York. His Hudson River seat had once been the home of his eldest sister, and when it passed to Livingston in 1828, he had resumed residence in his native state. He visited Washington in January 1836 to argue a case with Webster before the supreme court and to offer Jackson his assistance in renewed negotiations with France. He spent most of the winter in New York before returning to Montgomery Place, where he died, on May 23, 1836, "of bilious cholic by reason of drinking Cold Water when heated the day but one before."

SOURCES: W. B. Hatcher, *Edward Livingston, Jeffersonian Republican and Jacksonian Democrat* (1940); C. H. Hunt, *Life of Edward Livingston* (1864); *DAB*; G. Dangerfield, *Chancellor Robert R. Livingston* (1960), esp. 114, 278-80, 301-303; *N.J. Gazette*, 3 Oct 1781 (commencement); P. M. Hamlin, *Legal Education in Colonial N.Y.* (1939), 215; *Mil. Min., Council of Appointment, St. of N.Y.*, I (1901), 109, 153, 185; *NYHS Coll.*, LXIII, xvi; J. A. Scoville, *Old Merchants of N.Y. City*, III (1865), 225; *First Census, N.Y.*, 121; A. F. Young, *Democratic Republicans of N.Y.* (1967), 421 ("Beau Ned . . . poor man's friend"), 560 ("Aristocratical"), passim; A. Evers, *The Catskills* (1972), 241, 335; *N.Y. Hist.*, 24 (1943), 189; P. D. Evans, *Holland Land Co.* (1924), 178-79; D. S. Freeman, *George Washington*, VII (1957), 348-53; J. C. Miller, *Federalist Era* (1960), 172-73; J. M. Smith, *Freedom's Fetters* (1956), 85 ("refinement upon despotism") 114-15, 121-22; L. J. Cappon, ed., *The Adams-Jefferson Letters* (1959), II, 300 ("naughty lad"); *Hamilton Papers*, xxv, 304-305, 314-15; S. I. Pomerantz, *N.Y., An American City* (1938), 135-37, 208, 337; *MCCCNY*, III, passim; W.C.C. Claiborne, *Official Letter Books* (1917), II, 26; *Territorial Papers of the U.S.*, IX (1940), 242 ("Rights of Louisiana"), and passim; J. T. Hatfield, *William Claiborne* (1976), passim; *La. Hist. Quart.*, 26 (1937), 399, 400, 407; 24 (1941), 698-728; T. P. Abernathy, *The Burr Conspiracy* (1954), 25, 73-74, 93; G. Dargo, *Jefferson's La.* (1975), esp. 18, 31-32, 55-63, 61 ("petty . . . tyrant, cowardly . . . magistrate"), 74-101, 85 ("have him arrested here"); *La. Hist.*, 15 (1974), 243-72; 16 (1975), 145-66; 7 (1966), 241-51; *Complete Works of Edward Livingston on Criminal Jurisprudence* (1873), I, 562-63 ("crime is the effect"); *Journal of Criminal Law, Criminology, and Political Science*, 54 (1963), 288-95; *APS Proc.*, 27 (1889), 150; R. V. Remini, *Andrew Jackson and the Bank War* (1967), 67, 72; W.

Lewis, *Without Fear or Favor* (1965), 141-42; F. Rawle, "Edward Livingston," in S. F. Bemis, ed., *Amer. Secretaries of State and their Diplomacy*, IV (1928), 207f.; J. A. Munroe, *Louis McLane* (1973), 415-20; *MHM*, 51 (1956), 283-86; *NYHS Quart.*, 56 (1972), 223; J. S. Bassett, ed., *Correspondence of Andrew Jackson*, IV (1929), 385.

MANUSCRIPTS: DLC, DNA, KyU, LU, MdHi, MHi, Miss. Dept. Arch. and Hist., MiU, MoHi, N, NHi, NN, NjP, PHi, PPAmP, ViH

PUBLICATIONS: see *STE* and *The National Union Catalog; Pre-1956 Imprints*, 336 (1974), 590-94

                                                                          GSD

Robert Smith

ROBERT SMITH, A.B., A.M. 1785, lawyer and public official, was born in Carlisle, Cumberland County, Pennsylvania on November 3, 1757, one of the eleven children of Mary Buchanan and her husband, John Smith, an Irish immigrant and merchant. When he was two years of age, Smith's family moved to Baltimore, Maryland, where his father and uncle William Buchanan built the port's largest wharf. John Smith was a civic leader in Baltimore, serving as a trustee and elder of the First Presbyterian Church, and before and during the Revolution as a member of the city's nonimportation, armaments, observation, and correspondence committees. He was elected to the state senate in 1781, but his political prominence was matched by a decline in his financial fortunes, as the depreciation of currency rendered him almost bankrupt.

The date of Robert Smith's enrollment in the College is uncertain. In the fall of 1777 he absented himself from his studies long enough to fight, as a private soldier, in the battle of the Brandywine. But those early studies might have been followed either at the College, in which case he would have been a freshman, or at the academy at Newark, Delaware, where he may have been prepared. In July 1781 he joined the Cliosophic Society, then reviving from a wartime hiatus, and through his talents as a public speaker, he was chosen to deliver the valedictory address at commencement exercises that year. After participating in a dialogue on the "Origin and comparative merits of poetry and eloquence," he spoke on "the advantages which the United States of America enjoy above other Republicks which have arisen in the world, for framing a wise system of civil policy."

From Princeton, Smith returned to Baltimore to study law and then to join the bar in that city. His practice, primarily in admiralty law and including the training of law students, was soon one of Balti-

Robert Smith, A.B. 1781
BY FREEMAN THORPE

more's largest, and combined with his family connections, it provided him an avenue to politics. Smith's older brother Samuel, a distinguished revolutionary officer, was on his way to becoming the outstanding political personality in Baltimore and, as he would be for the next several decades, Smith was his brother's faithful ally. Both men were ardent supporters of the Constitution, and in 1788 Robert Smith was chosen one of Maryland's eight presidential electors. He would be the last surviving member of that first electoral college.

Although President Washington did not doubt Smith's "abilities and good character," he believed him to be too young and inexperienced for a seat on the federal bench, in spite of the entreaties of Smith's influential friends. Instead, Smith was named one of the justices of the Baltimore County Court of Oyer and Terminer on March 6, 1790. He resigned from that position barely five weeks later, however.

By the end of 1790 the Smith brothers were involved in a political struggle that would ultimately divide Maryland Federalists and help foster the state's Republican party. Baltimore and the counties abutting it, centers of commerce and industry, opposed the situation of the national capital on the Potomac River. Even such firm Federalists as the Smiths thus found themselves allied with their recent anti-Federalist rivals against the Compromise of 1790 and behind a so-called "Chesapeake ticket" of candidates who swept the local elections. Supporters of the compromise, notably the rural oligarchy of the south and west, backed a "Potomac ticket." They retained control of the assembly and promptly altered the election law to reduce the representation of the port city. The "Chesapeake" party disappeared, but its supporters had been alienated from the federal government and many of them, including the Smiths, gradually moved to the Republican camp.

That conversion was still in the future in 1790, however. Smith's Federalist connections, in fact, were strengthened when on December 7 he married a distant cousin Margaret Smith, the daughter of Federalist congressman William Smith of Baltimore. One year after Smith failed in a bid for the Maryland General Court in August 1791, Washington very nearly appointed him as the federal district attorney for Maryland. The commission was sent to Smith in care of James McHenry. But the appearance of a more qualified candidate at the last minute led Washington to change his mind, and the commission was not delivered. That the president had even considered Smith was undoubtedly due in part to General Samuel Smith's candidacy for Congress in 1792 and to the general's well-known interest in furthering the careers of his relatives.

While his brother moved on the national scene, Robert Smith increased his own standing in local politics. He served on Baltimore's committee for the relief of refugees from Hispañola in the summer of 1793, shortly after he had been appointed to an unexpired term in the state senate. In August he wrote a stinging criticism of the French minister to the United States, Edmond Charles Genêt, which was printed in the Baltimore newspapers although Smith disclaimed any intention to publish it. As a member of the House of Delegates in 1796, he sponsored a resolution condemning Genêt's successor, Pierre Auguste Adet, reflecting a consistent opposition to revolutionary France that was not entirely synchronized with the opposition to Jay's Treaty that finally led his brother into Republicanism. In fact, as late as 1797, Robert Smith was a leader of the opposition to such Republican-backed measures as widening the franchise in Maryland. He played a major role in the passage of a new city charter for Baltimore that

year, the terms of which greatly enhanced the influence of the Federalist commercial oligarchy.

Smith's own conversion to Republicanism was accomplished by the
election of 1800. The political influence of Samuel Smith was such
that President Jefferson felt compelled to include the Maryland congressman in his Cabinet. Accordingly, he offered him the portfolio of
the Navy Department, an appointment that was politely refused. After
four more failures to fill the position, Jefferson prevailed on General
Smith to serve unofficially as secretary of the navy, without salary or
commission, until July, when Jefferson turned to the general's brother.
The president was not seeking an expert in the "reading of Coke-Little-
ton," he told Robert Smith, but he wanted a man who was "so familiar
with naval things, that he would be perfectly competent to select
proper agents and to judge their conduct." Urged on by his brother,
who wanted to protect the navy from the budget-paring tendencies of
treasury secretary Albert Gallatin, Smith left the Maryland Assembly
and his thriving law practice to accept the Cabinet post, much to the
relief of anxious Jeffersonians.

The appointment was no plum in 1801. The navy was an expensive
service, long associated with a powerful central government and more
recently with the Quasi-War against France, and as such was an obvious target for economy-minded, domestically oriented Republicans
of whom Gallatin was the best representative. With Jefferson's initial
support, the treasury secretary set out to reduce naval expenditures and
trim the numbers of ships and men. With a staff of only three clerks,
Smith undertook the day-to-day direction of naval affairs while at the
same time conducting a delicate defense of the service against Gallatin's budget-cutting. The tension between his program and Gallatin's
was unavoidable, but their personal relationship was amicable for most
of Jefferson's presidency. Gallatin was convinced of Smith's inefficiency
and incompetence, however, as naval costs continued to rise.

Smith, for his part, was determined to build up the navy, especially
after hostilities between the United States and Tripoli began in 1802.
He fought an uphill battle against the president's preference for small
budgets, until in 1804, after the capture of the frigate *Philadelphia*,
Jefferson agreed to send a squadron against Tripoli that would, in
Smith's words, "be able, beyond the possibility of a doubt, to coerce the
enemy to a peace on terms compatible with our honor and our interest."
And in spite of Gallatin's complaints to the contrary, Smith did his
best to keep costs to a minimum. Throughout his tenure as secretary of
the navy, Smith had the respect and loyalty of the naval officers, among

whom he was known as a firm disciplinarian who stood squarely for the best interests of the service. The political obstacles notwithstanding, he managed to direct the maintenance of an effective blockade more than 3,000 miles away and to see to the career advancement of some of the country's most honored naval heroes. How much of his good reputation among the officers was due to his substitution of native whiskey for rum in the daily ration is not clear.

Smith was also known as the best host in the Cabinet, and the social events at his home were always well attended. One of the most sensational occurred in January 1804, when Smith's niece Betsy Patterson of Baltimore married Jerome Bonaparte, the youngest brother of Napoleon. The Smiths, and perhaps even Jefferson, hoped that the marriage might improve relations with France, but the bride appeared at the reception in a gown that revealed too much of herself to permit any of the guests to concentrate on matters of state. One aspect of Smith's social life was the deepening feud between his wife and Hannah Gallatin, the treasury secretary's wife, an animosity that grew as their husbands became more and more antagonistic.

Smith sought some relief from the pressures of his position in January 1805, when he offered himself to Jefferson as a possible replacement for Levi Lincoln, the recently resigned Attorney General. "I have," he told the president, "no attachment to the duties of the office I have nor the honor of holding and . . . a law-appointment would be more pleasing to me. My education and the habits of my life have given me a strong passion and a high taste for law-disquisition. And I have not yet been able to acquire a taste for the details of the Navy Department." Even if the salary were lower, Smith said, he would be happy for the change. Jefferson was at first reluctant to comply, since he felt that a new Attorney General would be easier to find than a new navy secretary, but on March 2 he nominated Smith as Lincoln's replacement and Jacob Crowninshield as Smith's. The Senate quickly approved both nominations.

Crowninshield, who never really liked the arrangement, found good reasons to stay in Massachusetts while he appealed to the president to withdraw his appointment. Meanwhile, Smith undertook the duties of both offices. The attendant increase in his correspondence may explain his infatuation with the "polygraph," a multiple writing device to which Jefferson introduced him in May. By August the president had to accept Crowninshield's withdrawal. He then offered the post of Attorney General, "not yet permanently filled," to Senator John Breckinridge, whom Smith himself had recommended for the office in January. The senator from Kentucky, father of Joseph C. Breckinridge (A.B.

1810), was a longtime associate of the Smith brothers in land speculation in Kentucky and Georgia, enterprises through which Smith also
established a friendship with Henry Clay. In December Breckinridge
was confirmed as Attorney General, and Smith, without a new commission, simply returned to his role as secretary of the navy. His interest in the law did not wane, but he declined a nomination in early
1806 to be chancellor and chief judge of the district court in Maryland,
apparently pacified by Jefferson's occasional requests for his legal opinion. In December 1806, as the president was preparing the government's case against Aaron Burr (A.B. 1772), Smith urged him to request a suspension of the writ of *habeas corpus*—a request which
Jefferson made and Congress promptly refused.

Smith was never comfortable with the Non-Importation Act of 1807,
aimed at Great Britain. He and Gallatin agreed, for once, that the law
was a "mischief-making busybody." Nevertheless, Smith saw to it that
the navy's role in the embargo was scrupulously observed. Samuel
Smith, disappointed at not being chosen to negotiate with the English
himself, meanwhile feared that the administration was too pro-British.
He wanted the embargo tightened, confident that it would succeed in
forcing a change in London's policy. Now in the Senate, General Smith
regarded Gallatin's position as soft, and as the differences between
Gallatin and Robert Smith continued, the treasury secretary became
the symbol of the schism within the Republican party that opened with
the election of James Madison (A.B. 1771) as president in 1808.

In the Senate Samuel Smith was allied for a time with former classmate William Branch Giles (A.B. 1781) as the leader of an antiadmin-
istration cabal labeled the "Invisibles" by Congressman Nathaniel
Macon (Class of 1778) and the "Malcontents" by other administration
supporters. The first occasion for internecine warfare came in 1809
when Madison decided to appoint Gallatin as secretary of state. To pac-
ify the Smith faction, he offered to move Robert Smith to the Treasury
Department, but Gallatin would not tolerate that arrangement. Giles
probably hoped for the State Department appointment himself, and
so joined Smith against Gallatin. But when Madison, realizing that the
Senate might block any nomination of Gallatin for another post,
agreed to let the treasury secretary remain where he was and name
Robert Smith to the State Department, Giles also split from the Smiths.

Gallatin had reasoned that if he were named to State and Smith to
Treasury, he would have to do both jobs. With Smith at the State Department, however, Madison would be able to oversee the department,
acting as his own secretary of state. It was on that assumption, and only
to keep the Smith faction in line, that Madison nominated the navy

secretary to the State Department. But Gallatin never forgave his Cabinet rival. Their social intercourse ended, and Gallatin went out of his way to snub Smith. One rebuff left Smith so angry that he vowed that had it not been for appearances he would have "shot [Gallatin] the next morning."

Smith's appointment was received derisively by several factions of the Republican party and by most Federalists. Almost at once, however, the secretary of state concluded an agreement with the British minister, David Erskine, that seemed to be a major diplomatic coup. It contemplated an end to British restrictions on American commerce and reparations for the *Chesapeake* affair of 1807 in exchange for the lifting of American bans on British ships. The politically troubled administration was suddenly the object of almost unanimous praise. Unfortunately, Erskine had exceeded his instructions and was recalled, and the agreement was nullified by London on the excuse that Smith's last memorandum had included a paragraph insulting to the king. There were much more important reasons for the revocation of the Smith-Erskine accord, but Smith made sure that the "Invisibles" knew that it had been Madison himself who wrote the offensive paragraph. Erskine's successor proved much less interested in negotiating a settlement of the differences between the two nations and the president turned toward finding some accommodation with France.

Smith doubted the wisdom of that policy. In particular, he opposed the passage of the two bills named for Nathaniel Macon, the second of which lifted restrictions against both European belligerents and promised to renew them against whichever power was the last to remove its impediments on American commerce. Reports of confidential Cabinet conversations leaked out to the "Invisibles," and Madison and Gallatin assumed that Smith was the source. In the spring of 1810 Napoleon took advantage of what he saw as the desperation of the United States by promising in the vaguest possible terms to rescind the French restrictions. Smith instructed the American minister in Paris, John Armstrong (Class of 1776), to insist on firm commitments from France, but Armstrong's interest was in resigning his post as quickly as possible. He did not trust the emperor's word, but to speed his own departure he assured Madison that France had met the requirements of Macon's Bill No. 2. The president decided, therefore, to reimpose restrictions on trade with England in November.

Smith opposed the precipitateness of the decision. He did not understand, or refused to appreciate, Madison's gamble. The president believed that British policy was both more dangerous and more provocative than French and was trying to escape from the dilemma of being at odds with both European powers simultaneously. Smith, however, wanted specific promises from Paris, and when Madison refused him permission to pursue a tough line with the French minister, the secretary of state grumbled noisily to almost anyone who wanted to listen. Beset by rivals within his own party, Madison concluded that Smith was trying to sabotage the administration and possibly to cement a coalition with Armstrong that would capture the presidency in 1812.

Madison's suspicions seemed vindicated when Samuel Smith led the successful Senate opposition to rechartering the Bank of the United States. Gallatin, who had tried to discredit both Smiths in 1809 by supporting trumped-up charges of collusion between the Navy Department and Samuel Smith's commercial interests during the Barbary War, now determined to force a confrontation. In an atmosphere poisoned by rumor and newspaper attacks by one side against the other, Gallatin told Madison that he could not continue to serve in so divided a government. Unwilling to lose an able and loyal subordinate, convinced of Robert Smith's disloyalty, and eager to effect a rapprochement with James Monroe, Madison rejected Gallatin's resignation and decided to remove Smith from the Cabinet instead.

In late March 1811, Madison confronted Smith in the White House with a list of charges of ineptitude and dishonesty, ranging from poorly written diplomatic instructions to divulging Cabinet secrets. Smith denied everything, but the president insisted that he resign. To protect his reputation, Smith was offered the American mission in St. Petersburg. When he stated his preference for London or the Supreme Court, he was told that both posts required talents superior to his. At the end of the meeting, Smith agreed to go to Russia.

Madison advertised the break by nominating Joel Barlow to succeed Armstrong in Paris—a post openly coveted by Samuel Smith. The senator and his allies soon convinced Robert Smith that he had been betrayed by Madison and Gallatin, and the outgoing secretary of state thereupon changed his mind about exile in St. Petersburg. He refused to attend social gatherings at the White House, including a dinner for the Russian legation, and when he returned to see the president on April 1, 1811, he both resigned his Cabinet post and declined the diplomatic one. A few days earlier he had told a sympathetic friend that "the course I have taken, I am confident, will lead to the injury of Mr. Madison and to my advantage . . . His overthrow is my object, and most assuredly I will effect it."

Smith was too sanguine. Madison took advantage of the adjournment of Congress to give Monroe an interim appointment as secretary of state, thereby reuniting the most powerful party factions and reviv-

ing the specter of a "Virginia Dynasty," to which Samuel Smith, especially, was firmly opposed. To save his own name and discredit the
president, Robert Smith wrote a bitter *Address to the People of the
United States*, which appeared in pamphlet form in late spring. Madison employed Barlow to reply in the administration's organ, the *National Intelligencer*, but the response did less damage to Smith than
his own polemic had done. In a time of national crisis, Smith's charges
against the administration, whatever their basis, were generally received as divisive and disloyal. Like most people, Jefferson believed
that they would hurt Smith more than anyone else. Madison prepared
a detailed account of the events leading to Smith's resignation, but he
never had to use it.

No evaluation of Smith's brief tenure as secretary of state can be
made apart from the political currents of the time. The Erskine agreement was a breakthrough in Anglo-American relations, but one in
which the British government was not truly interested. Smith's distrust
of Napoleon was entirely justified, of course. And he cooperated fully
in Madison's secret efforts to turn the European war into an opportunity to extend American sovereignty over disputed land in the
Floridas. That Madison was his own secretary of state is beyond question, for he had always expected and intended to be. Much more significant to the assessment of Smith's performance is the question of his
communication of secret information to the administration's enemies
and to foreign diplomats. Appointed to Madison's Cabinet only because of his connection with the powerful senator from Maryland, he
undoubtedly served his brother's interests before he served those of the
Virginia Dynasty. More for reasons of politics than for reasons of state,
Madison had to remove him. And as Samuel Smith acknowledged in
May, it was he, and not his brother, against whom Madison had acted.
Once war with England began and the party united behind the administration, Madison had won. Robert Smith's political career had
never been more than an adjunct to that of his brother. His service in
the Navy Department was therefore surprisingly commendable. His
troubles at the State Department should have been no surprise at all.

His public life ended, Smith returned to Baltimore to practice law
and attend to commercial affairs involving roads, ferries, and iron
works. His substantial landholdings in the south and west provided
some income, as did a farm, which he apparently managed from his
urban residence on Mt. Vernon Place where his household retained its
tradition of lavish party-giving. In April 1813 he accepted the non-
salaried office of provost of the new University of Maryland. But he unfortunately regarded the position as purely honorary and failed to pro-

vide the vigorous leadership needed by the institution. He attended only two faculty meetings—in April 1813, to accept the post, and in May 1815, to resign it. He continued, however, to teach law in the university.

Also in 1813 Smith became president of an auxiliary of the American Bible Society. His church-related activities generally increased, and from 1822 to 1828 he was a trustee of Baltimore's First Presbyterian Church. When the Baltimore Agricultural Society was established in 1818, Smith assumed its presidency. Two years later he was elected to the Royal Italian Agricultural Society as well.

Smith and his wife had eight children, seven of whom died young. The survivor, Samuel W. Smith, entered the College in the Class of 1820 and joined the Cliosophic Society before he was withdrawn "at the request of his father" in March 1819, during a time of chaotic troubles for Nassau Hall. Smith's will was made on June 10, 1825, leaving his large landholdings to his son and his property in Baltimore to his wife. His wife died, however, on November 25, 1842, less than one day before he did.

SOURCES: *DAB*; J. S. Pancake, *Samuel Smith and the Politics of Business* (1972); F. A. Cassell, *Merchant Congressman in the Young Republic* (1971); J. T. Scharf, *Hist. of Md.* (1967), II; Scharf, *Chronicles of Balto.* (1874); W. Reynolds, *Brief Hist. of the First Pres. Chh. of Balto.* (1913), 120, 122; P. A. Crowl, *Md. During and After the Rev.* (1943), 37; H. S. Randall, *Life of Thomas Jefferson*, II (1858), 640-41 & n; C. R. Williams, *Clio. Soc.* (1916), 21; *N.J. Gazette*, 3 Oct 1781 (commencement), and 10 Oct 1785 (A.M.); *PMHB*, 45 (1921), 49; 28 (1904), 299; *Doc. Hist. Fed. Elec.*, 247-49; L. M. Renzulli, Jr., *Md., the Federalist Years* (1972), 109, 147-48 & nn, 151-54, 154-56 & nn; *Md. Arch.*, LXXI, 320; LXXII, 89, 96, 218; *Washington Writings*, XXX, 461, 471 ("abilities and good character"); XXXII, 111, 158; *MHM*, 7 (1912), 304; 66 (1971), 162, 164; 14 (1919), 305-22; B. C. Steiner, *Life and Correspondence of James McHenry* (1907), 133-35, 206, 498-99; *Hamilton Papers*, XII, 213; XV, 301 & n; Jefferson MSS, 1801-1808, esp. als T. Jefferson to RS, 9 Jul 1801 ("familiar with naval things"), and 3 Jan 1805, T. Jefferson to J. Breckinridge, 7 Aug 1805 ("not yet permanently filled"), T. Jefferson to U.S. Senate, 2 Mar 1805, and RS to T. Jefferson, 2 Jan 1805, H. Dearborn to T. Jefferson, 2 Jan 1805, J. Crowninshield to T. Jefferson, 11 Jan, 24 Jan, 20 Feb, 27 Mar 1805; G. Hunt, ed., *Writings of James Madison*, VI (1906), 426n; VIII (1908), 137-49; C. W. Goldsborough, *U.S. Naval Chronicle* (1824), 213-14, 245 ("a peace compatible with our honor"); I. Anthony, *Decatur* (1931), 103; F. R. Rodd, *Gen. William Eaton* (1932), 100-101; C. McKee, *Edward Preble* (1972), passim; D. F. Long, *Nothing Too Daring* (1970), 40, 42; C. O. Paullin, *Commodore John Rogers* (1910); L. D. White, *The Jeffersonians* (1951), 142, 270, 468; D. Malone, *Jefferson the President, First Term* (1970), 59, 99, 263n, 315; S. Edwards, *Barbary General* (1968), 126-28; R. Walters, Jr., *Albert Gallatin* (1957), 147-53, 186, 194, 200 ("mischief making busybody"), 213, 232, 241; M. Smelser, *Democratic Republic* (1968), 46-47, 55, 105, 119, 153, 155, 188, 199; R. Ketcham, *James Madison* (1971), 431-32, 482-87; L. H. Harrison, *John Breckinridge* (1969), 126-27, 187, 189; *Clay Papers*, I, 194-95, 487, 547, 563; U.S. Senate, *Journal of Exec. Proc.*, I (1828), 486; C. M. Wiltse, ed., *Papers of Daniel Webster*, I (1974), 77; N. K. Risjord, *The Old Republicans* (1965), 116; *WMQ* (3 ser.), 33 (1976), 562 ("shot him the next morning"), 562-85; C. C. Tansill, "Robert Smith," in S. F. Bemis, ed., *Amer. Secre-*

taries of State and their Diplomacy, III (1927), 151-97, 195 ("the course I have taken); A. Lowndes, ed., *Arch. of the Prot. Episc. Chh. . . . Gen. Convention*, VI (1912), 205; A. A. Lipscomb, ed.; *Writings of Thomas Jefferson* (1903), XII, 276, 286-87; XIII, 46-47, 55; C. C. Mooney, *William H. Crawford* (1974), 43-44; I. Brant, *James Madison, Secretary of State* (1953), 473; Brant, *James Madison, the President* (1956); Butterfield, ed., *Rush Letters*, II, 1,132; C. F. Adams, ed., *Works of John Adams*, X (1856), 4-9; A. J. Beveridge, *Life of John Marshall*, IV (1919), 34-38; *Cat. MdHi Manuscripts*, 267; G. H. Callcott, *Hist. of Univ. of Md.* (1966), 31, 34; D. M. Dozer, *Portrait of the Free State* (1976), 304; Md. Wills, book 19, 37.

MANUSCRIPTS: DLC, MdHi, PHi, MiU-C, PHC, DS, DN, Marine Hist. Assoc. in Mystic, Conn., Franklin D. Roosevelt Libr., Hyde Park, N.Y.

PUBLICATIONS: see text

CLASS OF 1782

Spencer Ball, A.B.

Lucas Conrad Elmendorf, A.B.

Peter Edmund Elmendorf, A.B.

John Andre Hanna, A.B.

John Johnston, A.B.

William Kennedy

William Mahon, A.B.

John Morton, A.B.

Robert Pearson, A.B.

Richard (Dirck) Ten Eyck, A.B.

Stephen Van Rensselaer

Richard N. Venable, A.B.

Samuel Wilson, A.B.

Spencer Ball

SPENCER BALL, A.B., planter, was born August 6, 1762, at the family home of "Coan" in Northumberland County, Virginia, the oldest son of Captain Spencer Mottrom Ball and his wife, Elizabeth Waring Ball. The family connections included George Washington's mother, Mary Ball. In the year Ball graduated from the College, his father owned eighty-three slaves. Two years later tax records indicate that he owned two dwellings, one apparently at Northampton Court House, and twenty-four other buildings. His will, proved early in January 1787, provided for the education of a second son through three years at Glasgow, Scotland. Captain Ball had served a number of years in the Virginia House of Burgesses, as had his father before him, and had been a vestryman of St. Stephen's Parish, sheriff of his county, and a signatory of the Virginia Non-Importation Resolution of 1770.

Where and by whom young Ball was prepared for college have not been discovered, nor can it be said how early he may have been enrolled in the College of New Jersey. A manuscript list of members of the Cliosophic Society gives 1781 as the year of his admission to that organization, but that was the year in which the society was revived from the moribund state into which it had fallen during the war years, so the date provides no real clue to the time of Ball's first arrival in Princeton. The only firm evidence of his attendance at the College, aside from this membership and his graduation, is the newspaper report of the commencement exercises on September 25, 1782, which credits him with participation in a forensic dispute on the question of whether "the idea of the beautiful, in the fine arts," had "any real standard in nature." On that question Ball took the affirmative position.

Ball's career after graduation seems to have been the relatively uneventful and pleasant life of a Virginia planter. His father's will assigned to him half of the home seat, and a full one-eighth share of the slaves and stock belonging to the estate. It also provided that the estate should remain intact for a period of some four years for the education and maintenance of the younger children. Perhaps Ball for a time after graduation was principally engaged in assisting his father in the management of the family's property, which included a mill and enough land away from the home seat to take care of two more sons. In 1788, apparently late in March, Ball made a very fortunate marriage to Betty Landon Carter, the fourth surviving daughter of Robert Carter of Nomini Hall. She had been taught by Philip Vickers Fithian (A.B. 1772) while he served as tutor in the Carter family and was a younger sister of Anne Tasker Carter who had married John Peck (A.B. 1774), Fithian's successor as the family's tutor. Fithian described her in the year she reached the age of nine as "quiet and obedient." Whether she retained these virtues indefinitely is not known, but she probably brought to the marriage the usual dowry for Carter's daughters—500 acres, ten slaves, and a substantial allotment of livestock, the whole having a value of about £1,000. She also seems to have had a claim of comparable value upon the estate of her grandmother Anne Tasker, of the Maryland family.

By inheritance and marriage Ball had significant holdings in both Northumberland and Prince William counties. Perhaps he alternated between two residences, for he is found as a justice of the peace in Prince William as early as 1793 and in Northumberland in 1801. The census of 1820 locates his residence in Prince William, and there on February 28, 1832, he died in a brick-gabled mansion that served in July 1861 as a hospital during the Battle of Bull Run and that was totally destroyed a little more than a year later in the Second Battle of Manassas. To his marriage to Betsy, as Fithian knew her, there were born seven children, three sons and four daughters. His wife lived until 1842.

SOURCES: H. E. Hayden, *Va. Geneal.* (1931), 116-17, 135; J. F. Lewis and J. M. Booker, *Northumberland Cnty. . . . Wills* (1964), I, 129-31; II, 116-17, 119; *First Census, Va.*, 38, 75; *VMHB*, 5 (1897-1898), 191; W. G. Stanard and M. N. Stanard, *Col. Va. Reg.* (1902), 181, 184, 186, 188, 191, 194; *Jefferson Papers*, I, 46; W. Meade, *Old Churches, Ministers, and Families of Va.*, II (1900), 468; MS Clio. Soc. membership list, PUA; *N.J. Gazette*, 9 Oct 1782 (commencement); *WMQ* (1 ser.), 15 (1906-1907), 188; *Fithian Journal*, I, 50, 71n, 85 ("quiet and obedient"); L. Morton, *Robert Carter of Nomini Hall* (1941), 220, 228, 229 & n; J. R. Felldin, *Index to 1820 Census of Va.* (1976), 20; Federal Writers Project, *Prince William* (1941), 125-26.

WFC

Lucas Conrad Elmendorf

LUCAS CONRAD ELMENDORF, A.B., lawyer and public official, appears to have been known while resident in the College by his middle name, Conrad. He was so identified in the minutes of the trustees recording the award of his degree in September 1782, in newspaper reports of that year's commencement, and thereafter in the published catalogues of the College, in these with the usual Latin form, "Conradus." His first cousin and classmate Peter Edmund Elmendorf, when writing from Princeton to a member of the family, might refer to him as Lucas, however, as do most references that have been found to his later public career. Fortunately, even though the family was large and much given to the repetitive use of such names as Lucas and Conrad, it has been possible to identify Conrad, the College alumnus, as one and the same with congressman Lucas Elmendorf.

Elmendorf was baptized on March 8, 1761, at Kingston, Ulster County, New York, the son of Jonathan Elmendorf and his wife, Helena Smeedes Elmendorf. The family was of Dutch extraction and long identified with the Dutch Reformed Church of Kingston. Jonathan Elmendorf served as a trustee of the town, signed the association for the boycott of British goods on July 1, 1775, and was commissioned a major in the county militia on October 25, 1775. In time he rose to the rank of lieutenant colonel.

Lucas probably began his training for college in the "English academy" established by the town of Kingston in 1774. The required mastery of the classical languages may have come through tutoring by some pastor of his family's faith. That he may have felt pressure for attendance at Queen's College (Rutgers) in New Brunswick, which was sponsored by the Dutch Reformed Church, is suggested by his confession in a letter of July 2, 1781 from Nassau Hall to Peter Elmendorf's mother that he was "prejudiced in favour of this colledge which in my humble opinion is preferable to Brunswick." There is evidence that Peter may have been first enrolled in the fall of 1780 or the winter of 1781, and this may also have been true of Lucas, but there was no exact parallel in their college careers. Peter became a member of the Cliosophic Society, and Ashbel Green (A.B. 1783) was later to recall that Conrad was one of those associated with him in reestablishing the American Whig Society in the summer of 1782. At commencement on September 25, 1782, "Mr. C. Elmendorf" took the affirmative in a three-way dispute of the question of whether "all the differences in shape and complexion among mankind be accounted for from natural causes, on the supposition of the whole race having descended from one original pair?" One suspects that Professor Samuel Stanhope Smith (A.B. 1769) had a hand in the preparations for this debate, for it was a question he would discuss a few years later before the American Philosophical Society at Philadelphia.

After graduation Lucas must have promptly begun studying law, though where and with whom have not been determined, for he was admitted to the bar in 1785, and in 1789 his name appeared on a list of attorneys of the supreme court of the state of New York. He may have had his residence at first in the town of Hurley, which adjoined Kingston on the west, and if he was the Lucas Elmendorf of that place at the time of the census of 1790, as seems likely, he began his career with a substantial stake. The household showed one male over sixteen, one free white female, and nine slaves. He is usually described as of Kingston, and the house he occupied there through many years apparently was built by him not long after 1790. Local historians mention him among the more prominent attorneys of the county, and at times he is described as Judge Elmendorf, a title derived from his service from 1815 to 1821 as head of the county court.

How early Lucas became active politically has not been discovered, but he became so astute a political leader that Martin Van Buren is said later to have claimed him as a preceptor. His political leanings were toward the Democratic-Republicans in their opposition to the Federalists. He first became a candidate for Congress in 1794, and was defeated, but two years later he was elected to the Fifth Congress and took his seat in 1797. After two reelections, he declined to run in 1802 and retired from Congress in 1803, having served a total of six years. In Congress he seems to have achieved no special prominence, to have attended regularly, and to have spoken infrequently, and then only briefly. On the critically important legislation enacted by the Congress during the spring and summer of 1798, he voted consistently with the Republicans. Although for some reason he seems not to have voted on the Act Respecting Alien Enemies or the Sedition Act, he opposed the establishment of a Navy Department and the bill authorizing the president to create a provisional army. Earlier he had voted against a bill for strengthening the defenses of ports and harbors, although he insisted that New York should have a fair share of the benefits of the measure. In the dangerous deadlock that followed the election of 1800, he was one of the six New York delegates who gave the vote of that state to Thomas Jefferson rather than to Aaron Burr (A.B. 1772).

After leaving Congress in 1803, Elmendorf served two years, 1804 and 1805, in the lower house of the state assembly. Subsequently, from 1814 into 1817, he sat for the middle district in the state senate. Finally, from 1835 to 1840, he was surrogate for Ulster County. During his service in the state senate he was a leading opponent of the plan to construct what became the Erie Canal, a position probably related to his own heavy commitment to the future prosperity of Kingston. Following his service in Congress, he became deeply involved in projects for the building of turnpike roads that would link Kingston and other points having access to the Hudson with the upper Delaware and Susquehannah rivers, as far west perhaps as modern Binghamton. There was a succession of disappointments and reorganizations, and the goal set was never fully achieved. Elmendorf has been recognized as the chief mover in these efforts, and he must have been the heaviest loser, for it has been estimated that he invested $40,000 in ventures that were in a state of collapse by 1819. The part of the turnpike that was completed was at times described as "Lucas' turnpike," which is said to have survived in the name of Lucas Avenue in Kingston.

The details of Elmendorf's private life remain unusually obscure. If the identification of Elmendorf with the resident of that name in Hurley in 1790 be correct, he possibly had been recently married and had as yet no children. But the record of the marriage of Lucas Elmendorf to Ann Waddell on January 30, 1797 that is found in the register of Trinity Parish, New York City, is the only such record that has been discovered. A New York City directory for 1797 shows no Lucas Elmendorf then resident in the city, and it is possible that the groom, perhaps in his second wedding, was the recently elected congressman from Kingston. No evidence of children has been found, thus at his death on August 17, 1843, it seems he left no direct descendents. There was, however, a nephew named Lucas, the son of Elmendorf's older sister Blandina and her husband, Daniel Brodhead. In 1820 Lucas Brodhead had been sent to Kentucky for the management of landed properties Elmendorf had acquired there. He settled at Frankfort, where he practiced law; he died in 1849, leaving a widow, who subsequently married Orlando Brown (A.B. 1820), and a son who also bore the name Lucas.

SOURCES: *NYGBR*, 20 (1889), 101-106; 46 (1915), 101-105; G. Anjou, *Ulster Cnty., N.Y. Probate Recs.* (1906), I, 148n; alumni file, Elmendorf Family file, Trustee Minutes, and College catalogues, PUA; M. Schoonmaker, *Hist. of Kingston, N.Y.* (1888), 341-47, 405-410, 446-47; Ulster Cnty. Hist. Soc., *Proc., 1937-1938*, 22-26; als LCE to M. Elmendorf, 2 Jul 1781, NjP; see Peter Edmund Elmendorf (A.B. 1782); Beam, *Whig Soc.*, 61-62; *N.J. Gazette*, 9 Oct 1782 (commencement); *BDAC*; *N.Y. City Directory 1789*; *First Census, N.Y.*, 170, 172; W. C. DeWitt, *People's Hist. of Kingston, Rondout and Vicinity* (1943), 132; N. B. Sylvester, *Hist. of Ulster Cnty., N.Y.* (1880), 102-103, 177, 108, 404-410; D. R. Fox, *Decline of Aristocracy in Politics of N.Y.* (1965), 47; A. F. Young, *Democratic Republicans of N.Y.* (1967), 561; *A/C*, VII, 304, 311, 323, 1,554, 1,772; VIII, 2,028, 2,171; X, 1,029, 1,032; *N.Y. Red Book* (1895), 325, 377, 378; A. T. Clearwater, *Hist. of Ulster Cnty., N.Y.* (1907), 217; *KSHS Reg.*, 49 (1951), 19.

MANUSCRIPTS: NIC, WHi, NHi

                                                                WFC

Peter Edmund Elmendorf

PETER EDMUND ELMENDORF (PETRUS EDMUNDUS ELMENDORPH), A.B., lawyer, was baptized September 23, 1764, the second son to bear this name of Peter Edmund Elmendorph and his wife, Mary Crook Elmen-

Peter Edmund Elmendorf, A.B. 1782
BY JOHN RAMAGE

dorph, of Kingston, Ulster County, New York. The father was a merchant who died at the age of fifty on July 13, 1765, when young Peter
had yet to reach a first birthday. Peter grew up under the care chiefly
of his widowed mother, who died at the age of seventy-three on August
15, 1794. Her husband, who had served as trustee and magistrate of
the town, left his entire estate to his wife for the term of her widowhood, and something of its value is suggested by the record of her
losses when the British burned the town on October 10, 1777; they
were listed as three houses, one barn, three barracks, and one store-
house or shop. Her political sentiments, and perhaps her spirit, are
reflected in the fact that on July 1, 1775 she signed the association for
the boycott of British goods, one of only two women in the town to do
so. It appears likely that she continued to run her husband's business
for a time. Whether ultimately she remarried has not been determined,
but she was not listed as a head of family in the census of 1790. Peter's
classmate Lucas Conrad Elmendorf was a first cousin.

Peter's letters from Nassau Hall to his mother indicate that their relationship was a close one. The earliest of these, dated July 7, 1781, also suggests that he only recently had entered the College, for he referred to it as his first from Nassau Hall. In fact, he may have been enrolled as early as November 1780 and was certainly enrolled by January 17, 1781 when Professor Samuel S. Smith (A.B. 1769) issued to him a receipt for the payment of £3, "the advance of his tuition for the present session." In the interim he probably had been living at some house in the village, awaiting the repairs on war-damaged Nassau Hall that would make available for him a room there. To his mother on the following July 7 he could write: "I am well pleased, the Place agrees admirably with my disposition, my Room tho' not yet finished, is decent, clean, and nobly situated, we have the finest Prospect that ever could be desir'd, in short we have everything comfortable in life." By that time he seems also to have been well established as a student, for a letter from his cousin Conrad on July 2 had assured Mary Elmendorph that she "need no longer be troubled about Peter," who was "esteemed by the Tutor to be among the foremost in class" and who had shown "a steady application to his books."

Peter wrote again on July 27, his chief concern then being the purchase of "a broad Cloth for a winters dressing Coat," which he considered "very necessary here as all the Students in general wear them." A letter of August 29 reported a visit by his brother, with whom "all Esopus Students" seem to have dined at the local tavern. The letter of November 30 reveals that he had been away during the fall vacation and that he had returned safely, though unhappy upon hearing of a new requirement that board and tuition be paid in advance. He protested that he minded, not so much because as a result he was out of funds, but rather because of the quality of the food served by the College's steward. "I often repent that I saw his face; after having paid him 24 pound and then to live in the way we do is the most provoking thing I ever met with." He continued:

> We eat rye bread—half dough and as black as it possibly can be, old oniony butter and sometimes dry bread, and thick coffee for breakfast, a little milk or cyder and bread, and sometimes meagre chocolate for supper, very indifferent dinners, such as lean, tough, boiled fresh beef with dry potatoes! and if this deserves to be called diet for mean ravenous people let it be so stiled, and not a table kept for Collegians! Thus we may be said to exist and not to live as it becomes persons of good extraction.

Having joined the large company of students who over the centuries have found a stimulus to eloquence in the food served them at college,

Peter softened the charge in his next letter. Writing on January 19, 1782, and referring to his letter of November 30, he confessed that it contained "some sentiments which are now not altogether just." The food had improved, but he was still short of money. By June he must have won permission "to board out of College," for on June 7 he wrote his mother: "I have changed my board and find the difference to be very great with respect to diet and politeness."

No evidence has been found regarding his preparation for college. A part of it must have been gained through attendance at the academy the town opened at Kingston in 1774, and reopened not long after the British raid in 1777, but it is not certain that plans for adding a Latin academy to the original English academy were fully implemented before Peter entered the College. While at Nassau Hall, he became a member of the Cliosophic Society. At commencement on September 25, 1782, "Mr. P. Elmendorf" addressed "a very polite and splendid assembly" on "The nature of happiness."

Although Elmendorf's activity immediately after graduation is not known, he presumably began to read law before long, for he had qualified to practice at some time before 1789 when a directory for New York City listed him and his cousin Conrad among the attorneys of the supreme court of the state. Unfortunately, in neither case is the date of admission given. A letter of May 22, 1788 to his sister Blandina Bruyn, the wife of Jacobus Severyn Bruyn (Class of 1775), had been written from New City (Lansingburgh), located a few miles above Albany on the eastern side of the Hudson, and his account of his involvement in efforts to secure a minister for the local church suggests that he had thoughts of a continuing residence in that community. Late in the following October, he wrote his mother from Albany of plans to accompany "little Johnny" to Princeton or "New York College" and of the boy's preference for Princeton. "Johnny" no doubt was John Bleecker (A.B. 1791), the son of Rutger Bleecker and Elmendorf's sister Catharine. Peter seems to have had a responsibility beyond that of delivering the boy to the College, for President Smith forwarded a bill for his board in April 1789 to Elmendorf and reported favorably on John's progress as a student. Whatever other plans Elmendorf at first may have had, he settled finally in Albany.

His decision to do so may have been related to his marriage there on March 14, 1793 to Elizabeth Van Rensselaer, daughter of Philip Van Rensselaer and his wife, Maria Sanders. Their residence on Pearl Street came to her through her mother. Elizabeth died in 1798, leaving two daughters. Elmendorf was married in September 1802 to another Elizabeth Van Rensselaer, the daughter of Kiliaen Van Rensselaer and his wife, Maria White. To this marriage, five sons and a daughter were born, of whom only two sons survived the parents. Of the two children by the first wife, only one survived her father. Elmendorf died on May 15, 1835, his second wife having died on the preceding April 26.

It is difficult to arrive at an estimate of Elmendorf's career. Local historians speak of him as an eminent attorney, and perhaps he was. Albany directories show him continuing to live on Pearl Street, though not always at the same number. He at times is listed as an attorney, at times not. No evidence has been found of significant political activity. He appears to have lived quietly and well, as persons "of good extraction" are often able to do.

SOURCES: *NYGBR*, 20 (1889), 101-106; 49 (1915), 347; *Som. Cnty. Hist. Quart.*, 6 (1916), 194-99; G. Anjou, *Ulster Cnty., N.Y. Probate Rec.* (1906), I, 145, 146-48; alumni file, Elmendorf Family file, MS Clio. Soc. membership list (which has PEE admitted to Clio. in 1778, but also mistakenly gives 1783 as the year of his graduation), PUA; *N.Y. Wills*, VI, 295; M. Schoonmaker, *Hist. of Kingston* (1888), 341-47, 518, 522, 528; als PEE to M. Elmendorf, 7 Jul 1781, 27 Jul 1781, 29 Aug 1781, 30 Nov 1781, 19 Jan 1782, 7 Jun 1782, 27 Oct 1788; PEE to B. Bruyn, 22 May 1788; L. C. Elmendorf to M. Elmendorf, 2 Jul 1781; S. S. Smith to PEE, 10 Apr 1789; MS "Bill for expense of taking Jnº R. Bleeker to Princeton;" MS receipts by S. S. Smith, 17 Jan 1781 ("advance of his tuition"), 20 May 1782 (for a 40 shilling payment of "chamber rent"), 30 Aug 1782 (for a £3 payment toward "his tuition for the current half year"), all in NjP. Only in the fall of 1781 were repairs to Nassau Hall sufficiently advanced to permit restoration of the requirement that all students "lodge in College" [see *NJA* (2 ser.), v, 303-305; Maclean, *History*, I, 330-31; *N.J. Gazette*, 9 Oct 1782 (commencement); J. Munsell, *Coll. on Hist. of Albany*, IV (1871), 98, 120].

MANUSCRIPTS: NHi

WFC

John Andre Hanna

JOHN ANDRE HANNA, A.B., A.M. 1785, lawyer and public official, was born about 1761 in Hunterdon County, New Jersey, the son of Reverend John Hanna (A.B. 1755) and his wife, Mary McCrea. He was one of thirteen children, including James Hanna (A.B. 1777) and William Hanna (A.B. 1790). The mother was a sister of John McCrea (A.B. 1762) and Robert McCrea (Class of 1776). The father served as pastor of a number of Presbyterian congregations in Hunterdon County prior to his death in 1801 and was also a practicing physician. It is likely that young John was prepared for college by his father, who in addition to his other careers taught school from time to time.

According to catalogues of the Cliosophic Society published in the nineteenth century, Hanna was admitted to its membership in 1779.

At the commencement exercises of 1782, he was one of three partici-
pants in a debate of whether "in a confederation like that of America
. . . large states, or small ones" were "the more favourable to union,
population and improvement in the arts." It was appropriate that
Hanna, as a native of New Jersey, "maintained that small states were
the more favourable to these ends."

Hanna must have begun reading law immediately after graduation,
for his was admitted to practice in Philadelphia on February 1, 1784.
By the spring of the following year, he had cast his lot with the newly
created Dauphin County, Pennsylvania, where at the very first court
of the county, in May 1785, he was qualified as a member of the bar.
Described as being at the time six feet tall, handsome, and well pro-
portioned, Hanna seems to have quickly prospered. Presumably at an
early date, he married Mary Read Harris, daughter of John Harris,
the founder of Harrisburg. Before Hanna's death in 1805, the couple
was to have nine children, all girls, of whom six lived to maturity.
Settled in Harrisburg, Hanna at the time of the census of 1790 headed
a household that included four free white males over sixteen years of
age, four free white females, and two slaves. His property undoubtedly
increased after the death of his father-in-law in 1791, for he is named
thereafter among the heirs of John Harris. His holdings were not
limited to Harrisburg or Dauphin County, either. As early as February
1788, he acquired a warrant for three hundred acres in Cumberland
County, and he may have entered into speculative ventures in still
other counties.

In the life of the Harrisburg community, Hanna became an active
leader. He was among the subscribers to a fund in 1787 for the building of a church and schoolhouse "for the use of the subscribers." He
himself probably worshiped, as did other Presbyterians in the place,
with the nearby Paxton congregation, until 1796 when a separate
congregation was organized in Harrisburg, with Nathaniel R. Snowden
(A.B. 1787) as its first pastor. Hanna has been credited with the authorship of the legislative act that in 1791 incorporated the town as a borough and fixed its name as Harrisburg, thereby settling a question in
favor of his father-in-law's firm choice. When in 1793 illness among
the inhabitants raised the specter of a yellow fever epidemic, a mill
pond on Paxton Creek was blamed for the trouble. The site had been
purchased from John Harris, and in 1795 his heirs, including Hanna,
paid the owners of the mill $1,600, presumably the original purchase
price, as part of a much larger sum collected to compensate them for
the destruction of the pond. In the same year Hanna became a director
of the newly organized Harrisburg Library Company. His standing in

the community is indicated by his selection as "President of the Day" for the 1796 celebration of the Fourth of July. By then he was commonly known as General Hanna because of the rank he had achieved in the state militia. In 1794 he had been charged as a brigadier general with command of the Second Brigade of the Second Division of Pennsylvania troops sent for the suppression of the Whiskey Rebellion. He is said to have marched as far as Bedford with a force drawn from three counties, and shortly to have returned to Harrisburg for the disbandment of his unit. On the evening of the return there was a great ball.

As his military rank suggests, Hanna had become a person of political significance in his own section of the state. He had been one of three delegates from the county sent to the state convention meeting at Philadelphia in November 1787 to consider ratification of the new federal Constitution. He took no prominent part in the proceedings, but he was among the twenty-three members who failed in an effort to delay action on ratification until the people had had time to consider amendments to the document and who then voted against ratification. He was not among the signers of the formal announcement of the convention's decision to ratify. Instead, he was one of the twenty-one members of the dissenting minority who signed a formal address to the public setting forth their objections to the Constitution and in effect announcing that the struggle to prevent its adoption without amendment would continue. In this continuing effort, Hanna would serve as secretary to a special convention of representatives, mainly from the western counties, meeting at Harrisburg in September 1788, several weeks after the Constitution had been given effect through the ratification of nine states. This convention proposed a number of amendments designed to strengthen the protection for state and individual rights. Hanna, whatever may have been his own part in the proceedings aside from performing the formal duties of a secretary, was well launched into politics as an anti-federalist.

He served one term in the lower house of the state assembly in 1791. His next call to political office seems to have come with his election in 1796 as a member of the Fifth United States Congress. He was to be reelected to the Sixth through the Ninth congresses, though his death before the last of these assembled in its first session in December 1805, limited his actual service to four terms. In Congress Hanna obviously was disinclined to take the floor or to assume the role of a leader. Through the earlier years of his service, he seems to have been regular in attendance and ready to cast his vote whenever the house divided. That vote normally showed his identification with the Jeffersonian

Republicans. It is noticeable that his name and that of Albert Gallatin were usually found in the same column, be it a list of the yeas or the nays. An exception was his vote in May 1798 for the provisional army, perhaps because he was an instrument for presentation to President Adams of an address from the inhabitants of Harrisburg adopted that month in favor of putting the country into a state of readiness to defend itself. But he voted against the Alien and Sedition Acts and measures designed to bring a complete break with France. To a friend he wrote on June 3, 1798: "In case of war with France we have much to lose and nothing to gain but *honor*, and that *honor* depends . . . upon the fate of war." When the election of 1800 brought a tie between Thomas Jefferson and Aaron Burr (A.B. 1772), Hanna cast his vote for Jefferson. He found some of the duties of office burdensome, and toward the end of his service his attendance seems to have been less regular.

Possibly his health was failing. Nothing has been found regarding the circumstances of his death, which occurred at Harrisburg on July 23, 1805. According to a newspaper report, he was then only forty-four years of age.

SOURCES: *Hist. Reg.* (Harrisburg, 1883), I, 81-85 ("*honor* depends . . . upon the fate of war"); *BDAC*; J. B. McMaster and F. D. Stone, eds., *Pa. and the Fed. Constitution* (1888), 731 (which credits Hanna with Rev. military service for which no confirmation has been found); *Som. Cnty. Hist. Quart.*, 7 (1918), 92; Clio. Soc. catalogues of 1845 and 1876; *N.J. Gazette*, 9 Oct 1782 (commencement); J. H. Martin, *Bench and Bar of Phila.* (1883), 275; G. H. Morgan, *Annals of Harrisburg* (1906), 80-81, 85, 88-98, 113-14; J. I. Mombert, *Hist. of Lancaster Cnty. Pa.* (1869), 430; *First Census, Pa.*, 86; *Pa. Arch.* (3 ser.), XXIV, 692; (2 ser.), IV, 765; I. D. Rupp, *Hist. and Topography of Dauphin . . . and Perry Counties, Pa.* (1846), 277-78, 233-34, 237-46, 288; M. Jensen, ed., *Doc. Hist. of Ratification of Constitution*, II (1976), esp. 589, 591, 599-600, 616, 617-39; *Doc. Hist. Fed. Elec.*, I, 258-64; *A/C*, VIII, 1,772, 1,796, 1,829, 1,866, 2,029; IX, 2,128, 2,171, 2,792; X, 531, 915, 1,032n; *PMHB* 3 (1879), 235.

WFC

John Johnston

JOHN JOHNSTON, A.B., participated in a debate at his commencement on the question, "can all the differences in shape and complexion among mankind be accounted from natural causes, on the supposition of the whole race being descended from one original pair." He denied that proposition, took his degree, and then, apparently, left Princeton and disappeared from the records of the College until 1827, when for the first time its triennial catalogue noted his death. In his manuscript "Memoirs of Nassau Hall graduates," composed before his death in

1865, G. M. Giger (A.B. 1841) not only omitted Johnston's name but also failed to leave his customary blank page for a graduate whose career was unknown.

SOURCES: *N.J. Gazette*, 9 Oct 1782 (commencement). The number of John Johnstons active in the U.S. at the end of the eighteenth century and the beginning of the nineteenth century is too great to permit a case-by-case examination in order to discover the alumnus of CNJ. The lives of three individuals are particularly inviting possibilities, however.

John, the son of David and Magdalen Walton Johnston, was born at his father's country estate, "Annandale," in Lithgow, Dutchess Cnty., N.Y. David Johnston was an influential merchant in N.Y. City and a wealthy landowner who was an active Whig and who in 1774 became president of the city's Soc. of St. Andrew. A cousin through his mother of the Beekmans of N.Y., John Johnston was born on 13 Jun 1762. He became a lawyer in the city and on 23 May 1792 married Susannah Bard, the daughter of Dr. Samuel Bard. Johnston settled in Dutchess Cnty. and in 1807 became the first judge of the County Court of Common Pleas. He died on 29 Aug 1850, twenty-three years after the death of the CNJ graduate was noted in the not always accurate triennial catalogues. The distinction of his career and the nearness of his residence to Princeton create serious doubts that the College could for so long have been totally ignorant of his activities, however. [*NYGBR*, 33 (1902), 249; 34 (1903), 34; F. Hasbrouck, ed., *Hist. of Dutchess Cnty., N.Y.* (1909), 77; W. M. Mac-Bean, *Biog. Reg. of St. Andrew's Soc. . . . of N.Y.* (1922), I, 12-13, 238; J. B. Langstaff, *Dr. Bard of Hyde Park* (1942), 183.]

John, the son of Capt. Archibald and Sarah Johnston, was born on 1 Jul 1762 at Salisbury, Conn. He studied medicine in Litchfield and in Sep 1783 married Mary Stoddard, the daughter of Dr. Josiah Stoddard. After practicing in Salisbury for a few years, he moved with his family between 1788 and 1790 to Washington, Mason Cnty., Va. (later Ky.). He was a trustee of the town at least in 1800. Widowed twice, Johnston married three times and fathered a total of nineteen children before his death on 25 Oct 1832. The possibility of his being the CNJ graduate is enhanced by the notice taken of his death by John Pintard (A.B. 1776), who recalled having known Dr. Johnston. But no confirmation of his attendance at CNJ has been found. [W. P. Johnston, *The Johnstons of Salisbury* (1897), 51-53, 154-55; G. G. Clift, *Hist. of Maysville and Mason Counties, Ky.* (1936), I, 142, 368.]

John, the son of Robert and Eliza Sproul Johnston, was born near Castle Derg, Ireland, on 16 Jun 1765. Four years later he came with his parents and two older brothers to Cumberland Cnty., Pa., where his father bought a farm near Chambersburg. According to the recollections of his grandson, Johnston was apprenticed to a watch- and clock-maker before his marriage in 1787 to Mary Reed of Franklin Cnty., Pa. They then moved to Pittsburgh, where Johnston built a three-story building as a combination residence and jewelry shop. An active member of the community, he was one of the lay judges for the Court of Quarter Sessions in 1788, the session that admitted Hugh H. Brackenridge (A.B. 1771) to the Allegheny Cnty. Bar. Johnston was a founder of the Pittsburgh Fire Dept. and a Republican candidate for coroner in 1800. In 1804 President Jefferson appointed him postmaster of Pittsburgh, an office he held for eighteen years. He was also a Mason and a trustee of the First Presbyterian Church of Pittsburgh. He died on 4 May 1827—in time for his death to be noted in the CNJ catalogue for that year—survived by his wife, his daughter, and his son. Once again, however, no evidence of his attending the College has been found. [W. G. Johnston, *Life and Reminiscences* (1901), 4-11; *WPHM*, 11 (1928), 123; 12 (1929), 45; 4 (1921), 87, 92; 2 (1919), 228; 8 (1925), 260-61; 49 (1966), 41.]

William Kennedy

WILLIAM KENNEDY was one of six "young gentlemen" who were graduated from the grammar school at Nassau Hall and admitted to the freshman class of the College on September 28, 1779, according to a report prefacing the account of the College's commencement on September 29 that was published in the *New Jersey Gazette* for the following October 13. Each of the six was identified by his place of residence, and Kennedy was described as being "of Philadelphia." There is no cause for doubting this identification, for newspaper accounts of commencement exercises were obviously written in Princeton by some officer of the College who was in a position to know the residence of any and all students. Not only did reports appearing in New York and Philadelphia newspapers repeatedly read word for word the same but it is evident that the College was inclined to be boastful of the wide geographical area from which its students were drawn—in this instance, from South Carolina, Virginia, Philadelphia, New York, and Princeton, to which two of the six belonged.

Unfortunately, the fact that Kennedy at the time of his admission to the College was a resident of Philadelphia appears to be very nearly the only firm piece of evidence regarding him that can be discovered. His admission to the freshman class carries no proof in itself that he actually returned to Princeton in the following November, or at some time thereafter, to begin his collegiate studies, nor can it be said with certainty, as it can be of his schoolmate John Drayton of South Carolina, that he did not return. When notice is taken of a William Kennedy who, according to the *Biographical Catalogue of the Matriculates* (1894) enrolled at the University of Pennsylvania, entered the college there in 1779 and graduated with the A.B. degree in 1782, one is inclined to assume that Kennedy's name should be stricken from the list of possible students attending the College of New Jersey. Authoritative advice indicates that William Kennedy was not actually enrolled at Pennsylvania before January 1781, however, which opens the possibility that he may have been a student in the College at Princeton for a year or more before his transfer to a more conveniently situated institution.

There unhappily the story has to be left. Not even the evidence provided by the records of the University of Pennsylvania that he probably was a brother to the presumably younger Alexander and George Kennedy has made possible a firm identification of the man. There were many Kennedys in the United States at the time, not a few of them in Pennsylvania, and more than one bore the name of William.

SOURCES: The author is indebted to Francis James Dallett, Archivist of the University of Pennsylvania, for the advice that the compiler of the *Biog. Cat.* of 1894 usually arrived at a date for a graduate's admission by simply subtracting three years from the time of graduation. That was the term that had been set as the goal for a program of study leading to the A.B. degree, but its use for measuring a student's actual term of residence obviously can be misleading. The record of payments for tuition indicates enrollment at Pennsylvania by William Kennedy from January 1781 to 21 March 1782. With some apparent assistance from Pennsylvania's *Biog. Cat.*, Kennedy has been identified in several works, including *BDAC*, as the congressman William Kennedy (31 July 1768-11 Oct 1834) who sat in the House of Representatives from North Carolina during the Eighth, Eleventh, Twelfth, and Thirteenth congresses. But this identification has been rejected by John B. Flowers III in a sketch prepared for the forthcoming *Dictionary of N.C. Biog.* Congressman Kennedy was a native of Beaufort County, N.C. and the son of a prominent planter and public official of the county and state—hardly a person to be described as "of Philadelphia" in 1779. The author of the present sketch is indebted to Mr. Flowers for a copy of his as yet unpublished sketch. See also S. M. Lemmon, *Frustrated Patriots: N.C. and the War of 1812* (1973), 163; D. H. Gilpatrick, *Jeffersonian Democracy in N.C., 1789-1816* (1931), 96, 241-42; R.D.W. Connor, ed., *A Manual of N.C.* (1913), 916-20, 959; and M. B. Meriwether, ed., *The Carolinian Florist* (1943), for John Drayton's explanation that his father's death had prevented his return to the College.

WFC

William Mahon

WILLIAM MAHON, A.B., Presbyterian minister and schoolmaster, almost certainly was born in Cumberland County, Pennsylvania, the son of Archibald Mahon and his wife, Jean Mahon. The date of birth has not been discovered. An older adopted sister was Hannah Mahon, who married James Carnahan and on November 15, 1775 became the mother of James Carnahan (A.B. 1800), president of the College from 1823 until his resignation in 1854. The family name is a familiar one in the records of the Presbyterian Church in western Pennsylvania, and there can be little doubt that William grew up with that religious affiliation. Where and by whom he was prepared for college has not been found, and the only evidence that may provide a clue as to the time of his admission to the College is in catalogues of the Cliosophic Society published in 1845 and 1876, which indicate that he became a member in 1779. As for William's standing as a student there can be no question, for in the commencement exercises of September 25, 1782 he enjoyed the highest honor of delivering the Latin salutatory address. He spoke on the "mischiefs of faction and party in a commonwealth." Later in the day, he participated in a triangular dispute of whether "the idea of the beautiful, in the fine arts" had "any real standard in nature." His assigned part was to support the negative.

At some time after graduation, Mahon went south to Virginia, where on June 23, 1784, he was appointed tutor for the sophomore and junior classes at Hampden-Sidney College in Prince Edward County. John Blair Smith (A.B. 1773) was president under the provisions of a charter that in the preceding year had elevated the former Prince Edward Academy to the status of a degree-granting college. It is likely that Mahon had the recommendation of Samuel Stanhope Smith (A.B. 1769), brother of John Blair Smith, former head of the academy, and since 1779 Professor of Moral Philosophy at Princeton.

Mahon's experience at Hampden-Sidney seems to have been prophetic in its revelation of personal difficulties that were to plague him throughout a brief and tragic career. In early 1785 President Smith expelled a student because of a dispute with Mahon, only to have the decision reversed by the trustees in April. This reversal was accompanied by the enactment of a rule imposing upon the entire student body the cost of compensating an officer of the college for property destroyed by an unidentified student, an action that hardly could have strengthened the standing of the tutor in question with the student body. When the trustees met in the following September, Mahon reported to them that he repeatedly had been insulted by students, some of whom threw stones at him and his house at night, and that he had been unable to identify the culprits. A decision by the trustees to postpone action, though explained as attributable to the seriousness of the situation and the lack of full attendance at that meeting, suggests that they may have entertained some doubts as to the real source of the problem. At the subsequent meeting in December, the trustees concluded that no action needed to be taken in view of the fact that the laws of the college were adequate to cover all cases in which the offenders were identified. In April 1786 President Smith presented to the board a petition signed by thirty students calling for Mahon's dismissal. He was allowed to resign.

He apparently had been reading theology under Smith's guidance for some time with a view to entering the ministry, and certainly Smith continued to sponsor him in the achievement of this aspiration. The Presbytery of Hanover as early as May 1786 reported to the New York and Philadelphia Synod that "Mr. William Mahan" had been licensed to preach. In the following September Mahon was accepted as a probationary member of the presbytery. Thereafter, he probably undertook some missionary assignment or served as a supply minister to particular congregations. That the latter was true for at least a part of the time is suggested by a petition received by the presbytery on October 10, 1788, from the Hat Creek, Concord, and Walker's congregation that Mahon be ordained. On the next day he preached a sermon judged to be acceptable on a text assigned him by Smith, and this was followed by his ordination. The formal ordination sermon was preached by the aging Robert Smith of Pequea, Pennsylvania, Princeton trustee who was then visiting his son John Blair Smith. Mahon was reported to the General Assembly of the Presbyterian Church as a "regularly settled" minister of the Hanover Presbytery as late as 1794. He moved to Kentucky in or about 1795, when he began to supply the New Providence church in Mercer County. In October 1796 he became its regular minister, with a pastorate combined with that of the Upper Benson congregation in Franklin County. It was in 1796 that he became a member of the Transylvania Presbytery.

Presumably Mahon moved to Kentucky with the wife he had found in Charlotte County, Virginia, a daughter of James Venable, one of the founding trustees of Hampden-Sidney and a member of one of the prominent families of the Prince Edward section of the state. Mahon purchased a ninety-five-acre farm on the Salt River, and in 1797 he opened a school intended to provide a supplement to the uncertain stipend his congregations were able to pay him. Robert B. McAfee, who formerly had studied at the Transylvania Seminary in Lexington and who would become a leading lawyer and politician in the state, was among his first students. In the memoirs McAfee later wrote of his life and of the Providence church community, it is obvious that he had fond memories of Mahon and great respect for his attainments as a scholar and a teacher. Said he: "The time I spent at this school was the happiest of my life." He recalled especially the "debating Society" organized by the students with Mahon's cooperation, which drew in "almost the whole neighborhood" for four or five miles around Providence, for discussion of such exciting contemporary issues as were posed by the Alien and Sedition Acts and "John Adams standing army as well as our relations with France." In this connection, McAfee revealed that Mahon was a Federalist and that he regarded Thomas Jefferson as an infidel. But it is maintained that Mahon was cautious in making his political opinions known, and evidently the troubles he soon experienced were mainly attributable to his own personal problems.

McAfee made no effort to cover up Mahon's shortcomings. Indeed, at times his account goes into almost embarrassing detail. He was inclined to place a heavy part of the blame for Mahon's problems upon an unhappy marriage to a wife, who "tho otherwise a pleasant good woman was Hypocondrial and seldom left her room," and who in the absence of her husband neglected the discipline of "the worst set of negroes I ever saw." But it becomes all too apparent that Mahon by disposition was contentious, that he frequently gave way to perhaps an uncontrollable temper, and that these characteristics were made worse by heavy use of hard liquor, which initially is described as having been a secret indulgence at home. In April 1798 he came before the Presbytery charged with whipping "his negro women unmercifully" and with "factious proceedings in the congregation, and was admonished to maintain a stricter guard over his temper." On complaint by the congregation at Providence, the connection was dissolved by the presbytery on October 5, 1798. In the spring of 1799 Mahon moved to Danville, where he conducted a school of some forty or fifty scholars, with McAfee serving for a time as one of two ushers. The latter's account continues: "My friend & Preceptor Mr. Mahan still continued to drink secretly every morning filling his Tea Pot with Whiskey from a closet adjoining our room." All too soon, the effects of his secret drinking became public, and on November 24, 1802, he was brought once more before the presbytery on charges of intoxication. Less than a year later, on October 10, 1803, he was suspended from the ministry.

Little success has attended efforts to follow him through his later years. He seems to have continued to teach, even to do some preaching, but an appeal in 1812 for restoration to good standing as a minister was denied. McAfee's account is that Mahon's drinking "eventually ended in his ruin and death on his son's farm ten miles south of Lebanon on the south Fork of the Rolling in Washington County." The general catalogues of the College first carried a notation of his death in 1824. At Princeton he was destined to be remembered chiefly for having become "a subject of Presbyterial discipline" and having died "under a cloud," and in Kentucky for the consequences of "taking his tea."

SOURCES: The identification of Mahon's parentage depends chiefly upon persuasive evidence found in the special file for President Carnahan, PUA, but see also the alumni file for Mahon. *Pa. Arch.* (3 ser.), XX, 319, 445, 599; *First Census, Pa.*, 120; see Samuel Wilson (A.B. 1782) for an Archibald Mahon of Shippensburg, Cumberland Cnty., who probably was William's father and also father of Wilson's wife; *N.J. Gazette*, 9 Oct 1782 (commencement); A. J. Morrison, Hampden-Sidney College, *Cal. of Board Min.* (1912), 32-34; H. C. Bradshaw, *Hist. Hampden-Sidney College*, I (1976), 68-69; *Rec. Pres. Chh.*, 516; Foote, *Sketches, Va.*, 494, 534; *Min. Gen. Assem.*, *1789-1820*, 19, 58, 83, 166, 265; R. Davidson, *Hist. of Pres. Chh. in . . . Ky.* (1847), 127, 369; *Filson Club Hist. Quart.*, 27 (1953), 226; 16 (1942), 228; *WMQ* (1 ser.), 15 (1906-1907), 248; *VMHB*, 7 (1900), 32; *KSHS Reg.*, 25 (1927), 139-41, 142 ("standing army"), 143 ("Hypocondrial"), 215-17 ("filling his Tea Pot"); 29 (1931), 13-14 ("ruin and death"); 54 (1956), 42; MS memo of Mahon by J. D. Shane, Draper MSS 14C146, WHi ("taking his tea"); Giger, Memoirs ("Presbyterial discipline"); Alexander, *Princeton*, 211.

WFC

John Morton

JOHN MORTON, A.B., merchant and newspaper publisher, was born in New York City on March 28, 1763, the second son of John Morton and his wife, Maria Sophia Kemper. He was a younger brother of Jacob Morton (A.B. 1778), and the older brother of George Washington Morton (A.B. 1792) and George Clark Morton (A.B. 1795). The father, a native of Ireland, had come to America in the capacity of a commissary with the British army in 1760 and subsequently had settled in New York where he became a prosperous merchant. In time he owned a large brick house on Water Street, close at hand to a wharf on the East River that housed a wide variety of imports. The mother was of a German family and had migrated with her parents to America when a young child. The record of their son John's birth and baptism on April 3, 1763 is found in the registry of the city's Presbyterian church.

Morton grew up and received most of his education midst the excitement of the Revolution. His earliest schooling probably was in New York, but his father became a "warm Whig" and in advance of the British occupation of the city in 1776, possibly as early as 1775, he moved to'Elizabethtown, New Jersey. In search of greater safety, the family moved westward by way of Springfield to Basking Ridge, Somerset County, where the father purchased a farm and house that would be occupied by his family until the end of the war. This was not far from Morristown, Washington's headquarters after the Battle of Princeton, and John's younger sister Eliza later recalled that "American troops were constantly passing and repassing, and the house frequently full of officers." She also recalled that the family of Elias Boudinot, trustee of the College since 1772, then lived half a mile away and that another neighbor and friend was Samuel Kennedy (A.B. 1754), pastor of the local Presbyterian church. It is possible that John had attended, at least briefly, the academy in Elizabethtown at which his brother Jacob had been prepared for college and that his studies may have continued with Kennedy, who had combined the practice of medicine and the conducting of a classical school with his duties as a minister. Perhaps Kennedy by this time no longer maintained a regular school, however, which may help to explain the following entry in a ledger of Reverend Jonathan Elmer (Yale 1747) of Turkey (New Providence) under the date of July 14, 1777: "John Morton Came here to School." Turkey lay near Springfield at no great distance from Basking Ridge, and there seems to be every reason for believing that this John Morton was the future graduate of the College. When Morton entered Nassau Hall is unknown, but it is unlikely that it was before the fall of 1778. Perhaps John was one of the few students continuously enrolled through the four years preceding his graduation at the age of nineteen in 1782.

Morton had a memorable part in the graduation ceremonies on September 25 of that year. While he was at home during the preceding spring vacation, the house at Basking Ridge had been invaded at night by an armed band of masked men who escaped with £30 in specie, recently received as part payment for the house that had been acquired in Elizabethtown, and much other valuable plunder. John's father was ill at the time, but he insisted early on the following morning upon an unsuccessful attempt to pursue the criminals, and his death within a week of apoplexy added to the sensational character of the event. His son had the honor of closing the commencement exercises as the valedictory orator. He appeared in full mourning dress and, according to a newspaper report, he spoke "with a natural and moving eloquence that melted the whole assembly into tears."

Morton's sister Eliza later recalled that John "was amiable and affectionate, but deficient in energy of character." It was a moral judgment and one made in the light of achievements attained by other members of the family. The father had managed to escape from New York at the beginning of the Revolution with enough of his worldly goods to permit his family to live through the war in relative comfort and style as exiles in the Jersey hills. John's brother Jacob not only prospered as a New York attorney and became one of the city's outstanding personalities, but as executor of his father's estate he shrewdly anticipated that the government securities in which his father had heavily invested would eventually be made good. As for Eliza herself, she enjoyed the friendship of the College's president, Samuel Stanhope Smith (A.B. 1769), in whose home she more than once visited, and by whom she was married in 1797 to Josiah Quincy of Massachusetts, a young man of family and fortune who later would become the president of Harvard.

A little more than a year after John's graduation, the family returned to New York City, shortly after the British evacuation of the place in November 1783. Jacob began the practice of law, and his mother attended the Presbyterian services presided over once more by John Rodgers, longtime trustee of the College. John joined the counting office of one of the city's merchants. The choice of a career for the new graduate obviously had been that of his father. Some of the real estate in New York having been sold to satisfy prewar debts to British merchants, and John having completed his apprenticeship, it was decided, presumably by Jacob, to send him to England, "with the final remittances" in order to lay more secure foundations for a new commercial "establishment for the benefit of himself and his family." The plan apparently was not fully implemented. John sailed for England in 1791, but instead of cultivating helpful business connections, according to Eliza, "he spent his time in travelling," and "on his return in 1793, he relinquished business as a merchant."

Here her memory must have failed her, for the firm of John Morton and Co., merchants, first appears in New York City directories in 1793, with an address on Queen Street. It is also found in a directory for 1794, when it was located at 181 Pearl Street. In 1795 the entry was changed to John Morton & Co., printers. It was in this year apparently that Morton became the principal owner of the *Daily Advertiser*, founded in 1785 and one of the earliest daily newspapers in New York City. From 1789 to 1794 it had been published by Francis Childs and John Swaine, a partnership that ended in 1794, leaving Childs as the publisher. Apparently Morton purchased Swaine's share at some time in 1795, for after Childs had transferred his interest to Morton, the latter, in an editorial in the issue for January 25, 1796, stated that he had been the principal proprietor for the past year. His own name did not appear in the imprint, which read: "Printed by William Robins, for the Proprietor." This proprietorship must have included also the printing plant, for in September 1796 the city's Common Council ordered payment to him of more than £35 for printing and in the following December entered into an agreement with him to print certain public items in the *Daily Advertiser* and others separately. The venture into publishing was not so far removed from his business as a merchant as might be assumed, for the name of the paper provides a reasonably accurate description of its contents. At the time, such a paper was less a newspaper, in the modern sense of the term, than an advertising medium serving principally the commercial interests of the city.

It may be, however, that his sister was approximately correct in recalling that his trip to Europe was followed by abandonment of mercantile activity. She tells of accompanying him late in the summer of 1795 on a trip to Boston, undertaken by him for "the recovery of a debt due on his former mercantile concerns." This was the visit during which she met her future husband, and the details of the trip obviously remained vivid in her recollection. She speaks also of John's ultimate failure in his new venture, and there is confirmation enough in the record. His contract with the Common Council seems to have ended with a final payment of some £10 on August 6, 1798. The issue of the *Daily Advertiser* for July 10, 1798 had appeared with an imprint carrying only the name of Charles Snowden. In the directories from 1798 through 1800, Morton was listed simply as a merchant of 59 Broadway, which was the address also of his brother Jacob.

There is evidence that in 1798 Morton may have considered entering the military service at a time of increasing tension in relations with France, but instead on June 29, 1799, he received appointment as American consul at Havana in Cuba. He lived there for three years, according to a brief but informative article on the city of Havana that he wrote in 1803 for the New York *Medical Repository*. The editors thought so highly of the piece that they suggested that their readers might expect additional material drawn from the much fuller information Morton had collected. But this seems not to have occurred.

Indeed, the remainder of his life, even his residence after 1802, is obscure. It is said, on the authority of a member of the family, that he later lived in Philadelphia and died there in 1835 at the age of seventy, which seems to be off the mark by only two years. The College catalogues listed him as dead as early as 1830, perhaps because of some confusion with another John Morton, who was president of the Bank of North America from 1809 to 1822 and who died on April 23, 1828. Whatever may be the fact, the Princeton graduate seems never to have married.

Sources: *NYGBR*, 50 (1919), 143n; 5 (1874), 183; *Memoir of the Life of Eliza S.M. Quincy* (1861), 13-27, 24 ("full of officers"), 36-38, 42-43, 55-56 ("amiable and affectionate," financial remittances," "travelling"), 60-64 ("recovery of a debt"), 266; *NJHSP* (3 ser.), 3 (1898-1900), 179; *N.J. Gazette*, 9 Oct 1782 (commencement); *N.Y. Wills*, xii, 307-308; *DAB* (Josiah Quincy); C. Bridgham, *Bibliography of Amer. Newspapers* (1947), i, 620; *AASP* (n.s.), 27 (1917), 396-97; D. C. McMurtrie, *Hist. of Printing in U.S.*, ii (1936), 166-69; *NYSHA Proc.*, 17 (1919), 90-93; *MCCCNY*, ii, 278, 307-308, 400, 417, 461; *Hamilton Papers*, xxii, 93, 100, 529n; "Notices Respecting the City of Havana," *Medical Repository*, vi (1803), 228-34; als JM to T. Jefferson, 29 Nov 1802, Jefferson mss; Giger, Memoirs. Directories for Phila. throughout the period raise some doubt regarding his residence there and leave no room for mistakenly identifying him with John Morton, bank president, for whom see L. Lewis, Jr., *Hist. of the Bank of North Amer.* (1882), 119, 120.

WFC

Robert Pearson

Robert Pearson, A.B., A.M. 1785, lawyer, the son of Elizabeth Smith and her husband, Isaac Pearson, was born near Nottingham Township, Burlington County, New Jersey, where his father owned a sizable plantation and was also a successful investor in a variety of commercial enterprises. A vestryman of the Anglican St. Michael's Church in nearby Trenton, Isaac Pearson served on the Burlington County Committee of Observation in February 1775 and was then a member of the Provincial Congress of New Jersey and of the New Jersey Committee of Safety. The date of his son's birth is unknown, but it was probably late in 1762, for the bond of Isaac and Elizabeth Pearson's marriage was posted on December 7, 1761, and Robert Pearson was the older of their two living children in 1775 when his father made a will.

Very little has been discovered about Pearson's life before he entered the College, where he reportedly joined the Cliosophic Society in 1779. At the commencement exercises of 1782, he participated in a forensic dispute on the question of whether "the idea of the beautiful, in the fine arts, has any real standard in nature," in which he defended the proposition. He then delivered an address on "the advantages of a liberal education." He received his second degree in 1785, probably while he was reading law. Admitted to the state bar in April 1789 while practicing in Nottingham, he was listed as a counselor in May 1794.

In 1790, Pearson signed the successful petition of Robert Fitch to the New Jersey legislature for a monopoly on all steamboat transit on the east side of the Delaware River. Eight years later Pearson inherited a substantial amount of property from his father, including two slaves. In 1800-1801, and in 1810-1811, he, like his father, served on the vestry of St. Michael's Church, and he was a member of its board of trustees from 1801 to 1809.

After his last term on the vestry, and certainly by 1815, Pearson moved to Woodbury, Gloucester County. He continued his legal practice there. No evidence of his having married has been found. He died in Woodbury on April 23, 1825.

SOURCES: Alumni file, PUA; H. Schuyler, *Hist. of St. Michael's Chh., Trenton* (1926), 104; *N.J. Wills*, x, 344-45; *N.J. Gazette*, 9 Oct 1782 (commencement); 10 Oct 1785 (A.M.); Trenton Hist. Soc., *A Hist. of Trenton, 1679-1929* (1929), I, 135, 232; *Min. of the Prov. Cong. . . . of N.J.* (1879), 183, 194, 197, 325; T. Cushing and C. E. Sheppard, *Hist. of the Counties of Gloucester, Salem, and Cumberland, N.J.* (1883), 169; *Trenton Federalist*, 2 May 1825.

Richard (Dirck) Ten Eyck

RICHARD (DIRCK) TEN EYCK, A.B., physician, was the fourth of eight children and the second son of Matthew Ten Eyck, of Hurley, Ulster County, New York, and his wife, Cornelia Wynkoop. He was born February 1, 1762 and baptized six days later in the Dutch Reformed Church at nearby Kingston.

The Ten Eyck family had been farmers in the area since at least 1708 when Richard's great-grandfather Mathys Ten Eyck was granted land in Hurley. The exact occupation of Richard's father is unknown, but he possessed fourteen slaves in 1790 and was probably a landowner of some substance. The elder Ten Eyck was active locally as a member of the county convention electing delegates to the Provincial Congress in April 1775, and he served on the Ulster County Committee of Safety. Being over fifty years old, he was among those organized into the Hurley company of "Associated Exempts" in August 1778. He also held the position of speaker or president of the Hurley trustees and freeholders, and in this capacity, presented an address of welcome to George Washington in November 1782 when the general passed through the town.

Before coming to the College at an uncertain date, Richard Ten Eyck served for a time as a private in the First or Northern Regiment of Ulster County. He may also have attended the newly founded academy at Kingston, which in time boasted both an English and a Latin school. At Princeton, Ten Eyck was known by the Dutch form of his name and appears as "Derrick" among the graduate members of the American Whig Society, which he joined upon its reconstitution in 1782. On his diploma, however, his name was latinized to "Richardus." In the commencement exercises of September 25, 1782, Ten Eyck made the reply in a debate on the question whether large or small states were "more favourable to union, population, and improvement in the arts."

When and where Ten Eyck received his medical training have not been discovered, but it may have been in the area of New Jersey. That he earned the M.D. degree can only be inferred from his gravestone inscription. His wife, Janet Baker, whom he presumably had married before the birth of their first child in February 1787, was the daughter of a Somerset County man, Matthias Baker. The fact that Ten Eyck was named a coexecutor of his father-in-law's will, dated March 10, 1789, may indicate that he was still in the neighborhood then. In June 1790, though, his second child was baptized in the Dutch Church at Kingston, New York, and according to the census of 1790, Ten Eyck was settled in Hurley with three slaves in a household of seven. Over the next sixteen years, three more children were born, for a total of three daughters and two sons.

By all appearances, Ten Eyck lived his long life quietly as a country doctor. In 1798-1799 he was the town supervisor of Hurley, and a year or two later he signed a petition to the Consistory of Kingston, urging the establishment of a new Reformed church at Hurley. But when the Medical Society of the County of Ulster was formed in 1806, Ten Eyck was not among its founders, and he seems never to have been a member, although in 1808 his name was included in a catalogue of physicians in the county.

His wife Janet died in 1823, and it is said that he himself was blind for several years before his death on February 15, 1851. He was buried in the churchyard at Hurley.

SOURCES: Alumni file, PUA; *NYGBR*, 14 (1883), 275-76, 285; 61 (1930), 227; A. T. Clearwater, *Hist. of Ulster Cnty., N.Y.* (1907), 151, 262; *Washington Writings*, xxv, 346; *NYHSA Proc.*, 29 (1931), 129-40; Beam, *Whig Soc.*, 61; *N.J. Gazette*, 9 Oct 1782 (commencement); *N.J. Wills*, vii, 17; *First Census, N.Y.*, 170; N. B. Sylvester, *Hist. of Ulster Cnty. N.Y.* (1880), 121-22, 149-51.

JMR

Stephen Van Rensselaer

STEPHEN VAN RENSSELAER, A.B. Harvard 1782, LL.D. Yale 1822, public official, soldier, philanthropist, and one of the wealthiest men in the United States, was born on November 1, 1764, in New York City in the home of his maternal grandfather, Philip Livingston, signer of the Declaration of Independence. His mother, Catherine Livingston Van Rensselaer, was the sister of Philip Philip Livingston (A.B. 1758) and Peter Van Brugh Livingston, Jr. (A.B. 1766). His father, Stephen Van Rensselaer (Yale 1763), was the hereditary lord of the huge family estate, which in 1767 included more than 700,000 acres and 281 tenant families in New York.

The Van Rensselaers moved into a newly built manorhouse at Watervliet in Albany, New York in 1765. On October 19, 1769, the elder Stephen died at the age of twenty-seven, leaving the manor and most of the estate in trust to his namesake and elder son, and leaving instructions to his widow that their children were to be educated "in a manner suitable to their birth." The youngsters' guardian was to be their mother's kinsman Abraham Ten Broeck, a leading upcountry Whig, husband of the dead patroon's sister, and brother of Dirck Ten Broeck (Class of 1758).

Young Van Rensselaer received his earliest education at the school run by John Waters in Albany. At the wish of the Livingston family, he attended the academy in Elizabethtown, New Jersey, which was supervised in succession by Joseph Periam (A.B. 1762) and Francis Barber (A.B. 1767). The Revolution drove the boy and his family to sanctuary in Kingston, New York, where his education continued in a

Stephen Van Rensselaer, Class of 1782
BY GILBERT STUART

classical school under the direction of the Scottish immigrant John
Addison. In the summer of 1779 President Witherspoon stopped at
Kingston on his way south after having investigated New Hampshire
land grants for the Continental Congress. When he resumed his journey, Witherspoon took Van Rensselaer with him to be enrolled in the
grammar school in Princeton, where his father had preceded him some
fifteen years before.

Although he was a student in the grammar school for barely two
months, Van Rensselaer delivered the English valedictory address at
the school's commencement exercises on September 28, 1779. A lengthy
discourse on the Aristotelian injunction to "Know Thyself," the
speech was notable for its persistent warnings against the blandish-
ments of wealth and luxury. Along with five other graduates, Van
Rensselaer was then admitted "into the Freshman Class" at the College.

In Princeton, Van Rensselaer resided with the family of Professor
Samuel Stanhope Smith (A.B. 1769). His valedictory sentiments notwithstanding, and within the limits imposed by war and rural location,

he continued to live according to his ample means—so much so that he must have been one of the students about whose extravagance and ostentation Witherspoon complained in the summer of 1779. That August, for example, the young patroon paid more than £367 for the making of one green suit of clothes from Philadelphia.

At the end of the academic year in the fall of 1781, probably at the urging of relatives who feared that Princeton was still a dangerous place to be in time of war, Van Rensselaer applied for admission to Harvard College. It is likely that he had acquired some advanced standing while at Nassau Hall, for he applied to Harvard as a "Senior Sophister." On October 1 the faculty in Cambridge agreed to consider his application after he had undergone a period of "private instruction, in Mathematical and Metaphysical knowledge, and produced testimonials from Princetown College, of his regular standing & good behaviour there." On March 1, 1782, armed with a certificate from Witherspoon and fortified by several months of tutoring by Professor Samuel Williams, Van Rensselaer entered the senior class at Harvard.

He may have found the discipline in Cambridge less rigorous or the company more boisterous than in Princeton, for while there is no record of any disciplinary problem in his days at Nassau Hall, Van Rensselaer was among a group of Harvard men who were fined £15 each for patronizing a tavern on a Saturday night and then causing a commotion in the Yard that ended with the breaking of a few windows. Apparently, he continued his extravagant style of life, for when he graduated in September 1782 he left behind him a lengthy list of debts. To pay them he sent a bag of gold to his close friend Harrison Gray Otis (Harvard 1783). Van Rensselaer's own attitude toward the college may be inferred from a letter written to him by Otis during the latter's senior year in which the young Bostonian called upon Time to "hasten the desired Period when I shall bid adieu to the Sophisticated Jargon of a superstitious Synod of pension'd Bigots."

On June 6, 1783, Van Rensselaer married Margaret Schuyler, the daughter of another great New York landowner and revolutionary general, Philip Schuyler, at her father's seat in Schuylerville. Her sister was the wife of Alexander Hamilton, thus Van Rensselaer was united with the most powerful members of what would become the state's Federalist establishment. The newlyweds could not yet move into the mansion at Watervliet, which was occupied by Van Rensselaer's mother and her second husband, Dominie Eilardus Westerlo, pastor of the Dutch Reformed Church in Albany. Until his twenty-first birthday, Van Rensselaer and his wife lived in the church parsonage; they then simply exchanged residences with the Westerlos.

Shortly before Van Rensselaer attained his majority, the New York legislature abolished hereditary lordships and manors. Technically, therefore, he was merely the landlord of his gigantic holdings, but he was known almost universally as the "Patroon," and he regarded his responsibilities and prerogatives in virtually the same way as his ancestors had for more than a century. He was, however, prone neither to autocratic behavior nor to the unlimited aggrandizement of his personal wealth. When he became a communicant of the Dutch Reformed Church in the spring of 1787, he pledged himself to a life of temperance and simplicity, and he undertook to abide by that pledge in his dealings with his tenants. Mindful of the resentment that renters often feel toward landlords, and eager to populate and cultivate the full expanse of his property, Van Rensselaer replaced traditional leases with agreements that were tantamount to freehold contracts modified by restrictions on alienation and by the reservation of a relatively nominal perpetual rent. Almost all of his tenants were thus enfranchised, and the patroon was able to proclaim in a broadside advertisement in 1789 that no other "hired lands . . . [were] let on as favorable terms" as his own. Although the perpetual rent remained a potential cause for tenant discontent, Van Rensselaer was lenient in foreclosing and in the collection of arrearages. While his tenants paid lower fees than many, the proliferation of renters and the "quarter sale" system that the patroon adopted, possibly at the suggestion of his brother-in-law Hamilton, insured him a large and growing annual income. The generous terms and his reputation for philanthropy, while they did not defuse all tenant hostility, did tend to postpone the most extreme confrontations between landlord and renter until after Van Rensselaer's death.

One complaint against the patroon that was never entirely silenced was that he, like other great landlords, exerted "undue . . . influence" on his tenants' politics. Van Rensselaer was consistently active in public affairs after 1788, when he stood unsuccessfully for election to the state convention that was to consider the new federal Constitution. His district in Albany County was then heavily antifederalist. But once the Constitution was ratified, he and fellow Federalists were able to dominate the politics of the Upper Hudson Valley, and Van Rensselaer's own electoral victories in his district were so lopsided that his denials of using pressure on his tenants ring hollow.

With his father-in-law, Van Rensselaer led the parade in Albany that celebrated ratification in August 1788, and the next spring he was elected to his first term in the state assembly. In 1791 the patroon moved to the state senate, where he was among the minority who voted for Schuyler's reelection to the United States Senate against Aaron Burr (A.B. 1772). In 1792, as the running mate of John Jay, Van Rensselaer campaigned for the office of lieutenant governor. He served as election inspector for his own district during the contest, and Chancellor Robert Livingston, who supported the incumbent Clinton administration, charged Van Rensselaer with using special paper for the ballots cast by his tenants so that he could know how they voted. The election was extremely close, but Clinton won after a heated dispute over canvassing irregularities. During the debate, Van Rensselaer avoided a duel with one of the canvassers only by issuing a last-minute apology for having called the man a rascal.

Although party organization was fairly primitive in 1792, the election had reinforced the identity of federalism and property in New York. Given his youth and inexperience, Van Rensselaer's candidacy had underlined that point and provided the Clintonians with a perfect target for status-oriented politics.

Van Rensselaer and Jay successfully unseated the Clintonians in 1795. But while the patroon received nearly 70% of the votes of his own tenants, he won the lieutenant governorship by fewer than 700 of the 25,000 votes cast. In 1798, however, he was the nominee of both parties for reelection, and so won unanimously. Supported by the Federalists for governor in 1801, Van Rensselaer was able to call for support upon the likes of Jay, Hamilton, Schuyler, Rufus King, and Gouverneur Morris. Nevertheless, the New York Federalists shared the fate of their party nationwide, and the patroon was defeated.

After Schuyler's death in 1804, Van Rensselaer was the most prominent member of the ancient class of Dutch landlords, and his political influence remained commensurately strong. Yet his growing personal, business, and philanthropic concerns limited the amount of his time available for politics.

A semi-invalid for many years, Margaret Schuyler Van Rensselaer had died during the campaign of 1801. A son, Stephen (A.B. 1808), was the only survivor of their three children. In May 1802, Van Rensselaer married Cornelia Paterson, the daughter of Justice William Paterson (A.B. 1763). Together they were to have nine children.

Van Rensselaer's many interests included the Massachusetts Historical Society, of which he became a member in 1797; the German Society; the Albany Bible Society; the Bank of Albany, of which he was the first president of the board in 1792; and the city's orphan asylum. A passionate advocate of internal improvements, he served on the state commission that surveyed the route and supervised construction of the Erie Canal, and he was ultimately president of the canal commission for fourteen years. That work brought him into regular contact with DeWitt Clinton, who remained his "warmest friend."

The patroon's greatest enthusiasm, however, was reserved for the science of agriculture and for the conduct of education. In 1791 he had helped establish the Society for the Promotion of Agriculture, Arts, and Manufactures, which became the Society for the Promotion of Useful Arts in 1804. As president of the Albany Lyceum of Natural History, he was elected to head the Albany Institute when it was created in 1824. His influence in the state legislature, to which he was elected again from 1807 to 1810, and in 1816, was regularly used in the service of agriculture, and he was the first president of the state's Board of Agriculture in 1820. It was under his leadership that the board sponsored valuable surveys of New York farmland by Professor Amos Eaton, the results of which were published at Van Rensselaer's expense and were sent by him personally to Thomas Jefferson and James Madison (A.B. 1771). The patroon then sponsored Eaton on a lecture tour along the survey route, the first step in an educational effort that culminated in the establishment of an experimental school at Troy, New York in 1824. As president of the board of trustees of what became Rensselaer Polytechnic Institute, Van Rensselaer paid faculty salaries, hired staff, and purchased books and equipment. He was a friend and patron to other educational institutions as well: a trustee of Rutgers College, Williams College, and the Albany Academy, a regent and then Chancellor of the state university of New York; a major donor to the Albany Medical College and Hamilton College; and a leader of Yale's first major fundraising drive in 1831-1832. He maintained a cordial correspondence with Samuel Stanhope Smith after the latter's elevation to the presidency at Princeton, but whether and to what extent Nassau Hall may have benefited from his generosity remain unclear.

Van Rensselaer's first military appointment had been as a major in the Albany County Militia in 1786. He was promoted to lieutenant colonel and regimental commander in 1788, and in 1801, while lieutenant governor, he was given the rank of major general commanding the state's division of cavalry. Governor Daniel Tompkins's decision to appoint Van Rensselaer to command the New York militia during the War of 1812 was largely based on the fact that the patroon was the likely Federalist contender for Tompkins's office in 1813. The governor may have hoped to divide Federalist opponents of his party and the war by such an appointment, or he may have hoped to saddle his political rival with the onus of military defeat. Certainly, Van Rensselaer faced a difficult assignment in assembling and equipping his ill-trained troops during the summer of 1812, and he complained regularly that his men were not ready for combat. Whatever his personal attitude toward the war might have been, and in spite of his own lack of experience on the line, he abandoned partisanship and dedicated himself to his command. In early October, while camped at Lewiston on the Niagara frontier, he wrote to Rufus King that an immediate American victory was essential to erase the ignominy of recent defeats. Persuaded that he could not keep his 6,000 men under control without action, he launched a surprise attack on Queenstown, Canada on the night of October 11, and the town was quickly taken. Van Rensselaer's green troops soon lost their ardor, however, and refused to cross the river to reinforce Queenstown against a counterattack. Although the battle had been won, and in spite of the best efforts of Van Rensselaer, his kinsman Colonel Solomon Van Rensselaer, and Lieutenant Colonel Winfield Scott of the United States Army, the British recaptured the settlement. On October 23 Van Rensselaer resigned his command. He returned to Albany to a hero's welcome on October 31.

Accusing Tompkins of insensitivity toward the officers who had served at Queenstown, the Federalists nominated Van Rensselaer for governor in 1813. In a close election, Tompkins won. The patroon, who regularly criticized the conduct of the war by the state and federal governments, nonetheless resolutely abstained from any partisan or sectional attempts to weaken the national resolve or to end the war less than honorably for the United States.

During the "Era of Good Feeling," while political parties split, shifted, and realigned, Van Rensselaer continued a devout Federalist under various partisan labels. As an "Independent Republican," he was elected to the state constitutional convention in 1821, during which he managed to maintain friendships with both DeWitt Clinton and Martin Van Buren while standing firmly and futilely for limited suffrage. It was as a Clinton-style Republican that he was elected to succeed Solomon Van Rensselaer in the United States House of Representatives early in 1822, and his voting record in Congress was almost quaintly Federalist. In February 1825, after having apparently pledged to support William H. Crawford for president when the election was thrown to the House, Van Rensselaer ultimately voted for John Quincy Adams, thereby putting New York in Adams's column. It was one of the two or three crucial votes cast in that election, and it was a decision that was as difficult as any Van Rensselaer had ever made. By voting as he did, he alienated himself from the other residents of his boarding house at a time when such groupings were the fundamental units of congressional politics. One of his housemates, Van

Buren, ultimately forgave him, but the aging patroon was sent to "coventry" by many other colleagues in spite of his tearful apologies. Some charged him with lying, others with being weak or a fool. And he was as deeply distressed by having to make the choice as any other members were by the choice he made. For weeks he had been beset by supporters of Adams, Crawford, Henry Clay, and Andrew Jackson, and he had variously indicated that any one of them would be acceptable to him. Perhaps the best explanation for his decision was made more than a year before the vote was cast when, in a letter to Solomon Van Rensselaer, he explained that he had "worked against the Stream" until he was "exhausted." Now, he said, he was "disposed to glide with the Stream." His choice at least gained him friends among Adams's allies, including Daniel Webster, who not only offered to share his room with the patroon in the next session but also briefly paid court to Van Rensselaer's daughter Catherine.

Van Rensselaer retired from Congress in 1829, when he was chairman of the House Committee on Agriculture. He did not lose his interest in politics or in public issues, as his ongoing correspondence with Van Buren makes clear, and even his old fashioned Federalism may finally have yielded slightly to the pressures of a new era. But his health was gradually failing and he preferred to devote himself to his "benevolent" causes rather than to "appear again before the public in any other character than that of a Christian whose remnant of life I wish to spend promoting the extension of the Redeemer's Kingdom." The patroon summered at the spa in Saratoga Springs and he continued his charitable efforts to the regular enhancement of his reputation. He withdrew from active Freemasonry after declining reelection as Grand Master in Albany in 1826.

In 1832 Van Rensselaer prepared his will, dividing his holdings among his ten children, many of whom had been educated by Joseph Henry before that scholar moved on to the faculty at Albany Academy and then to Nassau Hall. Young Stephen Van Rensselaer, prohibited by law from inheriting the title of patroon, was given the manor house at Watervliet and most of the west manor. His half-brother William received the bulk of the east manor. One provision in the will required both heirs to collect rents still in arrears at the patroon's death, which came on January 26, 1839. Their efforts to assert the authority that their father had relaxed for so long produced the so-called Helderberg War, one of the most violent outbursts of tenant rebellion in the century. The ancient manorial system was defended by such authors as James Fenimore Cooper, an occasional guest in the old patroon's home, but the agitation led directly to provisions in the new state constitution of 1846 that abolished all feudal tenures and converted the Van Rensselaer estate into freeholdings with mortgage deeds. The body of Stephen Van Rensselaer, the last patroon, was buried in the family plot and later reinterred in Albany's Rural Cemetery.

SOURCES: *DAB; BDAC*; D. D. Barnard, *Discourse on . . . Stephen Van Rensselaer* (1839); J. B. Holgate, *Amer. Geneal.* (1848), 43, 51-54; C. Reynolds, *Hudson-Mohawk Geneal. and Family Memoirs*, I (1911), 14-19; Dexter, *Yale Biographies*, III, 53-54; T. E. Vermilye, "Funeral Discourse Occasioned by the Death of Hon. Stephen Van Rensselaer" (1839); W. Barlow, "Character and Reward of a Just Man" (1839); G. W. Bethune, "True Glory: A Sermon . . . on the . . . death of . . . Van Rensselaer" (1839), PPPrHi; *Princetonians, 1748-1768*, 188, 252; D. R. Fox, *Decline of the Aristocracy in Politics of N.Y.* (1965), passim; J. Judd, ed., *Correspondence of Van Cortlandt Family* (1977), 26, 507, 527-30; A. F. Young, *Democratic Republicans of N.Y.* (1967), passim; W. B. Fink, "Stephen Van Rensselaer: The Last Patroon," Ph.D. dissert., Teacher's College, Columbia Univ. (1950); *N.Y. Wills*, VIII, 290-92 ("suitable to their birth"); V. L. Collins, *President Witherspoon* (1925), II, 42, 117; SVR, "A Valedictory Oration . . . at the Grammar School, Sept. 28, 1779," als W. Pollard to SVR, 3 Aug 1780, in NjP; *NJA* (2 ser.), III, 669 ("Freshman Class"); Harvard Univ. *Faculty Records*, IV, 272-73 ("Senior Sophister"); V, 6-7 [with the permission of the Harvard Univ. Arch. and through the kind assistance of Ms. Jennifer Zukowski, which are gratefully acknowledged]; S. E. Morison, *Harrison Gray Otis* (1969), 36 ("pension'd Bigots"), 37; D. M. Ellis, *Landlords and Farmers in the Hudson-Mohawk Region* (1946), 36-38, 39 ("hired lands"), 40, 98-99, 128-29, 141-42, 231-35; Duke de la Rochefoucault Liancourt, *Travels Through the U.S.A.* (1799), I, 388; C. Z. Lincoln, *Constitutional Hist. of N.Y.* (1906), II, 16; E. W. Spaulding, *N.Y. in the Critical Period* (1932), 64; W. Strickland, *Journal of a Tour in the U.S.A.* (1971), 171 ("undue . . . influence"); A. Kass, *Politics in N.Y. State, 1800-1830* (1965), 59, 104; L. G. DePauw, *Eleventh Pillar* (1966), 112, 135; N. E. Cunningham, *Jeffersonian Republicans* (1957), 35-38; J. Munsell, *Annals of Albany*, III (1852), 152, 165, 171, 210; V (1854), 28; F. Monaghan, *John Jay* (1935), 405, 416; W. B. Hatcher, *Edward Livingston, Jeffersonian Republican and Jacksonian Democrat* (1940), 74-75; *Hamilton Papers*, XI, 378; XXI, 60, 101; XXIII, 43; XXIV, 212; XXV, 342-43, 348-49; *NJHSP* (n.s.), 16 (1931), 187; *MHSP* (2 ser.), I, 104, 201; J. A. Krout and D. R. Fox, *Completion of Independence* (1944), 378; *NYHS Coll.*, LXXIII, 11 ("warmest friend"); D. Bobbé, *DeWitt Clinton* (1933), 166, 249, 269; R. E. Shaw, *Erie Water West* (1966), 45; D. M. Ellis et al., *Hist. of N.Y. State* (1967), 170; N. Miller, *Enterprise of a Free People* (1962), 15; als SVR to T. Jefferson, 15 Feb 1825, and T. Jefferson to SVR, 20 Feb 1825, in Jefferson MSS; J. Madison to SVR, 14 Mar 1822, 11 Feb 1823, 6 May 1824, and SVR to J. Madison, 4 Feb 1823, in Madison MSS; *Centennial Celebration of Rensselaer Polytechnic Institute* (1825), 62-64, 104; H. B. Nason, *Bio. Rec. of the Officers and Graduates of Rensselaer Polytechnic Institute, 1824-1886* (1887), 19, 26, 27; B. M. Kelley, *Yale: A History* (1974), 152-54; *N.Y. Hist.*, 21 (1940), 276-77, 279; 32 (1951), 324-29; 50 (1969), 31-32; 35 (1954), 416; R. W. Irwin, *Daniel Tompkins* (1968), 101, 169, 170; als S. S. Smith to SVR, 22 Sep 1815, NjP; *Mil. Min., Council of Appointment, St. of N.Y.*, II, 1,403, 2,429; J. Richardson, *War of 1812* (1902), 129; H. L. Coles, *War of 1812* (1965), 59-63, 66; G. Tucker, *Poltroons and Patriots* (1954), 183-92; C. R. King, ed., *Life and Correspondence of Rufus King*, V (1898), 286-87; VI (1900), 250-51, 308-309; C.V.R. Bonney, *Legacy of Hist. Gleanings*, I (1875), passim, esp. 409 ("glide with the Stream"); L. L. Babcock, *War of 1812 on the Niagra Frontier* (1927), 37-39, 44-51; S. Van Rensselaer, *Narrative of the Affair of Queenstown* (1836); *NYHSA Proc.*, 3 (1909), 14-22; N. H. Carter et al., *Reports of the Proc. and Debates of the Convention of 1821* (1821), 182-83, 667, 668; *A/C*, XXXIX-XLII, passim; *Reg. of Debates in Congress*, I-VI; als SVR to M. Van Buren, 14

May 1824, 2 Apr 1834 ("Redeemer's Kingdom"), and passim, Van Buren mss; S. Liv-ermore, *Twilight of Federalism* (1962), 152, 172-83; G.G. Van Deusen, *Henry Clay* (1937), 191; J. S. Young, *Washington Community, 1800-1828* (1966), 104-105; A. Nev-ins, ed., *Diary of John Quincy Adams* (1951), 339-40; G. Hunt, ed., *First Forty Years of Washington Soc.* (1906), 176, 184-85 ("coventry"), 191-92; C. M. Wiltse and H. D. Moser, eds., *Papers of Daniel Webster*, II (1976), 138, 387, 413-14; J. S. Bassett, *Correspondence of Andrew Jackson*, V (1931), 479; B. Tuckerman, ed., *Diary of Philip Hone* (1910), 34-35, 59; *NCHR*, 15 (1938), 160; D. T. Miller, *Jacksonian Aristocracy* (1967), 65; T. A. Glenn, *Some Colonial Mansions* (1899), 142, 159, 160, 163, 164.

MANUSCRIPTS: N, NNC (DeWitt Clinton mss)

PUBLICATIONS: See Sabin, #98549; or *Cat. of Books in the Libr. of Stephen Van Rens-selaer, Manor House, Albany* (1834)

[handwritten: as well as a cousin of Henry Edward Watkins (A.B. 1801)]

Richard N. Venable

RICHARD N. VENABLE, A.B., lawyer, planter, and public official, was born January 16, 1763, in Prince Edward County, Virginia, the third son of Nathaniel and Elizabeth Woodson Venable. He was a younger brother of Samuel Woodson Venable (A.B. 1780) and Abraham Bed-ford Venable (A.B. 1780) and the older brother of Nathaniel E. Ven-able (A.B. 1796). The father, a leading resident of the county, was a founder and lifelong trustee of Prince Edward Academy, later Hamp-den-Sidney College, and there seems to be no reason for doubting that Richard, like his older brothers before him, had been prepared for college at the academy, which only in 1783 acquired by state charter the right to grant degrees. No doubt, too, it was the influence of Sam-uel Stanhope Smith (A.B. 1769), first rector of the academy who in 1779 returned to Nassau Hall as Professor of Moral Philosophy, that brought Richard to Princeton for the completion of his education. When he matriculated is uncertain. A later manuscript list of mem-bers of the Cliosophic Society gives 1781 as the date of his admission to that society, which presumably would have been on or after July 4, 1781, when the society is said to have been revived following a period of virtual inactivity imposed by wartime conditions. At his commence-ment on September 25, 1782, Richard delivered an English oration on the subject of agriculture.

Venable has been listed as a student in the College of William and Mary under the year 1785, which supports the tradition that after graduating from Princeton he studied law with the celebrated George Wythe, professor of law and police in that college since 1779. In July 1786 Richard was qualified as an attorney for practice in Prince

Richard N. Venable, A.B. 1782
BY JAMES PEALE

Edward County. He apparently qualified in other more or less neighboring counties, and for a time his residence was at Peytonsburg in
Pittsylvania County. The published fragment of a diary he kept shows
that he engaged in the usual itinerant practice of a lawyer moving
from courthouse to courthouse. Thus, under the date of January 22,
1791, he records: "Went to Henry Court 85 miles, from then[ce] to
Franklin C. H. 37 miles, returned by Sam Calland's to Peytonsburg,
55 miles, from there to Prince Edward 60 miles and returned to Peytonsburg 11 February." More than once he was in Richmond, since
1780 the capital city of the state. "This surely is the seat of law learning," he wrote, "courts of justice are here sitting almost from one end
of the year to the other." "Just five years since I began practice of the
law" is the entry under the date August 6, 1791. Eventually, he settled
permanently in his home county, though just when is uncertain, and
it has been suggested that thereafter his active interests were more
those of a planter than of a lawyer.

Although the published part of the diary is only a small fragment, it reveals a good deal of the man's character. When in Richmond, he attended the theater, and on one occasion, was "much entertained with the scenery and painting representing a shipwreck." Under May 4, 1791, the entry reads: "Came home, 25 or 30 miles, much devoted to reflection." The quality of his ruminations is suggested by the following notation of January 12, 1792: "I see through the window the ox that draws our firing wood. See how he holds down his head to the weather, and, as he slowly moves through the snow with gravity and humility, joins all nature in acknowledging that this is winter." He seems too to have loved books, and on a Sunday he might stay home from church to read Milton. Benjamin Latrobe, after traveling with him in the summer of 1796, described him as a man of "good sense" and a natural "mildness of temper." Latrobe noted of a company seemingly given to the use of "grog" that "Mr. Venable and myself are water drinkers." Venable's own diary entries were always brief, but he could lend life to a scene he observed, as when he described the "great anxiety in the people to see Gen'l Washington" when in June 1791 he passed through Charlotte Court House. "Strange is the impulse," he remarked, "which is felt by almost every breast to see the face of a great good man—sensation better felt than expressed."

Venable's diary reveals that he had a very active interest in the speculative, and ultimately abortive, venture of the Virginia Yazoo Company, as did his brother Abraham. The company was one of three (the others being the South Carolina and Tennessee Yazoo Companies) that in 1789 sought to purchase from Georgia some seven million acres of western lands for above $93,000. Negotiations with the state of Georgia fell through in advance of an act of the legislature in 1795, which resulted in sales commonly described as the Yazoo Fraud. Much more enduring was his identification as stockholder and officer of the Upper Appomattox Company incorporated by the Virginia legislature in 1795 to implement a project, inaugurated in 1787, for extending and improving the navigation of that stream. It was as a consulting engineer for this undertaking that Latrobe was brought into Venable's company during the summer of 1796. As late as 1835 Venable was one of the company's superintendents. He is said to have taken an active interest in a variety of other "internal improvements."

The most enduring of his commitments perhaps was to Hampden-Sidney College. Elected in 1792 to its board of trustees, on which his father and brothers Samuel and Abraham already sat, and to which his cousin Joseph Venable (A.B. 1783) was elected on the same day, Richard served until his death. Through much of the period from 1813 until his resignation as treasurer in 1832, he carried a special responsibility for the finances of the college, and it has been suggested that he and other members of his family were generous over the years in helping the college pay its bills. The duties of a trustee in these earlier years involved much more than attendance at the stated meetings of the board, and the variety of special assignments given to Richard Venable, including in 1828 membership in a committee charged with writing a history of the college, indicate that he was regarded as one of the more dependable of the trustees.

From time to time, he answered a call for service in public office, but there is little in the overall record to suggest that he was politically ambitious. He represented the county in the lower house of the state assembly in 1797-1798, 1820-1821, and 1830-1831. In 1820 he became a member of the board of school commissioners charged with the administration of that part of the state's literary fund assigned to the county for assistance in the education of poor children, and from 1823 to 1825 he carried the heavier responsibilities of treasurer to the board. He probably shared with his brother Abraham the convictions that made of the latter an active member of the Jeffersonian party. He himself served in 1816 on the Republican committee for Prince Edward County. In 1828 he seems to have been among the anti-Jackson men who failed by a large margin to carry the county. In that year he sat in a special convention presided over by James Madison (A.B. 1771) and was designated a member of the committee that drafted proposals for a broad program of state-sponsored internal improvements intended as a recommendation to a forthcoming constitutional convention. He sat as a member of the Constitutional Convention of 1829-1830, which effected moderate, though by no means extensive, reforms in the government of the state.

Venable seems not to have been a man inclined toward precipitate action. He did not marry until March 5, 1797, when he was wed at the age of thirty-four by Reverend Archibald Alexander, recently elected president of Hampden-Sidney, to Mary Morton, who was just over half his own age and the daughter of Colonel William Morton of Charlotte County, Virginia. At some time after the death of Venable's father in 1804, the couple took up residence on the family's Slate Hill plantation. They seem to have had at least two children: a daughter later married to Reverend J.H.C. Leach, and Richard N. Venable, Jr. The exact date of Richard, Sr.'s death has not been found, but it occurred in 1838, apparently of a heart attack, for the body was found face down in a very shallow stream.

SOURCES: See Abraham B. Venable (A.B. 1780); E. M. Venable, *Venables of Va.* (1925), 36; MS Clio. Soc. membership list, alumni file, PUA; *N.J. Gazette*, 9 Oct 1782 (commencement); *Tyler's Quart.*, 2 (1920-1921), 135-38 (diary fragment from which all quotations are taken except as cited below); J. D. Eggleston, *Historic Slate Hill Plantation* (1945), 18 ("this is winter"); B. H. Latrobe, *Diary of Benjamin Latrobe* (1905), 18 ("good sense"), 20 ("water drinkers"); S. G. McLendon, *Hist. of Public Domain of Ga.* (1924), 35-39; *Cal. Va. St. Papers*, VIII, 421; A. J. Morrison, *Hampden-Sidney College, Cal. of Board Min.* (1912), passim; H. C. Bradshaw, *Hist. of Hampden-Sydney College*, I (1976), 93, 96, 108, 110, 113, 145, 187, 198, 454; H. C. Bradshaw, *Hist. of Prince Edward Cnty., Va.* (1955), 169, 183, 187, 287-95, 325, 687, 832; *Journals, House of Delegates*, for 1797, 1820, and 1830; D. F. Wulfeck, *Marriages of Some Va. Residents*, VII (1967), 132.

MANUSCRIPTS: Hampden-Sydney Library

WFC

Samuel Wilson

SAMUEL WILSON, A.B., Presbyterian clergyman, was born in 1754 in Letterkenny Township, Cumberland (later Franklin) County, Pennsylvania, the son of John Wilson, farmer, and his wife, Sarah Reid Wilson. The relatively advanced age at which Wilson graduated raises questions not easily answered. In the case of students who subsequently entered the ministry, a likely explanation is a late "call to preach," perhaps the result of a late conversion experience. In this period, of course, the possibility of a delay imposed by military service during the war also has to be considered, but no unmistakable evidence of such service by Wilson has been found. Militia records show that there were two Samuel Wilsons enrolled in the Cumberland County Militia toward the end of the war, and one of them probably was the Princeton student. Tax records for the years from 1778 to 1782 reveal that one of the two, possibly three, Samuel Wilsons in Cumberland County held property in Letterkenny Township and suggest that Wilson was farming for at least part of the time before his admisison to the College. Perhaps the modest acreage listed had been inherited from his father, who reportedly died in 1773.

The only evidence regarding the possible date at which Wilson entered the College that has been found is in catalogues of the Cliosophic Society published in 1845 and 1876. Each of these dates his membership in the society from the year 1779. Unhappily, the validity of this record has been called into question by Wilson's great-grandson, Joshua Wilson Sharpe (A.B. 1873), who in 1915 stated that he then had in his possession Wilson's diploma from the American Whig Society. It was not impossible at this early date for a student to have belonged, at one time or another, to both societies, but it does seem to have been unusual. A more probable explanation is that the record itself is faulty.

Wilson became the victim of an even more serious error in the record of his graduation. There is no reason for doubting that at the commencement of September 25, 1782 he participated, as reported in the *New Jersey Gazette*, in a three-way debate of the question, "can all the differences in shape and complexion among mankind be accounted for from natural causes, on the supposition of the whole race having descended from one original pair?" He closed the exercise with an affirmative answer. The error is found in the list of that year's graduates, where Wilson's baptismal name was mistakenly given as William. At first glance, one assumes that this was a typographical mistake by the *Gazette*'s printer, but a check of the minutes of the trustees shows that there too the name is William Wilson. In time, the name William was struck out and Samuel inserted above the line. Some guess as to when the correction was made is possible by reference to the general catalogues of the College, where for the first time in the catalogue for 1815 he is listed as Samuel Wilson. Theretofore, in the periodically published catalogues he had remained William, or in the Latin customarily used, "Gulielmus" Wilson. The correction came sixteen years after his death, but the fact that he had died was not indicated in the catalogue in 1815. That indication is found first in the catalogue for 1818, when also for the first time the name was italicized to indicate that he had been a minister of the gospel.

Fortunately, Wilson's career after graduation poses few questions. He is said to have read theology with Reverend Robert Cooper (A.B. 1763) of the Middle Spring Church, Cumberland County. He was licensed to preach on April 14, 1785 by the Donegal Presbytery, which dismissed him to the Carlisle Presbytery on May 22, 1786. The Big Spring Congregation in Newville, west of Carlisle in Cumberland County, had been without a pastor since 1784 when William Linn (A.B. 1772) departed for Maryland, and 204 members of the congregation on March 21, 1786, had issued a call to Wilson, promising to pay "on his being ordained to be our minister" an annual salary of "one hundred and fifty Pounds, Pennsylvania Currency, in specie, and allow him the use of the dwelling-house, barn, and all the clear land on the glebe, possessed by our former minister, also plenty of timber for rails and fire-wood, likewise a sufficient security for the payment of the above-mentioned sums during his incumbency." He seems not to have been installed and ordained as pastor until June 20, 1787, but he presumably served the congregation during the interval. He continued as pastor of the Big Spring Congregation until his death at Newville on March 4, 1799.

Not long after assuming his first and only pastorate, Wilson was married to Jane Mahon, daughter of Archibald Mahon of Shippensburg, Pennsylvania, and probably a sister of Wilson's classmate William Mahon. The census of 1790 shows that "Revd. Samuel Wilson" headed a family of two free white males of sixteen years or above, one free white female, and one slave. The couple seem to have had two children, a son born in 1793 who died in 1809, and a daughter named Jean or Jane who married Dr. William M. Sharp of Newville. Wilson's widow in 1803 was married to John Heap of Shippensburg "at the seat of David Mahon," her brother, "near Shippensburgh."

SOURCES: *Centennial Memorial of the Presbytery of Carlisle* (1889), I, 106, 108, 114, 199, 426, 454; II, 71-72; Alexander, *Princeton* (which records a tradition that Wilson in 1788, no doubt a typographical error for perhaps 1778, "was farming his father's farm, when his youngest brother" came home from the army "sick with camp fever and died"; Samuel also contracted the illness, the account continues, and during his sickness "he resolved, if his life was spared, to devote it to the service of God in the work of the Christian ministry." Accordingly, on recovery he went to Princeton); Giger, Memoirs; *Pa. Arch.* (3 ser.), XXIII, 693, 706; XX, passim; Trustee Minutes, General Catalogues of College; alumni file, PUA; *N.J. Gazette*, 9 Oct 1782 (commencement); *Rec. Pres. Chh.*, 508, 543; *Min. Gen. Assem.*, *1789-1820*, 18, 89, 101, 121, 141, 170; *Hist. of Cumberland and Adams Counties* (1886) [Cumberland], 209; A. Nevin, *Churches of the Valley* (1852), 52-53, 323-26; *First Census, Pa.*, 77; *PGM*, 19 (1952-54), 119, 124n7d.; see William Mahon (A.B. 1782).

WFC

CLASS OF 1783

Samuel Beach, A.B.

William Clements, A.B.

Timothy Ford, A.B.

Ashbel Green, A.B.

Obadiah Holmes, A.B.

James (Green, Greene) Hunt, A.B.

Nathaniel Lawrence, A.B.

Jacob LeRoy, A.B.

Jacob Radcliff (Radclift, Radcliffe), A.B.

Joseph Riddle, A.B.

James Rock

Martin Roosevelt

Gilbert Tennent Snowden, A.B.

Edward Taylor, A.B.

Joseph Venable, A.B.

John Thornton Wood

George Whitefield Woodruff, A.B.

Samuel Beach

SAMUEL BEACH, A.B., A.M., tutor and perhaps a lawyer, was born on June 28, 1761, in Hanover Township, Morris County, New Jersey, the son of Enoch Beach and his first wife, Susan Day Darling Beach. He probably was prepared for college in the school conducted at Hanover by the Reverend Jacob Green (Harvard 1744), a charter trustee of the College of New Jersey from 1748 until his resignation in 1764 and the father of Beach's classmate Ashbel Green, later president of the College. Ashbel Green's autobiographical *Life* makes it evident that he and Samuel Beach were acquainted before they entered Nassau Hall in the spring of 1782. Indeed, Beach seems to have been in part responsible for Green's enrollment at Princeton instead of Yale, for he was the friend, as Green later recalled, who visited Nassau Hall and returned to Hanover with a report that determined Green's decision in favor of Princeton. In Nassau Hall they became roommates, and it seems safe to conclude that Beach was admitted at entrance to the junior class, as was Green, for they both graduated as members of the same class on September 24, 1783.

It is difficult to be certain regarding activities other than study in which Beach engaged before entering the College. He has been credited with military service during the Revolution, and this is possible, though standard authorities fail to provide confirmation. He first became liable for duty as a militiaman at the age of sixteen in 1777, and perhaps thereafter he responded to the recurring alarms that brought out the militia in the upper part of the state for the kind of adventures, including occasional clashes with British troops, that Ashbel Green was fond of recalling in his old age. But it has been assumed also that he was the Samuel Beach who late in the war taught a school near Newark in Essex County, and under state law, schoolteachers might be exempted from military service, as apparently was Beach by the county court in 1780. It can be added only that Beach may have been the schoolmaster who, according to tradition, on the occasion of an alarm, closed his school and went to war. That he might teach school before going to college was at the time in no way remarkable. So too did Ashbel Green.

His stay in the College was chiefly marked by the part he took in collaboration with Green in bringing about in June 1782 the revival of the American Whig Society, and on the day of his graduation, Beach was a noticeably active participant in the commencement exercises. Early in the program, he delivered an "English oration on the dangers and advantages of popular elections." And this oration was followed

Samuel Beach, A.B. 1783
BY ROBERT FULTON

immediately by his participation in a three-way "forensic disputation" of the question, "Is there any sufficient reason in the state of society, and the improvement of the human mind, why a more cool and dispassionate eloquence should be cultivated among us than was among the ancients?" Aside from the recognition thus given his talent, no special honors were assigned to him.

Samuel Beach and Ashbel Green passed at once, and together, from the status of undergraduates to that of tutors in the College. They assumed the full duties of the office in November 1783. Beach found these duties rewarding and at the same time burdensome, in part perhaps because he was beginning the study of law, probably with the guidance of the younger Richard Stockton (A.B. 1779). In a letter to a member of his family written on January 18, 1784, he outlined his daily routine by way of apology for not having written earlier:

I rise in the morning at 5 or half after 5 o'clock and attend prayers in the hall. From that until 8, I study to prepare for having a recitation. At 8 we breakfast, and from 8 till 9 some walk and idle about, but I generally sit down to study. At 9 o'clock I attend the recitation of the Junior class which generally employs me an hour and a half, and sometimes two hours. From eleven till one, I am preparing to hear the afternoon recitation. At one o'clock we dine, and after dinner we generally walk and divert ourselves untill 2. Then I attend the recitation of the Sophomore class untill 4 but this is only every other day. After which I study until 5—then go to prayers. After prayers we divert ourselves according to our several inclinations until 6 o'clock. We sup at six. After six, all must be in their rooms at their studies. I go to bed at 11, sometimes at twelve. Besides this I have to visit all the rooms in my entry three times a day, that is in the forenoon afternoon and in the evening—and likewise hear a private recitation, Thus almost, or indeed I may say quite all my time is employed.

The burdens of the job may have seemed the heavier because Beach suffered an uncertain state of his health, which in another decade would bring his death from what was known at the time as "a consumption."

In his letter of January 1784 he was able to report that the pain in his chest was almost gone, but before the year was out, his condition obviously had worsened. Although he may have begun the second year of his appointment as tutor, on December 19, 1784, he sailed from Philadelphia for Charleston, South Carolina, in quest of the benefits of a warmer climate. The passage was rough, and after seventeen days he reached Charleston on January 5, 1785. There he placed himself immediately under the care of Doctor David Ramsay (A.B. 1765) in the hope that he might return to his duties at the College in the spring. This he probably did, for Ashbel Green in his memoirs speaks of Beach as having spent the winter in Charleston, and credits him with "my first invitation to a settlement in the ministry." It was a call to become the assistant pastor of the Independent (Circular) Church of Charleston, to which Ramsay and other alumni of Nassau Hall belonged. Although Green declined the call, Beach returned to Charleston, where he would live out the short remainder of his life.

His permanent commitment to the Charleston area probably came before the winter of 1785 had passed. In Charleston he became a member of the Independent Church. There too he married Mary Lamboll Thomas, daughter of Reverend John Thomas, pastor of that church before his death in 1771. The date of the marriage is given as January 26, 1786, and to it were born four children, all girls, the first on July

6, 1787, the last on September 17, 1792. The two girls born between these dates, both named Susannah, died in infancy. Beyond these personal details, little has been discovered regarding Beach's life in South Carolina. It might be assumed that he managed to complete his studies in the law, and so to enter into its practice, but no confirmation has been found. He held at least one public office, that of a commissioner for an issue of paper money in 1789. But a directory for Charleston in 1790 did not even list his name.

And yet, after his death on May 11, 1793, a Charleston newspaper published the following unusually warm and lengthy tribute:

> Died. Samuel Beach, Esq.; from whose highly cultivated understanding and truly benevolent disposition, his family and friends had grounds—to expect a large harvest of comfort and usefulness. Early in life he rose to distinguished eminence in literature, and with great reputation discharged the duties of a tutor in the college of New Jersey; but his juvenile studies laid the foundation of a consumptive complaint, which proved fatal, after having been parried, for upwards of eight years, by the most guarded regimen.

Beach was buried in the churchyard of the Independent Church.

SOURCES: Alumni file, PUA, is helpfully supplemented by *Life of Ashbel Green* (1849), especially pp. 22, 58, 96, 107, 119-20, 130, 139, 149; Beam, *Whig Soc.*, 61-62; *Pa. Gazette*, 8 Oct 1783 (commencement); als SB to Mrs. H. Beach, 18 Jan 1784, AM 8504, and als SB to father, 15 Jan 1785, AM 2193, Gen. MSS. (misc.), NjP; *SCHGM*, 21 (1920), 157 (obituary); 29 (1928), 307 (tombstone inscription); 33 (1932), 158, 159 (baptism of two daughters). The assumption that Beach may have studied law with Richard Stockton is based on Green's statement (*Life of Ashbel Green*, 147) that Stockton offered to train Green in the law. J. B. O'Neall, *Bench and Bar of S.C.* (1859), II, 599, does not list Beach among the attorneys of Charleston.

WFC

William Clements

WILLIAM CLEMENTS, A.B., has not been identified. He was enrolled in the College at some time before June 1782, when according to an account by his classmate Ashbel Green, he was one of those who were instrumental in the revival of the American Whig Society. The minutes of the trustees indicate that he sustained with the other members of his class the usual August examination for the first degree, and the journal of another classmate, Gilbert Tennent Snowden, reveals that Clements was assigned the role for the coming commencement of replicator in a "dispute" between Joseph Venable and Jacob Radcliff of the question, "Can any measure that is morally evil be politically good?" But for reasons not explained, Clements was absent on commencement day, and so did not participate in the exercises. Except for the earliest notation of his death in the triennial catalogue of 1851, which in itself suggests that he meanwhile may have been lost sight of, no further record of his identification with the College has been found.

Clements may have been William, the son of John and Mary Clements, born on May 28, 1760, in Bristol Parish and presumably Prince George County, Virginia, but no connection of this William Clements with the College has been established. In Virginia the family, with the variant spellings of Clements, Clemens, Clemmonts, Clemmons, Clemonds, was an especially numerous one and the name William all too evidently popular. This is hardly less true of the Clements living in Maryland, and especially in Charles County. In New Jersey the family name was noticeably common in Gloucester County, and it was found in other states as well, but no clue as to the identity of the Princeton student has rewarded a search of the usual sources.

SOURCES: Beam, *Whig Soc.*, 61-62; Trustee Minutes, 24 Sep 1783, triennial catalogues, PUA; *Pa. Gazette*, 8 Oct 1783 (commencement); *Princeton Univ. Libr. Chron.*, 14 (1953), 76; C. G. Chamberlayne, *Vestry Book and Reg. of Bristol Parish, Va.* (1898), 302; P. Slaughter, *Hist. of Bristol Parish, Va.* (1879), 135; L. C. Bell, *Cumberland Parish, Lunenburg Cnty., Va.* (1930), 305, for marriage of William Clements on 26 Jan 1786 to Anne McCulloch. In Md. an interesting possibility is William Clements of Frederick Cnty. who is listed among the Federalists in a poll for the presidential election of 1796 and subsequently was a Federalist candidate for the office of sheriff [G. M. Brumbaugh, *Md. Recs.*, II (1967), 129, 138, 639.] Among the ratables in Gloucester Cnty., N.J., in 1779-1780 was William Clemmens, a single man with horse [*GMNJ*, 46 (1971), 140.]

WFC

Timothy Ford

TIMOTHY FORD, A.B., A.M. 1789, soldier, lawyer, and public official, was born in Morristown, Morris County, New Jersey, on December 4, 1762, the eldest of six children of Jacob Ford and his wife, Theodosia Johnes. Two of his three brothers, Gabriel (A.B. 1784) and Jacob (A.B. 1792), were in their turn both graduates of the College and lawyers.

The Ford family had moved to New Jersey from Duxbury, Massachusetts around 1701. Timothy's grandfather, Jacob Ford, a tavern-owner and iron manufacturer, was a representative to the New Jersey Assembly in 1772 and later active on the local committee of corre-

Wm Johnes (Class of 1776) was his uncle, and
Stevens Johnes Lewis (A.B. 1791) was a cousin,

spondence. Timothy's father in 1762 married Theodosia, the daughter of Timothy Johnes, minister of the Morristown Presbyterian Church, and settled in Morristown around 1773. In 1775 the father became a colonel of the local militia and afterwards was involved in skirmishes with British forces. He also operated a local gunpower mill and provided Washington's army with shot and shell before dying of pneumonia in January 1777.

Timothy Ford apparently received preparatory schooling in Morristown during the war but then joined the army as a private soldier in 1778 or 1779. He took part in an expedition to Staten Island in early 1780 and that June was at the front of a charge made by Lieutenant Colefax's troop in skirmishing at Springfield. In this second encounter, he was twice wounded in the thigh but made a speedy recovery. He probably came to Princeton not long thereafter. An 1845 catalogue of the Cliosophic Society dates his membership from 1780. At the commencement exercises of September 27, 1783, he was among those graduates who did not speak.

After graduating Ford studied law in the office of Robert Morris in New York and was admitted to the bar there. In 1785 he went south, taking the opportunity afforded by his sister Elizabeth's marriage to South Carolinian Henry William DeSaussure, lawyer, legislator, and briefly director of the United States Mint. Ford went with the newlyweds and his future bride, DeSaussure's sister Sarah Amelia, to Charleston, traveling on the way through Princeton, where he visited "many of my college & other acquaintances with whom I . . . renew[ed] the round of unpleasant feelings incident to parting with friends."

Ford initially found South Carolina somewhat uncongenial. He admired the quiet of Charleston's streets but thought the countryside lacking in variety and ill-provided with accommodations. The "dronish ease & torpid inactivity" of the inhabitants, which he attributed to the presence of slaves, led him to doubt that the state would ever be "enabled to stand by itself unconnected with, or unsupported by others." Slavery itself upset him; he noted that the large numbers of black slaves in the population of Charleston "begets a strange confusion of ideas & contradiction of principles—the general rule is Liberty, but the exceptions form a majority of 5 to 1." Yet despite misgivings, and after a return trip to New Jersey, Ford nonetheless settled in South Carolina, joining the bar in 1786 and entering into legal practice with his brother-in-law, DeSaussure.

Always a strong patriot and supporter of the federal Constitution,

The following year he visited his family in Morristown, returning to Charleston in early November.

Ford was founding secretary of the Charleston American Revolution Society in 1792. The same year he wrote *An Enquiry into the Constitutional Authority of the Supreme Federal Court*, refuting a pamphlet by James Sullivan (Harvard 1762), then attorney general of Massachusetts, which had opposed extending federal court authority over the states. In December 1792 Ford began the first of his three terms in the lower house of the general assembly, where he sat until 1797 as one of Charleston's fifteen representatives. Predictably he supported the low-country interests there, especially opposing the proposals for reapportionment of the legislature advanced by the democratic societies of Carolina and their upcountry allies. In a series of articles appearing in the local papers in 1794 under the name "Americanus" (later collected in a pamphlet), Ford argued in favor of the current apportionment, which he felt appropriately reflected the distribution of property within the state. Mere population, he said, should not be the only basis on which to fix representation; weight had to be given as well to property and to the prior occupancy of the land by the low-country men, whose initial settlement entitled them to a greater voice. Moreover, the existing division of seats had been established by a constitutional convention whose decisions were not, in Ford's eyes, liable to alteration without critical reason. While arguing this case, Ford also commented that the present system of representation posed no threat to citizens' liberty, especially since "the constant example of slavery stimulates a free man to avoid being confounded with the blacks." His views on slavery had obviously shifted since 1785.

Ford's flurry of political activity did not last beyond the 1790s, and he thereafter returned to his primary occupation as a lawyer, though at some time he served on the Charleston City Council. He was married twice, first on January 22, 1793 to Sarah DeSaussure, with whom he had one daughter. Sarah died in May 1799, and ~~little over a year later~~ Ford married Mary Magdalen Prioleau, whose father Samuel was a respected Charleston gentleman. This marriage produced two more daughters.

Ford was an active citizen in more than politics. He was the original recording secretary and on the board of managers of the Bible Society, the members of which seem at first to have been drawn largely from the Independent Church in Charleston, the church attended by David Ramsay (A.B. 1765) and other Princeton graduates. From 1802 to 1813 Ford acted as secretary and treasurer of the College of Charleston, serving later as a trustee, and he died while president of both the

Charleston Library Society and the Literary and Philosophical Society
of South Carolina. An address on chemistry that he delivered in 1817
before the latter group subsequently appeared in print.

Ford continued the practice of law to the end of his life, with apparent success. Early in his career, he was joined by his brother Jacob,
and later, when his brother-in-law was elevated to the bench, the
office of DeSaussure & Ford became Ford & DeSaussure. Ford had a
part in actions arising out of the Luxembourg Claims case in 1807 and
1808. Toward the end of his career, he spent most of his time in the
Court of Equity. He died December 7, 1830. According to the memorial of the Charleston Bar, he was learned, diligent, and cautious
in his work, sociable with his colleagues, unruffled, well respected,
and "of unsullied and excellent character."

Sources: DAB (father and DeSaussure); *Hist. of Morris Cnty., N.J.* (1914), I, 43-44;
alumni File, PUA; J. B. O'Neall, *Bench and Bar of S.C.* (1859), II, 150-55; Washington Writings, XVIII, 486n; *SCHGM*, 10 (1900), 101, 103-104; 13 (1912), 132-47, 181-
204 (which is TF's diary, 1785-86, quotations from pp. 134, 142-43); 32 (1931), 80;
Sibley's Harvard Graduates, XV, 312; J.S.R. Faunt et al., *Biog. Directory of S.C. House
of Reps.*, 1 (1974), 238, 243, 248; *NCHR*, 18 (1941), 259-77; J. H. Easterby, *Hist. of
College of Charleston* (1935), 57; D. Ramsay, *Hist. of Independent or Congregational
Chh. in Charleston* (1815), 26; Charleston city directories.

Manuscripts: SCHi   ND HsP 61 (1943), 197

Publications: see STE, #s 24324, 26987; Sh-Sh, #44056; Sh-C, #24557

Ashbel Green

Ashbel Green, A.B., A.M. 1785, D.D. University of Pennsylvania 1791,
LL.D. University of North Carolina 1812, Presbyterian clergyman,
eighth president of the College, writer and editor of religious works,
was born on July 6, 1762 at Hanover, New Jersey, the third son of
Jacob Green (Harvard 1744) and his second wife, Elizabeth Pierson
Green. Their youngest son was John Wickliffe Green (A.B. 1788).
The mother was a daughter of the Reverend John Pierson (Yale 1711)
of Woodbridge, New Jersey, one of the College's founders, and a
granddaughter of Abraham Pierson (Harvard 1668), the first rector
of the collegiate school in Connecticut that later became Yale College.
While an undergraduate at Harvard, Green's father was swept up in
the revivals conducted by the great evangelists George Whitefield and
Gilbert Tennent, the latter an original trustee of the College of New
Jersey. Afterward he studied for the ministry with the College's future
president Aaron Burr. In 1746 the elder Green was installed as min-

Ashbel Green, A.B. 1783

ister to the Presbyterian Church at Hanover, where he remained for the rest of his life. His congregation was a poor one, and Green added to his stipend by milling, distilling, and sometimes acting as a lawyer and physician to his neighbors. A trustee of the College for many years, his reputation for erudition was widespread. After President Jonathan Edward's death in 1758, Green took charge of the College and its grammar school for eight months. Over the years he published several widely circulated and influential works on theological issues.

Ashbel grew up in a strict, intensely pious, but not unkindly home. His father intended him to become either a farmer or a mechanic and hired a member of his congregation to instruct him and one of his brothers in agriculture. But the father also ran a school on his property; young Ashbel attended it, and developed decidedly literary tastes.

During the Revolution, Ashbel served in the state militia, rising to the rank of orderly sergeant, and participated in a few actions. But for most of the war years, he kept first an English, then a Latin school. Since a college education was useful in both of the professions he had in view, the law and the ministry, he shut up his school in November

1781 and returned to study with his father in preparation for college. Ashbel's choice of a college seemed unclear, however. After having been used as a barracks during the war, Nassau Hall was almost derelict. But a neighbor and friend, Samuel Beach (A.B. 1783), made an expedition to Princeton, decided that the College was salvageable, and both youths entered the junior class as roommates in the spring of 1782.

Ashbel discovered that aside from geometry he had been so well prepared for college that he had a remarkable amount of free time. He spent part of it reading, and an even larger part helping to revive the American Whig Society, which had been dormant during the war years. The members of Whig and the Cliosophic Society then embarked on a vigorous "paper war" to which Ashbel contributed his share. In the fall of 1782 President Witherspoon resigned his seat in Congress in order to do fuller justice to his duties at the College, and Ashbel immediately fell under his spell. "Alas! Nassau how art thou fallen!" he scribbled in his diary after hearing Witherspoon preach. "College is a mine of temptation—it is almost impossible here to preserve that strictness of morals which is necessary not only for the character of a Christian but a man of common probity." Ashbel was not all provincial prig, however. He unbent enough to take the part of Alexander the Great in a school play in the spring of his senior year. Nevertheless, Witherspoon's influence then and afterwards was decisive on the young man. In later years he would edit Witherspoon's writings, write his life, and—as well as he could—model his conduct on what he imagined Witherspoon's to have been.

Green's relative maturity and experience in teaching must have impressed Witherspoon favorably, for he spent half of his time during his senior year teaching in the College's grammar school. And in the spring of 1783, when Congress fled mutinous troops in Philadelphia to reassemble again in Princeton, Green found a wider stage for his talents. The Fourth of July saw him addressing an audience that included many members of Congress on "The superiority of a republican government over any other form." When time came for commencement in September, it was Green, as class valedictorian, who delivered the oration before members of Congress, representatives from foreign nations, and General Washington himself, who afterwards complimented the young orator on his performance.

After commencement Green was appointed a tutor in the College. He was still uncertain about the choice of an occupation. Richard Stockton, Jr. (A.B. 1779) offered to train him *gratis* for the law, and his fiancée wanted him to become a lawyer. But after consultation with Witherspoon, Green had a long talk with Samuel Stanhope Smith (A.B. 1769), Professor of Moral Philosophy at the College. "Theology is not the road to either fame or wealth," Smith explained; "the law, in this country, leads to those objects. But if you wish to do good, and prefer an approving conscience before all other considerations, I have no hesitation in saying that you ought to preach the gospel." Ashbel thereupon consulted his conscience (always a devastatingly demanding one) and decided to become a minister.

A calling chosen, Green turned to more tender matters. On November 3, 1785, he married Elizabeth Stockton, daughter of Robert Stockton, member of a prominent Princeton family who lived about a mile from Nassau Hall. The couple took up residence in an apartment in the Stockton home. By the end of the month, Green assumed a new responsibility when he was appointed Professor of Mathematics and Natural Philosophy in the College. He studied divinity with President Witherspoon and in February 1786 was licensed by the Presbytery of New Brunswick. Escorted by Witherspoon, Green preached his first sermon in the Presbyterian church in Princeton. Stanhope Smith introduced him about Philadelphia, and Green was shortly invited to assume the copastorship of that city's Second Presbyterian Church. Waiting to move to Philadelphia, he continued his studies and his teaching and supplied regularly at the Presbyterian church at Lawrenceville. Overwork shortly brought on a physical and nervous collapse. Green recovered quickly, but both physical and nervous ailments would continue to plague him regularly for the next sixty-two years.

The senior minister at Green's new church was James Sproat (Yale 1741). Like Green's father, Sproat had been drawn toward a career in the ministry while a student in college by the preaching of the New Light evangelist Gilbert Tennent, to whose Philadelphia pastorate he had succeeded. Green's appointment to the church was intended to heal the ancient but still real division between New Light and Old Light factions within Philadelphia Presbyterianism. When Green was ordained and installed in his new church in May 1787, John Ewing (A.B. 1754), a leading Old Light and minister of the First Presbyterian Church, preached the sermon, while George Duffield (A.B. 1752), a leading New Light and minister of the Third Presbyterian Church, delivered the charge to the pastor and people.

Pastoral duties engrossed Green's early years in Philadelphia, and his life was confined to the narrow orbit of New Jersey and Pennsylvania. He was elected to membership in the American Philosophical Society, publicly opposed the legalization of theatres in Philadelphia, helped David Ramsay (A.B. 1765) by reading proof for his *History of the American Revolution* (1789), and became a trustee of the College in 1790. In that year he introduced to the Presbyterian General Assembly a motion calling for closer relations between Presbyterians and New England Congregationalists. The motion was adopted, and in 1791 Green made a long trip to New England, where he became acquainted with many of the most noted political and religious figures of the day. The connections established on the trip served Green in good stead for many years to come. He also became wary of certain tendencies within New England Calvinism; when Jedidiah Morse, a leading New England minister, suggested that Presbyterians and Congregationalists unite, Green responded: "Our ministers and people would never endure your preachers of *liberal sentiments*." The trip brought Green to more than local prominence. On November 5, 1792, he was elected, along with Episcopalian bishop William White, as co-chaplain to Congress, a post he held until the capital was transferred to Washington in 1800. His preaching was apparently congenial to congressmen: "In the pulpit he might convince, but he kindled no man to rapture," an early Presbyterian historian remarked.

Green, in fact, presented something of a paradox to his contemporaries. One who knew him late in life, Reverend Nicholas Murray of Elizabeth, once made an assessment of Green that seems to have been applicable over much of his career:

> He was a man pre-eminently of two characters, public and private, and to form a right estimate of him, he must be known in both. To those who only knew him as a public man, he was stern, unyielding, dictatorial, and repulsive; to those who knew him both in public and in private, he was mild, pliable, and peculiarly attractive. Hence, by one class he was respected, but disliked; whilst by another he was uncommonly beloved, and regarded as an oracle.

Green's diary, in fact, demonstrates an astonishingly volatile inner life, one that swung from intense activity driven by unyielding conscience to prostrating depressions. It is perhaps not surprising that he collaborated with his friend Dr. Benjamin Rush (A.B. 1760) in the treatment of mentally ill persons.

After 1800 Green began to take a larger share in the affairs of his denomination and of the College. When President Smith left on an extended fund-raising tour after the burning of Nassau Hall in 1802, Green renewed his acquaintance with the College by overseeing its operation for several months. He delivered an address to the trustees and students on the necessity of the union of science (by which he meant "liberal knowledge in general") and religion that was published shortly thereafter.

During the latter part of 1806, both Green and his wife fell ill, and in January of the following year she died. Green slipped into a deep depression. His melancholy can only have been enhanced when a serious student riot occurred in the College in March 1807. As chairman of a committee of trustees appointed to write to suspended students' parents and to explain the matter to the public in the press, Green's actions can only be considered to have been disastrous for the College. He accused the ousted students of causing disturbances because of their bad morals, overindulgence in liquor, and too plentiful a supply of spending money. Such washing of dirty linen in public was hardly calculated to attract parents' favorable attention toward the College. And indeed, it did not. Enrollments appear to have declined over the succeeding few years, and President Smith's reputation received a blow from which it never fully recovered. Something of Green's regard for the College over the next few years is indicated by the fact that he sent his third son, James, to Dickinson College, while his second son, Jacob, graduated from Queen's (Rutgers) in 1812.

Bad publicity for the College came at a crucial moment not only for Green but for the Presbyterian church and its clergy as well. As the population grew and the frontier moved westward, almost all American religious denominations began to suffer severe shortage of ministers. At one point early in the century, it was estimated that fifty percent of Presbyterian pulpits were unfilled. The problem was viewed as not only one of recruitment but one of training as well. The Presbyterian Plan of Government, adopted in 1788, recommended that all candidates for the ministry possess a college degree and demanded postgraduate studies of at least two years under the direction of an approved minister. In 1792 the General Assembly had even suggested a *three*-year minimum period of postgraduate theological study. After 1800 a new wave of religious revivals, often under a Methodist or Baptist aegis, rose first on the frontiers and then swept swiftly eastwards. Many Presbyterians feared that unless new pools of trained ministers could be formed and tapped the church would be swept aside in a Second Great Awakening. As early as 1805 Reverend Samuel Miller, an influential Presbyterian leader in New York City who became a trustee of the College in 1807, persuaded Green to present an overture to the General Assembly calling for heightened recruitment, assistance, and overseeing of ministerial candidates. "It appears to me," Miller wrote to Green on March 12, 1805, "that we ought, forthwith, either to establish a new theological school in some central part of our bounds; or direct more of our attention to extend the plan and increase the energy of the Princeton establishment."

At the very moment that Miller and Green were considering new measures for ministerial training among Presbyterians, Orthodox and Hopkinsian Congregationalists in Massachusetts were pressing for similar measures there. Green, Miller, and others were in close contact with developments to the north, and some of their activities appear to have been decisively influenced by Congregationalist example. A brief look at this example helps place Green's activities over the next few years in perspective.

In 1805 and 1806 Harvard College was taken over by men who would soon be known as Unitarians. The majority of Massachusetts Congregationalists, faced like the Presbyterians with a need for trained ministers in an expanding population, were thereby deprived of one of their main sources of "orthodox" ministerial candidates. Orthodox Congregationalists, led by, among others, Green's old friend Jedidiah Morse, regrouped forces in Andover, Massachusetts. There in 1778 the Phillips family had established an academy for boys, and on the foundations of the academy, the Congregationalists erected another institution, Andover Theological Seminary. Sharing a common board of trustees with the existing academy, the theological seminary thoroughly overshadowed the academy for most of its existence. Generously endowed by the Phillips family and others, the seminary began operation in 1808. It was extremely successful for much of the nineteenth century and provided a model for professional ministerial training for other denominations.

As Presbyterians began their search for a new and more productive type of ministerial education, they had the developing model of Andover constantly before them. Like the Congregationalists with the Phillips Academy, they looked to the College at Princeton as a possible foundation for their new plans. But the College presented problems not apparent in the academy, ones that caused Presbyterians to view it with considerable suspicion. Some of the disquiet was due to the first stirrings of the great changes that would redraw the map of knowledge during the nineteenth century. "It is much to be doubted whether the system of education pursued in our colleges and universities is the best adapted to prepare a young man for the work of the ministry," Archibald Alexander, a prominent Philadelphia clergyman, declared to the General Assembly in 1808. He continued: "The great extension of the physical sciences, and the taste and fashion of the age, have given such a shape and direction to the academical course, that I confess, it appears to me to be little adapted to introduce a youth to the study of the sacred Scriptures." Although Alexander's words have sometimes been seen as an expression of clerical opposition to science, such was not the case. The difficulty was a general one, faced by all educators of the age. As the sheer volume of scientific knowledge exploded during the century, conscientious educators felt it necessary to include each new field in the undergraduate course of study. By the 1850s college curricula bulged with course after course of scientific subjects and the study of science seemed to leave little room for the study of anything else. A separate, postgraduate institution for the study of divinity was a natural solution.

The leaders of the movement for postgraduate ministerial education were not, moreover, completely certain that Princeton was the best place to locate the new institution. "I doubt whether a divinity-school there, with ever so able and eminent a professor at its head," Samuel Miller wrote to Green in May 1808, "could be made, in the present state of the college, to command the confidence and patronage of the Presbyterian Church. . . . I fear the theological students could not be the better for habitual intercourse with the students in the arts." Both Miller and Green were concerned too about the attitude of many clergymen, almost all of whom had received their training under the apprenticeship system, to the very notion of a theological school. Both men determined to proceed slowly. In 1809 Green's presbytery introduced to the General Assembly an overture proposing either the establishment of a central theological school for the Presbyterian church, two such schools, one in the north and one in the south, or separate schools in each synod. The various synods considered the different options over the following year. The results were inconclusive, but the committee in charge, headed by Miller, maneuvered the outcome toward the first option. In 1810 Green was appointed head of a committee to draw up a plan for a theological school. He consulted closely with Miller, Alexander, and others, and in 1811 presented a plan (one that owed not a little to Andover) to the General Assembly. In the meantime, the trustees of the College, including Green and Miller, proposed that the new institution be created as a separate department of the College itself, free to use the already existing facilities in Princeton (precisely who engineered this offer is uncertain). Miller, as we have seen, wanted a separate institution—not only because of the state of the College but because he wanted the seminary always to remain completely under Presbyterian control, which the College, because of the nature of its charter, was not. In any case, the General Assembly adopted Green's plan and decided to locate the new institution in Princeton. It elected Green's colleague in the Philadelphia Presbytery, Archibald Alexander, as the seminary's first professor. Green himself was elected chairman of the seminary's board of directors, a post he held until his death. (The directors were an advisory body; the seminary later was run by a board of trustees established in 1822.)

Most of the Presbyterian laity and clergy seem to have been indifferent to the establishment of the seminary. Its founding, and its location in Princeton, represented a farseeing, patient piece of clerical politicking on the part of Miller, Green, Alexander, and a very few other clergymen. But to Green would fall a special opportunity to assist in its establishment. When the new institution began operation in 1812, Samuel Stanhope Smith would have left the College, replaced by a new president—Ashbel Green.

On August 14, 1812, Smith resigned as president of the College, and trustee Samuel Miller polled the board, which immediately and unanimously elected Green president. Green later claimed that his election came as a complete surprise. It may well have been such. But since Miller, Green, and Alexander had been working closely together for years to assure the establishment of the theological seminary, and since Green's presidency of the College would assure vigorous assistance to the new institution, President Smith's resignation and Green's election may well have been more than a happy coincidence.

Green went to Princeton under a double charge—one explicit, the other implicit. The first required the reformation of the College and restoration of its reputation. The second involved the firm foundation of the theological seminary. Over the years Green devoted much of his time to the latter goal. He made the College's facilities available to the seminary's students, particularly in its early years, donated land to the institution, and spent considerable effort in raising funds for it. Such activities in no way implied a neglect of the affairs of the College. His presence brought an immediate change in the life of the institution. "Dr Smiths works have all been expelled, and others substituted in their room," one student reported home on December 2, 1812. He went on to note: "This no doubt will have a tendency greatly to injure the Dr's feelings. There appears to subsist between these ministers of Christ but little harmony or love." The student understated the matter. In his first report to the board of trustees, Green made a savage attack on his predecessor's administration. An excerpt is worth quoting at length:

> The majority of those who have received degrees with us for a
> number of years past, could not possibly have translated their own

diplomas into english. If classical learning was brought to the college by some who entered the Junior class, it was, in a measure, lost, before the end of the course. In that class, not a word of the classics, so far as I can find, has ever been read since the American revolutionary war.

Green also claimed that while mathematics, which he considered absolutely essential for an understanding of science, had not been neglected to the same degree, "what was learned was very imperfectly learned."

Decades later this report would return to shape Green's reputation for the worse. It remained in the College's records, and when President John Maclean came to write his massive history of the College in the 1870s, he discovered it. Every negative word that Green wrote reflected not only on Stanhope Smith but on Maclean's father, who had been a professor in the College under Smith, and Maclean went far out of his way to paint as rosy a picture as possible of Smith's later years and to refute Green. Maclean's generally negative appraisal of Green's administration was in turn adopted by later historians of the College and of American higher education.

On assuming his post, Green immediately set out for himself an elaborate series of fifteen "resolutions" as a guide to his conduct. Heavily paternalistic and moralistic, a part of the first gives the flavor of the rest: "I am to endeavour to be a father of the institution. I am to endeavour to the utmost to promote all its interests as a father does, in what relates to his children and property." It was a difficult task. "My first address to the students produced a considerable impression; insomuch that some of them shed tears," Green later recalled. He continued: "This greatly encouraged me; but the appearance was delusive or fugitive. Notwithstanding all the arrangements I had made, and the pains I had taken to convince them that their own good and the best interests of the institution were my only objects, I had the mortification to find that the majority of them seemed to be bent on mischief." Green was fifty years old when he assumed his post, and all his adult life had been spent as a pastor. It was hardly surprising that he saw his role not so much as an educator but as an evangelical clergyman, intent on restoring order and harmony through religious suasion. By April 1813 he was reporting to the trustees that morals and order among the students had been improved immeasurably by having the students from the theological seminary live in the College. Green added the study of the Bible to the College's curriculum for the first time in its history and founded a student Bible society.

Green's task could not have been made easier by several personal misfortunes that befell him early in his presidency. His first wife and the mother of his favorite son, Robert Stockton Green (A.B. 1805), had died in 1807, and the son died in 1813. On October 16, 1809, he had married Christiana Anderson, daughter of Colonel Alexander Anderson of Philadelphia, who bore him one son, also named Ashbel, but in 1814 she died from the complications of a miscarriage. (In October 1815 Green married Isabella McCulloh of Philadelphia, who died late in 1817.) Moreover, during the late winter and spring of 1814, the College again exploded into riot. The privy roof was set afire and a large bomb was set off in Nassau Hall. Green solved the problem by bringing criminal proceedings against the leaders and instituting a grand jury investigation into the affair. "Govern always but beware of governing too much," President Witherspoon had once warned Green. It was advice that Green, with the best of intentions, was constitutionally incapable of following.

The next year conditions improved, at least from Green's point of view. Beginning in January 1815, a revival (which Green attributed to his introduction of Bible study) swept the College. "Nothing like it has been seen here for more than forty years," Green reported happily to a friend. He went on: "The house is literally a house of prayer. Yet all is still and silent. No noise, no extravagance, no enthusiasm. . . . Surely there was scarcely ever so altered a place as our college,—comparing the last months with the present. Instead of meetings and plots and conspiracies, we have now nothing but meetings for religious conferences, and fervent social prayer." With the trustees' approval, he shortly published an account of the revival. It must have seemed to many evangelicals that order and morality had been finally restored to Nassau Hall.

Most of the conversions had been among members of the senior class, however. In 1816 they were gone, and in January 1817 the College was torn apart by still more student rioting. Widely publicized, the affair quickly undid any favorable impression the revival had made. "There appears to be 'something rotten in the constitution of Denmark' something fundamentally wrong in the discipline of this College," commented John Pintard (A.B. 1776) from New York City. He continued: "The truth I take it is that the professors & tutors are too rigid & inexperienced in life, know not how to enforce the laws or to relax with discretion. We were turbulent eno' in my day. But Doctor Witherspoon understood human nature & we never had such dreadful explosions. He always was the boys friend & he conciliated our affections & commanded our love & reverence."

Granting that Green was no Witherspoon, his experience was hard-

ly unique among American college presidents of the time, as his predecessor's later years might indicate. From the late 1790s through the
1820s, student unrest and rioting was a common occurrence not only
at Princeton but at many other American colleges. At Princeton certain immediate conditions existed that help in some measure to explain the various riots. For one thing, Nassau Hall was extremely over-
crowded; youths were jammed three or four together into the small
rooms. Green complained about this situation to the trustees constantly. To overcrowding was added the strain not only of strict discipline but of confinement as well. As one student wrote home in
February, 1813: "It has not ceased to snow almost every day for a
month, & if it continues any longer I shall be forced to run away; for
I can not live without exercise, & Dr. Green has forbidden any noise
or romping in the college—I was in hopes that we should have sufficient exercise in dancing and fencing." But neither dancing nor fencing was forthcoming at Green's Princeton. The ingredients for a po-
tentially explosive situation seem obvious. Moreover, this period
brought a change in the character both of students and faculty.

Until the American Revolution, most American college students—
not the majority, but normally the largest single group within a particular college class—had ended by becoming clergymen. Very often
"poor but pious" youths who had decided upon pursuing a career in
the ministry before attending college, they supplied a stable ballast
among a heterogenous undergraduate population. Temperament and
ambition demanded that they live lives circumscribed by thoughts of
future professional usefulness and advancement. The initial stages of
their postgraduate careers would be heavily dependent on the impres-
sions made on the college's clerical authorities during their undergraduate years. In the decades after the Revolution at some colleges,
Princeton among them, such students formed a decidedly smaller percentage of the student body. The tone of some colleges was now set primarily by youths from merchant or planter families who had little interest in pursuing clerical or even professional careers. And at the
same time, the character of the clergymen who staffed the colleges
changed. Very often they were no longer men of broad-based social
contacts and wide-ranging interests like John Witherspoon or Samuel
Stanhope Smith. They were instead much more "professional" in the
narrow sense of the term—considerably more focused on the affairs of
their churches and on religious concerns and thought in general than
had been the case with earlier generations of clergymen. And in many
American colleges, the world of a more narrowly religious clerical profession came into direct conflict with the world of a student body con-

siderably more secular than had been the case in previous years. The often explosive situations that resulted would not begin to be defused until the 1830s and 1840s, when the modern and secular academic profession began gradually but decisively to emerge from its clerical parent.

Surprisingly, despite the student rebellion of 1817, the College's enrollment increased the following year—from 150 in November 1817 to 164 in December 1818. Green and the trustees developed ambitious plans for an enlargement of Princeton's plant and faculty. They hoped to erect a new college building that would permit a substantial increase in the number of students, thus not only relieving overcrowding but providing more funds from tuition, which would in turn allow for the expansion of the faculty. Part of the scheme was fulfilled almost immediately. In 1818 Jacob Green, the president's son, was appointed to the newly created position of Professor of Experimental Philosophy, Chemistry, and Natural History, at a salary of $100 per year. But the Panic of 1819 intervened, and the plan was aborted. Moreover, a chain of events was set in motion then that would lead in 1822 to Ashbell Green's resignation.

The immediate circumstances surrounding Green's departure from office in 1822 are plain enough. They are clearly indicated in a letter that Green wrote to his son Jacob on April 12, 1822:

> We have had, what appear to me, strange doings in the board of trustees. Among other things, they have resolved that after next fall, the professorships of Mathematics & Chemistry shall be again united. Now, as you are not a great mathematician, & never intend to become so, you, of course, will not choose to become a candidate for the new appointment. This was, no doubt, not only foreseen, but intended by the projectors of this business,—a business, in my opinion, full of absurdity, if not some worse quality. I have heard no allegations made to your disadvantage; but without question, it was no objection to this measure, with some of the concerned, that it might probably wound both your feelings and mine. In this, however, I hope that they will obtain, at most, but a partial success. The less you & I feel & regard it, the better. . . . My principal concern is for the interests of the institution, which I am confident are not considered in this. . . . say and do nothing that can injure the coll[e]ge,—already too much injured by those who ought to have been its guardians & defenders.

Green, obviously, was being boxed into a well-nigh untenable position. Precisely how this came about is difficult to say; academic politics leave little written records and thus are normally almost impossible to reconstruct.

In this case, however, we have a partial explanation of the course of events by a witness to the affair, President John Maclean, at the time a young tutor in the College. According to Maclean, late in 1821 Green unintentionally slighted Henry Vethake, Professor of Mathematics and Mechanical Philosophy. One of the trustees, a close friend of Vethake (and not, alas, named by Maclean), on April 9, 1822 introduced to the board a resolution calling for an investigation into the composition of the faculty, into student discipline, and querying "whether any loss of reputation has been sustained by the institution, and, if so, what has caused it." The last item was a direct insult to Green. The resolution was passed, and a committee was appointed to look into the issues. Its report, among other things, recommended that the professorships of Mathematics and Natural Philosophy be combined. The latter position, as we have seen, was held by Jacob Green, who was in effect maneuvered out of his professorship. Green himself held his tongue until the eve of commencement on September 25. He then announced his resignation.

The affair is a curious one; it resembles the resignation of a later president of Princeton, Woodrow Wilson, who was also maneuvered out of his post through an obscure course of academic intrigue. All one can say at this distance is that Green had not kept his political fences mended. If he had been able to quash the trustees' resolution of April 9, if he had been able to block the acceptance of the resulting committee's report, if he had been able to muster an overwhelming show of support among the trustees when he proferred his resignation in September—if he had been able to do any or all of these things, he might well have died in office as President Witherspoon did. But one of the trustees exercised infinitely more influence over the board than did President Green.

Whether Green's ouster resulted from anything more than personal animosities is uncertain. The number of students in the College had been steadily declining, however—from 164 in 1818 to 142 in 1819, 121 in 1820, and a low of 114 in 1821-1822. The reasons for the decline are obscure. Princeton's reputation in 1822 was neither better nor worse than it had been for the preceding few years. The decline might have been caused by the financial panic of 1819, by the great increase in the number of colleges available in this period, or by Princeton's relatively high costs. A clue to the trustees' ready acceptance of Green's resignation may lie in their immediate election on September 26 of John Holt Rice as his successor. Rice was the leading Presbyterian

clergyman in Virginia, at the moment involved in an attempt to establish in his state another Presbyterian theological school. Rice refused
the post, but if he had accepted, more southern students would surely
have been attracted to the College, and, perhaps not coincidentally, a
potential rival of the Princeton Theological Seminary would have
been forestalled. But the question of whether such considerations entered into Green's ouster must remain conjectural.

One historian of the College has called Green's administration
"Princeton's nadir." Such was not the case; Princeton's nadir came in
the years after Green's departure. Despite the occasional student disturbances, his administration compares favorably with those of many
contemporary college presidents. His strong encouragement of religious activities among the students was completely in keeping with the
main cultural currents of the time and in no way signaled indifference
to the scientific advances of the day. Reviewing his Princeton presidency many years later, Green wrote that "in one thing I made a pal-
pable mistake, I had thought that if the College was once reduced to a
state of entire order, it would be likely to remain in that state. I did
not consider that all the students of the institution are changed every
four years." As president, Green in fact seems to have behaved much
as did Witherspoon in his later years. Then, the day-to-day operations
had been handled by vice-president Samuel Stanhope Smith. Witherspoon exercised a general supervisory role and pursued his broader
interests. Unfortunately for Green, none of his succession of vice-
presidents was as capable as young Smith had been. While Green left
the College in sound financial condition, his most lasting monument
in Princeton would be the theological seminary.

Green moved to Philadelphia in the fall of 1822 and at the age of
sixty-one, began a new career. He assumed the editorship of an almost
moribund religious periodical, *The Presbyterian*, renaming it *The
Christian Advocate* and managing it successfully for twelve years. The
journal brought to a wide audience (though not as wide as Green had
originally hoped) the latest news not only of religious matters but of
literature, science, and world affairs as well. During the 1820s and 1830s
Green gradually became one of the elder statesmen of the Presbyterian
Church, a unique link between the age of the Revolution and the Romantic era. He served as moderator of the General Assembly in 1824
and on many church boards as well. He saw his son Jacob become a
successful professor at Jefferson Medical College in Philadelphia and
carve out for himself a distinguished niche in the annals of American
science.

During the 1830s Green played one final major role in church affairs. In 1837 the Presbyterian church was torn once again by schism. Over three decades earlier, in 1801, Presbyterians had united in a Plan of Union with Connecticut Congregationalists. Both denominations agreed to cooperate on a wide spectrum of activities—missionary work, church staffing, and so forth. Green was among the main supporters of the 1801 plan. As the frontier moved westward, however, it seemed to many that Congregationalists more than Presbyterians were the main beneficiaries of the plan. Moreover, Presbyterians and Congregationalists began to diverge on theological matters. Some Presbyterians were more and more attracted to the conservative seventeenth-century theology of François Turretin. Some Congregationalists fell more and more into the "liberal" (but not Unitarian) circuit of thought represented by the contemporary New Haven theologian Nathaniel William Taylor. In the early 1830s "Old School" Presbyterians, centered in the middle states, instituted a series of heresy trials aimed at "New School" Presbyterians, who were very often of Congregationalist or New England background. From his position as an influential editor and revered elder of the church, Green was among the leaders in the Old School's attack on the New. The points at issue were extraordinarily complex. They involved differences over the meaning of confessionalism, over church polity, the relations of the church to voluntary societies, methods of revivalism, as well as theology. Judging by the scanty remaining evidence, Green seems to have been most concerned with maintaining the integrity of traditional Presbyterian ecclesiastical organization. Whatever Green's weaknesses as an academic politician, he and his Old School allies showed themselves accomplished clerical politicians: they succeeded in carrying their views by splitting the Presbyterian church right down the middle.

Green spent his final years revising his *Lectures on the Shorter Catechism* and writing a biography of President Witherspoon. Though the latter did not see publication until 1973, in manuscript it long remained a principal source of information on Witherspoon. During these years Green acted as informal minister to a Negro church in Philadelphia. His last sermon was delivered in the Negro Presbyterian church in Princeton. Green died in Philadelphia on May 14, 1848 and was buried in the Princeton cemetery near his presidential predecessors.

SOURCES: *Sibley's Harvard Graduates*, XI, 504-516; *DAB*; Sprague, *Annals*, III, 479-96; R. E. Lewis, in *JPHS*, 35 (1957), 141-56. The main source, and the one from which most of the quotations are drawn, is J. H. Jones, ed., *The Life of Ashbel Green, V.D.M. Begun to be Written by Himself in His Eighty-Second Year and Continued to his Eighty-Fourth* (1849). All other quotations from Green are drawn from MSS in the Green Family Papers, Firestone Library, NjP, and from the MS Minutes of the Board of Trustees, MS Minutes of the Faculty, and other miscellaneous MSS in PUA, Mudd Library, NjP.

Other sources are: Beam, *Whig Soc.*; Maclean, *History*, II; Wertenbaker, *Princeton*; Miller quotations from Samuel Miller, *Life of Samuel Miller* (1869), I, 192, 241; Alexander quotation from J. W. Alexander, *Life of Archibald Alexander* (1854), 315; L. Woods, *Hist. of Andover Theological Seminary* (1885); N. A. Naylor in *Hist. Ed. Quart.*, 17 (1977), 17-30; T. D. Bozeman, *Protestants in an Age of Science* (1977); C. Hislop, *Eliphalet Nott* (1971), 67; als W. McDougall to J. McDougall, 2 Dec 1812, Gratz Coll., PHi ("ministers of Christ"); Green, *Witherspoon*, 136 ("govern too much"); letter from Pintard to Eliza P. Davidson, 28 Jan 1817, in *Letters from John Pintard to His Daughter, NYHS Coll.* (1937), I, 51; als J. Garnett to "Mother," 13 Feb 1813, NjP ("ceased to snow"); E. H. Gillett, *Hist. of the Pres. Chh.* (1864), I, 560, for "no man to rapture" quote; *Min. Gen. Assem., 1789-1820*, and *1821-1835*, passim; *JPHS*, 13 (1928-1929), 117-74; E. A. Smith, *Pres. Ministry in Amer. Culture* (1962), 107-176; G. M. Marsden, *Evangelical Mind and New School Pres. Experience* (1970), esp. 59-87.

Mss: NjP, PHi, PPPrHi, and various items scattered in scores of other collections

PUBLICATIONS: see Maclean, *History*, II, 224-25

JMcL

Obadiah Holmes

OBADIAH HOLMES, A.B., farmer, in the general catalogues of the College was first listed as dead in 1797, and this notation helps to identify him as the Obadiah Holmes of Middletown Township, Monmouth County, New Jersey whose will was drawn on November 11, 1795 and proved on the following December 23. He bore the name of one of the original patentees of the Monmouth Grant of 1665, the son of Reverend Obadiah Holmes, pastor of the First Baptist Church of Newport, Rhode Island, from 1652 until his death in 1682. The family in New Jersey through successive generations tended to perpetuate the name Obadiah and the connection of its members with the Baptist church.

The Princeton graduate was the son of Obadiah Holmes, also of Middletown, whose will was dated December 2, 1775 and proved on February 12, 1776. In the will the elder Holmes described himself as a yeoman, and the inventory of his personal holdings indicates that he was a more than ordinarily prosperous yeoman. The estate included at least seven Negroes, more than £500 in loans at interest, a substantial number of horses and cattle, and household furnishings to match other evidences of his status. The total value was over £1,786. To his only son, he left all of his land, five of the Negroes, and much of the stock and furniture, under an obligation to pay each of his two sisters £150 when he attained the age of thirty. In the meantime, the daughters each received, in addition to horses, cattle, and household goods, a

Negro girl. The father obviously was a literate man, and one suspects that on the side he was something of a preacher. More than two weeks after executing his will, he added, on December 20, a codicil bequeathing to his son Bunyan's two volumes "in folio," Wilson's Christian Dictionary, a concordance, Bailey's Dictionary, Eschard's Gazetteer, the four volumes of Thomas Crosby's *History of the English Baptists* (1738-40), and three volumes of the "Independent Whig." For some reason, he omitted the two volumes of Bishop Gilbert Burnet's "History," which turn up in the later inventory.

It is possible that the codicil may have expressed the father's hope for his son's career, or perhaps it merely indicates that the boy already had displayed a love of books. Whatever the fact, his background obviously was such as to leave no room for surprise over his later enrollment in the College of New Jersey. No date of birth for the son has been found, but he obviously was still a minor at the time of his father's death, for he was not made an executor of the estate. The Obadiah Holmes, Jr. who was one of three executors was another person then living in Freehold Township.

In the absence of matriculation records, it is impossible to determine just when Holmes first came to Nassau Hall. The Cliosophic Society has dated his membership in that organization from 1780. In view of the assumed moribund state of that society before its revival in July 1781, his admission to the College actually may have come somewhat later. The one point that is above debate is that at his commencement in September 1783 he enjoyed the highest honor of delivering the Latin salutatory oration. He spoke "on the union of learning and religion."

It is probably significant that Holmes did not take the "second degree in arts," as the A.M. often was described at the time. Instead of heading toward qualification for practice in one of the professions, he seems to have turned his attention to the management of his not insignificant inheritance. It is said that his marriage to Catherine (Caty in his will) Remsen, also of Monmouth County, came as early as October 1783. When he died hardly more than twelve years after his graduation, there were six children: three daughters, Sarah (Sally), Catherine (Caty), and Maria, and three sons, Remsen, Obadiah, and William. The will left the property in control of the mother and two other executors. Catherine had the choice of a Negro man, a Negro woman, and a Negro boy for her own use during the period of her widowhood. She also was entitled in the ultimate division of the estate to one share, as were each of the daughters. Each of the three sons was to receive two shares, but it was stipulated that there was to be no division of the estate until the youngest son was twenty-one years old. It is difficult to say whether the estate had been increased over that of his father. The overall valuation placed upon it by the inventory of £1,462, rendered also as $3,657, was lower, but a comparative reading of monetary terms over the course of the last quarter of the century is not easy. There were nine slaves. Like his father, Holmes had money invested at interest, and his farm obviously was well stocked and equipped. Among the notes he held was an overdue one against the "Trustees Academy," perhaps the academy at Freehold, where Joseph Clark (A.B. 1781) had once taught, and where Holmes himself may have been prepared for college. An entry for "a quantity of books" at £4 tells little, but there is interest in the separate entry for two volumes of "Bunyans Works." Perhaps the folio volumes willed by his father made a special impression on the appraisers.

Holmes's widow may have run into early difficulties, for a guardian had been appointed for the children, none of whom as yet had reached the age of fourteen, by the spring of 1798. She died intestate by November 6, 1801, and Henry I. Remsen of New York City, a merchant, was appointed administrator of her estate, which included four Negro children. Later in the same month, Remsen became the guardian for Sally, oldest of the Holmes children.

Sources: Alumni file, ms Clio Soc. membership list, general catalogues, PUA; *Pa. Gazette*, 8 Oct 1783 (commencement); *N.J. Wills*, v, 251 (father); viii, 182; x, 222, 223. The original wills in the State Libr. at Trenton carry much helpful detail omitted from the abstracts found in the foregoing citations. For Reverend Obadiah Holmes, see E. S. Gausted, *Baptist Piety: The Last Will and Testimony of Obadiah Holmes* (1978).

WFC

James (Green, Greene) Hunt

JAMES (GREEN, GREENE) HUNT, A.B., lawyer and public official, was born in Cecil County, Maryland, the son of Ruth Hall and her second husband, the Reverend James Hunt (A.B. 1759). During young James's youth, his father served in several Maryland communities as a Presbyterian clergyman and schoolmaster, whose lesson plans in rhetoric included "field trips" for his students to the local courthouse. James and his younger brother William Pitt Hunt (A.B. 1786) probably received their preparatory education and acquired their interest in the law from him, and subsequent attendance at their father's alma mater would have been logical.

It has not been discovered when young James began his collegiate career. All that is known is that he joined the American Whig Society in the summer of 1782 and, for some unexplained reason, was absent from his class's graduation exercises in September 1783. His classmate Jacob Radcliff took Hunt's part in a rhetorical dispute, but Hunt was awarded the first degree with the rest, indicating that he had passed the required examinations given the previous month. Perhaps he was on a journey to claim his diploma when he visited Philadelphia at the end of October. His classmate Gilbert Snowden noted in a private journal that Hunt appeared on October 25: "He invited himself to my father's, forced his way as it were to stay with me, & all in such a mean servile way, as made me despise him." Snowden endured Hunt's company until the latter's departure on October 30, even though Hunt "was one whom I little valued, who had been my enemy in college, & whose temper & conduct had given me a disgust not easily to be forgotten." This hatred may have stemmed in some part from Snowden's membership in the Cliosophic Society, the rival of the Whigs.

The name of this graduate appears in all extant College records simply as "James Hunt," and using that name, Samuel Alexander, an early biographer of Nassau Hall alumni, wrote that Hunt later returned to Maryland to assist in his father's classical school. A genealogist of his mother's family, however, later identified him as "James Green Hunt," a South Carolina attorney and public official, an identification supported, interestingly enough, by Snowden's journal. In his first entry, Snowden listed all the members of the 1783 graduating class, and there Hunt is identified as "James G." The hypothesis gains strength from the will of the South Carolina man, which mentions a brother, William Pitt Hunt, and an estate in Maryland. The use of middle names was not a common practice in the eighteenth century, but since Hunt's younger brother had one, it is quite possible that James had been given one too, although he may have decided not to use it when matriculating in the College.

Hunt indeed may have taught school in Maryland for a short time after graduation, but it is likely that he studied law in Virginia where several of his half-brothers had settled. Family tradition holds that he entered the office of Edmund Randolph, then attorney general for the state, who also maintained an active private practice in Richmond. The future governor of Virginia certainly took on an assistant sometime during 1784, probably a law student, and that assistant may well have been Hunt.

Hunt first appears in the South Carolina records as an attorney in Charleston in 1786. Sometime during the next few years, he moved his practice to Columbia, the new state capital in Richland County. It was probably there that he married Sarah Taylor, eldest child of Thomas and Ann Taylor and sister of John Taylor (A.B. 1790). The political influence of a father-in-law who had been a member of South Carolina's two provincial congresses, a colonel in the Revolution, and later a state senator and Privy Council member in 1789 and 1790 was probably invaluable in helping Hunt launch a political career.

Hunt was a member of the convention called in 1790 to draft a new state constitution, and the following year he was elected to the South Carolina House of Representatives. To qualify for such election at the time, candidates had to meet a property requirement that they own five hundred acres of land and ten slaves or real estate worth a minimum of £150. Since Hunt's household only consisted of three white males over sixteen and two white females, according to the 1790 census, he must have been qualified by the value of his land.

Hunt served in two assemblies of the lower house. There, joined at times by his former classmate Timothy Ford, he figured prominently on committees assigned to revise the state's judicial system, investigate possibilities for a public school system, and prepare the articles of impeachment of Alexander Moultrie, a former state attorney general accused of misappropriation of funds. He was present for virtually all roll call votes during his tenure, supported a ban on the importation of slaves, and also voted to urge the state's congressmen to repeal the whiskey taxes.

In December 1791 Hunt was appointed a justice of the peace for Richland County, a position he held concurrently with his legislative post. Presumably he resigned from both offices after his election by the lower house as a judge of the Court of Equity on May 12, 1794. Chancellor Hunt was not destined for a long career on the bench, however. He presided over the June term of the court in 1794, during which time he filed no reports. He died the following August 10, apparently soon after the death of his wife.

Hunt's will, proved in Richland County on August 20, 1794, was to be executed by his father-in-law, other members of the Taylor family, and also his brother William. A half-brother, Richard Hall, also asked permission to "administer on his estate as one of the heirs." Hunt and his wife probably had no surviving children. His death was noted in newspapers as far away as Boston but was not indicated in the College's triennial catalogues before 1808.

SOURCES: Alexander, *Princeton*, 216; *Princetonians, 1748-1768*, 268-70; *WMQ* (1 ser.), 22 (1913-1914), 139 ("one of the heirs"); Beam, *Whig Soc.*, 62; G. T. Snowden, MS Journal 1783-85, PPPrHi; J. J. Reardon, *Edmund Randolph* (1974), 70; *First Census,*

S.C., 27; Y. Snowden, *History of S.C.*, I (1920), 505-511; J.S.R. Faunt et al., *Biog. Directory of S.C. House of Reps.*, I (1974), 231, 237; E. L. Green, *Hist. of Richland County, S.C.*, I (1932), 175-76, 230; MS Journals of the Ninth and Tenth General Assemblies, S.C. House of Reps. 1791-1794, passim; J. B. O'Neall, *Bench and Bar of S.C.* (1859), I, 232; II, 597 (has misprint), 601; *Columbian Centinel*, 17 Sep 1794. The assistance of N. Louise Bailey, coeditor of the *Biog. Directory of the S.C. House of Reps.*, is also gratefully acknowledged.

JW

Nathaniel Lawrence

NATHANIEL LAWRENCE, A.B., lawyer and public official, in normal times probably would have received his degree at an earlier date. The trustees in their annual commencement meeting of September 24, 1783, having as usual accepted the report of the final examination given members of the senior class, and having awarded them their degrees, then adopted the following resolution:

Capt. Nathaniel Lawrence, formerly a student in this institution, but interrupted in his collegiate course by the war, sollicited the degree of Batchelor of Arts, of which he had been deprived by the late confusions—The Trustees, finding that he has uniformly sustained an amiable character for good morals & diligence since he left the college—Resolved, that he be admitted to this honor with the present class.

For several years—in fact, well past the catalogue of 1797, which first recorded his death—the published general catalogues of the College continued to recognize the abnormality of the degree by listing Lawrence out of alphabetical order at the end of the Class of 1783.

In September 1783 Lawrence only recently had reached the age of twenty-two. He had been born on July 11, 1761, at Newtown, Queens County, Long Island, New York, the eldest child and son of Thomas Lawrence and his wife, Elizabeth Fish Lawrence. The father was a prosperous farmer and sometime seaman, who is said to have commanded in the "old French war" a vessel of eighteen guns that made several voyages, no doubt as a privateer, and who later became a justice of the county. The mother was also of Newtown, a sister of Peter Fish (A.B. 1774) and a cousin of Nicholas Fish (Class of 1777). One of Lawrence's sisters later married John Wells (A.B. 1788).

According to Philip Lindsley (A.B. 1804), Professor of Languages at Princeton from 1813 to 1824 and later president of the University of Nashville, who married Lawrence's sole surviving child Margaret

Elizabeth, Nathaniel had entered the College in May 1776, when he was not quite fifteen years old. Presumably, he returned in the following November, and so was among the students dismissed by President Witherspoon at the end of the month because of the rapidly deteriorating military situation in the state. Whether he was included in the handful of students who returned to their studies during the summer of 1777, or whether he may have been in residence through the winter and spring that followed are not known. It can be said only that on June 1, 1778, he was commissioned a second lieutenant in the Second Regiment of the North Carolina Continental Line, a unit commanded until late in the preceding November by Colonel Alexander Martin (A.B. 1756).

The special circumstances opening the way for this youthful adventure, at a time when Lawrence had yet to reach his seventeenth birthday, have not been discovered. No more can be said than that the North Carolina Line at the time was seriously understrength and some of its officers had been sent home for the purpose of recruitment. The army was getting ready to break camp at Valley Forge and would soon follow the British, after their withdrawal from Philadelphia, across New Jersey to the indecisive action at Monmouth Court House on June 28. With British forces once more concentrated at New York, Washington's troops subsequently were deployed along the Hudson. There, after a long winter, and exactly one year after he had been commissioned, Lawrence became a prisoner of war, on June 1, 1779, when the garrison at Fort LaFayette, below West Point and across the river from Stony Point, was forced to surrender after a stubborn defense to a superior British force. He remained a prisoner, most of the time on Long Island, until March 28, 1781, when he was exchanged.

According to his own account, Lawrence reported to Washington for orders and was referred to General Nathanael Greene, who as successor to Gates in command of the Southern Department then controlled Lawrence's unit. He wrote to Greene, who in August replied that the North Carolina Line was in so "deranged" a state that it was impossible to advise him on his current status and advised that he stay where he was until he heard further. Exactly where he was is not stated. By the spring of 1782, the North Carolina Line had gone through a reorganization, and Lawrence, having heard from a delegate to the Congress that Brigadier General Jethro Sumner was in command, wrote to him from Philadelphia on August 29, explaining that he had not heard further from Greene and had meanwhile joined the staff of General Robert Howe, also of North Carolina. He expressed the hope that he might be allowed to continue in that capacity. He wrote again to Sumner on February 24, 1783, this time from Princeton, reporting with some evident agitation that he had just received "your order of 17th Sept., 1782" and that he assumed that the altered "State of affairs" since that date would justify him in considering the order as not "obligatory." He mentioned the termination of operations in the south, the prospect of an early peace, and also the need his family, residents of Long Island, might have for his assistance. No response by Sumner has been found, but one more piece of correspondence regarding Lawrence's wartime record deserves mention. It is a letter from Doctor Hugh Williamson, North Carolina congressman, dated on September 17, 1783, at Princeton, where the Congress was then sitting, to Alexander Martin, who had become the governor of North Carolina. Lawrence had been much disturbed on checking a late return of officers of the North Carolina Line in the office of the secretary at war to discover that his name had been omitted. Williamson gave the details of Lawrence's service and imprisonment, reported the correspondence with Greene and his later service with Howe, and asked Martin to investigate lest Lawrence suffer an injustice.

These details of Lawrence's experience after his imprisonment have some bearing on several points of interest. Williamson's letter was written only a week before the trustees of the College agreed to award Lawrence the degree, which suggests that Lawrence's petition for it may have been made in person. The correspondence shows too that Lawrence was in Princeton in late February of 1783, and this raises the intriguing question of whether at some time after his imprisonment he may have returned to his studies in the College. If this had been the case, however, there seems to have been no reason why Williamson should not have mentioned it. Instead, he states that after Lawrence's service with Howe "the campaign being inactive Mr. Lawrence returned to live with some of his friends in the Country." How long that service may have lasted is suggested by Howe's role in the suppression of the mutiny of Pennsylvania troops that had driven the Congress from Philadelphia to a refuge in Princeton. Howe had arrived in Princeton on June 30, 1783 with some 1,500 troops dispatched from Newburgh in New York. He was ordered on to Philadelphia by Congress on July 1, and by July 5 was going into camp outside the city at Germantown. By September the danger had passed, courts-martial had been held, a policy of clemency toward those convicted had been agreed upon, and on September 13 Congress congratulated General Howe for the prudence he had shown throughout an operation involving a delicate consideration of the need to assert national authority without giving undue offense to the government of Pennsylvania. By then perhaps Lawrence was free to visit his friends in the country.

Whatever the fact may be, his apprehension of a failure by North Carolina to credit him with service rendered the state seems to have been unfounded. Surviving records indicate that he actually was included in the new "arrangement" of the North Carolina Line and that he was credited with service to the end of the war. Whether toward or in its termination he received a promotion to captain is less certain. More specific is the testimonty of Philip Lindsley in 1849 that Lawrence had received from North Carolina two land grants, of 2,560 acres each, one of them then in the possession of a grandson named Nathaniel Lawrence Lindsley.

It must have been not long after the commencement of 1783 that Lawrence began the study of law with Egbert Benson at Poughkeepsie, New York, for he was admitted to the bar of the supreme court of the state of New York on August 1, 1786. Through a part of his study at least, he was a fellow apprentice of the later jurist and law writer Chancellor James Kent of New York, and of his classmate Jacob Radcliff. By 1789, and perhaps earlier, he was a practicing attorney in New York City.

His first public office appropriately was that of a captain in the New York County Militia in 1787. In the next year he was one of the four delegates who represented Queens County in the convention meeting at Poughkeepsie to consider ratification of the Constitution of the United States. He has been identified as an antifederalist, together with the other Queens delegates, but on the critical final vote for unconditional ratification of the Constitution, the entire Queens delegation voted in the affirmative. However, Lawrence was counted among the leaders who on October 30, 1788, at Fraunces' Tavern launched a short-lived protest in behalf of a second federal convention.

In politics, the friends of Alexander Hamilton considered Lawrence to be a protégé of Aaron Burr (A.B. 1772), who was reported in the fall of 1791 as wanting Lawrence as his successor in the office of attorney general for the state. Writing to Hamilton on September 30, 1791, Nathaniel Hazard (A.B. 1764) declared: "Lawrence looks up to Burr with Veneration, has formed a favorable Opinion of you, but is shy. He is honest, but very wary & cold blooded for a young Man." Hazard advised that Lawrence disliked Governor George Clinton and that Hamilton's support of Lawrence's candidacy for the attorney general's post would provide "*indubitable* Proof of your sincere Good Will to Burr & himself." In the following November, the job went rather to Morgan Lewis (A.B. 1773), but it is significant that when Lewis was promoted to the state supreme court, in reward for his support of Clinton in the election of 1792, Lawrence became attorney general by a commission dated December 24, 1792. Obviously, Lawrence had come to terms with the Clintonian opponents of Hamilton.

It is obvious too that Lawrence was an ambitious young man who dared to set his sights high. Had his life been longer, he might have become a prominent figure in the politics of the state. As it was, he resigned as attorney general in November 1795, citing the increasing burdens of the office and his declining health. Prior to his appointment, he had represented Queens through two sessions of the lower house of the legislature in 1791 and 1792, and he sat again for the county in 1795 and 1796, a service ending in April of the latter year. His appointment by Governor John Jay as assistant attorney general for the district embracing Queens and four other counties in February 1796 may suggest that he was not irrevocably aligned with either of the emerging political parties of the time. He died at Hempstead, Long Island, on July 5, 1797, a victim of consumption, according to his son-in-law, which the family not surprisingly attributed to his imprisonment during the war.

Lawrence had been married on April 11, 1787 to Elizabeth Berrien, daughter of John Berrien, trustee of the College and justice of the supreme court of New Jersey before his death in 1772. She was an aunt of John McPherson Berrien (A.B. 1796), later United States senator from Georgia, and her death came on October 16, 1799. Of the children born to the couple, all died in their infancy except for Margaret Elizabeth, who married Philip Lindsley on October 14, 1813 and died in Nashville, Tennessee on December 5, 1845.

SOURCES: Als P. Lindsley to B. F. Thompson, 26 Feb 1849, Trustee Minutes, alumni file, general catalogues, all PUA; B. F. Thompson, *Hist. of Long Island* (1918), III, 618-19; J. Riker, Jr., *Annals of Newtown, Long Island* (1852), 288; *St. Rec. N.C.*, XIII, 480-81; XVI, 71, 72, 575, 576, 607, 608, 647-48 (NL to Sumner, 29 Aug 1782), 881-82 (Williamson to Martin, 17 Sep 1782), 939-40 (NL to Sumner, 24 Feb 1783), 1,002, 1,105; XVII, 64, 189; H. F. Rankin, *N.C. Continentals* (1971), 169-70; V. L. Collins, *Continental Congress at Princeton* (1908), 60-66, 143-46; N.Y. directories 1789-1792, 1794-1795; *Mil. Min., Council of Appointment, St. of N.Y.*, I, 133; E. W. Spaulding, *N.Y. in Critical Period* (1932), 225-26, 267, 269; L. G. DePauw, *Eleventh Pillar* (1966), 216, 249; *Hamilton Papers*, IX, 246-47 (Hazard to Hamilton, 30 Sep 1791); A. F. Young, *Democratic Republicans of N.Y.* (1967), 122, 200, 332; *N.Y. Red Book* (1915), 396-98, 531. According to a classmate, Gilbert T. Snowden, Lawrence was "formerly a member of the College & had been as far as the Junior class, being driven by the times into the army was admitted to a degree of B.A. with us" (see *Princeton Univ. Lib. Chron.*, 14 (1952), 76).

WFC

Jacob LeRoy

JACOB LEROY, A.B., merchant and public official, was born in New York City on November 19, 1763, the son of Jacob and Cornelia Rutgers LeRoy. Jacob LeRoy, Sr. was a prominent merchant of Huguenot descent who had emigrated from Amsterdam about 1750. Once in New York he established a partnership with Captain Anthony Rutgers, whose sister he married. Young Jacob was their sixth child. After his mother's death, his father married again in May 1766, this time to Catharine Rutgers, another of his partner's sisters.

The father's formal association with Anthony Rutgers ended in January 1769, but his business continued to grow. His establishment on Queen Street opposite Burling slip was described in 1775 as having a "varied assortment of hemp, cordage, yarn, dry goods (and) hardware." He apparently tried to maintain a neutral profile during the Revolution, for, though he freely reported to the New York Provincial Congress in March 1776 on rumors he had heard about the extent of foreign troops being sent to the colonies, by the end of that year he had fled north with his family and that of Captain Rutgers to Staatsburgh in Dutchess County. From there he petitioned the New York Committee of Correspondence several times for permission to return to the city to secure certain business papers, but when the matter was referred to General Washington in April 1777, permission was denied because LeRoy's political principles were suspect. This suspicion was deserved, for the elder LeRoy was also communicating that year with William Smith, the Tory brother of Thomas Smith (A.B. 1754), confined on parole at the nearby Livingston Manor. Perhaps their meetings were only incidental, since LeRoy's daughter Maria Anna had married a Livingston in May 1775, and apparently Smith did not believe much of the information received from LeRoy. By May 1778 Smith noted in his diary that he had less confidence in the LeRoys than earlier, and no further entries relating to them exist.

Presumably young Jacob remained with his family until beginning his collegiate studies. His father may originally have intended that his sons attend King's College, since he had donated an organ to that institution by 1770. But an older son, Herman, had been sent to Holland for a commercial education, probably with relatives, and by the time Jacob was ready for college, King's was closed and the war made passage to Holland dangerous at best. He may have arrived at Princeton in 1780, the year given in an early Cliosophic Society catalogue as his admission date, although other evidence indicates that the society was not revived until the following year. Nothing additional has been discovered concerning LeRoy's college career except that he was so unwell when he arrived for commencement that he returned home without participating in the exercises. His part was read for him by his classmate Gilbert Snowden.

After graduation LeRoy settled permanently in New York City, where he probably resided initially with his family. Originally he planned to become a lawyer, and with that in mind he clerked with Alexander Hamilton. Hamilton's bill to LeRoy's father for £150 had been cancelled by May of 1784, however, because "Mr. LeRoy did not continue his clerkship." Instead he entered the family business.

Throughout his life, Jacob was overshadowed by his brother Herman, who first achieved prominence in 1786 as the Dutch Consul General in New York, and who by 1788 had formed his own company in partnership with a brother-in-law, William Bayard, and for a time with his sister Elizabeth's husband, Gulian McEvers. The commercial house of LeRoy, Bayard, and Company became one of the largest in New York City in the early part of the nineteenth century, based largely on its early connections and successes buying securities for a Dutch banking house. Herman also played an important role for a time as a state legislator, an advocate of the right of foreigners to purchase land in New York state, and as an ally of Federalist politicians, including Secretary of the Treasury Alexander Hamilton. For his support he was chosen as a director of the Society for establishing Useful Manufactures and was elected to the first board of directors of the Bank of the United States. Later on he became president of the Bank of New York and founder in 1813 of LeRoy, New York in the large tract he owned in what is today Genesee County.

Jacob, on the other hand, remained with his father's firm, which had been called Jacob LeRoy and Sons since at least as early as 1784. Its shop at 31 Maiden Lane specialized in Dutch imports: "Russia duck, swedes iron, copper in sheets, twine, brimstone in rolls, chintzes, Callicoes, and a variety of Dry Goods." The name of the firm did not change at the father's death in early 1793, but its character may have, for late eighteenth-century city directories list it as a "counting house."

Jacob LeRoy, Sr.'s will named son Jacob and Captain Anthony Rutgers as executors. Their assignment in that capacity was somewhat unusual, however: they were to purchase two lottery tickets, one in England and one in Holland; then the prize money was to be added to the rest of the estate and divided equally between the widow and five surviving children. Apparently this was done in the hope of making up for what were going to be some heavy losses in French funds. A letter from Herman to Alexander Hamilton written in March 1793 suggests that compensation be made by deducting such amounts from this country's war debt to France.

Aside from a brief period of public service, the surviving record contains disappointingly little on Jacob LeRoy. It is known that on October 4, 1786 he was appointed a lieutenant in the New York militia and on January 26, 1792 was married to Martha Banyer, with whom he had at least one daughter. He was chosen an election in-spector for the city's Fourth Ward in 1798 and also held the post in April 1802. Late that year he was elected an assistant alderman for the Fourth Ward, and in 1803 held that position for the Third Ward. He won his highest public office, alderman for the Third Ward, on November 24, 1806, and served one term.

As a member of the city's common council, LeRoy sat on a variety of committees, the most important of which planned and supervised the building of the new city hall. His voting record was unwavering in its support of the city's mercantile interests. In May 1807 he was re-warded for his service to his home town when the Common Council named a newly acquired street for him. He was the only alderman so honored.

During this period LeRoy may also have been a vestryman of Trinity Church and a director of the Bank of New York. The last mention of him in the public record is his request made July 2, 1813 for water rights on the Hudson River. Such a grant was finally issued June 1, 1818, but since the petitioner had died on February 13, 1815, he did not profit from it personally. At the time of his death, his business had been moved to Washington Street at the corner of Rector, and he resided in a home he had had built a decade before on Liberty Street. His widow, a member of the Fifth Avenue Presbyterian Church since 1813, outlived him by fourteen years.

SOURCES: E. A. LeRoy, *Geneal. Chart and Hist. of the LeRoy Family* (1933), 2-3, and passim (confuses the careers of Jacob, Sr. and Jacob, Jr.); A. DuBin, *LeRoy Family* (1941), 5-6; *NYGBR*, 10 (1879), 48; 107 (1976), 99; *N.Y. Marriages*, 231; J. A. Scoville, *Old Merchants of N.Y. City*, III (1865), 88, 175; N.Y. Mercantile Libr. Assoc., *N.Y. City During the Amer. Rev.* (1861), 33 ("varied assortment"); Force, *Am. Arch.* (4 ser.), V, 385; *Cal. N.Y. Hist. Manuscripts, War of Rev.* (1868), I, 681; *Hamilton Papers*, I, 225, 228; III, 7 (clerkship); W.H.W. Sabine, *Hist. Memoirs of William Smith*, II (1958), 249, 380; E. B. Livingston, *The Livingstons of Livingston Manor* (1910), 546; *Hist. of Columbia Univ.* (1904), 35; *Clio. Soc. Cat.* (1845), 5; G. T. Snowden, MS Journal, 1783-1785, 11, PPPrHi; Davis, *Essays*, 185, 370-72, 392-94, 456; *N.Y. Directory 1786*, facsimile reprint (n.d.), 44, 101 ("Russia duck"); *Mil. Min., Council of Appointment, St. of N.Y.*, I, 110; *N.Y. Wills*, XIV, 225-26; A. M. Hamilton, *Intimate Life of Alexander Hamilton* (1910), 313; *MCCCNY*, II, 430, 717; III, 87, 150, 394, 244-45, 409-411; IV, 301, 423; VII, 506; IX, 675.

JW

Jacob Radcliff

JACOB RADCLIFF (RADCLIFT, RADCLIFFE), A.B., lawyer and public official, was born in Rhinebeck, New York and baptized in the German
Reformed Church there on April 29, 1764. He was the eldest son of
Sarah Kip and her husband, William Radcliffe, a Dutchess County
landowner, town supervisor, and state legislator, who also rose to the
rank of brigadier general in the New York militia. The family name
has been spelled variously in correspondence of the period, but Jacob
was himself using the simplified version in letters he penned in 1798,
and thus the name appears in the public record thereafter. Jacob was
one of five sons, four of whom became college graduates. William
graduated from the College in 1784 and two younger brothers were
Yale graduates of the early 1790s.

It is uncertain when Jacob began his collegiate studies, although
he was probably in Princeton by 1781 when a catalogue of the Cliosophic Society notes his admission to the organization. At his commencement he took part in a three-way debate comparing ancient and
modern abilities to cultivate "cool and dispassionate eloquence," and
in another, discussing whether "any measure that is morally evil [can]
be politically good." In both Radcliff took the negative position. He
then gave an oration for James Hunt who was absent from the proceedings.

The following spring Radcliff's classmate Gilbert Snowden noted
in his private journal an exchange of letters between the two young
men, and an entry of September referred to Radcliff as "a person for
whom I have a great esteem . . . worthy the regard of any man." Radcliff was then in Poughkeepsie, New York where he had moved shortly
after commencement. There he and another classmate, Nathaniel
Lawrence, studied law with Egbert Benson (King's 1756), attorney
general of New York state, and in due course were admitted to the bar
in 1786. That year Radcliff opened a law office in Poughkeepsie, was
appointed lieutenant in an artillery company of the Dutchess County
Militia, and on November 9, married Juliana Smith, daughter of
Reverend Cotton Mather Smith (Yale 1751) of Sharon, Connecticut.
The couple had three sons and two daugthers born to them between
1789 and 1801. In 1790 the census taker recorded six people in the
Radcliff household, including two slaves.

Radcliff apparently had a typical country law practice. The cases
he handled were those of his neighbors and concerned such matters
as minor boundary disputes and stolen cows. That routine was en-
livened October 3, 1792 by a visit from President Ezra Stiles of Yale

Jacob Radcliff, A.B. 1783
BY JOHN TRUMBULL

College, who was on a journey to Albany and may have stayed in Poughkeepsie because Radcliff's father-in-law had once been his student. Radcliff may have attended his younger brother's commencement in New Haven a few weeks before, and he might have invited Stiles to his home at that time.

In 1792 Jacob's father served a term in the New York Assembly representing Dutchess County, and was succeeded in the following two sessions by his eldest son, who was a member of committees to analyze the existing laws of the state as published in 1789 and to revise the criminal code. Young Radcliff's decidedly Federalist views were reflected in his votes to promote the mercantile interests in New York and in his strong personal animus toward those he regarded as enemies of the country. In July 1798, in a letter to the Reverend Jedidiah Morse (Yale 1783) of Charlestown, Massachusetts, he could not resist complimenting New England on its recent political stands and added: "there still remains among us (at least in this state) a hostile, malignant & dangerous French faction whom I do not hesitate to say, in case of a war . . . ought to be exterminated or banished from our Country. . . . I view a good citizen and a Jacobin as two incompatible beings, incapable of living in the same community or of breathing the same air in harmony—."

Under the governorship of John Jay, Radcliff was appointed assistant attorney general for Dutchess, Ulster, and Orange counties, serving from February 1796 to January 1798. In 1798 he moved his law practice to New York City, much to the dismay of other upstate Federalists like Philip Schuyler. "I hope every exertion will be made In Your quarter to insure Mr. Jay's Election," the latter wrote to his son-in-law, Alexander Hamilton, in March 1798 before the next gubernatorial contest. He added: "I fear the result in Dutchess County as I [do] not recollect Since Mr Radcliffs departure thence that we have any Active Influential friend here. I wish Mr Radif [sic] could go into that County—or at least that he would write to his friends." Radcliff apparently complied, for in the following December, Jay appointed him a justice of the New York supreme court, a post he was to hold for over five years.

On the bench Radcliff joined his former mentor Egbert Benson and another one-time student of Benson's and Dutchess County advocate, James Kent (King's 1781), giving the Federalists a majority of the five judgeships. The new appointees won early respect from their fellow attorneys. Robert Troup, a prominent New York lawyer, described them favorably in 1800, although his own clients had just lost a case in their courtroom: "They are young—well grounded in education—ambitious to distinguish themselves—and laborious—and no men can have juster notions of our system of things & its rational tendency." Together Radcliff and Kent's most important contribution was their codification of state laws published in 1802, which remained standard until 1813.

Although Kent remained on the bench for many years and rose to become its chancellor, Radcliff resigned in early 1804. He returned to his New York City legal practice to which he devoted most of the remainder of his life. In 1805 he also became a trustee of Columbia University, a position he held until 1817.

Radcliff either had a very successful legal practice or had received generous gifts from his father, who would live until 1813. He was an early stockholder in the Merchants Bank of New York, a Federalist institution founded in 1803. More important, he was one of three prominent New York lawyers who founded Jersey City, New Jersey. In 1802 the site was inhabited by only thirteen people, although a ferry to New York had been established there earlier. The new owners formed the Associates of the Jersey Company, a venture headed by nine directors, laid out a town of one thousand lots, each of which was sold for one hundred dollars, and obtained the town's designation as a port of delivery in 1806. The Associates ruled Jersey City until its incorporation in 1820.

In July 1808 Egbert Benson, as a retired federal judge, was busy forming Federalist committees of correspondence to support the election of Federalists in the fall elections in the north, to have the nation's capital moved back to Philadelphia, and to hold a northern convention. Radcliff was recruited for the New York committee and the convention secretly held in New York City that August. At the meeting, Charles C. Pinckney and Rufus King were renominated as candidates for president and vice-president, although these choices were not made public for several months. In spite of dissension among the Republicans, primarily over the embargo, this ticket was easily defeated by James Madison (A.B. 1771) and George Clinton. The Federalists, however, were more successful on the state level, and in 1809 they won control of the New York legislature for the first time in ten years. During this period, that body was empowered to fill many important local offices in the state through the Council of Appointment. When this council met in early 1810, after much disagreement, Radcliff was selected for the lucrative position of mayor of New York City.

Radcliff took the oath of office on March 5, 1810, but served only one year, because the Federalists soon lost control in the assembly and in the Council of Appointment. Before the return of DeWitt Clinton as mayor in 1811, however, Radcliff had introduced a measure to regulate the sealing of weights and measures and served on a committee considering police and court reform. He was required to vote only five times, all on minor issues. His salary was $7,000 for the year, which was paid in quarterly installments.

New York state politics remained a kaleidescope of competing factions and shifting alliances during the War of 1812. Radcliff's brother Peter had been named to the Council of Appointment, and in 1813 he renominated Jacob for the New York City mayoralty. Members of his own party bypassed Radcliff, however, in favor of the incumbent Clinton, who many had recently supported for the presidency in spite of his being a Republican. Radcliff and other hard-line Federalists were incensed. In 1814 one of them, Gulian C. Verplanck, writing under the name "Abimelech Coody," lampooned Clinton and his supporters in the local papers. The Washington Federalists, a splinter party formed by the anti-Clintonians, were consequently dubbed the "Coodies" by their opponents, and, though they received little support in that year's assembly elections, their efforts contributed to Clinton's dismissal in 1815. At that point a deal was struck. John Ferguson, grand sachem of the Tammany Society, was appointed mayor with the understanding that he would resign shortly and be replaced by Radcliff, who was duly sworn on July 10, 1815.

The second Radcliff administration lasted almost three years but was hardly more eventful than the previous one. On the city council, the mayor had an opportunity to cast only one important vote, that on ferry fares. At this time, he was also president of the Trustees of the Sailors Snug Harbor, a charitable institution for retired seamen, and he represented their interests to the council on at least one occasion. Perhaps the high point of his career was his welcome of President James Monroe to New York City in June 1817.

Radcliff's last political role was as a delegate to the state's constitutional convention of 1821, along with Stephen Van Rensselaer (Class of 1782), Peter Robert Livingston (A.B. 1784), and his former benchmate James Kent. While on the committee on suffrage, he was concerned about the Constitution's definition of equality of rights. Radcliff believed that the phrase referred to civil, and not to political rights, as did many Americans before passage of the Fourteenth Amendment, but he supported measures to extend the franchise. He also favored loosening restrictions on the establishment of corporations and introducing methods other than impeachment for removing judges. Perhaps his most important contribution was his successful campaign for the appointment of officials of New York City by its Common Council rather than by state bodies.

Radcliff apparently maintained an active law practice in New York City until shortly before his death. An 1842 city directory places his office at 118 Nassau Street and also lists him as a commissioner in bankruptcy, one of seven in the city. He died at the home of one of his daughters in Troy, New York, on May 6, 1844, having outlived his wife and at least one son.

SOURCES: *DAB; NYGBR*, 80 (1949), 210; E. M. Smith, *Hist. of Rhinebeck, N.Y.* (1881), 207; Dexter, *Yale Biographies*, v, 35, 81 (for brothers); *Clio. Soc. Cat.*, (1845), 5; *Pa. Gazette*, 8 Oct 1783; G. T. Snowden, MS Journal, 1783-1785, PPPrHi; *Mil. Min., Council of Appointment, St. of N.Y.*, I, 70; *First Census, N.Y.*, 92; J. T. Horton, *James Kent* (1939), 50-51, 112; Stiles, *Literary Diary*, III, 476; als JR to J. Morse, 2 Jul 1798, DeCoppett Coll., NjP ("there still remains among us"); *Hamilton Papers*, XXI, 388 ("every exertion"); J. Goebel, Jr., *Law Practice of Alexander Hamilton*, II (1969), 88 ("They are young"); J. D. Hammond, *Hist. of Pol. Parties in . . . N.Y.*, I (1842), 112, 201, 346-49, 397-98; D. S. Alexander, *Political Hist. of the St. of N.Y.*, I (1906), 68-69; P. G. Hubert, Jr., *Merchants National Bank* (1903), 43; W. H. Shaw, *Hist. of Essex and Hudson Counties, N.J.*, II (1884), 1,141, 1,146; R. Ernst, *Rufus King* (1968), 319; S. E. Morison, *Harrison Grey Otis*, II, (1913), 315; D. R. Fox, *Decline of the Aristocracy in the Politics of N.Y.* (1919),

111, 174, 203; *MCCCNY*, vi, 93, 236, and passim; viii, 261, 277, 749; ix, 194, 262, 317; M. J. Lamb, *Hist. of the City of N.Y.*, iii (1896), 553; A. Kass, *Politics in N.Y. State, 1800-1830* (1965), 75; J. G. Wilson, ed., *Mem. Hist. of the City of N.Y.*, iii (1893), 298; C. Z. Lincoln, *Constitutional Hist. of N.Y.* (1906), i, 631, 662; ii, 64; iv, 559; N. H. Carter, W. L. Stone, and M.T.C. Gould, *Reports of the Proc. and Debates of the Convention of 1821* (1821), passim; *N.Y. City Directory, 1842-1843* (1842), 265, 377; *N.Y. Daily Tribune*, 8 May 1844.

PUBLICATIONS: *Laws of the St. of N.Y.* (1802)

MANUSCRIPTS: NjP, MHi

JW

Joseph Riddle

JOSEPH RIDDLE, A.B., merchant, was born on April 5, 1763, the son of James Riddle, a York County, Pennsylvania farmer who had emigrated from Donegal, Ireland in the early 1750s. Joseph was the fifth of nine sons, but only he and his older brother James (A.B. 1779) are known to have attended college. Little is known about Joseph's stay in Princeton, only that he was a member of the American Whig Society and that sickness prevented him from attending his commencement in September 1783. His part in a rhetorical dispute was taken by his classmate Joseph Venable. Riddle's absence did not prevent his being awarded the first degree with the rest of his class, however.

Nothing has been discovered regarding Riddle's activities in the years immediately following his graduation, but he was married September 12, 1789, and by the following year was an established merchant in Alexandria, Virginia where he remained at least twenty years. During this period Alexandria was expanding, primarily because of its importance as a center for trade in grain. Riddle was prominent among the merchants of the port involved in the trade, but like most of them, his business was probably not confined to that. At one time he is known to have formed a business connection with James Dall (or Dahl) of Baltimore. Riddle named a son after his associate in 1796, and in 1798 the firm of Riddle and Dahl filed a suit before the Fayette County, Kentucky circuit court.

Riddle's presence in Alexandria was evident also from his other activities. He joined the Sun Fire Company in 1790 and in 1797 was one of its subdirectors. Later that year his name was among those on the roster of the Relief Fire Company. His concern for the frame structures of the town led his company to insure its two buildings in 1794 for $3,500, and by 1803 at least one of these had been replaced by a three-story brick building roofed with copper. By then Riddle also

Joseph Riddle, A.B. 1783
BY CEPHAS THOMPSON

owned a three-story brick warehouse. He played a role in the cultural
life of Alexandria as well, as a member of the local chapter of the St.
Andrew's Society and a patron of the New Theatre. In 1797 he was
among the twenty-nine who contributed two hundred dollars each for
its new building and thus became eligible for free admission for one
season.

By 1806 Riddle's fortunes may have taken a turn for the worse. That
May he wrote to Henry Clay, asking him to secure a debt from a Kentucky resident. The request was signed "for Self and Late Co." In spite
of improvements in Alexandria's accessibility to inland grain sources,
thanks in part to the efforts of the Potomac Canal Company to bypass
the obstacles of that river, the city's grain trade had suffered in the
previous few years. A bumper British harvest was complemented by a
poor one in Virginia and the effect was something of a setback for Virginia producers and merchants.

Riddle was still in Alexandria in 1810 when the last of his eleven
children was born. Riddle's wife, the former Sarah Morrow Kearsley
of Shepherdstown, Virginia, died that April, and he moved the family

to Richmond, perhaps soon after. There he probably continued to pursue mercantile interests, although all that is certain is an address on E Street listed in the city's 1819 directory. At a later date he and at least three of his children moved again, this time to Woodville, Mississippi. Riddle served for a time as that town's postmaster before his death in 1844.

SOURCES: Mrs. John H. Guy, Jr. and Dr. Herbert A. Claiborne, Jr. of Richmond, Va. have provided much of the information contained in this sketch, from the Claiborne family papers at ViHi. Their contribution is gratefully acknowledged. See also G. T. Snowden, MS Journal, 1783-1785, PPPrHi; G. M. Moore, *Seaport in Va.* (1949), 28, 46, 153, 155; M. G. Powell, *Old Alexandria* (1928), 240; *NCHR*, 4 (1927), 404-413; *Clay Papers*, I, 221, 237; *Richmond Directory* (1819), 65; Alexandria Assoc., *Our Town* (exhibition catalogue) (1956), 46-47. Scattered references are found to "Joseph Riddle" in the *Pa. Arch.* for mil. service between 1776 and 1782 in Washington, Lancaster, Cumberland, and Northumberland cnties. It is possible that one or more listings relates to the CNJ graduate.

JW

James Rock

JAMES ROCK of Princeton, New Jersey, according to a newspaper account of the commencement exercises of September 29, 1779, was one of six young men who after examination were graduated from the grammar school and admitted to the freshman class in the College on the preceding day. In the evening of September 28, the "College-Hall was lighted up," and the six newly admitted freshmen entertained "a numerous assembly of gentlemen and ladies" with orations. No positive evidence that Rock actually began his collegiate studies in the following November when a new term began has been found, but there also is no known proof that he did not, as is the case with one other of the six young men, John Drayton of the prominent South Carolina family. Drayton later explained that the death of his father had prevented his returning from his home to the College. In view of the absence of any such evidence in Rock's case, and of the very incomplete records that have survived for reconstruction of the College's history at this time, it has to be assumed that Rock probably matriculated. That assumption is strengthened by the fact that he lived in Princeton as the above cited newspaper account makes unmistakably clear.

Rock no doubt was the son of James Rock, local artisan, carpenter, and craftsman (it was not an age of the modern type of specialization), who from time to time had been employed by the College for repairs to Nassau Hall and its furnishings. A number of accounts for work done by him have survived, and they show that he supplied or repaired bedsteads, mended tables and once a large picture frame in the prayer hall, or took care of damage to doors and installed locks where needed. The range of his skills is suggested by the ledger of a local merchant which records payments to him in November 1775 for a chest and the repair of a gunstock. Where the elder Rock was born and how long he lived in Princeton is not known, but it can be said that his services to the College date from the earliest years of the Witherspoon administration.

Although the family name was not common in New Jersey, there seem to have been two James Rocks living at the time of the Revolution in the neighborhood of Princeton, and the fact that the village sat astride the line between Somerset and Middlesex counties complicates the problem of identification. Tax records for 1778 show a James Rock living in Windsor Township of Middlesex County, and the other as a resident of the western precinct of Somerset County, which included Princeton. The former does not appear on the tax list for 1780, and there is additional evidence that he may have died before the end of the Revolution. James Rock of Somerset may also have died by that time, or at some time before the younger James finished his studies in the grammar school. On October 13, 1783, a meeting of local residents, disturbed by indications that the Congress, which had been sitting in the village since the preceding June, might move to another place, resulted in a list of persons offering to make quarters available in the hope that Princeton might continue to serve as the seat of "the supreme Legislature of America." Among the subscribers was a Mrs. Rock, a listing strongly suggesting that she was a widow. She considered that her home, which had one fireplace, could hardly accommodate a member of Congress, but that the two beds with breakfast and tea for two would be adequate for "Attendants." Mrs. Rock is found too among the communicants of the local Presbyterian church in 1792, and again as late as 1807. A visitor to the town in 1804 recalled much later that her residence was located on the Main Street (Nassau) across from the northeast corner of the College grounds.

Unfortunately, little more can be said regarding the younger James Rock, who is not numbered among the graduates of the College. Perhaps his father's death cut short his education. Perhaps his parents' ambition for him outran his own. Perhaps he simply dropped out, as did others. No indication has been found that he rendered military service. Among the tax ratables of the western precinct of Somerset County in 1793 were a James Rock and a Mary Rock. Whether the latter was the name of a wife, or that of the mother, must be left to speculation. Perhaps the James Rock who evidently died intestate and whose estate was inventoried at a value of $511.75 on November 5, 1815 by James F. Rock, administrator, was the former student at Princeton.

SOURCES: *NJA* (2 ser.), III, 669-70 (graduation). Ms collections at NjP contain a number of accounts, receipts, etc. for father's services to the College, as does the Patterson Acct. Bk. See also K. Stryker-Rodda, *Rev. Census of N.J.* (1972), 247; *GMNJ*, 51 (1976), 131; *N.J. Wills*, v, 503; vi, 317; x, 375 (1805 inventory); *Cat. of N.J. St. Libr. Manuscripts Coll.* (1939), #476; V. L. Collins, *Continental Congress at Princeton* (1908), 195-99; Hageman, *Princeton*, I, 92, 104, 211; J. S. Norton, *N.J. in 1793* (1973), 401. For Drayon, see M. B. Meriwether, ed., *The Carolinian Florist* (1943), xxviii.

WFC

Martin Roosevelt

MARTIN ROOSEVELT, the fourth son and eighth child of Isaac Roosevelt, a merchant in New York City, was born at two o'clock in the morning on May 22, 1765. Two weeks later he was baptized at the "old Dutch Church" in the city. His godfather, Anthony Hoffman, Jr., was the scion of the wealthy family from Dutchess County, New York, into which Martin's mother, Cornelia Hoffman Roosevelt, had been born. James Roosevelt (A.B. 1780) was an older brother.

James and Martin were the only sons among their parents' ten children who survived beyond infancy. In 1772 the family moved from their home on Wall Street to a more spacious house on Queen Street. They remained there until 1775, when they sought refuge from the city at the Hoffman family estate near Rhinebeck. After a hiatus of some three years, James resumed his studies at Nassau Hall, and it is possible that during his senior year he was joined by his younger brother.

Martin Roosevelt certainly was in residence at the College at the close of the 1780-1781 academic year, but in the late summer of 1781 he fell ill. After suffering from what his father called a "Lingrin disorder" for "abt. 2 months," young Roosevelt died in Princeton on September 19. He was buried in Princeton.

SOURCES: C. B. Whittelsey, *Roosevelt Geneal., 1649-1902*; K. Schriftgiesser, *Amazing Roosevelt Family* (1942), 119. The author gratefully acknowledges the cooperation and assistance of Joseph W. Marshall, Supervisory Librarian of the Franklin D. Roosevelt Library (in which are located pages from the family Bible that are the source for the quotations used here); and of John A. Gable, Executive Director of the Theodore Roosevelt Association.

Gilbert Tennent Snowden

GILBERT TENNENT SNOWDEN, A.B., A.M. 1786, tutor and librarian of the College, and Presbyterian clergyman, was born in Philadelphia on April 25, 1763, the son of Isaac Snowden and his second wife, Mary Cox McCall. The father was a prominent merchant, quartermaster in the Revolution, and treasurer of the city and county of Philadelphia. He was also an active member of the Second Presbyterian Church of Philadelphia and the Presbyterian General Assembly in its formative years and was a trustee of the College of New Jersey from 1782 until he resigned in 1808. Gilbert was the second of five sons to graduate from the College, the others being Benjamin Parker Snowden (A.B. 1776), Samuel Finley Snowden (A.B. 1786), Nathaniel Randolph Snowden (A.B. 1787), and Charles Jeffry Smith Snowden (A.B. 1789). A sixth brother, Isaac Snowden, was a non-graduate member of the Class of 1785.

It is not clear when Gilbert first came to Princeton, although it is known that he had had some prior education in Philadelphia. In June 1782 he was one of the original members of the newly revived American Whig Society, but he was expelled two weeks later, apparently for some derogatory remarks about it made while on a visit home. He was soon admitted to the rival Cliosophic Society, and this action led to a "paper war" centering around Snowden, the results of which he felt for years. A later historian of the Cliosophic Society reported that a lampoon of Snowden written by his classmate Ashbel Green survived, and when the former found himself appointed tutor some years later, "he was annoyed by hearing this song sung by the rogues of the College, whom he had offended." Tradition holds that the original conflict only ended after Snowden asked his father to intercede on his behalf. The societies' rivalry continued, however. On July 4, 1783, a public audience was invited to hear an oration from each organization, and Snowden was chosen to represent the Cliosophic Society. Ashbel Green spoke for the Whigs. At his commencement almost three months later, Snowden spoke "on the subject of female education" and gave an additional oration for an absent classmate.

His memories of the day, along with those of the next year and a half, are preserved in a journal he kept for his self-improvement. He reported that after the graduation ceremony a class dinner was held, and later, a ball attended by "about 25 ladies & between 50 and 60 Gentlemen." Unfortunately, he had developed a severe headache during the ceremonies that "rendered me more fit for a bed than a ball room; but necessity obliged me to go to the latter. After 2 I began to feel much better & danced untill 5 with great satisfaction." Some proposed drinking till dawn, but Snowden finally went to bed instead. He also wrote at length about how shy and unsure of himself he had felt through the whole affair, but the next day his good friend Samuel Bayard (A.B. 1784) assured him that the ladies had been quite impressed with him.

Snowden went home within a few days and found himself at loose ends. Only sixteen, he had not as yet decided on a career. For several weeks he enjoyed the company of fellow alumni whenever possible, and some of them stayed at his home on trips through Philadelphia. During this time he began an extensive correspondence with many other College friends.

By the end of November he was back in Princeton, having decided "to spend the winter in studying such authors as will always be of use to me in any profession." He promptly moved into a room at the home of Doctor Samuel Stanhope Smith (A.B. 1769), already residing in the president's house, and renewed old acquaintances and his interest in the Cliosophic Society, meetings of which he attended regularly. With Smith's help, he developed an organized course of study, which included readings in ancient history and philosophy and French grammar and literature. He established a full daily schedule for himself, highlighted by a few hours in the College each evening, which he wrote were important for his improvement in the social niceties. These gatherings often lasted more than their allotted time, however, and with constant interruption from his two "roommates," Joseph Clay (A.B. 1784) and John Read (A.B. 1787), and from other friends, Snowden became increasingly disappointed at his lack of self-discipline. He finally began to study in earnest in March, by which time he had resolved to return home where he hoped that the quiet of his own room and the variety of the city might allow him to make better progress with his reading.

Instead, Snowden made great progress in finding diversions. He attended the theater and art exhibitions, visited young ladies, went riding with friends, indulged in voice lessons, and usually slept late. His journal, when he kept it, professed a growing disgust with himself over his bad habits, laziness, and lack of reading. By August he had returned to Princeton determined to make up for lost time, but two months later he was back in Philadelphia, about to become the law student of William Bradford (A.B. 1772).

Blackstone's *Commentaries*, the essential text of an eighteenth-century American legal education, apparently did not appeal to Snowden as much as he had hoped. More importantly though, he was suffering from overwhelming self-doubt, which led him to spend much of his time in meditation and prayer. This was brought on, according to the oration given at Snowden's funeral by Samuel Stanhope Smith, by the death of a prominent member of the Philadelphia bar. After consultation with parents, friends, and clergymen, including his mentors at Princeton, he finally settled on a career in the ministry.

While Snowden's journal ends abruptly in the midst of the spiritual turmoil that preceded this decision, much is known about his remaining twelve years. In late 1785 he was employed to teach the freshman class at the College, replacing his classmate Samuel Beach, and he was elected tutor by the trustees at their next meeting the following April. In September 1786 he was appointed College librarian and overseer of repairs, with a salary of £5 a year. College historians have assumed that when he resigned as tutor in April 1787 he also gave up these additional posts. Presumably during this time his ministerial training was advancing under the guidance of Smith and Witherspoon.

Snowden was originally licensed to preach by the Presbytery of Philadelphia, although its records do not indicate the date. He was transferred on November 24, 1790 to the Presbytery of New Brunswick, when he was ordained as pastor of the First Presbyterian Church of Cranbury, New Jersey, where he had preached the previous summer. There he succeeded Thomas Smith (A.B. 1758). Earlier he had married Ruth Lott of Princeton, and by 1794 they had two daughters.

Snowden flourished in Cranbury. His predecessor's salary had been raised to £100 shortly before his death, and this was apparently what the new minister received as well. The congregation also had a new church building. The late Reverend Mr. Smith had not been well for a long time, however, and Snowden found that much had been neglected. The church records were in great disorder, and he quickly set to work organizing and preserving them. He also busied himself instructing the children, visiting church members, and regularly reporting on their religious state and admonishing them on their behavior. The discipline that he formerly lacked himself he now tried to encourage in others. He required strict attendance and promptness at meetings, he appointed frequent fast days, and, as reported by a later historian of the church, "[t]okens were ordered to be distributed among those desiring to come to the Lord's table." Not surprisingly, not all members adapted well to this routine, and more than one case of discipline had to be settled by the presbytery, or Snowden's successor. Snowden was himself an active member of the presbytery, serving first as its clerk and later as treasurer. He was also a representative to the General Assembly of the Church in 1792.

This enthusiastic career ended abruptly with Snowden's death on February 20, 1797. Shortly before, he had visited New York, and while there, he contracted yellow fever. He left no will, but a £1,521 inventory reveals additional information. Dissatisfied with the parsonage allotted to him, Snowden had had a house built for his family in 1794 that was fully furnished and, with its three fireplaces, apparently comfortable enough for his parents to occupy shortly after his death. In addition to all its furnishings, his possessions included surveying instruments, two spy glasses, books valued at £500, and three slaves. He was succeeded at the Cranbury church by George Spafford Woodhull (A.B. 1790), and his widow eventually married the Reverend Andrew King (A.B. 1773).

SOURCES: Alumni file, Trustee Minutes, PUA; G. T. Snowden, MS Journal, 1783-1785, PPPrHi; *Princeton Univ. Libr. Chron.*, 14 (1952), 72-90; Beam, *Whig Soc.*, 61-63; C. R. Williams, *Clio. Soc.* (1916), 89 (lampoon); J. H. Jones, *Life of Ashbel Green* (1842), 142; *Pres. Encyc.*, 842; GMNJ, 27 (1952), 55; 28 (1953), 24; *Princetonians, 1748-1768*, 246; *Rec. Pres. Chh.*, 48, and passim; J. G. Symmes, *First Pres. Chh. of Cranbury, N.J.* (1869), 14-19 (tokens); W. B. Walsh, *Cranbury Past and Present* (1975), 67f., 73, 468, 518; S. S. Smith, *A Discourse delivered . . . at the Funeral of the Rev. Gilbert Tennent Snowden* (1797). *N. R., Snowden MS Diary, 1788-89, Phi's Clio. Minute Book, PUA.*   JW

Edward Taylor

EDWARD TAYLOR, A.B., physician, was born in Upper Freehold Township, Monmouth County, New Jersey, possibly on May 27, 1762. The Taylor family was a large one in the county, and the name Edward was common, thus it is not possible to be certain of the College graduate's parentage. He was probably the son of the farmer of that name, however, and not the son of the Baptist public official of nearby Middletown who was accused of aiding the British during the Revolution. In the late 1770s Taylor's father paid taxes on 250 acres, substantial holdings in livestock, and two slaves, probably the same two whom he bequeathed to his son Edward, along with all of the real estate and a silver tankard, in a will proved in October 1794. Other bequests totaling approximately £1,600 were also mentioned in that document. It is likely that young Edward's mother was Hannah Forman of Upper Freehold, who applied for a marriage license with Edward Taylor of that town on May 24, 1762.

According to an early catalogue of the Cliosophic Society, Edward Taylor was admitted to membership in that society in 1780, and it is possible that his collegiate education began during that year. His classmate Gilbert Snowden later noted in a private journal that Taylor had a part in the debates at commencement, but he did not mention his topic.

After graduation Taylor prepared for a career in medicine. He studied first with Dr. James Newell of Allentown, New Jersey and then moved to Philadelphia. There he attended lectures at the University of Pennsylvania, visited the wards of local hospitals, and may have been apprenticed for a time to Doctor Benjamin Rush (A.B. 1760). Although medical historians have credited him with earning an M.D. degree at the University of Pennsylvania, no record of such an award has been found. He was admitted to membership in the New Jersey Medical Society in November 1787.

Taylor first established a medical practice in Pemberton, Burlington County, New Jersey but moved to his native town within a short time. From Upper Freehold he developed a large country practice, which is said to have extended from the Atlantic Ocean to the Delaware River, much of which he covered on horseback. He married a woman named Sarah, had at least one child, and was active in both state and local medical associations. A founder of the Monmouth County Medical Society, he was its first vice-president in 1816 and its president in 1820, the same year in which he read a paper entitled "The Causes and Treatment of Pneumonic Inflammation."

Taylor and his wife were also active Quakers in Monmouth County. He witnessed countless wills and prepared even more inventories for local Friends through the years, and in 1801 he was chosen by the Robins Meeting as one of the executors for the will of Mingo, a freed black slave of Upper Freehold Township. Perhaps he had freed his own slaves by this time, although it would not have been as a result of New Jersey legislation, which did not require full emancipation until much later. In 1823 Taylor moved to Frankfort, Pennsylvania, where he served for nine years as superintendent of a Quaker institution for the insane. Apparently he returned to Upper Freehold before his wife's death in 1832.

Taylor was reputed to have been in excellent health all his life, in spite of the demands of his practice. He was also remembered as a teetotaller, as "conscientious and scrupulously correct" in his business, and as a man of "refined and cultivated taste" who found great pleasure in books. He died May 2, 1835 after a brief illness and was buried next to his wife.

SOURCES: Alexander, *Princeton*, 217; *GMNJ*, 32 (1957), 3; 50 (1975), 92; *N.J. Marriages*, 391; *N.J. Wills*, VIII, 351; X, 311-12; *Clio. Soc. Cat.* (1845), 5; *Princeton Univ. Libr. Chron.*, 14 (1952), 76; N.J. Med. Soc., *Rise, Minutes, and Proceedings* (1875), 54, and passim; Wicks, *Hist. of Medicine N.J.*, 419-20 (for quotations); F. Ellis, *Hist. of Monmouth Cnty., N.J.* (1885), 324.

JW

448

Joseph Venable

JOSEPH VENABLE, A.B., lawyer, was born in Lunenburg (later Charlotte) County, Virginia, on June 28, 1761, the son of James Venable and his wife, Judith Morton Venable. He was a first cousin of Abraham B. Venable (A.B. 1780), Samuel W. Venable (A.B. 1780), Richard N. Venable (A.B. 1782), and Nathaniel E. Venable (A.B. 1796). His father served as a justice of the peace for Charlotte County, as an elder in the Presbyterian church, and as a founding trustee of the Prince Edward Academy, which in 1783 became Hampden-Sidney College. He continued as one of the academy's trustees until his resignation in December 1795, on the eve of his move from Virginia to Kentucky. There is every reason for believing that Joseph was prepared for college at this academy, and that, as with his cousins, it was the influence of Samuel Stanhope Smith (A.B. 1769), first rector of the Prince Edward Academy and after 1779 Professor of Moral Philosophy at Princeton, that brought him to Nassau Hall. No degrees were granted at Hampden-Sidney before it received its charter in 1783.

The only clue as to the time of Joseph's admission to the College at Princeton is found in a list of the early members of the Cliosophic Society, which dates his membership from 1780. There may be some question as to the accuracy of this date, in view of the loss of the original records and the assumption that the society had been moribund for some time before its revival on July 4, 1781. If the family tradition that he at some time acted as a courier for Lafayette be accepted, there is ground for further doubting the accuracy of the records, for the likeliest opportunity for such service would have been during Lafayette's operations in Virginia in 1781. Moreover, given the opportunity Joseph had to secure a more than adequate preparation for college at the local academy, it seems unlikely that he would have been in residence at Princeton for anything like three full years before his graduation on September 24, 1783. In the commencement exercises of that day, Venable participated in a "dispute" of the following question: "Can any measure that is morally evil be politically good?" Newspaper reports of the day's proceedings give no indication of the side in this debate that was assigned to him.

Following his graduation Joseph evidently studied law, though where or with whom has not been discovered. It can only be said that the minutes of the Prince Edward County court show that in August 1789 he presented a license to practice law in the "Superior and Inferior Courts of this State." The same source indicates that he already had been recommended to the state's attorney general for appointment as deputy for the county, in succession to his cousin Abraham B. Venable. Joseph received the appointment and served as deputy attorney for the commonwealth until June 1810. It was an office that imposed no serious limitation upon his own private practice in Prince Edward and the neighboring counties of Charlotte, Cumberland, and Buckingham. On January 20, 1791, he married Elizabeth Watkins, sister of Henry E. Watkins, (A.B. 1801) and daughter of Francis Watkins, who then and for many years thereafter was the clerk of the Prince Edward County court. On August 21, 1792, Joseph was elected to the board of trustees for Hampden-Sidney College joining his father, and father-in-law, and his cousins Samuel Woodson Venable and Abraham B. Venable. Richard N. Venable was elected to the board on the same day as was Joseph, who served until his resignation in 1812.

Undoubtedly the reason for this withdrawal from what had become practically a family obligation was that he had moved his residence from Virginia to Kentucky in or about the year 1810. Apparently, like his father he settled with his family in Shelby County. It is difficult to find details regarding Joseph's career in Kentucky. Presumably he practiced law, and according to family tradition, he became a judge, though at what level of the judicial system is not said. There was a Judge Venable who in July 1825 presided at a banquet held at Shelbyville in honor of Henry Clay. As had his father, Joseph became an elder in the Presbyterian church, and two of his sons after attending the Princeton Theological Seminary became Presbyterian ministers. The family evidently was a large one, with perhaps as many as twelve children. Their mother died in 1832. Joseph Venable's death followed quickly, on July 28, 1833, while on a visit to Prince Edward County, Virginia, where he was buried.

SOURCES: Alumni file, PUA, which contains a short sketch of Joseph's life by J. D. Eggleston, former president of Hampden-Sidney; E. M. Venable, *Venables of Va.* (1925), 20-22, 25, 35-37; *WMQ* (1 ser.), 15 (1906-1907), 246-49; *Tyler's Quart.*, 17 (1935-1936), 197-98; *Bulletin Va. St. Libr.*, 14 (1921), 70, 87, 96, 99, 108; H. C. Bradshaw, *Hist. of Prince Edward Cnty., Va.* (1955), 145, 149, 247, 761, H. C. Bradshaw, *Hist. of Hampden-Sidney College* (1976), 56, 93, 113, 126, 135; MS Clio. Soc. membership list, PUA; *Pa. Gazette*, 8 Oct 1783 (commencement); D. F. Wulfeck, *Marriages of Some Va. Residents*, VII, 131; Hampden-Sidney College, *Gen. Cat.* (1908), 13-15; *VMHB*, 6 (1898), 175, 179; *Clay Papers*, IV, 515; *KSHS Reg.*, 9 (1911), 67.

WFC

John Thornton Woodford

JOHN THORNTON WOODFORD, planter and public official, was born July 29, 1763 in Caroline County, Virginia, the oldest son of William Woodford and his wife, Mary Thornton Woodford. He belonged to a family established in Virginia by his grandfather, also named William, who had emigrated from England, with advantageous connections there that included the Norton family of shippers and tobacco importers. John's father, a native Virginian, was a warden of St. Mary's Parish, a justice of the county court, and a friend and political associate of Edmund Pendleton, for whom he was an alternate delegate to the second Virginia convention of July 1775 until Pendleton's return from the Continental Congress early in August. William Woodford, who had served in the French and Indian War, was given command of one of the regiments raised for the colony's defense, and in the fall of 1775 the committee of safety, led by Pendleton, chose Woodford over Patrick Henry for command of an operation against Lord Dunmore at Norfolk that forced Virginia's last royal governor to find refuge aboard a British warship. Hero of the moment, Woodford was commissioned a colonel in the Continental Army on February 13, 1776 and promoted to the rank of brigadier general on February 21, 1777. His wife belonged to another prominent and well-connected Caroline County family.

John Thornton Woodford was one of six young men in the grammar school who were examined and admitted to the freshman class in the College on September 28, 1779. For his performance, he was awarded first prize "in extemporary exercises in Latin Grammar and Syntax." That evening "the College-Hall was lighted up," and the six new collegians entertained an audience that included the state's governor with orations. To Woodford fell the highest honor of delivering the Latin salutatory address. He probably had come to Princeton for completion of his preparatory studies in the fall of 1778, for letters from Pendleton to his father indicate that he was in Virginia prior to that time. Another letter of April 1, 1779 implies that the father may have taken advantage of a recent visit home by the son to send a letter to Pendleton. At first glance, it might be assumed that the visit, if actually made, had fallen during the spring vacation, but in a letter of the following May 10, Pendleton observed that "Master Woodford has made a judicious choice of the amusement of his Vacation, in coming to Headquarters, where good Company will teach him the world and give a Polish to his severe Studies." Presumably, the headquarters was that at Middlebrook, New Jersey, where Washington had his winter camp from February to June 1779.

Whether John enjoyed a similar reunion with his father during the fall vacation that followed his admission to the College cannot be said, but it is known that he returned to the College for his freshman year, probably when it opened a new academic term on November 8. Probably too he soon enjoyed at least a brief visit at Nassau Hall by his father, for a newspaper story dated at Trenton on December 15, 1779 reported that "most of the troops of the Virginia line" recently had arrived there "on their way to the southward" under General Woodford's command. Their mission was to reinforce the defenses of Charleston, South Carolina, where upon the capitulation of the city to the British on May 12, 1780, General Woodford became a prisoner of war. Having been transferred as a prisoner to New York, he died there on the following November 13 and was buried in the Trinity churchyard.

This tragic development put an end to his son's studies at Princeton. How early after his father's capture he may have gone home to the family's plantation on the Rappahannock River, about ten miles below Fredericksburg, Virginia, has not been determined. A letter of condolence written in November 1780 by President Witherspoon to the widowed mother suggests that John may have dropped out of school much earlier, for it states that he had written previously to her on the subject of her son's return to the College. He now advised that the gentleman who brought word of her husband's death reported that "the particular Request of General Woodford" was that "his Son should finish his Studies." The president added the assurance that he and his son-in-law, Professor Samuel Stanhope Smith (A.B. 1769), would give "all possible Attention" to her son's "Improvement." No evidence has been found to indicate that this appeal was successful.

Instead, John Woodford, although only seventeen at the time of his father's death, apparently elected to assume the responsibilities of head of the family. Whatever career he may have had in mind upon entering the College, he was destined to lead through many years the life of a well-placed planter. On May 4, 1786, he was married to Mary Turner Taliaferro of another prominent Virginia family. His name headed a list of those nominated by the Caroline County justices in July 1793 for addition to the county's commission of the peace, and on August 21 of that year, he and his younger brother William Catesby Woodford, whose name bespoke a family connection with the eminent naturalist Mark Catesby, were sworn as justices of the peace.

John, the son and grandson of soldiers, had been prompt in becoming active in the militia, and in 1795 he was commissioned as a captain of a troop of cavalry. In 1804 he was serving as a major in the state's Second Cavalry Regiment, and in 1814 and 1815 he was on active duty as a major, and possibly a lieutenant colonel, with dragoons apparently enlisted in the service of the United States during the nation's second and last war with Great Britain. Meantime, he had sat for his county in the House of Delegates from 1802 to 1806. He would return to the state's General Assembly as a member of the lower house in the session extending from December 1817 to February 1818.

Soon thereafter, apparently in 1819 or 1820, he moved with his family to Clark County, Kentucky. He had claims to land in that state, perhaps for as much as 13,000 acres, that depended basically upon his father's military service in the Revolution. In Kentucky Woodford seems to have left no marked impression upon the state's history, unless it was his love of finely bred horses, demonstrated before he left Virginia, that was responsible in part for the fact that the name Woodford would be long remembered in the history of Kentucky thoroughbreds. A member of the order of Masons as early as 1781, Colonel Woodford had a prominent part to play in the breakfast given by the Masons for Lafayette upon the latter's visit to Kentucky in 1825; Woodford presented a sash worn by his father in the Revolution to the guest of honor. He was numbered among the supporters of Henry Clay at about the same time and probably became a Whig in the politics of the state. Back in Virginia, his relatives considered him to be a very rich man who lived in grand style.

He died in Clark County, Kentucky, on January 31, 1844. By his marriage to Mary Taliaferro, he had become the father of eleven children, one of whom was married to the son of John Taylor of Caroline before the family moved to Kentucky. One of his own sons had died in 1818. His first wife having died not long after the move, he married a second wife, Mrs. Mary Lane Miller. No children were born to the second marriage.

Sources: C. W. Stewart, ed., *Woodford Letter Book, 1723-1737* (1977), esp. 3-48; *Life of Brig. Gen. William Woodford* (1973), esp. I, 214, 234; also II, 1,221-28; T. E. Campbell, *Colonial Caroline* (1954), 348, 433, 469; M. Wingfield, *Hist. of Caroline Cnty.* (1924), 184-90, 232, 275; D. J. Mays, *Edmund Pendleton* (1952), II, 32-33, 52-55, 64, 71-76; D. J. Mays, ed., *Letters, and Papers of Edmund Pendleton* (1967), I, 228n, 218, 227, 250, 262, 272, 277, 281 ("Master Woodford"); *NJA* (2 ser.), III, 669-70 (admission to CNJ); IV, 97 (father at Trenton); V. L. Collins, *President Witherspoon* (1925), II, 111 ("particular request"); *PMHB*, 23 (1899), 457; W. G. Stanard and M. N. Stanard, *Colonial Va. Reg.* (1902), 203; *VMHB*, 5 (1898), 191; *WMQ* (2 ser.), III, 233; *Cal. Va. St. Papers*, VI, 491; IX, 404, 409, 471; E. G. Swem and J. W. Williams, *Reg. of Gen. Assem. of Va.* (1918), 62, 64, 66, 95;

J. F. Hopkins, ed., *Clay Papers*, IV, 431; V, 563-66; *KSHS Reg.*, 34 (1936), 73; 40 (1942), 272; *Filson Club Hist. Quart.*, 25 (1951), 10; G. G. Clift, *Ky. Obituaries* (1977), 137.

WFC

George Whitefield Woodruff

GEORGE WHITEFIELD WOODRUFF, A.B., A.M. 1786, lawyer and farmer, was born in Elizabethtown, New Jersey on March 16, 1765, the second of three sons born to Elias and Mary Joline Woodruff. His father was steward of the College, serving intermittently between 1773 and 1788. His older brother Aaron graduated in 1779, and another brother, Abner, in 1784. He probably was also a relative of Benjamin and Joseph Woodruff (both A.B. 1753) and Hunloke Woodruff (Class of 1772). He attended the grammar school affiliated with Nassau Hall and in September 1779 was one of six of its students admitted to the freshman class. Like Aaron, George became a member of the Clio-sophic Society, and he maintained an interest in the organization that lasted at least until March 13, 1786, when an undergraduate member recorded discussing with him an inflammatory letter just sent to the Whigs.

Classmate Gilbert Snowden also took some note of Woodruff. He wrote in a private journal that George "spoke an oration on sensibility of affection" at their 1783 commencement, and during Snowden's return to Princeton the following winter, he and Woodruff took a long walk together. Since George's father was still the College steward at this time, it is likely that the young graduate had decided to live at home for awhile after graduation, perhaps like Snowden, in order to pursue graduate studies, for he was awarded a second degree by the College in 1786. He was probably encouraged to become a lawyer by his older brother, who had recently been admitted to the bar and was establishing a practice in nearby Trenton. It is not known with whom George studied law, but his admission to the New Jersey bar took place in 1788. Then, instead of trying to compete with his brother, who would soon hold several prominent positions in the state, he decided to strike out on his own in the relatively undeveloped state of Georgia.

In 1796 the Duc de la Rochefoucauld-Liancourt described Savannah, where Woodruff had been settled for over five years, as "unpleasant because of its burning and irritating sand, its climate and location . . . the spirit of license and anarchy is shocking." He also made several observations relating to the legal profession in the state: "The laws are printed in part, slowly, and with no set pattern. The number of barristers who own a complete collection of them perhaps amounts to two or three in the state. . . . They are borrowed from them when a debate or question about these laws arises." And finally, "Courts do not sit regularly; juries are empanelled with difficulty; but the legal profession is nonetheless one of those that can be pursued in this land with the greatest assurance of making money." And no wonder. The rapid increase in population in the decade following the signing of the Treaty of Paris and the expansion of cultivation of such cash crops as cotton and rice, to say nothing of the displacements of land and persons provided by the war, there was ample opportunity for those with some legal background.

Woodruff was not the first Princetonian to take advantage of this situation. Matthew McAllister (A.B. 1779), originally admitted to the bar in Philadelphia, had already been Georgia's attorney general, a member of the state legislature, and was the federal attorney for the district. He, as well as Joseph Clay (A.B. 1784), also a lawyer, were friends of Woodruff's and probably helped him make important contacts. Woodruff was appointed the first solicitor general of Georgia on June 23, 1795 and was the federal district attorney under the Adams administration. He was also an alderman of the city of Savannah in 1805. In 1794 he joined the Union Society, a charitable organization composed of the most respected men in the city. Meanwhile, he, along with virtually everyone else of some means, was dabbling in land speculation, having bought shares in one of the companies exploiting the Yazoo region. Fortunately for his political reputation as well as his financial position, he had sold these by June of 1796 before passage of the act rescinding the fraudulent second Yazoo sale. This was not to be his last investment in real estate, however.

Perhaps Woodruff's most successful venture in Savannah culminated in his marriage on March 30, 1796 to Jean (also known as Jane) Houstoun, eldest daughter of the late Sir George Houstoun, Baronet. Her family was one of the most prominent in the state, having been established there since Sir Patrick Houstoun, her grandfather, emigrated with Oglethorpe. This ancestor had been a member of the royal governor's council, but at least two of his sons were ardent patriots. John Houstoun was a member of the colony's first provincial congress and a delegate to the second Continental Congress. He was not in attendance, however, when the Declaration of Independence was signed, having returned home to try to control the actions of the Tory-leaning delegate, John Joachim Zubly, father of David Zubly

(A.B. 1769). He was later twice governor of Georgia, a state chief justice, and mayor of Savannah when George Woodruff arrived there. John's younger brother William, who married Mary Bayard, daughter of Nicholas Bayard (A.B. 1757), was a member of the Continental Congress between 1784 and 1786 and a delegate to the Constitutional Convention. Patrick Houstoun (A.B. 1745) was Jean Woodruff's younger brother.

Woodruff's father-in-law, a successful merchant, was one of the more conservative scions of the family. Although a member of the provincial congress in 1775, he lost his citizenship and some of his property in 1782 for the support he gave the English when they occupied Savannah during the Revolution. Later he served as Grand Master of the Georgia Masonic lodges and held several other local political and social offices. At his death in 1795, Jean inherited 413 acres and one-sixth of the remaining property.

The details of Woodruff's career have not survived in published records, but an extensive collection of family papers provides some insight into his activities over the years. His position as district attorney required frequent absences from home, in part because the seat of government of Georgia was still not permanently fixed. His private practice must have been highly successful, for he wrote to his brother Aaron in 1805 that he was taking four or five young students into his office at once. Like his brother, his politics bore a Federalist stamp, as he also wrote of his resentment of taxes imposed on the new banks, and later, of the extreme hardship the embargo acts were placing on the wealthy planters and merchants of Georgia. Since his wife's family had substantial holdings in cotton that no longer had access to European markets, and since his brother Abner had recently settled as a merchant in Savannah, Woodruff could not avoid suffering, at least indirectly, from the interruption of trade.

Woodruff's family life was also full. He and his wife ultimately had eleven children, including George Houstoun Woodruff (A.B. 1815), Robert James Woodruff (A.B. 1824), and Aaron Dickson Woodruff (A.B. 1836). The Woodruffs, along with other members of the close Houstoun clan, usually summered "on the Salts" at White Bluff, an estate once owned by John Houstoun that Woodruff and another in-law purchased in 1799 in trust for Houstoun family heirs.

Another visitor to Georgia, John Lambert, wrote in 1808 that Savannah was inhabited by "adventurers" residing there "merely for the purpose of accumulating a speedy fortune in trade; and [who] then retire . . . to some other part more congenial to health and comfort." Woodruff again seems to have followed a trend. As early as 1802 he was planning for the eventual resettlement of his family in

New Jersey. With Aaron's help, he purchased a 126-acre tract of land north of Trenton in what is today Ewing Township to establish a residence and farm for his family. The planning and building of Oaklands, as the resulting home came to be called, was a consuming interest of these widely separated brothers over six years. Along with the concerns of the main house and one for a tenant's family, letters are filled with discussion of the placement of various out-buildings, numerous plants, and orchards of fruit trees. Abner also played a role in this project; after resigning from the navy in 1803 he helped with the barn-raising, fence-building, and early tree-planting.

Meanwhile, Woodruff had also given his older brother charge of his two oldest children, George and Elias. They were living with Aaron's family while attending school in Trenton, but they often returned to Savannah for holidays. The expense of feeding, clothing, and educating two growing boys, along with the outlay of funds sometimes necessary for the building of Oaklands, eventually placed a strain on family finances. At first George did not find these expenses a hardship, but after the first embargo act was passed, he had great difficulty obtaining bills of exchange to defray mounting costs. He was also forced to sell some of his property in 1808 to make up for some funds he had loaned to Abner.

During the summer of 1808, George's family moved into Oaklands, although it was then unfinished. The house became a showplace of the area and the farm prospered. When an inventory was made of Woodruff's New Jersey property in 1815, it listed nine out-buildings in addition to the main stone house, five slaves, and household contents that included several large lots of silver and china. In addition to the produce of the farm, the family relied on regular shipments of rice, sweet potatoes, and oranges from Savannah. The Woodruffs also maintained close ties with their Houstoun relatives through what were apparently seasonal migrations. Jean Woodruff's mother spent every summer at Oaklands until she died in 1822, and letters written through the 1830s were filled with descriptions of the most recent eight-day sea voyage or the somewhat longer overland trip between Trenton and Savannah.

The most frequent traveler in the family continued to be George Woodruff. Only a few months after settling his family in the north, he returned to Georgia to attend to business affairs. In January 1809 he was among those who attended the organizational meeting of the Savannah Public Library, and the following fall he was in Millidgeville, Georgia where the legislature as well as the court was in session. While in Savannah, he generally lived with Abner. These yearly and lengthy trips continued at least until 1823 when he paid sixty dollars to Savannah's Christ Church for a pew for the year. By then, most of his business seems to have involved family matters such as settling his mother-in-law's extensive estate. If letters portray an accurate picture, Woodruff did not relish these journeys, and although his southern relatives were devoted to him, he came home as soon as possible.

Woodruff's later years were relatively quiet although marred by the sudden deaths of his sons Elias in 1819 and George, who had become an Episcopal deacon, in 1822. Aside from an occasional favor, such as the attempt he made to obtain a pension for a relative in 1830, he seems to have abandoned his legal practice. A letter to his wife, then on a visit to Savannah, revealed his chief interests, new issues before the New Jersey legislature and the concerns of his farm. He had also just subscribed to two more periodicals, the *Church Register* and the *Journal of Health*.

Woodruff's last major trip may have been the one he made to Washington with his only surviving daughter Mary in 1835. His business there is not reported, but Mary enjoyed visiting a session of the Senate along with attending many parties. His wife's niece wrote in 1837 hoping to persuade Woodruff to visit the south once more: "Tell my dear Uncle *he is the only one* who thinks he is *so old*—I hear everyone express surprise at his age, they say he is such a hole [*sic*], hearty looking man." It is not known whether he felt hearty enough to comply.

On September 10, 1838, Woodruff was elected president of a newly founded though short-lived lyceum, the Trenton Institute. He delivered a lengthy acceptance speech on the advantages of acquiring knowledge. Among these advantages, he mentioned pursuit of knowledge as a means for *"amusing us* in *old age*, when, from our Infirmities, we cannot enjoy the Scenes of active life, and when the *Friends* of our *Youth* are *no more*." He remained thus amused until his death on September 3, 1846, at which time he was the oldest member of the New Jersey bar. He was survived by his wife, who lived another two years, and four sons. His heirs received in addition to the New Jersey property, stock in the Planters Bank of Savannah and real estate in Chatham, McIntosh, and Bullock counties, some of which had once belonged to the Houstoun family.

SOURCES: C. N. Woodruff and M. R. Herod, *Woodruff Chronicles*, II (1971), 49-50; E. D. Johnston, *The Houstouns of Ga.* (1950), 160-61, 191, 335, and passim; *NJHSP*, 68 (1950), 83-92; *NJA* (2 ser.), III, 669; E. F. Cooley, *Geneal. of Early Settlers of Trenton and Ewing, N.J.* (1883), 313; C. R. Williams, *Clio. Soc.* (1916), 91; M. Lane, ed., *The Rambler in Ga.* (1973), 15 ("burning and irritating sand"), 7 ("laws are printed"), 9 ("Courts do not sit regularly"), 45 ("accumulating a speedy fortune"); *Princeton Univ. Libr. Chron.*, 14 (1952), 76; *DAB* (for John Houstoun); M. Farrand,

Rec. of Fed. Convention, III (1911), 97; R. G. Killion and C. T. Waller, *Ga. and the Rev.* (1975), 111; C. C. Jones, Jr., *Hist. of Savannah, Ga.* (1890), 435, 527, 556; E. M. Coulter, *Short Hist. of Ga.* (1933), passim; A. D. Woodruff to GWW, 5 Jun 1796, and GWW to A. D. Woodruff, 2 Jan 1805, 21 Jul 1806 ("on the Salts"), 8 Mar 1808; GWW to J. H. Woodruff, 6 Jan 1830, 17 Dec 1829, 28 Jan 1835; G.A.M. Houstoun to J. H. Woodruff 26 Oct 1837; MS Acceptance Speech, 1838; all in Woodruff Family Papers, NjP.

MANUSCRIPTS: NjP

JW

APPENDIX

BY JANE E. WEBER

PLACE OF BIRTH*

British Isles

William Richardson Davie '76

Connecticut

Eliphaz Perkins '76 — Matthew Perkins '77

Georgia

Andrew Johnston '76

Maryland

William Halkerston '78 — Daniel Jenifer '77
Robert Jenkins Henry '76 — John Jordan '77
James Hunt '83

Massachusetts

Jacob Conant '77 — David Hyslop '76
Levi Hopkins '77

New Jersey

William Barber '77 — Robert McCrea '76
Samuel Beach '83 — James McDonald '78
Bartholomew Scott Calvin '76 — Robert Martin '76
Joseph Clark '81 — George Merchant '79
Lardner Clark '76 — Richard Mount '76
Samuel Coles '80 — Benjamin Olden '76
Jonathan Dayton '76 — Robert Pearson '82
Timothy Ford '83 — Andrew Pettit '78
Ashbel Green '83 — Cyrus Pierson '76
Samuel Reading Hackett '77 — Aaron Rhea '76
Luther Halsey '77 — John Rhea '80
James Hanna '77 — James Rock '83
John Andre Hanna '82 — Joseph Rue '76
Robert Rosbrough Henry '76 — Joseph Scudder '78
Obadiah Holmes '83 — Benjamin Brearley Stockton '76
William Johnes '76 — Ebenezer Stockton '80
John Leake '76 — Richard Stockton '79
Richard Longstreet '77 — Edward Taylor '83
Samuel McConkey '76 — Daniel Thatcher '78

* As parents of subjects were often mobile, birth records of the period were incomplete. The above listing may be a best guess or an indication of where a subject spent most of his formative years. For example, Richard Mount '76 is listed as a New Jersey resident on a Cliosophic Society list during his college years. Since the family had been established in the state for over a century, it has been assumed that he was born there as well.

Samuel Vickers '77
Nehemiah Wade, Jr. '76
Peter Wilson '78

Aaron Dickinson Woodruff '79
George Whitefield Woodruff '83

New York

Theodorus Bailey '77
Abraham Bancker '77
James Beekman, Jr. '76
Nicholas Dean '76
Lucas Conrad Elmendorf '82
Peter Edmund Elmendorf '82
Nicholas Fish '77
Alexander Graham '77
John Graham '77
Nathaniel Lawrence '83
Jacob LeRoy '83
Edward Livingston '81
Henry Philip Livingston '76
Jacob Morton '78

John Morton '82
John Young Noel '77
John Pintard '76
Jacob Radcliff '83
James Roosevelt '80
Martin Roosevelt '83
John Rutherford '76
Lewis Allaire Scott '77
Abraham Smith '77
William Smith '78
Richard Ten Eyck '82
Stephen Van Rensselaer '82
William Van Ingen '80
John White '77

North Carolina

Nathaniel Alexander '76
Benjamin Hawkins '77
Joseph Hawkins '77
Tristrim Lowther '77

Nathaniel Macon '78
George West '79
James Lewis Wilson '76

Pennsylvania

John Armstrong, Jr. '76
Andrew Bayard '79
James Ashton Bayard '77
George Blewer '77
William Boyd '78
William Coates '76
Benjamin Dunlap '78
John Evans Finley '76
Joseph Washington Henderson '76
Adam Hoops, Jr. '77
William Kennedy '82
John Wilkes Kittera '76
Matthew McAllister '79
Thomas Harrison McCalla '77

William Mahon '82
Archibald Campbell Read '76
James Riddle '79
Joseph Riddle '83
Alexander Russell '80
Nathaniel Welshard Semple '76
Samuel Shannon '76
Robert Smith '81
Benjamin Parker Snowden '76
Gilbert Tennent Snowden '83
Gilbert Tennent, Jr. '77
Robert Wharry '78
Samuel Wilson '82
Matthew Woods '78

Rhode Island

George W. Hazard '77

William H. Vernon '76

Virginia

Spencer Ball '82
Richard Bibb '77
John Brown '78
William Brown '80
James Crawford '77
William Crawford '81
Benjamin Erwin '76

William Branch Giles '81
Francis Jefferson James '81
Joseph Flavius Lane '76
Richard Bland Lee '79
Charles Lewis '76
Thomas Parker '76
William Ramsay '76

James Ramsey '76
Abraham Bedford Venable '80
Joseph Venable '83

Richard N. Venable '82
Samuel Woodson Venable '80
John Thornton Woodford '83

West Indies

John Trotman '78

Unknown

John Brown '78
John Brownfield '77
William Clements '83
John Ellet '78
George Faitoute '76
John Johnston '82
Samuel King '76
John McAllister '76

Moses McCandless '76
Samuel McGee '76
Elisha Neil '76
William Ross '78
Jesse Smith '78
John Smith '78
William Stephens '78
Samuel Thane '77

PLACE OF PRIMARY RESIDENCE*

Connecticut

Matthew Perkins '77

England

Robert McCrea '76

Georgia

Andrew Johnston '76
Matthew McAllister '79
John Young Noel '77

Samuel Vickers '77
George Whitefield Woodruff '83

Kentucky

John Brown '78
James Crawford '77
Benjamin Erwin '76
John Evans Finley '76

James Hanna '77
William Mahon '82
Samuel Shannon '76

Louisiana

Edward Livingston '81

Maryland

William Halkerston '78
Robert Jenkins Henry '76
James Hunt '83

Daniel Jenifer '77
John Jordan '77
Robert Smith '81

Massachusetts

Jacob Conant '77

David Hyslop '76

*Since many subjects moved several times during their lives, no listing of this nature can be definitive. For instance, Edward Livingston '81 was an important public servant in the state of New York as well as Louisiana.

New Jersey

William Boyd '78
Bartholomew Scott Calvin '76
Joseph Clark '81
Jonathan Dayton '76
Nicholas Dean '76
Samuel Reading Hackett '77
Robert Rosbrough Henry '76
Obadiah Holmes '83
William Johnes '76
John Leake '76
Richard Longstreet '77
Benjamin Olden '76
Robert Pearson '82
Cyrus Pierson '76

Aaron Rhea '76
Joseph Rue '76
John Rutherford '76
Joseph Scudder '78
Gilbert Tennent Snowden '83
Ebenezer Stockton '80
Richard Stockton '79
Edward Taylor '83
Samuel Thane '77
Daniel Thatcher '78
Nehemiah Wade, Jr. '76
Peter Wilson '78
Aaron Dickinson Woodruff '79

New York

John Armstrong, Jr. '76
Theodorus Bailey '77
Abraham Bancker '77
William Barber '77
James Beekman, Jr. '76
Lucas Conrad Elmendorf '82
Peter Edmund Elmendorf '82
George Faitoute '76
Nicholas Fish '77
Luther Halsey '77
Nathaniel Lawrence '83
Jacob LeRoy '83
Henry Philip Livingston '76

George Merchant '79
Jacob Morton '78
John Morton '82
John Pintard '76
Jacob Radcliff '83
James Roosevelt '80
Martin Roosevelt '83
Lewis Allaire Scott '77
Abraham Smith '77
Benjamin Brearley Stockton '76
Richard Ten Eyck '82
William Van Ingen '80
Stephen Van Rensselaer '82

North Carolina

Nathaniel Alexander '76
William Richardson Davie '76
Benjamin Hawkins '77
Joseph Hawkins '77

Tristrim Lowther '77
Nathaniel Macon '78
James Lewis Wilson '76

Ohio

Eliphaz Perkins '76

Pennsylvania

Andrew Bayard '79
James Ashton Bayard '77
George Blewer '77
William Coates '76
Ashbel Green '83
John Andre Hanna '82
Joseph Washington Henderson '76
Adam Hoops, Jr. '77
John Wilkes Kittera '76
Andrew Pettit '78

Archibald Campbell Read '76
James Riddle '79
Alexander Russell '80
Nathaniel Welshard Semple '76
Benjamin Parker Snowden '76
Gilbert Tennent, Jr. '77
John White '77
Samuel Wilson '82
Matthew Woods '78

Rhode Island

George W. Hazard '77   William H. Vernon '76

South Carolina

Samuel Beach '83   William Smith '78
Timothy Ford '83   Robert Wharry '78
Thomas Harrison McCalla '77

Tennessee

Lardner Clark '76

Virginia

Spencer Ball '82   Charles Lewis '76
Richard Bibb '77   Thomas Parker '76
William Brown '80   William Ramsay '76
William Crawford '81   James Ramsey '76
Benjamin Dunlap '78   Joseph Riddle '83
William Branch Giles '81   Abraham Bedford Venable '80
Levi Hopkins '77   Joseph Venable '83
Francis Jefferson James '81 Richard N. Venable '82
Joseph Flavius Lane '76   Samuel Woodson Venable '80
Richard Bland Lee '79   John Thornton Woodford '83

Unknown

John Brown '78   James McDonald '78
John Brownfield '77   Samuel McGee '76
William Clements '83   Robert Martin '76
Samuel Coles '80   Richard Mount '76
John Ellet '78   Elisha Neil '76
Alexander Graham '77   John Rhea '80
John Graham '77   James Rock '83
John Johnston '82   William Ross '78
William Kennedy '82   Jesse Smith '78
Samuel King '76   John Smith '78
John McAllister '76   William Stephens '78
Moses McCandless '76   John Trotman '78
Samuel McConkey '76   George West '79

PROFESSIONAL OCCUPATIONS

Ministry

ANGLICAN/EPISCOPALIAN
James Lewis Wilson '76

PRESBYTERIAN
William Boyd '78   Ashbel Green '83
Joseph Clark '81   Joseph Washington Henderson '76
James Crawford '77   William Mahon '82
Benjamin Erwin '76   Joseph Rue '76
George Faitoute '76   Nathaniel Welshard Semple '76
John Evans Finley '76   Samuel Shannon '76

Gilbert Tennent Snowden '83
Daniel Thatcher '78

Peter Wilson '78
Matthew Woods '78

Law

Theodorus Bailey '77
John Brown '78
William Richardson Davie '76
Jonathan Dayton '76
Lucas Conrad Elmendorf '82
Peter Edmund Elmendorf '82
Timothy Ford '83
William Branch Giles '81
John Andre Hanna '82
John Wilkes Kittera '76
Nathaniel Lawrence '83
Richard Bland Lee '79
Edward Livingston '81
Matthew McAllister '79
Jacob Morton '78
John Young Noel '77

Robert Pearson '82
Jacob Radcliff '83
James Riddle '79
John Rutherford '76
Lewis Allaire Scott '77
Joseph Scudder '78
Abraham Smith '77
Robert Smith '81
Richard Stockton '79
Abraham Bedford Venable '80
Joseph Venable '83
Richard N. Venable '82
Nehemiah Wade, Jr. '76
Aaron Dickinson Woodruff '79
George Whitefield Woodruff '83

Medicine*

Nathaniel Alexander '76
William Brown '80
Robert Rosbrough Henry '76
Daniel Jenifer '77
Thomas Harrison McCalla '77
Eliphaz Perkins '76
Cyrus Pierson '76
William Ramsay '76
James Ramsey '76

Benjamin Parker Snowden '76
Benjamin Brearley Stockton '76
Ebenezer Stockton '80
Edward Taylor '83
Richard Ten Eyck '82
Gilbert Tennent, Jr. '77
Samuel Vickers '77
Robert Wharry '78
John White '77

Business

Andrew Bayard '79
James Ashton Bayard '77
James Beekman, Jr. '76
Richard Bibb '77
Lardner Clark '76
Adam Hoops, Jr. '77
Jacob LeRoy '83
Tristrim Lowther '77
John Morton '82

Thomas Parker '76
Andrew Pettit '78
John Pintard '76
Joseph Riddle '83
James Roosevelt '80
Alexander Russell '80
Samuel Woodson Venable '80
William H. Vernon '76

Education

Bartholomew Scott Calvin '76
Luther Halsey '77

George Merchant '79

* Lines between the traditional divisions of the medical profession were indistinct in eighteenth century America. This listing includes men who functioned as apothecaries, surgeons, and physicians.

HOLDERS OF MAJOR PUBLIC OFFICES

Members of State Constitutional Conventions

James Crawford '77
William Branch Giles '81
Nathaniel Macon '78

Jacob Radcliff '83
Stephen Van Rensselaer '82
Richard N. Venable '82

Members of State Legislatures

Nathaniel Alexander '76
Theodorus Bailey '77
Abraham Bancker '77
Richard Bibb '77
John Brown '78
William Richardson Davie '76
Jonathan Dayton '76
Lucas Conrad Elmendorf '82
Timothy Ford '83
William Branch Giles '81
John Andre Hanna '82
Benjamin Hawkins '77
Joseph Hawkins '77
Joseph Flavius Lane '76
Nathaniel Lawrence '83

Richard Bland Lee '79
Edward Livingston '81
Matthew McAllister '79
Nathaniel Macon '78
Jacob Morton '78
John Pintard '76
Jacob Radcliff '83
James Roosevelt '80
John Rutherford '76
Robert Smith '81
Stephen Van Rensselaer '82
Abraham Bedford Venable '80
Richard N. Venable '82
John Thornton Woodford '83
Aaron Dickinson Woodruff '79

State Governors

Nathaniel Alexander '76
William Richardson Davie '76

William Branch Giles '81

State Judges

Matthew McAllister '79
Jacob Radcliff '83

James Riddle '79

State Attorneys-General

Nathaniel Lawrence '83
Matthew McAllister '79

Aaron Dickinson Woodruff '79

Other High State Offices

Abraham Bancker '77
William Barber '77
Nicholas Fish '77
Nathaniel Lawrence '83
Jacob Radcliff '83

John Rutherford '76
Lewis Allaire Scott '77
Stephen Van Rensselaer '82
Joseph Venable '83
George Whitefield Woodruff '83

Members of the Continental Congress

John Armstrong, Jr. '76
John Brown '78

Jonathan Dayton '76
Benjamin Hawkins '77

Members of the Constitutional Convention of 1787

John Armstrong, Jr. '76
William Richardson Davie '76

Jonathan Dayton '76

Members of State Ratifying Conventions

Abraham Bancker '77
William Richardson Davie '76
John Andre Hanna '82

Benjamin Hawkins '77
Nathaniel Lawrence '83

Members of U.S. Senate

John Armstrong, Jr. '76
Theodorus Bailey '77
John Brown '78
Jonathan Dayton '76
William Branch Giles '81
Benjamin Hawkins '77

Edward Livingston '81
Nathaniel Macon '78
John Rutherford '76
Richard Stockton '79
Abraham Bedford Venable '80

*Members of U.S. House of
Representatives*

Nathaniel Alexander '76
Theodorus Bailey '77
John Brown '78
Jonathan Dayton '76
Lucas Conrad Elmendorf '82
William Branch Giles '81
John Andre Hanna '82

John Wilkes Kittera '76
Richard Bland Lee '79
Edward Livingston '81
Nathaniel Macon '78
Richard Stockton '79
Stephen Van Rensselaer '82
Abraham Bedford Venable '80

U.S. Attorneys-General

Robert Smith '81 (acting)

U.S. Secretaries of State

Edward Livingston '81

Robert Smith '81

U.S. Secretaries of War

John Armstrong, Jr. '76

U.S. Secretaries of the Navy

Robert Smith '81

U.S. District Judges

Richard Bland Lee '79

U.S. District Attorneys

Edward Livingston '81
Matthew McAllister '79

Richard Stockton '79
George Whitefield Woodruff '83

Presidential Electors

William Branch Giles '81
John Rutherford '76
Robert Smith '81

Richard Stockton '79
Aaron Dickinson Woodruff '79
George Whitefield Woodruff '83

THOSE PERFORMING SOME FORM OF MILITARY SERVICE
DURING THE WAR OF INDEPENDENCE

Nathaniel Alexander '76
John Armstrong, Jr. '76
Theodorus Bailey '77
William Barber '77
Richard Bibb '77
George Blewer '77
William Bostwick '76
John Brown '78
Joseph Clark '81
William Richardson Davie '76
Jonathan Dayton '76
Nicholas Dean '76
Timothy Ford '83
Ashbel Green '83
Samuel Reading Hackett '77
Luther Halsey '77
Joseph Hawkins '77
George W. Hazard '77
Robert Rosbrough Henry '76
Adam Hoops, Jr. '77
Levi Hopkins '77
Daniel Jenifer '77
John Jordan '77
John Wilkes Kittera '76
Nathaniel Lawrence '83
Henry Philip Livingston '76

Richard Longstreet '77
Thomas Harrison McCalla '77
James McDonald '78
Nathaniel Macon '78
Thomas Parker '76
Andrew Pettit '78
John Pintard '76
William Ramsay '76
Archibald Campbell Read '76
Aaron Rhea '76
James Riddle '79
Alexander Russell '80
Samuel Shannon '76
Robert Smith '81
Benjamin Parker Snowden '76
Benjamin Brearley Stockton '76
Ebenezer Stockton '80
Richard Ten Eyck '82
Gilbert Tennent, Jr. '77
John Trotman '78
Samuel Woodson Venable '80
Samuel Vickers '77
George West '79
Robert Wharry '78
John White '77
Samuel Wilson '82

Professed Loyalists

Andrew Johnston '76
Robert McCrea '76

William Smith '78

INDEX

BY RUTH L. WOODWARD

A single date within parentheses indicates the Class to which a Princetonian belonged. The names of all matriculates for whom a sketch is included in this volume are listed in italic type, as is the location of the sketch, which follows immediately after the class identification. In the case of identical family names, the relationship to the College of New Jersey matriculate is indicated. Non-family members with identical names are identified by profession or place of residence. Place names are often made specific by including within parentheses the name of the county.

Library of Congress Cataloging in Publication Data

Harrison, Richard A., 1945-
  Princetonians, 1776-1783.

  "Third volume in the series of biographical
dictionaries of Princetonians"—Pref.
  Includes bibliographical references and index.
  1. Princeton University—Alumni—Biography.
I. Title.
LD4601.H38   378.749'67 [B]   81-47074
ISBN 0-691-05336-7   AACR2